MEDIEVAL RELIGION

Constance Hoffman Berman presents an indispensable new collection of the most influential and revisionist work to be done on religion in the Middle Ages in the last couple of decades. Bringing together an authoritative list of scholars from around the world, the book provides a valuable service to students of religious history in providing a compilation of the most important new work. The collection includes considerations of gender, "otherness," the body, and diversity of beliefs between the eleventh and fifteenth centuries. *Medieval Religion: New Approaches* is essential reading for all those who study the Middle Ages, church history, or religion.

Constance Hoffman Berman is Professor of History at the University of Iowa where she has taught since 1988. She has published widely on medieval religious women, reform religion in the twelfth century, and the Cistercian Order. Her books include *The Cistercian Evolution* (2000).

REWRITING HISTORIES
Series editor: Jack R. Censer

MEDIEVAL RELIGION

New Approaches

Edited by
Constance Hoffman Berman

Routledge
Taylor & Francis Group

NEW YORK AND LONDON

First published 2005
by Routledge
270 Madison Ave, New York, NY 10016

Simultaneously published in the UK
by Routledge
2 Park Square, Milton Park, Abingdon, Oxon OX14 4RN

Routledge is an imprint of the Taylor & Francis Group

Typeset in Palatino by
Florence Production Ltd, Stoodleigh, Devon
Printed and bound in Great Britain by
MPG Books Ltd, Bodmin

Library of Congress Cataloging in Publication Data
Berman, Constance Hoffman
Medieval religion: new approaches/Constance Hoffman Berman.
p. cm. – (Re-writing histories)
1. Church history – Middle Ages, 600–1500.   2. Religion – History.
I. Title.   II. Series.
BR270.B47 2004
270.3–dc22   2004015899

British Library Cataloguing in Publication Data
A catalogue record for this book is available from the British Library

ISBN 0–415–31686–3 (hbk)
ISBN 0–415–31687–1 (pbk)

FOR OUR SON
BENJAMIN, HIS GOOD HEALTH,
AND HIS GOOD HUMOR

CONTENTS

FIGURES

SERIES EDITOR'S PREFACE

Rewriting history, or revisionism, has always followed closely in the wake of history writing. In their efforts to re-evaluate the past, professional as well as amateur scholars have followed many approaches, most commonly as empiricists, uncovering new information to challenge earlier accounts. Historians have also revised previous versions by adopting new perspectives, usually fortified by new research, which overturn received views.

Even though rewriting is constantly taking place, historians' attitudes towards using new interpretations have been anything but settled. For most, the validity of revisionism lies in providing a stronger, more convincing account that better captures the objective truth of the matter. Although such historians might agree that we never finally arrive at the "truth," they believe it exists and over time may be better approximated. At the other extreme stand scholars who believe that each generation or even each cultural group or subgroup necessarily regards the past differently, each creating for itself a more usable history. Although these latter scholars do not reject the possibility of demonstrating empirically that some contentions are better than others, they focus upon generating new views based upon different life experiences. Different truths exist for different groups. Surely such an understanding, by emphasizing subjectivity, further encourages rewriting history. Between these two groups are those historians who wish to borrow from both sides. This third group, while accepting that every congeries of individuals sees matters differently, still wishes somewhat contradictorily to fashion a broader history that incorporates both of these particular visions. Revisionists who stress empiricism fall into the first of the three camps, while others spread out across the board.

Today, the rewriting of history seems to have accelerated to a blinding speed as a consequence of the evolution of revisionism. A variety of approaches has emerged. A major factor in this process has been the enormous increase in the number of researchers. This explosion has reinforced and enabled the retesting of many assertions. Significant ideological shifts have also played a major part in the growth of revisionism. First, the crisis of Marxism, culminating in the events of Eastern Europe in 1989, has given rise to doubts about explicitly Marxist accounts. Such doubts have spilled over into the entire field of social history which has been a dominant subfield of the discipline for several decades. Focusing on society and its class divisions implied that these are the most important elements in historical analysis. Because Marxism was built on the same claim, the whole basis of social history has been questioned, despite the very many studies that directly had little to do with Marxism. Disillusionment with social history, simultaneously opened the door to cultural and linguistic approaches largely developed in anthropology and literature. Multi-culturalism and feminism further generated revisionism. By claiming that scholars had, wittingly or not, operated from a white European/American male point of view, newer researchers argued that other approaches had been neglected or misunderstood. Not surprisingly, these last historians are the most likely to envision each subgroup rewriting its own usable history, while other scholars incline towards revisionism as part of the search for some stable truth.

Rewriting Histories will make these new approaches available to the student population. Often new scholarly debates take place in the scattered issues of journals which are sometimes difficult to find. Furthermore, in these first interactions, historians tend to address one another, leaving out the evidence that would make their arguments more accessible to the uninitiated. This series of books will collect in one place a strong group of the major articles in selected fields, adding notes and introductions conducive to improved understanding. Editors will select articles containing substantial historical data, so that students – at least those who approach the subject as an objective phenomenon – can advance not only their comprehension of debated points but also their grasp of substantive aspects of the subject.

The history of the late medieval Church once focused on papal and male initiatives and ignored or downplayed the contribution of lower levels of the priesthood and women. This collection restores individual initiative by men and women at all levels, and shows the way that, despite the efforts of the clergy to establish hierarchical privilege, women in particular played an active role in medieval religion. Furthermore, papal and clerical efforts to establish adherence to their own vision of Christianity had a negative impact on those outside the faith, especially on Jews and Muslims. Berman's volume highlights these effects, which too have been overlooked or treated in isolation. New research included in this volume has provided the material to solidify these new interpretations.

CONTRIBUTORS

Anna Sapir Abulafia is Vice President and College Lecturer in History at Lucy Cavendish College, Cambridge University. She has had published: *Christians and Jews in the Twelfth-Century Renaissance* (London: Routledge, 1995); *Christians and Jews in Dispute: Disputational Literature and the Rise of Anti-Judaism in the West c.1000–1150* (Aldershot: Variorum, 1998); *The Works of Gilbert Crispen, Abbot of Westminster* (London: Oxford University Press, 1986); *An Attempt by Gilbert Crispin, Abbot of Westminster at Rational Argument in the Jewish–Christian Debate* (Barcelona: Abadia de Montserrat, 1984); and has edited *Religious Violence Between Christians and Jews: Medieval Roots, Modern Perspectives* (New York: Palgrave, 2002).

Constance Hoffman Berman is Professor of History at the University of Iowa. Other books by Constance Hoffman Berman are: *Medieval Agriculture, the Southern-French Countryside, and the Early Cistercians: A Study of Forty-three Monasteries* (Philadelphia, PA: American Philosophical Society, 1986); *The Cistercian Evolution. The Invention of a Religious Order in Twelfth-Century Europe* (Philadelphia, PA: University of Pennsylvania Press, 2000); *Women and Monasticism in Medieval Europe: Sisters and Patrons of the Cistercian Order*, original sources translated and edited (Kalamazoo, MI: Medieval Institute Publications, 2002); and, co-edited with Judith Rice Rothschild and Charles W. Connell, *The Worlds of Medieval Women: Creativity, Influence, Imagination* (Morgantown, WV: West Virginia University Press, 1985).

Caroline A. Bruzelius is the A. M. Cogan Professor of Art and Art History at Duke University. Books by Caroline A. Bruzelius include: *The Thirteenth-Century Church at Saint-Denis* (New Haven, CT: Yale University Press, 1985); *The Brummer Collection of Medieval Art: The Duke University Museum of Art* (Durham, NC: Duke University Press, 1991); *Paesaggi Perduti: Granet a Roma 1802–1824, exh. cat., 30 ottobre 1996–12 gennaio 1997, American Academy in Rome* (Milan: Electa, 1996); and *L'apogée de l'art gothique: l'église abbatiale de Longpont et l'architecture cistercienne au début du XIIIe*, trans. Marie-Françoise Brunet (Saint-Nicholas-les-Cîteaux, France: Cîteaux, 1990); and *The Stones of Naples, Church Building in the Angevin Kingdom, 1266–1343* (New Haven, CT: Yale University Press, 2004).

Caroline Walker Bynum has taught at Harvard University, the University of Washington, and Columbia University, where she has won three awards for outstanding teaching. Her work has been awarded prizes by the Berkshire Conference of Women Historians, the Renaissance Society of America, the American Philosophical Society, and the Phi Beta Kappa Society. She is currently Professor in the School of Historical Studies at the Institute for Advanced Study in Princeton. Books by Caroline Walker Bynum include: Docere verbo et exemplo: *An Aspect of Twelfth-Century Spirituality* (Missoula, MT: Scholars Press, 1979); *Jesus as Mother: Studies in the Spirituality of the High Middle Ages* (Berkeley, CA: University of California Press, 1982); *Holy Feast and Holy Fast: The Religious Significance of Food to Medieval Women* (Berkeley, CA: University of California Press, 1987); *Fragmentation and Redemption: Essays on Gender and the Human Body in Medieval Religion* (New York: Zone Books, 1991); *The Resurrection of the Body in Western Christianity, 200–1336* (New York: Columbia University Press, 1995); *Metamorphosis and Identity* (New York: Zone Books, 2001); edited with Stevan Harrell and Paula Richman, *Gender and Religion: On the Complexity of Symbols* (Boston, MA: Beacon Press, 1986); and edited with Paul Freedman, *Last Things: Death and the Apocalypse in the Middle Ages* (Philadelphia, PA: University of Pennsylvania Press, 2000).

Giles Constable is Professor Emeritus in the School of Historical Studies at the Institute for Advanced Study in Princeton. Books by Giles Constable include: *Monastic Tithes: From their Origins to the Twelfth Century* (Cambridge: Cambridge University Press, 1964); *The Letters of Peter the Venerable*, 2 vols (Cambridge, MA: Harvard University Press, 1967); *Medieval Monasticism: A Select Bibliography* (Toronto: University of Toronto Press, 1976); *Cluniac Studies* (London: Variorum Reprints, 1980); edited with Robert Benson *et al.*, *Renaissance and Renewal in the Twelfth Century* (Cambridge, MA: Harvard University Press, 1982); with Alexander P. Kazhdan, *People and Power in Byzantium* (Washington, DC: Dumbarton Oaks, 1982); *Monks, Hermits, and Crusaders in Medieval Europe* (London: Variorum Reprints, 1988); *Three Studies in Medieval Religion and Society Thought* (Cambridge: Cambridge University Press, 1995); *The Reformation of the Twelfth Century* (Cambridge: Cambridge University Press, 1996); *Culture and Spirituality in Medieval Europe* (Aldershot: Variorum, 1996); *Religious Life and Thought (Eleventh–Twelfth Centuries)* (London: Variorum Reprints, 1979); *"Love and Do what you Will:" The Medieval History of an Augustinian Precept* (Kalamazoo, MI: Medieval Institute Publications, 1999); *Cluny from the Tenth to the Twelfth Centuries: Further Studies* (Aldershot: Ashgate, 2000); edited with Bernard Smith, *Libellus de diversis ordinibus et professionibus qui sunt in aecclesia* (Oxford: Oxford University Press, 1972; rev. edn 2003); edited, *Consuetudines benedictinae variae* (Siegburg: F. Schmitt, 1975); edited with Theodore Evergates, *The Cartulary and Charters of Notre-Dame of Homblières* (Cambridge, MA: Medieval Academy of America, 1990); *The Letters between Bernard Berenson and Charles Henry Costes* (Florence: L. Olschki, 1993).

Dyan Elliott is Professor of History at Indiana University, also Adjunct Professor of Religious Studies. Books by Dyan Elliott are: *Spiritual Marriage: Sexual Abstinence in Medieval Wedlock* (Princeton, NJ: Princeton University Press, 1993); *Fallen Bodies: Pollution, Sexuality and Demonology in the Middle Ages* (Philadelphia, PA: University of Pennsylvania Press, 1999); and *Proving Woman: Female Spirituality and Inquisitional Culture in the Later Middle Ages* (Princeton, NJ: Princeton University Press, 2004).

Fiona J. Griffiths is Assistant Professor of History at New York University. She is currently completing a book in which she examines the *Hortus deliciarum* of Herrad of Hohenbourg as evidence for women's involvement in Reform and Renaissance during the twelfth century.

Dominique Iogna-Prat is a Senior Research Historian for CNRS in Paris and teaches History at the University of Burgundy in Auxerre. Books by Dominique Iogna-Prat include: *Order and Exclusion: Cluny and Christendom Face Heresy, Judaism, and Islam, 1000–1150* (Ithaca, NY: Cornell University Press, 2002), which first appeared in French as *Ordonner et exclure. Cluny et la société chrétienne face à l'hérésie, au judaïsme et à l'islam: 1000–1150* (Paris: Aubier, 1998); *Agni immaculati. Recherches sur les sources hagiographiques relatives à saint Maïeul de Cluny (954–994)* (Paris, 1988); with Robert Delort, *La France de l'an mil* (Paris: Éditions du Seuil, 1990); *Religion et Culture: Autour de l'An Mil: Royaume capétien et Lotharingie* (Paris: Picard, 1990); with Colette Jeudy and Guy Lobrichon, *L'École carolingienne d'Auxerre: de Murethach à Rémi, 830–908* (Paris: Comité des travaux historiques et scientifiques, 1991); with Barbara H. Rosenwein, Xavier Barral i Altet, and G. Barruol, *Saint Maïeul, Cluny et la Provence* (Salagon: Les Alpes de Lumière, 1994); with Christian Sapin, *Millénaire de la mort de saint Maïeul, 994–1994* (Auxerre: CNRS, 1994); with Eric Palazzo, *Marie: Le culte de la Vierge dans la société médiévale* (Paris: Beauchesne, 1996); *Études Clunisiennes* (Paris: Picard, 2002); edited with Danièle Sansy, *La Rouelle et la croix: destins des juifs en occident* (Saint-Denis: Presses Universitaires de Vincennes, 2002); and edited with Patrick Corbet and Monique Goullet, *Adélaïde de Bourgogne: Genèse et représentations d'une sainteté impériale* (Paris/Dijon: Université de Dijon, 2002).

Katherine Ludwig Jansen is Associate Professor of History at The Catholic University of America, Washington, DC. She is author of *The Making of the Magdalen: Preaching and Popular Devotion in the Later Middle Ages* (Princeton, NJ: Princeton University Press, 2000).

Jo Ann McNamara is Professor Emerita of History at Hunter College, Columbia University, New York. Books by Jo Ann McNamara include: *Gilles Aycelin: The Servant of Two Masters* (Syracuse, NY: Syracuse University Press, 1973); *A New Song: Celibate Women in the First Three Christian Centuries* (New York: Harrington Parks Press, 1985); *The Ordeal of Community and* (edited with John Halborg) *The Rule of Donatus of Besançon* (Toronto:

Peregrina, 1985); *Sisters in Arms: Catholic Nuns through Two Millennia* (Cambridge, MA: Harvard University Press, 1996) – in Spanish, *Hermanas en armas: dos milenios de historia de las monjas católicas* (Barcelona: Herder, 1999); translation and introduction, *The Life of Yvette of Huy by Hugh of Floreffe* (Toronto: Peregrina, 2000); edited and translated with John E. Halborg, *Sainted Women of the Dark Ages* (Durham, NC: Duke University Press, 1992); and edited with Barbara J. Harris, *Women and the Structure of Society: Selected Research from the Fifth Berkshire Conference on the History of Women* (Durham, NC: Duke University Press, 1984).

Maureen C. Miller is Associate Professor of History at the University of California, Berkeley. Books by Maureen C. Miller include: *The Formation of a Medieval Church: Ecclesiastical Change in Verona, 950–1150* (Ithaca, NY: Cornell University Press, 1993); *The Bishop's Palace: Architecture and Authority in Medieval Italy* (Ithaca, NY: Cornell University Press, 2000); with Paolo Golinelli, *Chiese e Società in Verona medievale* (Verona: Cierre edizione, 1998) and *Power and the Holy in the Age of the Investitures Conflict: A Brief Documentary History* (New York: Bedford/Saint-Martin's, 2004).

David Nirenberg is Professor of History and of Romance Languages and Literatures at Johns Hopkins University, Baltimore, where he holds the Charlotte Bloomberg Chair in the Humanities and directs the Leonard and Helen Stulman Jewish Studies Program. Books by David Nirenberg are: *Communities of Violence: Persecution of Minorities in the Middle Ages* (Princeton, NJ: Princeton University Press, 1996); and, edited with James Clifton and Linda Neagley, *The Body of Christ in the Art of Europe and New Spain, 1150–1800* (Munich and New York: Prestel, 1997).

Jonathan Riley-Smith is Professor of Church History at Cambridge University. Books by Jonathan Riley-Smith include: *The Knights of Saint John and Cyprus, c.1050–1310* (London: Macmillan, 1967); *The Feudal Nobility and the Kingdom of Jerusalem, 1174–1277* (Hamden, CT: Archon Books, 1973); *What Were the Crusades?* (Totowa, NJ: Rowman and Littlefield, 1977); *The Crusades: Idea and Reality* (London: E. Arnold, 1981); *The First Crusade and the Idea of Crusading* (Philadelphia, PA: University of Pennsylvania Press, 1986); *The Crusades: A Short History* (New Haven, CT: Yale University Press, 1987); *The Atlas of the Crusades* (New York: Facts on File, 1991); *The Oxford Illustrated History of the Crusades* (Oxford: Oxford University Press, 1995); *The First Crusaders: 1095–1131* (Cambridge: Cambridge University Press, 1997); *The Oxford History of the Crusades* (Oxford: Oxford University Press, 1999); *Hospitallers: The History of the Order of Saint John* (London: Hambledon Press, 1999); *The Sovereign Military Order of Malta: A Short History* (London: BASMOM, 2001); *The Experience of Crusading* (Cambridge: Cambridge University Press, 2003).

Miri Rubin is Professor of History at Queen Mary College, University of London. Books by Miri Rubin include: *Charity and Community in Medieval*

Cambridge (Cambridge: Cambridge University Press, 1987); *Corpus Christi: The Eucharist in Late Medieval Culture* (Cambridge: Cambridge University Press, 1991); and *Gentile Tales: The Narrative Assault on Late Medieval Jews* (New Haven, CT and London: Yale University Press, 1999). She has also co-edited, with David Abulafia and Michael J. Franklin, *Church and City, 1000–1500: Essays in Honour of Christopher Brooke* (Cambridge: Cambridge University Press, 1992), and, with Sarah Kay, *Framing Medieval Bodies* (Manchester: Manchester University Press, 1994), and has edited *The Work of Jacques Le Goff and the Challenges of Medieval History* (Woodbridge: Boydell Press, 1997). She is currently working on *The Penguin History of Britain, 1314–1485* (forthcoming, 2004).

Norman Zacour is Professor Emeritus of History at the University of Toronto, Ontario, Canada. Books on medieval history by Norman Zacour are: *A Note on the Papal Election of 1352: The Candidacy of Jean Birel* (New York: Fordham University Press, 1957); *Talleyrand: The Cardinal of Périgord* (Philadelphia, PA: American Philosophical Society, 1960); *An Introduction to Medieval Institutions* (New York: Saint-Martin's Press, 1969); *Petrarch's Book Without a Name: A Translation of the* Liber sine nomine (Toronto: Pontifical Institute of Medieval Studies, 1973); with Harry Hayard, *The Impact of the Crusades on the Near East* (Madison, WI: University of Wisconsin Press, 1985); and *Jews and Saracens in the* consilia *of Oldradus de Ponte* (Toronto: Pontifical Institute of Medieval Studies, 1990).

ACKNOWLEDGMENTS

Permission has been granted for reproducing texts by American University Press for Jo Ann McNamara, "Canossa and the Ungendering of the Public Man," *Render Unto Caesar. The Religious Sphere in World Politics*, ed. Sabrina Petra Ramet and Donald W. Treadgold (Washington, DC: American University Press, 1995), pp. 131–50; American Church History Society (Yale University) and the University of Pennsylvania Press for Constance Hoffman Berman, "Were There Twelfth-century Cistercian Nuns?" *Church History* 68 (1999): 824–57 (from complete article, pp. 824–64), and *The Cistercian Evolution* by Constance Hoffman Berman; Cambridge University Press for Giles Constable, *Three Studies in Religious and Social Thought* (Cambridge, 1995), pp. 251–66, 289–304; Cornell University Press for Dominique Iogna-Prat, "Creation of a Christian Armory against Islam," reprinted from *Order and Exclusion. Christian Society Faces Heresy, Judaism and Islam, 1000–1150*, translated by Graham Robert Edwards. Original French edition, *Ordonner et Exclure*, © 1998 by Aubier, Paris, all rights reserved. English translation © 2002 by Cornell University, used by permission of the publisher, Cornell University Press (Ithaca, NY: Cornell University Press, 2002, pp. 338–57); Maureen C. Miller, "Secular Clergy and Religious Life in Verona, 950–1150," reprinted from Maureen C. Miller *The Formation of a Medieval Church. Ecclesiastical Change in Verona, 950–1150*, copyright © 1993 by Cornell University. Used by permission of the publisher, Cornell University Press (Ithaca, NY: Cornell University Press, 1993), pp. 50–62, 71–4, 76–93; The Ecclesiastical History Society for Miri Rubin, "Desecration of the Host. The Birth of an Accusation," from *Christianity and Judaism. Studies in Church History*, ed. Diana Wood (1992), vol. 29, pp. 169–85; *Harvard Theological Review* for their permission to reproduce Caroline Walker Bynum, "Jesus as Mother and Abbot as Mother. Some Themes in Twelfth-century Cistercian Writing," *Harvard Theological Review* 70 (1977): 257–84; *History*, for Jonathan Riley-Smith, "Crusading as an Act of Love," *History* 65 (Blackwell Publishing, 1980): 177–92; The International Center for Medieval Art, The Cloisters, New York, Publishers of *Gesta* for Caroline A. Bruzelius, "Hearing is Believing. Clarissan Architecture, ca. 1213–1340," *Gesta* 31 (1992): 83–91; Manchester University Press for Anna Sapir Abulafia, "Bodies in the Jewish–Christian Debate," from *Framing Medieval Bodies*, ed. Sarah Kay and

Miri Rubin (Manchester: Manchester University Press, 1994), pp. 123–37; The Pontifical Institute of Mediaeval Studies for Norman Zacour, "The Cardinals' View of the Papacy," from *The Religious Roles of the Papacy. Ideals and Realities, 1150–1300*, ed. Christopher Ryan (Toronto: PIMS, 1989), pp. 413–38, © 1989 by The Pontifical Institute of Mediaeval Studies, Toronto; Princeton University Press for Katherine Ludwig Jansen, "The Vita Contemplativa," from *The Making of the Magdalen. Preaching and Popular Devotion in the Later Middle Ages* (Princeton, NJ: © Princeton University Press, 2000), pp. 116–29, 135–42, and David Nirenberg, "The Two Faces of Secular Violence," chapter 7 from *Communities of Violence. Persecution of Minorities in the Middle Ages* (Princeton, NJ: © Princeton University Press, 1996), pp. 200–30; University of Pennsylvania Press for Dyan Elliott, "The Priest's Wife," *Fallen Bodies: Pollution, Sexuality, and Demonology in the Middle Ages* (University of Pennsylvania Press, 1999), pp. 81–106 plus notes; and for Fiona J. Griffiths, "Men's Duty to Provide for Women's Needs." Abelard, Heloise, and their negotiation of the *cura monialium*," from *The Journal of Medieval History* 30 (2004): 1–24. All articles are reproduced with the kind permission of the authors. Every effort has been made to trace and contact copyright holders, but if you are aware of any omissions please contact Routledge with the additional information.

Permission for plates and illustrations has been provided by Roberto Hüner, photo of Santa Maria in Trastevere; Boston's Isabella Stewart Gardner Museum, "Madonna with Child Enthroned with Saints (1307)," by Guiliano da Rimini; Caroline Bruzelius, Duke University; Cambridge University Library, ff. 1.27, p. 238, diagram illustrating Gilbert of Limerick, *De statu ecclesiae*; London, British Library, MS Harley 7026, fol. 13r, marginal illustration; Naples, Soprintendenza dei Beni Culturali e Monumentali, Santa Chiara, Naples plan; Rome, Bibliotheca Vaticana, Barbarini Latin 592, membrane 1, Mater Ecclesia in eleventh-century Exultet Roll; and Massimo Velo, photos of Santa Chiara in Naples.

The editor would like to thank the contributors for their kindness and patience; they have provided inspiration, support, and friendship. She also thanks Victoria Peters and Jane Blackwell at Routledge for patience and hard work, Jack Censer for his queries and discussions of shared concerns, and her students in UI classes on the History of the Medieval Church for testing and commenting on chapters. Special thanks also go to Malcolm Barber for excellent suggestions and to graduate students, Renée Goethe, who provided research assistance, Pamela Stucky Skinner, for Latin expertise, and Melissa Moreton for help getting the cover photograph, as well as to Roberto Hüner who took that photo. She thanks Dale Kinney, who is the expert on Santa Maria in Trastevere, and Birgitta Wohl; the content of their NEH summer seminar at the American Academy in Rome in summer 1999 is apparent throughout these pages. The editor wishes to acknowledge a long friendship with the late Dr Barbara Kreutz, *magistra nobilissima*, who supported so many projects and will be so much missed. None of the above, is, of course, responsible for any of the errors or shortcomings of this book. Finally, the volume would not have been completed without David Berman's help and support, and without the expertise and care of a host of doctors and staff at UIHC and of many friends in Iowa City who saw us through a child's illness, and it is dedicated to that child, Benjamin Berman, a Stoic, a sensitive cellist, and a terrific son.

ABBREVIATIONS

AASS	*Acta Sanctorum* (Paris: Victor Palmé, 1865–)
ACA	Arxiu de la Corona d'Aragó:
	C Cancelleria Reial
	cr. cartes reials
	RP Reial Patrimoni
ACV	*Archivio Capitolare, Verona*
ADG	Arxiu Diocesà de Girona
AHCG	Arxiu Històric de la Ciutat de Girona
AMVil	Archivo Municipal de Vilareal
Annales ÉSC	*Annales: Économies, Sociétés, Civilisations* (Paris: 1946–)
ARV	Archivo del Reino de Valencia
ASF	*Archivio di Stato, Florence*
ASV	*Archivio Segreto Vaticano*
ASVR	*Archivio di Stato, Verona*
BAV	Bibliotheca Apostolica Vaticana
BC	Biblioteca Civica, Verona
BHL	*Bibliotheca hagiographica latina antique et mediae aetatis*, 2 vols. *Subsidia hagiographica*, no. 5, Brussels: Société Bollandistes, 1898–1901, and *Bibliotheca hagiographica latina: Novum supplementum*, ed. H. Fros, *Subsidia hagiographica*, no. 70, Brussels: Société Bollandistes, 1986
Bibl. Clun.	Bibliotheca Cluniacensis
BL	British Library
BN	Bibliothèque nationale
BS	*Bibliotheca Sanctorum*, 12 vols and index. Rome: Città nuova, 1961–70
CC:CM	*Corpus Christianorum, Continuatio Mediaevalis* (Turnhout: Brepols, 1966–)
CC:SL	*Corpus Christianorum, Series Latina* (Turnhout: Brepols, 1953–)
CDV	*Codice Diplomatica Veronese*, ed. Vittorrio Fainelli (Venice: Deputazione di storia patria per le Venezie, 1940–63)

CIC	*Corpus iuris canonici*, 2 vols, ed. Emil Friedberg (Leipzig: Bernhard Tauchnitz, 1879–81)
CSS	Peter the Venerable, *Contra sectam Sarracenorum*, ed. Reinhold Glei, in *Petrus Venerabilis Schriften zum Islam*, Corpus Islamico-Christianum, series latina I (Altenberge: CIS Verlag, 1985)
DDC	*Dictionnaire de droit canonique*, 7 vols (Paris: Letouzey et Ané, 1935–65)
DHGE	*Dictionnaire d'Histoire et de Géographie Ecclésiastique* (Paris: Letouzey et Ané, 1912–)
Ep., Epp., Epist.	Letter(s), when following name of author, except in Epist. for those of Abelard and Heloise, as cited on p. 307, note 2.
FC	*Fathers of the Church*, New York: Cima, Fathers of the Church *et al.*, 1947
LP	*Liber pontificalis*, in *Raccolta degli Storici Italiani*, 2, 3, ed. Ludovico A. Muratori (Bologna: Nicola Zanichelli, 1924) or ed. Duchesne, *Le Liber pontificalis*, texte et commentaire par Louis Duchesne (Paris: E. Thorin, 1884, rep. 1981)
Mansi	*Sacrorum conciliorum nova et amplissima collectio*, ed. Giovanni D. Mansi, 53 vols (Florence and Venice: Antonius Zata, 1759–98)
MGH	*Monumenta Germaniae Historica:*
Briefe	*Die Briefe der deutschen Kaiserzeit* (Weimar, 1949; Munich, 1983)
Cap.	*Leges in quarto ii, Capitularium regum francorum* (Hanover, 1883–97)
Conc.	*Leges in quarto, III: Concilia* (Hanover, 1893)
Const.	*Leges in quarto, IV: Constitutiones et acta publica imperatorum et regum*, 5 vols (Hanover, Hahnianus, 1893–)
Dipl.	*Diplomatum regum et imperatorum Germaniae* (Berlin: Weidmanns, 1879–)
Leges (*folio*)	*Leges in folio*, vols 1–5 (Leipzig: Hiersemann, 1925–)
Libelli	*Libelli de lite imperatorum et pontificum, saeculis XI et XII conscripti* (Hanover, 1891–7)
SS	*Scriptores in folio et quarto*, ed. C. H. Pertz *et al.* (Hanover, 1826–)
SS rerum Germ.	*Scriptores rerum Germanicarum in usum scolarum separatim editi* (Hanover and Berlin, 1871–)
SS rerum Lang.	*Scriptores rerum Langobardicarum et Italicarum, saec. VI–IX* (Hanover, 1878–)
SS rerum Merov.	*Scriptores rerum Merovingicarum* (Hanover, 1884–)

PL	*Patrologiae cursus completus . . . series Latina (Patrologia Latina)*, comp. J. P. Migne, 221 vols (Paris: Garnier Fratres et J.-P. Migne, 1844–64)
RHC	*Recueil des Historiens des Croisades*, ed. Académie des Inscriptions et Belles-Lettres (Paris, 1941–)
RHC Oc.	*RHC Historiens occidentaux* (Paris, 1844–95)
RHGF	*Recueil des historiens des Gaules et de la France* (Paris, 1738–)
RIS	*Rerum Italicarum scriptores*, ed. Ludovico A. Muratori, 25 vols (Milan: Societas Platinae, 1723–51)
RLS	*Repertorium der lateinischen Sermones des Mittelalters, für die Zeit von 1150–1350*, ed. Johann Baptist Schneyer (Münster: Aschendorff, 1969–90)
SC	*Sources chrétiennes*, Paris Editions du Cerf, 1940
"Summary"	Peter the Venerable, *Summa totius haeresis Sarracenorum*, ed. Reinhold Glei, in *Petrus Venerabilis Schriften zum Islam*, Corpus Islamico-Christianum, series latina I (Altenborge: CIS Verlag, 1985)

Cover and frontispiece Christ and the Virgin Mary from Santa Maria in Trastavere, twelfth-century apse mosaic (photo: Roberto Hüner).

INTRODUCTION

Constance Hoffman Berman

Traditionally, the history of religion in the central Middle Ages has charted the rise of papal power vis-à-vis the Emperor in the eleventh century, followed in the twelfth century by a movement of religious reform characterized by a single group of reformers, the Cistercians. Beginning in the thirteenth century, Innocent III consolidated papal power along with a new urban-based religion preached by charismatic practitioners of apostolic poverty like Francis of Assisi who founded one of the mendicant orders. Also in that century, the Dominican and Franciscan preachers created the theological syntheses of the universities. A modern Catholic historiography has looked to the thirteenth century, epitomized by the *Summae* of Thomas Aquinas, as the pinnacle of religious development in the Middle Ages. Indeed until this last century medieval history was taught primarily as the history of theology and medieval religious movements, much of it the realm of Catholic historians, whereas non-Catholic historians tended to concentrate on the Reformation and its attack on the medieval Church.

This changed in the early twentieth century, particularly in North America, where a new understanding of medieval history developed out of a Protestant and secular American context.[1] Such new understandings were particularly associated with Charles Homer Haskins, who was interested in the origins of our separation of Church and State in the Investiture controversy of the late eleventh century, and in the origins of European science in what he called the twelfth-century Renaissance.[2] But Haskins' *Renaissance of the Twelfth Century*, while arguing that the Middle Ages were not dark, gave little attention to religion per se. Often work on medieval religion continued in old grooves. The history of religious orders remained written only by modern monks (and an occasional nun) usually lacking training as historians; their understanding of modern monastic life was often read back into the past. Theology in particular was a Catholic monopoly held by papally appointed commissions of scholars who edited by committee the definitive works of Thomas Aquinas and other medieval theologians. In that traditional history of medieval religion, outsiders to Catholicism were not usually welcome. Whereas once the standard historiography had emphasized the developments of the mendicants in the thirteenth century as the triumph of the Church,

1

recent study has seen the twelfth century or even the eleventh as the central period of interest because of its innovations. In this period of the "Reformation" of the central Middle Ages, as Giles Constable has called it,[3] an increasing array of religious services were offered by specialized groups. There arose religious orders that specialized in ransoming captives, in aiding the sick, in ministering to the urban poor, wider participation in religious movements such as pilgrimage, Crusades, and religious confraternities; adult conversion to the religious life was possible for more and more people. The newest work either expands the boundaries of the study of medieval religion to look at these understudied groups or to consider the participation of women in religious groups, or looks at the consequences of administrative structures, theology, and canon law on the interaction between insiders and outsiders, such as Jews or pagans.

Recent changes in the history of medieval religion derive from demographic shifts in the historical and religious studies professions themselves, for the recruiting of women and minorities into academe has coincided with new interests in gender, multiculturalism, and non-elites. The work of many of the contributors to this volume has created a new and wider view of what religion meant not only for medieval Christians, but for their neighbors who were not Christians. These selections are written by established academics in Europe and North America who study religion as part of the culture of the past, rather than because they subscribe to a specific belief system. Such historians have begun crossing the departmental barriers between history, art, and religion, and between histories of Christianity, Judaism, and Islam, as well as crossing temporal boundaries between the medieval and early modern world. The selections in this book point to the many new questions to be explored before we fully understand the impact of such developments on the Christian message and Christian institutions. These selections draw on new archival research, or on a reinterpretation of sources once dismissed as uninteresting or irrelevant. These challenges to old paradigms found here are ones that are only gradually being incorporated into more standard surveys. Their questions open new doors to future investigation by researchers whose work will be conducted not just in established document collections, but in obscure archives and libraries and in archeological spaces, not just in Latin and Greek sources, but increasingly in Hebrew and Arabic ones.

Often the rewriting of institutional history requires new forays into the archives to add to the range of sources available, but it also involves applying the source criticism of nineteenth-century positivists to cherished texts that earlier had been exempt from such scrutiny. So the latest generation of medieval historians of religion finds themselves needing the technical skills to work in the archives and libraries at the same time that they are applying the gender analysis, deconstruction, and new historicism of the late twentieth century. Surprising as it may seem, we often still find ourselves, as French historian Michel Parisse recently commented, *trapped* by our lack of authenticated and well-dated documents.[4] Such revisionism in the history of institutions can meet with considerable resistance, however. It upsets a dominant narrative that had supported the prestige of certain medieval institutions that have continued into the present. Most work on the twelfth-century Cistercians (whose successors include the modern-day Trappists), for instance, left out women because at some moment in the later twelfth century monastic association with women came to be equated with the welcoming of women into heretical sects. Accounts of early Cistercian history leave out women almost entirely and, when Cistercian nuns are included, they are cited as examples of apostasy (in this context the breaking of monastic vows).[5] Those accounts also assumed that the Cistercian Order expanded by colonization from a Burgundian center. My own work has shown that women were there, that much of the Cistercian expansion was by incorporation of earlier groups, and that the texts cited to support the standard narrative are not eyewitness accounts, but self-promoting narratives whose claims to authority do not hold up.[6]

The expansion of Western European Christianity in the central Middle Ages can no longer be presented as a benign process when the history of outsiders to Christianity is included. Although the process has been slow, accounts of medieval Christian atrocities against the Jews or their holy books (once confined to the work of historians of Judaism housed in separate departments or separate institutions) have begun to be incorporated into our discussion. We now ask how we should judge the adept theologian William of Auvergne, bishop of Paris, a great intellectual, who nonetheless oversaw the burning of two dozen cartloads of Talmuds in 1242.[7] Our students are exposed to the accounts of indiscriminate murder and rapine by those taking Jerusalem in 1099, or hear the words of the leader of the Crusade against Cathar heretics in thirteenth-century southern France, Arnold Amalric, abbot of Cîteaux, who apparently told the French knights outside besieged Béziers to "kill them all for God would know which are the heretics."[8]

Historians who once studied the Crusades or the Reconquest of Spain as series of military and diplomatic victories or setbacks for Christian forces now consider how Crusades and Reconquest affected Muslims, and that Crusaders often began their campaigns to the East by attacks on Jewish communities in the West. We consider how an initial Crusading victory followed by many unsuccessful Crusades may have led Western Christians to attribute their initial victories to God's perception of the purity of their society, and later defeats to its ungodliness. Defeat in the Crusades hence could lead to concern about purifying their own society, and too often that meant ridding it of outsiders or heretics. Thus, as lines between heresy and orthodoxy were drawn by able university-trained theologians, many from the new mendicant orders, those individuals were also drawn into preaching against heresy and soon into inquiring into its spread as the Inquisition came to be born c.1229.[9] The development of a uniform Christian orthodoxy at the universities of Paris and Bologna did not only lead to advances in Christian theology, but provided the training for bishops, preachers, and investigators for the

Inquisition (also often associated with mendicant orders), which was aimed at converting Jews and Muslims, and reintegrating heretics into the Church or else condemning them to execution. The consequences for those not considered Catholic Christians could be devastating when either clerics or powerful secular rulers became convinced of the universal applicability of the Christian message and the necessity that orthodoxy be preserved "for the salvation of souls," even at the price of violent repression. The traditional triumphant history of medieval Christianity disappears as historians ask how and why institutions such as Crusade and Inquisition could so easily be diverted to inappropriate ends, or how such developments in the medieval Church perverted the original meaning of Christianity.

This new scholarship, which has emphasized the role of cultural interactions with "others" or the participation of women in medieval religion, has discussed as well the consequences of a new affectivity in the mind-set of medieval Christians. This is exemplified by an intense consideration of charitable love, or *caritas* within religious communities, an interest in love that paralleled that of courtly love poetry or romances about knightly love in this period.[10] This new affective piety is seen both in the writings of monastic authors and in art depicting the humanity and suffering of Christ, much of it showing his very human relationship with his mother. Such emphasis on the humanity of Christ is exhibited, for instance, in the apse mosaic from the church of Santa Maria in Trastevere in Rome, as described by art historian Dale Kinney:

> Its iconography is unusual, for it shows not exactly a Coronation of the Virgin but a co-enthronement in which Christ embraces his already coronated mother. Its patronage is also exceptional: as part of the new construction that replaced the ancient church of Santa Maria in Trastevere under the sponsorship of Pope Innocent II (1130–43), it is the only example of direct papal patronage of monumental imagery surviving from the twelfth century.[11]

A detail is reproduced on the cover and in the frontispiece illustration here.

Kinney goes on to examine the iconography in the entire mosaic, the central image of which is of Christ, with his mother just to his right.[12] She suggests that it is difficult to know if a medieval pilgrim entering this church when it was filled with the flickering light of candles could have read the inscription: "His left hand is under my head, and his right hand shall embrace me," which is found on the Virgin's scroll (from the Song of Songs 2.6, 8.3), or the text held by Christ: "Come my chosen one and I will place in you my throne," which comes from the medieval liturgy for the Feast of the Assumption of the blessed Virgin Mary.[13] These texts seem to be incorporated to justify the unusual iconography of the mosaic. Its content might be thought to reflect some of the concerns of twelfth-century religious thinkers about the Virgin Mary and her precise relationship to her son, or how she exercises her power

4

in heaven, but also suggests to the modern viewer many of the ambiguities about the relationship of Christ to the Church, of papal authority within the clerical hierarchy, of clergy to laity, and of men to women within Christendom. Despite Christ being in the center of the mosaic, it is noticeable when one visits the church today that, unless one is standing precisely in the processional center aisle, the images of Jesus and his mother appear to share centrality in the mosaic. This mosaic, with its ambiguity about relationships and its blurring of categories – with an image of Christ and his mother more typical of lovers in Old Testament images than of New Testament personages – suggests some of the richness and variety of medieval religious thought and practice found in this volume.[14]

The selections in this volume are presented in four parts. Part I looks at how Christians of the central Middle Ages thought about themselves within specific institutions, often creating new ones to accommodate changing self-images. It begins with Caroline Walker Bynum's "Jesus as Mother," a consideration of how abbots in the newest and most successful religious movement of the twelfth century, the Cistercian Order, described their caring roles by using feminine imagery. Bynum has been at the forefront in tracing women's spirituality in the later Middle Ages; in this selection she carefully shows that uses of feminine language among the Cistercians does not indicate a softening of Cistercian monastic attitudes toward women. Jonathan Riley-Smith, in "Crusading as an Act of Love," looks at how the preaching of Crusade, and its interpretation as a series of battles won or lost because of God's favor or disfavor toward Christian forces, distorted Christianity, creating violence and intolerance toward others which have consequences for the present day.[15] Giles Constable describes social organization as viewed by the clergy of the time in "The Orders of Society;" he discusses their efforts to draw lines or make charts, to categorize, and to define just where everyone fit in Christendom, an enterprise that became more difficult as society became more mobile and urbanized in the later Middle Ages.

Part II's selections revise traditional narratives of developments within the institutional church. Jo Ann McNamara's re-envisioning of the conflict of church and state, "Canossa and the Ungendering of the Public Man," describes the reform efforts of the eleventh century (often called the Gregorian Reform) as a conflict about gender. As Dyan Elliott shows in "The Priest's Wife," reform of the clergy included a well-known campaign against clerical marriage which contributed to the growing misogyny of the later Middle Ages. Such change was associated with an increased separation of the clergy from the laity, and on a theological elevation of the Eucharist as not just shared food representing Christ, but the very body and blood of Christ. Elliott underlines the demonization of priests' wives as an element in the campaign against clerical marriage. In "Secular Clergy and Religious Life in Verona, 950–1150," Maureen C. Miller reinterprets the effects of the Gregorian reform in a local context, showing how established Benedictine communities evolved into mixed-gender religious communities ruled by abbesses, hospitals ruled by the lepers themselves, or training centers for the new parish priests needed in a diocese with a rapidly growing population. Miller agrees with John van Engen that historians' discussion of the so-called "crisis" of the old monasticism (in which it was believed that Cluniac monasticism became bankrupt and had to be replaced by Cistercian and other new reform movements) has depended too heavily on the rhetorical "grandstanding" of self-interested treatises written by those "new monks" rather than on actual evidence of decline among traditional monks.[16] Norman Zacour, in "The Cardinals' View of the Papacy, 1150–1300," problematizes our assumptions about papal power by suggesting that the medieval papal curia often had a corporate view of the Papacy in which the cardinals had considerable advisory power for the Pope.

In Part III monasticism and the religious life are considered in studies that concentrate on religious women (who had been much neglected in earlier scholarship) and the necessary interactions of their lives with those of medieval men within reformed monastic institutions that were once thought to have included only men. Each chapter represents not only the most innovative new scholarship, but uses different bodies of evidence: legal transactions, saints' lives, sermons, art and architectural evidence, letters, and theological treatises. Constance Hoffman Berman, in "Were There Twelfth-Century Cistercian Nuns?," provides evidence that there were women within the early Cistercian movement. Her consideration of why women were left out of the story has led to more general conclusions about the Cistercian and other religious reformers of the twelfth century and about the very creation of that new institution of the time, the religious order. Katherine Ludwig Jansen, in "Mary Magdalen and the Contemplative Life," a selection from her *The Making of the Magdalen*, shows how mendicant men and women in their consideration of the conversion to the religious life could identify with a feminine image of humanity and weakness – "the ultimate sinner," Mary Magdalen. Jansen's work and that of Caroline Bruzelius, in "Hearing is Believing," consider how both the Eucharist and women saints, like Mary Magdalen, inspired devotion, not only among penitential women, but also among men, particularly those associated with the mendicant orders. Bruzelius looks at the architectural consequences of female enclosure and female devotion to the Eucharist among the followers of Saint Clare. In "Men's Duty to Provide for Women's Needs," Fiona Griffiths, by reassessing the evidence from the letters of Heloise and Abelard and other writings by Abelard usually considered only in the context of an intellectual history too often unconcerned with women's history, challenges the traditional view that the care of souls for female religious was seen as a serious burden by religious men. In fact men could find a means to their own salvation in the duty of supporting religious women.

Part IV considers the establishment of Christian doctrinal positions about Jews and heretics, as well as popular beliefs about such "others." In "The Creation of a Christian Armory," Dominique Iogna-Prat considers abbot Peter the Venerable of Cluny's treatise against the Muslims and assesses the reality of the standard interpretation, associated with Haskins and the twelfth-century Renaissance historiography, that abbot Peter was a liberal-minded churchman, who, by disputing with Jews, heretics, and Muslims, was in fact tolerant of non-Christians. Although in comparison to many others Peter the Venerable may have been tolerant, the argument for Peter's open-mindedness has been based on a very superficial reading of Peter's treatises. In fact, as Iogna-Prat shows, in his "Against the Saracens," Peter was creating an "arsenal" of arguments against these "out-groups"; he neither attempted to understand them nor to accept that they might have different versions of religious truth than he. Anna Sapir Abulafia, in "Bodies in the Jewish–Christian Debate," turns to the attitudes toward Jews among a group of early twelfth-century theologians that includes Peter the Venerable. Her discussion here considers the opposing Jewish/Christian notions of an embodied deity and how those notions of embodiment informed their inability to accept one another's beliefs. Abulafia's ability to move back and forth between Jewish and Christian viewpoints is one of the hallmarks of her important work on Christian/Jewish relations. Miri Rubin's "Desecration of the Host," treats the fictions about Jews and attacks on the Eucharistic wafer, or Host, that are traceable to mid- to late-thirteenth-century sources; she describes the unfolding of violence against Jews that was associated with the telling of these stories. Rubin shows how Christians are divided from non-Christians or heretical Christians by lines of inclusion or exclusion drawn by a hegemonic clergy. She argues that the clergy, in making such "others" less than human, can be seen as causal agents even when that violence was "popular." David Nirenberg also looks at specific instances of an increasingly well-documented violence against Jews, in this case in late medieval Spain during Easter Week in "The Two Faces of Secular Violence against Jews," where he describes how young clerics used the stoning of the Jewish quarters to prove their devotion to Christ. While Abulafia and Rubin suggest a slowly deteriorating situation with regard to the hostility of Christians toward Jews, Nirenberg is much less convinced that violence against Jews actually increased in the late Middle Ages, as opposed to being simply better documented.

There is much work still to be done – about religious women and their ability to reject the misogyny of the clergy, about the conflict between center and periphery in the institutional Church, or about the rhetoric and popular tales that inspired Christian violence. Particularly with regard to the effect of Christian attitudes toward outsiders, we need to ask searching questions not only about sources of intolerance, but about who benefitted from such intolerance. What institutions gained from the ritualized violence against Jews across Europe during Holy Week, or from the elaboration in publicly displayed and recited works of art and literature, of tales about the desecration of the Eucharistic wafer by Jews? What did some Christians gain by refusing a life of *convivencia*, or peaceful coexistence, with their Muslim neighbors? In offering opportunities for penitence from sin in such activities as founding new religious communities or going on Crusade, did clerical and monastic authorities not only perpetuate violence against non-Christians in the Crusading movement, but make *all* violence capable of being excused by Church authorities if proper penitential acts were undertaken? It is such difficult questions as these that the selections in this volume have begun to address.

NOTES

1　Gabrielle M. Spiegel, "In the Mirror's Eye: The Writing of Medieval History in North America," *The Past as Text: The Theory and Practice of Medieval Historiography* (Baltimore, MD: Johns Hopkins University Press, 1997), pp. 57–80.

2　Charles Homer Haskins, *Renaissance of the Twelfth Century* (Cambridge, MA: Harvard University Press, 1927); Robert L. Benson and Giles Constable, with Carol Lanham, *Renaissance and Renewal in the Twelfth Century* (Cambridge, MA: Harvard University Press, 1982).

3　Giles Constable, *The Reformation of the Twelfth Century* (Cambridge: Cambridge University Press, 1996).

4　Michel Parisse, "Conclusions," in *Unanimité et diversité cisterciennes*, ed. Nicole Bouter, p. 698 (Saint-Etienne: Publications de l'université de Saint-Etienne, 2000).

5　In the standard medieval account of Cistercian origins, Conrad d'Eberbach's *Le Grand Exorde de Cîteaux ou Récit des débuts de l'Ordre cistercien* (trans. Anthelmette Piébourg, intro. Brian P. McGuire), the only women referred to are Benedict's sister, Scholastica (who is not named), another unnamed woman from centuries earlier accused of having caused the pollution of a Carolingian priest, and the anonymous women among the army of the dead or the possessed; in narratives written by Cistercian monks in twelfth- and thirteenth-century England discussed by Elizabeth Freeman, *Narratives of a New Order: Cistercian Historical Writing in England, 1150–1220* (Turnhout: Brepols, 2002), Cistercian nuns are only mentioned as examples of breaking vows and running away from the community.

6　On conservative resistance, see reaction to Berman, *The Cistercian Evolution: The Invention of a Religious Order in Twelfth-Century Europe* (Philadelphia, PA: University of Pennsylvania Press, 2000), which filled 101 pages in *Cîteaux* 51 (2000): 285–386, and her response in *Cîteaux* 53 (2002, appeared fall 2003): 333–7.

7　Leslie Smith, "William of Auvergne and the Jews," *Christianity and Judaism: Studies in Church History* 29, ed. Diana Wood (1992): 107–17.

8　The source is a Cistercian, Caesarius of Heisterbach, writing some years later; see further discussion in Peter of les Vaux-de-Cernay, *The History of the Albigensian Crusade*, trans. W. A. Sibly and M. D. Sibly (Woodbridge: Boydell, 1998), appendix B, pp. 289–93.

9　Henry Charles Lea, *A History of the Inquisition of the Middle Ages* (New York: Macmillan, 1906–9); Richard Kieckhefer, *Repression of Heresy in Medieval Germany* (Philadelphia, PA: University of Pennsylvania Press, 1979); Robert E. Lerner, *The Heresy of the Free Spirit in the Later Middle Ages* (Notre Dame, IN: University of Notre Dame Press, 1991); Walter L. Wakefield, *Heresy, Crusade, and Inquisition in Southern France, 1100–1250* (London: G. Allen & Unwin, 1974); and David Burr, *The Spiritual Franciscans: From Protest to Persecution in the Century after Saint Francis* (University Park, PA: Penn State University Press, 2001).

10　On the romances as well as concern about the Virgin, see Penny Shine Gold, *The Lady and the Virgin; Image, Attitude, and Experience in Twelfth-Century France* (Chicago, IL: University of Chicago Press, 1985); on secular love in southern France, see

Fredrik L. Cheyette, *Ermengard of Narbonne and the World of the Troubadours* (Ithaca, NY: Cornell University Press, 2001).

11   Dale Kinney, "The Apse Mosaic of Santa Maria in Trastevere," in *Reading Medieval Images: The Art Historian and the Object*, ed. Elizabeth Sears and Thelma K. Thomas (Ann Arbor, MI: University of Michigan Press, 2002), pp. 18–26, here p. 19.

12   There is reference here, then, to the Christian Trinity:

> Nearly all of the axial elements refer to Christ: ... the only other referents on the axis are God the Father, whose hand holds a wreath above Christ's head, and the Holy Spirit, represented by the dark ray above God's hand. ...

Kinney, "Santa Maria in Trastevere," pp. 22–3.

13   Kinney, "Santa Maria in Trastevere," *passim*; she provides these translations on p. 24.

14

> The Virgin Mary, already seated in the Lord's throne, has preceded other mortals to his presence and partakes of his divinity in a uniquely intimate way. ... Christ's own gesture is much more unusual, and startling, in this context: his right arm wraps behind the Virgin to embrace her, his fingers closing on her shoulder. Characteristic of lovers, this motion was often depicted in illustrations of Old Testament couples but is rarely seen in New Testament Iconography and never in apse mosaics.
>
> Kinney, "Santa Maria in Trastevere," p. 24.

15   Edward Said, *Orientalism* (New York, 1978), esp. pp. 58–61, argued that medieval Christian notions of Islam contributed to modern Western/Islamic conflict. While there are inaccuracies in some of its details, Said's study nonetheless signals a shift in the discourse.

16   See John van Engen, "The 'Crisis of Cenobitism' Reconsidered: Benedictine Monasticism in the Years 1050–1150," *Speculum* 61 (1986): 269–304.

Part I

RELIGIOUS SPECULATION AND SOCIAL THOUGHT

Introduction

Two rival descriptions have often been used to characterize the intellectual developments in Western Europe during this period. One already mentioned was the notion of a twelfth-century Renaissance, which was popularized by Charles Homer Haskins in the 1920s. This response to early modernists' frequent dismissal of the Middle Ages as "Gothic" focused on the twelfth-century revival of the learning of pagan antiquity, particularly in the cathedral schools and urban centers.[1] A different description was that introduced by Jean Leclercq in his famous study, *The Love of Learning and the Desire for God*, which stressed an opposition between the twelfth-century innovations of the new urban schools and the more traditional biblical commentary or exegesis of the monasteries.[2] What were once predominant characterizations of the period – that of a twelfth-century Renaissance, and that of a clear demarcation between rural/monastic and urban/scholastic learning – have been modified, however, in the latest scholarship on twelfth-century religious and intellectual history, as this part's selections show.

According to existing scholarship, Christianity came under the control of an increasingly powerful clergy in the late eleventh through thirteenth centuries. What was orthodoxy and what was heresy became more clear than ever before, and there was considerable reorganization within the Church. Since late antiquity two wings of the Church – the clerical (priests who had administered early urban churches with a bishop at their head) and the monastic (those who sought to escape the political fray to live contemplative lives) – had vied for authority and precedence. The process was a contentious one, carrying with it major issues of political power. Both clerics and monastics sought to distinguish themselves from seculars. Particularly after the turn of the first millennium, monastic claims to greater purity and asceticism pulled the clerical branch toward such practices as celibacy. At the same time monks were also increasingly ordained as priests and the celebration of anniversary masses

11

for patrons became a more important part of monastic life.[3] Monks and clerics moved closer together in their claims to purity and began to see themselves as a "clerical order" superior to those men and women who constituted the "order of the laity." As Christians began to categorize and define their beliefs and practices more precisely, important issues of doctrine were debated and there were great advances in speculative theology which would culminate in the theological *Summae* of the thirteenth century. Central to these developments was an intellectual revolution among religious thinkers based on methods borrowed from ancient philosophy, which allowed a systematic clarification of religious doctrine. Using the same tools of logic and reason, scholars also began to systematize Church or canon law. The methods they used, which would come to be called "scholasticism," were developed primarily in the cathedral schools and came to full flowering in the medieval universities, but were also employed in monastic communities. For instance, among the early leaders in subjecting faith to the methods of reason was Anselm, abbot of the Norman monastery of Bec (d. 1109), whose scholarship had been conducted primarily in that monastic setting before he became archbishop of Canterbury.[4]

The twelfth century in earlier scholarship was believed to be a period that had a suddenly cultural flourishing with the birth of Gothic cathedrals with their tall slender windows, incredible stained glass, and flying buttresses, with a parallel growth in intellectual life centering on the growing communities of scholars who flocked to Bologna to study law and to Paris to study liberal arts and theology, with the growth of "scholastic methods" (see pp. 13–14) in the urban schools which paralleled in its complexity and structure the intricacies and the sharp distinctions and relief of the ages' rising cathedrals. The twelfth-century intellectual revival, like that of the fifteenth-century Renaissance, was seen as a re-energizing of the learning of the ancient world, both in newly enhanced study of the classics of Latin antiquity and a revival, often by way of Arabic, or Hebrew translations, of Greek speculative thinking. It was at the same time the period in which "courtly love" and the songs of the troubadours came to the fore, in which sculptural art had a reawakening, and in which the first murmurings of secular and vernacular literature are found. Recently, however, some scholars, like C. Stephen Jaeger, have suggested that the term "Renaissance" has as much to do with the education in the cathedral schools of the eleventh century as with the period of greater "grandeur" of the twelfth, and that if we look beyond Paris we have a very different view of what and when a medieval "Renaissance" occurred.[5]

The most important aspect of the twelfth-century "rebirth" was its flowering of interest in the religious life. Its debates about the Christian life and Christian doctrine were aimed at making the entire world into a monastery, and living a Christian life characterized by charitable love, or *caritas*. As Giles Constable remarks, it constituted a "set of values . . . at the heart of the movement of reform which can be seen as an effort to monasticize first the clergy, by imposing on them a standard of life previously reserved for monks, and then the entire world."[6] Religious reform was missing in the earlier views of

Haskins, and the mixing of monastic and clerical lives, of urban scholastic and monastic Bible-study, are more prominent than Jean Leclercq posited.

It has long been recognized that scholastic methods began to be used in the twelfth century to reorganize medieval religious thought into questions that could be resolved by affirmative propositions or their negatives, but in a new wave of thinking we are realizing that monastic authors used scholasticism and that urban clerics came from or returned to monastic settings. The scholastic method is epitomized in the work of the most famous of the twelfth-century teachers, Peter Abelard (d. 1142), whose textbook for theological reasoning, *Yes and No (Sic et Non)*, laid out the methods of dialectical or systematic reasoning to be used in theological analysis.[7] Although Abelard made himself unpopular because of the arrogant ways in which he put such methods to work, much of the scholarly activity of the twelfth century consisted of just such sorting out, categorizing, and defining. By mid-century, several other textbooks had undertaken the same kind of analysis. One was a collection of canon (or Church) law, Gratian's *Decretum*, the *Concordance of Discordant Canons* (c.1140), which became the standard text from which canon law would be studied. Another was Peter Lombard's mid-twelfth-century *Four Books of Sentences*, a highly influential text on the Bible on which new candidates in the study of theology were expected to write commentaries as part of their initial training.[8] While today work on theology and intellectual history topics continues on traditional lines, recent work on such authors as Abelard has stressed the ways in which intellectuals' activities crossed the boundaries between scholastic and monastic concerns, for instance, with regard to women's religious lives (see Chapter 11).[9]

Mixing of categories is everywhere apparent, for the intellectual revolution of the twelfth century embraced not only those urban-trained clerics who remained in the schools, but those who had retreated from urban contexts to the rural monastic life, and those who had been brought up from childhood as monastics, including women.[10] Heloise (d. 1164), Peter Abelard's student, lover and wife, whose intellectual efforts were so intertwined with his, retreated to the monastic life after their disastrous marriage. So did Abelard, but, while he returned to his urban teaching, Heloise became the abbess of the new community he had founded, the monastery called the Paraclete in the countryside of Champagne, and Heloise and Abelard would debate at length the form of life which should be lived there (see Chapter 11). This soon became an important reform community of nuns with a number of daughter-houses. Heloise's training had been in the shadow of the cathedral of Paris, and her education was very similar to that of Peter Lombard (d. c.1160) or Hugh of Saint-Victor (d. 1141) or Abelard himself.[11] Monastic contexts thus often overlapped with urban "scholastic" ones, and not only for nuns.

The most famous monastic counterpart to the urban Peter Abelard was Bernard, abbot of Clairvaux (d. 1153), an early leader among the Cistercians; his powerful intellect and charisma were responsible for much of the order's success. Bernard was an early recruit to this group and his life epitomizes the phenomenon of adult religious conversion in the twelfth century. Bernard's education, like that of many other twelfth-century monks, had not begun in the monastery. Apparently, he had been trained in an urban school before converting as an adult to the religious life. His preaching attracted many individual men to the monastic life at Clairvaux, and caused many independently founded reform communities to seek affiliation with Clairvaux as daughter-houses.[12] Bernard preached against heresy in southern France, and in support of the second Crusade, but made efforts to prevent attacks on the Jews by Crusaders. Although often presented by members of his own order as being opposed to religious women, Bernard was an important supporter of the religious community of nearby Jully where many of his female relatives were nuns.[13] Throughout his life Bernard seems to have been torn between his abbatial duties at Clairvaux and his role in international affairs; his complaints about the difficulty of combining the active life of preaching against heresy and his own urge to return to the contemplative life of prayer and scriptural study at Clairvaux anticipated the concerns of thirteenth-century mendicants about the active versus the contemplative life.

Bernard's conflict with Peter Abelard, in which Bernard was particularly harsh and uncompromising, suggests an element of personal rivalry between these two charismatic leaders, rather than a great contrast between monastic and scholastic methodologies. Many of Bernard's positions on doctrine were not far removed from those of Abelard.[14] Bernard's attack on Abelard, indeed, may have reflected not so much Bernard's fear of Abelard's theology, as Bernard's fear of the potentially heretical, anti-clerical leaders of urban revolts against bishops, whom Abelard seemed to support.[15] By the second half of the twelfth century the scholastic education propounded by Abelard was rapidly becoming routinized. The community of scholars teaching the liberal arts and studying theology in Paris had organized themselves into a guild of clerical scholars, called a *universitas*, or university. They sought licenses to teach from the chancellor of the cathedral of Paris from at least the 1160s, and by the early thirteenth century had various statutes and privileges issued by the bishop of Paris, the Pope, and the King of France. Parisian masters and teachers would often advise Kings and Popes on particular doctrinal issues – most famously, almost all the legislation for the Fourth Lateran Council of 1215 had been crafted by members of the Parisian scholarly community.[16] The colleges or *studia* of the Dominicans and Franciscans would become famous for their teaching and for their resident masters, including among them the Dominican Thomas Aquinas, and the Franciscan Bonaventure (both of whom died in 1274). Increasingly monastics came to the urban schools for their education.[17]

The following chapters consider topics discussed by monastic and clerical thinkers of the eleventh through thirteenth centuries which have tended to be ignored by traditional theological work. Chapter 1, by Caroline Walker Bynum, considers how abbots in the newest and most successful religious group of the twelfth century, the Cistercians, used feminine imagery to describe their roles within the monastic community and their relationships to

God. In their monastic humility such writers sought to have the Jesus to whom they prayed act as a mother for them, but that maternal imagery was also transferred to their own activities of authority. Cistercian sermons in particular are filled with images of the Virgin Mary as the merciful mother, of her motherly concern for her children, of Jesus or an abbot described as a mother holding and nursing her children at her breasts. Bynum underlines that the use of maternal language and imagery among the Cistercians is not a proto-feminist one – it in no way necessarily indicates a softening of monastic attitudes toward women. Bynum discusses these views primarily in the works of Bernard of Clairvaux, but underlines that her discoveries are not limited to Bernard alone, nor are these images exclusively Cistercian. This new emphasis on the maternal side of monastic authority was widespread among male monastic writers of the twelfth century. In describing their abbatial roles as acting in mothering ways, we see Bernard and his colleagues searching to insert Christian charity, *caritas*, into the monastic worlds in which they live and breath.

The intellectual advances of the twelfth- and thirteenth-century university were accompanied by a generalized assumption of Christian superiority over the rest of the world that may be associated with the Crusading movement and the resort to direct military actions on the part of the Church was growing. It is, however, important to realize that Crusading grew out of Western attitudes and did not create them. That it should be Churchmen who decided what were the proper military objectives for Christian knights, moreover, had been implicit in the movements known as the Peace and Truce of God, which attempted to limit warfare in Western Europe by allowing battles only at certain times, condemning attacks on noncombatants (women, children, and priests), outlawing the burning of fields and buildings, and establishing a code of good conduct for the Christian knight.[18] Certainly even before the first Crusade, the Church encouraged reconquest in Spain by Christians who were promised immediate salvation if they died fighting the Muslim Infidel; indeed in some senses the Iberian Crusades were the successful ones.[19] Whatever earlier doubts there may have been about Christianization by force disappeared with the early twelfth-century victories. The taking of Jerusalem in 1099 was followed by the establishment of Latin kingdoms in the East, with several thousand Crusaders staying there to rule. It is easy to say in hindsight that Crusader victories had more to do with political disarray among the Muslims than any Western superiority, but Crusaders, Papacy, and much of Christian Europe viewed the victories in the East, won without any of the promised support from the Byzantines, as a sure sign that God was on the side of the Western Church.[20] Discussion of the Crusades reveals that the rhetoric of affective piety and charity which Bynum sees articulated in Cistercian descriptions of Jesus as mother could have a darker side. As Jonathan Riley-Smith shows in Chapter 2, it was a rhetoric of "love of God and love of neighbor" that motivated Crusaders departing for the East, as Riley-Smith finds from an examination of the texts that influenced

Crusaders to take the cross and those in which Crusaders described their own actions. The injunction to love God and love your neighbor as yourself was a powerful means of inciting violent campaigns against those who were construed as "other" by western Catholic Christians. This theme permeated the papal encyclicals of the time, as illustrated in one from Innocent III in 1215 which Riley-Smith quotes:

> How does a man love according to divine precept his neighbor as himself when, knowing that his Christian brothers in faith and in name are held by the perfidious Muslims in strict confinement and weighed down by the yoke of heaviest servitude, he cannot devote himself to the efficacious work of liberating them?[21]

It is shocking to realize how the concern with charity that inspired Bernard of Clairvaux to describe himself as a mothering abbot could be used as a justification for violence, and how love of God and neighbor inspired Christians to depart on Crusades against pagans and Moslems.

Riley-Smith turns to the Latin father, Augustine, to locate this "Christian tradition of violence," in which violence was used to correct out of love, not hate:

> To Augustine, the intentions of those who authorized violence and of those who participated in it had to be in favor of justice, a virtue which for him assigned to everyone his due, working through love of God and love of one's neighbor.[22]

Such love, as Riley-Smith points out, was a one-sided love and he suggests that more generous definitions of love can be found in the writings of the Church fathers. Moreover, as he points out, the twelfth-century equation of love with crusading and killing went against the original message of Christianity, and reflects an ethnocentric assumption of Western and Christian righteousness seen even to this day.

Whatever "grandeur" could be found in this period of change, of enormous social mobility or dislocation, and struggles between traditional authorities and new groups, was accompanied by a general sense of unease associated with rapid population and economic growth. Clergy and monks alike attempted to bring their world under control by organizing it into categories. What they found instead were increasingly hybridized institutions, like the military-religious orders or recruits of peasant/monks and nuns, the lay-brothers and lay-sisters.[23] In Chapter 3, Giles Constable discusses the difficulties of categorization in the diversity of monastic and clerical views of how society was divided into "orders" or ranks, and organized in hierarchical ways. The most commonly cited model of such medieval "orders" was that of the "Three Orders": "those who work," "those who fight," and "those who pray." Constable, however, discusses the many alternatives to these three orders – in particular the division between clerical and lay found in such works as those by Bernard of Clairvaux. Such texts tended to number their points by reference to well-known biblical duos, triads, or quartets. Constable gives the following example:

WITHDRAWN

> In his ninth sermon "On diverse things," Bernard combined two tripartite models based on the people, saints, and the converted in Psalm 84.9 with a bipartite model based on two other biblical texts. "We are accustomed to understand in these words the three types to whom alone God spoke peace, just as the other prophet [Ezechiel] foresaw that only three men would be saved, Noah, Daniel, and Job, expressing in a different order the same orders of the continent, the prelates, and the married." He then proceeded to give another inter-pretation of the categories in Psalms 84. . . .[24]

Such biblical numerology, using references to already familiar triads, provided a means by which monastic thinkers tried to bring order out of the chaos of a world undergoing great change. Constable discusses in this regard the hier-archical schemes found in the writings of Gilbert of Limerick, and particularly the illustrations found in early manuscripts of Gilbert's work. (See Figure 3.2 on p. 74.) In such discussion the word "order" denotes the major distinc-tion in ways of life (the most frequent meanings of the term "ordo" at this time): that between those who had been elevated to the clergy and those who had not.

It is against such a background that twelfth-century thinkers worried about how parts of society fit together, or how religious leaders needed to have maternal characteristics, and how to justify Crusades as acts of charity. In these three studies we see twelfth-century intellectuals valiantly developing new concepts of the divisions of society, how individuals should perceive themselves, and how Christian charity and empathy with a suffering and increasingly human Christ could best be achieved.

NOTES

1   See pp. 1–2.
2   Jean Leclercq, *The Love of Learning and the Desire for God: A Study of Monastic Culture*, trans. Catherine Misrahi (New York: Fordham University Press, 1961).
3   On this see, for example, the abbey of Cluny, discussed by Barbara H. Rosenwein, *To Be the Neighbor of Saint Peter: The Social Meaning of Cluny's Property, 909–1049* (Ithaca, NY: Cornell University Press, 1989).
4   Generally, see Marcia L. Colish, *Medieval Foundations of the Western Intellectual Tradition, 400–1400* (New Haven, CT: Yale University Press, 1997).
5   C. Stephen Jaeger, "Pessimism and the Twelfth-Century 'Renaissance'," *Speculum* 78 (2003): 1151–83 and Jaeger, *The Envy of Angels: Cathedral Schools and Social Ideals in Medieval Europe, 950–1200* (Philadelphia, PA: University of Pennsylvania Press, 1994).

WITHDRAWN

SPRING CREEK CAMPUS

6   Giles Constable, *The Reformation of the Twelfth Century* (Cambridge University Press, 1996), p. 6.

7   Such methods were not Abelard's alone. Indeed Abelard was probably not the most successful practitioner of them; he rushed to hasty conclusions without completely treating certain issues. As a consequence of this, as well as because his arrogant manner made him unpopular, a number of his works were condemned as heretical. He was required by the Council of Soissons in 1121 to burn his treatise on the Trinity, for instance; see Colish, *Medieval Foundations*, p. 208; Grover A. Zinn, "Abélard, Peter (1079–1142)," in *Medieval France: An Encyclopedia*, eds William W. Kibler and Grover Zinn, with John Bell Hennemann, Lawrence Earp, and William Clark (New York: Garland, 1995), pp. 2–3; and Constant J. Mews, "The Council of Sens (1141): Abelard, Bernard, and the Fear of Social Upheaval," *Speculum* 77 (2002): 342–82.

8   Beryl Smalley, *The Study of the Bible in the Middle Ages*, 3rd edn, rev. (Oxford: Blackwell, 1983).

9   The distinctions are between old and new methods. Whereas once theological studies had focused on either a single topic (The Trinity, or Creation, for instance) or on a single biblical book (The Book of Job, or The Song of Songs), the new twelfth-century work commented on topics organized by compendia such as Peter Lombard's *Sentences*. Colish, *Medieval Foundations*, pp. 229ff.

10 One of the foremost twelfth-century monastic intellectuals was the abbess, Hildegard of Bingen, who had been brought up since childhood in the monastic life and whose many writings were created by a mysticism drawing on her attention to scriptural reading and the liturgy. She presented her views as those of an untutored woman through whom God spoke. Despite having no training in the urban schools, she was nonetheless consulted by other scholars on theological questions and was an important preacher against heresy. Colish, *Medieval Foundations*, p. 226. Similarly, Herrad of Landsberg, abbess of Hohenburg near Strasbourg (r. 1167–d. 1195), directed the creation in her monastic *scriptorium* of a massive encyclopedia containing all of human knowledge organized for easy consultation by her nuns, the *Hortus Deliciarum (The Garden of Delights)*. *Herrade des Landsberg: Hortus Deliciarum*, with commentary and notes by A. Straub and G. Keller (Strasbourg: Imprimerie Strasbourgeoise, 1879–99).

11 On Heloise and the Paraclete, see *Listening to Heloise: The Voice of a Twelfth-century Woman*, ed. Bonnie Wheeler (New York: St Martin's Press, 2000); her correspondence with Abelard indicates that she knew both Greek and Hebrew and was well-read in the writings of the Christian and pagan authors of antiquity.

12 On Bernard of Clairvaux, see Colish, *Medieval Foundations*, pp. 227ff.; on the expansion of Clairvaux, see Marcel Pacaut, "La Filiation claravallienne dans la genèse et l'essor de l'Ordre cistercien," *Histoire de Clairvaux: Actes du Colloque de Bar-sur-Aube/Clairvaux, 22–23 juin, 1990* (Bar-sur-Aube, 1991), pp. 135–47.

13 On Jully, see below, pp. 218–19.

14 Colish, *Medieval Foundations*, pp. 279ff.

15 A revolt against the Archbishop of Reims and Arnold of Brescia's aid in the revival of the ancient Roman Senate were at issue: see Mews, "The Council of Sens," and on Arnold of Brescia and revived Senate in Rome, Robert L. Benson, "Political *Renovatio*: Two Models from Roman Antiquity," in *Renaissance and Renewal in the Twelfth Century*, eds Robert L. Benson and Giles Constable (Cambridge, MA: Harvard University Press, 1982), pp. 339–86.

16 See Jane Sayers, *Innocent III, Leader of Europe 1198–1216* (London: Longman, 1994), and John Baldwin, *Masters, Princes, and Merchants: The Social Views of Peter the Chanter and his Circle* (Princeton, NJ: Princeton University Press, 1970).

17 For instance, for a Cistercian college in Paris, see Maurice Dumolin, "La censive du collège des Bernardins," *Bulletin de la Société de l'histoire de Paris et de l'Ile de France* 62 (1935): 25–58.

18 *The Peace of God: Social Violence and Religious Response in France around the Year 1000*, eds Thomas Head and Richard Landes (Ithaca, NY: Cornell University Press, 1992).

19 Joseph F. O'Callaghan, *Reconquest and Crusade in Medieval Spain* (Philadelphia, PA: University of Pennsylvania Press, 2003).

20 After the initial victories in the East, however, there were few signs of God's favor for the crusaders; see Jonathan Riley-Smith, *The Crusades: A Short History* (New Haven, CT: Yale University Press, 1987); John France, *Victory in the East: A Military History of the First Crusade* (Cambridge: Cambridge University Press, 1994), and volumes by Riley-Smith cited in the list of contributors; on military orders specifically see Malcolm Barber, *The Military Orders: Fighting for the Faith and Caring for the Sick* (Aldershot: Variorum, 1994) or Barber, *The New Knighthood: A History of the Order of the Temple* (Cambridge: Cambridge University Press, 1994). On the Fourth Crusade which ended up attacking the Christian city of Zara on the Adriatic coast before sacking Constantinople, see Donald E. Queller and Thomas F. Madden, *The Fourth Crusade: The Conquest of Constantinople, With an Essay on Primary Sources by Alfred J. Andrea*, 2nd edn, rev. (Philadelphia, PA: University of Pennsylvania Press, 1997). See also Norman Housley, *The Italian Crusades: The Papal-Angevin Alliance and the Crusades Against Christian Lay Powers, 1254–1343* (Oxford: Clarendon Press, 1982).

21 See p. 57.

22 See p. 58.

23 On hybrids, see Caroline Walker Bynum, *Metamorphosis and Identity* (New York: Zone Books, 2001), ch. 1.

24 See p. 81.

1

JESUS AS MOTHER AND ABBOT AS MOTHER

Some themes in twelfth-century Cistercian writing

Caroline Walker Bynum

In many ways the new approaches to medieval religion that this volume documents can be traced to a ground-breaking paper by Caroline Walker Bynum presented in May 1977 at a Cistercian Studies Conference in Kalamazoo; the article that grew out of that paper is what is included here. Bynum's careful and systematic reading of well-known texts on medieval monastic spirituality showed that there was much more to discover about the spirituality of reformed monasticism than just about the various modes of ascent of the soul toward God on which earlier historians had been focusing. The language and images she uncovered had been ignored as they were thought irrelevant because they had to do with "feminine" aspects of behavior, or irreverent (in the sense of not in appropriate good taste for academic discourse), because they discussed bodily functions such as nursing and body parts such as a mother's breasts.

Bynum treats with great sensitivity the nuances of such medieval treatments of body and gender that often had been marginalized in earlier readings. She carefully distinguishes, moreover, between a feminization of language and imagery that is related to the "affectivity" among male authors of the Cistercian Order, and their often intolerant stances toward women in monastic communities and beyond. These were, after all, men who had dedicated themselves to monastic celibacy and the purity of the monastic life; they were concerned about suppressing their sexuality and keeping themselves away from female sources of temptation and contamination. So it is perhaps not surprising that twelfth-century monastic authors like Bernard of Clairvaux were apt to integrate the most hateful remarks about women taken from the writings of the early Latin Fathers, like Jerome. Yet Bernard could be sympathetic to individual religious women, and was devoted to the Virgin Mary. Indeed there is some debate about whether he inspired, or was inspired by, the image of Jesus and his mother in the apse mosaic at Santa Maria in Trastevere found on the cover and in the frontispiece of this volume.

It is such images of maternity as those found in Bernard's writings about God and about monastic authorities that Bynum treats here. She has continued to lead research on medieval spirituality, the affective spirituality of Cistercian nuns, the association of food and fasting with women, both religious and secular, and bodily issues such as fragmentation, resurrection, and transformation. This selection first appeared in Harvard Theological Review 70 (1977): 257–84, *and is reproduced with permission from that volume. It was later expanded as part of a collection of essays,* Jesus as Mother: Studies in the Spirituality of the Central Middle Ages.

*　*　*

A number of scholars in this century have noticed the image of God or Jesus as mother in the spiritual writings of the central Middle Ages.[1] The image has in general been seen as part of a "feminine" or "affective" spirituality, and neither of these adjectives is incorrect.[2] The idea of God as mother is part of a widespread use, in twelfth-century spiritual writing, of woman, mother, characteristics agreed to be "feminine," and the sexual union of male and female as images to express spiritual truths; the most familiar manifestation of this interest in the "female" is the new emphasis on the Virgin in doctrinal discussions and especially spirituality.[3] And the frequency of references to "mother Jesus" is also part of a new tendency in twelfth-century writing to use human relationships (friendship, fatherhood or motherhood, erotic love) in addition to metaphysical or psychological entities to explain doctrinal positions or exhort spiritual growth.[4] But characterizations of the "mother Jesus" theme as "feminine" or "affective" are also somewhat misleading. The use of characteristics agreed to be "maternal" to talk about God emerges very strongly in male writers of the twelfth century and is part of a broader tendency to attribute "maternal" characteristics to male religious authorities; to call this usage "feminine" is therefore confusing and may obscure an important contrast with the later Middle Ages, a period in which such imagery was very popular with female writers.[5] Moreover, simply to describe this particular image as part of the "affectivity" of later medieval religious life not only ignores the patristic roots of the image and of the general twelfth-century interest in the human Christ. It also fails to note the particular characteristics of the twelfth-century theme, which puts much less emphasis than the later medieval image on suffering and birth-as-separation, and much more emphasis on breasts and nurturing, the womb, conception, and union as incorporation.[6]

In this chapter I want to suggest that the use of maternal imagery to describe God and Christ, who are usually described as "male," was more widespread in twelfth-century spiritual writing than has previously been noticed[7] and that the image itself is far more complex. I shall do this by discussing the Cistercians: Bernard of Clairvaux, Aelred of Rievaulx, Guerric of Igny, Isaac of Stella, Adam of Perseigne, and Helinand of Froidmont; William of Saint-Thierry, a black Benedictine who became a Cistercian only late in life; and the Benedictine Anselm of Canterbury, from whom certain of these later writers perhaps borrowed their maternal imagery.[8] I concentrate on these authors not because the image occurs nowhere outside them (it appears casually in a number of works and contexts)[9] but because I have not found it developed at such length in other twelfth-century writers.[10] But my purpose is not just to describe the image. I want also to suggest that we can understand why it occurs only if we look at its context as well as its sources. As André Cabassut pointed out a number of years ago, maternal imagery was applied in the Middle Ages to male religious authority figures, particularly abbots, bishops, and the apostles, as well as to God and Christ.[11] Moreover, the use of maternal imagery to talk about "male" figures is developed in the twelfth century by cloistered authors with particular reference to a cloistered setting. Thus in order to explain this particular image, it is necessary to explore generally (and to suggest some conclusions about) twelfth-century religious language and twelfth-century life.

I

Let me begin by giving six examples of twelfth-century authors who use the idea of motherhood (physiological or psychological) to talk about figures usually described in "male" language. Anselm of Bec (d. 1109), later archbishop of Canterbury, in his *Monologion* objects to calling God "mother" both because male is superior to (i.e. stronger than) female and because (according to his understanding of biology) the father contributes more to the child than the mother in the process of reproduction.[12] Nonetheless he speaks in a particularly lyrical prayer of both Paul and Jesus as "mothers" to the individual soul. In this passage Anselm associates "mother" as well as "father" with "engendering" and stresses the mother as one who gives birth, even dying to give the child life; but the contrast which he draws between Jesus as father and Jesus as mother stresses the father as one who rules and produces, the mother as one who loves. In an association of images that continues throughout the twelfth century,[13] Anselm describes the consoling, nurturing Jesus as a hen gathering her chicks under her wing (Matthew 23.37) and suggests that mother Jesus revives the soul at her breast:

> You [Paul] [are] among Christians like a nurse who not only cares for her children but also gives birth to them a second time by the solicitude of her marvelous love.
>
> Gentle nurse, gentle mother, who are these sons to whom you give birth and nurture if not those whom you bear and educate in the faith of Christ by your teaching? . . . For, as that blessed faith is born and nurtured in us by the other apostles also, how much more by you, because you have labored and accomplished more in this than all the others . . . . O mother of well-known tenderness, may your son feel your heart [viscera] of maternal piety . . . .
>
> But you, Jesus, good lord, are you not also a mother? Are you not that mother who, like a hen, collects her chickens under her wings?

22

Truly, master, you are a mother. For what others have conceived and given birth to, they have received from you. ... You are the author, others are the ministers. It is then you, above all, Lord God, who are mother.

Both of you [Paul and Jesus] are therefore mothers .... For you accomplished, one through the other, and one through himself, that we, born to die, may be re-born to life. Fathers you are then by result, mothers by affection; fathers by authority, mothers by kindness; fathers by protection, mothers by compassion. You [Lord] are a mother and you [Paul] are also. Unequal by extent of love, you do not differ in quality of love .... You have given birth to me when you made me a Christian, ... You [Lord] by the teaching coming from you and you [Paul] by the teaching he inspires in you ....

Paul, mother, ... lay then your dead son [i.e. the sinful soul] at the feet of Christ, your mother, for he is her son. Or rather throw him into the bosom [sinus] of Christ's love, for Christ is even more his mother. Pray that he may revive this dead son, not so much yours as his. Do, mother of my soul, what the mother of my flesh would do ....

And you also, soul, dead by yourself, run under the wings of your mother Jesus and bewail your sorrows under his wings.

Christ, mother, who gather under your wings your little ones, your dead chick seeks refuge under your wings. For by your gentleness, those who are hurt are comforted, by your perfume the despairing are reformed. Your warmth resuscitates the dead; your touch justifies sinners .... Console your chicken, resuscitate your dead one, justify your sinner. May your injured one be consoled by you; may he who of himself despairs be comforted by you and reformed through you in your complete and unceasing grace. For the consolation of the wretched flows from you, blessed, world without end. Amen.[14]

Bernard of Clairvaux (d. 1153), whose use of maternal imagery for "male" figures is more extensive and complex than that of any other twelfth-century figure, uses "mother" to describe Jesus, Moses, Peter, Paul, prelates in general, abbots in general, and, most frequently, himself as abbot.[15] To Bernard, the maternal image is almost without exception[16] elaborated not as giving birth or even as conceiving or sheltering in a womb but as nurturing, particularly suckling. Breasts, to Bernard, are a symbol of the pouring out toward others of affectivity or of instruction and almost invariably suggest to him a discussion of the duties of prelates or abbots. Interestingly enough, Bernard not only develops an elaborate picture of the abbot (he usually has himself in mind) as mother, contrasting *mater* with *magister* (or *dominus*) and stating repeatedly that a mother is one who cannot fail to love her child;[17] he also frequently attributes "maternal" characteristics, especially suckling with milk, to the abbot when he refers to him as "father." He does not, however, reject the conception of the "father" as disciplinarian.[18]

Many of Bernard's references to himself as mother occur casually in letters. He admonishes the parents of Geoffrey of Péronne when he enters the monastery of Clairvaux:

> Do not be sad about your Geoffrey or shed any tears on his account, for he is going quickly to joy and not to sorrow. I will be for him both a mother and a father, both a brother and a sister. I will make the crooked path straight for him and the rough places smooth.[19]

He explains to his own monks his absence and his love for them:

> Sad is my soul until I shall return, and it does not wish to be comforted until I come to you . . . . Behold this is the third time, unless I am mistaken, that my sons have been torn from my heart, little ones, weaned before their time.[20]

To abbot Baldwin of Rieti he writes: "As a mother loves her only son, so I loved you, when you clung to my side pleasing my heart."[21] To Robert, whom he fears he has driven away by harshness, he explains (weaving together images of "father" and "mother"):

> Who else would not scold your disobedience and be angry at your desertion . . .? But I know your heart. I know that you can be led more easily by love than driven by fear . . . .
> And I have said this, my son, not to put you to shame, but to help you as a loving father because if you have many masters in Christ, yet you have few fathers. For if you will allow me to say so, I begot you in Religion by word and example. I nourished you with milk when, while yet a child, it was all you could take . . . . But alas! how soon and how early were you weaned . . . . Sadly I weep, not for my lost labour but for the unhappy state of my lost child . . . . My case is the same as that of the harlot Solomon judged, whose child was stealthily taken by another who had overlain and killed her own. You too were torn from my breast, cut from my womb. My heart cannot forget you, half of it went with you . . . .[22]

His letters also contain passing references to the motherhood of God:

> Do not let the roughness of our life frighten your tender years. If you feel the stings of temptation, . . . suck not so much the wounds as the breasts of the Crucified. He will be your mother, and you will be his son.[23]

But Bernard's most complex use of maternal imagery occurs in his sermons on the Song of Songs (Song of Solomon). Here he repeatedly chooses to explain references to breasts that are erotic in the biblical text with lengthy discussions of the obligation of prelates, especially abbots, to "mother" the souls in their charge. Commenting on the verse "For your breasts are better than wine, smelling sweet of the best ointments" (Song of Solomon 1.1–2), he first associates nursing with Christ the bridegroom:

> She [the bride, i.e. the soul] would seem to say to the bridegroom [Christ]: "What wonder if I presume to ask you for this favor, since your breasts have given me such overwhelming joy?" ... When she said, then, "Your breasts are better than wine," she meant: "The richness of the grace that flows from your breasts contributes far more to my spiritual progress than the biting reprimands of superiors."[24]

From this he moves to a discussion of "those who have undertaken the direction of souls":

> how many [of them] there are today who reveal their lack of the requisite qualities! ... They display an insatiable passion for gains. ... Neither the peril of souls nor their salvation gives them any concern. They are certainly devoid of the maternal instinct .... There is no pretense about a true mother, the breasts that she displays are full for the taking. She knows how to rejoice with those who rejoice, and to be sad with those who sorrow (Romans 12.15), pressing the milk of encouragement without intermission from the breast of joyful sympathy, the milk of consolation from the breast of compassion.[25]

A number of sermons later Bernard returns to a discussion of "breasts," which suggest to him the subject of "mothers"; and once again "mothers" suggest to him the responsibility of prelates:

> Here is a point for the ear of those superiors who wish always to inspire fear in their communities and rarely promote their welfare. Learn, you who rule the earth (Psalms 2.10). Learn that you must be mothers to those in your care, not masters; make an effort to arouse the response of love, not that of fear; and should there be occasional need for severity, let it be paternal rather than tyrannical. Show affection as a mother would, correct like a father. Be gentle, avoid harshness, do not resort to blows, expose your breasts: let your bosoms expand with milk, not swell with passion .... Why will the young man, bitten by the serpent, shy away from the judgment of the priest, to whom he ought rather to run as to the bosom of a mother? If you are spiritual, instruct him in a spirit of gentleness ....[26]

And, still later, Bernard returns to breasts and nursing as symbols of preaching:

> Take note however that she [the bride] yearns for one thing and receives another. In spite of her longing for the repose of contemplation she is burdened with the task of preaching; and despite her desire to bask in the bridegroom's presence she is entrusted with cares of begetting and rearing children. [Just as once before, she is reminded that] she [is] a mother, that her duty [is] to suckle her babes, to provide food for her children . . . . We learn from this that only too often we must interrupt the sweet kisses to feed the needy with the milk of doctrine.[27]

In contrast to Bernard, William of Saint-Thierry (d. 1148) avoids explicit references to God as "mother," using "father and child" or "bridegroom and bride" to describe the soul's relationship to God. But, like Bernard, William expounds the references to breasts in the Song of Songs as descriptions of Christ feeding and instructing the individual soul:[28]

> it is your breasts, O eternal Wisdom, that nourish the holy infancy of your little ones . . . . Since that everlasting blessed union and the kiss of eternity are denied the Bride on account of her human condition and weakness, she turns to your bosom; and not attaining to that mouth of yours, she puts her mouth to your breasts instead . . . .[29]

Like Bernard, William uses such references to breasts as opportunities to discuss the burdens of the abbacy.[30] And elsewhere in his works, despite the fact that "Eve" or "woman" is frequently for him a symbol of weakness or of the flesh,[31] he includes references to Christ nursing his children, to the fostering wings of Jesus, and references (perhaps with "womb" overtones) to the soul entering the side of Christ:

> It was not the least of the chief reasons for your incarnation that your babes in the church, who still needed your milk rather than solid food, who are not strong enough spiritually to think of you in your own way, might find in you a form not unfamiliar to themselves.[32]

> Those unsearchable riches of your glory, Lord, were hidden in your secret place in heaven until the soldier's spear opened the side of your Son our Lord and Savior on the cross, and from it flowed the mysteries of our redemption. Now we may not only thrust our fingers or our hand into his side, like Thomas, but through that open door may enter whole, O Jesus, even into your heart, the sure seat of your mercy . . . .

... Open to us your body's side, that those who long to see the secrets of your Son may enter in, and may receive the sacraments that flow therefrom, even the price of their redemption.[33]

Lord, whither do you draw those whom you thus embrace and enfold, save to your heart? The manna of your Godhead, which you, O Jesus, keep within the golden vessel of your all-wise human soul, is your secret heart .... Blessed are the souls whom you have hidden in your heart, that inmost hiding place, so that your arms overshadow them from the disquieting of men and they hope only in your covering and fostering wings.[34]

Guerric, abbot of Igny (d. 1157) is, after Bernard, the Cistercian who makes most frequent and complex use of maternal imagery to speak of God and male authority figures. Guerric uses "motherhood" to describe the relationship of Christ, Peter and Paul, and prelates in general to the soul of the individual believer; he also reverses the image, using "maternity" to describe the birth or incorporation of Christ in the individual soul:[35]

Give to the church, he [Solomon] says, the living infant, for she is its mother. Whoever does his will [Christ's], he is his mother and brother and sister.

Lord Solomon, you call me mother .... And indeed I will show myself a mother by love and anxious care to the best of my ability. ...

Brethren, this name of mother is not restricted to prelates, although they are charged in a special way with maternal solicitude and devotion; it is shared by you too who do the Lord's will. Yes, you too are mothers of the child who has been born for you and in you, that is, since you conceived from the fear of the Lord and gave birth to the spirit of salvation.[36]

Unlike Bernard, Guerric is fascinated by images of pregnancy and of the womb. He not only speaks at length of the soul hiding in the wounds and heart of Christ; he also explicitly associates heart and womb[37] and produces a bizarre description of the soul as child incorporated into the bowels of God the father:

He [God the father] draws them [the wretched] into his very bowels and makes them his members. He could not bind us to himself more closely, could not make us more intimate to himself than by incorporating us into himself.[38]

He [Christ] is the cleft rock ... do not fly only to him but into him. ... For in his loving kindness and his compassion he opened his side in order that the blood of the wound might give you life, the warmth of his body revive you, the breath of his heart flow into you. . . . There you will lie hidden in safety . . . . There you will certainly not freeze, since in the bowels of Christ charity does not grow cold.[39]

Thus, to Guerric, the maternity which is associated with the womb is a symbol of fertility, security, and union more than a symbol of separation, suffering, or sacrifice. And Guerric, like Bernard, uses maternal attributes to expand and change what he means by "father.[40] But Guerric also, when he contrasts "fathering" and "mothering," associates "engendering" and "authority" with the father, "nursing" and "loving" with the mother;[41] and his most extensive images are images of breasts and milk:

> The Bridegroom [Christ] . . . has breasts, lest he should be lacking any one of all the duties and titles of loving kindness. He is a father in virtue of natural creation . . . and also in virtue of the authority with which he instructs. He is a mother, too, in the mildness of his affection, and a nurse . . . .
>
> But behold all at once the Holy Spirit was sent from heaven like milk poured out from Christ's own breasts, and Peter was filled with an abundance of milk. Not long afterwards Saul became Paul, the persecutor became the preacher, the torturer became the mother, the executioner became the nurse, so that you might truly understand that the whole of his blood was changed into the sweetness of milk, his cruelty into loving kindness.[42]

The image of God as mother is less important to Aelred of Rievaulx (d. 1167) than to Guerric; meditation on the infancy and childhood of Jesus is more important. But Aelred elaborates the idea of Jesus as nursing mother as well as the image of Jesus our brother suckled at the Virgin's breasts:[43]

> On your altar let it be enough for you to have a representation of our Savior hanging on the cross; that will bring before your mind his Passion for you to imitate, his outspread arms will invite you to embrace him, his naked breasts will feed you with the milk of sweetness to console you.[44]

In a complex discussion of John reclining on Jesus' breast, Aelred says that John drinks the wine of knowledge of God whereas the soul of the ordinary believer feeds on the milk which flows from Christ's humanity.[45] The blood which flows from the wound in Christ's side becomes wine, the water becomes milk; and the soul not only draws nurture from Christ but also flees for refuge into the wound (and possibly womb?) in the wall of his body:

> Then one of the soldiers opened his side with a lance and there came forth blood and water. Hasten, linger not, eat the honeycomb with

your honey, drink your wine with your milk. The blood is changed into wine to gladden you, the water into milk to nourish you. From the rock streams have flowed for you, wounds have been made in his limbs, holes in the wall of his body, in which, like a dove, you may hide while you kiss them one by one. Your lips, stained with his blood, will become like a scarlet ribbon and your word sweet.[46]

And Aelred, like other Cistercian authors, moves naturally from a discussion of parents and nursing to a discussion of the heavy burdens borne by religious leaders:

But while the holy soul lingers in these delights [i.e. the child Jesus remains behind in Jerusalem] its mother and foster-father grieve; complain and search; when at length they find it they upbraid it with gentle reproaches and take it back to Nazareth. This can be applied in particular to those spiritual men who have been entrusted with preaching God's Word and caring for souls. Further, our foster-father I would interpret most readily as the Holy Spirit and nothing is better fitted to serve as our mother than charity. These cherish and make us advance, feed and nourish us, and refresh us with the milk of twofold affection: love, that is, for God and for neighbor.[47]

His biographer reports that his dying words to his own monks were: "I, love you all . . . as earnestly as a mother does her sons."[48]

Adam, abbot of Perseigne (d. 1221), is the only twelfth-century Cistercian writer to emphasize the pains of labor when he uses maternal imagery or to draw extensively on the biblical reference to the woman in travail (John 16.21). In this he is closer to Anselm than are the earlier Cistercian writers. But in contrast to Anselm's stress on Christ's suffering for the soul, Adam's use of giving birth as an image is almost completely restricted to discussion of the soul's fertility in good works or of the solicitude of abbots (or bishops) for their charges.[49] Adam insists that a good father must also be a good mother (i.e. prelates must give birth to as well as engender).[50] When he turns to the soul's relationship to God, however, it is nursing not giving birth that becomes the dominant image; and, to Adam, the nurse is usually the Virgin. We, the children, drink Christ, the milk, at the Virgin's breasts and so become the brothers of Christ in a special sense, that is, those who nurse at the breast alongside him.[51] "Do you think," writes Adam, "that this most loving of all children would refuse to his nursing brothers the womb or the breasts of his mother, when he has chosen her precisely for mother so that she may be the nurse of the humble?"[52] Moreover, Adam also speaks of the prelate as nurturing, using the hen-and-chicks metaphor (which he supplements with references to the strength of eagles).[53] To the bishop of Le Mans, he writes:

Besides, in what way are you yourself named father or mother of little ones, you who do not jealously watch over your chicks with tender affection as a hen does, or like an eagle provoking her chicks to fly flutter over them and bear upwards in your wings both by word and example those little ones commended to you?[54]

II

Modern scholars and editors have often been embarrassed by these elaborate and physiologically explicit images.[55] But if we attempt to analyze them rather than explain them away, two clear patterns emerge. First of all, the images assume certain sexual stereotypes – that is, they show that, to these religious writers, certain personality characteristics were seen as female and certain characteristics as male. Throughout these texts, gentleness, compassion, tenderness, emotionality and love, nurturing, and security are labeled female (or "maternal"); authority, judgment, command, strictness, and discipline are labeled male (or "paternal"); instruction, fertility, and creativity are associated with both sexes (either as begetting or as conceiving). Moreover, these stereotypes remain the same whether they are evaluated as negative or positive. Thus to Adam of Perseigne, the maternal and female is strong;[56] to William of Saint-Thierry the female is a symbol of both weakness and penitence.[57] And Helinand of Froidmont (d. *c.*1229) gives a complex and repeated explanation of *mulier* as related to *mollis* ("soft" in the sense of "weak") and *malleus* ("hammer" in the sense of "scourge") – an explanation which is intended to interpret the tenderness of women in a very pejorative light.[58] Because these sexual stereotypes are constant throughout the literature, it seems clear that authors spoke of "fathers" as "nursing" or joined "mother" to "father" in their descriptions (whether of God, the apostles, prelates, or of themselves) in order to add a specific dimension to their general conception of leadership, authority, and pastoral concern.

A second pattern unites these images which is as obvious as the first. Both in references to earthly authority figures and in reference to God, a maternal image is an image of dependence or union or incorporation. Breasts and nurturing are more frequent images in this literature than conceiving and giving birth. And where birth and the womb are dominant images, the mother is usually described as one who conceives and carries the child in her womb, not as one who ejects the child into the world, suffering pain and possibly death in order to give life. Conceiving and giving birth, like suckling, are thus images primarily of fertility, return or union, security, protection, dependence, or incorporation, not images of alienation, sacrifice, or emergence in the sense of separation. References to God as mother usually occur, not in the context of castigation of sinners or elaboration of the gulf between human and divine, but rather as part of a general picture of the believer as child or beginner, totally dependent on a loving and tender God. Indeed descriptions of the soul as nursing child are even more common than explicit references to the breasts of God: when the soul is described as Christ's brother, for example, it is usually seen as a brother of the nursing not the adult Christ.[59] Descriptions of prelates as mothers are more likely to refer to birth pangs than are maternal images of God. But even when the pain of giving birth is used to describe abbots or bishops, it is not an image which denotes separation or alienation of prelates and their charges; it is rather a description of the extreme difficulty of being a good father/mother in the practice of pastoral care.

III

Why then do twelfth-century spiritual writers make repeated use of a network of maternal metaphors that has been almost completely absent in modern devotion? And why do the images have the particular characteristics they have? An answer to these questions must begin with a discussion of sources, for the use of "maternal" or "female" images to describe "male" figures was not uncommon in earlier Christian literature. In the Old Testament, God speaks of himself as a mother, bearing the Israelites in his bosom, conceiving them in his womb (Isaiah 49.1 and 66.3).[60] In the New Testament, such imagery is nonexistent.[61] But Christ is described as a hen gathering her chicks under her wings (Matthew 23.37). And the contrast drawn in the Epistles between milk and meat as a symbol of types of instruction and levels of spiritual growth (1 Corinthians 3.1–2; Hebrews 5.12; 1 Peter 2.2) seems to have suggested to later writers that the apostles responsible for the Epistles, Peter and Paul, themselves provided the milk for beginners and should therefore be seen as mothers. Cabassut has noted that the apocryphal *Acts of Peter* in the third century addresses Christ as "father," "mother," "brother," "friend," and "servant" (although the Latin translator suppressed "mother" in his version).[62] Elaine Pagels, in a recent article, has pointed out the use of "God as mother" in Clement of Alexandria (d. 215) and Origen (d. 254), connecting the theme to Gnostic conceptions of God.[63] The *Regula magistri* and later monastic texts refer to the abbot as "mother";[64] and there are scattered references throughout the Fathers, Greek and Latin, to God and Christ as maternal.[65] The more popular theme of the church as (virgin) mother, common in the early patristic period probably because it expressed so perfectly the nature of an entity withdrawn from the world (virgin) yet expanding and converting (mother), was used in the eleventh and twelfth centuries by reformers to express very different concerns.[66] Although it is not a "female" theme applied to "male" figures, it suggested to twelfth-century authors an association of instruction and pastoral responsibility with maternity and nurturing.

Furthermore, inversion of language and therefore of values is a New Testament literary technique ("Hath not God made foolish the wisdom of this world?," 1 Corinthians 1.20; "But many that are first shall be last," Mark 10.31; etc.), which twelfth-century authors such as Adam and Bernard used quite consciously. Bernard writes:

> I rightly apply to myself those words of the Prophet: . . . "Play the mountebank I will . . . ." A good sort of playing this . . . by which we become an object of reproach to the rich and of ridicule to the proud. In fact what else do seculars think we are doing but playing when what they desire most on earth, we fly from; and what they fly from, we desire? [We are] like acrobats and jugglers, who with heads down and feet up, stand or walk on their hands . . . . And we too play this game that we may be ridiculed, discomfited, humbled, until he comes who puts down the mighty from their seats and exalts the humble.[67]

When he distinguishes monks and clergy by calling monks "women" and clergy "men," Bernard means to suggest that monks have a weakness and unworldliness that is valued in God's eyes as humility.[68] Thus sexually inverted images (i.e. calling men "women") were part of a larger pattern of using inverted language to express personal dependence and the dependence of one's values on God.

But the mere existence of earlier literary techniques or "maternal" texts does not explain why twelfth-century authors chose to borrow them. And closer exploration reveals some basic differences between patristic and twelfth-century uses of the theme of God as mother. By far the fullest patristic elaboration of the theme (fuller in fact than any of the twelfth-century references) occurs in Clement of Alexandria's *Paedagogus*, but Clement nowhere moves from a discussion of Christ as pedagogue and mother to a discussion of the responsibilities of prelates or clergy.[69] And Origen's commentary on the Song of Songs, which opens with a discussion of levels of knowledge as "milk" and "meat," does not elaborate these references into a discussion of either prelates or Christ as mother; nor does Origen choose to explain the breasts of the bridegroom (Song of Solomon 1.2) as a nursing image, let alone use it, as do Bernard and William, to introduce a discussion of the burdens of pastoral responsibility.[70]

Certain twelfth-century assumptions about family and about physiology may help to explain why some texts were borrowed and interpreted as they were. It is obvious that family relationships are very natural images and symbols in any pre-industrial society. Moreover, twelfth-century people assumed that breast milk was processed blood and also that the ideal child-rearing pattern was for the mother to nurse her own child; thus, according to their physiological theory, the loving mother did feed her child with her own blood.[71] Clement of Alexandria in the second century goes to great lengths to explain the relationship of breast milk to the blood supplied to the foetus. He does this in order to link biblical passages about Christ offering milk to the young and meat to adults with the establishment of the sacrament of bread (flesh) and wine (blood). The entire discussion is an elaboration of the theme of Christ as mother. In Clement's extended exegesis we find spelled out the connection between the blood flowing from Christ's side and the milk flowing from maternal breasts that lies behind many twelfth-century metaphors.[72] Although legends of the lactation of Saint Bernard by the Virgin Mary appear only at the very end of the period I am considering, it is significant that one of the earliest versions associates the blood flowing from Christ's heart with the milk flowing from the Virgin's breasts as parallel offers of comfort to the praying Bernard.[73] Moreover the association of biblical texts and images that lay behind the emergence in the twelfth and thirteenth centuries of the devotion to the sacred heart of Jesus appears to have maternal overtones in a physiological sense. Out of the idea that John reclining on Christ's breast "drinks wisdom" and those passages in the Song of Songs which refer to the "wounds of love" and the "clefts in the rock where the dove hides," twelfth-century authors such as Hildegard of Bingen (d. 1179) and Aelred of Rievaulx construct the idea that the soul enters Christ's side, nurses from it as if from a breast, and is born from it as from a womb.[74] Thus legends of lactation and the emerging devotion to the sacred heart probably both contributed to and expressed a general tendency to associate birth and suckling with the figure of Jesus.

Modern scholars have sometimes suggested that imagery mirrors life, that the use of "marriage" or "mothering" as images for spiritual truths reflects a positive evaluation of these institutions in society or even that a maternal conception of God reflects a greater equality for women in society or theology.[75] The twelfth-century situation is, however, more complicated. While there was some new emphasis in theology on the spiritual equality of women,[76] some renewed interest among male leaders in the spiritual direction of women,[77] and some tendency in hagiography and monastic writing to stress the influence of actual mothers and of "maternal" qualities on the spiritual development of children,[78] there was certainly in the general society no "mystique" of motherhood; both medical texts and exhortations to virginity dwell on the horrors of pregnancy and the inconveniences of marriage.[79] Not only do discussions of asceticism warn against family ties; even authors who speak of the parent–child relationship as a kind of love see it as a lower form; lower, that is, than friendship or the love of husband and wife.[80] And those same authors who equate "motherhood" or the Virgin Mary with compassion and nurture also use "woman" as a symbol of physical or spiritual weakness, of the flesh, of sin, of inability to bear burdens or resist temptation.[81] By the end of the twelfth century, the wave of misogyny was strong enough to bring a sharp curtailment in the places for women in the most important of the new religious orders.[82] Indeed it may be that twelfth-century cloistered males felt comfortable using "feminine" imagery for themselves only because they were cut off completely from the temptation of women in their lives. Bernard of Clairvaux certainly links receptivity to the "mothering" of Jesus with renunciation of earthly mothers. The passage from letter 322 quoted on p. 24 (". . . suck not so much the wounds as the breasts of the Crucified . . .") continues:

He [Christ] will be your mother . . . . But "a man's household are his own enemies." These are they who love not you but the satisfaction they derive from you . . . . And now hear what blessed Jerome says: "If your mother should lie prostrate at the door, if she should bare her breasts, the breasts that gave you suck, . . . yet with dry eyes fixed upon the cross go ahead and tread over your prostrate mother and father. It is the height of piety to be cruel for Christ's sake." Do not be moved by the tears of demented parents who weep because from being a child of wrath you have become a child of God.[83]

Isaac of Stella (d. 1169) links the parenthood of God with even harsher rejection of earthly family:

For myself I declare that I am a stranger and pilgrim here below . . . . I am not a son of man but a son of God hidden under the appearance and resemblance of man; henceforth I am not the son of my father and mother, nor the brother of my brother, even if they say, affirm and swear falsely that I am theirs. If they produce witnesses and if they signal with recognizable marks on my skin and in my flesh, I have awareness myself of my origin and I persist in denying; I protest that I am not what they say . . . . Indeed we are all orphans; we have no father on earth for our father is in heaven and our mother is a virgin. It is from there that we have our origins . . . .[84]

Thus in some cases monastic idealizing of maternal qualities may reflect hostility toward rather than admiration of real mothers.[85]

It therefore seems to me that we should not read the somewhat sentimentalized maternal imagery of twelfth-century spiritual writing as an indication of a new respect for women or for mothers. Nor do I wish to turn the argument around and see in such imagery merely hostility toward real women or alienation from family.[86] Rather I wish to reject any approach which isolates imagery from context and then relates the isolated image directly to the world outside the cloister. Images can be understood only by discovering the other images among which they occur and the basic problems about which they are intended to speak. And, in the writings analyzed above, maternal imagery is used, to put it very simply, to talk about authority (good and bad) and dependence (good and bad). In the remainder of this article I shall therefore argue that the answer to the question "why did twelfth-century Cistercians speak of Jesus as mother?" lies in two things: in the ambivalence of these authors (all of them abbots) about the exercise of pastoral responsibility, and hence about authority in general, and in their deep sense of the life of the cloister as cut off from the world. To say this is not to propose that their conception of God is a projection of their own psyches. But it is to say that the language in which they chose to describe their relationship to God expressed the particular ideals and problems of the form of religious life they practiced.

In order to expand and substantiate this argument, I must now turn, one by one, to the two general aspects of maternal imagery noted in Section II (pp. 30–1).

IV

Twelfth-century authors have extraordinarily consistent stereotypes of "male" and "female," "father" and "mother." "Father" is associated with discipline, decision, and authority; "mother" with nurture and affectivity. When these authors apply maternal imagery to individuals not ordinarily considered female, they frequently use the phrase "father and mother" or "master (*magister, dominus*) and mother," thus clearly supplementing discipline with love. Even when the paired designation is not explicitly used, maternal imagery is almost invariably attached to those male figures whom both medieval and modern readers would see as authority figures: Moses, Peter and Paul (in their capacity as teachers), abbots, prelates, Jesus, God. Almost invariably such imagery adds something to these figures qua rulers or fathers; and the "something" it adds is always nurturing and affectivity. Thus the specific context in which maternal imagery appears suggests that twelfth-century authors saw God, abbots, and prelates as rulers, and that rule, to them, was problematic – i.e. that it needed to be complemented or corrected by something else. These authors appear to have supplemented their image of God with maternal metaphors because they needed to supplement their image of authority with that for which the "maternal" stood: emotion and nurture.

That the need to supplement authority with love is the motive behind much maternal imagery is perhaps clearest in the case of Bernard of Clairvaux. Gammersbach has suggested that the reason for Bernard's parallel descriptions of Christ and abbot lies in an explicit conception, found in the Benedictine Rule itself, of the abbot as image of Christ to his monks.[87] This is certainly correct. But this concept by itself would not explain why the description of both Christ and abbot has the content it does. More must be said. As I have already pointed out, Bernard's mind frequently leaps to the topic of responsibility when it finds feminine imagery; it leaps to maternal imagery when it must discuss rule or discipline (either human or divine). The addition of "mother" to "father" in these descriptions of God and prelates is not an exclusion of "fatherly" qualities (stern but caring discipline) from Bernard's image of authority any more than his addition of "father" to "judge" and "lord" is an elimination of rule and judgment.[88] But the fact that almost any biblical or passing reference to "mothering" or the "feminine" triggers in Bernard an agonized discussion of the burdens of pastoral care suggests that the exercise of authority is a problem for him which "being maternal" in some way alleviates.

Bernard reveals himself in his letters as a person who worried more about whether he loved adequately than about whether he was loved;[89] some of his need to supplement images of rule or command with images of nurture and affectivity may express his own psychological makeup. But the concern to add affectivity to rule appears in William, Guerric, Aelred, Adam, and Isaac of Stella as well. As I demonstrated in Sections I and II, these authors all use images of fertility, giving birth, and breast-feeding to stress the difficulties of being a good abbot, and images of fostering, protecting, nursing, and teaching to describe the good bishop.[90]

Moreover, in several of these authors, the effort to expand or supplement the conception of rule (divine and human) occurs in conjunction with intense and articulated ambivalence about their own exercise of leadership. William of Saint-Thierry several times expressed feelings of exhaustion and a desire to leave his abbacy, a desire upon which he finally acted.[91] Bernard often wished to renounce the cares of pastoral responsibility and return to contemplation, yet he issued violent rebukes to other abbots who acted upon such yearnings. His ambivalence is at times acute enough to seem a self-hatred, an antagonism toward the gift for administration and preaching which he knows himself to possess.[92] And even Aelred, who appears to have had a sunnier disposition than Bernard or William, expresses different views of the value of administration and pastoral responsibility depending on his audience. At least when writing for recluses, he rejects such activity in strident language.[93]

There are also institutional indications that the abbatial role was seen as a heavy burden in the twelfth century. The number of resignations was large. They are usually described in the hagiography as a search for solitude and contemplation, a description which may cover a multitude of motives but which is itself significant as an indication of what was admired.[94] And by the thirteenth century many of the new orders began to move toward a new institutional arrangement, election of abbots for a limited term rather than for life – clearly a response to twelfth-century feelings that lifelong rule was too great a burden both for the abbot and for his sons.[95]

The reasons for this ambivalence about rule are complex. Anxiety about taking on pastoral care (often expressed as a debate between the active and contemplative lives) was part of the monastic tradition. Some twelfth-century Cistercians, especially Aelred, began to make creative use of the traditional texts in a way that points toward a conception of one "life" which alternates between action and contemplation;[96] and almost every twelfth-century Cistercian author struggles toward a conception of "service" of neighbor that defines service as largely affective.[97] The concern of abbots about their role is thus part of a far larger Cistercian concern and ambivalence about the meaning of "love of neighbor" in monastic life.

Moreover, as the institution of child oblates was rejected and a greater emphasis was placed on adult choice and conversion,[98] it is possible that more demands were put on abbots to offer spiritual guidance to sensitive souls who worried about the quality of their inner life. Aelred of Rievaulx writes, drawing on his own experience as novice master, of the novice who worries because his gift of tears has dried up upon entering the monastery. Both Bernard and Adam of Perseigne speak of similarly delicate problems of spiritual direction.[99] It seems possible that adult or adolescent converts, whose awareness of having made a personal choice could be acute, needed fewer rules (or "discipline") and more advice (or "nurture") than the young children common in monastic houses a hundred years earlier. In any case, twelfth-century discussions of spiritual direction indicate that abbots were in fact called upon to respond with qualities men of the period considered "feminine." The large number of resignations, the unhappy musings of William and Bernard over the burdens of rule, the statement of even so temperate a man as Aelred that service of others is a fall from Christ[100] suggest that some abbots felt taxed or even trapped by the intense emotional response they now considered to be a necessary part of the "father/mother" role.

Considered in this context, it does not seem surprising that twelfth-century Cistercian authors articulated a new conception of authority (both the authority of God and the authority of the monastic superior), nor is it surprising that they used "maternal" imagery to express this concept.[101] The image of "mother" stood consistently for nurture and love throughout the literature of the period; the image of "woman" stood generally, although not universally, for "weakness." "Maternal" images could thus have negative or at least ambiguous connotations despite their consistent denotation of unflagging love. To speak of God, of apostles and bishops, abbots and novice masters, and of oneself, as *mater et pater* perfectly expressed an ideal of discipline plus affectivity. But it is also possible that describing themselves as "mothers" in their capacity as rulers was a good way for twelfth-century Cistercian males to express the ambivalence they felt about the necessity to rule, even if (perhaps especially if) the rule included nurture and emotional response.

V

But why was the image of God as mother used so frequently to express dependence, union, and incorporation? The answer to this question lies partly in certain fundamental characteristics of twelfth-century spirituality and theology. Despite the large amount of modern scholarship which stresses the "pessimism" of twelfth-century spiritual writing (i.e. pessimism about the value of the world, concern with sin, etc.),[102] the monastic writing of the period is better described by the characterizations of Robert Javelet and Richard W. Southern: "humanism," "personalism," and "dynamism."[103] Whatever particular theological issue is under discussion, a twelfth-century spiritual writer (at least when addressing monks) is apt to use it to describe the route to God. Thus, for example, both predestination and free will are used to convince readers that God is a goal toward which they are in fact moving. Such an attitude tends to use references to "sin" to stimulate not despair or guilt but a sense of progress toward and dependence on God. Whatever basic assumptions lie behind this optimism (and some of them are clearly neo-Platonic) it is well captured in the idea of God's motherhood as Bernard understood it: a mother cannot fail to love her child; sin is a tarnishing of what the child should be, a naughtiness, but the fundamental bond of mother–child remains.[104] Moreover, the traditional emphasis on monks as "beginners in the school for the service of God" certainly influenced Cistercian authors to elaborate for their fellow monks a picture of the soul at the very first stage of growth (for which the unweaned infant is an obvious metaphor).[105] Adam of Perseigne, for example, suggests that when the soul is itself a "child" it contemplates the humanity of Christ as a nursing baby; awareness of suffering and crucifixion (the adult Christ) can come only when the soul is an adult, ready for "meat" not "milk."[106]

But the general optimism of twelfth-century theology is only part of the context against which we should locate the concern for dependence on God that the theme "mother Jesus" expresses. We must also understand this concern against the background of cloistered, especially Cistercian, life. For, in the particular authors considered here, dependence on God is expressed in a number of relational and bodily images, some of which are not "feminine"; and the more concerned an author is with images of dependence and incorporation, the more likely he is to stress detachment from, independence from, and withdrawal from the world. Thus maternal imagery is part of a broad concern with dependence/independence, incorporation/withdrawal (or, to put it another way, with "true" and "false" dependence). And this concern lies behind not only the language that these authors employ but also their way of life.

If we look at the structure of Cistercian monasticism as it emerges in the early twelfth century we find a concern for independence from "the world" coupled with a concern for intense and humble dependence within church and cloister. In their economic and administrative arrangements, Cistercians tried to withdraw from power relationships with laity (as embodied in property relationships); yet they submitted themselves to episcopal authority, refusing at least initially to seek exemptions. They stressed solitude and withdrawal to the desert: of the authors studied here, Guerric was attracted to the solitary life; Isaac of Stella withdrew to a tiny, austere island community; and Adam of Perseigne and William of Saint-Thierry both changed orders in adulthood to seek a life of deeper withdrawal from the world.[107] Again and again their writings stress the renunciation of all family ties. Yet Cistercians in general opposed the eremitical movement, emphasizing the importance of dependence and interdependence within a community – interdependence in which all are servants and learners, not masters and teachers.[108]

Thus Cistercians seem to have viewed themselves as renouncing dependence on the world in order to embrace dependence within religious community as a way of learning dependence on God. Aelred of Rievaulx draws explicitly the connection between perfect detachment from the world and perfect union with both neighbor and God in love.[109] It is exactly this sense of renunciation of false dependence (on the world) in order to create true dependence (on God and community) that the imagery of Cistercian writings conveys. Each of the authors analyzed above emphasizes physical withdrawal from and renunciation of the world. Each uses maternal imagery to express an intense emotional dependence of the child-soul on God, a dependence for which the affective bond of abbot and monk is preparation. Several authors choose images which express the relationship of the soul to God in a way which also joins the soul with other souls (as, for example, nursing brothers of Christ). Indeed it seems no accident that the twelfth-century Cistercian author who writes with the greatest passion of the necessity for solitude and for the austere isolation of a tiny community – Isaac of Stella – has the most radical imagery of incorporation.[110] Isaac, who also uses images of bride (the soul) and bridegroom (Christ), mother (the Virgin Mary) and child (the soul),[111] develops a complex metaphor of the mystical body of Christ which goes so far as to claim that Christ himself is not complete until we are all incorporated into him.[112] Similarly, when Aelred of Rievaulx writes of Christ on the crucifix feeding the soul with milk, he immediately associates this feeding with the virginity of the watching soul, symbolized by John and Mary, and suggests that Christ from the cross gives the two virgins to each other for mutual love and comfort. This complex passage thus joins virginity (renunciation of the world), the motherhood of Christ, and the union of virgin souls in love not only with Christ but also with each other.[113]

One final piece of evidence (a sort of exception that proves the rule) may be adduced to support the argument that the Cistercian fondness for maternal imagery is related to their intense concern with dependence and independence. In contrast to every author studied above, a somewhat later Cistercian, the former troubador Helinand of Froidmont, shows no interest in the cloister as withdrawn or isolated, writes with little affectivity, and uses little imagery of incorporation (and little "feminine" imagery).[114] Helinand, who is far more interested in the organization of the church and the life of the clergy, is fond of the kind of building imagery that was popular with some regular canons.[115] It is significant that a Cistercian who lacks the intense interiority and sense of incorporation with God that characterizes other Cistercians lacks also any interest in the cloister either as solitude or as community. Thus it seems that those Cistercian authors who use maternal imagery for God develop it as part of an interest in affectivity and dependence which is tied to their sense of the cloister as independent of the world.

*   *   *

I have attempted in this chapter to talk about the ways in which one image (which turns out to be a cluster of images) expresses some of the basic values that are implicit in the life of a religious community. Cistercians drew their maternal imagery from earlier literature, particularly Anselm and the Bible. But I have tried to argue here that they used it to express immediate concerns: a need for affectivity in the exercise of authority and in the creation of community, and a complex rhythm of renouncing ties with the world while deepening ties within the community and between the soul and God. My analysis does not, I realize, answer all possible questions about maternal imagery in twelfth-century spiritual writing.[116] It does not try to say what in society or in the depths of the human psyche led to the consistent association of women with tenderness or of mothers with closeness, nor does it say why values such as emotionality and dependence on God, among others, became central in a religious community intended to renounce the values and ties of worldly society. To answer those questions would be to write another essay – one which would have to consider a far greater range of phenomena than I have explored here. But at least this analysis should make clear why we cannot isolate an image from its intellectual or its institutional context and why we cannot take it as literal comment on the objects or situations from which the metaphors are constructed. The maternal imagery of medieval monastic treatises tells us that cloistered males in the twelfth century idealized the "mothering" role, that they held consistent stereotypes of femaleness as "compassionate" and "soft" (either "weak" or "tender"), and that they saw the bond of child and mother as a symbol of closeness, union, or even the incorporation of one self into another. But it would be dangerous to argue that this imagery tells us what monks thought of actual women or of their own mothers. If religious symbols express the values of communities which use them and if those communities consciously transmute or invert the values of the world, then the monastic idea of mother Jesus tells us, at least directly, only what monks thought about Jesus and about themselves.

NOTES

1 I would like to thank Peter Brown, Giles Constable, and Judith Van Herik, who read earlier drafts of this article and made suggestions. I would also like to thank the students in Church History 224 at the Harvard Divinity School, especially Sharon A. Farmer, John Martin, Catherine Mooney, and Carol G. Rucker, whose papers suggested to me ideas or citations. None of these people is responsible for the opinions expressed here. A short paper, using material from Sections II and IV of this article, was presented at the Seventh Cistercian Studies Conference at Kalamazoo, Michigan, May 5–8, 1977.

2 André Cabassut, "Une dévotion médiévale peu connue: la dévotion à 'Jésus Notre Mère,'" *Mélanges Marcel Viller, Revue d'ascétique et de mystique* 25 (1949): 234–45; Giles Constable, "Twelfth-Century Spirituality and the Late Middle Ages," *Medieval and Renaissance Studies 5, Proceedings of the Southern Institute of Medieval and Renaissance Studies, Summer, 1969* (1971): 27–60; John Bugge, *Virginitas: An Essay in the History of a Medieval Ideal* (The Hague: Archives Internationales d'Histoire des Idées, 1975), esp. pp. 100–5; Eleanor C. McLaughlin, "'Christ My Mother': Feminine Naming and Metaphor in Medieval Spirituality," *Nashota Review* 15 (1975): 228–48. (See also

Ritamary Bradley, "The Motherhood Theme in Julian of Norwich," *Fourteenth-Century English Mystics Newsletter* 2.4 [1976]: 25–30, which came to my attention too late for use in this article.)

3   See Hilda C. Graef, *Mary: A History of Doctrine and Devotion*, 2 vols (New York: Sheed and Ward: 1964), vol. 1, esp. pp. 210–64.

4   See Robert Javelet, *Image et ressemblance au douzième siècle, de saint Anselme à Alain de Lille*, 2 vols (Paris: Université de Strasbourg, 1967), esp. vol. 1, pp. 451–61; Joseph A. Jungmann, "The Defeat of Teutonic Arianism and the Revolution of Religious Culture in the Early Middle Ages," in his *Pastoral Liturgy* (New York: Herder and Herder, 1962), pp. 48–63.

5   Hildegard of Bingen is the only female writer from the twelfth century whom I have found to use maternal imagery, although the point needs further investigation; for the later period see Cabassut, "Une dévotion médiévale," pp. 239–45, and E. McLaughlin, "'Christ My Mother,'" pp. 235–40. Bugge, *Virginitas*, pp. 100–5, suggests without proof that male writers are more apt to use feminine imagery when writing to women. It is true that Aelred's *De institutione inclusarum*, which uses maternal imagery, was written for anchoresses (see nn. 43–6) and that Adam of Perseigne uses such imagery in writing to women (see Adam of Perseigne, *Correspondance d'Adam, abbé de Perseigne [1188–1221]*, [ed. Jean Bouvet; *Archives historiques du Maine* 13, fascicules 1–10; Le Mans, 1951–62]; letters 45 and 55, 441–4 and 571–80; *Patrologia Latina* [hereafter *PL*], vol. 211, cols 623–4 and 659–64). But I find in the twelfth century no general pattern of using female imagery especially when addressing women.

6   On this point I differ from Cabassut who felt that Christ's death as a giving birth was the fundamental idea behind the "mother Jesus" theme wherever it occurred.

7   For the twelfth century, E. McLaughlin and Cabassut discuss only Bernard of Clairvaux.

8   This was Cabassut's conclusion, "Une dévotion médiévale," p. 239. The general influence of Anselm, particularly Anselm's prayers, on the Cistercians is well known: see J. Lewicki, "Anselme et les doctrines des Cisterciens de XIIe siècle," *Analecta Anselmiana* 2 (1970): 209–16; S.Vanni Rovighi, "Notes sur l'influence de saint Anselme au XIIe siècle," *Cahiers de civilisation médiévale* 8 (1965): 46–50. Of the texts studied here, Guerric of Igny's treatment of Peter and Paul (see n. 35) is so close to Anselm's (see n. 14) as to suggest that the similarity cannot be coincidental.

9   For example, God or Jesus as mother: Hugh Lacerta, *Liber de doctrina vel liber sententiarum seu rationum beati viri Stephani primi patris religionis Grandmontis*, CC:CM 8 (Turnhout, 1968), chs 10, 14; *Ancrene Riwle: The English Text of the Cotton Nero A.XIV*, ed. Mabel Day (London: Early English Text Society, 1952), p. 103. The bishop as mother: Gerhoh of Reichersberg, *Liber de aedificio Dei*, ed. E. Sackur, *MGH, Libelli*, vol. 3, p. 201.

10 This analysis is thus not an argument that the theme "mother Jesus" is an exclusively or peculiarly "Cistercian" theme; the fact that it occurs in some form in Anselm, William of Saint-Thierry, and Stephen of Muret (see n. 9) would refute this argument. But in the twelfth century the theme occurs in its fullest elaboration in Cistercian authors and, as I suggest below, there are aspects of Cistercian life and spirituality that explain this fact.

11 Cabassut, "Une dévotion médiévale," p. 235.

12 Anselm, *Monologion*, ch. 42, *Opera omnia*, ed. Francis S. Schmitt (Edinburgh, 1946) vol. 1, p. 58. This view of the respective male and female contributions to reproduction was the common one in the Middle Ages; see Vern L. Bullough, "Medieval Medical and Scientific Views of Women," *Viator: Medieval and Renaissance Studies* 4 (1973): 487–93.

13 See nn. 34 and 54. Even in Helinand of Froidmont, who uses less "feminine" imagery, the hen-and-chicks reference occurs to describe both Christ's advent in the

human heart and the parallel roles of Christ and abbot: see Helinand de Froidmont, sermons 6 and 14, *PL*, vol. 212, cols 531D and 591–4.

14   Anselm, prayer 10 to St Paul, *Opera omnia* ed. Schmitt, vol. 3, pp. 33 and 39–41; see also *Méditations et prières de saint Anselme*, trans. A. Castel, introduction by A. Wilmart (Paris and Maredsous: Collection Pax, 1923), pp. i–lxii and 48–61.

15   JESUS: Bernard of Clairvaux, letter 322, "Epistolae," ed. Jean Mabillon, *PL*, vol. 182, col. 527C; Bernard, *Sermones super Cantica Canticorum, S. Bernardi Opera Omnia*, vols 1 and 2, ed. Jean Leclercq, Charles H. Talbot, Henri M. Rochais (Rome: Editiones cistercienses, 1957) I, sermon 9.5–10 and sermon 10.1–4, 45–50. MOSES: *Super Cantica* 1, sermon 12.4, 62–63. PETER: letter 238, *PL*, vol. 182, col. 429C–D. PAUL: *Super Cantica* I, sermon 12.2, 61; ibid. 2, sermon 85.12, 315. PRELATES OR ABBOTS: *Super Cantica* 1, sermon 9.9, 47; sermon 10.2–3, 49–50; sermon 23.2 and 7–8, 139–40 and 142–4; ibid. 2, sermon 41.5–6, 31–2. SELF: letter 1, *PL*, vol. 182, col. 76A–B; letter 71, col. 183B–84A; letter 110, col. 253; letter 146, col. 303B–C; letter 152, col. 312A; letter 201, col. 369B–C; letter 258, cols 466B–67A; and *Super Cantica* 1, sermon 29.6, 207. See also Suibert Gammersbach, "Das Abtsbild in Cluny und bei Bernhard von Clairvaux," *Cîteaux in de Nederlanden* 7 (1956): 85–101, and Gervais Dumeige, "Bernard de Clairvaux, 'Père et Mère' de ses moines," *Études* 277 (1953): 304–20. Extensive discussions of CHARITY AS MOTHER are found in: letter 2, *PL*, vol. 182, cols 79D–81A, and letter 7, cols 93D–94C.

16   Passages in which Bernard sees "mothering" as "giving birth with pain": Bernard of Clairvaux, letter 146, *PL*, vol. 182, col. 303B–C; *Super Cantica* 1, sermon 29.6, 207. In letter 144, col. 301A–B, Bernard refers to the pain of having children torn away before the proper time for weaning, but this is clearly a nursing image.

17   Bernard of Clairvaux, *Super Cantica* 1, sermon 12.4, 62–63; sermon 23.2, 139–40; sermon 26.6, 173; letter 258, *PL*, vol. 182, cols 466A–67A; letter 300, cols 502A–C.

18   Bernard of Clairvaux, letter 1, *PL*, vol. 182, cols 67–79; letter 238, cols 427B–31A; *Super Cantica* 1, sermon 16.4–8, 91–4.

19   Bernard of Clairvaux, letter 110, *PL*, vol. 182, col. 253; trans. Bruno Scott James, *The Letters of Saint Bernard of Clairvaux* (London and Chicago, 1953), letter 112, 169.

20   Bernard of Clairvaux, letter 144, *PL*, vol. 182, cols 300B and 301A.

21   Bernard of Clairvaux, letter 201, *PL*, vol. 182, col. 369B–C.

22   Bernard of Clairvaux, letter 1, *PL*, vol. 182, cols 72 and 76A–C; trans. James, letter 1, 3, and 7, with my changes.

23   Bernard of Clairvaux, letter 322, *PL*, vol. 182, col. 527.

24   Bernard of Clairvaux, *Super Cantica* 1, sermon 9.5–6, 45–6; trans. Kiliam Walsh, *The Works of Bernard of Clairvaux* 2: *On the Song of Songs* 1 (Spencer, MA: Cistercian Fathers, 1971), pp. 57–8.

25   Bernard of Clairvaux, *Super Cantica* 1, sermon 10.3, 49–50, trans. Walsh, *Song* 1, pp. 62–3.

26   Bernard of Clairvaux, *Super Cantica* 1, sermon 23.2, 139–40; trans. Walsh, *Song* 2, p. 27.

27   Bernard of Clairvaux, *Super Cantica* 2, sermon 41.5–6, 31–2; trans. Walsh, *Song* 2, p. 208.

28   William of Saint-Thierry, *Exposé sur le Cantique des Cantiques*, ed. Jean-M. Déchanet (Paris: Editions du Cerf, 1962), chs 37–8, pp. 120–4; chs 44–6, pp. 132–6; and ch. 52, p. 144 (cf. ch. 83 on the breasts of the bride, pp. 200–2).

29   William of Saint-Thierry, *Sur le Cantique*, ch. 38, pp. 122–4; trans. Mother Columba Hart, *The Works of William of Saint-Thierry* 2: *Exposition on the Song of Songs* (Spencer, MA: Cistercian Fathers, 1970), p. 30.

30   William of Saint-Thierry, *Sur le Cantique*, ch. 52, p. 144, and see n. 91 below.

31   William of Saint-Thierry, *Meditativae Orationes*, nos. 4 and 5, *PL*, vol. 180, cols 216A and C and 221C; see also William, *La contemplation de Dieu: l'oraison de Dom*

Guillaume, ed. J. Hourlier (Paris: Sources chrétiennes, 1959), ch. 3, p. 64; and William, *Epistola ad fratres de Monte-Dei*, 1.37, *PL*, vol. 184, col. 332B.

32 William of Saint-Thierry, *Meditativae Orationes*, no. 10, *PL*, vol. 180, col. 236A; trans. Sister Penelope, *The Works of William of Saint-Thierry* 1: *On Contemplating God . . .* (Spencer, MA: Cistercian Fathers, 1971), pp. 152–3.

33 William of Saint-Thierry, *Meditativae Orationes*, no. 6, *PL*, vol. 180, cols 225D–6A; *Works* 1, p. 131. See n. 39 below.

34 William of Saint-Thierry, *Meditativae Orationes*, no. 8, *PL*, vol. 180, col. 230C; *Works* 1, p. 141.

35 Guerric of Igny, *Sermons*, ed. John Morson and Hilary Costello, 2 vols (Paris: Editions du Cerf, 1970 and 1973), vol. 1, third Christmas sermon, chs 4–5, pp. 196–200; first Epiphany sermon, ch. 6, p. 250; vol. 2, second sermon for Lent, ch. 2, p. 30; fourth sermon for Palm Sunday, ch. 5, pp. 210–14; second sermon for SS Peter and Paul, chs 1–6, pp. 380–94; second sermon for the Nativity of Mary, chs 3–5, pp. 490–6.

36 Guerric of Igny, *Sermons* 1, third Christmas sermon, chs 4–5, p. 198, as well as Guerric of Igny, *Liturgical Sermons*, trans. by the monks of Mount Saint Bernard abbey, 2 vols (Spencer, MA: Cistercian Fathers, 1970–1), vol. 1, p. 52.

37 Guerric of Igny, *Sermons* 2, second sermon for the Annunciation, ch. 4, p. 140; see also second and third sermons for the Annunciation, pp. 126–62 *passim*.

38 Guerric of Igny, *Sermons* 2, second sermon for Lent, ch. 2, 30; *Liturgical Sermons* 1, p. 142.

39 Guerric of Igny, *Sermons* 2, fourth sermon for Palm Sunday, pp. 212–14; *Liturgical Sermons* 2, pp. 77–8. In psychoanalytic theory, "bowels" is a standard womb symbol; see Sigmund Freud, "On the Sexual Theories of Children" (1908), *The Complete Psychological Works of Sigmund Freud*, ed. James Strachey and Anna Freud (London: Hogarth Press, 1959), pp. 207–26, esp. p. 219.

40 Guerric of Igny, *Sermons* 2, second sermon for Lent, pp. 26–36.

41 Guerric of Igny, *Sermons* 2, second sermon for SS Peter and Paul, pp. 380–94, and first sermon for the Assumption, pp. 414–26.

42 Guerric of Igny, *Sermons* 2, second sermon for SS Peter and Paul, ch. 2, pp. 384–6; *Liturgical Sermons* 2, p. 155.

43 Aelred of Rievaulx, "De Jesu puero duodenni," *Opera omnia* 1: *Opera ascetica*, ed. Anselm Hoste and Charles H. Talbot, *CC:CM* 1 (Turnhout, 1971), ch. 3.31, pp. 277–8 (cf. ibid., ch. 3.30, p. 276); and Aelred of Rievaulx, *De institutione inclusarum*, ch. 26, in Aelred, *Opera omnia* 1, p. 658, and ch. 31, vol. 1, pp. 668–71.

44 Aelred of Rievaulx, *De institutione*, ch. 26, *Opera omnia* 1, p. 658; trans. M. P. Mcpherson in *The Works of Aelred of Rievaulx* 1: *Treatises and Pastoral Prayer* (Spencer, MA: Cistercian Fathers, 1971), p. 73.

45 Aelred of Rievaulx, *De institutione*, ch. 31, *Opera omnia* 1, p. 668.

46 Aelred of Rievaulx, *De institutione*, ch. 31, *Opera omnia* 1, p. 671; Mcpherson, *Works* 1, pp. 90–1.

47 Aelred of Rievaulx, *De Jesu puero*, ch. 3.30, *Opera omnia* 1, p. 276; trans. Theodore Berkeley, *Works* 1, as cited in note 44.

48 Walter Daniel, *The Life of Ailred of Rievaulx*, trans. Frederick M. Powicke (London: Nelson, 1950), p. 58.

49 Adam of Perseigne, *Correspondance*, ed. Jean Bouvet, letter 2, pp. 20–2; letter 11, pp. 77–8; letter 41, p. 410; letter 50, p. 519, and *PL*, vol. 211, col. 623.

50 Adam of Perseigne, *Correspondance*, letter 2, pp. 20–2.

51 Adam of Perseigne, *Correspondance*, letter 35, pp. 305–7, and *PL*, vol. 211, cols 602–3; letter 45, p. 443, and *PL*, vol. 211, col. 624; letter 48, pp. 471–4 and 477, and *PL*, vol. 211, cols 635–6 and 638; letter 53, pp. 541–3 and 545–6, and *PL*, vol. 211, cols 604–5 and 607; letter 54, pp. 553–5. See also letter 64, pp. 629–30, and *PL*, vol. 211, col. 651, which refers to Christ at the Virgin's breast but says that we receive our milk from the Word itself.

52 Adam of Perseigne, *Correspondance*, letter 53, p. 542.

53 Adam of Perseigne, *Correspondance*, letter 2, p. 22; letter 4, p. 30.

54 Adam of Perseigne, *Correspondance*, letter 4, p. 30. In addition to the authors discussed above, Gilbert of Hoyland, *Sermones in Canticum Salomonis*, sermon 5, *PL*, vol. 184, col. 32C, sees Jesus as the nurse preparing pap for the child.

55 See Eleanor McLaughlin, "'Christ My Mother,'" pp. 246–7.

56 Adam of Perseigne, *Correspondance*, letter 2, pp. 20–2; Adam here associates woman with strength and fecundity. But in letter 30, pp. 221–2, he gives the standard exegesis of Eve as the lower part of the soul, Adam the higher.

57 For the use of "woman" or "Eve" or the "feminine" as a symbol of spiritual weakness (although often combined with penitence) see n. 31 above. In William of Saint-Thierry, *Sur le Cantique*, ch. 63, p. 162, *mulier* is related to *molis*, which seems to mean "weak" as well as "delicate."

58 Helinand of Froidmont, sermon 20, *PL*, vol. 212, cols 646–52; and *Epistola ad Galterum*, col. 753B. (The etymology is borrowed from Varro.) See also sermon 27, col. 622B, and n. 68 below.

59 See n. 51.

60 See Cabassut, "Une dévotion médiévale," pp. 236–7, and Phyllis Trible, "God, Nature of, in the Old Testament," *The Interpreter's Dictionary of the Bible, Supplementary Volume* (Nashville, TN: Abingdon Press, 1976), pp. 368–9.

61 Mark 3.25, where Christ refers to any faithful follower as his mother or brother, is a very different use of "mother" as symbol.

62 Cabassut, "Une dévotion médiévale," p. 237.

63 Elaine H. Pagels, "What Became of God the Mother? Conflicting Images of God in Early Christianity," *Signs: Journal of Women in Culture and Society* 2 (1976): 293–303.

64 Cabassut, "Une dévotion médiévale," p. 235. For a Carolingian example of the abbot as mother, see Paschasius Radbertus, *Vita sancti Adalhardi*, ch. 71, *PL*, vol. 120, col. 1543D.

65 For example: John Chrysostom, *In Matthaeum homiliae*, 76.5, *Patrologia Graeca* 58, col. 700, see Cabassut, "Une dévotion médiévale," p. 237; Irenaeus, *Adversus haereses*, 3.24. I, *Patrologia Graeca* 7, cols 966–67; Ambrose, *De virginibus*, 1.5, *PL*, vol. 16, col. 205; Augustine, *In Iohannis Evangelium Tractatus CXXIV*, chs 15.7, 16.2, 18.1, and 21.1, *CC:CM* 36 (Turnhout, 1954), pp. 153, 165, 179, and 212. I am grateful to Karl Morrison for the Augustine references.

66 See Jungmann, *Pastoral Liturgy*, pp. 48–63; see also Mary Douglas, *Purity and Danger: An Analysis of Concepts of Pollution and Taboo* (New York/Washington: Praeger, 1966), p. 157.

67 Bernard of Clairvaux, letter 87, *PL*, vol. 182, col. 217C–D; trans. James, letter 90, 135.

68 Bernard of Clairvaux, *Super Cantica* I, sermon 12.9, 66 (he compares monks to women who remain at home spinning while their husbands, i.e. bishops, go out to war). See also ibid., sermon 12.8, 65–6, where Bernard calls himself a woman as an indication of his weakness and of his need for contemplation. For a discussion of inverted imagery used by women, see Jo Ann McNamara, "Sexual Equality and the Cult of Virginity in Early Christian Thought," *Feminist Studies* 3 (1976): 145–58.

69 Clement of Alexandria, *Paedagogus*, 1.6, in *Clemens Alexandrinus* 1, ed. Otto Stählin (Leipzig, 1936; Berlin: Akademie-Verlag, 1972 reprint), pp. 104–21; see also *Paedagogus*, 1.5, 96–104.

70 Origen, *Commentarium in Canticum Canticorum*, prologue and book 1, and *Homilia in Canticum Canticorum*, homilia prima, ch. 5, in *Origenes Werke* 8, ed. W. Baehrens (Leipzig: Hinrichs, 1925), pp. 61–70, 90–5, and 34–5.

71 Mary Martin McLaughlin, "Survivors and Surrogates: Children and Parents from the Ninth to the Thirteenth Centuries," *The History of Childhood*, ed. Lloyd DeMause

(New York: Psychohistory Press, 1974), pp. 115–18; Michael Goodich, "Barthol-omaeus Anglicus on Child-rearing," *History of Childhood Quarterly: The Journal of Psychohistory* 3.1 (1975): 80.

72 Clement, *Paedagogus*, 1.6, ed. Stählin, 1, pp. 104–21.

73 Léon Dewez and Albert van Iterson, "Le lactation de saint Bernard: Légende et iconographic," *Cîteaux in de Nederlanden* 7 (1956): 165–89. We should also note in this connection the legend, found in a work attributed to John Chrysostom and repeated by Guerric, that the apostle Paul bled milk rather than blood when he was beheaded (see Guerric of Igny, *Liturgical Sermons* 2, p. 154, n. 7). Moreover, lacta-tion as an act of filial piety (an adult female offering the breast to a parent or an adult in a desperate situation) was a solemn theme in the literature and religion of pagan antiquity; see Adolphe de Ceuleneer, "La Charité romaine dans la littérature et dans l'art," *Annales de l'Académie Royale d'archéologie de Belgique* 67 (Antwerp, 1919): 175–206.

74 Jean Leclercq, "Le sacré-coeur dans la tradition bénédictine au moyen âge," *Cor Jesu; Commentationes in litteras encyclicas Pii PP. XII 'Haurietis aquas,'* ed. Augustin Bea (Rome: Herder, 1959), pp. 3–28; see also Cyprien Vagaggini, "La dévotion au sacré-coeur chez sainte Méchtilde et sainte Gertrude," ibid., pp. 31–48.

75 Mary M. McLaughlin, "Survivors and Surrogates," pp. 101–81 *passim*; Constable, "Twelfth-Century Spirituality," pp. 42 and 51; Pagels, "What Became of God the Mother?," pp. 293–303. None of these arguments is incorrect as far as it goes, but only Mary McLaughlin takes into account the ambivalence which a seemingly posi-tive image may reflect. John Anson, "The Female Transvestite in Early Monasticism: The Origin and Development of a Motif," *Viator: Medieval and Renaissance Studies* 5 (1974): 1–32, takes an approach to inverted sexual imagery somewhat similar to my own.

76 See Mary McLaughlin, "Peter Abelard and the Dignity of Women: Twelfth-Century 'Feminism' in Theory and Practice," *Pierre Abélard, Pierre le Vénérable: Les courants* . . . (Paris: CNRS, 1975), pp. 287–333; John Benton, "Fraud, Fiction and Borrowing in the Correspondence of Abelard and Heloise," ibid., pp. 469–506; and Eleanor McLaughlin, "Equality of Souls, Inequality of Sexes: Women in Medieval Theology," in *Religion and Sexism: Images of Women in the Jewish and Christian Traditions*, ed. Rosemary Ruether (New York: Simon and Schuster, 1974), pp. 213–66.

77 See the works cited in n. 82.

78 M. McLaughlin, "Survivors and Surrogates," pp. 124–39.

79 M. McLaughlin, "Survivors and Surrogates," pp. 124–39; Alice A. Hentsch, *De la littérature didactique du moyen âge s'adressant spécialement aux femmes* (Cahors: Coueslant, 1903); Philippe Delhaye, "Le dossier anti-matrimonial de l'*Adversus Jovinianum* et son influence sur quelques écrits latins du XIIe siècle," *Medieval Studies* 13 (1951): 65–86; Bullough, "Medieval Medical and Scientific Views," pp. 485–501; Goodich, "Bartholomaeus Anglicus," p. 80. See also Hildegard of Bingen, *Hildegardis Causae et Curae*, book 2, ed. P. Kaiser (Leipzig: Bibliotheca Teubneriana, 1903), pp. 104–5 and 108–9.

80 See William of Saint-Thierry, *De natura et dignitate amoris*, PL, vol. 184, cols 379–408 *passim*, esp. ch. 7, cols 391A–C. The same view is expressed later by Bonaventure, *Commentarium in Ioannem* 15.20, *Opera Omnia* 6 (Quaracchi, 1893), p. 450.

81 See nn. 56–8 and 68.

82 For a summary, see Richard W. Southern, *Western Society and the Church in the Middle Ages* (Harmondsworth: Pelican, 1970), pp. 309–31. See also Simone Roisin, "L'efflorescence cistercienne et le courant féminin de piété au XIIIe siècle," *Revue d'histoire Ecclésiastique* 39 (1943): 342–78, and Brenda M. Bolton, "*Mulieres Sanctae*," *Studies in Church History* 10 (1973): 77–95.

83 Bernard of Clairvaux, letter 322, *PL*, vol. 182, col. 527C–D; trans. James, letter 378,

p. 449, with my changes; see n. 23 above. See also Bernard's letter 104, *PL* 182, col. 240A–C.

84 Isaac of Stella, *Sermons,* ed. Anselm Hoste and Gaston Salet, 3 vols (Paris: Editions du Cerf, 1967 and 1974), vol. 2, sermon 29, p. 172 (cols 1785C–D).

85 Psychoanalysts note that a close relationship between mother and son is connected with hostility toward women; while it is hard to know how such theory would relate to individual medieval men about whose childhoods we know little, such a theory certainly suggests that a literary tradition of misogyny and a literary tradition of idealizing motherhood are not in any way inconsistent. See Karen Horney, "The Dread of Women: Observations on a Specific Difference in the Dread Felt by Men and by Women Respectively for the Opposite Sex," *International Journal of Psychoanalysis* 13 (1932): 348–60, and Douglas, *Purity,* pp. 166–87.

86 David Herlihy has suggested that medieval religious movements are part of a general rebellion against the family: "Alienation in Medieval Culture and Society," *Alienation: Concept, Term, and Meanings,* ed. Frank Johnson (New York: Seminar Press, 1973), pp. 125–40; a similar approach is taken by Michael Goodich, "Childhood and Adolescence among the Thirteenth-Century Saints," *History of Childhood Quarterly* 1 (1974): 285–309. While the argument is attractive, it seems to me to somewhat oversimplify a complex phenomenon.

87 Gammersbach, "Das Abtsbild in Cluny," pp. 85–101.

88 Bernard describes himself as a father who delivers the scourges "of a friend," (Bernard of Clairvaux, letter 281, *PL,* vol. 182, col. 487C); elsewhere he contrasts father and judge (letter 65, cols 170D–72D), rejects the term "father" in favor of "brother" (letter 72, col. 186D), or retains the term "father" while applying to it nursing imagery (see n. 22 above). Bernard also retains royal and even judgmental or angry images of God (*Super Cantica* 1, sermon 16.4–8, pp. 91–4).

89 We see this especially in Bernard of Clairvaux, letter 85, *PL,* vol. 182, cols 206C–10A; letter 87, cols 211–17; letter 258, cols 466–67; and letter 73, cols 187–8, where Bernard says that loving ought to be difficult. Bernard's own ambivalence comes out clearly in letter 72, col. 186D, where he admits that he is the father but refuses fatherly authority because, he says, he and all the monks are brothers.

90 See nn. 30, 35, 36, 40, 41, 47, 48, 50, 53, and 54; and Isaac of Stella, *Sermons,* ed. Hoste, vol. 2, sermon 27, pp. 150–2 (col. 1780D); in the same passage Isaac also describes the abbot as executioner and flagellator.

91 William of Saint-Thierry, *De natura et dignitate amoris,* ch. 8, *PL,* vol. 184, cols 393–5; William, *Meditativae Orationes* 11, *PL* 180, cols 237–42; and William, *Sur le Cantique,* ch. 52, p. 144.

92 Bernard of Clairvaux, letter 87, *PL* 182, cols 211–17, and letter 233, cols 420–1; see also the citations from *Super Cantica* in nn. 17 and 24–7 above; and *Super Cantica* 2, sermons 52 and 53, 90–102.

93 Compare Aelred of Rievaulx's tolerant view of the demands of administration in *De Jesu puero,* ch. 3.31, *Opera* 1, 277–8, with his harsh description of it as a "dung heap" in his *De institutione,* ch. 28, *Opera* 1, 660–1.

94 Pierre Salmon, *The Abbot in Monastic Tradition: A Contribution to the History of the Office of Religious Superiors in the West,* trans. Claire Lavoie (Washington, DC: Cistercian Studies, 1972), pp. 46–104, esp. pp. 95–9.

95 Salmon, *The Abbot,* pp. 95–9; see also François Chamard, "Les abbés au moyen âge," *Revue des questions historiques* 38 (1885): 71–108.

96 C. Dumont, "L'équilibre humain de la vie cistercienne d'après le bienheureux Aelred de Rievaulx," *Collectanea ordinis Cisterciensium Reformatorum* 18 (1965): 177–89; Aelred Squire, "Aelred of Rievaulx and the Monastic Tradition Concerning Action and Contemplation," *The Downside Review* 72 (1954): 289–303; Constable, "Twelfth-Century Spirituality," pp. 40–5.

97 I have discussed Cistercian conceptions of community and Cistercian ambivalence about love of neighbor in "The Cistercian Conception of Community: An Aspect of Twelfth-Century Spirituality," *Harvard Theological Review* 68 (1975): 273–86.

98 See M. McLaughlin, "Survivors and Surrogates," pp. 130–3.

99 Aelred of Rievaulx, *De speculo caritatis*, 2.17, *Opera Omnia* 1, pp. 86–91. See Louis Bouyer, *The Cistercian Heritage*, trans. Elizabeth A. Livingstone (Westminster, MD: Newman Press, 1958), p. 139, and Aelred Squire, "The Composition of the *Speculum caritatis*," *Cîteaux* 14 (1963): 229–30. Adam of Perseigne, *Correspondance*, letter 24, pp. 169–73. Bernard, *Super Cantica* 1, sermon 9.2, p. 43.

100 Aelred of Rievaulx, *De speculo*, 3.37, *Opera Omnia* 1, pp. 153–6.

101 l would explain the fact that these authors also use maternal imagery for bishops and other prelates as a reflection of this general concern and ambivalence about authority and about the active life, toward which some of them were drawn; see nn. 96 and 97.

102 Robert Bultot, *Christianisme et valeurs humaines: La doctrine du mépris du monde en Occident de saint Ambroise à Innocent III* (Louvain: Nauwelaerts, 1963–4); Jonathan Sumption, *Pilgrimage: An Image of Mediaeval Religion* (Totowa, NJ: Rowman & Littlefield, 1975), esp. pp. 11–21.

103 Javelet, *Image* 1, 451–61; Richard W. Southern, *Medieval Humanism and Other Studies* (New York: Harper & Row, 1970) pp. 29–60; see also Colin Morris, *The Discovery of the Individual, 1030–1200* (New York: Harper & Row, 1972).

104 See Bernard, *De diligendo Deo*, 7.17, in *Tractatus et Opuscula, S. Bernardi opera* 3, ed. Jean Leclercq and Henri M. Rochais (Rome: Editiones cistercienses, 1963), p. 134 (lines 10–11), where Bernard gives as examples of love that does what it freely desires: a hungry man eating, a thirsty man drinking, and a mother nursing her child. See also the references cited in n.17 above; letter 300 is addressed to a woman and discusses maternal affection literally.

105 The fact that the authors considered in this article were writing for those already in the cloister undoubtedly contributes to the tone of optimism.

106 See n. 51.

107 See Bouyer, *Cistercian Heritage*. On Adam of Perseigne, see J. Bouvet, "Biographie d'Adam de Perseigne," *Collectanea ordinis Cisterciensium Reformatorum* 20 (1958): 16–26 and 145–52.

108 See Bynum, "The Cistercian Conception of Community," pp. 273–86.

109 Aelred of Rievaulx, *De institutione*, ch. 28, *Opera Omnia*, p. 661. This is all the more remarkable because it occurs in a work addressed to recluses, not to the cloistered.

110 See Isaac of Stella, *Sermons*, ed. Hoste, vol. 1, sermon 2, pp. 98–102 (cols 1693D–94D); vol. 1, sermon 14, pp. 276–80 (cols 1737A–38A); vol. 1, sermon 15, pp. 286–93 (cols 1739B–40D); vol. 2, sermon 18, pp. 18–20 (cols 1752A–B): vol. 2, sermon 37, pp. 296–304 (cols 1816A–17D); and sermon 50, *PL*, vol. 194, col. 1858B–62A, for Isaac's intense sense of renunciation of the world. See also Franz J. P. Bliemetzrieder, "Isaak von Stella, Beiträge zur Lebensbeschreibung," *Jahrbuch für Philosophie and spekulative Theologie* 18 (1904): 1–35.

111 See Isaac of Stella, *Sermons* 1, sermon 11, 242–4 (cols 1728B–D); sermon 42, *PL*, vol. 194, col. 1832B; sermon 45, *PL*, vol. 194, col. 1841C–D; sermon 51, *PL*, vol. 194, col. 1863A.

112 Isaac of Stella, *Sermons* 2, sermon 29, 166–80 (cols 1784B–87C); 2, sermon 34, 232–54, esp. 234 (col. 1801A–B); sermon 42, *PL*, vol. 194, col. 1829D; sermon 51, *PL*, vol. 194, cols 1862–63A. We should note that vol. 1, sermon 14, 270–80 (cols 1735B–8A) joins in the same discussion the "corps mystique" theme and almost frantic exhortation to renounce the world. It is no accident that Isaac sees sin, the loss which is the opposite of union (incorporation) with God, as fragmentation.

113 Aelred of Rievaulx, *De institutione*, ch. 26, *Opera Omnia* 1, pp. 658–9.

114 See Helinand of Froidmont, *Sermons, PL,* vol. 212, cols 481–720. The description of Helinand in François Vandenbroucke, *La morale monastique du XIe au XVIe siècle* (Louvain and Lille: Editions Nauwelaerts, 1966), p. 165, which has become standard in reference works, seems to be based entirely on the first Christmas sermon: "Helinand . . . atteste un attachement en quelque sorte chevaleresque à Marie." If all the sermons are considered together, a very different picture emerges.

115 Helinand of Froidmont, sermon 23, *PL,* vol. 212, cols 670–1; sermon 25, cols 685–7; sermon 26, cols 693–7 (and cf. sermon 11, col. 580B–C); sermon 27, cols 700–2; sermon 28, vols 71–116. See Gerhard Bauer, *Claustrum Animae: Untersuchungen zur Geschichte der Metapher vom Herzen als Kloster* I (Munich: Fink, 1973). Helinand is also fond of military imagery. Building and military images occur in his sermons for clergy, references to the Virgin in his sermons for monks.

116 In addition to its place in the history of devotion, which I have treated here, the theme of the "motherhood of God" has implications for the theology of the Atonement, the Incarnation, and the Trinity. I hope to deal in a later article with the role of the idea in the history of doctrine – a topic for which Clement of Alexandria, Anselm, and Julian of Norwich are more important than these twelfth-century Cistercians.

2

CRUSADING AS AN ACT OF LOVE

Jonathan Riley-Smith

This was Riley-Smith's inaugural lecture for The Royal Holloway College, University of London, in May 1979 (published in History *65 (1980): 177–92). In that same year the publication of Edward W. Said's* Orientalism *made clear to many as never before that the Crusade has been a major factor in the centuries-long distrust between East and West, particularly in the Middle East. Today's charged connotations for the word "Crusade," along with the fact that our own recent anti-war movements have had slogans like "make love not war," means that calling "crusading" "an act of love" is highly ironic. With such irony, however, Jonathan Riley-Smith quickly convinces his audience of a profound insight all too easily missed: Crusades unlike wars today were not motivated by governmental policy, but by many individual, personal decisions to take the sign of the cross.*

Riley-Smith makes clear that crusaders, moreover, were aroused to battle by a message of love, not hate. It was not hatred of "others" that motivated such Christians, but the sense that they were participating in the acting out of God's plan for humanity. In this plan "others" like Moslems were not to be destroyed in episodes of violence, hatred, and intolerance (although that is what happened), but were to be converted to Christianity. Western knights at this time were taught that to be good Christians meant undertaking great acts of Christian love or charity – caritas – the greatest of these being "love of God" and "love of neighbor." Only by departing to defend the Holy Land could such knights truly act out that love to which they were enjoined. Obviously crusaders acted out of more than a desire to carry the Cross for Christ – opportunism, yearning for adventure, or even simply the obligation to follow one's Lord into battle were all present, but the rhetorical message was love. Love of God and fear of the Last Judgment if that love was not acted on were the message of Crusade preaching. "Fired by the zeal of love," Christian soldiers, who were subject to excommunication if they failed to perform the Crusade once they had taken the sign of the Cross, went to considerable personal risk and expense to make the pilgrimage to Jerusalem to defend the Holy Places.

Today we can see the danger of such rhetoric, of believing that killing could ever be an act of love, and we realize that in the Middle Ages that message inspired crusaders not only to defend the Holy Places by violence against the Muslims, but to act violently towards Jews and heretics in the West. The notion that Christian love could encompass the killing of non-Christians was, as Riley-Smith notes, completely at odds with the real message of Christianity, which was tolerance. Given how convinced Christians would come to be that such actions were enjoined by their religion, however, it is no wonder that Crusades are still seen by non-Christians as the epitome of intolerant Western military adventures.

Note that the papal letters and decrees referred to in this selection are identified by their opening Latin words, for instance Quantum praedecessores, *which are untranslatable in their abbreviated form.*

* * *

In his encyclical *Quantum praedecessores* of December 1145, Pope Eugenius III (1145–53) wrote of those who had answered the call to the First Crusade that they had been "fired by the ardor of charity."[1] In an *excitatorium* (a rousing speech to inspire those on crusade) of the late 1180s, Peter of Blois (d. 1205) argued that Christians would gain merit if, "Fired by the zeal of charity, they fight fiercely those who blaspheme against Christ, pollute the sanctuary of the Lord and in their pride and unbelief abase the glory of our Redeemer."[2] In the 1260s, the French poet Rutebeuf, lamenting the failure of his countrymen to move themselves to recapture Jerusalem, exclaimed that "the fire of charity is cold in every Christian heart."[3] These writers used the theological word *caritas, charitei* (charity) for Christian love, heightened it in a traditional Christian way with the words "fired" or "fire," and linked it to the crusades. Since love has always been held to be fundamental to all Christian ethics, including the ethics of violence, it is worth asking how representative they were of the apologists for the crusading movement. I hope to show that the idea of the crusader expressing love through his participation in acts of armed force was an element in the thinking of senior churchmen in the central Middle Ages. An understanding of this can help us place the crusades in the context of the spiritual reawakening of Western Europe that accompanied the eleventh-century reform movement. Christian love, however, was presented to the faithful in a way that they would understand, rather than in the form that would have reflected the complexities of the relationship between violence and charity as understood by theologians and canon lawyers. My discussion is limited to the justification of crusades to the East, although crusaders were not by any means only to be found in expeditions launched to recover or aid the Holy Land; they also campaigned in Spain, along the shores of the Baltic and even in the interior of Western Europe.[4]

Christian charity encompasses love of God and love of one's neighbor, and both these expressions of love were touched on by apologists for the crusades: in September 1096, Pope Urban II (1088–99) promised the indulgence to those Bolognese who joined the First Crusade, "seeing that they have committed their property and their persons out of love of God and their neighbor";[5] and

Bernard of Clairvaux (d. 1153), writing in the 1140s of news of Muslim victories in the East, asked, "If we harden our hearts and pay little attention . . . where is our love for God, where is our love for our neighbor?"[6]

It was believed that crusaders particularly expressed their love of God in the way they became literally followers of Christ. From the first, they were treated as "soldiers of Christ," who had joined an expedition out of love for him. And the taking of the cross, the sewing of a cross on a man's garments as a symbol of his vow to crusade, was seen as a response to Christ's statement: "Whosoever doth not carry his cross and come after me cannot be my disciple" (Luke 14.27). It is notoriously difficult to establish exactly what occurred at the Council of Clermont in November 1095, but it is possible that Pope Urban II preached the First Crusade on the basis of this text. The author of one of the accounts of the council mentioned that he had done so when he ordered the crusaders to sew crosses on their clothes.[7] Another witness also referred to it, in a narrative in which Urban was made to remind his audience of Christ's words:

> He that loveth father or mother more than me is not worthy of me. And everyone that hath left house or father or mother or wife or children or lands for my name's sake shall receive an hundredfold and shall possess life everlasting (Matthew 10.37, 19.29).[8]

There is evidence that, whatever Urban actually said, a chord was struck in the hearts of those who responded to him. The anonymous author of the *Gesta Francorum* (*The Deeds of the Franks*) took part in the First Crusade, and opened his narrative with a moving reference to the subject:

> When already that time drew nigh, to which the Lord Jesus draws the attention of his people every day, especially in the Gospel in which he says, "If any man will come after me, let him deny himself and take up his cross and follow me" (Matthew 16.24), there was a great stirring throughout the whole region of Gaul, so that if anyone, with a pure heart and mind, seriously wanted to follow God and faithfully wished to bear the cross after him, he could make no delay in speedily taking the road to the Holy Sepulchre.[9]

The German Ekkehard of Aura (d. *c*.1125), who was himself in the East in 1101, compared the crusaders to Simon of Cyrene, who had helped Jesus carry his Cross,[10] and the twelfth-century chaplain of the French King, Odo of Deuil, began his account of the Second Crusade with the words:

> In the year of the Incarnation of the Word 1146, at Easter at Vezelay, the glorious Louis, . . . King of the Franks and Duke of the Aquitanians, . . . undertook to follow Christ by bearing his cross in order to be worthy of him.[11]

An anonymous twelfth-century poet wrote:

> You who love with true love
> Awake! Do not sleep!
> The lark brings us day
> And tells us in this hideaway
> That the day of peace has come
> That God, by his very great kindness,
> Will give to those who for love of him
> Take the cross and on account of what they do
> Suffer pain night and day
> So that he will see who truly loves him.[12]

This seam of devotion was richly worked by authority. In *c*.1144, in a bull that was often to be reissued, Pope Celestine II (1143–4) wrote that the Templars, "new Maccabees in this time of Grace, renouncing earthly desires and possessions, bearing his cross, are followers of Christ."[13] And the image of the crusader denying himself and actually taking up Christ's cross was particularly strongly expressed at the turn of the twelfth and thirteenth centuries by Pope Innocent III (1198–1216)[14] to whom God was a benefactor of all, owed by all many profound and unrepayable debts of gratitude:

> Who would refuse to die for him, who was made for us obedient unto death, a death indeed on the cross?[15]

> If God underwent death for man, ought man to question dying for God?[16]

Innocent expanded his discussion on the relationship between the crusader and the cross in his great encyclical *Quia maior*, which launched the Fifth Crusade (1217–21):

> We summon on behalf of him who when dying cried in a great voice on the cross, made obedient to God his father unto death on the cross, crying so that he should save us from the eternal crucifixion of death; who, indeed, for his own sake summoned us and said, "If any man will come after me, let him deny himself and take up his cross and follow me" (Matthew 16.24). And in this clearly he said, "Whoever wishes to follow me to the crown should also follow me to the battle, which is now proposed to all as a test."[17]

In a letter of 1208 to Leopold of Austria, Innocent had also stressed the insignificance of the crusader's action when compared to that of Christ:

> You receive a soft and gentle cross; he bore one that was sharp and hard. You wear it superficially on your clothing; he endured it really

in his flesh. You sew on yours with linen and silk threads; he was nailed to his with iron and hard nails.[18]

His pontificate marks a climax in the use of this imagery, but the love of God expressed by crusaders may still have been a popular theme in thirteenth-century sermons. The *Ordinacio de predicacione S. crucis in Anglia* (*Instructions for Preaching the Holy Cross in England*) of c.1216, obviously following Innocent, referred to those entering the service of the cross as observing the commandment to love God with all one's heart,[19] and Cardinal Odo of Châteauroux, who in 1245 was given the task of preaching and organizing a new crusade from France, devoted a homily to the subject. Preaching on the text, "Amen I say to you that ... you who have followed me ... shall also sit (alongside) ... when the Son of Man shall sit on the seat of his majesty" (Matthew 19.28), Odo enjoined his audience to forsake everything for the love of God: true conversion could only come about through love of God rather than of earthly things and a man could love his neighbor only as an expression of his love of God. He went on to tell his listeners:

> It is a clear sign that a man burns with love of God and zeal for God when he leaves country, possessions, house, children and wife, going overseas in the service of Jesus Christ. .... Whoever wishes to take and have Christ ought to follow him; to follow him to death.[20]

There can be little doubt that the audiences addressed by popes and preachers saw the expression of love for God in terms that were real to them, above all in the light of their relationship with and the loyalty they owed to secular rulers. And these rulers were also feudal lords. At the time the ties between vassals and their lords were regarded as being so close and were held in so emotional a way that feudal terminology was used by the poets of courtly love to describe the devotion of the perfect lover to his lady.[21] To the crusaders, Christ was a king and lord who had lost his inheritance to the pagans: indeed the image of the Holy Land as Christ's inheritance, which was an old one, was used in one of the accounts of Pope Urban's speech at Clermont[22] and often thereafter; even as late as 1274, Pope Gregory X (1271–6) wrote in his *Constitutiones pro zelo fidei* (*Edicts for the Zeal of the Faithful*) of the feelings of charity that should be aroused in Christian hearts at its loss.[23] It was the duty of Christ's subjects to fight for the recovery or in the defense of Christ's heritage as they would for the domains of their own lords, and the anonymous twelfth-century poet, from whose crusade song I have already quoted, expressed a common opinion when he wrote that "he who abandons his lord in need deserves to be condemned."[24]

Faced by a world that saw things in such concrete terms the popes tended to express themselves on this matter in a cloudy way, probably because theologians could not bring themselves to use too explicitly the feudal relationship, with its notions of contract and reciprocal obligations, as a means of describing man's relationship to God. The modern German medievalist Carl Erdmann has drawn attention to the ambiguous way in which, as he turned for help to the feudal knighthood in the 1070s and 1080s, Pope Gregory VII (1073–85) used the feudal terms *miles* (knight or soldier), *fidelis* (faithful), and *servitium* (service),[25] and the same was true of Gregory's successors. But popes could also on occasion specifically use the images of the everyday world to bring home to people what was meant by loving God. Innocent III, for instance, was fond of referring in this way to Christ as a king:

> Consider most dear sons, consider carefully that if any temporal king was thrown out of his domain and perhaps captured, would he not, when he was restored to his pristine liberty and the time had come for dispensing justice, look on his vassals as unfaithful and traitors against the crown and guilty of *lèse majesté* unless they had committed not only their property but also their persons to the task of freeing him? . . . And similarly will not Jesus Christ, the king of kings and lord of lords, whose servant you cannot deny being, who joined your soul to your body, who redeemed you with his precious blood, who conceded to you the kingdom, who enables you to live and move and gave you all the good things you have . . . condemn you for the vice of ingratitude and, as it were, the crime of infidelity if you neglect to help him?[26]

At about the same time the great preacher James of Vitry (d. 1240) developed what Innocent was saying in one of his sermons, although he was careful to point out that man's relationship with Christ was not a feudal one:

> When a lord is afflicted by the loss of his patrimony he wishes to prove his friends and find out if his vassals are faithful. Whoever holds a fief of a liege lord is worthily deprived of it if he deserts him when he is engaged in battle and loses his inheritance. You hold your body and soul and whatever you have from the Supreme Emperor and today he has had you called upon to help him in battle; and though you are not bound by feudal law, he offers you so many and such good things, the remission of all sins, whatever the penalty or guilt, and above all eternal life, that you ought at once to hurry to him.[27]

Later in the century, Odo of Châteauroux (d. 1273), in the sermon to which I have already referred, asked his audience a question colored by the aspirations and feelings of the world in which they lived: "What is loving God if it is not desiring his honor and glory?"[28] Churchmen, therefore, could portray the crusader's love of God in terms that laymen could recognize as being analogous to their regard for their earthly superiors. But the presentation of theology in everyday terms is revealed even more strikingly in the expression of the idea of love for fellow-men.

The belief that crusading expressed love of one's neighbor as well as love of God also dated from the First Crusade. It has long been accepted that an important element in Pope Urban's thinking when he preached the cross was the opportunity he saw of bringing fraternal aid to Christians in the East, oppressed by or in danger from the Muslims.[29] The twelfth-century Baldric of Dol, in his account of the sermon at Clermont, laid emphasis on the supposed suffering of the eastern Christians and made Urban make a typical distinction between the barbarisms of internal strife in France and the virtues of helping the East:

> It is dreadful, brothers, dreadful, for you to raise thieving hands against Christians. It is much less evil to brandish the sword against the Muslims; in a particular case it is good, because it is charity to lay down lives for friends.[30]

The development of the idea of violence expressing fraternal love can be illustrated from the sources for the history of the Military Orders, which were linked closely to the crusades, even if the brothers in them were not technically crusaders.[31] The founding of the Order of Knights Templar is a remarkable event in the history of the religious life. One of the chief attractions of the First Crusade, which followed closely on a change in the Church's thinking on the role of laymen,[32] was that now at last the laity had a task to perform, pleasing to God, for which they were especially equipped and which professed religious were not permitted to undertake. In a well-known passage in his history of the crusade, Guibert of Nogent (d. *c*.1124) welcomed the fact that now laymen could attain salvation through works without entering a monastery;[33] and the sudden realization that the leading crusader Tancred, torn between "the Gospel and the world," had of the new role for Christian warriors, and his enthusiastic response to it,[34] is evidence for the force of this idea, as is the emphasis on the "new knight" still to be found in the writings of Bernard of Clairvaux half a century later.[35] But so dominant was the appeal of the religious life and so superior was its status that, within twenty years of the capture of Jerusalem, professed religious were themselves taking on the role of warriors, usurping the special function of the laity. All contemporaries were struck by the fact that a new kind of religious life had come into being, in which the brothers could hardly have acted in a more secular way. The compilers of the Templar rule wrote:

> We believe that by divine providence this new kind of religious order was founded by you in the holy places, so that you combine soldiering with the religious life and in this way the order can fight with arms and can without blame smite the enemy.[36]

The association in the Templar life of both religious and military practices was a point also made in Bernard of Clairvaux's treatise, the *De laude novae militiae* (*In Praise of the New Knighthood*),[37] and in the early thirteenth century, by which time the Hospitallers had also taken on military responsibilities and the Spanish and German Military Orders had been founded, James of Vitry wrote of the brothers:

> Concerning whom the Lord says, "I will encompass my house with them that serve me in war, going and returning" (Zechariah 9.8). Going in time of war, returning in time of peace; going by means of action, returning by means of contemplation; going in war to fight, returning in peace to repose and devotion to prayer, so that they are like soldiers in battle and like monks in convent.[38]

The appearance of followers of a religious rule who were dedicated to war was bound to lead to controversy. In the 1160s and 1170s Pope Alexander III (1159–81) was worried by the transformation of the Hospital of Saint John into a Military Order,[39] and as early as the 1120s someone, perhaps Hugh of Saint Victor (d. 1141), had to answer on the Templars' behalf critics who maintained that a monastic profession to defend with arms the faith and Christendom was "illicit and pernicious" and that it would lead the Templars into sin because war was activated by hatred and greed:

> I say to you that you do not hate, which is unjust, because you do not hate man but iniquity. Again I say, you are not greedy, which is unjust, because you acquire that which should justly be taken on account of sins and that which is justly yours because of the work that you do.[40]

But the real reply was given in 1139 by Pope Innocent II (1130–43) in *Omne datum optimum*, the papal charter for the Templars, and it was a reply that drew attention to the love shown by the brothers:

> As true Israelites and most instructed fighters in divine battle, filled with the flames of divine charity, you carry out in deeds the words of the Gospel, "Greater love than this no man hath, that a man lay down his life for his friends."[41]

In 1155 this was re-emphasized by Pope Adrian IV (1154–59) in *Sicut sacra evangelia*, in phrases that were often to be repeated in later papal letters:

> The knights of the Temple ... are especially called to the service of the omnipotent God and are numbered with the heavenly host. This is indicated by their reverend habit and is shown by the sign of the cross of Our Lord which they wear on their bodies. Indeed they have been founded for this purpose, that they do not fear to lay down their lives for their brothers.[42]

The same attitude was to be found with regard to the Hospitallers as they took on military duties. The first reference to a military wing in their statutes treated it as an extension of their charitable work: "These elemosynary grants have properly been established in the holy Order of the Hospital, except for the brethren-at-arms, whom the holy Order keeps honorably, and many other bounties."[43] And in 1191 Pope Celestine III (1191–8) referred to the Hospitallers, fighting the infidel and looking after the poor, as "the children of peace and love . . . servants in Christ of the holy poor of Jerusalem and of all lands everywhere."[44] In this respect the Military Orders sprang from the same stem as did the other new orders of the time, demonstrating in their own fashion the concern for charitable work and the care of one's neighbor that so many of them showed.

The idea that crusading expressed fraternal love was, of course, also put forward in encyclicals directed chiefly at the laity. In 1169, Pope Alexander III, responding to a request for aid from the Kingdom of Jerusalem, published a major appeal with the widest possible circulation. He began it by stressing the role of love:

> Among all the means that Divine Wisdom has provided for the exercise of charity in the midst of temporal affairs, it would be difficult to find a field of action in which this charity could be expressed with more glory with regard to virtue, and with better results with regard to rewards, than in aid to relieve the needs of the Church in the East and the faithful of Christ, by defending them against the onslaught of the pagans, so that both the cult of the Divine Name does not fail and the virtue of brotherhood shines forth praiseworthily.[45]

In 1215 Innocent III returned to the theme of love in *Quia maior*, this time love for Christians in territories occupied by the Muslims:

> How does a man love according to divine precept his neighbor as himself when, knowing that his Christian brothers in faith and in name are held by the perfidious Muslims in strict confinement and weighed down by the yoke of heaviest servitude, he cannot devote himself to the efficacious work of liberating them? In this he transgresses the command of that natural law which the Lord declared in the Gospel. "All things . . . whatsoever you would that men should do to you, do you also to them" (Matthew 7.12). Is it by chance that you do not know that among them (the Muslims) many thousands of Christians are held in servitude and in jail, tortured with innumerable torments?[46]

Now, the striking thing about these references to love is that they are one-dimensional and therefore not truly Christian. Love of neighbor was always treated in crusade propaganda in terms of fraternal love for fellow-Christians, never in terms of love shown for enemies as well as friends. And this one-sided view of love did not properly reflect Christian teaching in the past or at the time. One has only to read the *Sentences* of Peter Lombard (d. *c*.1160) to find a contemporary theologian putting before his readers a more fully rounded view. By neighbor, Peter stressed, one must mean all mankind. Certainly, he argued, fellow-Christians ought especially to be loved and, in that we cannot *show* equal love to all, they should come first, since they are members of the same body and recognize the same Father. It is, moreover, sufficient to love enemies straightforwardly and not to hate them; in this respect love of enemies comes last in a scale of expressions of love. But he emphasized that enemies must be included in our love for all men and he quoted Augustine of Hippo (d. 430) to the effect that it is more virtuous to love enemies than friends.[47]

The Christian tradition on violence, moreover, the foundations of which had been laid by the Fathers, naturally stressed the role of love, for enemies as well as friends, in the use of force. Augustine had treated the matter comprehensively. To him, just violence required right intention on the part of the imposers of force as an essential prerequisite. In his treatise on the Sermon on the Mount, containing one of his earliest essays on the subject, he stressed that the intention behind punishment designed for the purpose of correction had to be to make the offender happy; it had to be imposed out of love by those who had in this matter overcome hatred. Christ had denounced hatred seeking vengeance, not love desiring to correct the object of love. Further, many noble and saintly men had in the past inflicted death as a punishment for sins. Those put to death had suffered no injury from it; rather, they were already being injured by their sins and their state might have become far worse had they been allowed to live. Augustine referred here to the prophet Elijah killing on authority from God and he drew attention to the apostle Paul delivering a sinner over to Satan for the destruction of his flesh, so that his spirit might be saved (1 Corinthians 5.5). He admitted that he did not really understand the meaning of the words Paul had used, but he maintained that it was clear that, whatever Paul did mean, he intended to save a soul; in other words that this was a punishment imposed through love.[48] To Augustine, the intentions of those who authorized violence and of those who participated in it had to be in favor of justice, a virtue which for him assigned to everyone his due, working through love of God and love of one's neighbor.[49] It being often more loving to use force than indulgence, it followed that just violence had love for those on whom it was meted out as the mainspring of action; and this kind of motivation would mean that one would be careful to employ only such violence as was necessary.[50] Augustine often wrote of the way parents could express their love for their children by correcting them,[51] and he also referred to the violence sometimes needed in healing the sick or in rescuing men from physical danger against their wills.[52] The scriptures were combed by him for references to acts or expressions of violence, motivated by love, perpetrated by Moses and Elijah,[53] by the apostle Paul,[54] by a loving

God, and even by a loving Christ, as when he scourged the stall-keepers out of the Temple and blinded Paul on the road to Damascus.[55] All of this provided a basis for his justification of the repression of heresy. It was right, and a sign of love and mercy in imitation of Christ, for a loving Church, in collaboration with a loving state, to force heretics from the path of error for their own benefit, compelling them to goodness in the same way as the host at the wedding feast in Christ's parable had sent out his servant to force those in the highways to come to the banquet.[56]

Augustine's thought was very influential in the central Middle Ages. On most of the criteria for Christian violence crusading ideas followed his. But they did not on love. One explanation might be that since Augustine devoted most of his writing on violence to justifying the suppression of heresy – and made little distinction between force associated with war against external foes and force used internally to repress heretics – his approach was one that could lead more naturally to an emphasis on love as a disciplinary force, for which parallels could be drawn with family life. But, in fact, writers at the time of the crusades also treated violence against external and internal injurers under the same general heading. And since they did not distinguish the forms of violence, at least as far as the justification of force went, one would not expect crusade propagandists to have done so either.

It might also be pointed out that certain premises in Augustine's thought were alien to the theology of the central Middle Ages and that this might explain why the justifiers of crusading violence did not follow him on the issue of love of enemies as well as friends. In particular, he had a very negative attitude toward free will, and this led him to have a pessimistic view of the ability of most of mankind truly to act through love. The fact was that those whom love restrained were less numerous in this world than those who had to be restrained by terror. Fear, instilled by the penal laws of the Roman emperors against heresy, forced men to truth, and many were brought to the true faith and to salvation who otherwise would not have known it. Moreover, fear gave the faint-hearted the excuse to break with heresy.[57] Augustine could, therefore, compare just and unjust persecution: the Roman state, in alliance with the Church, imposed a just persecution, while the pagan emperors and the wicked persecuted unjustly.[58] He argued that Christ had promised blessedness for those persecuted for justice's sake, but had said nothing about those persecuted for the sake of injustice. Nobody became a martyr merely by suffering for religion: "It is not the penalty that makes a martyr, but the cause."[59] So the essential thing was the justice of the cause for which one suffered, and an image Augustine used was that of Christ, unjustly crucified, hanging on the cross between the two thieves, who had been justly condemned.[60] Playing down free will it was, of course, fairly easy to justify violence in terms of love shown to those incapable of motivation to good except by fear. But it was far less easy to do so if one shared the highly developed notions of free will that were common in the central Middle Ages, since coercion potentially limited the operation of free will in the coerced. In a formal pronouncement, or *dictum*, in his important *Causa XXIII* on violence, the canonist Gratian (fl. 1130–40), writing *c*.1140, showed anxiety about this matter.[61]

Augustine's approach to free will, moreover, resulted in an indifference to the salvific value of works.[62] In fact he did not really believe that any special merit attached to the participants in this violence. He wrote that Abraham had shown "praiseworthy" compliance with God's order to sacrifice Isaac,[63] but he seems to have regarded even acts of violence on God's specific command – a category of force to which he paid special attention – as being merely blameless.[64] One would be quite wrong to refuse such an order, but only doing one's duty if one obeyed it. In fact the man who owed obedience to the giver of a command, whether God himself or God's minister, did not himself kill: he was an instrument in the hand of the authorizer.[65] To the apologists for the crusades, on the other hand, merit, which of course stemmed from the dominant position held by the concept of free will, played so large a part that a recent historian of the crusades has defined holy war in terms of its meritoriousness.[66]

But, apart from Gratian's *dictum* to which I have already referred, theologians of the time of the crusades do not seem to have found it difficult to graft ideas of free will and merit on to Augustinian thought. Indeed, if there is one feature of their treatment of love and violence it is how Augustinian it is; and quotations from Augustine, including those which emphasized love of enemies, predominate in their writings. It was Anselm of Lucca (d. 1086), a supporter of Pope Gregory VII, who in books XII and XIII of his *Collectio canonum*, written in *c*.1083, collected the basic Augustinian texts on violence, including those on force and love, and passed them on to his successors as authorities for the arguments that the Church did not persecute but expressed love when she punished sin; that Moses, using force on orders from God, did nothing cruel; that punishment could be imposed not out of hatred but out of love; and that wars could be benevolent in intention.[67]

Anselm was followed by Ivo of Chartres (d. 1116) who, in his *Decretum* and *Panormia*, written in France in *c*.1094 on the eve of the First Crusade,[68] used his authorities to demonstrate that love of neighbor demanded that in normal circumstances one should not kill.[69] One should not embark on punishment unless one had personally overcome hatred; indeed penalties could be imposed on those who killed out of hate and not out of zeal for justice.[70] But Ivo stressed, in an Augustinian passage that was later to be used by Gratian, that the exercise of Christian forbearance did not entirely rule out necessary fighting.[71] Love, in fact, could involve physical correction, in the same way as a father punished a son or a master a servant.[72] To coerce one's neighbor could be to love him and the man who punished evil did not persecute but loved.[73] Indeed in the *Panormia*, which was a popular work,[74] three chapters were devoted to the arguments, taken entirely from Augustine, that neighborly love demanded that men prevent their neighbors from doing evil and that Christians could, in fact, sin if they did not persecute those engaged in evil works.[75] Ivo maintained that wars fought by true Christians were in fact acts of pacification, since their aim was peace.[76]

The works of Anselm of Lucca and Ivo of Chartres foreshadowed that of Gratian, but in no way approached the subtlety and honesty of Gratian's treatment of force in Causa XXIII of his *Decretum*, written *c*.1140. He began by facing up squarely to the passages in the New Testament that appeared to forbid Christians to use violence of any kind, but he then took his readers through a mass of material that gradually revealed the Christian justification of violence. On the issue of love, including love of enemies, he was, like Anselm and Ivo, fundamentally Augustinian. The use of force was not entirely forbidden in the precepts of forbearance,[77] for while they should be interpreted as meaning that clemency and tolerance should be shown, bad sins ought to be punished, as in the cases of Ananias and Sapphira on the condemnation of Saint Peter – this was a favorite example of the Fathers and of those writing on violence in the central Middle Ages – of Elymas who was blinded on the word of Saint Paul, and of the sinner whom Saint Paul handed over to Satan.[78] Evil must not be rendered for evil and one should love enemies, not persecute them,[79] but Augustine's analogies of the doctor prescribing for patients and the heads of households correcting sons and servants were drawn on.[80] Out of maternal love the Church could prescribe medicine for sinners, and in any case better the wounds of a friend than the kisses of an enemy.[81] Men were bound to love their enemies, to pray for them, and show mercy to them, but the demands of love should mean that they could not allow others to sin with impunity. Acts of mercy could themselves be unjust, and one such act could lead to universal harm.[82] And so the restless were usefully corrected by the office of public power. It was better to love with severity: persecution was not always culpable for it could serve love.[83] And the wicked could be forced to goodness: men had the example of Christ to follow here; nobody loved more than he did, yet he forced the apostle Paul on to the path of righteousness. Moses, too, punished the Israelites not out of cruelty but out of love. Correction was an attribute of mercy, as could be found by reading not only the Old Testament, but also the New, although the examples in it were more rare.[84] Gratian believed that he had established from his authorities that punishment in itself was permitted and did not necessarily involve hatred.[85]

As a final example of the treatment of love and violence at the time of the crusades one might look at Thomas Aquinas's (d. 1274) early polemical treatise *Contra impugnantes*, written in 1256.[86] This again was Augustinian in its approach and it repeated the argument that Christ only gave the apostles, who were simple and uneducated men, power to authorize punishment by means of force after he had taught them to love their neighbors absolutely.[87]

Reading these works one glimpses what seems to be a different world to that portrayed in crusading propaganda. Instead of the one-dimensional notion of fraternal love for fellow-Christians, violence is treated in the context of love for all mankind, enemies as well as friends. For all its obvious faults, one is bound to admire the subtlety and learning of the canonists' treatment of force and to recognize that it has an authentic place in the Christian ethical tradition. But it must be stressed that theologians and canonists and the popes and curial clerks who wrote the calls to crusade did not live in different worlds. Pope Alexander III, for instance, in whose name was issued one of the encyclicals from which I have quoted, was himself a canonist and the author of a commentary on Gratian's *Decretum*.[88] It is not believable that the popes who proclaimed crusades and the more respectable preachers who whipped up enthusiasm for them did not grasp the complexity of the Christian position. They must have presented their one-sided version of love deliberately, with a view to the audience they were addressing.

It could be that they dared not do otherwise. A feature of the attitudes of twelfth-century lay society as revealed in its vernacular poetry was its blind, uncomprehending hatred of the infidel, expressed, for instance, in Charlemagne's famous declaration in the *Song of Roland* [written down in the late eleventh century] that "Never to paynims may I show love or peace." Through the epics runs the theme of an implacable war of conversion against non-Christians, a theme that expressed itself in the slaughters that accompanied the conquests of the First Crusade and the forced conversions that were perpetrated in the East and in Spain.[89] Only toward the end of the twelfth century did the picture of the "noble heathen," the pagan who was capable of good actions, begin to take hold among ordinary laymen.[90] Given this feeling, it was hardly possible for crusade propagandists to write in terms of love of enemy; on the contrary, crusading literature and propaganda played on the existing xenophobia by the use of emotive terms – enemies of God, servants of the Devil, servants of the Anti-Christ – to describe the Muslims.[91]

But this negative explanation is not sufficient. The popes and their representatives must have brought up the subject of love because of the positive feelings they knew would be aroused in those who listened to their appeals. I believe that, as with love of God, we find here echoes of the secular world. It will have been noticed that in the sources from which I have quoted the words most commonly used to refer to fellow-Christians are brothers and friends. And at this time the word friend as often as not meant kinsman, as well as simply friend, as in a French eleventh-century document which referred to "his friends, that is to say his mother, his brothers, his sisters and his other relatives by blood or by marriage."[92] Men hearing these words would be encouraged to think of fellow Christians as their relatives and the specific use of this kind of imagery is to be found in one of the reports of Pope Urban's sermon at Clermont, in which he was said to have referred to the eastern Christians as "your full brothers, your comrades, your brothers born of the same mother, for you are sons of the same Christ and the same Church."[93] It is well-known that in the central Middle Ages kinship was regarded as creating the same sort of binding obligations as vassalage. The family was a source of strength to the individual, and ties of kinship took precedence, along with vassalage, over all others. It looks as though crusade propagandists decided to present crusading love to laymen in the same terms as love of family. And if one accepts the modern French historian Georges Duby's belief that in twelfth-century knightly families "the patrimony seemed indeed to have been the essential support for the recollection . . . of family consciousness,"[94] then the idea of Palestine as the hereditary patrimony of Christ takes on a new meaning. In an age obsessed by family land-holdings, Christ's children were being aroused by threats to their father's inheritance.[95]

My suggestion that crusading charity was presented to the laity as an example of family love leads to a further point. French historian Marc Bloch has written that "the Middle Ages, from beginning to end, and particularly in the feudal era, lived under the sign of private vengeance."[96] The history of the eleventh, twelfth, and thirteenth centuries is punctuated by violent vendettas. The Church was naturally opposed to them, but it looks as though in its preaching of crusades it was not averse to using the imagery of the family feud to attract knights. Vengeance on the infidel who had oppressed Christians' brothers and seized their fathers' patrimony was a theme in crusade propaganda;[97] and when in 1198 Pope Innocent III referred to crusaders being summoned "as sons to take vengeance on an injury to their father and as brothers to avenge the destruction of their brothers,"[98] everyone must have known what he meant. The crusade was in this sense a blood-feud waged against those who had harmed members of Christ's family.

But I would also argue that love, even in the debased form in which it was presented to potential crusaders, was theologically essential to the crusading movement, because for Christians in all ages sacred violence cannot be proposed on any grounds save that of love. And the idea of such charity, in the sense of love, contributed to the crusades' attraction in that, while all sorts of motives and feelings conditioned the response of Latin Christians to the popes' appeals to take the cross, contemporaries really did feel that they were engaging in something morally satisfying. In an age dominated by the theology of merit this explains why participation in crusades was believed to be meritorious, why the expeditions were seen as penitential acts that could gain indulgences, and why death in battle was regarded as martyrdom. In the 1930s Carl Erdmann, in his influential book on the origins of the movement, linked it to the eleventh-century reformers who were, he explained, "the very men who stood for the idea of holy war and sought to put it into practice."[99] His association of the reform movement with the development of the crusading idea was one of the most striking features of a brilliant study, but it can be argued that he did not take things far enough; that, although he gave evidence for a relationship between reform and sacred violence, he did not explain why such a relationship existed. In fact, as manifestations of Christian love, the crusades were as much the products of the renewed spirituality of the central Middle Ages, with its concern for living the *vita apostolica* (the life in imitation of that of the Apostles) and expressing Christian ideals in active works of charity, as were the new hospitals, the pastoral work of the Augustinians and Premonstratensians, and the service of the friars. The charity of Saint Francis may now appeal to us more than that of the crusaders, but both sprang from the same roots.

NOTES

1 Eugenius III, "Epistolae et privilegia," *Patrologia Latina* (hereafter *PL*), vol. 180, col. 1064.

2 Peter of Blois, "Epistolae," *PL*, vol. 207, col. 533.

3 Rutebeuf, *Onze poèmes concernant la croisade*, ed. Julia Bastin and E. Faral (Paris: P. Genthner, 1946), p. 63.

4 See Jonathan S. C. Riley-Smith, *What Were the Crusades?* (London: Macmillan, 1977), pp. 13–15.

5 *Epistulae et chartae ad historiam primi belli sacri spectantes*, ed. Heinrich Hagenmeyer (Hildesheim, 1901; reprint New York: G. Olms, 1973), p. 137. See also *Papsturkunden in Spanien. I. Katalonien*, ed. Paul Kehr (Berlin: Weidmannsche, 1928), p. 287; *Epistolae et chartae*, ed. Hagenmeyer, pp. 178–9 (a letter from Pope Paschal II [1099–1118]).

6 Bernard of Clairvaux, "Epistolae," *PL*, vol. 182, no. 364.

7 Baldric of Dol, "Historia Jerosolimitana," *Recueil des Historiens occidentaux des croisades* (hereafter *RHC Oc.*) 4, p. 16. See also Baldric of Dol, *Epistolae et chartae*, ed. H. Hagenmayer (Heidelberg: Carl Winters Universitätbuchhandlung, 1913), p. 164; Ekkehard of Aura, "Hierosolymita," *RHC Oc.* 5, p. 15. Quotations from scripture are given in the "Douai" translation.

8 Robert of Rheims, "Historia Iherosolimitana," *RHC Oc.* 3, p. 728; and see also p. 850; Fulcher of Chartres, *Historia Hierosolymitana*, ed. H. Hagenmeyer (Heidelberg: Carl Winters Universitätbuchhandlung, 1913), pp. 115–16, 163; Gaufridus, "Dictamen," *RHC Oc.* 5, p. 349; Henry of Huntingdon, "De captione Antiochiae a christianis," *RHC Oc.* 5, p. 374. For the case put another way about a century later, see Cardinal Henry of Albano, *Tractatus de peregrinante civitate dei*, *PL*, vol. 204, col. 361.

9 *The Deeds of the Franks and the Other Pilgrims to Jerusalem*, ed. Rosalind Hill (London: Thomas Nelson and Sons, 1962), p. 1. See Paul Rousset, *Les origines et les caractères de la première croisade* (Neuchâtel: Bacconière, 1945), p. 99.

10 Ekkehard of Aura, "Hierosolymita," p. 39 and p. 34, "Historia de translatione," *RHC Oc.* 5, p. 257.

11 Odo of Deuil, *De profectione Ludovici VII in orientem*, ed. Virginia Gingerick Berry (New York: Norton, 1948), p. 6.

12 *Les chansons de croisade*, ed. Joseph Bedier and Pierre Aubry (Paris: H. Champion, 1909), p. 20. Friedrich-Wilhelm Wentzlaff-Eggebert, *Kreuzzugsdichtung des Mittelalters* (Berlin: De Gruyter, 1960), p. 325, has suggested that vernacular poetry reflected the themes of crusade preaching. I am inclined to think that the traffic of ideas was two-way.

13 *Papsturkunden für Templer und Johanniter*, ed. Rudolf Hiestand (Göttingen: Vandenhoeck and Ruprecht, 1972), no. 8.

14 Innocent III, *Die Register Innocenz III*, eds Othmar Hageneder and Anton Haidacher (Graz: Bölhaus, 1964), vol. 1, nos. 13, 302, 407; Innocent III, "Opera omnia," *PL*, vol. 215, cols 1339–40; Innocent III, "Quia maior," ed. Georgine Tangl, *Studien zum Register Innocenz III* (Weimar: Bölhaus, 1929), pp. 88–9; Roger of Howden, *Chronica*, ed. William Stubbs (London: Longman, 1868–71), vol. 4, pp. 165–6.

15 Innocent III, *Register*, no. 302; see also Innocent III, "Opera omnia," *PL*, vol. 215, col. 1339.

16   Roger of Howden, *Chronica* 4, p. 72. This echoes Urban II at Clermont as reported by Baldric of Dol, "Historia," p. 15.
17   Innocent III, "Quia maior," p. 88.
18   Innocent III, "Opera omnia," *PL*, vol. 215, col. 1340.
19   *Quinti Belli Sacri Scriptores minores*, ed. Reinhold Röhricht (Geneva: Typis J. G. Fink, 1879), p. 4.
20   Odo of Châteauroux, "Sermones de tempore et sanctis," ed. Jean-Baptiste Pitra, *Analecta novissima* (Paris, 1888), vol. 2, pp. 310–15. For an even later example, see Rutebeuf, *Onze poèmes*, pp. 121, 128.
21   Marc Bloch, *Feudal Society* (London: Routledge and Kegan Paul, 1961), p. 233.
22   Guibert of Nogent, "Historia quae dicitur Gesta Dei per Francos," *RHC Oc.* 4, p. 137. See also Baldric of Dol, "Historia," p. 14.
23   "Constitutiones pro zelo fidei," ed. Heinrich Finke, in *Konzilienstudien zur Geschichte des 13. Jahrhunderts* (Münster: Regensberg, 1891), p. 113.
24   *Les chansons de croisade*, ed. Bedier and Aubry, p. 20.
25   Carl Erdmann, *The Origin of the Idea of Crusade* (Princeton, NJ: Princeton University Press, 1977), pp. 201–10. See also Ian S. Robinson, "Gregory VII and the Soldiers of Christ," *History* 58 (1973): 177–84.
26   Innocent III, "Opera omnia," *PL*, vol. 214, cols 809–10; and 215, col. 1500; Innocent III, "Quia maior," pp. 89–90.
27   James of Vitry, "Sermones vulgares," ed. J. B. Pitra, *Analecta novissima* (Paris: Typis tusculanis, 1888), vol. 2, p. 422.
28   Odo of Châteauroux, "Sermones," pp. 310–11.
29   Erdmann, *Origin*, pp. 349–50, 355ff.
30   Baldric of Dol, "Historia," pp. 13–15. See also Hugh of S. Maria, "Itineris Hierosolymitani Compendium," *RHC Oc.* 5, p. 363; "Narratio Floriacensis," *RHC Oc.* 5, p. 357.
31   See Riley-Smith, *What Were the Crusades?*, pp. 70–1.
32   Robinson, "Gregory VII," pp. 169–92.
33   Guibert of Nogent, p. 124. See also Pope Urban II's letter to Vallombrosa, "Papsturkunden in Florenz," ed. W. Wiederhold, *Nachrichten von der Gesellschaft der Wissenschaften zu Göttingen* (1901), p. 313.
34   Radulph of Caen, "Gesta Tancredi," *RHC Oc.* 3, p. 606. See Erdmann, *Origin*, pp. 336–7.
35   Rousset, *Origines*, pp. 154–5, 159–63.
36   *Die ursprüngliche Templerregel*, ed. Gustav Schnürer (Freiburg: Herder, 1903), p. 147.
37   Bernard of Clairvaux, "De laude novae militiae," *Opera Omnia*, eds Henri Rochais and Jean Leclercq (Rome: Editiones cistercienses, 1963), vol. 3, pp. 219–22.
38   James of Vitry, "Sermones," p. 406.
39   Jonathan S. C. Riley-Smith, *The Knights of St. John in Jerusalem and Cyprus* (London: Macmillan, 1967), p. 76.
40   "Un document sur les débuts des Templiers," ed. Jean Leclercq, *Revue d'histoire ecclésiastique* 52 (1957): 87. For the authorship, see Marie Luise Bulst-Thiele, *Sacrae Domus Militiae Templi Hierosolymitani Magistri* (Göttingen: Vandenhoeck und Ruprecht, 1974), p. 23.
41   *Papsturkunden für Templer*, ed. Rudolf Hiestand (Göttingen: Vandenhoeck und Ruprecht, 1972), no. 3, pp. 205–6. See also *Cartulaire général de l'ordre de Temple 1119?–1150*, ed. Marquis d'Albon (Paris: H. Champion, 1913), vol. 1, no. 4: "Such eminence of charity and grace of praiseworthy honesty are seen to abound among the devoted knights of the Temple of Jerusalem."
42   *Papsturkunden für Templer*, no. 27; and nos. 38, 54, 75, 93.
43   *Cartulaire général de l'ordre des Hospitaliers de St. Jean de Jérusalem (1100–1310)*, ed. Joseph Delaville Le Roulx (Paris: E. Leroux, 1894–1906), no. 627.

44 *Cartulaire des Hospitaliers*, no. 911.
45 Alexander III, "Opera omnia," *PL*, vol. 200, col. 599, and cols 601–2. For the background, see R. C. Smail, "Latin Syria and the West, 1149–1187," *Transactions of the Royal Historical Society*, 5th series, 19 (1969): 13–14.
46 Innocent III, "Quia maior," p. 90.
47 Peter Lombard, "Sententiarum libri quatuor," *PL*, vol. 192, iii, D. xxvii, *c*.4, DD. xxix–xxx.
48 Augustine, "De sermone Domini in monte," *CC:SL* 35, I, xx §§ 63–5.
49 For instance, Augustine, *De civitate Dei*, *CC:SL* 47–8, XIX, vii, xxi.
50 Augustine, "Epistolae," *PL*, vol. 33, no. xciii § 8. But cf. R. S. Hartigan, "St Augustine on War and Killing: The Problem of the Innocent," *Journal of the History of Ideas* 27 (1966): 201–4.
51 Augustine, "De sermone Domini in monte," I, xix § 63; "In epistolam Joannis ad Parthos tractatus," *PL*, vol. 35, VII § 8; *De civitate Dei*, XIX, xvi; "Epistolae," nos. lxxxix § 2, cxxxviii § 14, cliii §17, clxxxv §§ 7, 21.
52 Augustine, "Epistolae," nos. xciii §§ 2–4, clxxxv §§ 7, 33–4.
53 Augustine, "De sermone Domini in monte," I, xx § 64; "Contra Faustum Manichaeum," *PL*, vol. 42, xxii § 79; "Contra litteras Petiliani," *PL*, vol. 43, II, lxxxvi § 191.
54 Augustine, "De sermone Domini in monte," I, xix § 65; "Contra Faustum Manichaeum," xxii § 79; "Contra epistolam Parmeniani," *PL*, vol. 43, iii § 3; "Contra litteras Petiliani," II, xx § 44.
55 Augustine, "Contra litteras Petiliani," II, xix § 43, lxxx § 177; "Epistolae," nos. xciii § 7, clxxxv § 22.
56 Augustine, "Epistolae," nos. lxxxix § 6, xciii §§ 1, 6, c §§ 13, 16, cxxxviii §§ 14–15, clxxiii §§ 3–10, clxxxv §§ 23–4, 46; "Contra Gaudentium," *PL*, vol. 43, i § 28; "Sermones" *PL*, vol. 38, no. cxii § 8.
57 Augustine, "Epistolae," nos. xciii §§ 1–3, 17–19, cliii § 16, clxxiii § 2, clxxxv §§ 7, 13–15, 21, 29, 32.
58 Augustine, "Epistolae," nos. xciii § 5, clxxxv §§ 8–11. See also "Contra epistolam Parmeniani," i §§ 13–15; "Contra litteras Petiliani," II, xix–xx §§ 43–4, lxxxvi § 191, lxxxviii § 195; "Epistolae," nos. xciii § 50, c §§ 7, 11, cviii § 14.
59 Augustine, "Epistolae," nos. lxxxix § 2, cciv § 4. See "De sermone Domini in monte," 1, v § 13; "Contra epistolam Parmeniani," i §§ 13–15; "Contra litteras Petiliani," II, lxxxiv § 186; "Epistolae," nos. xciii §§ 8, 16, clxxxv § 9.
60 Augustine, "Epistolae," no. clxxx § 9.
61 Gratian, "Decretum," ed. Emil Friedberg, *Corpus iuris canonici*, 1 (Leipzig: ex officina Bernhardi Tauchnitz, 1879), C. 23, q. 6, c. 4 d.p.c.
62 Etienne Gilson, *The Christian Philosophy of Saint Augustine* (London: Victor Gollancz, 1961), pp. 154–5.
63 Augustine, "Contra Faustum Manichaeum," xxii § 73.
64 Augustine, "Contra Faustum Manichaeum," xxii § 75.
65 Augustine, *De civitate Dei*, 1, xxi, xxvi; and also "Contra Faustum Manichaeum," xxii § 75; "Quaestiones in Heptateuchum" *CC:SL* 33, VI, x.
66 James A. Brundage, *Medieval Canon Law and the Crusader* (Madison, WI: University of Wisconsin Press, 1969), pp. 21, 29 and Brundage, "Holy War and the Medieval Lawyers," *The Holy War*, ed. Thomas Patrick Murphy (Columbus, OH: Ohio State University Press, 1976), p. 116.
67 Anselm of Lucca, *Opera Omnia*, *PL*, vol. 149, cols 532–4; A. Stickler, "Il potere coattivo materiale della Chiesa nella riforma Gregoriana, secondo Anselmo da Lucca," *Studi gregoriani* 2 (1947): 235–85; Erdmann, *Origins*, pp. 244–5.
68 Pierre Fournier and Gabriel Le Bras, *Histoire des collections canoniques en occident* (Paris: Recueil Sirey, 1931–2), ii, pp. 82–3, 96–7.
69 Ivo of Chartres, "Decretum," *PL*, vol. 161, x cc. 4, 157.

70   Ivo of Chartres, "Decretum," x c. 60; "Panormia" *PL*, vol. 161, viii c. 9.
71   Ivo of Chartres, "Panormia," viii c. 42.
72   Ivo of Chartres, "Decretum," x cc. 60, 76, 77; "Panormia," viii c. 22.
73   Ivo of Chartres, "Decretum," x cc. 62, 76, 95; "Panormia," viii c. 36.
74   Fournier and Le Bras, *Histoire*, ii, p. 97.
75   Ivo of Chartres, "Panormia," viii cc. 15–17; and see also c. 58.
76   Ivo of Chartres, "Decretum," x c. 105.
77   Gratian, "Decretum," C. 23, q. 1 c. 2.
78   Gratian, "Decretum," C. 23 q. 4 c. 26 d.p.c.
79   Gratian, "Decretum," C. 23 q. 4 c. 16 d.p.c.
80   Gratian, "Decretum," C. 23 q. 4 c. 24; q. 5, c. 36.
81   Gratian, "Decretum," C. 23 q. 4 cc. 25, 37.
82   Gratian, "Decretum," C. 23 q. 4 cc. 32 d.p.c., 33.
83   Gratian, "Decretum," C. 23 q. 4 c. 37.
84   Gratian, "Decretum," C. 23 q. 4 cc. 43–4, 51.
85   Gratian, "Decretum," C. 23 q. 4 c. 54 d.p.c.
86   See James A. Weisheipl, *Friar Thomas d'Aquino* (Oxford: Blackwell, 1974), pp. 383–4.
87   Thomas Aquinas, "Contra impugnantes Dei cultum et religionem," *Opera omnia iussu Leonis XIII P.M. edita*, 41 (Rome: Ex typographia Polyglotta, 1948, 1970), cap. xvi, esp. § 4.
88   Alexander III, *Summa*, ed. Friedrich Thaner (Innsbruck: Wagner, 1874), esp. pp. 88–98.
89   Pierre Boissonade, *Du nouveau sur la Chanson de Roland* (Paris: Champion, 1923), pp. 291–2; Rousset, *Origines*, pp. 110–33.
90   For a recent survey of the literature, see Rainer Christoph Schwinges, *Kreuzzugsideologie und Toleranz* (Stuttgart: Hiersemann, 1977), pp. 102–8.
91   For the terms used at the time of the First Crusade, see Rousset, *Origines*, pp. 104–5.
92   Bloch, *Feudal Society*, pp. 123–4, and p. 231, where he argued that the word *friend (amicus)* was also often used of a vassal. For references to *amici*, perhaps in this sense, see Fulcher of Chartres, *Historia*, p. 137; Henry of Albano, "Tractatus," cols 360–1. For the use of the terminology of mercenaries with reference to crusaders, see Fulcher of Chartres, *Historia*, p. 136; Baldric of Dol, "Historia," p. 15.
93   Baldric of Dol, "Historia," pp. 12–13. See also Fulcher of Chartres, *Historia*, pp. 132–3, for a reference to the eastern Christians as "confratribus vestris."
94   Georges Duby, *The Chivalrous Society* (London: Arnold, 1977), p. 146.
95   Or their mother's inheritance: see, for instance, Peter of Blois, "De Hierosolymitana peregrinatione acceleranda," *PL*, vol. 207, col. 1063.
96   Bloch, *Feudal Society*, p. 125; and pp. 123–33.
97   For the First Crusade, see Rousset, *Origines*, pp. 105–6; and for ideas of vengeance in the epics, p. 126.
98   Innocent III, *Register*, no. 302. See also Roger of Howden, iv, p. 165; Innocent III, "Quia maior," p. 90.
99   Erdmann, *Origins*, p. 143 and *passim*.

3

THE ORDERS OF SOCIETY IN THE ELEVENTH AND TWELFTH CENTURIES

Giles Constable

When we teach the Middle Ages, we often present a notion of the "Three Orders": "Those who work," "Those who fight," and "Those who pray," in the formulation of the bishops Adalbero of Laon (d. 1031) and Gerard of Cambrai (d. 1051). There was a much broader concern in the Middle Ages about "orders" that went far beyond the socio-political orderings of the Golden Age posited by Adalbero and Gerard. This selection from Constable's longer work on "The Orders of Society" describes the eleventh- and twelfth-century commentary that divided society into two, three, four, or even seven parts, often at the same time. Constable discusses the ordo monasticus *or the* ordo clericus *as "ways of life" which are not yet separated into monastic or religious orders or administrative institutions. The "ideas of hierarchy and authority," and the practice among monastic and clerical writers of looking for "a deeper meaning in the observable world," as Constable puts it, led medieval writers, almost all of whom were clerical or monastic, to describe their world using comparisons to biblical duos, triads, and quartets. Such biblically based schemes of social organization allowed eleventh- and twelfth-century clergy to discuss "orders" in terms of their relative purity and aided in the elevation of the clergy that was central to Church reform in this period when clerics assimilated the monastic virtues into their own order. These efforts can be recognized as part of the intellectual ferment of the twelfth-century's program to organize its sources and ideas. Such formalized schemes also had political significance when they both separated clergy from laity and placed the Church or the Pope at the top of both diagrams, as we see in Figures 3.1 and 3.2. This selection comes from "The Orders of Society," in Giles Constable, Three Studies in Religious and Social Thought (Cambridge, 1995), pp. 251–66, 289–304; notes have been renumbered.*

* * *

The attention that has been given by scholars in recent years to the three orders of "those who prayed (*oratores*)," "those who fought (*bellatores*)," and "those who worked (*laboratores*)" has tended to obscure the fact that society was ordered in other ways, especially in the early Middle Ages.[1] The most common division was into a different three orders: first, of clerics, who ruled the church and were also called prelates, fathers, rectors, and doctors; second, of monks, nuns, and hermits who left the world to serve God; and, third, of laymen and -women who lived and worked in the world. These were parallel to the orders of the continent, who abstained from sexual activity and were sometimes equated with widows and widowers; the virgins; and the married. . . .[2] Over the years the clerical and monastic orders tended to amalgamate into a single clerical order, with two branches: one secular, which lived in the world, and the other regular, which followed a rule and lived a life of withdrawal. Society was therefore often seen as consisting of two orders of the clergy and laity. Meanwhile, however, the lay order divided into the orders of fighters and workers, which formed the basis of the second and third estates, and in the late Middle Ages into the many occupational and professional groups out of which eventually emerged the class structure of modern society.

The significance of these divisions and their relation to the actual conditions and changes of society are debated by scholars. While some of them were clearly more realistic than others, and they all to some extent reflected actual social conditions and developments, historians cannot expect to find in them an accurate picture of society.[3] The writers of almost all the works cited here were monks, nuns, or clerics, and very few of them, aside from an occasional scribe who classified the witnesses to charters, sought to give a factual description of medieval society. Their background and training accustomed them to look for a deeper meaning in the observable world around them and to apply to it the patterns they found in the Bible and other traditional sources. The differences between darkness and light, night and day, and sleep and awakening, for instance, or between reptiles, fish, and birds were of greater interest to them as part of God's plan than as natural phenomena, and the ordering of society was an essential part of that plan. They moved with relative ease between the patterns found in the sources and the world of observation and found correspondences which for them contained an inner truth. These views were embodied in sermons and other types of works addressed to a wider audience, and they were probably shared by many members of the non-literate public, who also saw society as divided into orders. . . . It is often hard to tell in exactly what sense *ordo* was being used, and especially to distinguish the social and sacramental senses of the term; but its root meaning remained row, rank, or grade, usually in a collective sense, which distinguished it from an individual honor or dignity as these terms are now used. One entered into rather than received an order, which was marked by a way of life and an internal discipline as well as exterior distinctions and obligations.[4]

Before studying the application of this concept of "orders" to society in the Middle Ages, several questions need to be asked, even if they cannot be fully answered. First, on what were they based? Augustine gave a broad answer in the *Enchiridion*, where he classified the "men to be saved" in I Timothy 2.4 into various groups of twos and threes: royal and private; noble and non-noble; lofty and humble; learned and unlearned; healthy and weak; gifted, slow-minded, and foolish; rich, poor, and middle; male and female; infants, boys, and adolescents; young, grown-up, and old; and as differing in languages, customs, crafts, professions, and in their wills and consciences.[5] An Anglo-Norman lawyer in the early twelfth century wrote that "There is a distinction of persons in condition, in sex, according to profession and order, according to the law to be observed, which should be kept in mind by judges in dealing with all matters."[6] An individual's position in society thus depended on various factors, and distinctions could be made on many grounds, which are themselves an indication of the concerns of society.

Second, did they include everyone? Some in theory did, and others did not, but most of them applied only to Christians. The famous canon "There are two types (*genera*) of Christians" in the collection of canons called the *Decretum* of Gratian (fl. 1140) was attributed to Jerome (d. 420), though it probably dated from the eleventh century, and Rupert of Deutz (d. 1125) referred to "the three orders of those who believe in Christ."[7] Most writers were aware of the existence of Jews, Moslems, and pagans, and a few made specific allowance for an order of those outside the church or of the unfaithful.[8] According to Bruno of Segni, abbot of Montecassino (d. 1123) in his commentary on the Psalms, all members of the church were encompassed by Galaad, Manasses, and Ephraim, who stood respectively for the doctors and teachers, the seekers for heavenly things, and "those who render the fruit of good work to God."[9] Bruno apparently excluded those who were idle (presumably in a spiritual sense) or were not members of the church, and the borders even between comprehensive categories like Christians and non-Christians, married and unmarried, and free and unfree were blurred by the existence of converts, of widows and widowers, and of freedmen who came between the free and the slave.

A third question is whether the divisions were mutually exclusive. As a rule a person could not belong to more than one group within a system, but many systems overlapped. In a charter for Cluny in 1107 a donor established four categories of people who were forbidden to infringe his gift: "a man or woman, from those close to me or from among strangers, free or servile, cleric or lay."[10] Each of these divisions was exclusive, but some categories could be combined with others. A man could thus be a stranger, free, and lay, but a cleric could not be a woman or servile. As time went on the categories tended to break down. The distinction in a charter of 971 between "faithful clerics and noble clerics" reflected the imposition on the clerical order of the division of the lay order into "faithful" and "nobles."[11] Distinctions based on birth, position, wealth, and power cut across other social categories. In the eleventh and twelfth centuries, many people were puzzled by the emergence of what may be called cross or anomalous orders, like the military orders and lay brothers, who were both lay and religious, and the *ministeriales*, military followers of the German kings who were both knights and unfree.

Fourth, how were the orders evaluated? Nearly all social divisions involved some measure of ranking, and some were clearly hierarchical and served as a basis of social stratification. The equation of order with hierarchy by Denis the pseudo-Areopagite (*c*.500 CE) was cited by Thomas Aquinas (d. 1274) in the *Summa theologia*, and within each category one group was commonly ranked above or below the others.[12] In the early Middle Ages monks were usually ranked above clerics and laymen, and "those who prayed," above "those who fought" and "those who worked." In corporate and organic models of society, some parts of the body were usually esteemed more than others, as the head and heart more than the feet, though they were based on a view of the interdependence of the various parts, all of which were necessary to the proper functioning of the whole body. Several writers in the twelfth century recognized that the rank or esteem of individuals did not depend exclusively on the prestige of their order. Gerhoh of Reichersberg (d. 1169) said that no order or way of life was holier than another and that a deacon might be holier than a priest and a layman than a monk, and Peter of Blois (d. 1205) maintained that each order of humanity deserved eternal life, though there were differing roads to salvation.[13] The thirteenth-century Bonaventure wrote that the orders should be distinguished according to their degree of perfection, which varied in terms of their loftiness, productivity, and discipline and that, "the comparison is according to status, not according to persons, since a lay person is sometimes more perfect than a religious person."[14] As time went on there was a tendency to reassess the value of the orders, and some authors ranked the clergy, and some even the laity, highest.

The possibility of moving from one order to another also posed a problem. ... Laymen and clerics could become monks, according to a follower of Anselm, "but a monk may never leave his order." Robert Pullen (d. 1147) on the other hand, maintained that laymen could become monks and both laymen and monks could become prelates, but prelates could not become monks, and neither prelates nor monks could become laymen.[15] Bonaventure argued on the analogy of the Trinity that the laity like the Father was productive, the clergy like the Son was both productive and produced, and the monks like the Holy Spirit were only produced. Laymen could therefore become clerics or monks, clerics could become monks but not laymen, and monks could not become either clerics or laymen. He left the way open, however, for a cleric who was in lower orders and "totally unsuitable" to revert to the lay order.[16] In fact, under special circumstances, both clerics and monks were sometimes laicized.[17] Andrew the Chaplain (often known to students as Andreas Capellanus, (d. 1186) distinguished three parallel orders of men and women – common, noble, and more noble – and a fourth order of most noble men, whom he equated with the clergy. He asserted that people should keep, and especially marry, within their order, saying that "the distinction of orders" had always existed "so that everyone may remain within the limits of their type and may be satisfied for all things within the boundaries of their order." Andrew referred repeatedly to the "boundaries" of the ranks and orders, but he knew in fact both that men and women married outside their orders and that women took their husbands' orders and also that rulers could make a common man noble on account of his probity and way of life.[18]

The position of women in the medieval orders of society was unclear.[19] Women were indeed not specifically mentioned in many categories and were excluded from some, above all the clergy. But it would be untrue to say that they were never mentioned in the descriptions of social orders. No one doubted that women prayed, occasionally fought and governed, and above all worked, even if their role was invisible. The divisions based on gender and on sexual activity clearly included, and sometimes gave priority to, women. Tertullian (d. 245) described three grades of virginity made up of virgins from birth, from rebirth in baptism, and from refusal to remarry, and Ambrose (d. 397) in his treatise *On Widows* described "the triple virtue" of conjugal, widowed, and virginal chastity.[20] These categories applied to men as well as women, but Wolbero of Saint-Pantaloon in the twelfth century referred to virgins "who hold the highest rank."[21] A charter from Béziers in 1057 listed "any bishop, any cleric, any man, either great or small, or any types of women;" Ortlieb of Zwiefalten (d. 1163) mentioned "many nobles and middling men and men of lesser fortune and of both sexes"; Abbo of Fleury (d. 1004), Gilbert of Limerick (d. 1147), and Andrew the Chaplain listed parallel orders of men and women; and James of Vitry (d. 1240) in the early thirteenth century addressed some of his sermons to women, including nuns, female serfs, widows, and virgins.[22] A woman holding a child is in the front row of the "people" (populus) in an illustration (see Figure 3.1) of the church in an eleventh-century Exultet Roll [a roll containing the text, with illustrations, of Easter praises called "Exultet"].[23] Even more explicit is the diagram (see Figure 3.2) in manuscripts of Gilbert of Limerick's *On the State of the Church*, which dates from the early twelfth century, and shows the three orders of prayers (oratores), ploughers (aratores), and fighters (bellatores) marked respectively O, A, and B, with a V for *viri* and an F for *feminae* on either side. In the associated commentary Gilbert wrote that "I do not say that it is the office of women to pray, to plough, or certainly to fight; but they are associated with and serve those who pray, plough, and fight."[24] This puts it in a nutshell. Women were not excluded from the orders of society, but their role was subordinate to that of men. They existed primarily in relation to men and were subsumed into the orders which were seen as essentially male. . . .

The principal social divisions were distinguished by differences which were recognized and accepted by people at the time, and some of them were enforceable by law. Among the questions Charlemagne (768–814) posed to the bishops and abbots in 811 was what it meant "to leave the world" and

Figure 3.1 Illustration of *Mater Ecclesia* in eleventh-century Exultet Roll. Rome, Bibliotheca Vaticana, Barbarini Latin 592, top third of membrane 1 (© Biblioteca Apostolica Vaticana).

whether arms-bearing and public marriage were the only differences between those who left the world and those who cleaved to it.[25] According to a twelfth-century Italian commentary, "On Invention," people were separated by their differing modes of life and ways of living, and it went on to distinguish soldiers, clerics, and tanners, who presumably stood for all those who worked with their hands.[26] The "modes of life" included the declared objective and intention, which for a monk was withdrawal from the world and dedication to God, for a cleric service of the church, and for a layman work in the world.

As time went on, distinct codes of behavior developed for each order, like chivalry for knights, and sermons *ad status* (addressed to particular estates, orders or groups) spoke to the special obligations and needs of almost

Figure 3.2 Diagram illustrating Gilbert of Limerick's *De statu ecclesiae*. Cambridge University Library, folio 1.27, p. 238 (reproduced by permission of the Syndics of Cambridge University Library).

every occupational group in medieval society. In the eleventh century Gobert of Laon, in his treatise *On the Tonsure and Clothes and Life of Clerics*, said that a cleric was distinguished by his name, which meant "elect of God," and that "The tonsure and status and clothing also express this."[27] Appearance, clothing, diet, and way of life were all important indications of order and rank.[28] A monk was set off by what he ate as well as by his habit, tonsure, shaved beard, and life of prayer. Nobles were expected both to look and to behave like nobles, and in the late Middle Ages the clothes worn by the different ranks of society, and by their servants, were regulated by sumptuary laws.[29]

A good example of the importance attached to the concept of order and of "knowing one's place" in medieval society is found in the treatise *On the Institution of Clerics*, which was written in the middle of the twelfth century by the regular canon Philip of Harvengt (d. 1183): "It is good for a man to know the order in which he is constituted and its limit or boundary so that he may neither insolently exceed the clear boundaries nor weakly shrink from them by retiring to the side." Correct behavior is based on knowing the boundaries between the orders, Philip continued. . . . In this passage Philip of Harvengt referred to *ordo* and *ordinare* almost thirty times and used three characteristic classical examples and four biblical quotations on the need for order. Without ever precisely defining them, he stressed the limit, boundary, and fixed borders of the orders, and their truth, dignity, and sanctity. For him this was a matter of practical as well as theoretical importance, since as a regular canon, and hence a cleric, he was concerned to protect the prerogatives of his order, especially parochial rights and revenues, from the encroachments of monks.[30]

Philip barely scratched the surface of the opportunities offered by the Bible to assert the need for clearly defined social orders. In addition to the explicit references to order in the apostle Paul and other places, there were countless pairs and triplets which were used as prototypes or parallels for the various orders of society. The best known were Noah, Daniel, and Job (Ezekiel 14.14–20), who were considered the exemplars respectively of clerics, monks, and laymen (or occasionally of laymen, monks, and clerics) and of the continent, virgins, and married. . . . Noah's ark, Solomon's temple, and the types of sacrifice in Exodus and Leviticus were all rich sources of bipartite, tripartite, and quadripartite models, as were the animals in the books of Genesis and Job.[31] The groups of three in the New Testament were headed by the Trinity, followed by the three Marys; the three dead people raised by Christ; the three groups of angels, shepherds, and kings at the nativity; Lazarus (or Jesus Himself), Mary, and Martha; Mary, Joseph, and Simeon; and Peter, James, and John. The way, the truth, and the life in John 14.6 and the good, the acceptable, and the perfect in Romans 12.2 were also used. . . . The Gospel of Matthew furnished Judea, the house, and the field (24.16–8), the master who gave five talents, three talents, and one talent respectively to his servants, "to every one according to his ability" (25.15), and the sower who sowed on stony ground, thorns, and good ground and received harvests of a hundred-, sixty-, and thirtyfold (13.3–8), which were cited as evidence of the rewards awaiting the different orders in heaven. The four animals and seven seals of the Apocalypse were much used in prophetic works, less frequently as social models. The most important pairs were Peter and John and Mary and Martha. Pairs of people of whom "one shall be taken and one shall be left" are found in the Gospels both of Matthew (24.40–1), where there are two pairs, one in the field and one at the mill, and of Luke (17.34–5), where there are three pairs, one each in bed, grinding, and in the field, which were compared to monks who prayed and meditated, clerics who served the church, and laymen who worked, though opinions differed over whether the clerics or the laity were in the field or at the mill.[32]

Parallels like these may seem far-fetched, not to say fanciful, but the use of the Bible in this way was common practice in the Middle Ages, and still is among certain groups of Christians. It was the task of theologians and especially commentators to discover the truths contained in ancient texts, which were covered by the integument (the external skin or coating), as it was called, both of literal meaning and of allegory, and by the patina of age and neglect. . . . The very number and variety of biblical prototypes for social orders therefore shows the importance attached in the Middle Ages to the concept of the division of society into distinct orders. No single system of social orders prevailed in the eleventh and twelfth centuries, when there were any number of different, and frequently overlapping, schema for dividing people into two, three, four, or sometimes more, categories. . . .

The revival of interest in Antiquity, especially Calcidius's (*c*.4 CE) translation of the *Timaeus*, where Plato divided society into priests, laborers, and soldiers, and in the *Celestial Hierarchy* and *Ecclesiastical Hierarchy* of Denis the pseudo-Areopagite, introduced various ancient schemes of social order into Western thought.[33] Calcidius equated Plato's divisions with the highest, middle, and lowest and these in turn with heavenly, angelic, and earthly; wise men, military men, and common men; the head, chest, and lower parts; and reason, energy, and desire. The medieval commentators (including Thomas Aquinas) were attracted by the model of the city-state and saw the divisions as powerful men, honest citizens, and tradesmen – sometimes typified by tailors – as the upper, middle, and lower (suburban) parts of a town, and as greater men, soldiers, and saddle-makers. . . .

It is impossible to study here all the systems that were put forward at this time, of which some were highly idiosyncratic. Bishop Fulbert of Chartres (d. 1028/9) who was an experienced administrator and level-headed man, wrote to king Robert of France (972–1031) in 1027 – the same time that bishops Adalbero of Laon (d. 1037) and Gerard of Cambrai (d. 1051) expounded the functional tripartition of society – that a recent rain of blood, which washed easily off wood but not off rock or human flesh, stood for three types of men:

wood for the pious and chaste, rock for the impious, and flesh for the forni-cators; and in his poem "On Fear, Hope, and Love," of which there are three versions, Fulbert equated the fear of punishment to God's servant or groom, the hope for reward to His vassal or soldier, and the love of virtue to His likeness and offspring, or to a king or the son of a king. Together they consti-tuted "the triple order of men."[34] In one of the *Similitudes* attributed to Anselm of Bec (d. 1109, abbot of Bec, later Archbishop of Canterbury) men were divided into angels, good men, and mercenaries, who served respectively, like the followers of a king, for the lands they already held, in the hope of recov-ering lands lost by their parents, and only for money; and in another they were divided into the orders of prayers, husbandmen, and defenders, to whom God assigned differing offices in the world, in the same way the head of a household makes use of sheep, cows, and dogs.[35]

The ideas of hierarchy and authority, the distinctions between the earthly orders, and their correspondence with the heavenly orders were emphasized in the works of Denis the pseudo-Areopagite. Humbert of Silva Candida (*c*.1000–61) followed Denis in *Against Simoniacs*, where he cited the nine vari-eties of men which corresponded to the orders of angels.[36] Later in this work Humbert used an organic model and compared the clerical order, lay power, and the lowly (*vulgus*) to the eyes, chest and arms, and lower parts of a body, and in an eleventh-century poem written in Humbert's honor the traditional model of Noah, Daniel, and Job was applied to the three "series" of men who fight, who preach and lead the celibate life, and who marry – "The third order gives associates by good marriage."[37]

The parallel between the orders of angels in heaven and of men on earth was also brought out by Botho of Prüm or Prüfening (d. *c*.1170) in *On the State of the House of God*, where he compared the heavenly orders of princi-palities, archangels, and angels to the earthly orders of monks, rulers, and priests, and in the *Gregorianum* of Garnier of Saint-Victor (d. 1170), who said that the earthly, like the heavenly, hierarchy rose from the priests, who paral-leled the angels, to those who rejected all earthly things and like the seraphim rested in the love of God.[38] This theme is also found in the works of Bernard of Clairvaux (d. 1153), Alan of Lille (d. *c*.1202), and other Cistercian writers, and, in the thirteenth century, of William of Auvergne (d. 1249) and Thomas Aquinas (d. 1274).[39] These and other works reflected the tendency to divide the lay order along the lines not only of occupation, as between the fighters and workers or rustici and burgenses, but also of social rank, wealth, legal status, and even, occasionally, ethnic origin.[40]

The division of the lay order was paralleled by the tendency to combine the orders of monks and clerics into a single order of churchmen variously known as clerics, prayers (*oratores* or *orantes* in the *Similitudes* of Anselm of Bec), or those who preach and lead a celibate life, according to the poem in honor of Humbert of Silva Candida. The distinctiveness of the monastic order in the early Middle Ages depended upon the fact that most monks were not ordained, but this began to break down in the Carolingian period. As more and more monks took orders, and many of them functioned as priests, it was natural to regard them as the regular branch – those members who lived under a rule – of the clerical order.[41] In the eleventh century the differences between the clerical and monastic orders were further reduced by ecclesiastical reformers who imposed on clerics the rules of celibacy, and sometimes also of the common life, which had previously characterized monks.

The division of society into two rather than three orders had ancient roots and is found in many Carolingian sources, including royal, papal, and conciliar decrees as well as the works of theologians. Abbot Odo of Cluny (927–42) in his *Conferences* distinguished between good men and bad, who went back respectively to Cain and Abel and were perpetuated in Jerusalem and Babylon, between overt evil-doers and hidden evil-doers, "who assume the habit of religion but subject themselves to many vices publicly or to a few secretly," and between the perfect and the less perfect, "who are unable to penetrate spiritual things and deprive the five bodily senses." He compared the orders of the church to the animals in the Book of Job and said that Christ is served by His family, "that is, the entire collection of the elect, who live either in riches or in poverty in the clerical or in the lay order." Elsewhere in the *Conferences*, Odo suggested that society was divided into clerics, monks, and laymen, and in his sermon on Saint Benedict referred to the country-people and town-folk "joined to noble men and adorned with the honest people of clerics," who came to his tomb, but Odo also accepted a bipartite view of society.[42]

Two "ways" were combined with three "orders" in the reply given by abbot Martin of Jumièges, who lived in the mid-tenth century, to the question "Why does the Christian religion fill the church with a three-part order?" Martin had said, according to Dudo of Saint-Quentin (d. c.1043), writing in the early eleventh century, that "Everyone receives his reward according to his labor. ... The sum of the Christian religion is divided into a three-way order by the service of laymen and canons and by the disciplined labor of monks." He went on to distinguish two ways, to which he applied the Greek terms practical (or canonical), by which the lay order lived, and theoretical (or apostolic) "which we sinners strive to follow."[43] The Cluniac historian Ralph Glaber (d. c.1044) also suggested a bipartite within a tripartite division when he wrote that "The middle and lesser men sank to great disgraces on the example of the great men" after "the leaders of both orders" performed deeds of violence and rapine.[44] The two orders here were lay and clerical, within each of which were ranks of majors, middles, and minors. Anselm of Laon (d. 1117), in his commentary on the parable of the sower, said that it designated the three orders of the church, "namely the married, the continent in the active life, and the continent in the contemplative life," but he went on to say:

> The main division ought to be [between] the just [of whom] some are contemplative and some active. The actives are subdivided, however, some married and some continent. The thirty-fold and sixty-fold fruit is given to the actives and the hundred-fold to the contemplatives.[45]

This therefore combined three bipartite divisions into the married and continent, the active and contemplative, and the just and damned.

For many churchmen and writers in the eleventh and twelfth centuries, even when they were themselves monks, the basic social division was between the clergy and the laity. In the illustration already cited (Figure 3.1, p. 73) to an eleventh-century Exultet Roll from Monte Cassino (the monastery founded by Saint Benedict), the figure of Mother Church stands under an arch in the center with the clergy on one side and the people on the other. The clerics include figures both with and without visible tonsures (perhaps standing for monks and secular clerics), and two of them carry books. In the front rank of the people are a man and a woman holding a child.[46] Monks increasingly lost their status as a separate order of society. Herbert of Losinga (d. 1119), who was bishop of Norwich under English Kings William II (1087–1100) and Henry I (1100–35), wrote that "The prerogative of this [clerical] order . . . has been entirely transferred to monks" and that "A monk is the same thing as a cleric."[47] Archbishop Lanfranc of Canterbury (d. 1089) wrote to Pope Alexander II (1061–73) in 1072 that the council of Winchester was attended by "bishops, abbots, and others from the sacred and lay order," and Bonizo of Sutri (d. 1090) said in his *Book on the Christian Life*, which was completed *c.* 1090:

> Some Christians are clerics [and] others laymen, and some in these conditions are subordinate and some superior. Of the superiors placed in the clerical order, some are bishops, others priests of the second order, some abbots, [and] some provosts. But in the lay order some [are] kings, some judges.[48]

Here (as in the Homblières charter from 971 cited above, note 11) the division of rank cut across the division into laymen and clerics, who included monks, since abbots and provosts were among the superiors and simple monks presumably among the subordinates.

The classic formulation of this bipartite view of society was the canon "There are two types of Christians," which almost certainly dates from the eleventh century, although it was attributed to the fourth-century Christian Father Jerome in Gratian's *Decretum* (*c*.1140). . . .[49] The clergy was described as dedicated to contemplation and prayer. Their tonsure was a sign of their rule in the kingdom of God and their renunciation of worldly possessions.

By requiring poverty and common life of clerics this canon both promoted their assimilation with monks and underlined their difference from laymen, who owned property, married, and engaged in worldly activities.[50]

The legal distinction between the clerical and lay orders is found especially in the works of canon lawyers. Ivo of Chartres (d. 1116) wrote to the bishop of Orleans, protesting the participation of ecclesiastical judges in a judicial duel, that "otherwise we would be usurpers of the other order and will obtain the merit neither of our [clerical] office, which we will have put aside, nor of the other [lay office], which we shall have usurped."[51] The two orders were here therefore identified with ecclesiastical and secular jurisdictions. Stephen of Tournai (1128–1203), in his *Summa* on the *Decretum* of Gratian, wrote:

> There are two peoples in the same city under the same king, and two lives according to the two peoples, and two governments according to the two lives, and a double order of jurisdiction proceeds according to the two governments. The city [is] the church; the king of the city, Christ; the two peoples, the two orders in the church, of clerics and laymen; the two lives, spiritual and carnal; the two governments, the priesthood and the kingdom; the double jurisdiction, divine and human law. Render to each its own, and all things will fit.[52]

The ancient political doctrine of the priestly and royal powers was thus transformed into a social doctrine distinguishing two types of people, clerical and lay.

The concept of a separate order of monks, beside and in addition to the clergy and laity, did not disappear in the face of this emphasis on bipartition. The reform movement of the eleventh and twelfth centuries was indeed to some extent inspired by a desire to reform the monastic order, which was thought to have fallen into disrepair, and to assert its influence among the clergy and laity. . . .[53]

The twelfth-century Cistercian, Bernard of Clairvaux, deserves special study on account of the richness of his use of the concept of *ordo*, which he applied not only to monks but to society, the church, and human affairs generally.[54] "Order (*ordo*)," he said in the treatise *On Consideration*, was the opposite of "confusion (*confusio*)," and within a few pages of his treatise called *The Apology* he used the term to apply to the order and orders of monks, the divisions of society, and the proper relation of the body and the spirit.[55] He described Peter Abelard in a letter to cardinal Ivo as "a monk without a rule, a prelate without a cure, [who] neither holds order nor is held by order."[56] "He set in order charity in me" from the Song of Songs was one of Bernard's favorite biblical texts,[57] together with Paul's "Every one in his own order" and the triads of Noah, Daniel, and Job from Ezekiel and three kings and three shepherds at the Nativity. Among texts which were less usually applied to social orders Bernard cited several from the Psalms, including the princes of Judah, Zabulon, and Nephthali (Psalms 67.28), Ephraim, Benjamin, and Manasses (Psalms 79.3), and the people, saints, and "them that are converted to the heart" (Psalms 84.9), and the bed, beam, and rafters and the plants in the garden from the Song of Songs 1.15–6 and 4.13. He used these to illustrate the division of society into the orders of clerics, monks, and laymen and of the clergy (priests, prelates, and rectors), the penitent or continent, and the married or faithful populace, and, more rarely, into other tripartite divisions, as in the seventh sermon on the Song of Songs, where he identified Judah, Zabulon, and Nephthali with the confessors, continent, and contemplatives. In the forty-sixth sermon he referred to Christian princes "of both orders," meaning secular and ecclesiastical, but in other works he insisted on the distinction between monks and both the clergy and the laity, and in a Bernardine text from the abbey of Orval the "states" in the church were described as secular but catholic, religious, and perfect.[58]

In his ninth sermon "On diverse things," Bernard combined two tripartite models based on the people, saints, and the converted in Psalms 84.9 with a bipartite model based on two other biblical texts:

> We are accustomed to understand in these words the three types to whom alone God spoke peace, just as the other prophet [Ezekiel] foresaw that only three men would be saved, Noah, Daniel, and Job, expressing in a different order the same orders of the continent, the prelates, and the married.

He then proceeded to give another interpretation of the categories in Psalms 84, of which the first and third applied to monks: the people were "the brothers with offices who are occupied with external and as it were popular affairs" and the converted were "the cloistered monks who are hampered by no occupation and are freely at leisure to see 'that the Lord is sweet' [Psalms 33.9]." He declared that God speaks peace to these groups "because they strive for the same thing," but by different paths, which Bernard compared (shifting to a bipartite model) to the musical instruments, the psaltery and harp, in Psalms 56.9, of which one gave a higher and the other a lower note, and to Martha and Mary, who chose the best part "although the humble behavior of Martha was perhaps not of less merit with the Lord." The saints who came between these two types in the Psalms, Bernard concluded (moving back to the tripartite model), were the prelates, "for whom both lives are necessary" and who serve both groups and will receive "a greater abundance and overflowing measure of peace" if they minister well.[59] . . .

Bernard excelled at imaginative forays into the realms of imagery and association. In his first sermon on the Nativity, for example, commenting on "Who hath loved us and washed us of our sins" in Apocalypse 1.5, he defined the four uses of water as washing, drinking, irrigating (without which new plantations, he said, "either are less successful or totally perish out of dryness"), and cooking, and he associated these with the four fountains of mercy, wisdom, grace, and love, from which come the waters of remission, discretion, devotion, and emulation, with which we "cook" our affections. Christ demonstrated these qualities during His lifetime and, Bernard added later, promised a fifth fountain of life "after this age." These five fountains corresponded to His wounds, and three of the first four corresponded to the three orders of the church as represented by Noah, Daniel, and Job, and the fourth to all, since everyone needs the fountain of mercy and the cleansing water of remission. Job the layman was associated with wisdom and the drinking water of discretion; Daniel the monk with grace and the irrigating water of devotion; and Noah the prelate with love and the cooking water of emulation."[60]

Bernard moved with ease between the social, institutional, moral, and spiritual applications of his illustrations and texts, which he interpreted in unusual and sometimes unexpected ways, ranging from the sublime, if not to the ridiculous, at least to the down-to-earth, like the allusions to irrigation and cooking in this sermon. . . . Bernard divided monks into the beginners, the advancers, and the perfect in his first sermon on Saint Andrew, where he said that fear of God was the beginning of wisdom, hope the middle, and love the fullness.[61] In other texts the three categories of monks, or sometimes of all men, were described as penitents or beginners, as advancers or initiates, and as completed, arrived, promoted, or persevering. . . .[62] This sort of moral categorization of society was popular in the twelfth century, especially among Cistercians but also with other authors. . . .

According to Hildegard of Bingen (d. 1179), the four living creatures of Apocalypse 4.7 stood for the orders of society: the lion for monks, the calf for clerics, the man for the laity, and the eagle for a fourth order of "men who keep themselves from sins . . . [and] rise to continence from previous laymen."[63] This fourth order thus imposed a division into sinners or sinless on the lay order, or perhaps on all three orders. Elizabeth of Schönau (d. 1164), in one of her visions, saw three paths which expressed "the quality of the three orders in the church, that is, of the married, the continent, and the rectors." The way of the married was surrounded by snakes; the way of the continent was adorned with flowers and free of snakes; and "the middle way between the former two, broader than these, is that of the rectors."[64]

The regular canons also examined the nature of the orders and stressed their moral as well as their social character. Hugh of Saint-Victor (d. 1141) divided men in terms of their attitudes toward the world into those who use it, those who flee and forget it, and those who are oblivious to it.[65] Philip of Harvengt, whose description of the importance of order in society was cited above, returned to the topic at several points in his *Six Treatises on the Institution of Clerics*. All Christians were divided into orders, Philip said, "for among them the clerical order is one thing, the monastic order another, and the military [order] another, each of which is named by its qualities in such a way that they are distinguished by characteristics as by name." He acknowledged that the terms were sometimes used loosely, as when a lettered knight or monk, or even a woman, was called a *clericus* in the sense of literate or knowing letters, but when a *conversus* (converted one, often a lay-brother) was called a *laicus* because he was illiterate; but monks, clerics, and knights were distinguished essentially by what they are, not by their accomplishments or occupations, which might overlap. ... Within the course of his treatise, therefore, Philip shifted from a tripartite division into clerics, monks, and knights, to a bipartite division between the clergy, who included monks and clerics, and the people, who included knights and husbandmen.[66]

This type of division, often with further categories, was common in less formal sources in the twelfth century. "A multitude of nobles, clerics, laymen, husbandmen, and women" grieved at the death of Gerald, abbot of La Sauve Majeure, in 1095, and of clerics, monks, peasants, poor, and all men at the death of count Charles of Flanders in 1127.[67] The canonization [in *c*.1201] of Gilbert of Sempringham (d. 1189) was witnessed by "both religious and seculars, both clerics and laymen, both men and women."[68] The archbishop of Magdeburg in 1107/8 addressed his appeal for a campaign against the Slavs not only to the great magnates but also "to all the faithful of Christ, bishops, abbots, monks, hermits, recluses, provosts, canons, clerics, princes, soldiers, servile knights (*ministeriales*), clients, and to all greater and lesser men."[69] A charter from Saintes in 1137 listed the knights "and many others of both the clerical order and the lay," and Otto of Freising (d. 1158) distinguished the three orders of captains, vavassors (or lower knights), and commoners in north Italy in the middle of the twelfth century. . . .[70]

Underneath many of these lists lay a basic bipartite vision of society, which left an increasingly smaller place for monks. Honorius Augustodunensis (d. 1157) in the *Summa gloria* divided "the university of the faithful" into the clerics who occupied themselves with the speculative life and the people who applied themselves to the active life. A king must be either a cleric or a layman, Honorius said later, adding that "If he is neither a layman nor a cleric then he is a monk," which is impossible because monks neither marry nor bear arms.[71] Hugh of Saint-Victor, in his influential *On the Sacraments*, distinguished the orders of laymen and clerics and the lives of earth and the body and of heaven and the spirit,[72] and Peter Comestor (d. 1178), in his eighteenth sermon, identified the two types of men with the wells dug for men and beasts by Isaac in Genesis 26.[73] . . .

Many writers continued to divide society on ethical, moral, and religious grounds, such as the good and the evil and the elect and the damned.[74] Goscelin of Saint-Bertin (d. 1107) defined the four orders at the Last Judgment as two of the elect (the saints and less perfect) and two of the damned (bad Christians and pagans), and the two worst orders for Guibert of Nogent (d. 1124) were those who acted evilly and those who did not want to act well, whom he compared respectively to Her and Onan.[75] The author of a late twelfth-century treatise on ecclesiastical rhetoric divided men into the two distinctions of the non-Christian infidels, who included pagans and Jews; and faithful Christians, who included apostates, heretics, and schismatics who were under the power of the church and could be compelled to return "to the obligation of their profession."[76] . . .

These texts show that the distinct status of monks was still recognized, even when they were included in the clerical order or regarded as something of an anomaly, as by Honorius Augustodunensis. There are countless references to the decline and restoration of the monastic order in the chronicles, charters, letters, histories, saints' lives, and other types of sources in the twelfth century. The author of the twelfth-century treatise *On the Profession of Monks* stressed that the special blessing of monks marked the distinctiveness of their order, and the monk-bishop Otto of Freising referred with satisfaction to the growing vigor in his own times "both in the monastic and in the clerical order."[77] Abbot Suger of Saint Denis (d. 1151) had a biographer also named Suger, who said in his apologetic dialogue, written in 1154, that "our republic rests principally on two orders, that is the monastic and the military" and that at the time he was writing, when "the state of things and the whole course are staggering," men "from both orders" must be found to bear their portions of the burden.[78]

Joachim of Fiore, who died in 1202, built his system of successive ages on the distinction between laymen, clerics, and monks, whom he called spiritual men and who would dominate the coming spiritual age. "In the first age the order of married men was authorized by God the Father," Joachim wrote in his *Book of Concord of the New and Old Testaments*. "In the second [age] the order of clerics was glorified by the Son. In the third [age] the order of monks will be glorified by the Holy Spirit."[79] "Just as the order of married men, which shone in the first age, seems to belong to the Father by the property of likeness," Joachim wrote in his *Exposition on the Apocalypse*, "the order of preachers, . . . which [shone] in the second, [belongs] to the Son; so the order of monks to which the final great times are given, [belongs] to the Holy Spirit."[80] In his *Treatise on the Four Evangelists* Joachim equated each order with one of the gifts brought by the magi and one of the trees in Isaiah 60.13: the box-tree, which is law, with the laity; the pine-tree, which burns easily and gives light, with monks; and the fir-tree, with its spreading branches, with the clergy.[81] Joachim combined with this tripartite structure of orders a bipartite division based on Esau and Jacob, who stood for the clerical and monastic orders in the second age, and on many other biblical pairs.[82] Jacob's daughters stood for the divisions among monks, "since there is one monastic order," Joachim said, "but many spiritual orders of monks."[83]

The types of social divisions discussed here and the variety and occasional idiosyncrasy of the biblical and other models, might suggest that society was seen in the eleventh and twelfth centuries in almost as many ways as there were writers. The growing curiosity about the surrounding world, and perhaps also its growing diversity, fostered a wide range of speculation about the natures of society. But, in addition to these many different views, and to some extent underlying them, was a broad measure of agreement on the basic structure of society, and indeed with the persistence of the three traditional tripartite divisions into virgins, continent, and married, into virgins and continent together, pastors, and married, and into monks, clerics and laymen, and to a lesser degree, the more recent division into prayers, fighters, and workers.

NOTES

1   Among general works, see Jacques Le Goff, "Note sur société tripartite, idéologie monarchique et renouveau économique dans la chrétienté du IXe au XIIe siècle," in *L'Europe aux IXe–XIe siècles: Aux origines des états nationaux*, eds Tadeusz Manteuffel and Aleksander Gieysztor (Warsaw: Varsovie Panstwowe Wydawn Naukowe, 1968), pp. 63–71. Georges Duby, *Les trois ordres ou l'imaginaire du féodalisme* (Paris: Gallimard, 1978); published in English as *The Three Orders: Feudal Society Imagined*, trans. Arthur Goldhammer (Chicago, IL: University of Chicago Press, 1980); Ottavia Niccoli, *I sacerdoti, i guerrieri, i contadini: Storia di un'immagine della società* (Turin: G. Einaudi, 1979); and Elizabeth A. R. Brown, "Georges Duby and the Three Orders," *Viator* 17 (1986): 51–64.

2   On chastity and celibacy as distinguishing marks of social groups in late Antiquity, see Edward Arthur Judge, "The Earliest Use of *Monachos* for 'Monk' and the Origins of Monasticism," *Jahrbuch für Antike und Christentum* 20 (1977): 72–89, esp. 75–6, and Peter Brown, *The Body and Society: Men, Women and Sexual Renunciation in Early Christianity* (New York: Columbia University Press, 1988), and generally, John W. Baldwin, "Five Discourses on Desire: Sexuality and Gender in Northern France around 1200," *Speculum* 66 (1991): 797–819.

3   The reasons for the predominance of tripartite divisions are obscure. The modern historian Arnaldo Momigliano, in refuting the idea that functional social tripartition had ancient Indo-European or classical roots, maintained that "the Middle Ages are trifunctional because they are Christian," but this may beg the question. See Arnaldo Momigliano, "Georges Dumézil and the Trifunctional Approach to Roman Civilization," *History and Theory* 23 (1983): 312–30, esp. 329. On the idea of the *triquadrus orbis*, which is found in Orosius, see Joseph Armitage Robinson, *The Times of Saint Dunstan* (Oxford: Clarendon, 1923), p. 58, and *The Regularis concordia*, ed. Thomas Symons (Edinburgh: Nelson, 1953), p. 37, and on the tripartite divisions of time, Giles Constable, "Past and Present in the Eleventh and Twelfth Centuries: Perceptions of Time and Change," in *L'Europe dei secoli XI e XII fra novità e tradizione: Sviluppi di una cultura. Atti del decima settimana internazionale di studio, Mendola, 25–29 agosto 1986* (Milan: Università cattolica del Sacro Cuore, 1989), pp. 135–70, here pp. 149–50, and Paul Dutton, "The Materialization of Nature and Quaternary Man in the Early Twelfth Century," *Sewanee Medieval Studies 6: Man and Nature in the Middle Ages*, read in typescript (1991), and the texts by Joachim of Fiore cited in notes 79–81, and of language, Irvin M. Resnick, "Lingua Dei, lingua hominis: Sacred Language and Medieval Texts," *Viator* 21 (1990): 51–74; here 60–72. Bruno of Segni, *In Genesim*, 9–10, in *PL*, vol. 164, 185BD, equated the three sons of Noah with Hebrew, Greek, and Latin, and Hugh of Saint-Victor, *Miscellanea* 3, 34, in *PL*, vol. 177, 1815CD, said that Egyptian was spoken by bad men, Canaanite by good men, and Hebrew by angels.

4   On the variety of medieval definitions, see Charles du Fresne Du Cange, *Glossarium ad scriptores mediae et infimae Latinitatis* (Paris: Librairie des sciences et des arts, 1840–50), vol. 4, pp. 728–31, who listed eight distinct meanings for *ordo*. See Luise

Manz, *Der Ordo-Gedanke* (Stuttgart and Berlin: W. Kohlhammer, 1937); Pierre-Marie Gy, "Remarques sur le vocabulaire antique du sacerdoce chrétien," in *Études sur le sacrement de l'ordre* (Paris: Éditions du Cerf, 1957), pp. 125–45, here 126–33; Marie-Dominique Chenu, *La théologie au douzième siècle* (Paris: J. Vrin, 1957), p. 130, who gave seven applications of *ordo*; H. Marton, "De sensu termini 'Ordinis' in fontibus saeculi duodecimi," *Analecta Praemonstratensia* 37 (1961): 314–18; George C. Waterston, *Une étude sémantique du mot "ordre" ... dans le français du moyen âge* (Geneva: Librairie Droz, 1965), pp. 24–33, who distinguished the four basic meanings as sacerdotal, rank, distribution, and military discipline; Yves Congar, "Les laïcs et l'ecclésiologie des 'ordines' chez les théologiens des XIe et XIIe siècles," in *I Laici nella "Societas Christiana" dei secoli XI e XII. Atti della terza settimana internazionale di studio, Mendola, 21–27 agosto 1965* (Milan: Università del Sacro Cuore, 1968), pp. 84–5; Paul Antin, "*Ordo* dans S. Jérôme," in his *Recueil sur saint Jérôme* (Brussels: Latomus, 1968), pp. 229–40; Pierre Van Beneden, "Ordo: Über den Ursprung einer kirchlichen Terminologie," *Vigiliae Christianae* 23 (1969) and Van Beneden, *Aux origines d'une terminologie sacramentelle: Ordo, ordinare, ordinatio dans la littérature chrétienne avant 313* (Louvain: Spicilegium sacrum Lovaniense, 1974), who concentrated on the sacramental meaning; Roland Mousnier, "Les concepts d''ordres,' d''états,' de 'fidélité,' et de 'monarchie absolue' en France de la fin du XVe siècle à la fin du XVIIIe," *Revue historique* 247 (1972): 289–312, and Ursula Keudel, "*Ordo* nel 'Thesaurus linguae latinae,'" in *Ordo: Atti del II Colloquio internazionale ... Roma, 7–9 gennaio, 1977*, eds Marta Fattori and Massimo Bianchi (Rome: Edizioni dell'Ateneo e Bizzarri, 1979), vol. 1, pp. 13–22.

5   Augustine, *Enchiridion*, 27, 103, in *CC:SL*, 46, 105. Ratherius of Verona, *Praeloquia*, 6, 20 in *CC:CM*, 46A, 187, listed rich, middle, and poor; healthy and infirm; young, old and infants; sinners and just; and clerics and laymen in addition to every order, condition, sex, age, and profession.

6   *Leges Henrici* 9.8, in *Die Gesetze der Angelsachsen*, ed. Felix Liebermann (Halle: Niemeyer, 1903–16), vol. 1, p. 555. See Austin Lane Poole, *The Obligations of Society in the XII and XIII Centuries* (Oxford: Ford Lectures, 1946), p. 2.

7   Gratian, *Decretum*, c. XII, q. i, c. 7, ed. Friedberg (Leipzig: Tauchnitz, 1879), col. 678, and Rupert of Deutz, *De sancta trinitate*, 31: *In Hiezecihelem*, II, 23, in *CC:CM*, 23, 1719.

8   See Regensburg Letters, 6–7, in *MGH, Briefe*, vol. 5, 291 and 298, and nn. 216–17 for Goscelin of Saint-Bertin and a twelfth-century, rhetorical treatise. Jews and gentiles were mentioned as objects of charity in a letter dated 964 in the Saint-Gall Collection, no. 24, in *MGH, Leges* (folio), vol. 5, p. 410.

9   "In these are understood both clerics and laymen, both male and female, both rich and poor, both free and serfs, and all others who are not idle but who labor faithfully in the vineyard of the Lord," Bruno of Segni, *In Psalmos*, 107, in *PL*, vol. 164, 1117C–18A. See Réginald Grégoire, *Bruno de Segni exégete médiévale et théologien monastique* (Spoleto: Centro italiano di studi sull'alto medioevo, 1965), p. 375 and n. 277.

10   *Recueil des chartes de l'abbaye de Cluny*, ed. Auguste Bernard and Alexandre Bruel (Paris: Imprimerie Nationale, 1876–1903), vol. 5, p. 212, no. 3862.

11   *The Cartulary and Charters of Notre-Dame of Homblières*, ed. Theodore Evergates, Giles Constable, and William M. Newman (Cambridge, MA: Medieval Academy, 1990), p. 56, no. 14.

12   See René Roques, in *Théologie de la vie monastique: Études sur la tradition patristique* (Paris: Aubier, 1961), pp. 287–96; David E. Luscombe, "Conceptions of Hierarchy before the Thirteenth Century," in *Soziale Ordnungen im Selbstverständnis des Mittelalters* (Berlin and New York: De Gruyter, 1979), pp. 1–19 on Denis; Paul Rorem, *Pseudo-Dionysius: A Commentary on the Texts and an Introduction to their Influence* (New York and Oxford: Oxford University Press, 1993), pp. 107–14, on the clerical and

lay orders (including monks) in the *Ecclesiastical Hierarchy*; and n. 358 on Thomas Aquinas, who cited Denis's *Celestial Hierarchy*, 3, 7–9, and *Ecclesiastical Hierarchy*, 5, i.

13   Gerhoh of Reichersberg, *In Psalmos* 3, *Gerhohi Praepositi Reichersbergnesis, Opera Inedita*, ed. Damien and Odulphus van den Eynde and Angelinus Rijmersdael (Rome: Apud Pontificium Athenaeum Antonianum, 1955–6), and Peter of Blois, Ep. 102, *Petri Blesensis Bathoniensis archidiaconi opera omnia*, ed. John A. Giles (Oxford: Parker, 1847–8), vol. 1, p. 328.

14   Bonaventura, *In Hexaemeron* (Vatican version), 22, 23, in *S. Bonaventurae . . . opera omnia*, v (Quaracchi: 1891), p. 441; cf. (Siena version), 4, 3, 20–3, ed. Ferdinand Delorme (Quaracchi: 1934), p. 256. The Vatican version is based on the edition of 1588–99 and seven manuscripts; the Siena version is based on Siena, Bibl. Mun. MS U. V. 6.; the two versions have different numberings and, in many places, different texts.

15   Robert Pullen, *Sententiae* 7, 19–24, in *PL*, vol. 186, 931A–8C.

16   Bonaventura, *In Hexaemeron* (Vatican version), 22, 16–17, in *Opera omnia*, 5, 440.

17   Gislebert of Mons, *Chronicon Hanoniense*, 134, ed. Léon Vanderkindere (Brussels: Commission royale d'histoire, 1904), p. 199, records that archdeacon Albert of Liège was made a knight in 1187. See also Jean Dunbabin, "From Clerk to Knight: Changing Orders," in *The Ideals and Practice of Medieval Knighthood*, ed. Christopher Harper-Bill and Ruth Harvey (Woodbridge: Boydell, 1988), vol. 2, pp. 26–39.

18   Andrew the Chaplain, *De amore*, 6, A–C, ed. E. Trojel (Munich: Eidos Verlag, 1964), pp. 18–19, 40–1, 47, 51, 60, 61, 64.

19   Some scholars have said that they were entirely omitted and constituted, as it were, a separate order or estate; for example, Shulamith Shahar, *The Fourth Estate: A History of Women in the Middle Ages*, trans. Chaya Galai, 2nd edn (London and New York: Methuen, 1984).

20   Tertullian, *De exhortatione castitatis*, 1, 4, in *CC:SL*, 2, 1015, and, on widows and virgins, *Ad uxorem*, 1, 8.2, in *CC:SL*, 1, 382. See Jo Ann McNamara, *A New Song: Celibate Women in the First Three Christian Centuries* (New York: Haworth Press, 1983), esp. pp. 99–100, saying that "Tertullian was the first Christian to attempt the structuring of a celibate order," and p. 123. For Ambrose, see her n. 63. On female virginity and celibacy see Brown, *The Body and Society*, and, in the twelfth century, Thomas Renna, "Virginity and Chastity in Early Cistercian Thought," *Studia Monastica* 26 (1984): 43–54.

21   Wolbero of Saint-Pantaloon, *Super Canticum Canticorum, Ep. ded.*, in *PL*, vol. 195, 1007A. The feminine *quae* (who) shows Wolbero had women in mind. See also Rupert of Deutz, *De sancta trinitate*, 12: *In Numerum*, 2, 21, in *CC:CM*, 22, 993, who referred to the three orders of married, continent, and widows and virgins together "according to either sex."

22   *Cartulaire de Béziers (Livre Noir)*, ed. Jean-Baptiste Rouquette (Paris and Montpellier: Picard, 1918–22), p. 86, no. 70, and Ortlieb of Zwiefalten, *Chronicon*, 1, 2 in *MGH, SS*, 10, 84, ed. Luitpold Wallach, Erich König, and Karl Otto Müler, *Schwäbische Chroniken der Stauferzeit* 2 (Sigmaringen, 1978), p. 86. For the other writers, see above nn. 31, 36, and Abbo of Fleury, *Liber apologeticus*, in *PL*, vol. 139, 466C–467A, and James of Vitry, "Sermones vulgares," in *Analecta novissima. Spicilegii Solesmensis altera continuatio*, ed. Jean-Baptiste Pitra (Paris: Gregg, 1885–8), vol. 2, pp. 344–442.

23   See note 46.

24   On Gilbert of Limerick, *De statu ecclesiae*, in *PL*, vol. 159, 997C–8A. See Roger A. B. Mynors, *Durham Cathedral Manuscripts to the End of the Twelfth Century* (Oxford: Oxford University Press for Durham Cathedral Dean and Chapter, 1939), pp. 41–2 and pl. 32; Aubrey Gwynn, *The Twelfth-Century Reform*, vol. 2.1 of *A History of Irish Catholicism* (Dublin: Gill, 1968), pp. 36–8; and Duby, *Les trois ordres*, pp. 345–6. One text and diagram (not reproduced here) are found in MSS Durham, Cathedral

Library, B. II. 35, fol. 36v (*c*.1166) and another in Cambridge, University Library, MS ff. 1.27, p. 238 (*c*.1200 which may be a copy of the Durham manuscript) (see Figure 3.2, p. 74); neither is Gilbert's original, which probably consisted entirely of triangles and pyramids that were transformed into arches in the process of copying. *V(iri)* and *F(eminae)* above and below, and on either side of, *O(ratores)* – prayers), *A(ratores)* – plowers), and *B(ellatores)* – fighters) can be seen on the five lower levels of the Cambridge diagram (Figure 3.2, p. 74). The arches marked *M(onasterium)* have only *O(ratores)*. Gilbert's use in the text of *conjugati* and *conjugatae* (once with specific reference to the (*oratores*) is puzzling, since it can hardly be thought to mean "married." He may have had in mind nuns, as in the bottom line of the Cambridge diagram, where *moniales*, or nuns, is spaced out between the letters for *canonicales* and *universales* (see *PL*, vol. 159, 997A), or perhaps "double" houses of men and women. I am indebted to Robert Benson for help with this material.

25 *MGH, Cap.*, 1, 163, no. 72.4.
26 Mary Dickey, "Some Commentaries on the 'De Inventione' and 'Ad Herennium' of the Eleventh and Early Twelfth Centuries," *Mediaeval and Renaissance Studies* 6 (1968): 1–41, esp. 19.
27 Gobert of Laon, *De tonsura et vestimentis et vita clericorum*, ed. M. Hélin, in *Le Musée belge Revue de philologie classique* 34 (1930): 146.
28 On food as an indication of social rank, see George Fenwick Jones, "The Function of Food in Mediaeval German Literature," *Speculum* 35 (1960): 78–86, who said (p. 85) that "Mediaeval man thought that people ate what they did because of what they are."
29 See Eusèbe-Jacob de Laurière, *Ordonnances des roys de France* (Paris: Gregg Press, 1723–1849), 1, 541–3, for the sumptuary legislation of Philip the Fair in 1294. I owe this reference to Elizabeth A. R. Brown.
30 See Philip of Harvengt, *De institutione clericorum*, 4: *De continentia clericorum*, 86, in *PL*, vol. 203, 791A–2C. The first four treatises were dated about 1140/50 by G. P. Sijen, "Les oeuvres de Philippe de Harveng, abbé de Bonne-Espérance," *Analecta Praemonstratensia* 15 (1939): 129–66, here 150–1, and the remainder after Philip became abbot of Bonne-Espérance by A. Erens, in *Dictionnaire de la théologie catholique* (1903–50), vol. 12.1, 1409. In his *Ep.* 13, in *PL*, vol. 203, 1058, Philip said that people should know their grade or order and obey the way of life associated with it.
31 See François Chatillon, "*Tria Generum Hominum*: Noe, Daniel et Job," *Revue du moyen âge latin* 10 (1954): 169–76; Georges Folliet, "Les trois catégories de Chrétiens: Survie d'un thème augustinien," *L'année théologique augustinienne* 14 (1954): 81–96, and Folliet, "Les trois catégories de Chrétiens à partir du Luc (17.34–6), Matthieu (24.40–1), et Ezéchiel (14.14)," in *Augustinus Magister: Congrès international augustinien, Paris, 21–24 septembre 1954* (Paris: Études augustiniennes, 1954), vol. 2, pp. 631–44, esp. pp. 636–7; Henri de Lubac, *Exegèse Médiévale* (Paris: Aubier, 1959–64), 2.1, 283; Congar, "Les laïcs," p. 85 and n. 189. Noah usually stood for the prelates or rectors but he was occasionally identified with the married, as by Hildebert of Lavardin, "Serm. 70," in *PL*, vol. 171, 715C, and even with the life of monks, as in Jean Leclercq, "Sermon ancien sur la persévérance des moines," *Analecta monastica* 2 (1953): here 22–3, and Leclercq, *Otia monastica. Études sur le vocabulaire de la contemplation au moyen âge* (Rome: Herder, 1963), p. 97, n. 17.
32 See Antonio Quacquarelli, *Il triplice frutto della vita cristiana: 100, 60, e 30 (Matteo XIII-8, nelle diverse interpretazionei)* (Rome: Herder, 1953, rep. 1989), who studied the use of the parable in the works of various writers from the fathers to modern times; Giovanni Miccoli, *Chiesa gregoriana. Ricerche sulla riforma del secolo XI* (Florence: La Nuova Italia, 1966), pp. 5–6; and Congar, "Les laïcs," pp. 86–9.
33 Plato, *Timaeus* 17C, and Calcidius, *Commentaries*, 232–3, ed. J. H. Waszink (London and Leiden: Warburg Inst., 1962), pp. 8 and 246–7. See Tilman Struve, *Die Entwicklung der organologischen Staatsauffassung im Mittelalter* (Stuttgart: Hiersemann, 1978),

pp. 67–71 (on Calcidius), and pp. 116–22; Luscombe, "Conceptions of Hierarchy"; Paul Dutton, "'Illustre civitatis et populi exemplum:' Plato's *Timaeus* and the transmission from Calcidius to the End of the Twelfth Century of a Tripartite Scheme of Society," *Mediaeval Studies* 45 (1983): 79–119, esp. 84–5; and Rorem, *Pseudo-Dionysius*, esp. pp. 73–83, 124–6, 167–74, and 214–25. On the use of the term *ordo* in the twelfth century, see Marton, "De sensu termini 'Ordinis.'"

34 Fulbert of Chartres, *Epp.* 125 and 137–9, ed. Frederick Behrends (Oxford: Oxford Medieval Text Series, 1976), pp. 226 and 248–50.

35 Anselm of Canterbury, *De humanis moribus per similitudines*, 80 and 127, in *Memorials of Saint Anselm*, ed. Richard W. Southern and Franciscus S. Schmitt (London: Oxford University Press, 1969), pp. 70 and 87; cf. the versions in *PL*, vol. 159, 651A–2A and 679A.

36 Humbert of Silva Candida, *Adversus simoniacos*, 3, 3, in *MGH*, *Libelli*, 1, 201.

37 Humbert of Silva Candida, *Adversus simoniacos*, 3, 29 (p. 235), and K. Francke "Zur Characteristik des Cardinals Humbert von Silva Candida," *Neues Arkiv* 7 (1882): 614–19, here 618. See Harmut Hoffmann, "Die beiden Schwerter im hohen Mittelalter," *Deutsches Archiv* 20 (1964): 78–114, esp. 82–3.

38 Botho of Prüm, *De statu domus Dei*, 4, 16, and 5, 7–9, in *Maxima bibliotheca veterum patrum*, ed. Marguerin de la Bigne (Lyons: Apud Arissonios, 1677), 21, 509B, 512C–13A; Garnier of Saint-Victor, *Gregorianum*, 1, 2, in *PL*, vol. 193, 26C–30A.

39 Luscombe, "Conceptions of Hierarchy," pp. 11–17.

40 In the Rigsthula, for example, the three sons of Rig were born of different mothers in different houses, one poor, one richer, and one luxurious. They had different colored skin and hair – dark, red, and pale – and were said to stand for slaves, freeholders, and nobles. *Edda. Die Lieder des Codex Regius nebst verwandten Denkmälern*, ed. Gustav Neckel and Hans Kuhn, 5th edn (Heidelberg: C. Winter, 1983), pp. 280–7, and trans. Lee M. Hollander, *Edda Saemundar: The Poetic Edda*, 2nd edn (Austin, TX: University of Texas Press, 1962), pp. 140–9. See Jones, "The Function of Food," p. 79, and Edward O. G. Turville-Petre, *Myth and Religion of the North* (New York: Holt, Rinehart and Winston, 1964), p. 150, on the date of this work, which some scholars assign to the tenth/eleventh and others to the twelfth/thirteenth centuries. I owe these references to Ruth Mellinkoff. Honorius Augustodunensis, in the *Image of the World*, divided all men at the time of Melchizedek into freemen, soldiers, and serfs, whom he compared to Noah's three sons, and Bonizo of Sutri (c.1045–90) divided the "people" into artisans, merchants, and husbandmen. Honorius Augustodunensis, *Imago mundi*, 3, ed. Valerie I. J. Flint, in *Archives d'histoire doctrinale et littéraire du Moyen Age* 49 (1982), p. 125 (= *PL*, vol. 172, 166AB), and Bonito of Sutri, *Liber de vita christiana*, 8, 1, ed. Ernst Perels (Berlin: Weidmannsche Buchhandlung, 1930), p. 252. Similar divisions are found in charters and other types of sources. The monastery of Sauve was founded in 1029 at a meeting of monks, clerics, soldiers, and laymen; all men were either "free or unfree" in a charter of 1035/70; and Peter of Mercoeur was elected bishop of Le Puy in 1053 by "the clergy, people, and militia." The decision of early eleventh-century Count Burchard of Vendôme (d. 1005) to leave "the secular militia" and to enter "the monastic life" was greatly regretted, according to his *Life* written in 1058 by Odo of Saint-Maur de Fossés, "by all the leading men of the French, by monks, by clerics, by widows, and by all the orders of both sexes and ages. . . . All the knights wept, all the poor lamented." Only the cenobitic servants of God rejoiced that so great a knight became a monk. Respectively, Claude de Vic and Josephe Vaissete, *Histoire générale de Languedoc* (Paris: Privat, 1730–45), vol. 2, pp. 184 and 220, nos. 164 and 199, in second edition by Auguste Molinier (Toulouse: Privat, 1871–1904), vol. 5, pp. 391 and 468, nos. 191 and 234; Marc Bloch, *Mélanges historique* (Paris: S.E.V.P.E.N., 1963), vol. 1, p. 327, n. 2. Odo of Saint-Maur, *Vie de Bouchard le Vénérable, comte de Vendôme, de Corbeil, de Melun, et de Paris (Xe et XIe siècles)*, published with an introduction by

Charles Bourel de la Roncière (Paris: Picard, 1892), pp. 26–7 (*Bibliotheca hagiographica latina*, 1481).

41   This tendency has been reversed in the second half of the twentieth century, when some monks have not taken orders and have reasserted the concept of a distinct monastic order: see Olivier Rousseau, *Théologie* (1961): 275.

42   Odo of Cluny, *Collationes*, 1, 14 and 35–40, and 3, 1, in *Bibliotheca Cluniacensis* (hereafter *Bibl. Clun.*), ed. Martin Marrier and André Duchesne (Paris: Protat, 1614), cols 170A, 183B–5C, and 220E–1B; and 3, 7, in *Bibl. Clun.*, col. 225B, and *Serm. 3 de sancto Benedicto*, ibid., col. 139A. See Paolo Lamma, *Momenti di storiografia cluniacense* (Rome: Nella sede dell'Istituto, 1961), pp. 55–76, esp. pp. 62–4. Liutprand of Cremona, *Historia Ottonis*, 1, ed. Joseph Becker (*MGH, SS Rerum Germ.*, 41; Hanover and Leipzig, 1915), p. 160, after mentioning two bishops who were "not of the other order," meaning the lay order.

43   Dodo of Saint Quentin, *De moribus et actis primorum Normanniae ducum*, 58, ed. Jules Lair (Caen: F. Le Blanc – Hardel, 1865), pp. 200–1. See Duby, *Les trois ordres*, pp. 108–12.

44   Ralph Glaber, *Historiae*, 4, 5, 17, ed. Maurice Prou (Paris, 1886), p. 105 = ed. John France (Oxford: Oxford Medieval Texts, 1989), p. 198. The phrase *utriusque ordinis, professionis*, or *gradus*, meaning clerical and lay, is found in Ordericus Vitalis, *Historia ecclesiastica*, 12, 27, and 13, 12, ed. Marjorie Chibnall (Oxford: Clarendon Press, 1969–80), 6, 306–7 and 422; *MGH, Const.*, 1, 165, no. 112; and *Urkunden der Markgrafen von Meissen und Landgrafen von Thüringen 1100–1195*, ed. Otto Posse (Leipzig: Ciesecke und Devrient, 1889), p. 65, no. 82.

45   Anselm of Laon, *In Matthaeum*, 13, in *PL*, vol. 162, 1370AC. See Franz Bliemetzrieder, *Anselms von Laon systematische Sentenzen* (Münster: Aschendorff, 1919), pp. 134–5, and Heinrich Weisweiler, *Das Schriftum der Schule Anselms von Laon und Wilhelms von Champeaux in deutschen Bibiliotheken* (Münster: Aschendorff, 1936), p. 153, on the three orders of married, continent, and virgins in Anselm's treatise on marriage.

46   Rome, Biblioteca Vaticana, MS, Barb. lat. 592. See Myrtilla Avery, *The Exultet Rolls of South Italy* (Princeton, NJ: Princeton University Press, 1936), vol. 2, pp. 34–5 and pl. 149; Yvonne Labande-Mailfert, "L'iconographie des läics dans la société religieuse aux XIe et XIIe siècles," in *I Laici* (cited in note 4 above), pp. 513–15; and, generally, Piotr Skubiszewski, "*Ecclesia Christianitas, Regnum* et *Sacerdotium* dans l'art des Xe–XIe s. Idées et structures des images," *Cahiers de civilisation médiévale* 28 (1985): 133–79, esp. 137 and 170 on representations of social orders and 144, n. 74 on the church as a building, and Hélène Toubert, *Un art dirigé. Réforme grégorienne et iconographie* (Paris: Éditions du Cerf, 1990), pp. 37–63 (56 and fig. 14 on this manuscript).

47   Herbert of Losinga, *Ep.* 60, ed. R. Anstruther (Brussels and London: Caxton Society, 1846), p. 106. See Edward M. Goulburn and Henry Symonds, *The Life, Letters and Sermons of Bishop Herbert of Losinga* (Oxford: Parker, 1878), vol. 1, pp. 266–8, dating this letter about 1114.

48   Lanfranc of Canterbury, *Ep.* 4, ed. Helen Clover and Margaret Gibson (Oxford: Oxford Medieval Texts, 1979), p. 50, and Bonizo, *Liber de vita christiana*, 2, 3, ed. Perels, p. 35 (xxi on the date, citing Paul Tournier), on which see Carl Erdmann, *Die Entstehung des Kreuzzugsgedankens* (Stuttgart: Kohlhammer, 1935), pp. 719–37; Luigi Prosdocimi, "Lo stato di vita laicale nel diritto canonico dei secoli XI e XII," in *I Laici* (cited in note 4 above), p. 67; and Robert I. Moore, *The Origins of European Dissent* (London: Saint-Martin's Press, 1977), p. 78.

49   Gratian, *Decretum*, c. xii. q. 1, c. 7 (ed. Friedberg, col. 678). See Ronald J. Cox, *A Study of the Juridic Status of Laymen in the Writing of the Medieval Canonists* (Washington, DC: Catholic University, 1959), pp. 20–6 (p. 21 on the date); Gilles Couvreur, *Les pauvres ont-il les droits?* (Rome and Paris: Libreria editrice dell'Università Gregoriana, 1961), p. 196, n. 167; Prosdocimi, "Chierici e laici nella

società occidentale del secolo XII: A proposito di Decr. Grat. c. 12 q.I. d.7: 'Duo sunt genera Christianorum,'" in *Proceedings of the Second International Congress of Medieval Canon Law* (Vatican City: S. Congregatio de seminarii et studiorum universitatibus, 1965), pp. 105–22 (106–7 on the date), and Prosdocimi, "Lo statu di vita laicale," pp. 69–71.

50 See Jean Leclercq, François Vandenbroucke, and Louis Bouyer, *La spiritualité du moyen âge* (Paris: Aubier, 1961), p. 127; Prosdocimi, "Chierici," pp. 111–14; and on tonsure, Cox, *A Study*, pp. 30–8.

51 Ivo of Chartres, *Ep.* 247, in *PL*, vol. 162, 254C; in *Ep.* 739 (col. 146D) Ivo espoused the tripartite division into married, continent, and rectors, whom he compared to Noah, Daniel, and Job.

52 Stephen of Tournai, *Summa*, intro., ed. J. F. von Schulte (Giessen: 1891), pp. 1–2. See Robert W. Carlyle and Alexander Carlyle, *A History of Mediaeval Political Theory in the West* (Edinburgh and London: Barnes & Noble, 1950), vol. 2, pp. 198–9 and 225, who saw this passage as a restatement of the Gelasian theory, and Prosdocimi, "Chierici," and Prosdocimi, "Lo statu di vita laicale," pp. 72–5. On the various uses of the Gelasian doctrine in the eleventh and twelfth centuries, see Robert L. Benson, "The Gelasian Doctrine: Uses and Transformations," in *La Notion d'autorité au moyen âge: Islam, Byzance, Occident* (Paris: Presses universitaires de France, 1982), pp. 13–44.

53 See Charles Dereine, "Chanoines (des origines au XIIIe s.)" in *Dictionnaire d'Histoire et de Géographie Ecclésiastique* 12 (1953): 353–405, esp. 364–5 and 375–6.

Already in the tenth century, John of Salerno, in his *Life* of Odo of Cluny, wrote that "As the order of monks diminished among us, so it was also corrected and is often corrected by many prodigies, so that it may with the support of God survive." John of Salerno, *Vita Odonis*, 3, in *Bibl. Clun.*, col. 45D (*Bibliotheca hagiographica latina*, 6292–5). Peter Damian (d. 1072), in his *Life* of the monastic reformer Romuald of Ravenna (d. 1027), wrote that the emperor Otto III (980–1002) was "very kind to the monastic order" and that Romuald "was thought to want to turn the whole world into a hermitage and to associate the entire multitude of the people with the monastic order"; Peter Damian, *Vita beati Romualdi*, 25 and 37, ed. Giovanni Tabacco (Rome: 1957), pp. 53 and 78 (*Bibliotheca hagiographica latina*, 7324). Martinien of Rebais or Marmoutier at the turn of the eleventh century deplored "the ruin of the monastic order," of which he traced the origins to the order of the apostles, "Whence it is said among the people that on the day of judgment a monk will be either with the apostles or like the traitor Judas"; Martinien, *Exhortatio*, vol. 1, 8, ed. Henri Roux, in *Mélanges bénédictins publiés à l'occasion du XIVe centenaire de la mort de saint Benoît par les moines de l'abbaye de Saint-Jérôme de Rome* (Abbaye S. Wandrille: Éditions de Fontenelle, 1947), p. 339; see also vol. 2, 27, p. 344.

54 See Manz, *Der Ordo-Gedanke*, pp. 37–8; Folliet, "Les trois catégories," pp. 89–90 (on Bernard's use of Noah, Daniel, and Job); Hans Wolter, "Bernhard von Clairvaux und die Laien," *Scholastik* 34 (1959): 161–89; and Placide Deseille, in *Théologie* (1961): 519–24. See also the Old French translation of Bernard's sermon *Ad abbates*, in *Li sermon saint Bernart*, ed. Wendelin Foerster (Erlangen: A. Deichart, 1885), no. 41.

55 Bernard of Clairvaux, *De consideratione*, 3, 5, 20, in Bernard of Clairvaux, *Opera Omnia*, ed. Henri Rochais and Jean Leclercq (Rome: Editiones cistercienses, 1963–), vol. 3, pp. 447–8, and *Apologia*, 3, 5–6 and 9, 19, ibid., pp. 84, 87, and 96–7.

56 Bernard of Clairvaux, *Ep.* 193, *Opera Omnia*, vol. 8, p. 44. On the distinction between the monastic and clerical orders in Bernard's works, see also Marie-Anselme Dimier, "Saint Bernard et Saint Jérôme," *Collectanea ordinis Cisterciensium reformatorum* 15 (1953): 216–22.

57 There are twenty-eight references to Cant. 2.4, including those in Bernard of Clairvaux, *Serm. 49–50 super Cantica*, *Opera Omnia*, vol. 2, pp. 73–83, in the type-script "Index des citations scripturaires dans les oeuvres de saint Bernard" drawn up by the Administratief Centrum of the Bernardus-Konkordans at Bergeyk in

1982–3. See also Bernard's references to the theme of ordered love in *Serm. 50 de diversis*, 2, *Opera Omnia*, vol. 6.1, p. 271; *De diligendo Deo*, 8, 25, and 14, 38, ibid., 3, 139–40 and 151; and *Epp*. 8, 1; 11, 7; 85, 3; and 87, 10, ibid., 7, 48, 58, 222, 230.

58   Bernard of Clairvaux, *Serm. 46 super Cantica*, 2, *Opera Omnia*, vol. 2, p. 56: "Christiani ... utriusque ordinis principes." This comes in the middle of a passage comparing the bed, beams, and rafters in Cant. 1.15–16 to the orders of monks, rulers, and clerics; see also Jean Leclercq, "Inédits bernardins dans un manuscrit d'Orval," *Analecta monastica* 1 (1948): 152.

59   Bernard of Clairvaux, *Serm. 9 de diversis*, 3–5, *Opera Omnia*, vol. 6.1, pp. 119–20. The phrase *"contrario quidem ordine"* is translated "in a different order" rather than "in a contrary order" because Daniel invariably stood for the continent even if the roles of Noah and Job varied. It is not clear whether the second group of prelates were like those referred to earlier in the sermon (i.e. the clergy) or were monastic superiors who served both the *officiales fratres* and the *claustrales*. Cf. Henri-M. Rochais and Irène Binont, "La collection de textes divers du manuscrit Lincoln 201 et saint Bernard," *Sacris erudiri* 15 (1964): 44–5.

60   Bernard of Clairvaux, *Serm. 1 in nativitate*, 5–8, *Opera Omnia*, vol. 4, pp. 247–51.

61   Bernard of Clairvaux, *Serm. 1 in natali S. Andreae*, *Opera Omnia*, vol. 5, p. 430.

62   H.-M. Rochais, "Inédits bernardins dans le manuscrit Harvard 185," *Analecta monastica* 6 (1962): 81–2 and 134, nos. 28 and 42, and Rochais and Binont, "Collection," (n. 190), pp. 45, 133, and 123 (Luke 6.22, and 23), and p. 199.

63   Hildegard of Bingen, *Ep*. 51, in *PL*, vol. 197, 262A–7C.

64   Elizabeth of Schönau, *Liber viarum Dei*, 5, ed. Roth, p. 90 = Ekbert of Schönau, *Vita s. Elisabethi Schonaugiensis*, 6, 90, in *PL*, vol. 195, 166C–7A.

65   Hugh of Saint-Victor, *De arcs Noe morali*, 1, 4, in *PL*, vol. 176, 630B. In his *Serm. 72* on John the Baptist, in *PL*, vol. 177, 1128–9, Hugh compared the valleys, plains, and hills to lowly subjects, married people, and contemplatives.

66   Philip of Harvengt, *De institutione clericorum* in *PL*, vol. 203, 665–1206. At the beginning of the first treatise, *De dignitate clericorum*, 1 (coll. 667–8), he asserted the antiquity and superiority of the clerical or apostolic order; see also *De continentia clericorum*, 106–18 (coll. 1810–26; quote on 826C), and *De obedientia clericorum*, 39 (coll. 927A).

67   *Vita Geraldi Silvae Maioris*, 27, in *PL*, vol. 147, 1041C (*Bibliotheca hagiographica latina* 3417), and Walter, *Vita Caroli comitis Flandriae*, 43, in *MGH*, *SS*, 12, 557 (*Bibliotheca hagiographica latina*, 1573).

68   *The Book of St. Gilbert*, ed. Raymonde Foreville and Gillian Keir (Oxford: Clarendon, 1987), p. 172; see also the *Epistola de canonizatione*, 26–7 (ibid., pp. 242 and 248).

69   *Urkunden der Markgrafen von Meissen*, ed. Posse, p. 18, no. 22.

70   *Cartulaire de l'abbaye royale de Notre-Dame de Saintes*, ed. Th. Grasilier (Niort: L. Clouzot, 1871), p. 136, no. 113, and Otto of Freising, *Gesta Friderici*. 1, 11, 13, ed. Georg Waitz and Bernhard von Simson (*MGH*, *SS rerum Germ.*, 46; Hanover and Leipzig, 1912), p. 116. On towns, see Robert S. Lopez, "Still Another Renaissance?" *American Historical Review* 57 (1951–2): 1–21, here 12, on *maiores, milites,* and *negotiatores* in Italian towns. The witnesses to Cluniac charters still tended to be described as monks, clerics, and laymen, but a few were witnessed by categories described as soldiers, townsmen, servants, freemen, and serfs. Peter the Venerable (1092–1156), abbot of Cluny in the mid-twelfth century, divided the nobility in Burgundy into dukes, princes, counts, knights, and castellans, and the non-noble lay society into merchants, townsmen, peasants, husbandmen, poor men, widows, orphans, and every type of low person; he divided society in the Auvergne into lords of castles, lesser knights, townsmen, peasants, and every type of layman; see *Cartulaire de Cluny*, vol. 5, pp. 212, 229, and 593, nos. 3862, 3874, and 4239. Lucius II in 1144 and Urban III in 1186 referred to "all the monks, clerics, and laymen living within the boundaries of Cluny," in Pierre Symon, *Bullarium sacri ordinis Cluniacensis*

(Lyons: Antonium Jullieron, 1680), pp. 52 and 83 (Jaffé 8621 and 15574). See the references to the orders of monks, clerics (or canons), and laymen in *Cartulaire de Cluny*, vol. 5, pp. 22, 298, and 365, nos. 3670, 3944, and 4009, and to the monastic order in vol. 3, p. 803, vol. 4, p. 756, and vol. 5, p, 69, nos. 2779, 3598, and 3724, and Peter the Venerable, *Epp.* 171, 173, and 191, in *The Letters of Peter the Venerable*, ed. Giles Constable, 2 vols (Cambridge, MA: Harvard Historical Studies, 1967), vol. 2, pp. 1, 406, 410–11, and 442. Elsewhere, as in *Epp.* 16 and 150 (1, 24, and 370), Peter distinguished monks, clerics, and laymen.

71   Honorius Augustodunensis, "Summa gloria," 1 and 9, *MGH*, *Libelli*, vol. 3, 64 and 69.

72   Hugh of Saint-Victor, *De sacramentis*, 2, 2, 3–4, in *PL*, vol. 176, 417–18, and trans. Roy J. Deferran (Cambridge, MA: Mediaeval Academy of America Publ. 58, 1951), pp. 255–6. See Gy, "Remarques," pp. 130–1, who said that Hugh introduced the technical distinction between *ordo* and *dignitas*, and Prosdocimi, "Chierici," pp. 119–21, and Prosdocimi, "Unità et dualità del popolo cristiano in Stephano di Tournai e in Ugo di S. Vittore: 'Duo populi' et 'Duae vitae,'" *Études d'histoire du droit canonique dédiées à Gabriel le Bras* (Paris: Sirey, 1965), pp. 673–80, here pp. 676–8, where he said this passage may be an interpolation, and Prosdocimi, "Lo statu di vita laicali," pp. 71–2.

73   For according to the hierarchy of Denis [the pseudo-Aeropagite], there are two types of faithful in the church of God. The first which is called God-seeing, the other which is called following; the God-seers we call the ministers of the church . . . the followers we call the people of the multi-tude, which sits at the feet of the God-seer.

Peter then compared the ministers to the Aaronites and ploughing bulls and the people to the Caathites and asses, and said that "The mother church speaks to these two but to each with its own and separate admonition," Peter Comestor, *Serm. 18*, in *PL*, vol. 198, 1770BD. See Jean Longère, *Oeuvres oratoires de maîtres de Paris parisiens au XIIe siècles* (Paris: H. Champion, 1975), vol. 1, p. 111, and, on the sources, vol. 2, pp. 92–3. In Guernes of Pont-Sainte-Maxence, *La Vie de Saint Thomas Becket*, ed. Emmanuel Walberg (Paris: H. Champion, 1936), p. 96, no. 623, lines 3111–12, the two orders of people in the church were the "people" and the "clergy."

74   Artur Michael Landgraf, *Dogmengeschichte der Frühscholastik* (Regensburg: Friedrich Pustet, 1952–6), vol. 4.1, p. 10, n. 10, citing from a sermon attributed to Peter Comester in Leipzig, Universitätsbibliothek, MS Lat. 381, fol. 139.

75   Goscelin of Saint-Bertin, *Liber confortatorius* 4, ed. C. H. Talbot, in *Analecta monas-tica* 3 (1955): 110–11 (see p. 8, dating this work 1082/3), and Guibert of Nogent, *Liber quo ordine sermo fieri debeat*, in *PL*, vol. 132, 22C.

76   *Die rhetorica ecclesiastica*, ed. Ludwig Wahrmund (Aalen: Scientia Verlag, 1906), pp. 50–1.

77   *De professionibus monachorum*, in Martène (1736–8), vol. 2, pp. 469–96 (see André Wilmart, "Les ouvrages d'un moine de Bec. Un débat sur la profession monastique au XIIe siècle," *Revue bénédictine* 44 (1932): 21–46, esp. p. 30 on the title); Otto of Freising, *Chronica*, 7i, 9, ed. A. Hofmefster (*MGH*, *SS rerum Germ.*, 45; Hanover and Leipzig, 1912), p. 321.

78   Suger, *Dialogus*, 6, ed. André Wilmart, in *Revue Mabillon* 32 (1942): 90–1. Tener may be a misprint for tenor. See Hubert Glaser, "Wilhelm von Saint-Denis: Ein Humanist aus der Umgebung des Abtes Suger und die Krise seiner Abtei von 1151 bis 1153," *Historisches Jahrbuch* 85 (1965): 257–322; 285 on the date and 287.

79   Joachim of Fiore, *Concordia novi ac veteris Testamenti*, vol. 5, 21 (Venice: 1519, repr., 1964), folio 70v. See Marjorie Reeves, *The Influence of Prophecy in the Later Middle Ages: A Study of Joachimism* (Oxford: Clarendon, 1976), p. 13. E. Randolph Daniel dated the work between 1182 and 1198 in his edition of Books 1–4 (Philadelphia:

Transactions of the American Philosophical Society 73.8, 1983), p. xxvi, where he argued (p. xxiv) that Book 5 belongs with Joachim's works on the Gospels and the Apocalypse. For other references to the lay (married), clerical, and monastic (contemplative) orders in Joachim's works, see Morton W. Bloomfield, "Joachim of Flora: A Critical Survey of his Canon, Teachings, Sources, Biography and Influence," *Traditio* 13 (1957): 249–311, here 266, n. 76.

80   Joachim of Fiore, *Expositio in Apocalypsim*, prol. (Venice, 1527, repr. Minerva, 1964), folios 5r–v; see also vol. 1, 2 (folio 37v).

81   Joachim of Fiore, *Tractatus Super Quatuor Evangelia*, ed. Ernesto Buonaiuti (Rome: Tipografia del Senato, 1930), pp. 76–7. He went on to say that the three orders were distinguished by fear, love of God, and love of neighbor.

82   See Bloomfield, "Joachim of Flora," p. 266, n. 74, on triplets, and Reeves, *The Influence of Prophecy*, p. 11, on pairs.

83   Joachim, *Concordia*, 5, 47–9, edn cited in note 79, folios 82r–83v (quote on 83v).

Part II

REFORM AND GROWTH IN THE CLERICAL HIERARCHY

Introduction

The most striking thing about religion in the medieval centuries is that Western Europe was subject to a single religious institution, the Catholic Church, which came increasingly under the leadership of the bishop of Rome, the Pope. The medieval Church included, of course, the entire community of the faithful, but those who led it and increasingly enunciated its law and doctrine consisted of a clerical or priestly hierarchy headed by the Pope, and those monks and nuns who had retreated from the world to live more perfect lives and whose authority derived from their saintliness. Only from c.1050, however, did the Pope begin to emerge as the supreme clerical power within the Western Church. Contributing to this was an elevation in all clerical status along with an emerging concern about the purity of the clergy that was associated with the newly articulated doctrine of transubstantiation, which asserted that at the instant of consecration the Eucharist was transformed from shared food into the very body and blood of Christ even though its outward appearance did not change. Once consecrated, the Eucharistic wafer or "Host" became a relic of Christ.

In the eleventh century the reform movement began to give attention to the interference of the laity in church affairs, which culminated in the late eleventh-century battle between Pope Gregory VII (1073–85) and Emperor Henry IV (1056–1106). The principal concerns of the eleventh-century reformers, whose activities we call the Gregorian Reform, would be simony, the buying and selling of Church office or of the sacraments and related lay investiture into Church office, but a number of reformers also began an attack on clerical marriage, the sin of nicolaitism. Not surprisingly the most virulent opposition to clerical marriage came from the monastic wing of the Church, which thought that all clerics should live like monks. In the early Middle Ages, kings and emperors in the West, as well as counts, countesses, and other lords, had exercised considerable control over Church institutions within their realms. Starting in the eleventh century, secular rulers in the West, and in particular the Emperor (who traditionally received the imperial crown from the Pope in Rome), became concerned about who was the incumbent of the Papacy. A sense developed that the Church had fallen under the control of powerful families, particularly in Rome, where those who controlled papal elections comprised a few families of Roman nobles more interested in family prestige and power than in good Church administration. By the eleventh-century not just the Emperor, but clerics who were reformers, began to object to the inter-ference in Church affairs by non-clerics, regarding with dismay the use of the Church to promote local secular interests. Not only in Rome, but throughout the West, laymen made appointments to Church office and reformers denounced such interference in the affairs of the ecclesiastical hierarchy as the sin of simony. Increasingly it was asserted that canonical election required that ecclesiastics be elected by the group over which they would have authority. Thus, the clergy of a cathedral would elect their bishop, the monks or nuns of an abbey would elect their abbot or abbess, with the pope being elected by the cardinals (see pp. 98–9). Such election was not to be influenced by secular individuals, and lay patrons could not simply appoint family members or sell an office to the highest bidder.

Church reform and what came to be called the Investiture Controversy, in which Pope and Emperor fought for supremacy, were closely related, the issue of investiture being a specific part of the attack on simony. The initial impulse for reform, ironically as it turned out, came from the German Emperor Henry III (1039–56). He seems to have refused to accept fees for appointments and supported canonical elections of ecclesiastics, but also viewed it as wholly appropriate that an emperor should concern himself with clerical appointment. In 1046 Henry intervened in the local politics of the election of the bishop of Rome at the Synod of Sutri, which deposed three rival popes and elected a new Pope, who died in 1049; Henry then placed his own candidate on the papal throne as Leo IX (1049–54). Leo IX, how-ever, insisted on his own canonical election by the Romans and began his own program of reform under papal, not imperial, direction. Once the initia-tive was seized by the popes, reformers like Gregory VII actively fought for independence from the interference of emperors themselves.

The first major clash came when Emperor Henry IV (1056–1106), using the traditional power to name abbots and bishops that his father, Henry III, had exercised, was deemed by Pope Gregory VII to have subverted papal claims to authority. The opening battle between the two was over the investiture of the archbishop of Milan in northern Italy. Henry IV undertook to invest the new archbishop in office against Gregory's prohibition. The war and propaganda campaign that ensued led to Gregory VII's proclamation of Henry's deposition and the papal announcement that Henry's vassals were released from service owed him. The confrontation reached its dramatic high point when Henry came as a penitent to Canossa in 1077 (see the introduction to Chapter 4, pp. 102–3), but conflict continued into the twelfth century and only in 1122 were differences between Emperor and Pope ironed out with the Concordat of Worms. Claims of papal power over the entire Church, which were clearly laid out by Gregory VII in a private memo called *The Dictates of the Pope* (*Dictatus Papae*), paralleled claims of emperors and kings to increasing power over their subjects.[1] Increasingly, the Pope acted like a secular ruler reigning as he did over the city of Rome, the papal territories and other properties belonging to the papacy, most of them in Italy, and making claims to rule over the entire Western Church.[2] Although the papacy and emperor remained rivals, both were interested in increasing the power of their respective institutions and both in insulating themselves from the intervention of women and family.

In Chapter 4, Jo Ann McNamara brings feminist and gender analysis to the dramatic events of Canossa, the meeting of the Pope and the Emperor in 1077, placing those events in the larger context of "institution-building." Rulers and reformers alike sought to decrease the personal, familial aspects of either Empire or Papacy, Church or State. In her view, their aim was to elevate these institutions and their incumbents into disembodied entities whose power was so far above that of mere mortals that those who ruled them became "men" without the "gendered" characteristics of men. The principle invoked by secular and ecclesiastical rulers was election of the most fit over any consideration for inheritance or appointment. While childless secular rulers were not successful in imposing such a program of "ungendered rulership" in their realms, the Church did wrest control of most ecclesiastical elections from the hands of its secular patrons, including women. Reformers also successfully placed the election of the Pope firmly in the hands of the college of cardinals. What is new here is McNamara's recognition that such institution-building was at the cost of women and their power – in its denunciation of the matriarchs of the Roman families, of mothers as regents for kings and emperors, and even of monastic women. Lost was an earlier Rome, in which a married priest might eventually be elected Pope and simply take vows of celibacy along with his wife, Marozia. Clerics increasingly insisted on their own celibacy and chastity as a means of elevating themselves above laymen who led lives in which gender, sexuality, and inheritance by heirs remained important. Canossa and Gregory VII's humbling of Henry IV can be seen as a great turning point in the Investiture Controversy, that great conflict between eleventh-century Church and State, which was part of the larger Gregorian reform.

This reform movement had other aspects, however. To assert a clerical superiority over the laity meant internal reform of the clergy, in particular by the condemnation of nicolaitism, the "sin" of clerical marriage. In Chapter 5, Dyan Elliott turns to postmodern theory to investigate, by a careful rereading of the sources, the progressive demonization of clerical wives by such reformers. Her focus is a series of lives of an early Italian archbishop, Saint Severus of Ravenna, who had been married and had a daughter when he was elected. There were several accounts of his life. By the time of that written by the famous reformer and polemicist of the Gregorian reform of the late eleventh century, Peter Damian, the discomfort felt by such reformers about such a married bishop was apparent. Such reformers changed all parts of clerical society by enforcing the ban on clerical marriage from the very top of the hierarchy down to the parish level and they did so remarkably successfully.[3]

Reforms of the papacy would have repercussions for local dioceses. In Chapter 6, Maureen C. Miller looks at the Gregorian reform as it played out in a single diocese of northern Italy, that of Verona. This diocese and its ecclesiastical appointments had long been fought over by emperor and pope, but it was among the secular clergy that reform seems to have first spread. As population and prosperity increased in the diocese in the eleventh century, we see better education of clergy, the ending of clerical marriage, the organization of clerics as well as monks and nuns into new communities, and the creation of new types of institutions – hospitals for strangers or lepers, for instance. For the bishop, canonical election replaced a patronage system in which supporters of emperor and pope had vied. The dramatic changes seen in Verona were very specific to its political and economic circumstances and local reforms of monastic and related institutions were little influenced by international trends.

All these developments within the Church of the central Middle Ages meant that the clerical branch went from being one in which nearly all bishops were equals, to one in which popes and their courts had priority; from one in which bishops were married, to one in which clerical wives were repudiated and to one increasingly represented by men only and, indeed, by celibate men alone. The rhetoric of the clerical and monastic orders began to place barriers between clerics and all women, even nuns. As clerical marriage was banned, priests' wives were increasingly demonized and clerical families split up; formerly married priests and their families may have sought the religious life in new eremitical communities.[4] As men came to be more and more in charge, the issues shifted as to which men were in charge. Did both the Pope and the Emperor have authority over the Church, or the Pope alone, or the Pope and his cardinals and other agents? To what extent did those agents (the papal legates) who were sent to act in the Pope's name override the authority of local bishops and archbishops, abbots and abbesses? Meanwhile, as the clerical branch became more hierarchical, it was claimed that even monastics were to answer to the clerical branch – either to local bishops or, more often, directly to the Papacy. Many of the Gregory VII's eleventh-century claims with regard to Papal power within the Church and against the Emperor were still premature and did not bear fruit until somewhat later.

Like claims to papal primacy, the origins of a college of cardinals are obscure, although their role in elections was clarified with a series of election decrees, announced at synods or councils. The earliest, in 1059, gave power to elect the Pope to a college of fifty-two members: cardinal bishops, cardinal priests, and cardinal deacons. Cardinal priests were those responsible for serving the four major churches of Rome. The cardinal deacons served the smaller diaconate churches located throughout the city. Local bishops from the region around Rome were promoted to the status of cardinal bishops, in effect elevating the Pope to the status of an archbishop over the region. These cardinals as a group not only elected new popes, but assisted in the daily papal business of the papal court (the *curia*). They were employed as witnesses to the papal letters, called papal bulls because of the lead seals with images of Saints Peter and Paul attached, assisting the Pope at councils and synods, supporting the codification of Church or canon law, particularly at the University of Bologna, and the issuance of new papal legislation as additions to that law, and undertaking administrative tasks. They also deputized as papal legates and were sent to resolve disputes and assert papal interests outside Rome.[5] Despite reform, twelfth-century papal elections still often were influenced by the great Roman families whose rivalries helped foment schism – the election of two rival popes to fill a vacancy with neither of them immediately recognized by all of Christendom.[6]

With the considerable increase in papal business over the twelfth century came an enormous increase in the number of papal letters or bulls issued and the development of a bureaucracy in the papal chancery to handle the copying and issuance of such documents. The papal curia was particularly important in its functions of resolving disputes and offering dispensations – the latter, for instance, to legitimize sons of priests or to allow the illegitimate to be ordained as priests. Of particular note in the development of the business of the papal court was its claim to be the court of last appeal in all cases, including many that involved seculars. The Papacy also expanded its purview enormously by claiming authority over anything having to do with such sacraments as marriage, including dissolution, questions of the legitimacy of children, or the degrees of consanguinity within which marriage could be celebrated. Secular lords seeking papal dispensations on marital disputes brought vast numbers of disputes before the papal curia. The production of documents for litigants and petitioners from throughout Europe brought money into Rome because gifts and payments were required for the issuance of judgments and privileges.

Within this growing court and the wealth that it produced, the question was raised by the cardinals, as Norman Zacour shows in Chapter 7, about what the Papacy was. Was it the pope alone? Was it the pope and his court – that is, the pope and the cardinals who elected him? Most theorists of the time (not surprisingly many of them cardinals themselves), opted for the corporate definition: that is, that the cardinals were themselves part of the institutionalized power which was the Papacy. They defined themselves in many ways, including puns on the Latin words cardinal (*cardinales*) and the Latin word *cardines*, meaning hinges. Zacour lists:

some well-developed metaphors about the successors of the apostles: pillars of the church of God; part of the pope's body; the *cardines* – the hinges – upon which the great door of the universal church swings; senators of the church, reminiscent of the senators of the Roman empire now absorbed into the Christian body politic; *patres conscripti* – enlisted fathers . . . of the Christian church.[7]

Zacour's discussion provides an insight into the increasingly complex nature of power in the papal curia in the late Middle Ages, when the pope became a territorial prince as well as continuing to come from one of the ruling families of the city. Thus, the Papacy came to the height of its power. Beginning with Alexander III, most notably with Innocent III, and continuing right up to the pontificate of Boniface VIII (1294–1303), the authority of the Papacy was on the ascendant.

The following four chapters provide a different view of the medieval Church from that of earlier, often very triumphant, accounts of the expanding powers of the Papacy and the Church in the Middle Ages. Such traditional interpretations once measured the success of the medieval Church and of medieval religion by the victories of eleventh-century Popes in their struggle with the Emperors. But such interpreters forgot all too easily that the principle of canonical election (election of bishop or abbot by the community he served) that were asserted and defended by eleventh-century reformers would be subverted by the Papacy itself by the fourteenth century. By then popes claimed the right to appoint virtually all members of the Church hierarchy and many heads of religious communities as well.[8] As popes gained in power and prestige often at the expense of the rest of the Church, the papal court came to appear more and more like that of a secular prince rather than that of the pious leader of an international institution.

NOTES

1   The most complete treatments are found in Ian S. Robinson, *The Papacy: 1073–1198: Continuity and Innovation* (Cambridge: Cambridge University Press, 1990), Gerd Tellenbach, *The Church in Western Europe from the Tenth to the Early Twelfth Century*, trans. Timothy Reuter (Cambridge: Cambridge University Press, 1993), and Uta Renate Blumenthal, *The Investiture Controversy: Church and Monarchy from the Ninth to the Twelfth Century* (Philadelphia, PA: University of Pennsylvania Press, 1988); Brian Tierney, *The Crisis of Church and State, with Selected Documents* (Englewood Cliffs, NJ: Prentice Hall, 1964), has a number of the relevant documents, including one about the buying of a bishopric, pp. 29–30, and the *Dictatus Papae*, pp. 49–50.

2   The rise of the papal curia paralleled that of secular governments; see, for instance, complex papal ceremonial for papal coronations or religious processions on feast days within the city of Rome. See Agostino Paravicini-Bagliani, *The Pope's Body* (Chicago, IL: University of Chicago Press, 2000), and Paravicini-Bagliani, *La cour des papes au XIIIe siècle* (Paris: Hachette, 1995).

3   As Elliott (see Chapter 5, pp. 124–5) says:

> The measures taken against clerical wives in and after the eleventh century were severe in the extreme: some canons went so far as to suggest enslavement. But considering the number of married clergy and their vigorous resistance to the new order – resistance that is described in detail for cities such as Milan – the success of the program was quite remarkable. This is certainly true for the long term. . . . But even in the short run, it is uncanny how the wives contemporary with the Gregorian Reform seem to have melted away.

4   See the example of Valmagne in Berman, *Cistercian Evolution: The Invention of a Religious Order in Twelfth-Century Europe* (Philadelphia: University of Pennsylvania Press, 2000), p. 205, and of Obazine in Berman, *Women and Monasticism in Medieval Europe: Sisters and Patrons of the Cistercian Order* (Kalamazoo, MI: Medieval Institute Publications, 2002), pp. 77ff.

5   Many twelfth-century cardinals had training in Bologna or Paris. They served for life and, when one died, his successor was named by the incumbent pope; new popes were hence frequently chosen from among the cardinals; see Bernhard Schimmelpfennig, *The Papacy*, trans. James Sievert (New York: Columbia University Press, 1992).

6   Several survivors of such schism, the twelfth-century Popes Innocent II (1130–43) and Alexander III (1159–81), once having successfully overcome their rivals, consolidated their power in Rome and throughout the Church by calling great ecumenical councils, Lateran II in 1139 and Lateran III in 1179 respectively. At the first a variety of doctrinal and disciplinary issues concerning heresy, usury, and the marriage of clergy were ironed out. We also know that Innocent II's successful return to Rome c.1140 led to the renovation of Santa-Maria-in-Trastevere. See discussion of this church's apse mosaic on pp. 4–5. In 1179 the Third Lateran Council's first piece of business would be to declare that a pope could only be elected by a vote of two-thirds of the cardinals and other issues regarding papal elections were also clarified. The Fourth Lateran Council in 1215 was called not because it ended a schism, but because Pope Innocent III (1198–1216), with the assistance of Parisian theologians, had compiled a great program of reform legislation to be enacted, a program that reshaped the church more significantly than any other council before the end of the Middle Ages. On the first three Lateran Councils, see Robinson, *The Papacy*, 121ff.; on the fourth, see Jane Sayers, *Innocent III, Leader of Europe, 1198–1216* (London, Longman, 1994).

7   See p. 184.

8   See Schimmelpfennig, *Papacy*, 198ff.; on the effects on monasticism, see Nicole de Peña, *Les moines de l'abbaye de Moissac de 1295 à 1334: entre coutumes clunisiennes et nécessités économique*, Cahiers Mabillon I (Turnhout: Brepols, 2001).

4

CANOSSA AND THE UNGENDERING OF THE PUBLIC MAN

Jo Ann McNamara

The central event in traditional accounts of the Gregorian reform is Canossa, the larger-than-life meeting of the German ruler Henry IV and Pope Gregory VII ensconced in the castle of that name in Italy in 1077. The castle belonged to Gregory's powerful supporter, the Countess Matilda of Tuscany, and Henry traveled there in secret during the winter of 1076–7. There he presented himself as a penitent (possibly standing for three days outside in the snow) because he had been excommunicated by Gregory in the previous year and was threatened with rebellion in Germany after the Pope announced that Henry's vassals no longer owed him loyalty. In appearing before the gates of Canossa as a penitent Henry forced the Pope's hand, for once the penitent ruler appeared before him Gregory VII could not avoid lifting the excommunication decree and reintegrating Henry into the Church. Although Gregory supposedly hesitated, his first duty, not as Pope but indeed as a simple priest, was to reconcile the truly penitent. Henry humbled before the Pope had nonetheless retained his throne. Perhaps humiliation had been turned into victory. McNamara, a leader in the feminist reassessment of the history of the early and medieval Church and State, here suggests that Canossa, from the perspective of gender history, represents a particular moment of male history, part of a larger movement (the Gregorian reform) in which male clergy attempted to "ungender" themselves by ending clerical marriage and strictly excluding women from participation in Church affairs. These moves to "ungender" the clergy were particularly unfortunate for the former wives of clergy and their children (as we see in Chapter 5, by Elliott), but they set a model in the creation of a public sphere restricted only to men. This trend is also seen in the secular sphere, where attacks on women's public roles undermined the power they had formerly enjoyed within the family context. McNamara's feminist rereading of the traditional history of Rome and its bishops in the tenth century brings into question the characterization of that period as a "pornocracy," as it was called by bishop Liutprand of Cremona, a northern Italian chronicler who was appalled by the power of the Theophylact family in Rome and that of its matriarchs, Theodora and Marozia. We can now see that part of Liutprand's fixation on how badly Rome was ruled may have been caused by his own bitterness about personal betrayal – Hugh of Provence, once Liutprand's patron, had abandoned him and Hugh's marriage with Marozia provided an easy target. This article by Jo Ann McNamara was originally published *in* Render Unto Caesar: The Religious Sphere in World Politics, *eds Sabrina Petra Ramet and Donald W. Treadgold (Washington, DC: American University Press, 1995), pp. 131–50.*

* * *

The conflict between Church and state has long been the grand focus of traditional medieval history, with Canossa as the hinge upon which European history turns. No single word so swiftly evokes the great traditional debate over religion and politics. There at the gate of the mighty castle on its craggy peak, the Holy Roman Emperor, Henry IV (1056–1106) knelt kissing the pastoral ring of the Roman Catholic Pope, Gregory VII (1073–85), the defining moment of the struggle for right order in the European world.[1] Church and state came to Canossa in 1077 to determine whether a divinely appointed king or the Vicar of Christ would ultimately act as God's legitimating agent in a Christian polity. The question remains open. The grandeur of the rhetoric flows on. The majestic competition of the twin institutional pillars of society still magnetizes our attention.

However, this clash of institutions masks the fundamental unity of Christian faith and Christian culture that secured the collective adherence and loyalty of the many peoples of medieval Europe. Christian religion gave the emerging European civilization its unifying conceptual framework. The Church–state conflict that so long divided the European conscience tends to distract our attention from the basic harmony of their goals. In 1076, Europe was entering its decisive formative period and, as dedicated "reformers," both contenders for its leadership agreed that the civilization to come would reflect the order established once and for all in the Garden of Eden by God and nature.

Let us look again at Canossa in the light of recent feminist Heidi Hartmann's formulation of male dominance as dependent on male hierarchy and male solidarity.[2] Two men met at Canossa, each at the peak of his own hierarchy. Henry and Gregory contested for mastery of the world. The women who had brought them there were invisible on the completed canvas. The owner of the castle itself, Matilda of Tuscany (d. 1115), whose armies guarded the Alpine passes for Gregory, is nowhere to be seen. Gone out of memory is Henry IV's regent-mother, the Empress Agnes of Poitou (regent at the outset for Henry IV, whose minority was 1056–65), whose pious enthusiasm for reform let slip the imperial prerogatives over papal election. There is no sign of the hundreds of powerful women who actively shared the public sphere in this age of noble power. Two men, their gender masked by their grand titles, their masculinity subsumed by the anthropomorphized institutions they claimed to represent, confronted each other at Canossa. Their meeting marks the culmination of a period of primitive institutionalization, when popes and emperors had collaborated to re-establish the rough boundaries that marked and protected their respective institutions from female encroachment. The peak and its castle and the world of power they represented had been transformed into a womanless space wherein men could play power games as though no queen had ever crossed the board.

In this world the formulation of the two cities by the Church Father, Augustine of Hippo (d. 430), remained the ideal for men who aspired to a well-ordered society. In the beginning of the tenth century, however, the institutional foundations of both Church and State were thoroughly sapped by the proprietary claims of noble families. They had gained the right of hereditary succession to public offices from the Carolingian King of Western Francia, Charles the Bald (843–77) at Quierzy in 877. Their military strength and the proprietary rights they drew from the endowment of churches gave them power over ecclesiastical offices and the estates that supported them.[3] They tended to value present advantage over future security, subordinating lineage to the horizontal kindred. Thus inheritance was broadly shared. Widows, children, siblings, and cousins were deployed as advantageously as possible. Daughters filled gaps in the male line, and widows acted as surrogates for their husbands in retaining offices and the property that went with them.

In most areas, the inheritance laws of the Germanic tribes that were exclusionary with regard to women had been softened and revised to allow women to inherit from both their natal and conjugal kin. The disadvantage of being placed below their brothers in the order of inheritance was nullified by an astonishingly high female survival rate.[4] Moreover, women took precedence over uncles on the natal side and over their own younger sons on the conjugal side.[5] When married, their inherited property continued to belong to them; when widowed, they continued to dispose of dowers and morning gifts as well as inherited property from their husbands. Women frequently appeared in the land market, selling and buying property for themselves.[6] Hereditary right to the property of both fathers and husbands gave them a unique capacity to concentrate power. They could take the legacy of one marriage into another marriage, creating new alliances as they went. They could pre-empt the inheritance of their first husbands' children for the benefit of children from their second marriages. As widows, they could draw everything together according to their own designs. The decisive influence of women was inescapable in the tenth century.[7] Between kindreds and kingdoms, women often acted as "peace-weavers," knitting up alliances as they moved through marriage and motherhood. Theoretically subsumed in a patriarchal system, passed from the power of a father to the authority of a husband, they ultimately identified themselves as daughters, sisters, wives, or mothers, according to their own purposes. In extreme cases, this meant joining together unrelated kingdoms and subverting the dynastic system. Women knitted up boundaries and tore apart centers. They drew their husbands into a private circle and withdrew them from institutional loyalties.

In this sense, form was being attacked and nearly destroyed by formlessness, a social chaos associated with the activities of women.

The porous kinship system also allowed tenth-century women passage into the sacred precincts of the Church. Dynastic strategy often dictated that family property in the hands of women should be secured through their appointment to monastic offices. From its inception, monasticism was a lay movement, and the Benedictine rule under which most regulars lived strongly discouraged the ordination of monks. Until the tenth century, the system was a model of near equality between women and men. The chanting of the offices was not gender specific, and monks and nuns shared the same Benedictine and Augustinian rules. Liturgies, processions, pilgrimages, and displays of relics were again common to both. The centrality of the sacraments was not so dominant in the tenth century as it would become in the central Middle Ages. Reservation of the Eucharist lessened the need to have a priest for its dispensation, and monastic confession was made to both male and female heads of communities.[8] Despite this lay status, the enjoyment of clerical exemptions and honors tended to join consecrated women with male regulars in the clerical order. Where powerful abbesses ruled, priests served them as chaplains, and, as in Rome, women sometimes undertook all but the most strictly sacerdotal functions of the higher clergy. The royal abbess Matilda of Quedlinburg (d. 999) ruled Germany as regent for her brother Otto II (973–83) and, exercising her powers as *metropolitana*, presided over an episcopal synod.[9]

The overwhelming majority of priests married, sometimes more than once, and their wives insisted on all the financial formalities that accompanied lay unions.[10] Clerical families, though almost invisible to historical documentation, were susceptible to the same patterns of female longevity and shared functions that often subverted the conventional gender system among the laity. An incident from the life of Peter Damian shows a priest's wife performing a pastoral role not dissimilar to the parish activities of modern Protestant ministers' wives.[11] Eleventh-century monks of Marmoutiers justified their tenth-century ejection of the original community by claiming that the sacristan's "concubine" and her son had taken charge of ringing the bell.[12] From various reforming prohibitions in the ninth century, we know that women sometimes acted as acolytes (assistants to the priests in performing the Mass, usually boys) and even occasionally ventured to say Mass themselves (though without consecrating the sacrament).[13] It seems likely, therefore, that priests' wives in smaller parishes performed similar services, encroaching on the sacred preserves of the priesthood as their secular sisters invaded the shrunken precincts of public power.

For centuries, a minority of churchmen had tried to eliminate priestly marriage.[14] In the early tenth century, their complaint was an institutional argument against clerical wives as consumers of Church goods and heirs of Church wealth.[15] The married clergy retaliated with assurances that their wives more than paid their own way by the work they did to support their husbands and families.[16] The active property transactions between priests and with the laity might appear to support the critics of clerical marriage, but such critics take no account of the property to support the couple and their children that a priest's wife might bring to the marriage. Moreover, particularly in the tenth and eleventh centuries, frequent land transactions of various sorts (whether involving clerics or not) might simply indicate good husbandry of resources and proper attention to networking among one's neighbors, following the impeccable example of the reforming monks of Cluny whose records of surviving transactions fill six large printed volumes.[17] There is no reason to suppose that a clergy with customary rights to inheritance would not be as devout and effective as a clergy appointed by political patronage. Care for the family inheritance would ensure that priest's wives acted like other mothers; they would not take property out of the Church, and their children – even daughters – would be as carefully deployed as the daughters of laymen for the common advantage of the family and its (in this case ecclesiastical) inheritance. Propertied clerical wives probably made transactions just as laywomen did. Priests' widows must have acted as "regents" for the humbler parishes, where an informal system of hereditary pastorates seems to have prevailed. In brief, clerical families probably behaved in about the same way as secular families. This was certainly the case in the Greek Church, where clerical marriage was legally imposed on the clergy.[18]

In the West, however, reformers believed that they saw the sacred boundaries of the Church being breached not only by clerical marriage but by the intervention of lay patrons who claimed rights of appointment to clerical offices based on their proprietary interests in Church estates. This was labeled simony, the sin or "heresy" of selling sacramental grace in the form of Church office. (Realistically, a self-reproducing clergy should have been the best corrective for the forms of simony involving lay intervention in appointment to Church office, but longstanding convention in the West ensured that the holders of the higher ecclesiastical offices were celibate.) But it was not just that the Church chose clerical celibacy. Lay lords too had a strong interest in clerical celibacy, perhaps stronger than that of most priests. Lay lords needed a steady supply of ecclesiastical offices to which they could appoint their own relatives – relatives whom they chose to keep unmarried so as to concentrate wealth back in a single line of the patrimony, rather than dissipating it among younger sons or cadet branches.[19] From the earlier period up to the eleventh and twelfth centuries at least at the highest ranks of such appointment, if a candidate for the episcopacy was married, his wife usually separated from him and invalidated their marriage by taking monastic vows. At a time when the lay aristocracy was becoming more powerful (sometimes at the expense of the Church), the upper levels of the ecclesiastical hierarchy were thus the only institutions in Western Europe that did not produce a hereditary aristocracy.

Women and men alike used familial powers to appoint Church officials.[20] The imperialist chronicler Liutprand of Cremona (d. 972) noted with despair that in Italy, from Lombardy to Rome, women were in power everywhere, not least of all in the papal city. In the ninth century, Liutprand begins by telling us, the last German Carolingian, supported by Pope Formosus (891–6) was thwarted by the Roman nobility led by Ageltrude, the widowed Duchess of Spoleto, whose husband Wido had usurped the imperial crown in 889. In the next generation, as Liutprand's pages tell us, even the papacy fell victim to female usurpation. Ambitious wives, widows, and mothers crowded Liutprand's pages with their struggles for control of Italy's crown.

In Rome in the early tenth century, according to Liutprand, Theodora, a woman widely praised for her religious devotion, domestic virtue, and charity, married Theophylact, the *magister militum*, leader of the Roman nobility against the imperialist and papal factions.[21] Together Theodora I and Theophylact would control the outcome of the papal election of Sergius III (904–11), whose union with their daughter Marozia had already produced the future John XI (931–5).[22] After Theophylact died in 916, his widow, Theodora I, instituted the fourteen-year reign of John X (914–28), who had so impressed her and her late husband by his effectiveness at Ravenna that they had, uncanonically, procured his transfer to the see of Bologna. Theodora, calling herself *senatrix*, shared her power with her two daughters, Marozia and Theodora II.

When Theodora died before the end of John X's reign, her daughter Marozia took her title as senatrix and married Alberic, marquis of Spoleto, who had meantime assumed Theophylact's military office in Rome. When Alberic died she was able to pass her father's offices on to a new husband, Guy of Tuscany. A papal bid for independence in 926 ended when the younger couple, Marozia and Guy, besieged the Lateran and deposed John X. Marozia, always according to Liutprand, appointed two more popes and then gave the office to her son, John XI, who was Pope from 931 to 935. He played the sacerdotal role while she continued to control the secular powers of the bishop and ruler of Rome.

Widowed once again, in 932, Marozia took a third husband, Hugh of Provence (d. 947). Hugh was the grandson of the Emperor Lothar (954–86) and his concubine Waldrada. But for the vagaries of Carolingian divorce laws which had prevented Lothar and Waldrada a legitimate union (but did produce a huge dossier about the attempt of Lothar to divorce), Hugh might have become emperor through strict inheritance.[23] By his own efforts, he had already in 926 gained the kingship of Italy. Hugh and Marozia were within reach of the imperial crown when Marozia's son from her first marriage, Alberic, denounced his mother's third marriage (to Hugh of Provence, who was Alberic's father-in-law) as incestuous.[24] This caused a riot in the city of Rome, and Marozia was imprisoned, while Hugh was driven from the city. The *senatrix* disappeared from history, but not her progeny.[25] Alberic's bastard son was crowned John XII and ruled from 955 to 963. Through Marozia's sister,

Theodora II, the line extended down to John XIX (1024–32) and Benedict IX (1032–45).

Seen through other eyes, the tenth-century episcopacy of Rome, the incipient papacy, represented the triumph of the Roman nobility. The papacy was neither particularly scandalous nor corrupt, but the nobles' narrow and pragmatic ambitions were to take what they could from a fragmented world. Marozia was simply a very effective agent of an extremely ambitious noble family. Her youthful liaison with the deacon who became Sergius III was apparently a public one and seems to have cast no shame on her as "first lady" of Rome. It may well have been viewed as a marriage, since Marozia contracted no other alliance until after Sergius died. Indeed, she seems quite properly to have allowed her conjugal life to lapse into continence when the path to the papacy opened up for her "husband." As his widow after Sergius's death, she in fact oversaw the office of bishop of Rome carefully until her son was old enough to take his father's place. Stripped of hysterical polemics and political factionalism, this is perfectly plausible. But for a thousand years, polemics have dominated the historical discourse, branding Marozia and her female contemporaries an infamous "pornocracy" or government by whores.

Tenth-century men were apparently shocked by the emergence of so many wicked stepmothers and merry widows. Perhaps they had taken male dominance for an incontrovertible fact of nature and forgotten that it depends on homosociability, or male bonding, and that it must be upheld by institutions and customs.[26] Not only had they lost their sense of allegiance to a larger commonwealth, they had also betrayed their gender solidarity. They had favored and promoted their daughters, their wives, and their sisters in the hope of deploying them for personal gain. In the process, they had overturned the right order of the world and sold themselves into unnatural servitude to women.[27] The ambition to rise had spurred people of every social level to seize what advantages they could from the prevailing anarchy. The same anxiety generated a fear of falling that drove them, at last, to "re-form" a stabler order.[28]

This profound sense of disorder predictably inspired a sense of pollution that was unequivocally associated with the rule of women in Liutprand of Cremona's history of tenth-century Italy.[29] In his pages, we hear nothing of the inheritance laws of Italy or the deployment of women for political advantage. Instead, he spins a fable of women who took advantage of men's inability to control their sexual drives by using fatal female charms to subjugate their natural superiors. Liutprand describes the early tenth-century Duchess Bertha, widow of the marquis of Tuscany – who refused to surrender her castles to her enemies – as having taken over his authority and support of his faithful "by cunning, lavish gifts and the pleasant exercises of the nuptial couch."[30] Liutprand describes how Bertha's daughter Ermengarde, widow of the marquis of Ivrea, "gained the chief authority in all Italy" because "she carried on carnal commerce with everyone, prince and commoner alike."[31] He accused Willa, the heroic and resourceful wife of Berengar, marquis of Friuli, who was elected King of Italy in 888, of unchastity with a chaplain described as "hairy, dirty and having a tail," and Liutprand said that she used sorcery to talk her husband into having the chaplain castrated when she was almost caught.[32] The same fear and hatred of women was expressed in the campaign of tenth-century bishops Rather of Verona and Atto of Vercelli against clerical marriage. In this atmosphere, the quintessential myth of pollution and disorder – the legend of Pope Joan – grew up and flourished.[33]

Most improbably Liutprand had characterized Theodora I, senatrix and wife of Theophylact, as a "shameless strumpet who ruled Rome in the manliest fashion."[34] He says that she procured the papacy for her son John "because she feared that she wouldn't be able to satisfy her lust often enough if he were two hundred miles away." She "forced him to comply with her desires again and again."[35] Liutprand marveled that her daughters, Marozia and Theodora II, surpassed her in "the exercises of Venus," and he likened Marozia to Herodias [niece, second wife, and sister-in-law of the Herod who had beheaded John the Baptist, she epitomized unrestrained lust]. Liutprand blamed Marozia for luring to Rome "like an ox to the sacrifice," her future husband, Hugh of Provence, a man described by Liutprand as having many good qualities that were marred only by his weakness for women.[36]

Liutprand was typical of most theorists of misogyny in that he opposed in his writing this "pornocracy" with stories of a saintly woman who typified the right order of things, but who also represented the party in opposition to those who had seemingly betrayed Liutprand himself. Thus, Hugh of Provence, Liutprand's original patron (later misguided enough not to support the writer) had, according to the writer, Liutprand, tried repeatedly to fulfill his imperial ambitions from the time of his election as king of Italy in 926 until he died in 947, but these ambitions would only be fulfilled through a saintly woman. Thus, after Hugh's son Lothar died in 950, the Lombard estates and the imperial claim inherited from Hugh by Lothar devolved upon the latter's widow, Adelheid, who was in fact the daughter of the person who had once been Hugh's chief rival, Raoul, or Rudolph, King of Burgundy (922–6). Adelheid found herself the unwilling target of greedy suitors from all over Italy and, after a heroic escape from the dungeon in which one of them had confined her, Adelheid chose as her second husband, Otto of Saxony (King Otto I, 936–73, emperor from 962), thus drawing the German king into the tangled affairs of Italy. Adelheid and Otto I would be anointed together as rulers of the Holy Roman Empire in 962 by Theodora I's grandson, John XII. Through the reigns of her son and grandson, sometimes with the competitive help of her Byzantine daughter-in-law Theophano (who had married Otto II in 972), Adelheid dominated the government of Germany (and served as regent for Otto III from 991 to 996), while the men pursued their imperial ambitions in Italy, but she is presented by Liutprand, the imperialist propagandist, as her husband's gracious spouse without mention of her political ambitions. Similarly, Odilo of Cluny (abbot, 994–1049), whose reforming monastery she favored with her charity, proclaimed Adelheid a saint.[37]

The documents of practice show that Theodora I's grandson (Marozia's stepson), John XII (955–63), governed the Church energetically, reforming and restoring several monasteries and resolving disputes about the privileges of German bishoprics. He also pursued the family's policy of resisting German imperialism, organizing a revolt against Otto I as soon as the Emperor was well away from Rome. But Liutprand framed the issue as a sexual one, attributing the Pope's rebellion to his fear that the emperor would attempt to correct his vices.[38] Liutprand accused Pope John XII of appointing as governor of many cities the widow of one of his vassals, because he was besotted with her. He characterized John's weakness for women as uncontrollable and indiscriminate, maintaining that the revolt that restored him after the Emperor's condemnation was no more than a riot by women who had shared his bed.[39] Liutprand's charges justified the rebellious clergy's allowing Otto I to judge and depose the Pope – a precedent that would support every imperial intervention of later times. However, the Romans continued to support the Theophylact family, canonically electing yet another member of the house, John XIII (965–72), son of Theodora II.[40] The family continued to lead the Roman nobility under "Crescentius, son of Theodora."[41]

Liutprand expressed the underlying unease that steadily persuaded men to sacrifice the advantages they derived from the deployment of women. His myth of male nature governed by uncontrollable lust argued the need for a woman-free space or institution if men were to pursue their lofty political concerns without genital distractions. In such an arena, elevated above their sexuality, they could become ungendered, generic "men." The Church was best equipped to accomplish this political reformation. The incontrovertible truths of the Catholic religion provided theoretical support for a woman-free space, and the ordained clergy had already formed a solid core from which it could expand. Sexuality, marriage, and the gender system were sturdily framed by the religious tradition of Christianity, which reshaped the Jewish legacy with Augustine's concept that the Fall came with the discovery of sexual desire. Thus the sin of disobedience, the cause of the primal disorder in human affairs, was linked to the presence of woman in the Garden of Eden. Eve alone bore the burden of human sexuality and its concomitant pollution, the fundamental cause of reproduction and death. Women's exclusion from the clergy restored the condition of Eden. Priests in their sacerdotal roles regained for Adam the innocence he had had before the creation of Eve made him a gendered being. The assumption, being hence fixed in the mysterious "nature of things," was that women could not perform sacramental functions. This thus assured men of a zone of "liberty" from female interference and sexuality outside the gender system.[42]

The Church also offered a means of expanding its womanless space by monasticizing the clergy and clericizing the monastic movement. The great Burgundian abbey of Cluny, founded in 909, took the lead. Uniquely, in that proprietary age, Cluny tried to free itself entirely from lay patronage, branding such lay interference as a form of simony. As its prestige grew, Cluny imposed its own monastic practices and a central discipline on houses that agreed to adopt its constitutions, securing their patrons' renunciation of proprietary rights on these subject abbeys and returning them to the system of election defined in the Benedictine rule. Canonical election by the community itself became the ideal agent of reform, not only for the Cluniacs but ultimately for the Church itself, because it created a sealed community from which all alien elements (lay patrons, particularly female patrons) could be excluded. Breaking with the traditions of the past in which female-headed houses were often seen, Cluny also steadfastly spurned women's houses, however well disciplined or well reputed, as partners in reform.

Odo of Cluny (abbot, 910–42) shared Liutprand's aversion to women. His misogyny was based on the same fearful myths that had from at least the time of Augustine identified lust as original sin transmitted from one generation to the next in the very act of conception.[43] According to Odo, lust represented a lack of control that threatened to unman its victim, to reduce him to an irrationality that subjected him to women. He maintained that all men would choose chastity if they could see the disgusting anatomy beneath a woman's skin, seeming to imply that men lacked the vulgar underpinnings of human biology. The monasticism of Cluny claimed the superiority of its reformed houses over the allegedly corrupt houses they were replacing. Hence, by virtue of their exclusion from the charmed Cluniac circle, women's religious communities came inevitably to be associated with the corruption not found at those houses reformed by Cluny. This tendency of Cluny not to include monastic women was reinforced by a growing tendency there (and elsewhere) for monks to embrace ordination, infusing their old devotions with the added benefit of sacramental powers, allowing them to celebrate masses for the dead. The growing emphasis on these masses, for which Cluny and its daughter houses became famous, seem to have further undervalued the prayers of women.

Beginning in the tenth century and despite its deleterious effect on their own patronage powers, wealthy donors hastened to assist the monastic reform epitomized by Cluny. And so did popes, including those associated with the Theophylact family. The chancery of the very same Sergius III to whom Marozia may once have been married seems to have issued Cluny's first papal exemptions at the time of the foundation in 909. It was Marozia's son, Alberic, who brought Odo of Cluny to Rome in the early tenth century to cleanse various corrupt Roman monasteries with Cluniac reforms. Such was the force of the new monastic spirituality, that even women appear to have internalized a belief in the inherent superiority of male spirituality.[44] We find in the documents of practice that the nun Marozia, possibly the *senatrix* herself, left goods to the abbot of Subiaco, "because the prayers of monks seem better to me than those of nuns."[45] Similarly, the German empresses were lured away from patronage of women's communities to the new reforms. Whereas after the death of Henry I (919–36) his widow, Queen Matilda (d. 968) had turned the royal monastery of nuns at Quedlinburg into a royal cult center, the wife of his successor Otto I, Empress Adelheid, became the mainstay not of houses of religious women but of Odilo of Cluny to whose obedience she submitted countless ancient monasteries.[46]

The great women's monastic houses, dependent so often for their financial survival on the dowries and inheritances that supported the nuns, began to smell of simony in the form of requests for dowries when women entered.[47] Even the language of virginity, once the clear preserve of women, was perverted to misogynistic uses. As Odo of Cluny suggested in his biography of the secular saint Gerard of Aurillac, the most innocent women tend to provoke men to rape.[48] While a generation later, the nun Hroswitha (d. c.1003) wrote a series of plays on women's chastity to refute the slanders of contemporary misogynists, hers was a strong voice, but she was crying in the wilderness.[49] Men's fear and misogynist hatred were driving religious women to the margins of the monastic order (and asserting that such margins were corrupt) at the same time they drove women, in a larger sense, to the margins of humanity itself.[50]

Cluny's separation of its eleventh-century monastic world from that of monastic women reinforced the monks' position that they were part of the increasingly elevated clerical world of ordained men. Moreover, the clergy as a whole began to monasticize as men (clerical and lay alike) were increasingly convinced that celibate monks were inherently more virtuous than the married secular clergy. Although clerical marriage was not discernibly damaging to the Church, it represented loss of control for that centralizing institution. According to their critics, clerical wives used the affections of their smitten partners to loosen their institutional loyalties to the Church. From the mid-tenth century, popes, bishops, and emperors sporadically joined forces to separate priests from their wives on the grounds that they formed a threat to Church property.[51] But institutional arguments had little hold over the majority of the clergy. They followed their sexual and affectionate inclinations and clung to their wives and children, successfully resisting reform by inertia, by pleading poverty without their wives, and they could do this by securing secular protection.[52] Leaving the spiritual excellence of chastity to the monastic orders, they were content to rest upon the modest virtues of marital fidelity. The *Rescript* of Ulrich, the defender of clerical marriage, condemned the reformers' reckless distortion of biblical citations to justify the innovation as "straining the breast of Scripture until it yielded blood in place of milk."[53]

Since practical arguments were unavailing, clerical marriage could be undercut only by religious theory. Odo of Cluny, with his Augustinian tendency to tie sin to sexuality and sexuality to women, showed the way. Monastic and secular clergy after him drew together to argue for the inherent dangers of the female presence to male purity and virtue. Their careless and intemperate language confused respectable conjugal union with the most shameless promiscuity and attempted to inspire priests with fear and revulsion for all women.[54] Further, the laity were encouraged to see married priests as "foul vessels of corruption" and to doubt that the sacraments performed by such corrupt priests could possibly be agents of salvation.[55]

Reform thus focused on the two breaches through which women threatened the institutional integrity of the Church: simony and clerical marriage, and, in 1049, clerical marriage was joined to simony in the reform agenda of Pope Leo IX (1048–54) and the Emperor Henry III (1039–56). The sacramental activities of the clergy gained a new centrality in Catholic devotion and became amalgamated with the purgative elements in monastic spirituality. The most ardent defender of clerical celibacy, Peter Damian (d. 1072), claimed that a man dedicated to God must be as virgin as God's mother herself if he were successfully to change the bread and wine into the body and blood of Christ.[56] Humbert of Silva Candida (d. 1061), best known for his attacks on the heresy of simony, also pronounced the Greek married clergy to be heretical.

The process of hereticizing clerical marriage depended heavily on allegory. The symbolism once firmly affixed to consecrated virgins was transferred to the Church as "Bride of Christ" and "Mother of all Christians."[57] Simony became rape and lay patrons were depicted as taking her by force.[58] Priests, as vicars of Christ, were transformed into the husbands of the Church and fathers of her children. Reforming rhetoric systematically classed priests' wives as whores and their husbands as adulterers. Priests were even charged with incest with the daughters of the Church, which was their bride (and mother). Neither the rigor of the theology nor the logic of the allegory stands up under close examination, but its terrifying and lurid imagery achieved its purpose. This anthropomorphized and feminized Church crowded biological women out. It allowed the allegorized clergy to preserve their technical manliness in the absence of the defining presence of women. At the same time, it allowed a subtle transformation. In this slippery thinking, the clergy became the Church. They tended to discard their gender as men became "man." In the tightening circle of Christian marriage, where two became one flesh, the Pope was transformed from an ambitious man into a depersonalized agent of a higher power.

It took a long time to inculcate disgust of ordinary sexual relations. A century passed between the tenth-century Atto of Vercelli's attacks and the first papal prohibition on clerical marriage, and it was nearly another century before the invalidation of priestly marriage at the Council of Pisa in 1135. But, long before that, the reformers had won the ideological battle.[59] By 1059, the Church needed only to eliminate imperial influence to complete its carefully bounded woman-free space. In that same year, Nicholas II (1058–61) prohibited clerical marriage and instituted the College of Cardinals as the canonical source of papal election. At Canossa in 1077 both parties agreed that what was insupportable was the thought of priests handling the sacred host with fingers polluted by the touch of their wives.

The Church and the State were, as Augustine had seen, natural partners. Until 1059, the emperors and the popes had the same goals. The emperors used their powers of appointment to Church office to secure the papacy from the influence of the Roman nobility. The popes, in turn, ratified imperial appointments of celibate, often monastic, clergy so as to secure somewhat those offices from the influence of the German nobility. Like the popes, the emperors sought to pull men free of the circles of family interest that weakened the magnetism of central government. The logic of transforming the imperial state from private to public power demanded modification of the reproductive cycle that enhanced the role of women and yoked women's power to the laws of inheritance. The imperial claims of Otto I (emperor 962–73) rested on his marriage to Adelheid in 951, and they were reinforced by the union of Otto II (973–83) in 972 with Theophano, who claimed kinship with the Byzantine emperor.

The newly liberated ecclesiastical hierarchy offered the secular power both a theory and a mechanism for breaking the yoke of biology. The Holy Roman Empire rested on a concept of fitness reinforced by the biblical models of Saul and David, liturgically expressed in the ceremony of coronation. The Germanic principle of election (from among claimants with royal blood) combined easily with Christian notions that election was an agent of divine will, the principles which guided the canonical election process by circles of internal electors. The German state could not define such a circle of electors as cleanly as the Church did, but electoral authority could block the passage of royal power through the hands of widows. The seal of consent provided by the assembled princes lifted the monarch above his kindred, and the mystique conferred by royal blood protected the kingship from the competitive ambitions of the noble electorate.

The Roman Empire, the institutional model for its German successor, had not always depended on biology for its survival. At the height of their powers the emperors had freely adopted qualified successors in the absence of an heir. To avoid the fragmentation of the state itself that had earlier dissolved the Carolingian Empire in fratricidal strife, the German emperors risked, and sometimes incurred, dynastic failure. They regularly appointed most of their sons and daughters to Church offices, pruning their family trees by favoring lineage over horizontal kindred.[60] The death of Otto III (983–1002) without heirs was followed by the election of Henry II (1002–24), who also died without heirs, perhaps inspired by design. Later biographers maintained that the sainted emperor Henry II and his Empress Cunegund (or Kunigunde) took a vow of chastity upon their marriage, relying on election and the fitness of a near relative to ensure continuity of the monarchy.[61] At Otto's death Cunegund herself carried the imperial insignia to the emperor-elect who succeeded her husband, Conrad (1024–39). Such policies, however, reinforced the importance of widows. Empresses Adelheid and Theophano did not like each other, but they held the empire together during the infancy of Otto III. Conrad associated his son, Henry III, in the monarchy; Henry III, in turn, crowned his son while the boy was still a child. This crowning of the heir while the current ruler was still alive, moreover, might have been an effective vehicle for replacing the partnership of queens with a partnership of father and son, if the Germans had only had the longevity of the French royal family. However, Henry IV was still a child when his father died and left him during his minority (1056–65) to the regency of Agnes of Poitou.

In the end, the German emperors ultimately lacked the courage or the will to wrest the empire entirely on the electoral system. Royal blood, indeed, was probably the only ingredient that could prevent the Holy Roman Empire from following its pagan predecessors down the dreary path of election by combat. However, inheritance of rulership tended to strengthen conjugal bonds. The Saxon dynasty (936–1024) was distinguished for its queens.[62] The destructive effects of these women's natal ties, moreover, were neutralized in that empire by the practice of choosing wives from distant royal lineages who tended to identify closely with the fates of their husbands and sons. The German empresses were devoted to the high purposes of the state. They shared royal anointment and played an active role in all the business of the realm. But even the military functions of the emperor were not totally secure against such female encroachment. In widowhood, they acted as regents, guarding the interests of their sons and of the monarchy. But the enchanted circle that held the royal family distanced the king from other men, and the power of women and family within the aristocracy had much the same effect as clerical marriage had on the Church.

The willingness of the Saxon empresses to identify themselves with the state and subsume their own interests into its development meant that they tended to share the emperors' conflations of themselves with the anthropomorphized state. This frustrated the process of "ungendering" within the ruling families.[63] During their successive regencies, Theophano (regent for Otto III, 983–91) and Adelheid (regent for Otto III, 991–6) tended to mask their own influence by depersonalizing the king, emphasizing the office above the man. The sanctity that had formerly been a characteristic of queenship as well as kingship was thus gradually transformed into support of the sacral kingship of the eleventh century.[64] The German emperors were set apart from "the laity" by the quasi-sacramental liturgies of coronation, complementary to priestly ordination. But the state lacked the religious reinforcement of the sacramental system, which uncompromisingly set ordained men apart from women. The empress was anointed jointly with her husband. Insofar as he lost his human characteristics, so did she, yet she kept him tied to biological mortality.

Unless the emperor could free himself from this union, he could not become "ungendered." But if he retained his gender, he could not draw other men from their families and private interests and weld them together to serve the state. Thus to some degree, the anti-sexual polemics that drove Church reform overflowed into the secular realm. Around 1022, when the emperor was promoting the cause of sacerdotal celibacy in Rome, heretics who condemned the flesh and its reproductive drives began to appear in palace circles (fore-shadowing the Cathars of the next century).[65] Perhaps men were beginning to see themselves as blighted by contact with women, who consistently outlived them and remarried. They began to evince fear of the polluting results of sexuality, which had once been a monastic phobia only. We see this in tenth-century Odo of Cluny's model lay saint, Gerald of Aurillac, who took a vow of virginity after being overcome by lust for a peasant girl whom he barely escaped raping.

Sacerdotal kingship implicitly drew the monarchy toward the standards of purity being demanded for the clergy. The chronicle of the eleventh-century bishop Thietmar of Merseburg (975–1018) included a tale of the Ottonian Henry I (919–36) getting drunk during Mass and making love to his wife in a diabolic manner, leading to the birth of a son doomed to sow discord among the family.[66] Perhaps fear of such outcomes was effective. Although most nobles continued to pursue a marriage pattern that assured them of children, the rulers did not.[67] Edward the Confessor of England (1042–66) and the Emperor Henry II (1039–56) actually merited canonization for their refusal to consummate their marriages. Their purity was in contrast to the evil gossip and suspicions of adultery that weakened popular opinion of their wives, though both women were vindicated. Cunegund was Henry's partner in sanctity as well as in government, but her childless state deprived her of the regency when he died.

Although the devices of such ungendering loosened the union of the royal couple, the emperors increasingly used the services of celibate clergymen to protect their estates and offices from the hereditary claims of the secular nobility. Before 1076, the concept of sacerdotal kingship had effectively exempted royal appointments to Church office from the charges of simony leveled at secular patrons. This enabled the emperors to disrupt the nobility's kinship networks by making celibacy the price of new appointment to royal offices. In effect, nobles who wanted to profit from royal service had to move out of their family circles into the expanding womanless space of the institutional ecclesiastical and royal "family," where they could interact together without reference to gender. This is what was happening when, having received Theophylactus's old offices from the Roman people, Henry III insulated the reforming papacy from the electoral politics of the Roman nobility until his death in 1056.

Ironically, even while the institutions that would eventually ensure their exclusion were being put in place, women were more prominent in the public sphere than ever. Agnes of Poitou, Henry's widow, was descended from the Duke of Aquitaine, who had originally launched the Cluniac reform. Like her contemporaries, she was powerfully drawn to the ideals of the reformers. Her correspondence with Peter Damian, the fanatical enemy of clerical marriage, foreshadowed the literary conventions of courtly love. Women had long led the way in renouncing sexuality. The rhetoric of virginity traditionally lauded virile women who were free of the gendering disabilities of reproduction.[68] Gregory VII himself felt so comfortable with Agnes of Poitou (regent for Henry IV, 1056–65) and with Mathilda of Tuscany, survivor of two unconsummated marriages, that he once contemplated joining with them in a Crusade against the Muslims.[69] Women were scandalously prominent among the heretics who condemned the flesh and its works. Countess Adelaide of Savoy, Henry IV's mother-in-law, drove married priests and their wives from her lands.[70]

Under Agnes's regency, the reformed papacy dealt a fatal blow to imperial influence in 1059 with the passage of the new election laws (coinciding with the passage of laws prohibiting clerical marriage). The institution of the electoral powers of the College of Cardinals opened the way to the complete sealing of clerical boundaries. "For Reason of Church" replaced the ordinary strictures of personal politics. The twenty-year march toward Canossa began. The emperor was accused of selling into prostitution the bride he was bound to protect.[71] Supported by the armed forces of Beatrice and Matilda of Tuscany, the reformed papacy set out to rid the Church of the last bastions of secular influence.

Such a combination of women and priests as we see with Matilda of Tuscany and Pope Gregory VII was an insupportable threat to the nobility.[72] The powers and privileges they had once bestowed on their women without hesitation were now seen as agents of their dynastic destruction. The male ranks of the German aristocracy swiftly closed around the young Henry IV, depriving Agnes of her regency and branding her "the tears of Germany." She was the first in a long line of queens who would be cursed as foreign intruders and alienated from their husbands' government.

Thus the Church led the way in the institutionalizing of Europe.[73] The Investiture Conflict limited secular control of Church offices, but monarchs soon offset the loss by appointing celibate clergymen to secular offices. The precincts of the developing schools came to be closed to all but boys in clerical orders. There they learned the secret codes and arcane skills that mysteriously qualified them to man the offices of the expanding bureaucracies of both Church and State. In the twelfth century, this institutional development provided the education and the assortment of career choices that promoted individualism among men.[74] These same clerically trained men could refine their collective identities within a variety of corporate bodies.[75]

The praise of virginity so popular in earlier monastic discourse virtually disappeared by the end of the twelfth century. The Church began systematically to urge the laity to marry and to stay married.[76] Marriage was elevated to the status of a sacrament and, for a while, the benefits of conjugal love were espoused while virginity was denigrated.[77] For the clergy, the operative condition was not, in fact, virginity but celibacy. As long as the clergy remained unmarried and without legitimate children, Mother Church tended to be indulgent to those clerics as her progeny. At the same time, twelfth-century romances warned of the threat of women and their powerful sexual attractions to the military and courtly institutions that were dependent on male bonding to make them work. The destructive fires of romantic love could be seen as a threat not only to the family but, in the classic Arthurian formulations, to Church and State as well.

Despite their superficial institutional conflict, the men who headed the hierarchies of religion and politics cooperated and supported one another in maintaining this new but basic social structure. They were at one in legitimating the gender system that allotted public space solely to men. The emperor had removed corrupting women from the clerical sphere. In turn, the Church provided the State with an ideology of misogyny, rituals of legitimation, and a celibate and ungendered clerical ministry. Together they constructed a secular womanless space that separated the real bodies of corporeal men from their functional identities. A century after Canossa, the re-formed patriarchy had regained firm control of women by an idealized brotherhood of man. It was already becoming possible for public men again to marry and sire children, for the structural barriers between men's and women's spheres had become firm. The area of women's action, movement, and influence had been safely restored to the margins of the "real world" of anthropomorphized institutions within which men masked their own male gender and presented themselves as if they were the whole of humanity.

NOTES

1   This is the commonly accepted view first delineated by Gerd Tellenbach, *Church, State and Christian Society at the Time of the Investiture Contest* (Oxford: Blackwell, 1959).

2   Heidi Hartmann, "Capitalism, Patriarchy and Job Segregation by Sex," in *Capitalist Patriarchy and the Case for Socialist Feminism*, ed. Zillah R. Eisenstein (New York and London: Monthly Review Press, 1979), p. 232, n. 1.

3   Émile Amann and Auguste Dumas, *L'Église au pouvoir des laïques (888–1057)*, Histoire de l'Église, vol. 7, ed. Auguste Fliche and Victor Martin (Paris: Blood and Gay, 1940), use their title to characterize the period as that of "the Church in the power of the laity."

4   This was so despite the ravages of infant mortality, early marriage, and child-birth, which should have balanced male mortality. Karl J. Leyser, *Power and Conflict in an Early Medieval Society: Ottonian Saxony* (Bloomington, IN: University of Indiana Press, 1979), pp. 53–4, shows that thirty-four wives listed in marriage charters outlived one or more husbands, compared with thirteen who did not. Among the same group, fourteen sisters compared with nine brothers are known to have survived.

5   Leyser, *Power*, p. 58, details the impressive inheritance records of mothers, daughters, and sisters in Saxony despite their disadvantages.

6   David Herlihy, "Land, Family and Women in Continental Europe, 701–1200," in *Women in Medieval Society*, ed. Susan Mosher Stuard (Philadelphia, PA: University of Pennsylvania Press, 1976), 13–46.

7   The effects of this power in England and France as well as in Germany and Italy are explored at some length by Jo Ann McNamara and Suzanne Wemple, "The Power of Women Through the Family" in *Women and Power in the Middle Ages*, ed. Mary Erler and Maryanne Kowaleski (Athens, GA: University of Georgia Press, 1988).

8   The deathbed accounts of female saints in early medieval convents emphasize communal chanting by the community of nuns; it is not always certain that priests were even in attendance. See various examples in Jo Ann McNamara, John E. Halborg, and E. Gordon Whatley, *Sainted Women of the Dark Ages* (Durham, NC: Duke University Press, 1992). Odilia of Hohenburg even gave herself communion on her deathbed: *Vita Odiliae abbatissae Hohenburgensis*, ed. W. Levison, vol. 6 of *MGH, SS rerum Merov.*, 22.

9   *Annales Quedlinburgensis*, ed. G. H. Pertz, vol. 3 of *MGH, SS*, 22–69, 72–90.

10 The foremost critic of clerical marriage, Peter Damian (d. 1072), recognized that clerical wives believed themselves to have made a solemn engagement fortified with legal provisions and religious rites. See Peter Damian, *Opusculum decimum octavum contra intemperantes clericus, dissertatio*, 2, c. 7; *Patrologiae Latina*, hereafter *PL*, vol. 144, c. 410.

11 John of Lodi, *Vita Petri Damiani*, in *PL*, vol. 144 (reprint in *CC:CM*, Turnhout: Brepols, 1979), pp. 111–46, here 144.

12 Sharon Farmer, *Communities of Saint Martin: Legend and Ritual in Medieval Tours* (Ithaca, NY: Cornell University Press, 1991), p. 97. "Concubine" was the standard reform terminology for a priest's wife.

13 The author of the *Vita Mathildis Reginae, MGH, SS*, 4, 282–302, actually praised her for carrying the bread and wine to the priest during mass.

14 Jo Ann McNamara, "Chaste Marriage and Clerical Celibacy," in *Sexual Practices and the Medieval Church*, eds Vern L. Bullough and James A. Brundage (Buffalo, NY: Prometheus Books, 1982), pp. 22–33.

15 Atto of Vercelli to the priests of his diocese, *c*.960, in *PL*, vol. 134, 115–19.

16 Anne L. Barstow, *Married Priests and the Reforming Papacy: The Eleventh-Century Debate* (New York: Edwin Mellen Press, 1982).

17 See Barbara H. Rosenwein, *To Be the Neighbor of Saint Peter: The Social Meaning of Cluny's Property, 909–1049* (Ithaca, NY: Cornell University Press, 1989).

18 Barstow, *Married Priests*, pp. 28–9.

19 Leyser, *Power*, p. 64.

20 Eleanor Searle, *Predatory Kinship and the Creation of Norman Power, 840–1066* (Berkeley, CA: University of California Press, 1988), has elaborated the idea that bastardy created the "right" kind of kindred – those who support the legitimate head of the family without challenging his leadership or inheritance rights. Celibate relatives fulfill such functions even more readily and, of course, any children of clergy would have been bastards.

21 From a letter of Vulgarius, a partisan of Sergius III, the earliest source for Theodora's history; see Amann and Dumas, *L'Église au pouvoir*, pp. 31–2.

22 Liutprand of Cremona's charge – that Marozia had a child with Sergius III – is echoed in the *Liber Pontificalis*, ed. Louis Duchesne (Paris: Bibliothèque des Écoles françaises d'Athènes et de Rome, 1884–92), 2:243, and in the more contemporary Flodoard, *Historia ecclesiae Remensis IV, 24*, eds J. Heller and G. Waitz, *MGH, SS*, 13, 409–599.

23 Lothar's efforts to legalize his relationship with Hugh's grandmother and divorce his wife Tetberga are detailed by Hincmar of Reims in *De Divortio Lotharii et Tetbergae*, in *PL*, vol. 125, 619–772, here 629ff.; and discussed in Jo Ann McNamara and Suzanne Wemple, "Marriage and Divorce in the Frankish Kingdom," in *Women in Medieval Society*, ed. Susan Mosher Stuard (Philadelphia, PA: University of Pennsylvania Press, 1976), pp. 95–124, here 108–11.

24 Hugh's daughter, Alda, was married to Alberic, a union that bore no fruit. Canon law had already stretched the boundaries of incest to in-laws and sacramental relatives as well as cousins to the seventh degree. See McNamara and Wemple, "Marriage and Divorce," *passim*.

25 Flodoard, *De Triumphis*, in *PL*, vol. 135, 832.

26   Eve Kosofsky Sedgwick, *Between Men: English Literature and Male Homosocial Desire* (New York: Columbia University Press, 1985).

27   Tellenbach's classic exposition in *Church, State and Christian Society* (cited in note 1) of this concern for right order defines liberty as service freely chosen. The changing vision of "order" itself has been explored by Georges Duby, *The Three Orders: Feudal Society Imagined*, trans. Arthur Goldhammer (Chicago, IL: University of Chicago Press, 1978). [See also Chapter 3 above, pp. 68–94.]

28   Barbara Rosenwein, *Rhinoceros Bound: Cluny in the Tenth Century* (Philadelphia, PA: University of Pennsylvania Press, 1982), linked tenth-century reform to a pervasive psychic depression, or *anomie*, caused by the decline of allodial landholding and the universal scramble to make the dependency of every class as advantageous as possible.

29   Mary Douglas, *Purity and Danger: An Analysis of the Concept of Pollution and Taboo.* (New York: Praeger, 1966), has classically explicated the fears associated with the dissolution of boundaries separating the pure from the polluted.

30   Liutprand of Cremona, *Anapodosis (Tit-for-Tat)*, 2:55, in *Works*, trans. F. A. Wright (New York: E. E. Dutton, 1930).

31   Liutprand, *Anapodosis* 3:7. See 3:10 for her defeat of Rudolph of Burgundy through a perfumed letter.

32   Liutprand, *Anapodosis* 5:32.

33   It was first recorded in 1086 by Mariano Scoto and Sigebert of Gembloux, as having distantly occurred in 855, but by the eleventh century it was already an old legend. See Cesare d'Onofrio, *Papessa Giovanna* (Rome: Romana Società Editrice, 1979). Clarissa Atkinson, *The Oldest Vocation: Christian Motherhood in the Middle Ages* (Ithaca, NY: Cornell University Press, 1991), calls it the epitome of disorder: a woman on the papal throne and a child in the pope's belly – surely a fitting metaphor for tenth-century Europe.

34   Liutprand, *Anapodosis* 2:48.

35   Liutprand, *Anapodosis* 3:19.

36   Liutprand, *Anapodosis* 3:44. In the absence of other sources, no one has thought to challenge Liutprand's estimate. Lea's estimate of Marozia as the epitome of all vices has been universally accepted, and the unchallenged perception of ecclesiastical corruption in the tenth century rests on such naive estimates. Henry C. Lea, *History of Sacerdotal Celibacy in the Christian Church* (London: Watt, 1932, reprint University Books, 1966), p. 144. [But see the recent Christina La Rocca *Italy in the Early Middle Ages 476–1000* (Oxford University Press, 2002).]

37   Odilo of Cluny, *Epitaphium Adalheidae Imperatricis*, PL, vol. 142, 974–5. [See the recent *Adélaïde de Bourgogne, Genèse et représentations d'une sainteté impériale*, eds Patrick Corbet, Monique Goullet, and Dominique Iogna-Prat (Paris/Dijon: Université de Dijon, 2002).]

38   Amann and Dumas, *L'Église au pouvoir*, p. 45, accept the charges that John was prone to riotous living but note that Liutprand, the main source, is hardly above suspicion. Two independent sources, *Le Liber Pontificalis, texte et commentaire*, ed. Louis Duchesne (Paris: E. Thorin, 1884, rep. 1981), and Benedict of San Andreas, *Chronicon*, MGH, SS, vol. 3, exist. While the *Liber* is also favorable to the German party, Benedict is less partisan, but he also says that the Pope was fond of worldly pleasures, hunting by day, attending banquets at night.

39   Liutprand of Cremona, *Liber de Rebus Gestis Ottonis*, 17–20, in *Works*, trans. Wright, pp. 229–30.

40   Amann and Dumas, *L'Église au pouvoir*, p. 57.

41   This assumes that Duchesne, editor of the *Liber Pontificalis* 2, 253, is right in believing that Crescentius was a brother of John XIII.

42   The difficulties of discovering the original reasons for the exclusion of women from the priesthood are discussed in Jo Ann McNamara, *A New Song: Celibate Women*

in the First Three Christian Centuries (New York: Haworth Press, 1983; New York: Harrington Park Press, 1985).

43 Odo of Cluny, *Occupatio* 7, 117, in *PL*, vol. 133.

44 Bernard Hamilton, "The Monastic Revival in Tenth Century Rome," in *Monastic Reform, Catharism and the Crusades 900–1300*, ed. B. Hamilton (London: Variorum Reprints, 1979).

45 Bernard Hamilton, "The House of Theophylact and the Promotion of the Religious Life for Women in Tenth Century Rome," in Hamilton, *Monastic Reform* [these were not the only religious communities she supported].

46 Amann and Dumas, *L'Église au pouvoir*, p. 61.

47 Eventually, the dowries themselves would be branded simoniac by the Fourth Lateran Council, although they could never be dispensed with by communities of nuns.

48 Odo of Cluny, *Vita Geraldi*, in *PL*, vol. 133.

49 Her emphasis on the saintly Ottonian queens in her history of Otto the Great may also have been an ideological counter to Liutprand, whose history of the same emperor must have been available to her.

50 Abbot Abbo of Fleury (988–97)'s vision of three social orders defined by male functions in public life implicitly excluded women from the monastic order and from the active laity as well. Duby, *The Three Orders*, p. 88. In a practical way, this is reflected in the severe decline in endowments for women's monasteries, even in Saxony, by the eleventh century. Moreover, women's monasteries destroyed by Vikings were frequently restored as male communities and other female communities were dissolved as "corrupt" in order to replace the nuns with men. [The foundation of a single community by Cluny for the sisters of monks among its leadership, that of Marcigny *c.*1054, did not begin to make up for the numbers of houses of religious women suppressed in this period; but it might be considered the beginning of an opening of the monastic reform to women in the twelfth century, as discussed by Miller, Chapter 6, and Berman, Chapter 8.]

51 See legislation and attempts at enforcement cited in Lea, *History*, pp. 149–50.

52 Lea, *History*, p. 150, believed that sacerdotal marriage was accepted as a necessity in many areas, as shown by its exclusion from the disciplinary questions addressed by the reforming councils of Saint-Denis in 995 and Dortmund in 1005.

53 See Barstow, *Married Priests*, for full coverage of the defense.

54 For an early example, Atto of Vercelli, *c.*960, in *PL*, vol. 134, 115–19, treated any relationship between women and priests as fornication and advised the priests of his diocese that it was the one sin they could not resist except through flight.

55 This rhetoric, familiar to all students of the Gregorian Reform, was most violently articulated by Peter Damian, *Liber Gomorrhianus*, in *PL*, vol. 145, 159–90.

56 Peter Damian, *Opusculum Decimum* 1:4, in *PL*, vol. 145, c. 393.

57 Tellenbach, *Church, State and Christian Society*, p. 127.

58 Rape still carried the connotation of theft or even elopement. See McNamara and Wemple, "Marriage and Divorce," *passim*.

59 Barstow, *Married Priests*, p. 76.

60 Leyser, *Power*, p. 27.

61 This chastity was not accepted without suspicion. See, for example, Raoul Glaber's *Chronicon*, in *MGH, SS*, vol. 7, 62. William of Malmesbury forthrightly impugned Edward the Confessor's motives for failing to consummate his marriage with Earl Godwin's daughter as an effort to direct the crown to his cousin in Normandy. *Gesta Regum Anglorum* of William of Malmesbury (London, English Historical Society, 1840; Vaduz: Kraus Reprint, 1964), vol. 2, c. 197, p. 239. Hugo Koch, *Die Ehe Kaiser Heinrichs II mit Kunigunde* (Köln: I. P Bachem, 1908), argued that Henry hoped to have children and that the chaste marriage was a later fabrication. See also

Philipp Oppenheim, *Die Consecratio Virginum als geistesgeschichtlichen Probleme* (Rome: Herder, 1943), p. 70.

62 Patrick Corbet, *Les saints ottoniens: sainteté dynastique, sainteté royale et sainteté féminine autour de l'an Mil* (Sigmaringen: Thorbecke Verlag, 1986), p. 258.

64 Leyser, *Power*, p. 44, notes the influence of the queens. For saintly queenship, see Jo Ann McNamara, "*Imitatio Helenae*: Sainthood as an Attribute of Queenship in the Early Middle Ages," in *Saints: Studies in Hagiography*, ed. Sandro Sticca (Binghamton, NY: Medieval and Renaissance Texts and Studies, 1996). For the broader aspects of saintly kingship in the eleventh century, see Marc Bloch, *Les rois thaumaturges. Études sur le caractère surnaturel attribué a la puissance royale, particulièrement en France et en Angleterre* (Paris: Armand Colin, 1961).

65 Duby, *The Three Orders*, pp. 129–31, associates these heretics with the chanceries of Europe.

66 Thietmar, *Chronicle* 1.31, in *MGH, SS*, vol. 3, 741, 742. He gives another example of misfortune following unusual coitus with one's wife.

67 Georges Duby, *Medieval Marriage. Two Models from Twelfth-Century France*, trans. Elborg Forster (Baltimore, MD: Johns Hopkins University Press, 1978), proposed that easy divorce for dynastic reasons represented an "aristocratic model" of marriage as opposed to the indissoluble ecclesiastical model.

68 Jo Ann McNamara, "Sexual Equality and the Cult of Virginity in Early Christian Thought," *Feminist Studies* 3 (1976): 145–58.

69 *The Correspondence of Pope Gregory VII*, ed. and trans. Ephraim Emerton (New York: W. W. Norton, 1960), p. 60.

70 Barstow, *Married Priests*, p. 59.

71 Tellenbach, *Church, State and Christian Society*, p. 131.

72 Robert I. Moore, "Family Community and Cult on the Eve of the Gregorian Reform," *Transactions of the Royal Historical Society* 5, no. 30 (1980): 49–69.

73 This process has been exposed in great detail by Harold J. Berman, *Law and Revolution: The Formation of the Western Legal Tradition* (Cambridge, MA: Harvard University Press, 1983).

74 Colin Morris, *The Discovery of the Individual, 1050–1200* (New York: Harper Torchbooks, 1972).

75 Caroline W. Bynum, "Did the Twelfth Century Discover the Individual?" in *Jesus as Mother, Studies in the Spirituality of the High Middle Ages* (Berkeley, CA: University of California Press, 1982), pp. 82–108.

76 Duby, *The Three Orders*, p. 134.

77 John Baldwin, "Five Discourses on Desire: Sexuality and Gender in Northern France Around 1200," *Speculum* 66 (1991): 797–819.

5

THE PRIEST'S WIFE

Female erasure and the Gregorian reform

Dyan Elliott

An issue of great concern to eleventh-century reformers was the sexual purity of the clergy, hence their concern with nicolaitism, or clerical marriage. Yet there had been a time in the Western Church when the marriage of priests, or at least of the lower clergy, was not yet disallowed. In this chapter Dyan Elliott explores the issues of clerical marriage and the worsening treatment of priests' wives by examining successive versions of the Life of Severus, *archbishop of Ravenna in the fourth century. This bishop had been married and had a daughter and was well known to have been buried next to them. One version of the life of Severus was written and commented on in the ninth century, but it was then rewritten in several forms during the eleventh century. Elliott's comparison of the various versions of this life brings the tools of critical theory to bear on their evidence of changes in attitudes toward the wives of priests up to the time of the Investiture Controversy and focuses on the harsh view of the famous polemicist of the Gregorian reform, Peter Damian (1007–72). We see the progressive demonization of those women who had once legitimately been married to priests and who had served important functions in the local church. Elliott stresses the sexual anxieties of a clergy on whom celibacy had been newly enjoined because of concern that the purity of priests affected the validity of sacraments, but also because of the economic burdens that the Church claimed were being placed on its property by clerical marriage and the children of priests. Much of the action in this chapter takes place in eleventh-century northern Italy, a region characterized by economic revival, rivalry between Pope and Emperor, and concern about ecclesiastical reform. This selection comes from Dyan Elliott,* Fallen Bodies: Pollution, Sexuality, and Demonology in the Middle Ages *(Philadelphia, PA: University of Pennsylvania Press, 1999), pp. 81–106; original Latin quotes have been eliminated from notes and text.*

*   *   *

In the eleventh century, the Western clergy, Europe's intellectual elite, reinvented itself – an imaginative act necessarily accompanied by efforts to eradicate evidence of past identity.[1] Elites are wont to do this, and, since they

123

command the communicative media with representational authority, they generally succeed. Reinvention is a faltering process, and the result is never seamless. There are always discontinuities, fissures, awkward persistences – historical anomalies that mark the difference between the official story and other rejected versions of the past. The eleventh century, particularly the period from mid-century onward known as the Gregorian Reform, is illustrative of this process in that the very boldness of the clergy's imaginative exercises left so palpable a residue of unwanted truths. Moreover, these remnants seem to coalesce around and reanimate arguably the most compelling, but certainly the most poignant, instance of historical debris from this period: the priest's wife. From the eleventh century onward, she would haunt the church's official story. She is with us still. Here I consider the priest's wife, both for her own sake and as a figure and stand-in for all those mundane, sexually active women who imperil sacerdotal and ritual purity. The very success of the Gregorian Reform makes the ordinary woman suspect in this generalized sense. Moreover, even as carnal woman may be construed as representing a rejected option for the clergy, the Virgin Mary is introduced as her purified substitute. Thus the designation that the priest's wife carried, of rejected womanhood, though constantly mutating to include categories like the saint or the witch, is also applied specifically to the clerical concubine. These different manifestations are unified by the distinctly female threat they present to sacerdotal ambitions, which in the aftermath of the reform will be most dearly symbolized in the cult around the Eucharist.

The conditions responsible for the spectralization of the priest's wife are well known. The reforming clergy wished to sever itself from and, in so doing, to raise itself above, lay society. The establishment of clerical celibacy as a mark of both difference and superiority was central to this project and part of a larger program to reify opposites such as clerical/lay, celibate/married, male/female.[2] These ends were, in part, achieved by a remarkable spate of pollution-laden rhetoric unequaled in the previous history of the Western Church and probably never matched in subsequent centuries.[3] The reformers needed every bit of the assistance that a heated polemic might confer: the delegitimization of clerical marriage, and its ultimate outlawing, constituted a formidable task that meant meddling with a long tradition.[4] Even though the church had never been comfortable with such unions, clerical marriage was nevertheless tolerated until the mid-eleventh century. While a priest was officially forbidden to marry after ordination, the marriage was still valid should he do so. Priests who were married at the time of ordination, on the other hand, were theoretically required to abstain sexually from their wives. But some of the most authoritative canons of the church forbade the married priest to separate from his wife, lest she be left destitute.[5]

The measures taken against clerical wives in and after the eleventh century were severe in the extreme: some canons went so far as to suggest enslavement.[6] But considering the number of married clergy and their vigorous resistance to the new order – resistance that is described in detail for cities such as Milan – the success of the program was quite remarkable.[7] This is certainly true for the long term. Studies such as Christopher Brooke's examination of church disciplinary activities show that clerical marriage was effectively stamped out in such backwaters of reform as England by the end of the twelfth century.[8] But, even in the short run, it is uncanny how the wives contemporary with the Gregorian Reform seem to have melted away. Where they went has been the subject of some historical speculation. The little bit we know about the actual women who were repudiated and disinvested is largely guesswork: thus Georges Duby and Jo Ann McNamara speculate that such women became a part of the growing number of rootless poor, while the mysterious "prostitutes" described amid the entourage of itinerant preachers such as Robert of Arbrissel may be a shorthand for rejected clerical wives.[9]

The most frequently avowed reason for suppressing the clerical wife was that her sexual presence polluted the minister of the altar. The frequently withheld reason was that she was a drain on church resources and her children would entail the alienation of church property.[10] Yet her potential for disturbing the symbolic order far transcended ritual or even economic concerns, striking at the heart of the reformers' classificatory system that was so essential to church hierarchy. Aspects of this particular transgression were consciously acknowledged. Thus Peter Damian (d. 1072), for example, wrote to Countess Adelaide of Savoy that God recognizes only three kinds of women: virgins, wives, and widows. Women who do not fit into one of these categories – and he argues that the clerical wife does not – do not arrive in God's presence.[11]

But the clerical wife's potential boundary crossing can clearly be pushed much farther than Damian's familiar triune division of women. As anthropologist Mary Douglas has so deftly demonstrated, the animals perceived as abominations in the Book of Leviticus are precisely those creatures that transgress against apprehended divisions among species: things that live in the sea, but crawl; and animals with cloven feet that refuse to chew their cud like the "clean" animals of the flock.[12] The priest's wife is a vivid representation of this kind of anomaly precisely because her mixed, hybrid, "impossible" status is ambiguous in a way that reveals the seams in classificatory categories. At a time when reformers were insisting on a strict division between clergy and laity,[13] she defies both categories as being neither entirely lay nor fully clerical. From ancient times she was referred to as *presbyteria* or *sacerdotissa*, and according to some rites even received a distinct garb and special blessing at the time of her husband's ordination.[14] She wobbles between heretical and orthodox, depending on the ideology of whoever discerns her.[15] To the reformers she was the image of overcranked lust.[16] To those opposing the reform she was the mainstay of clerical domestic economy.[17] In the event that she and her husband abstained sexually upon his ordination, in accordance with the disciplinary requirements of the early church, she hovers somewhere between marriage and celibacy. If sexually active, she was perceived as incestuous due to her relationship with her spiritual father – the priestly husband.[18] Though ineradicably female, she nevertheless challenges prescribed gender separation by her invasion of sacred space, now being rigorously redefined as masculine.[19] Her domination of her husband through money and sex was perceived as threatening to masculine ascendancy.[20] Moreover, as a result of reform measures, she takes a frightening status dive from respectable wife to concubine or whore in a relatively brief period, as do her children, who go from legitimate heirs to disinherited bastards.[21]

In the eleventh century she was already a living artifact attesting to an earlier truth – dangerous detritus ripe for disavowal. Thus she came to epitomize all of the practices that were targeted by the reformers in the course of this ideological struggle. In the reformers' very vehemence in disowning her, however, they frequently overstepped themselves, betraying some of their worst fears about the faith – often through enumerating aspects of the perceived threats she presented in an incomplete or unsuccessful effort to vanquish them. Therefore the priest's wife, as historical remainder or, to use my earlier image, as specter, deserves special notice for her capacity to unsettle the history of the Western Church. Not only is she a remembrance of what the church would like to forget but she also acts as a mechanism for eliciting threatening subtexts that the reformers would have consciously disowned.

Thus, even if the historical wives of priests have been effectively erased, I would nevertheless argue that their image remains as a kind of shadow text in a badly executed palimpsest, a text found beneath another text. So does the historical problem they present. The clerical wife's downward-shifting social trajectory and the conflicted positions she was forced to assume unleashed anxieties that challenged the very core of Christian doctrine. These anxieties were fought and temporarily increased by a theological focus on the material presence in the sacrament of the altar and the rise of the cult of the Virgin Mary. And yet the same fears would persist long after the occasion for their appearance had been officially banished. It is by following the trail of negation, disavowal, and doubt that the threatening image of the priest's wife, relegated to an effaced subtext, may be rendered historically visible.

Severus and the reiterative swerve

Polemical works denouncing clerical marriage in general or clerical wives in particular abound for the eleventh century and are doubtless the most direct route for identifying the kinds of anxieties identified above. But here I would like to consider sources that do not announce their interest – particularly renarrations of the past. A successful renarration wrought by the reforming camp would aspire to neutralize disavowed truths, discrediting them or delimiting their power to persuade. Alternatively, it would provide an opportunity to stabilize clerical identity by reiterating carefully chosen truths in a way that effaced or overwhelmed alternative possibilities. And yet, such efforts at containment or effacement are bound to fail at their intended purpose.[22]

Around the year 1070, at the very height of reforming ardor, two contemporary authors chose to renarrate the story of the fourth-century Saint Severus of Ravenna, who was not simply purported to be a married priest but a married archbishop.[23] From a small but distinguished cohort of saintly married clerics, only Severus attracted authorial interest as a married priest during the period of the Gregorian Reform.[24] His memory is more encumbered with the basic furniture of historicity than is the case with many of his celestial peers. He was present at the Council of Sardica (342) and underwrote its constitutions. He is depicted in Justinian's mosaics in Saint Apollinare in Classis. His name also appears in the earliest martyrologies.[25]

Agnellus's ninth-century account

The first attempt at any sort of vita for Severus seems to have been Agnellus's *Pontifical Book of the Church of Ravenna*, written between 830 and 832, which was the font for subsequent eleventh-century recastings of Severus's life.[26] The work as a whole is understandable in terms of the author's pride in Ravenna's unique ecclesiastical history, which distinguished it from the other archbishoprics of western Europe. Ravenna had been the headquarters of Byzantine rule in Italy. Although definitely part of the Latin as opposed to the Greek church, for some time it was outside the Germanic orbit. This changed when Ravenna was invaded by the Lombards in 751, soon to be reconquered by Pepin and given to the Pope in about 754 – a bequest that was confirmed by Charlemagne. Even so, the archbishops of Ravenna resisted any implication of subservience to Rome, while Agnellus himself exhibited hostility to Rome throughout his history.[27]

At the time that Agnellus wrote, Europe was experiencing an early series of attacks on clerical marriage under the auspices of the Carolingian Reform. Even Ravenna, with its relatively worldly clergy and its tradition of separateness from Rome, must have felt the tremors. Agnellus, though by no means a reformer himself, was seemingly aware of the ways in which the perceived decadence of the Ravennese clergy could further imperil its tenuous independence. He thus pays lip service to reform-inflected rhetoric when he criticizes the decadence of Ravenna's bishops – accusing them of hawking, singing dirty songs, and even driving priests away from their sacramental duties in church.[28] Agnellus is also attuned to the particular sensitivity of the subject of clerical marriage throughout his history, and he does his best to make any instances conform to the most estimable prototypes. In addition to Severus, the first example that Agnellus discusses, he also recounts the pontificates of two other bishops who were at some point married: Agnellus (556/7–69/70) and Sergius (ordained between 742 and 752). With respect to Bishop Agnellus, his chronicler-namesake is careful to underline that the bishop's wife had died before her husband was ordained deacon.[29] Even so, our chronicler is conscious that the mere mention of a bishop ever having been married still had the capacity to confound. He thus goes on to muse that one naturally wonders how a married man managed to secure such a prestigious position in the church, using this rhetorical occasion to remind his audience of the apostle's ordinance that a bishop may be married once (I Timothy 3.2). That the matter had not yet been brought to satisfactory closure and continued to rankle is suggested by Agnellus's promise to return to the question of clerical wives – a promise that he does not keep.[30]

According to Agnellus's testimony, Bishop Sergius, the other married bishop, had his wife ordained as a deaconess at the time of his elevation. We are even told that she remained in her habit for the rest of her life.[31] Despite this precaution, the account of Sergius's turbulent reign demonstrates Agnellus's awareness of just how irregular it was for a layman to be directly elevated to bishop in the eighth century – even with the vow of chastity implicit in the wife's reception of the veil. Bishop Sergius was, as we learn, imprisoned by the Pope, who questioned him closely about his marital status in an attempt to strip him of his title.[32] Agnellus's sensitivity on this score is even more apparent in a telling omission. He suppresses altogether from his narrative a second and failed attempt to elect a layperson as bishop, which occurred immediately after the reign of Sergius.[33]

Thus Agnellus was very much aware of clerical marriage, not simply as an undifferentiated issue in the wider context of clerical corruption, but as a singular problem that in recent history had threatened the independence of the entire Ravennese church. His treatment of Severus's life imbibes these tensions. From a chronological and narrative standpoint, the account anticipates and prepares the way for the discussion of the other married bishops. The very fact that Severus was a married bishop who was actually honored as a saint serves as a tacit exoneration of the married incumbents, particularly the beleaguered Sergius, whose sudden elevation from layman was exactly parallel to that of Severus.

Yet Agnellus's treatment of Severus, while in a certain sense capitalizing on his sainthood, does not conform to the typical chronological progression of hagiography; instead he prefers an idiosyncratic structure better suited to his purpose of acknowledging yet ultimately assuaging the sense of the wife as threat or problem. The events of Severus's life are related through a series of marvels.[34] These amount to a mere four and are treated in the following order: a mystical ecstasy, which Severus undergoes while performing Mass and during which time he attends the burial of his colleague Bishop Geminiano; a miracle at the funeral of his daughter, Innocentia; his own marvelous death;[35] and his heavenly election as bishop. With the exception of the ecstasy, his wife, Vincentia, plays a crucial role in these miracles. In fact, it is no exaggeration to say that she is at the center of his holy repertory.

At the time of the miracle at the burial of the daughter, the first in Agnellus's triad of conjugal miracles, his wife Vincentia is already dead and buried in the family tomb. When the tomb is opened for the daughter Innocentia's burial, the bystanders advise Severus that there is insufficient room in the grave. Severus tearfully reproaches his wife:

> Oh woman, why do you trouble me? Why don't you make a place for your daughter? Acknowledge what you carried, what was taken from your flesh; don't hesitate to receive her. Look, I entrust to you what you gave to me. Don't be stupid: from whence she came, she returned. Make room for her burial. Don't make me sad.[36]

This rather sharp address is not without effect. Vincentia's bones move with such great speed "that living bodies of humans can scarcely move faster," and the funeral proceeds apace.[37]

Severus's abrasive, even hectoring, tone is revealing, as is the source of his exasperation. The wife, even in death, is portrayed as taking up too much space. Her body's awkward over-presence may be understood in the context of external events that were transforming the clerical wife into a spiritual embarrassment. And this is implied in Agnellus's narration. The possible prototypes for this kind of miracle may be used as a gauge to measure the extent of uxorial angst.

First, there is the story recounted by Pope Gregory the Great (540–604) of a monk who is informed he will die and promptly begins digging his grave. When the abbot of the community sickens and bespeaks a place in the monk's grave, the monk at first refuses on the grounds of insufficient room. Although the abbot assures him that they will both fit, when the tomb is opened for the monk's funeral there is not enough space. When one of the monks acting as pallbearer calls out, "Father Abbot, what of your promise that the grave would hold both of you?," the body immediately turns on its side. If this was Agnellus's source, the attending monk's exasperation with the deceased abbot, now magnified in Severus's vita, was transferred to the deceased wife – which is significant in itself.[38] But if Agnellus was familiar with the graveside miracles related by the sixth-century Gregory of Tours, the exasperation expressed is even more at odds with this prototype – which was meant to emphasize the spiritual solidarity of the couple. According to Gregory of Tours, at the funeral of Riticius, a confessor saint, the recently dead husband revives just long enough to remind his long-dead wife of his promise (which he made in response to her tearful entreaties) that they should be buried together, using the most gentle address. Her body immediately moves to accommodate him.[39]

In the account of the death of Severus himself, the third marvel, Agnellus revisits the posthumous site of ambivalent family values, correcting (or at least containing) the saint's fractious tone heard earlier. The bishop is celebrating Mass and, just after receiving the body and blood of Christ, gives orders for the family sepulcher to be opened. Wearing his pontifical stole,

Severus enters the grave, lies between his wife and his daughter, and orders the seal to be replaced. Then, while in prayer, he expires.[40]

The final marvel, chronologically prior to these earlier miracles, is couched in the events surrounding his election to office. Severus, we now learn, was a humble weaver of wool. When it came time to elect a new bishop of Ravenna, he told his wife that he wished to be present in order to witness the predictable miracle that attended the appointment of all archbishops of Ravenna: a dove would descend from heaven and alight on the head of the bishop elect.[41] Vincentia's response is scornful: "Sit here and work; don't be so lazy. Whether you go or not, the people won't make you bishop. Get back to work."[42] When Severus persists, his wife changes the direction of her sarcastic sallies, replying that he is sure to be made bishop as soon as he arrives. Vincentia's words prove an ironic prophecy. Although Severus hides behind the doors to conceal his filthy clothes, the dove alights on his head, not once but three times. "When she heard what she had recently derided, she then rejoiced over him."[43] She had, after all, predicted his unlikely triumph.

By breaking with a normative temporal flow in his arrangement of the miracles, Agnellus has effectively foregrounded the wife of Severus as a disturbing surplus or superfluity. And yet his idiosyncratic chronology also seems to have been governed by a desire to begin with the miracle that incorporates, and therefore anticipates, the other two in his narrative. Thus, at the burial of Innocentia, the harsh words of Severus to the troublesome remains of his wife serve as a tacit response to her jibes on the day of his election – though this becomes clear only later. Her body's ready obedience, moreover, suggests that she has learned due conjugal submission. The image of mother and daughter at rest in the collective tomb anticipates the death of Severus himself. Any efforts to reconstruct the reasons behind this ordering of events are necessarily very tentative. But it is doubtless significant that Agnellus begins with the episode that literally and symbolically buries wife and daughter – those two most awkward vestiges of Severus's earlier life, which are causally and, in this instance, spatially linked. Indeed the daughter, the most significant fruit of the fraught union, is only mentioned in this anecdote – seemingly introduced into the narrative for the sole purpose of being buried. In a similar vein, it is extremely appropriate that in the first marvel the wife's body is immediately problematized for its recalcitrance. And yet, there can be little doubt that by putting Severus's acerbic remarks first and Vincentia's shrewish behavior on the day of his election last, the harsh contours of uxorial reproach are softened considerably by the time we reach the chronologically prior, but sequentially later, episode, From this perspective, conjugal quarrels on either side of the grave ultimately neutralize each other in this interesting triptych. Similarly, the tensions surrounding the clerical wife as a inherent problem are confronted and then dispelled. What remains at the center and also, in many ways, central to this account is the image of peace when the family is finally reunited in death.

Liudolph's ninth-century account

Agnellus does not discuss the necessary transition to chastity that a sudden elevation to bishop would entail. As in the instance of Sergius XL, whose ordination corresponded to his wife's consecration as deaconess, the transition from wife to sister is formulaic and goes without saying.[44] But the Frankish monk Liudolph, writing shortly after 858, who recounts the illicit translation of Severus's relics to Germany at the hands of a thief who specialized in relics, recognizes an affirmative possibility for emphasizing the transition to chastity and seizes upon it. Upon hearing about the election of Severus, both daughter and wife assume veils: the former's signifying virginity, the latter's signifying widowhood. That these symbols of sexual abstinence do not mark the separation of domiciles is evident from Liudolph's account of the death of Severus. In a conflation of the miracle at the daughter's funeral with the events surrounding the bishop's own demise, Liudolph omits Severus's rancorous words to his wife, preferring a gentler address directed to both wife and daughter: "Give me space for sleeping with you so that those who lived in this world in common may also use a common grave."[45] This rerendering also conveys a suppressed truth that was latent in Agnellus's account: that the wife was where she should be – however awkwardly and embarrassingly so – as was her offspring. The husband's place was with them.

Liudolph's account is based on his own inquiries in Italy, where he was at pains to understand the history behind the new relics just acquired. Never doubting that Germany was the beneficiary of not just one, but a conjugal cluster of saints, Liudolph attempted to learn from his informant, a monk at Classis, the actual feast days for the two holy women. The answer was disappointing: due to the various invasions, the precise dates for the deaths of mother and daughter were forgotten, so they were commemorated at the same time as Severus. But at least this confirmed the existence of a modest cult for mother and daughter alike. And the group commemoration underscored clerical marriage as the mechanism of sanctification. In other words, this dubious conjugal unit was still in the ninth century a potential springboard into grace. The accounts of both Agnellus and Liudolph present a compelling picture of sacerdotal conjugality according to the old school: a carnal union transformed into a spiritual marriage; a familial grave; graveside miracles projecting the continuation of the marriage bond beyond the grave;[46] a bishop completing Mass and descending into the grave to join his family in episcopal garb; and a nuclear family achieving sainthood.

The eleventh-century anonymous monk of Classis

For the latter part of the eleventh century, the story of Severus was undoubtedly volatile subject matter in uneasy times and required concerted efforts at stabilization and control. In addition to an anonymous life, probably written by a monk of Classis, two sermons were dedicated to Severus by Peter Damian, one of the standard-bearers of papal reform.[47] Clearly both authors had a particular investment in the saint's patronage. The monastery of Classis not only bore the saint's name but still continued to claim his relics.[48] In contrast, Peter Damian was born in Ravenna and took every opportunity to praise his native city, writing sermons to commemorate several of its archbishops.[49] But whatever degree of personal investment can be reconstructed on behalf of these authors, one of the factors encouraging a reconsideration of Severus was doubtless his marital condition. The fact that the spirited wife was something of a thorn in the bishop's flesh was especially apposite in this time of extraneous wives.

The anonymous author, writing in the eleventh century, rearranges the four marvels at the heart of Severus's life chronologically, but otherwise conforms closely to Agnellus's rendition. Nevertheless, whatever clarity a chronological structure might impart to the narrative is ultimately undercut by the texture of the vita in its entirety. The account of the saint's life is sandwiched between an introductory chapter treating Severus's fatherland, marriage, and work in general terms and two concluding chapters – appropriately rubricated as "digressions." The life as a whole, but especially these three sections framing its particulars, are ideological minefields, riven by the author's diatribes against imaginary foes, thus ultimately creating a troubled and self-interrupting narrative. For instance, the introductory chapter discusses Ravenna's venerable tradition of divine election through the descent of the dove, a sign associated with the city's first twelve pontiffs. But this symbol of grace sets the stage for a gratuitous denunciation of simony and the contemporary trafficking in ecclesiastical offices.[50] The later account of Severus's election proper likewise prompts a lively attack on those who criticize monks who preach – the connecting link allegedly being that both Severus and the monks are, in the author's eyes, enabled by the principle of divine election. These two areas of concern – certainly the question of simony but also the defense of uppity monks – would ostensibly mark the author as a supporter of aspects of the eleventh-century reform.[51] And yet a third, and certainly the most obsessive, area for self-interruption concerns the question of Severus's marriage. Here our author seems to break with any distinct reform platform.[52]

The author's tirades on marriage frame, but do not intrude on, the central events of Severus's *Life*. The introductory chapter blends the saint's commendable poverty (deduced by the fact that he ate by the labor of his own hands) with his marriage:

> In this spot if any supercilious individual with an enigmatic mind and tasteless objection detracts from the holy man because he was married when he acceded to the archbishopric of Ravenna, let him hear the Apostle responding: "That all things are pure to the pure [Romans 14.20]." Therefore just as the eating of foods does not pollute a man unless that schemer which is concupiscence precedes,

so indeed legal marriage does not pollute the Christian who in no
wise binds himself by a vow of virginity or continence unless earlier
that deceptress which is desire corrupts by the foment of obscene
love. But if anyone is bound by a vow, he is compelled to render; for
there it is written, vow and render [Psalm 75.12].[53]

The vow clearly alludes to the conjugal debt, which is premised on Paul's
insistence that husband and wife do not have autonomous control over their
own bodies but must submit to the other's sexual demands (I Corinthians
7.4). In other words, the purity of Severus's life is warrant against the
potentially dangerous pleasures inherent in eating and sex – two activities
that were related in ascetical tradition and in the minds of contemporaries of
the author.[54]

The digression immediately following the events of Severus's life proper
extends the premise based on the inherent purity of the individual that
animates the author's exculpation of a married person who accedes to a
bishopric. This principle, still guided by the metaphor of ingestion, is applied
not only as a commendation of Severus's purity, but also as a condemnation
of his potential critics – now designated as heretics:

Indeed no place of remonstrance is left to the heretics who judge
Severus, the blessed of the Lord, that to be tied in marriage is to the
dishonor of the church. Each one is covered in the feces of their own
obscenity, they are ignorant of the grace of the Holy Spirit, who do
not in any way recognize that grace in others because they feel [it]
so little in themselves. If a person therefore never will have tried the
taste of honey, he does not in any way know of its savor. But against
those who use wormwood alone, neglecting other herbs, the bitter
seems to them excessively sweet and they imagine the other herbs
to be equally bitter on account of their inexperience with the taste
[of honey].[55]

The author goes on to affirm the goodness of marriage when used legitimately. Moreover, he contends that the singular purity of Severus anticipated
his selection by the Holy Spirit's descent in the form of the dove and that
this event, in turn, confirmed his pre-existing purity. His state of innocence
is likened to the sexuality of Adam and Eve before the Fall, that is before
shame entered the world – a guarantee against incorrect usage:

And so blessed Severus with his dove-like eyes looking on all the
works of God, also understood marriage to be especially good, if
someone used it legitimately, because if it were not good, woman
would never have been created as helpmate by God. . . . Indeed the
first couple lost these [dove-like] eyes, when having completed their
prevarication, they were abandoned by God and the eyes of both

were opened. After, moreover, they lost these eyes of doves, they blushed immediately; because death entered through the windows of the carnal eyes.[56]

This evocation of the Fall, particularly the traditional association between sex and death, would have been an unmitigated indictment of marriage if Severus were not proof of the reversibility of this gloomy sentence. In his pristine state with his dovelike innocence, Severus is likened to a child who has yet to learn shame: "For he does not blush at his members ... thinks nothing unchaste; desires no illicit things because the Holy Spirit who inhabits him, who keeps him with an uncorrupted mind, knew nothing of these things."[57]

Thus was the enviable condition of Severus before, during, and presumably after marriage. To be sure, the anonymous Classis author ultimately backs away from his potentially daring contention regarding the innocence of correct usage in marriage, which if followed to its logical conclusion would challenge any moral argument for clerical celibacy. Instead, he proceeds to underline that Severus's marriage had preceded his election to the bishopric, after which his wife was turned into a sister, as was the case with the apostle Peter.[58] Even so, an argument for the possibility of purity in a sexually active marriage is implicitly advanced. Thus the final digression again emphasizes that Severus's eventual transition to chastity was anticipated by his high degree of continence in marriage – a claim vindicated by the dove's miraculous election:

> That we may confess the truth that the chastity and continence [of Severus] existed before the Episcopacy, the Holy Spirit itself clearly demonstrated through the dove in the election, which flew over many Priests and Deacons and assigned its beloved an inner place within itself.[59]

The miracle Severus performed at his daughter's funeral, when he ordered his wife's body to one side, is then interpreted as alluding to both his past married life and its chaste terminus:

> The most Holy Pontiff [bishop] of his church seems secretly to have satisfied his earlier reputation as husband. ... For it is believed that he remembered his earlier pristine life, when it is read that he was bound in marriage by Christian authority. That, moreover, he ordered with so imperious an authority that the body of his dead wife bend itself to the side clearly shows how secure he was from her touch, after he was made Bishop.[60]

The word "secretly," of course, speaks volumes. Even in the case of this near-apologist, an admission of the need for secrecy and discretion (and hence an acknowledgment of difficult external circumstances) slips in. In fact, most of

the turbulence of these various renditions results from this fitfully acknowledged aspect of "his earlier reputation as husband."

The monk of Classis displays no absolute political agenda on clerical
marriage. Certainly he is supportive of aspects of the contemporary reform
movement, as his condemnation of simony would suggest. But his possible
resistance to the reformer's position with respect to clerical marriage can be
gleaned, I would argue, from the rhetorical targeting of his fictive heretics.
There had been heretics in the early eleventh century who claimed that all
marriage was evil. These groups had, however, long disappeared, their zeal
for purity having seemingly been absorbed by the reforming platform. The
opponents that the anonymous author is instead addressing are probably
those ideologues who permitted (and sometimes even abetted) the riots
against married priests and ordered the laity to boycott their masses.[61] Yet
the anonymous author's main strategy against his imagined heretics was to
exaggerate their position by implying that their rigid standards would necessarily condemn a worthy saint like Severus – a rather confused rearguard
action. Given that around this time Bishop Ulrich of Imola had actually
written a treatise demanding the instant legalization of clerical marriage, the
monk of Classis's approach seems rather timid.[62]

Consciously or not, the monk of Classis had positioned himself at a couple
of junctures where he could have made a meaningful intervention in the
debate, if he had so chosen. The application of "all things are pure to the
pure" to the married condition, including that of priests, resonates with unrealized revolutionary content. Historical hindsight also teaches us what the
author's emphasis on election might imply or to what it might have applied.
In addition to his contention that certain monks are elected to preach,
the monk of Classis also argues that Severus was divinely elected to the
bishopric as a married man, while many (chaste) clerics were passed over.
This argument would be pushed further by the Norman Anonymous,
certainly the most original and defiant defender of clerical marriage writing
in about 1100 (that is, at least several decades after our hagiographer),
who had insisted that only the Holy Spirit made priests on the basis of divine
election – a contention with extreme predestinary overtones. Disciplinary
considerations, like chastity, were thus void.[63]

The overall impression that the eleventh-century anonymous life of Severus
leaves is one of agitation and confusion. The author's dueling with imagined
foes detracts from the image of conjugal sanctity which had been at the center
of the earlier narratives. Although the impulse to apologize for Severus's
married state is certainly one of the factors that provoked the monk of Classis
to write, his defense is, nevertheless, indirect rather than frontal – sacrificing
the wife by relegating her to relative obscurity rather than upholding her
position and reputation or fame. For not only does the anonymous author
fail to acknowledge the ancient cults of mother and daughter, but he even
suppresses the mother's name altogether.[64] Certainly, it was in keeping with
the spirit of the age to downplay female sanctity, since in this period of reform

the number of female saints plummeted to an all-time low. And the claims of a clerical wife must, necessarily, have been worse than negligible.[65]

Peter Damian and the priest's wife

If the position of the anonymous monk of Classis remains elliptical, Peter Damian's is clear. He was one of the major ideologues for the papal reform movement.[66] At papal behest, he undertook a mission to Milan directed against married and simoniac priests. He was also active against married clergy in other cities such as Lodi.[67] His virulent criticism of clerical marriage is well attested in his writings.[68] Indeed, the priest's wife seems to have occupied a special place in Damian's psychological development. According to his biographer, John of Lodi, Damian owed his life to the wife of a priest, since his mother, suffering from postpartum depression, initially refused to care for the infant Peter until a neighboring priest's wife intervened and began nursing the baby herself. Lester Little alerts us to the fact that this story could be apocryphal: that the child succored by a priest's wife would live to be the scourge of clerical marriage perhaps smacks of too much ironic symmetry to be entirely credible. If this is the case, John's invention backfired in certain ways. When characterizing the intervention of Damian's benefactress, he describes her as "the wife of a priest who performed the office of a priest when she softened the maternal disposition to piety."[69] In the act of evoking her in order to contain her, John lets the genie out of the bottle and finds it impossible to put her back.

Of particular interest is Damian's own account of the lasting impression he received of a clerical couple who lived next to him during his student days in Parma. The woman was "of lewd appearance, alluring in her shameless beauty."[70] The priest was a jolly man, well dressed, with a fine singing voice. This attractive couple filled their days with laughter and joking:

> From these passionate and abandoned goings-on, I could not distance myself mentally, because I was so physically near them. What could I do, since as I saw all this happening, I was so tempted by sexual excitement, that even after I came to the hermitage, the memory of this alluring scene often attacked me? I must confess that frequently the devilish enemy flashed these images before my eyes and tried to persuade me that people who live such delightful lives are the most happy and fortunate. But now that I have told of the beginning of this merry affair, let me also report on how it ended. ... After they had lived together in such wanton pleasure for almost twenty-five years, they were found in their house, dying together in the flames. And thus the heat of passion gained for them a fiery holocaust.[71]

Damian's description of their deaths constitutes a deliberately inverted hagiography. Whereas the handful of married saints of the early church are

frequently perceived as having achieved salvation through a shared martyrdom, anticipated in the common life of their carnal marriage, the united
death of the priest and his wife leads only to perpetual damnation – again a
projection of their sinful carnal union.[72]

In short, far from becoming the object of gratitude (if we believe the infancy
narrative) or sympathy, the priest's wife emerged as a target for Damian's
most intense hostility – a hostility exacerbated when the priest's wife rose
unbidden to his thoughts when "the devilish enemy flashed these images
before (his) eyes." Damian, a man who by his own admission experienced
extreme agitation at the sight of a pretty woman even when he was no longer
young, compared the way he guarded his eyes from young women with how
children are kept from fire[73] – an evocative image considering his memory of
the fire in Parma. His monastic conversion occurred around the age of twenty-
eight, long after his adolescence in Parma.[74] Since he spent a number of years
as a secular cleric, a wife would necessarily represent a rejected alternative
in a way that she would not have been for someone who had entered a
monastery as a child oblate. Damian's own agony over the apparent felicity
of the clerical couple attests to this. His commitment to celibacy was seemingly renewed with every vituperative return to the clerical wife in his
writings, the only occasion on which he permitted himself consciously to
evoke her otherwise banished image.

But, in addition to his interest in Severus and his leading role in the attack
on clerical marriage, Damian was possessed of certain personality foibles that
fostered inadvertent self-revelation. At one point he claims to write, "that I
might restrain my wandering and lascivious mind with a leash."[75] Elsewhere
he admits that he was especially prone to the vice of scurrility – a proclivity
for excessive, buffoonish, and perhaps even prurient talk. Through ascetical
practices, such as flagellation, he could temporarily repress his scurrility but
could never entirely conquer it.[76] Damian's verbal excesses, spurred by the
release he found in writing, constitute an imaginary archive of things better
left unsaid, as well as things just barely left unsaid.

If the reality of the priest's wife of Parma was too appealing, the specter
of Severus's sharp-tongued wife would be irresistible to Damian, given his
personal polemical needs. Indeed, in the first of his two sermons on Severus,
Vincentia receives pride of place, though once again her name is suppressed.
Damian begins this sermon with a reminder that Severus's feast day corresponds with the presentation of Christ in the temple – an event recalling that
original act of humility, the incarnation, which enabled humanity's subsequent elevation. The theme of the sermon is thus that those who humble
themselves shall be exalted (Luke 18.14).[77] Embarking on a terse recapitula-
tion of the events occurring on the day of the election, Damian presents
Severus as an exemplar of this salubrious humility. His general poverty, lowly
occupation, and squalid clothes all testify to this virtue.[78] But it is particularly the curmudgeonly wife who permits him to exercise his pre-eminent
forbearance.

Severus is described as being contented with the humble, even the womanly job of wool worker. He chose it as an opportunity to cultivate charity between himself and his wife, since by sharing the same work there would be no disparity between them. When she repaid him with biting words, he answered with the mildness of a dove. Nor did he seek to avenge himself, as would be in keeping with the power that he, as husband, rightfully exercised over his wife. Instead, he bore in mind the apostolic injunction to love his wife and not behave harshly to her (Colossians 3.19). Moreover, through a peculiar application of the apostle Paul's formulation of the conjugal debt (1 Corinthians 7.4) – a citation almost invariably reserved for sexual prerogative in marriage – Damian emphasized that Severus did not act as if he possessed autonomy over his person, but only departed to witness the election of the new bishop after his wife had given her begrudging permission.[79] In a burst of warm adulation, Damian invites his monastic audience to admire a man who, though able to be stubborn with any man, humbly obeys a subject woman; who, though capable of rendering evil for evil, tolerates his wife's jibes with equanimity; and who would avenge himself against those who harmed him, but not against his wife.[80]

Even as the long-suffering and feminized husband is presented as a vessel of grace, so the outspoken and domineering wife is described as an explicit agent of the devil:

> For the ancient enemy – who was not able to provoke him to impatience by poverty, the affliction of hard work, nor from the deformity of mean clothing – kindled the mind of the wife to inflicting abusive words and stimulated her tongue to the injury of biting rebukes.[81]

The stellar resistance of Severus is likened to a noble edifice besieged, which a hostile impetus cannot overthrow. Because the devil finds Severus virtually impregnable, he needs access. Thus the devil uses the woman as a siege ladder to assail the husband's heart. Again, through a specious use of scripture, Severus is described as rebuffing his wife's jibes by theoretically attending to the prohibition of women teaching (I Timothy 2.12).[82] And so the devil, who had conquered Adam, loses to this humble woolworker. The devil, moreover, is foiled, since he inadvertently set the wife – the flawed helpmate whom he had kindled to the abuse of bitter rebuke – on the path to learning patience. Moreover, Damian's use of the possessive pronoun in "his own helpmate" in itself creates doubt. While one assumes that the wife is Severus's helpmate in keeping with the designation of Eve in Genesis, "his own helpmate" could also be read as the devil's own helpmate. In fact, this latter reading, arguably more correct grammatically, is also vindicated by contexts.[83] The biblical patriarchs Job and Tobias are then invoked, since they too had successfully withstood the taunts of their evil-minded wives. Yet, in balance, Damian grants that there is a certain ironic justice in this wifely scourge, since Adam should never have listened to Eve in the first place.[84]

Damian's treatment of Vincentia certainly counteracted the allure of the priest's wife in Parma. But there was a danger in going too far, especially considering that Vincentia was (or had been) honored as a saint in some circles. Thus Damian winds up:

> But we do not say these things so that we may assert that the wife of the holy man perished with her womanly reproaches. For if he knew that she were excluded from the destiny of the elect, by no means would the man filled with the Holy Spirit wish to share a tomb with her. Their common burial indicates that a diversity of merits does not distinguish the souls of the blessed spouses.[85]

This delightfully grudging compromise nevertheless grants what Damian has hitherto only affirmed through negation. Damian's suppressed truth is that the wife is not only saved but is as deserving of veneration as the husband. To justify his concession, Damian notes that the wife did penance after the election when she became aware of her error. He also adds that she did, after all, congratulate her husband when he was elected. Still, Damian cannot resist noting in his second sermon on Severus that, when the bishop ordered the wife's body to one side, her prompt and necessarily wordless response was a divine judgment against her wordy insubordination in life.[86] The saint's exasperated reproach that provoked the miracle at the daughter's grave is not, however, recorded. Clearly it would be out of keeping with Severus's reputation for humble endurance.

The final marvel, in which Severus learns of his approaching death while saying Mass and enters the tomb in his episcopal stole to be reunited with his family, is, significantly, omitted. The immediate juxtaposition of the sacrament and the family tomb may have unnerved Damian. This omission is ideologically in keeping with the strict clerical/lay divide, which Damian maintained throughout his writings.[87] In any event, he was more interested in presenting a fractious and turbulent family life that was hardly in keeping with any image of eternal rest.

Peter Damian and the empty altar

While the monk of Classis had evoked an Adam and Eve of a prelapsarian sexual purity – a purity that Severus enjoyed and managed to retain in marriage – Damian's primordial couple was definitely postlapsarian, bequeathing a legacy of power struggles and petulant paybacks. By exaggerating Severus's forbearance and even distorting traditional biblical exegesis in order to suggest that this level of passivity is divinely mandated, Damian presents an unattractive picture of domineering wife and meek, cowering husband. The institution that would foster such reversals, moreover, is accordingly as comfortless as the relationship itself. The wife as the devil's helpmate radiates with an evil but as yet unrealized potential for even more extensive acts of malice.

Damian's recasting of Severus's vita is still only covertly hostile. The gloves come off in Damian's actual writings directed against the practitioners of clerical marriage. Two themes in particular seem coextensive with his sermons on Severus. The disturbing process of feminization, which Severus undergoes as a kind of spiritual discipline, achieves full visibility (and a more markedly negative valence) in Damian's portrayal of the female-dominated clergy. Similarly, Vincentia's domineering contumaciousness develops into an even more exaggerated alliance with the devil in Damian's polemical writings.

Damian presents contemporary priests' companions (from whom he withholds the title of wives) as unabashedly diabolical, even as their method of domination is explicitly sexual. With characteristic rhetorical panache, Damian gives vent to his scurrility:

> O you the clerics' charmers, devil's choice tidbits, expellers from paradise, virus of minds, sword of souls, wolfbane to drinkers, poison to companions, material of sinning, occasion of death. . . . You, I say: I mean the female chambers of the ancient enemy, of hoopoes, of screech owls, of night owls, of she-wolves, of blood-suckers . . . whores, prostitutes, paramours, wallowing pools of greasy hogs, bed chambers of unclean spirits, nymphs, sirens, lamiae, followers of Diana.[88]

In stark contrast to the monk of Classis's reflection on good and bad eating, that all things are pure to the pure, Damian subtly deploys the interconnectedness of gluttony and lust by tracing how these women's sinful relations with Satan implicate them in a diabolical food chain. The devil feeds on clerical concubines: "for on [them] he feasts just as on delicate viands, and is crammed by the exuberance of [their] lust."[89] In the case of the women, however, lust arises directly from their own feeding. They are, for instance, likened to tigresses who drink blood. This image is derived from the bestiary tradition, a genre in which Damian was clearly an adept, having written a bestiary of his own. He further associates the clerical wives with an assortment of mythological women (such as harpies and sirens) who feed on men.[90] The mythological series is rounded off by a reference to that most treacherous of female animals, the viper. A momentary glance at Damian's own bestiary reveals why the viper was, to his mind, apposite: "This species is also naturally endowed with this manner of intercourse . . .: the male thrusts its head into the mouth of the female. Impatient in her lovemaking, she bites off the head and swallows it."[91] Accordingly; Damian's parallel attack on clerical wives associates them with: "furious vipers who out of ardor of impatient lust decapitate Christ, the head of clerics, in [their] lovers."[92] After an interlude, during which the women in question are accused of "tear[ing] unfaithful men from the ministry of the altar which they enjoyed, so that [the women] suffocate them in the slippery glue of [their] love" and persuading their consorts to worship the Beast (Revelations 14.9–11),[93] Damian returns to the metaphor of eating:

> Just as Adam perversely chose the one forbidden fruit over all the licit foods in paradise, so from the entire multitude of humankind only those men who are entirely prohibited from every confederation of womanly desire are chosen by [these women]. . . . Meanwhile the ancient enemy pants to invade the summit of ecclesiastical chastity through [these women]. Let me clearly and not undeservedly acknowledge that [such women] are asps or serpents, who thus suck the blood from wretched and reckless men, as [the women] inflate [the priests'] guts with lethal poison.

Barely skipping a beat, Damian moves from the desecration of the chastity of the church's ministers to the very substance of their holiness:

> And by what audacity of mind are [the women] not horrified to touch the hands anointed by holy chrism or oil, or even [those hands] accustomed to [touch] the gospels or apostolic pages? The scripture says concerning the malign enemy that his food is elect [Habukkuk 1.16]. Through [these women], therefore, the devil devours his elect food, while he tears the very holy members of the church with his teeth just as with two millstones of suggestion and delectation, and when he joins [the priests] to [their sexual partners], he transposes [the priests] into his own guts.[94]

This diabolical digestive feat, by which the devoured priests are mysteriously decanted into the devil's belly from the bellies of his unholy female accomplices, will in turn introduce a justification of the ordinance of Pope Leo IX (1049–54) that the women of priests be enslaved to the Lateran palace. Damian reflects on the aptness of this arrangement: "Namely by the law of equity that those who are convicted of having raped the sacred altars of the servants of God should supply this servile offering of their forfeited rights immediately to the bishop."[95]

The clerical wives' demonically inspired cannibalism anticipates the horrors that would be alleged against witches centuries later – the main difference being that what was advanced at the level of metaphor in the eleventh century was by the fifteenth century being claimed as real. Real witches were believed to eat real people. Even so, Damian's cannibalism was arguably as real for him, albeit in a different register. The women in question are seen as consuming the priesthood by compromising what was "holy" in them according to the Hebrew Bible's sense of the word: what is set apart for God and what must remain whole and complete.[96] To Damian's mind, sexual purity was the *sine qua non* of sacerdotal holiness. And so the clerical concubine's sexual presence was a kind of rape of the altar in the double meaning of the verb *to rape* in medieval Latin – a sexual crime against the animate offering to God, the priest; and a theft perpetrated against the Christian community at large. The bifurcated nature of the concubine's offense is also implicit in the cannibalistic imagery. On the one hand, she is devouring the priest by contaminating what has been set apart for God. The act of eating, moreover, stokes her lust, so that she will continue to be an unsated, and hence ongoing, source of contagion. On the other hand, she is devouring what benefits should accrue to the community through the celebration of the Mass, a fact that is subtly suggested by the inverted and diabolical Eucharist that is at the center of the above invective.

At times Damian seems to perceive this change in terms of a distinct reversal of Christ's salvific work. The sacrifice of the altar was intended to be the source of grace. But when offered by a polluted priest, it inspired divine ire and possible punishment.[97] This substitution of a curse for a blessing was perhaps linked to Damian's frequent musings on the Pauline censure of those who receive the sacrament unworthily, therefore eating and drinking damnation rather than salvation (1 Corinthians 11.29).[98] Hence, in the imaginary indictment of a married bishop, Damian thunders:

> What business have you to handle the body of Christ, when by wallowing in the allurements of the flesh you have become a member of Antichrist? . . . Are you unaware that the Son of God was so dedicated to the purity of the flesh that he was not born of conjugal chastity, but rather from the womb of a virgin? And if that were not enough, that only a virgin should be his mother, it is the belief of the church that his foster father also was a virgin. . . . If he wished to be fondled by hands that were unsullied as he lay in the crib, with what purity does he now wish to surround his body as he reigns on high in the glory of the Father's majesty? . . . If you commit incest with your spiritual daughter, how in good conscience do you dare perform the mystery of the Lord's body?[99]

Here, as elsewhere, aspects of Mariology (as well as a precocious introduction of the cult of Saint Joseph) served to reinforce the sense of outrage implicit in so sacrilegious an offering.[100] Damian's reflection that the son of a virgin should be handled by a virgin, in fact, was repeated frequently in his writings.[101]

This citation might imply that the offending bishop was only risking his own safety, and thus his sin was of a personal nature. Elsewhere, for instance, Damian cites God's warning to Moses that those who pollute the temple with uncleanness may die in their own filth (Leviticus 15.31).[102] But the implications of a polluted priest performing Mass far exceed personal consequences. To his make-believe bishop, for instance, Damian alleges:

Since all ecclesiastical orders are accumulated in one awesome structure in you alone, you surely defile all of them as you pollute yourself by associating with prostitutes. And thus you contaminate by your actions the doorkeeper, the lector, the exorcist, and in turn all the sacred orders for all of which you must give an account before the severe judgment seat of God. As you lay your hand on someone, the Holy Spirit descends upon him; and you use your hand to touch the private parts of harlots.[103]

Moreover, a vitiated priesthood has dire consequences for the entire community, as is evident in his *Book of Gomorrah*:

To what purpose are you so eager to ensnare the people of God in the meshes of your own perdition? Is it not enough that you yourselves are plunging headlong into the depths of sin? Must you also expose others to the danger of your fall?[104]

The threat of a retributive justice visited on the entire community, in fact, still represents an assurance of God's power manifested through the Eucharist, albeit in reverse. But Damian's rhetoric also nervously skirts a possible absence at the center of the mystery, try as he may to disguise it. What, for example, does he mean when he implies that a bishop implicated in a sin contaminates all of the lesser orders in the church? Is he arguing that the episcopal power of ordination is in some way impaired? If this is the case, the sacraments administered by one whom he ordained may be worthless. Or, worse still, is he suggesting that a bishop's fall would harm not only those ordained subsequent to his fall but all of his spiritual clients retroactively – the kind of spiritual "domino effect" that was believed to occur in the later Cathar heresy when a Perfect fell from grace?[105] If, as Damian implies, the besmirched bishop's power to ordain to the priesthood is in some way impaired, how can he simultaneously maintain that the Holy Spirit still descends with the bishop's laying on of hands? On many occasions, Damian upbraids the polluted priests who continue to minister in their contagion when, as he argues, their sacrifices are spurned by God.[106] He also describes the married clergy as an illegitimate, soft, effeminate lot, degenerating from the genuine nobility of the order of priests.[107] At one precarious juncture, he even refers to those who abuse the body of Christ through whatever means – from sexual incontinence to using moldy bread in their celebration of Mass – as pseudo-priests who are destroying the work of the apostles.[108]

Damian's rhetoric of sacerdotal illegitimacy and potential inefficacy is best described as an emotional, as opposed to an intellectual, Donatism [see note 97]. His apparent ambivalence concerning the masses of married priests corresponds to aspects of the disciplinary measures mobilized in this period. In particular, the papacy, following the lead of the Milanese Patarenes, forbade married priests to say Mass and ordered the laity to boycott the masses of married priests – an interdict that could be construed as a covert recognition of the inefficacy of the sacrament when administered by unworthy hands.[109] Any Donatist tendencies in Damian are, however, muted by the more frequent motif of retributive justice. And yet, once aware of both aspects of Damian's rhetoric, the Donatist strains seem to rise unbidden even through his rather smug anticipations of divine vengeance. Thus in an imaginary appeal to the priests themselves, Damian marvels that priests "do not dread to touch the obscenities and impure contagion of women," since at the moment of consecration:

> The sky is opened, the highest and the lowest things rush together in one, and what sordid individual does not dread to hurl himself audaciously [into holy things]? Angelic powers assist with trembling, the divine power descends between the hands of those offering [the Mass], the gift of the Holy Spirit flows, and that pontiff, whom the angels adore, does not recede from the sacrifice of his body and blood [the host], and yet he [the married priest], whom the fire of hellish lust inflames, does not tremble to be present.[110]

In other words, Christ is present and the married priest should fear to be present. And yet, the rhetoric of retributive justice only barely conceals a worse possibility than a polluted altar, and that is an empty one – empty by virtue of a sacramental inefficaciousness, which Damian's rhetoric simultaneously denies and implies.

Damian's discursive responses to the married celebrant – the overt threat of retributive justice versus the covert and ultimately pessimistic fear of sacramental inefficacy – sustain one another in a creative tension. They are contradictory insofar as the sacrament's awesomeness could hardly sit easily with its potential worthlessness. Even so, they are an integral unit. Retributive justice not only presupposes sacramental efficacy but, with its heightened sense of sacrilege, is an implied guarantee of the miraculous nature of the sacrament. Such insistence on justice is necessary in order to quiet the numbing fear of sacramental inefficacy which would strike at the heart of the Eucharist: the fear that, when the priest says the appropriate words, there is only bread and wine – no change, no grace.

The increasing emphasis on the material presence of Christ in the sacrament of the altar opened up a huge chasm in the symbolic order, the very emphasis on "the divine presence" in the Eucharist conjuring up anxieties over absence. But eleventh-century Christendom was nevertheless provided with an excuse. The priest's wife, now cast in the role of devil's colleague and concubine, has metaphorically raped and plundered the altar and made off with the Host. The majority of the Western Christian world concurred with this assessment. The sacramental benefits rightfully belonging to the community were being siphoned off by someone. Somebody was stealing them, and the priest's wife was the most likely suspect. Thus, targeted by the mob through violent demonstrations and pious vandalism, she was exposed to vehement repression.[111]

NOTES

1 Elliott's chapter in *Fallen Bodies* includes an opening quote from Freud:

> "Now you'll think I mean to say something insulting, but really I've no such intention." We realize that this is a rejection by projection, of an idea that has just come up. "You ask who this person in the dream can be. It's *not* my mother." We emend this to: "So it *is* his mother."

See Sigmund Freud, "Negation," in *The Standard Edition of the Complete Psychological Works of Sigmund Freud*, ed. James Strachey (London: Hogarth Press, 1961), vol. 19, p. 235.

2 On this initiative, which Jo Ann McNamara sees as part of a much wider crisis in masculine identity, see her groundbreaking "The *Herrenfrage*: The Restructuring of the Gender System, 1050–1150," in *Medieval Masculinities: Regarding Men in the Middle Ages*, ed. Clare Lees (Minneapolis, MN: University of Minnesota Press, 1994), pp. 3–29, esp. pp. 5–12. Cf. Enrico Cattaneo's discussion of the reforming clergy's efforts to distance themselves from the laity both through creating a heightened aura around the priests and his liturgical function and, on a more concrete level, through proposed architectural change in the church – separating the clergy, laymen, and laywomen ("La liturgia nella riforma gregoriana," in *Chiesa e riforma nella spiritualità del sec. XI*, Convegno del Centro di studi sulla spiritualità medievale, 6 [Todi: Presso l'Accademia Tudertina, 1968], pp. 184–6); also see Giles Gerard Meersseman, "Chiesa e 'Ordo laicorum' nel sec. XI," in *Chiesa e riforma*, pp. 40–2, 68–74; and Dyan Elliott, *Spiritual Marriage: Sexual Abstinence in Medieval Wedlock* (Princeton, NJ: Princeton University Press, 1993), pp. 94–5, 98–104.

3 On tenth-century anticipation of this pollution-laden rhetoric, see Jo Ann McNamara, "Canossa and the Ungendering of the Public Man,"reprinted as Chapter 4, this volume.

4 See M. Dortel-Claudot, "Le Prêtre et le mariage: évolution de la législation canonique des origines au XIIe siècle," *L'Année canonique* 17 (1973): 319–44; and Anne Llewellyn Barstow, *Married Priests and the Reforming Papacy: The Eleventh-Century Debates* (New York: Edwin Mellen, 1982), pp. 19–45. Also see Jo Ann McNamara, "Chaste Marriage and Clerical Celibacy," in *Sexual Practices and the Medieval Church*, eds Vern Bullough and James Brundage (Buffalo, NY: Prometheus, 1982), pp. 22–33, 231–5. A married priesthood was, and still is, the practice of the eastern church.

5 Dortel-Claudot, "Le Prêtre et le mariage," pp. 336, 340.

6 This was enacted at a Roman council that took place in either 1049 or 1050 under Leo IX. Peter Damian alludes to this legislation with approval, as will be seen on p. 141. For an analysis of canonistic antecedents, particularly the Council of Pavia in 1022, see J. Joseph Ryan, *Saint Peter Damiani and His Canonical Sources: A Preliminary Study in the Antecedents of the Gregorian Reform* (Toronto: Pontifical Institute of Mediaeval Studies, 1956), no. 197, pp. 101–2.

7 On the Milanese reform led by the so-called Patarene movement, see Herbert E. J. Cowdrey, "The Papacy, the Patarenes, and the Church of Milan," *Transactions of the Royal Historical Society*, series 5, 18 (1986): 25–48. See particularly the impassioned account of Landulf the Senior, himself a married priest, in book 3 of his *Mediolanensis historiae libri quatuor*, ed. Alessandro Cutulo, *Rerum Italicarum Scriptores*, rev. edn

(Bologna: Nicola Zanichelli, 1942), 4, 2, pp. 81–128. One of the leaders of the reform, the deacon Ariald, was eventually murdered by his enemies. His body, described as creating a terrible stench that threatened to reveal where it was hidden, was handed over to his enemies – appropriately castrated (3.30, pp. 121–2). On Peter Damian's mission to Milan, see n. 67, below. It was possible that the married clergy attempted to buttress their practice by conciliar action. There is, however, no mention of any such efforts in Michael Stoller, "Eight Anti-Gregorian Councils," *Annuarium Historiae Conciliorum* 17 (1985): 252–321, but considering that Stoller was forced to reconstruct these legislative endeavors from fragments, and that very little of the *acta* remain, it is possible that there were such organized efforts. On a possible council of Trebur, see n. 67 below. For the literary defense of clerical marriage, see Barstow, *Married Priests*, pp. 105–73, and Augustin Fliche, *La Réforme grégorienne* (Louvain: Spicilegium Sacrum Lovaniense, 1937), 3, pp. 1–48.

8   Christopher Brooke, "Gregorian Reform in Action: Clerical Marriage in England, 1050–1200," *Cambridge Historical Journal* 12 (1956): 1–21, and 187–8.

9   Georges Duby, "Les pauvres des campagnes dans l'occident médiéval jusqu'au XIIIe siècle," *Revue d'histoire de l'église de France* 52 (1966): 28; McNamara, "The *Herrenfrage*," p. 12. Jacques Dalarun also assesses the early members of the monastic foundation of Fontevrault as casualties of the eleventh-century marriage crisis. See "Robert d'Arbrissel et les femmes,"*Annales ÉSC* 39 (1984): 1140–60. As Ruth Mazo Karras, *Common Women: Prostitution and Sexuality in Medieval England* (New York: Oxford University Press, 1996), pp. 86–138, demonstrates for a later period, it became routine to describe clerical concubines as prostitutes.

10 The question of pollution will be taken up later. With regard to clerical marriage as a drain on church resources, see Gregory VII's very pointed complaint to William the Conqueror against a bishop who used church property to dower his intended, Gregory VII, "Ep. 16," in *Epistolae Collectae*, ed. P. Jaffé, in *Monumenta Gregoriana, Bibliotheca Rerum Germanicarum* (Berlin, 1865; reprint Aachen: Scientia, 1964), 2, pp. 541–2. But usually property interests are rhetorically subordinated to other concerns. Peter Damian, for example, demonstrates considerable consternation over the depletion of church property when treating other subjects. See Peter Damian, Ep. 35, "To the Clergy and Laity of the Diocese of Osimo," ghostwritten on behalf of Leo IX, *Die Briefe des Petrus Damiani*, ed. Kurt Reindel, *MGH, Die Briefe der deutschen Kaiserzeit*, 4 (Munich, 1983), 1, pp. 336–9, hereafter *Briefe*; some are translated in *Letters*, trans. Owen J. Blum, *Fathers of the Church* (New York: Cima, 1947), Mediaeval Continuation, 2 (Washington, DC: Catholic University of America, 1990), 2, pp. 61–3, hereafter *Letters*; and Damian, Ep. 74, "To an Anonymous Bishop," *Briefe* 2, pp. 369–75; *Letters*, 3, pp. 151–6. This issue is tactically suppressed in his attacks on clerical marriage, however, except perhaps by innuendo. Thus he argues that the married priests are a bastard line who, like the illegitimate offspring of the patriarchs, will be separated from the true heirs. He also responds to the married priests' claims that they need wives because they cannot afford servants by reasoning that this was, in fact, an argument *against* marriage so as to avoid the additional drain of child-support (Damian, Ep. 162, "To Archpriest Peter," *Briefe* 4, pp. 154–5). The economic considerations are reflected in the hard line taken *against* the sons of priests, who were theoretically pronounced illegitimate and barred from the priesthood. See n. 21 below.

11 Damian, Ep. 114, "To Adelaide of Savoy," *Briefe* 3, p. 299. Damian returns to the question of categories toward the end of his letter when he somewhat tactlessly reassures Adelaide that "multivirae" – women who have been married many times, as had Adelaide – can be saved. He adds, however, that he does not mention this in order to inspire her to further nuptial escapades (p. 304). Adelaide had been married three times but was a widow when Damian wrote to her in 1064. See Francesco Cognasso's entry in *Dizionario biografico degli italiani* (Rome:

Società Grafica Romana, 1960), 1, pp. 249–51. Gregory VII wholeheartedly adopted Damian's sentiments and, indeed, his rhetoric in this matter; see Fliche, *La Réforme grégorienne*, 2, p. 156.

12   Mary Douglas, *Purity and Danger: An Analysis of the Concepts of Pollution and Taboo* (London: Routledge & Kegan Paul; Ark Paperbacks, 1966; reprint 1988), ch. 3, pp. 41–57. Robert I. Moore first applied aspects of Douglas's analytical framework to this period of reform in his "Family, Community, and Cult on the Eve of the Gregorian Reform," *Transactions of the Royal Historical Society*, series 5, 30 (1984): 49–69, esp. 66–9; cf. Moore, *The Formation of a Persecuting Society: Power and Deviance in Western Europe, 950–1250* (Oxford: Blackwell, 1987), esp. pp. 100–1.

13   Thus Damian argues that contact with the laity corrupts the secular priesthood:

> There is something else that displeases me regarding secular priests, namely, that since they associate with laymen by living amid the citizens of a region, many of them are no different from their neighbors in their way of life and irregular morals. They normally involve themselves in secular affairs, and show no restraint in taking part in idle and senseless conversation.
>
> (Ep. 47, "To an Unidentified Bishop," *Briefe* 1,
> p. 45; *Letters*, 2, pp. 254–5)

Note that Humbert of Silva Candida's insistence on a similar separation between clergy and laity is one of the cornerstones of his arguments against lay investiture. See *Libri III adversus simoniacos* 3.9, ed. F. Thaner, *MGH, Libelli*, vol. 1, p. 208. He is especially exercised over the fact that not only laymen but also laywomen control church property in this way (3.12, p. 212).

14   Suzanne F. Wemple, *Women in Frankish Society: Marriage and the Cloister, 500 to 900* (Philadelphia, PA: University of Pennsylvania Press, 1985), pp. 131–2; and Elliott, *Spiritual Marriage*, p. 87. Also see the entries for *presbyteria* and for *sacerdotissa* in Charles du Fresne Du Cange, *Glossarium ad scriptores mediae et infimae Latinitatis* (Paris: Librairie des sciences et des arts, 1840–50), 6, pp. 488–9 and 7, p. 255. On the possible quasi-sacerdotal functions of clerical wives, see McNamara, Chapter 4, this volume.

15   Damian, Ep. 112, "To Bishop Cunibert of Turin," *Briefe* 3, p. 286, argues that once the married priests attempt to defend their error, they become heretics. The married "heretics" were called Nicolaites, after the heretics described in Rev. 2.6 and 14–15. According to Barstow, *Married Priests*, p. 54, Cardinal Humbert of Silva Candida set a precedent for labeling the married clergy and their defenders heretics.

16   See the section on pp. 139–45, "Peter Damian and the Empty Altar."

17   See n. 10, above.

18   Damian, Ep. 31, "To Leo IX," *Briefe* 1, p. 299; *Letters*, 1, p. 19. Ep. 61, "To Nicholas II," *Briefe* 2, pp. 214–15; *Letters*, 3, p. 10. Ep. 162, "To Archpriest Peter," *Briefe* 4, p. 152.

19   See Ariald's dramatic rebuilding of a church with a high wall separating the choir (where the clergy was) from the laity – the laity's area being additionally divided between men and women (Andrew of Strumi, *Vita santi Arialdi*, c. 12, ed. Friedrich Baethgen, *MGH, SS*, vol. 30, 2 [Leipzig: Karl W. Hirssemann, 1934], p. 1058).

20   Cf. Damian's hyperbolic comments to married priests: "I convene you, o uxorious enticers, and enslaved by the riches of dominating women," Ep. 162, "To Archpriest Peter," *Briefe* 4, p. 147).

21   Clerical marriage was condemned, as was the ordination of priests' sons, at Bourges in 1031 (see Fliche, *La Réforme grégorienne*, 1, p. 99). But this stricture only really began to be enforced for the entire church in the 1070s under Gregory VII. See Barstow, *Married Priests*, pp. 65–77; and James Brundage, *Law, Sex, and Christian Society in Medieval Europe* (Chicago, IL: University of Chicago Press, 1987),

pp. 216–19. Note, however, that the classificatory confusion generated over the clergy's sexual partners persisted into the later Middle Ages; see Karras, *Common Women*, p. 30.

22 This contemporary truism, so frequently associated with a postmodern sensibility, was already a factor in Freud's analysis. Thus he described how a patient's defense mechanisms can be duped into reinstating repressed symptoms, characterizing this self-defeating response as "a good example of the rule that in time the thing which is meant to be warded off invariably finds its way into the very means which is being used for warding it off." The act of reiteration renders itself complicit with this reappearance, since its inevitable lapses, slips, and dodges open spaces within which the repressed can make a come-back. Controlled repetition is thus an impossible proposition. Foreign or repressed elements are introduced unwittingly, engendering a dangerous swerve from the professed telos. Freud, *Notes upon a Case of Obsessional Neurosis* (i.e. "Rat Man"), in *The Standard Edition* 10, p. 225. Aspects of the foreign particles introduced are indistinguishable from the disavowed material that returns, creating something like the "doubling" effect, which, according to Homi Bhabha's analysis of colonial discourse, invokes disavowed knowledges that return and destabilize authority. See "Signs Taken for Wonders: Questions of Ambivalence and Authority under a Tree Outside Delhi, May 1817," *Critical Inquiry* 12 (1985): 161. I am also influenced here by Jacques Derrida's concept of iterability in *Limited Inc*, trans. Samuel Weber (Evanston, IL: Northwestern University Press, 1988), app., pp. 127–9. Cf. Judith Butler's comments on the occasional discontinuities in the repeated acts that constitute gender in her *Gender Trouble: Feminism and the Subversion of Identity* (New York: Routledge, 1990), p. 141.

23 By the sixth century there is little mention of married bishops except in Gaul, where such unions are the source of considerable ambivalence. See Brian Brennan, "'Episcopae:' Bishops' Wives Viewed in Sixth-Century Gaul," *Church History* 54 (1985): 311–23.

24 Peter Damian did write a sermon commemorating the translation of the relics of Bishop Hilary of Poitiers – a saint who was married and purportedly had a daughter as well (Serm. 2, *Sermones*, ed. Giovanni Lucchesi, CC:CM, 57 [Turnhout: Brepols, 1983], pp. 3–7). No mention, however, is made of this fact. This sermon, based on a secondhand account by a monk who had read Hilary's life by St Fredolinus (*BHL* 3170), was probably an occasional piece written during Damian's mission to Gaul in 1063 (see Damian, Serm. 2, c. 3, *Sermones*, p. 4, and Lucchesi's introductory remarks on p. 2).

25 *AASS*, previous commentary, Ludolphus, February, 1: 78–9; Giovanni Lucchesi, *BS*, vol. 11, cols 997–8.

26 On Agnellus, see Paolo Lamma's entry in *Dizionario biografico degli italiani*, I, pp. 429–30; and Thomas Hodgkin, *Italy and Her Invaders*, 2nd edn (Oxford: Clarendon Press, 1892), 1, 2, pp. 900–16. For Agnellus's account of Severus's life, I have used Alessandro Testi Rasponi's edition of the *Liber pontificalis (hereafter LP)*, in *Raccolta degli Storici Italiani*, 2, 3, ed. Ludovico A. Muratori (Bologna: Nicola Zanichelli, 1924), based on the later but more prolix Codex Estense. Rasponi's superior but incomplete edition leaves off at ch. 103 of the 175 chapters. For later chapters, I have used Oswald Holder-Egger's edition in *MGH, Scriptores rerum Langobardicarum et Italicarum, saec. VI–IX* (hereafter *SS rerum Lang.*), pp. 265–391.

27 See Hodgkin, *Italy and Her Invaders*, 7, pp. 163, 197–200, 328–41.

28 On the worldliness of the church of Ravenna, see Agnellus, *LP*, c. 104, ed. Holder-Egger, p. 345. Also see T. S. Brown, *Gentlemen and Officers: Imperial Administration and Aristocratic Power in Byzantine Italy, A.D. 554–800* (Hertford: Stephen Austin and Sons for the British School at Rome, 1984), pp. 188–9. Brown overstates his case for worldliness, however, by arguing that many of the minor clergy were married –

hardly irregular for this period. Nor for that matter would the marriage of minor clerics be outlawed even after the eleventh-century reform. Brown also notes that some of the archbishops of Ravenna treated by Agnellus were married without qualifying this observation. This is rather misleading, as it implies that they continued to enjoy conjugal rights after ordination, which, as is clear from the following discussion, they were emphatically portrayed as relinquishing.

29 Agnellus, *LP*, c. 84, ed. Holder-Egger, p. 333.
30 Holder-Egger, the editor of the volume, also remarks that Agnellus does not, in fact return to this problem unless one takes ch. 97 into account (Agnellus, *LP*, c. 84, p. 334, n. 2). Ch. 97 is an indictment of men who are dominated by their wives, but it certainly does not seem to be addressed to a clerical audience, though Brown clearly reads it this way – possibly because at one point in Agnellus's narration he addresses his audience as "fratres" (Agnellus, *LP*, c. 97, p. 341; see Brown, *Gentleman and Officers*, p. 188, n. 23; note that, since Agnellus was a monk, "fratres" could signify an even more scandalous but different kind of laxness). In any event, since the author made it clear that the wife died prior to Bishop Agnellus's elevation, his skittishness on this subject suggests that for bishops to be married at any point in their careers was hardly routine.
31 Agnellus, *LP*, c. 154, ed. Holder-Egger, p. 377.
32 Agnellus, *LP*, c. 157, ed. Holder-Egger, p. 379.
33 Hodgkin, *Italy and Her Invaders*, 7, pp. 339–40.
34 These are, however, prefaced by some preliminary remarks, which include a discussion of the mystical meaning of Severus, an allusion to his miraculous election to office, and a terse mention of his presence at Sardica (Agnellus, *LP*, c. 11, ed. Rasponi, pp. 42–4).
35 This incident is followed by one miracle at Severus's grave (Agnellus, *LP*, c. 16, ed. Rasponi, pp. 50–1).
36 Agnellus, *LP*, c. 15, ed. Rasponi, pp. 47–8. Cf. Severus's slightly exasperated tone when the surrounding clergy, rouse him from his ecstasy: "O what did you do? Why do you disturb me?" (Agnellus, *LP*, c. 14, ed. Rasponi, p. 45).
37 Agnellus, *LP*, c. 15, ed. Rasponi, p. 48.
38 Gregory the Great, *Dialogues* 3.23, ed. Adalbert de Vogüé (Paris: Éditions du Cerf, 1979), 2, p. 360; Gregory, *Dialogues*, trans. Odo John Zimmerman (Washington, DC: Catholic University of America Press, 1959), p. 156.
39 See Elliott, *Spiritual Marriage*, pp. 70–1.
40 Agnellus, *LP*, c. 15, ed. Rasponi, pp. 48–9.
41 Giovanni Lucchesi thinks the fact that all the bishops of Ravenna were allegedly elected this way is suppressed in Agnellus but is more developed in Peter Damian's rendering: the latter refers to the dove's election as "the accustomed way." See "Il Sermonario di S. Pier Damiani," ed. Giovanni Lucchesi, in *Studi Gregoriani per la storia della "Libertas Ecclesiae,"* eds Alfonso M. Stickler and Giovanni Battista Borino. (Rome: Ateneo Salesiano, 1975), p. 54. But since, in Agnellus's characterization, Severus says ahead of time that he wants to see the miraculous descent of the dove, the tradition strikes me as implicit – compressed as opposed to suppressed.
42 Agnellus, *LP*, c. 17, ed. Rasponi, p. 51.
43 Agnellus, *LP*, c. 17, ed. Rasponi, pp. 51–2.
44 What is implied is, of course, the ecclesiastically endorsed ideal. On the difficulties surrounding a clerical transition to chastity, see Elliott, *Spiritual Marriage*, pp. 83–91.
45 Liodolphus, *AASS*, February, 1: 89.
46 See Elliott, *Spiritual Marriage*, pp. 69–70.
47 This dating is only approximate, but the rhetoric of reform clearly places it in the later eleventh century. Giovanni Lucchesi, an expert on both Peter Damian and the bishops of Ravenna, in his "Il Sermonario di S. Pier Damiani," pp. 55–6, tentatively dates Damian's sermons on Severus as 1069 or 1070, positing that the

anonymous vita of Severus was written between 1050 and 1070 (*Bibliotheca Sanctorum*, vol. 11, col. 1000).

48 Severus's relics, along with those of his wife and daughter, were taken to Germany by Otgar, Archbishop of Mainz. The translation occurred *c.*857 and is described in the contemporary account by the monk Liudolf (Liodolphus, *AASS*, February, 1: 90–1). This kind of theft was a common phenomenon. See Patrick Geary, *Furta Sacra: Thefts of Relics in the Central Middle Ages* (Princeton, NJ: Princeton University Press, 1978), generally; on Severus, p. 58. Seemingly undaunted by the widespread knowledge of this celebrated theft, however, the anonymous monk of Classis claims that the relics are in a marble sarcophagus in the basilica at Classis and alleges that they still work miracles. It does not inspire confidence, however, that his example of a contemporary miracle is lifted from Agnellus (Liodolphus, *AASS*, February, 1: 85; cf. Agnellus, *LP*, c. 16, ed. Rasponi, p. 50). Damian, however, does report contemporary miracles in the basilica, particularly water with healing powers emanating from the altar (Damian, Serm. 5, c. 9–10, *Sermones*, ed. Lucchesi, *CC:CM*, 57, pp. 30–1). Damian, cagily, does not specify which basilica – the one in Italy or Germany – although Lucchesi, "Il Sermonario di S. Pier Damiani," pp. 55–6, suggests that the miracles were part of the oral tradition, perhaps reported to him by pilgrims from Germany. Elsewhere Damian reports that the monastery possessed Severus's body but not his heart. See Damian's *Vita beati Romualdi*, c. 12, ed. Giovanni Tabacco (Rome: Sede dell'Instituto, Palazzo Borromini, 1957), p. 33. This may have been how the monastery finessed the embarrassing absence of its patron. Lucchesi gives 1042 as the date for Damian's vita of Romuald ("Clavis S. Petri Damiani," *Studi su S. Pier Damiano in onore del Cardinale Amleto Giovanni Cicognani*, Biblioteca Cardinale Gaetano Cicognani, 5 [Faenza: Seminario Vescovile Pio XII, 1970], p. 60).

49 Damian also wrote one sermon for Archbishop Eleucadius and three for Apollinarus, archbishop and martyr (Damian, Serms 6 and 30–2, *Sermones*, ed. Lucchesi, *CC:CM*, 57, pp. 34–43, 172–203). His anti-simoniacal work *Liber gratissimus*, moreover, is dedicated to Henry Archbishop of Ravenna. In the conclusion Damian alludes to Ravenna's series of saintly bishops as a kind of apostolic Senate (Damian, Ep. 40, "To Archbishop Henry of Ravenna," *Briefe* 1, p. 507; *Letters*, 2, p. 212). On Damian's affection for Ravenna, see Jean Leclerq, *Saint Pierre Damien: ermite et homme d'église* (Rome: Edizione di storia et letteratura, 1960), pp. 19, 161.

50 Liudolphus, 1.4–5, *AASS*, February, 1: 82–3.

51 On the reformers' initiative against simony, see Fliche, *La Réforme grégorienne*, 1, pp. 337–40; 2, pp. 136–41. On monks preaching reform, see Barstow, *Married Priests*, pp. 49–50.

52 Note that vita *BHL* 7864, a reworking of the anonymous life, omits the digressions on marriage discussed below, instead adding its own digression on Arianism – a more apposite concern for the fourth century. See the description of codex signatus XXXIX, G. S. III, 12, folios 152r–77, in "Catalogus codicum hagiographicorum bibliothecae Ambrosianae Mediolanensis," *Analecta Bollandiana* 11 (1892): 335–6. The manuscript in question is an eighteenth-century transcription.

53 Liudolphus, 1.3, *AASS*, February, 1: 82.

54 Cassian discusses how excess food results in nocturnal pollutions in *Collatio* 22.3 (*Conférences*, ed. E. Pichery, *Sources Chretiennes*, no. 64 [Paris: Éditions du Cerf, 1959], 3, pp. 116–17). Also see the interesting pairing of these two forms of indulgence by Honorius Augustodunensis. He poses the question of "Whether it is a sin to marry or to eat meat,"which he resolves in the negative. But he then asserts, "It is good not to touch a woman, and good not to eat meat,"*Libellus Honorii Augustodunensis presbyteri et scholastici*, ed. J. Dieterich, in *MGH, Libelli*, vol. 3, pp. 34–5. (I am deliberately leaving Honorius's name in its Latin form; cf. Valerie Flint,"Heinricus of Augsburg and Honorius Augustodunensis: Are They the Same Person?" *Revue bénédictine* 92 [1982]: 148–58.) Also see Damian's indictment of

married clerics for their presumed gluttony, Damian, Ep. 162, "To Archpriest Peter," *Briefe* 4, p. 160.

55 Liudolphus, 5.17, *AASS*, February, 1: 85.

56 Liudolphus, 5.18, *AASS*, February, 1: 85–6.

57 Liudolphus, 5.18, *AASS*, February, 1: 85–6.

58 Liudolphus, 5.18–19, *AASS*, February, 1: 85–6.

59 Liudolphus, 5.24, *AASS*, February, 1: 87.

60 Liudolphus, 5.24, *AASS*, February, 1: 87.

61 For an overview of some of these early heresies, all of which stressed sexual purity and sometimes included attacks on married clergy, see Malcolm Lambert, *Medieval Heresy: Popular Movements from the Gregorian Reform to the Reformation*, 2nd edn (Oxford: Blackwell, 1977; 2nd edn, 1992), pp. 9–32. On the connection between the cessation of heresy and the commencement of the reform movement, see Robert I. Moore, "The Origins of Medieval Heresy," *History* 55 (1970): 33–4.

62 See Barstow, *Married Priests*, pp. 107–16. Ulric's defense was written in 1060, in response to Nicholas II's reissuing of the ban on clerical marriage. This is the first of a series of eleventh-century defenses. The previous efforts had been in the fourth century.

63 Barstow, *Married Priests*, pp. 157–73.

64 The daughter's name, in contrast, emerges at her funeral as follows: "Erat autem eadem Virgo Innocentiae insignita vocabulo," Liudolphus, 4.12, *AA:SS*, February, 1: 84.

65 Jane Tibbetts Schulenburg, "Sexism and the Celestial Gynaeceum – from 500–1200," *Journal of Medieval History* 4 (1978): 124–6, demonstrates that the total number of female saints took a nosedive in the eleventh century and continued to plummet throughout the twelfth.

66 See Fliche, *La Réforme grégorienne*, 1, p. 256; 2, pp. 109–11, 140–1, 156, 240; and Jean Leclercq, *Saint Pierre Damien*, pp. 111–17.

67 Peter Damian describes his successful mission of 1059 against the married and simoniac clergy of Milan in Ep. 65, "To Archdeacon Hildebrand (the future Gregory VII)," *Briefe* 2, pp. 228–47; *Letters* 3, pp. 24–39. The oath pronounced by Guido, archbishop of Milan, which renounced the "heresies" of simony and nicolaitism (i.e. clerical marriage), was recorded by the reformer Ariald (*Briefe* 2, pp. 244–5; *Letters* 3, pp. 37–8). On Damian's mission to Milan see H. C. Lea, *A History of Sacerdotal Celibacy*, 2nd edn (Boston: Houghton Mifflin, 1884), pp. 213–14; and Constanzo Somigli, "San Pier Damiano e la Pataria," in *San Pier Damiano nel IX centenario della morte (1072–1972)* (Cesena: Centro studi, 1972), 3, pp. 193–206. On the documents and chronology for this mission, see Giovanni Lucchesi, "Per una Vita di San Pier Damiani," in *San Pier Damiano*, 1, pp. 141–5. Elsewhere, Damian describes a campaign in Lodi where he reports that the married priests threatened his life. They justified their married status by claiming its authorization at the Council of Trebur (Ep. 112, "To Bishop Cunibert of Turin," *Briefe* 3: 266–7). Damian claims he had never heard of this council, and modern scholars are likewise baffled. Ryan suggests that the reference to Trebur could be a confused reference to the Council of Trulla (692), the council that sanctioned clerical marriage for the eastern church (*Saint Peter Damian*, no. 193, p. 100).

68 Damian's writings against clerical marriage have attracted considerable attention. See Jean de Chasteigner, "Le Célibat sacerdotal dans les écrits de saint Pierre Damien," *Doctor Communis* 24 (1971): 169–83; Pietro Palazzini, "S. Pier Damiani e la polemica anticelibataria," *Divinitas* 14 (1970): 127–33; Barstow, *Married Priests*, pp. 58–64; Carlo Mazzotti, "Il celibato e la castità del clero in S. Pier Damiani," *San Pier Damiano*, pp. 343–56; and Fliche, *La Réforme grégorienne*, 1, pp. 206–13. My contribution is to focus on some of the imagistic underpinnings of Damian's rhetoric.

69 "Uxor presbytetri officio functa est sacerdotis, dum et maternum ad pietatem mollivit affectum," John of Lodi, *Vita S. Petri Damiani*, c. 1, *PL*, vol. 144, cols 115–16; also see n. 2. This is a strange slip for the biographer and disciple of a man who denied the legitimacy of such marriages, one that made the editor of Damian's vita in *Patrologia Latina*, the venerable Dom. J.-P Migne, scramble for cover. Migne hastily attached a footnote to John's overgenerous designation, remarking that elsewhere the priest's wife is referred to as "the sinful little woman" (*peccatrix muliercula*). This is a modest reminder of the *presbyteria*'s capacity to warp the woof of any text. Cf. Lester K. Little, "The Personal Development of Peter Damian," in *Order and Innovation in the Middle Ages: Essays in Honor of Joseph R. Strayer*, ed. William C. Jordan *et al.* (Princeton, NJ: Princeton University Press, 1976), pp. 322, 323–4. On John of Lodi, his vita, sources, and the manuscript tradition, see Lucchesi, "Per una Vita di San Pier Damiani" in *San Pier Damiano*, 4, pp. 7–66, esp. 8–22.

70 Damian, Ep. 70, "To Landulf Cotta of Milan," *Briefe* 2, p. 320; trans. Blum, *Letters* 3, p. 110. The letter was written to this particular Milanese reformer, a member of the lower clergy, to remind him of his unfulfilled vow to become a priest.

71 Damian, Ep. 70, "To Landulf Cotta of Milan," *Briefe* 2, p. 320; trans. Blum, *Letters* 3, p. 110. Also see Little, "Personal Development of Peter Damian," pp. 319–21, 333.

72 See, for example, the popular *passio* of Daria and Chrysanthus: "They were made companions in blood in their passion, just as they had been husband and wife in mind; as if in one bed, so then remained in one pit" (*AASS*, October, 11: 483); on this motif see Elliott, *Spiritual Marriage*, pp. 69–70. Cf. Damian's sermon on the martyrs St Vitalis and his wife, Valeria, of Ravenna. He argues that, since the city possesses the husband's relics, it must necessarily possess the wife's because a married couple who were two in one flesh would likewise be buried together (Serm. 17, 1, c. 8, *Sermones*, ed. Lucchesi, *CC:CM*, 57, p. 91). He extends this argument to include their two martyred sons, Gervasius and Protasius, who were mystically present in the body of their progenitor, Vitalis, though separated by burial sites.

73 Damian, Ep. 143, "To Countess Guilla," *Briefe* 3, p. 522; also see his letter on anger, which concludes with the admission of his own tendency toward anger and his ongoing struggle against lust (Ep. 80, "To an Unidentified Bishop," *Briefe* 3, p. 416; *Letters* 3, pp. 200–1). These letters were written in 1067 and 1060 respectively, when Damian was well into his fifties – elderly by medieval standards. On Damian's relations with women, see Jean Leclercq, "S. Pierre Damien et les femmes," *Studia monastica* 15 (1973): 43–55; also see Little, "Personal Development of Peter Damian," pp. 333, 335.

74 His monastic conversion occurred in 1035, and the usual date given for his birth is 1007. Little, however, contests this second date and other aspects of the traditional chronology given for Damian's life (see Little, "Personal Development of Peter Damian," pp. 318–21; also see Blum's introduction to *Letters* 1, pp. 4–5).

75 Damian, Ep. 62, "To Bishop Theodosius of Senigallia, and Bishop Rudolphus of Gubbio," *Briefe* 2, pp. 219–20; *Letters* 3, p. 14. He goes on to ask that these two men read his works carefully and censor anything inappropriate. Fortunately, his request seems to have gone unheeded – or perhaps his censors were not very censorious.

76 Damian, Ep. 138, "To His Brother Damian," *Briefe* 3, p. 474. See his panegyric in praise of flagellation, Ep. 161, "To the Monks of Monte Cassino," *Briefe* 4, pp. 135–44. Also see his concern over light and frivolous speech in Ep. 56, "To Petrus Cerebrosus," *Briefe*, 2, p. 154; *Letters* 2, pp. 361–2. Elsewhere, he argues that the hermitage is a cure for the vice of scurrility (Ep. 28, "To Leo of Sitria," *Briefe* 1, p. 276; *Letters* 1, p. 285. See Little, "Personal Development of Peter Damian," pp. 335–7, 340.)

77 Damian, Serm. 4, c. 1, *Sermones*, ed. Lucchesi, *CC:CM*, 57, pp. 16–17.

78 Damian, Serm. 4, c. 2, p. 17.

79 Damian, Serm. 4, c. 2, p. 18.

80 Damian, Serm. 4, c. 2, p. 18.

81 Damian, Serm. 4, c. 3, p. 19.

82 Damian, Serm. 4, c. 3, p. 19.

83 Damian, Serm. 4, c. 4, p. 19.

84 Damian, Serm. 4, c. 5, pp. 20–1.

85 Damian, Serm. 4, p. 21.

86 Damian, Serm. 4, c. 8, p. 30.

87 See n. 13 above. On Damian's contempt for lay life and his attitudes toward marriage, see Robert Bultot, *Christianisme et valeurs humaines. A La doctrine du mépris du monde, en Occident, de S. Ambroise à Innocent III*, vol. 4, *Le XIe siècle: 1. Pierre Damien* (Louvain: Nauwelaerts, 1963), pp. 53–62, 100–11. Also see Walter Ferretti, "Il posto del laici nella Chiesa secondo S. Pier Damini," *San Pier Damiano*, 2, pp. 246–7; and Owen J. Blum, *St. Peter Damian* (Washington, DC: Catholic University Press, 1947), pp. 91–7. Both of these authors point out that Damian in no way encouraged laypersons to aspire to higher levels of spirituality, reserving those heights for religious personnel.

88 Damian, Ep. 112, "To Bishop Cunibert of Turin," *Briefe* 3, p. 278. Barstow translates this and several of Damian's other lurid invectives in *Married Priest*, pp. 60–1.

89 Damian, Ep. 112, "To Bishop Cunibert of Turin," *Briefe* 3, p. 278.

90 Damian, Ep. 112, "To Bishop Cunibert of Turin," *Briefe* 3, p. 278. In Damian's own bestiary, the tigress may be tricked out of pursuit if hunters throw a glass ball in front of her, since she is liable to mistake her own reflection for that of her cub. He then continues to argue that the tigress is the devil. Humanity can throw off pursuit by showing the devil his true followers in the glass. These followers would be individuals who reflect the devil's own image and worship the beast (Rev. 14.9; Damian, Ep. 86, "To Desiderius, Abbot of Monte Cassino," *Briefe* 2, pp. 476–8). On Damian and the bestiary tradition, see Leclercq, *Saint Pierre Damien*, pp. 83–92.

91 Damian goes on to say that the children thus engendered gnaw through the mother's sides, killing her as they are being born, concluding, "and so they were parricides before they were offspring" (Ep. 86, "To Desiderius, Abbot of Monte Cassino," *Briefe* 2, pp. 490–1; *Letters* 3, pp. 284–5). Cf. Isidore of Seville, *Etymologiae* 12.4.10–11, *PL*, vol. 82, col. 413. Damian is also aware of the tradition whereby the male viper seeks illicit sexual union with the sea eel (murena), remarking that "the qualities of another strain are bred into the offspring of this venomous beast" (Ep. 86, "To Desiderius, Abbot of Monte Cassino," *Briefe* 2, p. 493; *Letters* 3, p. 286). On the murena, see Isidore, *Etymologiae* 12.4.43, *PL*, vol. 82, col. 455. The twelfth-century bestiarist relays all of the above information in his discussion of the viper and moralizes the male viper's defection from his violent wife in favor of the more accommodating murena into a warning to unruly wives (trans. T. H. White, *The Bestiary: A Book of Beasts* [New York: Putnam, 1954; Capricorn Books edn, 1960], p. 171).

92 Damian, Ep. 112, "To Bishop Cunibert of Turin," *Briefe* 3, p. 279.

93 Damian, Ep. 112, "To Bishop Cunibert of Turin," *Briefe* 3, p. 279.

94 Damian, Ep. 112, "To Bishop Cunibert of Turin," *Briefe* 3, pp. 279–80.

95 Damian, Ep. 112, "To Bishop Cunibert of Turin," *Briefe* 3, p. 281.

96 See Mary Douglas, *Purity and Danger*, pp. 49–52.

97 The theology implicit in the rape of the altar is not immediately clear, since at no time does Damian consciously assume a Donatist stance, which would be to urge deliberately that sacraments administered by an unworthy priest were invalid. Any such tendency was seemingly put to the test over the question of simony. In a work that Damian himself called *The Most Gratuitous Book* (*Liber gratissimus*), he had vigorously opposed the more radical view articulated by men such as Humbert of Silva Candida, who had argued that clerics purchasing their offices were devoid

of any sacerdotal efficacy. Damian explicitly denies that the Eucharist is any less efficacious when performed by wicked priests, extending his demonstration of God's willingness to work through unworthy priests to the example of Rainaldus, the bishop of Fiesole. This married simoniac with numerous concubines and progeny was still permitted to work miracles. (Damian, Ep. 40, "To Archbishop Henry of Ravenna," *Briefe* 1, pp. 411–12; *Letters* 1, pp. 130, 154. Humbert of Silva Candida's *Libri III adversus simoniacos* is cited in note 13. On the contested relation between these two adversial works, see Damian, *Briefe* 1, pp. 432–3, n. 82. For an analysis of Damian's attitude toward simony, see Fliche, *La Réforme grégorienne*, 1, pp. 214–30.)

Even so, as Damian's *Book of Gomorrah*, an unprecedented attack on homosexual practices among the clergy, would certainly indicate, Damian was obsessed with the question of sexual purity in all forms in a way that his fellow reformers, who had little or no interest in acting against homosexuals, were clearly not. (Damian, Ep. 31, "To Leo IX," *Briefe* 1, pp. 284–330; *Letters* 2, pp. 3–53. On Leo IX's tepid reception of this work, see John Boswell, *Christianity, Social Tolerance, and Homosexuality: Gay People in Western Europe from the Beginning of the Christian Era to the Fourteenth Century* [Chicago, IL: University of Chicago Press, 1980], pp. 210–12; and Blum, *St. Peter Damian*, pp. 20–1. He was also extremely concerned that the utensils used for celebrating Mass were clean. See Ep. 47, "To an Unidentified Bishop," *Briefe* 2, pp. 46–7; *Letters* 2, pp. 255–6.) His attachment to purity was not always negatively defined, however, as Damian's pivotal role in the promotion of the cult of the Virgin Mary would suggest.

In any event, given Damian's preoccupation with purity, it is natural that the issue of clerical marriage was perceived as more dangerous than the other two planks of the reforming platform: simony (which he was moderately concerned about) or lay investiture (which he cared very little about). Barstow argues, with reason, that Damian prioritized the problem of clerical purity over simony (*Married Priests*, p. 52). On Damian's relative indifference to lay investiture, see Fliche, *La Réforme grégorienne*, 1, p. 256. Cf. Conrad Leyser, who argues that Damian's focus on sexual purity was conditioned by his calculation that the war against simony was both quixotic and destructive to the church, in "Peter Damian's 'Book of Gomorrah,'" *Romantic Review* 86 (1995): 206. So Damian, while consciously opposing what he saw as Donatism, remained convinced that clerical impurity robbed the faithful by effecting an essential change in the intended effects of the sacrament.

98 References to this biblical passage are especially apparent in Damian's *Liber gratissimus* (Damian, Ep. 40, "To Archbishop Henry of Ravenna," *Briefe* 1, pp. 404, 412, 413, 453; *Letters* 2, pp. 124, 131, 132, 167). In the context of the *Liber gratissimus*, however, Damian is ultimately applying the text to a different purpose, arguing for the efficacy of the sacrament in spite of an unworthy celebrant and the possible punishment he might incur for partaking undeservedly. The Pauline passage was the basis for the Eucharist as a form of ordeal. See H. C. Lea, *Superstition and Force: Essays on the Wager of Law – the Wager of Battle – the Ordeal – Torture*, 4th rev. edn (Philadelphia, PA: Lea Bros, 1892), pp. 344–51.

99 Damian, Ep. 61, "To Nicholas II," *Briefe* 2, p. 214; *Letters* 3, pp. 10–11; cf. Ep. 162, "To Archpriest Peter," *Briefe* 4, p. 146, and Ep. 47, "To an Unidentified Bishop," *Briefe* 2, pp. 45–6; *Letters* 2, pp. 254–5.

100 Francis L. Filas, *Joseph: The Man Closest to Jesus* (Boston, MA: St Paul Editions, 1962), p. 99.

101 Damian, Serm. 45, c. 8, *Sermones*, ed. Lucchesi, CC:CM, 57, p. 269; Ep. 162, "To Archpriest Peter," *Briefe* 4, p. 146.

102 Damian, Ep. 112, "To Bishop Cunibert of Turin," *Briefe* 3, p. 271.

103 Damian, Ep. 61, "To Nicholas II," *Briefe* 2, pp. 215–16; *Letters* 3, p. 11.

104 Damian, Ep. 31, "To Leo IX," *Briefe* 1, p. 316; trans. Blum, *Letters* 2, p. 38. On the priest's responsibility for the people and the grievousness of celebrating unworthily, also see Chasteigner, "Le Célibat sacerdotal," pp. 175–7.
105 See Lambert's discussion of the kind of spiritual paranoia endemic to this group (*Medieval Heresy*, pp. 107–8).
106 Damian, Ep. 112, "To Bishop Cunibert of Turin," *Briefe* 3, p. 272; Ep. 31, "To Leo IX," *Briefe* 1, p. 317; *Letters* 2, p. 39.
107 Damian, Ep. 162, "To Archpriest Peter," *Briefe* 4, p. 153.
108 Damian, Ep. 47, "To an Unidentified Bishop," *Briefe* 2, p. 50; *Letters* 2, p. 260.
109 See Lea, *History of Sacerdotal Celibacy*, 1, pp. 194–6, 227, 256; Fliche, *La Réforme grégori-enne*, 2, pp. 139–40; and Barstow, *Married Priests*, pp. 53, 57. On the resistance to the lay boycott, see Barstow, *Married Priests*, pp. 118, 133, 149–50; and Lea, *History of Sacerdotal Celibacy*, 1, pp. 296, 308.
110 Damian, Ep. 162, "To Archpriest Peter," *Briefe* 4, p. 156.
111 I am influenced here by Slavoj Žižek's analysis of the skinheads' demonization of outsiders. This is motivated by a sense that the other

> appears to entertain a privileged relationship to the object – the other either possesses the object-treasure, having snatched it away from us (which is why we don't have it), or poses a threat to our possession of the object. In short, the skinheads' "intolerance" of the other cannot be adequately conceived without a reference to the object-cause of desire that is, by definition, missing.
>
> (*The Metastases of Enjoyment: Six Essays on Woman and Causality* [London: Verso, 1994], p. 71)

See Landulf the Senior's description of the mob violence against married priests in *Mediolanensis historiae libri quatuor* 3.10, p. 93.

6

SECULAR CLERGY AND
RELIGIOUS LIFE

Verona in the age of reform

Maureen C. Miller

Traditional presentations of the reform movement of the central Middle Ages depended heavily on the accounts written by members of the new religious orders of the twelfth century, in particular by the Cistercians who had by the early thirteenth century emerged as the primary "winners" among the new monastic reform groups in France and England. Cistercian accounts from the period, not surprisingly, stressed problems within the older monasticism and the necessity of reform. But were such accounts of crisis in the older monasticism accurate? In this chapter Maureen Miller argues that in the diocese of Verona in northern Italy there is little indication of a crisis in monasticism. Indeed, she confirms the importance of traditional practices among many groups of both secular and monastic clergy. In the context of a rapid demographic growth and the cessation of local repercussions from the investiture quarrel between Pope and Emperor, reform came to mean local election rather than appointment by outsiders. Bishops were no longer the puppets of distant authorities, but had more direct interest in local diocesan business. In the diocese of Verona the life of apostolic poverty was construed as that of the poor and sick, and the local reform movement encompassed the foundation of new houses for monk and nuns, hospitals for lepers and others in need, and the creation of hermitages by the most austere. Local officials including the bishops encouraged such communities. The selections in this chapter come from Miller's The Formation of a Medieval Church: Ecclesiastical Change in Verona, 950–1150 *(Ithaca, NY: Cornell University Press, 1993), pp. 50–62, 71–4, 76/7–93, with notes renumbered and Latin quotations omitted.*

* * *

Two areas of change are most striking in the development of the secular clergy in Verona and its countryside over the eleventh and early twelfth centuries. First, institutional change slowly transformed their organization. Secular clerics increasingly formed *scole* (not exactly schools, but communities of priests) and collegiate churches which had come together by the twelfth century to form guild-like congregations. Second, new ideas about the secular clergy – about the appropriate ways for them to live and act, about their relation to lay society, and about the importance of their pastoral functions – informed and amplified these institutional changes. By the mid-twelfth century these new ideas produced higher expectations for the secular clergy but also greater esteem. The institutional reorganization of the clergy is the most immediately apparent change revealed by Veronese charters, and, over the eleventh and early twelfth centuries, numerous *scole* appear. Their formation was particularly intense in the city, but also occurred in the countryside. By 1021 there was a *scola* at the urban church of Santa Maria Consolatrice, and at Santa Maria Novella and San Guisto by 1035.[1] By 1055 there was a *scola* dedicated to Santa Maria, Sant'Agata and Santa Cecilia, and by 1083 another at San Siro.[2] *Scole* also were formed in rural parishes. The clergy of San Floriano in the Valpantena formed a *scola* by 1054, and there was a *scola* at Cerea by 1061.[3]

Why were so many *scole* formed in the eleventh century? To understand this development we must first consider the tenth-century Bishop Ratherius (ruled 932–5, 946–7 and 961–8) and his attempts at reform. The chief result of the canons' failure to support the minor clergy adequately, according to Ratherius, was that young clerics "hastened illegally to Holy Orders," before they were prepared intellectually or spiritually for priestly duties.[4] This need for priests, as the number of new churches increased over the eleventh century, certainly encouraged the development of *scole*.[5] Although the formation of *scole* seems to respond to a need to train more priests, these institutions also offered the opportunity for fellowship advocated by reformers in order to promote both discipline and spiritual devotion in the clergy. They were communities as well as centers of education. Even churches not designated as *scole*, especially rural *plebes* or parishes, developed communities of secular clerics in the eleventh century.[6] While the incidence of collegiality increases over the eleventh and early twelfth centuries, it is impossible to say if the newly founded clerical communities were living the kind of communal life advocated by reformers. We do not know if their members shared a common table, slept in a common dormitory, and celebrated the hours together. Certainly, in outlying *plebes*, which were usually responsible for several smaller village churches, a strict communal life would have been impractical. In the early Middle Ages, rural clerics were expected to come together only on the first of the month. After a mass, they were to share a meal, sing hymns, have "religious conversation," and discuss "things that happen in their parishes." A ninth-century manuscript in the Capitular Library containing a song for such a gathering suggests that the Veronese clergy were following this custom.[7] What became of this practice in the eleventh and twelfth centuries is unknown.

The documented reform of one urban church, however, reveals at least one compromise considered suitable for the life and work of secular clerics.

In February of 1046, the abbot of Santa Maria in Organo issued a series of directives to the secular clergy of a church subject to his monastery, Santa Maria Antica. With the approval of his monks and the "good neighbors" of the church, he ordered the priests of Santa Maria Antica to eat and to sleep "communiter" in a room adjacent to their church during Lent. Only if they were outside of the city of Verona, or ill, or engaged in some activity not for their own enjoyment or benefit could they be excused.[8]

Our sources do not reveal whether other communities of secular clerics adopted similar arrangements. What we do know is that over the eleventh century *scole* and other churches of the secular clergy began to attract lay donors. Usually these donors lived near the church they patronized (like the "good neighbors" who supported the abbot's reforms), and often they asked the prayers of its clergy. These gifts suggest that lay persons perceived communities of secular clerics as worthy recipients of support and as worthy intercessors for their souls. Whether or not these clerics would have won the praise of Roman reformers, they appear to have won the confidence of local donors.

The chronology of the formation of clerical communities is especially significant: these changes among the secular clergy occurred across the tenth, eleventh, and early twelfth centuries. The gradual pace of change is particularly important in assessing its causes. First, the gradual spread of *scole* parallels the multiplication of churches within the diocese. As instructional and formative institutions of the clergy, the new *scole* arose to meet the demand for clerics in a period of demographic expansion. Second, if the new confidence of lay donors in the secular clergy does denote some reformation of clerical life in the spread of clerical communities, then the chronology of that development suggests that clerical reform in Verona was a movement of local origin, not a reaction to Rome.[9] The spread of both *scole* and communities of clerics indicates continuity with tenth-century attempts at reform under Ratherius and a steady development through the eleventh century. This reorganization of the secular clergy was not a sudden change accomplished during or after the investiture crisis, and it was certainly not imposed from outside the diocese. It may have been supported and influenced by reform currents in northern Italy. But if the adoption of collegiality is a mark of "reform," then the Veronese clergy began their reform well before papal pronouncements demanded it.

The fact that some reform was already underway by the mid-eleventh century is also important. It helps explain why Verona did not experience the violent clashes associated with the reform era in other cities. Local historians have interpreted the obvious loyalty to the emperor and the lack of popular risings against the imperial Church as a total lack of reform in the city.[10] Yet the spread of *scole* and clerical communities suggests a slow and moderate reformation of clerical life, despite Verona's imperial allegiance. The Veronese maintained their traditional alliance with the German emperors as well as a strong local ecclesiastical tradition.

The manuscripts of the capitular library, in fact, demonstrate that local ecclesiastical life developed independently of the city's political affiliations from the tenth century. Ties with south German monasteries were very strong in the era of Carolingian domination. The liturgical calendars, musical notation, and plainsong melodies used by the cathedral clergy show the influence of Reichenau and St Emmeram, monastic centers that supplied several of Verona's bishops as well. Although Verona continued to receive its bishops from north of the Alps, beginning in the tenth century its liturgical life was more influenced by Italian contacts. Cantors adopted Nonantolan and central Italian musical notation; they also used Italian plainchant melodies.[11] A liturgical calendar from Monza appears in an eleventh-century manuscript used at the cathedral, and manuscripts copied in the canons' scriptorium survive most numerously in Italian ecclesiastical collections.[12] Despite continued German political domination, the Veronese Church from the tenth century was decidedly Italian.

The independence of Veronese ecclesiastical life, however, was not isolation. If the reform of the secular clergy was occurring gradually from the tenth century, the chronology of several changes nevertheless indicates the influence of papal reform efforts. Which reforms advocated by Rome did the Veronese clergy adopt? Although there is no evidence of opposition to lay investiture within the diocese, other reform tenets made a deep impact upon the Veronese clergy. Generally, the reforming councils held at Rome from the 1050s aimed to purify the clergy and to delineate more clearly the sacred and the profane. The canons of these councils demanded, for example, that clerics should not charge fees for administering the sacraments, should not have wives, should not bear arms or follow worldly professions, and should not frequent taverns.[13] The intent was to produce a clergy more noticeably distinct in life and morals from the laity. Adherence to these canons is, of course, difficult to gauge. Veronese charters offer us evidence, however, that by the early twelfth century the clergy had a greater sense than before of membership in a distinct and separate ecclesiastical order. They also suggest that by the twelfth century there was either a decline in clerical marriage and concubinage or at least a greater reticence about it in documents.

Let us first consider the "mulierositas" – the tendency to be married – of the clergy. Clerical marriage and concubinage were never completely stamped out. Verona's bishops throughout the Middle Ages had to repeat decrees against both, but, after 1122, the wives, concubines, and sons of priests disappear from notarial documents.[14] Couples such as "Toto priest of the church of Santa Maria outside the gate of San Zeno at the place called Fratta, and the woman Dodolenda living in the city of Verona near the Arena" were commonly mentioned in notarial documents through the eleventh century, but such couples do not appear after 1102.[15] References to sons of priests remain common for another two decades, and then become rare.[16] While this does not mean that clerical concubinage and marriage was eliminated, it does indicate that at least the principle advocated by the reformers was accepted.

Other changes in Verona's secular clergy are revealed in notarial formulas. Before the 1080s, priests in the Veronese diocese professed the law of their "race" or "tribe": Lombard, Salic, or Roman. In a document of 1082, however, a new clause appeared for the first time. Persenaldus, priest of the church of San Siro, declared that he lived by the Roman law "according to the order of the churches."[17] That an actual change of law was being required of priests is illustrated by the declaration of the priest Siginzo, "who used to profess by his race to live by the Lombard law, but according to the order of the churches he was seen to live by Roman law."[18] This profession of a different law, the law of the Church, evinces both a greater corporate sense among the clergy and a separation of the individual cleric from his past, his family, and their law, when he received Holy Orders.[19]

Even the cathedral chapter, which Bishop Ratherius in the tenth century saw as the chief impediment to reform, had definitely adopted a communal life by the early twelfth century.[20] This process can be traced in the notarial clauses indicating where chapter documents were redacted.[21] These clauses through the early 1080s indicate that canons were still living in houses clustered around the cathedral. In 1079, for example, the archdeacon of the chapter, Isnardus, had a document concerning lands of the canons, drawn up "in the two-story house of the aforesaid Isnardus."[22] By 1090, however, the archdeacon and other leaders of the chapter were having documents redacted not in their houses, but in their "rooms."[23] Where were these rooms? A document of 1118 specifies the location: "in the canonry of the holy Veronese church in the room of a deacon of that place."[24] Notarial designations stabilized in the 1120s: from this period on, the chapter's documents were redacted in the canonry or cloister of the Veronese church. A document of 1120 reveals that this cloister had a refectory, and one of 1133 was drawn up "before the door of the canons' dormitory."[25] Archaeological excavations corroborate, in fact, that the cloister of the chapter dates from approximately the early twelfth century.[26] The chronology of the chapter's reform in Verona seems to be about average for northern Italian cities.[27]

In addition to coming together in new communities and to following the Roman law of the Church, the Veronese clergy exhibited an even more expansive sense of corporatism in the formation of urban and rural Congregations of Veronese clergy known as the *Clerus Intrinsecus* (the urban clergy) and *Clerus Extrinsecus* (the rural clergy). The Congregation of urban clergy was formed by the very beginning of the twelfth century and its rural counterpart by the century's close.

The urban Congregation first appears in a donation of 1102.[28] The early documentation of the Congregation reveals that it was headed by an archpriest assisted by several other officials called *primicerii*.[29] It also suggests some of the impulses behind its formation. Several of the churches whose clergy were most active in the Congregation were sites of well-established *scole*. Daniel, archpriest of San Pietro in Castello, appeared with the archpriest of the Congregation and its *primicerii* in a document of 1103.[30] Several early documents of the Congregation were drawn up at Santo Stefano.[31] Another church prominent in the Congregation's early history was San Giusto, the site of a *scola* by 1035.[32] The formation of the Congregation thus seems related to the ongoing spread of collegiality among the Veronese secular clergy and the establishment of *scole* to train clerics.[33]

When documentation of the Congregation's membership appears, it is clear that it included the secular clergy of urban churches generally, but especially those exercising care of souls. Forty-nine of the fifty-nine churches inscribed as members by the early fourteenth century were parochial churches. Even parochial churches whose clergy were appointed by local religious houses – such as Santissima Trinità and San Giorgio in Braida – participated in the Congregation: care of souls brought them under the *Clerus Intrinsecus*. This composition and the chronology of its development suggest that one of the key forces behind the Congregation's formation was the devolution of pastoral care in the city from the cathedral to neighborhood parishes. Before the millennium, the care of souls throughout the city rested with the cathedral, but urban expansion over the eleventh century led to the emergence of parishes in the twelfth century. And when the boundaries of the urban parishes were defined in the late twelfth century it was the archpriest of the Congregation who was assigned the task.[34]

The division of pastoral care among the urban clergy gave them more responsibility. Ultimately it gave them more power, and the Congregation became the institution through which this new power was exercised. The Congregations controlled appointments to churches, and in 1185 Pope Urban III (1185–87) confirmed to the urban Congregation its "third share" in the election of the bishop (the rural Congregation and the cathedral chapter held the other two thirds).[35] By forming the two Congregations, the majority of the secular clergy kept the elite cathedral chapter from dominating diocesan government. With the development of the Congregations, the immense power of the cathedral chapter was finally effectively curtailed.

Like the guilds that provided these services for lay artisans, however, the Congregation also represented the interests of its members. It is the representation of these interests, especially against those of the cathedral chapter, which is foremost in the early documentation of the Congregation. Its archpriest, for example, was present with many clerics from urban churches at a legal judgment against the canons' claim to control the church of Sant'Alessandro in Quinzano.[36] The Congregation's right to participate in the election of the bishop and its direct control of several urban churches figures prominently in this twelfth-century documentation. Confraternity may have been sought by the Congregation's members, but these secular clerics also sought authority and representation within the ecclesiastical constitution of the diocese.

The secular clergy not only won these new jurisdictions, but also gained the approbation and support of the ecclesiastical hierarchy and the laity.

The papal curia entrusted several disputes to the judgment of the Congregation's archpriest in the twelfth century. Pope Alexander III (1159–81) submitted a matrimonial case to the archpriest in 1176.[37] The Congregation's archpriest was also among the leading ecclesiastics Pope Lucius III (1181–85) asked to resolve a dispute between the monastery of Santa Maria in Organo and two of its subject churches.[38] Lay support for the secular clergy is demonstrated in donations to the institutions of the secular clergy: their *scole*, their churches, and their Congregations. Such donations became numerous only in the eleventh and twelfth centuries.[39]

In sum, the secular clergy of the mid-twelfth century were very different from their early medieval forerunners. The Veronese clergy before the millennium were loosely organized around the cathedral chapter. The chapter was the only institution representing the secular clergy, and yet its canons were hardly representative: they were extraordinarily wealthy while most clerics were extremely poor. This elite chapter dominated the city's secular clergy and by the tenth century had produced a clergy ill prepared to administer pastoral care.

The expansion of pastoral care necessitated by a growing population underscored the need for change and encouraged the development of institutional forms to bring it about. The spread of *scole* slowly diminished the dominance of the cathedral chapter, tied the clergy more firmly to the bishop, and fostered communal life, as well as meeting the demand for clerics as the Church grew. These institutional developments and the new ideas of the reform era transformed the secular clergy. By the mid-twelfth century, the secular clergy were no longer dominated by the cathedral chapter. Although this institution remained prominent and powerful, the majority of the secular clergy was represented within the diocese by the new urban and rural Congregations. A large part of the clergy lived in clerical communities, either *scole* or collegiate churches. They professed a separate law and had accepted, at least in principle, the ideal of a life separate from and more rigorous than the laity's. They enjoyed greater support from the laity and assumed a prominent and respected role in the governance of the Veronese Church. The challenge of tremendous growth and expansion had been met with institutional creativity and reform.

* * *

Similarly, there is little evidence of decadence and decline in Veronese Benedictine monasticism. Indeed, there is a great deal of positive evidence for the continued popularity and vitality of the Benedictine life through the mid-twelfth century.[40] Eleven new Benedictine monasteries were built between 1000 and 1500 (nine for men and two for women).[41] Most of these houses are mentioned only in passing in the documents that survive: a small group of monks at the church of San Mauro in Saline, a monastery on the river Mincio cataloged among the possessions of the Veronese episcopate, and a new foundation at Nogara supported by the monks of Nonantola.[42] Some monks, as was common in the eleventh century, were propelled out of their houses by a desire to emulate the Desert Fathers.[43] In 1027 a Veronese notary described a piece of land as bordered on the north by an encampment of hermits – hermits of Saint Benedict.[44]

Some of the new foundations were proprietary monasteries built by local noble families. The monastery of Santo Stefano donated to Cluny by Albert of Bonavigo and his son Henry was surely such a private foundation.[45] The most successful new monasteries, however, appear to have been episcopal foundations.[46] The monastery of Santi Pietro e Vito di Calavena emerged in the remote mountains northeast of the city in the mid-eleventh century.[47] Around the same time, a monastery was built at the church of Santi Nazaro e Celso just beyond the city's walls.[48] Foundation charters do not survive for either house, but both had strong early ties to the Veronese episcopate. Bishop Walther (1037–55) had built a castle at Calavena, and one suspects that he may have had a hand in founding the monastery too.[49] The jurisdiction of the abbey was confirmed to the see in 1145.[50] San Nazaro received significant support from the bishop in its early years. In 1036, "considering the church of the holy martyr of Christ Nazaro destitute of its own means to be restored by the brothers gathered there," Bishop John (1015–37) made a sizable donation to the monastery "in order that there may always be a house of monks there"; the locations of both monasteries' patrimonies also suggest episcopal involvement.[51]

Both these traditional Benedictine foundations were highly esteemed within and beyond the local community. Pope Lucius III, just before his death in 1185, made the difficult trek to Calavena to consecrate a new church there; he also took the monks under his protection.[52] San Nazaro received gifts from a wide spectrum of donors: emperors; Verona's comital family, the San Bonifacio, and other local nobles; the notarial and judicial families of the city; artisans; persons living near the monastery; and donors from communities where the monastery held lands.[53] Pope Adrian IV (1154–59) in 1158 took the monastery under the protection of the Holy See.[54] And when a German baron returning from the second crusade was on his deathbed, he called on the abbot of San Nazaro to hear his confession and entrusted to the monastery the relics of Saint Blaise which he had acquired during his years in the Holy Land.[55]

Another mid-eleventh-century foundation with episcopal support, the monastery of San Giorgio in Braida, did not fare as well as Calavena and San Nazaro. Its failure, however, impugns not Benedictine monasticism, but papal–imperial politics. The foundation had an auspicious start. Its founder Cadalus was a cleric from a wealthy Veronese family who was trained in the cathedral chapter and had served Bishop Walther as *vicedominus*. In 1046, just after having been made bishop of Parma, Cadalus returned to Verona, secured a site on the banks of the Adige from Bishop Walther, and arranged for a monastery to be built using his substantial family inheritance. He carefully provided for the spiritual and material well-being of the monks, insisting that the monks should elect their abbot from among themselves; no one from outside the community should be made abbot. He placed the monastery under the protection of the bishop, but explicitly stated that the bishop had no power over it and could not alienate any of its lands either through leases or benefices.[56] Subsequent events in the career of San Giorgio's founder, Cadalus, who was elected to the papacy, but remains treated in history as an anti-pope, may have impeded the development of the monastery.[57]

The failure of San Giorgio to attract monks may be read as some censure of Cadalus himself or his involvement in the schism following his nomination as Pope, but fears about the monastery's future may also have made it a poor risk for a lifelong vow. The security of the monastery's patrimony may well have been in question because San Giorgio's lands bordered on significant holdings of the house of Canossa, and Beatrix of Canossa, countess of Tuscany in the first half of the eleventh century, and her daughter Countess Matilda (d. 1115), both of whom were avid supporters of the Roman faction.[58] When a Benedictine community finally did appear at San Giorgio in the 1070s, one of its first acts was to seek protection for its holdings.[59]

Ongoing conflict between the emperor and Rome also adversely affected the development within Verona of new congregations of Benedictines advocating a stricter interpretation of the rule.[60] In the early 1070s there was support within the city for a Vallombrosian foundation. John Gualbert (d. 1073), the Florentine monk who inspired the strict Vallombrosian interpretation of the rule, was still alive and had already acquired a reputation for sanctity through his bold promotion of reform.[61] Enthusiasm for his ideas and uncertainty in the local political climate allowed the cornerstone of the church and monastery of Santissima Trinità in the diocese of Verona to be set in 1073.[62] Despite the reconciliation of its count, Verona was not completely reconciled with the papal party until the Emperor made peace in 1111. Only after this settlement of political tensions did work on Santissima Trinità begin again.[63] It seems significant, moreover, that the first donation to support the renewed construction of the Vallombrosian church and monastery came from the d'Este family so often cited as mediators in the papal–imperial struggle.[64] In 1115 it was the Marquis Falco d'Este, son of Adalbert Azzo, who donated lands and pasture rights to the church and monastery of Santissima Trinità.[65] The establishment of a monastery of the reformed Vallombrosian congregation in Verona was, indeed, the fruit of political mediation. The church and monastery were finally consecrated on January 12, 1117.[66]

Ties with Benedictine reform movements north of the Alps, on the other hand, did not occasion controversy. The ancient Veronese monastery of Santa Maria in Organo established ties with the south German house of Benedikt-beuern in the mid-eleventh century. At the instigation of Emperor Conrad II (1027–39), the royal abbey of Benediktbeuern had been reformed in 1031. A new abbot and twelve monks were sent from Tegernsee, a monastery itself reformed in 982 under the influence of Saint Emmeram in Regensburg. Within a decade of Benediktbeuern's reform, its influence was radiating further south. By 1041, Santa Maria in Organo had received a new abbot, Ingelbero, from Benediktbeuern.[67] Unfortunately, no documentation illumines Abbot Ingelbero's impact on monastic life within Santa Maria's cloister.[68]

None of these developments in the Benedictine life in Verona, however, suggest a "crisis" of monasticism.[69] Not only did Benedictine houses founded before the millennium survive, but new monasteries, both male and female, were founded in the city and in the countryside. They received strong support from the Veronese bishops and from local donors. Benedictine reform movements also took root in the city; but their development was very strongly influenced by papal–imperial politics. Indeed Veronese evidence suggests a modification of the crisis thesis. Traditional Benedictine monasticism was not in decline in Verona in the eleventh and twelfth centuries, but new interpretations of the religious life nevertheless were developing. The emergence of new kinds of institutions for the religious life surely did signal an end to the pre-eminence the Black Monks had enjoyed in the early Middle Ages. But even these new interpretations of religious life owed much to monastic ideals.[70] The life of Saint Gualfardus (d. 1127) illustrates these continuities.

Gualfardus came to Verona from Augsburg with a company of merchants. Seeing what an agreeable place Verona was, Gualfardus remained in the city when the rest of his company returned to Germany. He worked as a saddler outside the city walls and, "chaste as the snow, inflamed with charity, sober in his humility, free of anger, great in constancy, long-suffering by virtue of his patience, compassionate with pity," he began to give whatever he earned to the poor and destitute.[71] His desire for eternal life and his longing to flee the vanity of this world, however, prompted him to leave the city secretly and go off into the forest of Saltuclo (not far from Verona on the Adige). He lived an austere and holy life there for twenty years.

There came a time, however, when it was pleasing to God that the works of blessed Gualfardus be made known to men. So the Lord pointed out the holy man to certain sailors navigating on the Adige and they took him on their boat to the city. There Gualfardus went to several churches doing good works. He stayed for a while at San Pietro in Monastero (near the cathedral); then, after a flood of the Adige, he went to the Vallombrosian church of Santissima Trinità. Finally, he took up residence at the church of San Salvar, where he lived in a tiny cell, in constant prayer and fasting, for ten years. People began to flock to the holy man: he cured the sick of fevers and fatigues, gave sight to the blind, cast out demons, and healed cripples. Even nature recognized the virtue of Gualfardus. When he went down to the Adige to wash his hands and fill his cup, fish would come to him. They would touch his hands and swim into his cup, not wanting to be put back into the river when he rose to leave.[72] After his death, miraculous cures of all kinds occurred at his tomb.

Gualfardus spent most of his life as a hermit and a recluse. Both his flight into the woods and his life of austerity in the cell at San Salvar would have been entirely comprehensible to those who lived under Benedict's rule. But Gualfardus began his religious life caring for the poor outside the city walls, and, having been sent back to the city by God, he ended his life curing the sick, the crippled, the blind, and the deranged. These acts of mercy, which captivated his contemporaries, signal a new focus in religious life. While Gualfardus's sojourn in the wilderness recalls the tradition of Saint Anthony, his compassion for the poor, and even the fish touching his hands, presage a new spirituality, one usually attributed to the great mendicant orders of the thirteenth century. These new visions of the religious life were well established in Verona by 1150.

The subsequent history of Cadalus's troubled monastic foundation provides a good example of the new kinds of religious life which emerged in the early twelfth century. Although founded in 1046, it was not until after Cadalus's death that a monastic community appeared at San Giorgio in Braida. In a document of 1075 an abbess, not an abbot, is named.[73] Richarda governed the monastery from 1075 to at least 1096. She rented, exchanged, and sold its lands and received donations. She also sought and received renewed imperial support.[74] A charter of 1096 also reveals that the church of San Giorgio had been designated a *plebs* and that it was being administered by a *scola* of secular clerics headed by an archpriest.[75]

This community of cloistered women and the adjacent *scola* of secular clerics appears to have coexisted without problems under the leadership of the Abbess Richarda. After her death, difficulties seem to have arisen. A charter of November 1101 recorded Amharda as abbess, and then from 1109 to 1111, Armengarda. Suddenly in 1113 there was an abbot, Martin.[76] The next document concerning the monastery gives the first evidence of the bishop's intervention to reform the house. On July 22, 1121, Charles, the son of the monastery's longtime advocate Godo, was forced to renounce advocacy of the monastery and his fief into the hands of Bishop Bernard (1122–35). The reason given was the "very, very great evil which he very frequently committed against the venerated place of San Giorgio in Braida, and, finally because of the great plunder of mares which he had driven to Sabbion."[77]

Weak and changeable leadership after the death of Richarda seems to have allowed the supposed protectors of the monastery to take advantage of its patrimony. This was exactly the sort of lay behavior that Cadalus's foundation charter had tried to deter. A series of inventories of the lands of San Giorgio dating from this period indicate the first task facing the new leadership: the reconstitution of the monastery's patrimony.[78] Aided by a grant of tithes from the bishop, Peregrinus, the reformer hand-picked by the bishop to lead the monastery, began buying property and arranging advantageous exchanges of lands with other religious houses to accomplish this task.[79]

The formal charter outlining Bishop Bernard's reform of the monastery, however, alludes not only to temporal disarray, but also to moral decay. He characterized the house as "having been destroyed" in both a spiritual and temporal sense. "First," the bishop explained, "it had been a monastery of women and afterwards of monks. But in either case it was a brothel of Venus, a temple of the devil more than of God."[80] The bishop's solution to this problem, however, is most important. He did not turn to a "reforming" order, or any revamping of Benedictine monasticism at all, despite the stated wishes of the founder eighty years earlier that there should always be a house of Black Monks there. "Having therefore expelled the blasphemers of God from that place," wrote Bernard, "I ordained religious clerics in it who, by the grace of God, lead the celibate life of canons and observe the canonical rule." He named Peregrinus as *praepositus* of all the brothers serving God there.[81] In order to reform San Giorgio, Bernard instituted a house of regular canons.

What sort of religious life did these canons lead? How did it differ from Benedictine monasticism? Bishop Bernard, like other contemporaries, gives us only rather vague outlines. As noted above, they lived under and had the right of electing a *praepositus*. They observed a "canonical rule." According to this rule, they said Matins and the rest of the Hours and at these times they were allowed to ring bells. Bernard also relinquished authority over the temporal goods of the house, "in order that they may serve God more freely."[82]

To which "canonical rule" was Bernard referring? Most regular canons were identified as living by the Rule of Saint Augustine, but each congregation usually adopted a set of canonical practices or customs as well. Several of these sets of guidelines for houses of regular canons were in circulation in the early twelfth century, originating in the most successful foundations. Institutes from the houses of Saint Victor in Paris, Saint Ruf in Avignon, the canons of Saint John Lateran, and those of the Ravennese house of Santa Maria in Porto offered specific injunctions for the ordering of the religious life of canons.[83] In 1132 a bull of Innocent II described the canons of San Giorgio in Braida as living by the Rule of Saint Augustine.[84] In 1186 Urban III's bull confirmed at San Giorgio "the canonical order according to the Rule of Blessed Augustine and the institutes of the brothers of Porto."[85] The lives outlined by these canonical rules and the Rule of Saint Benedict differ only subtly. Both prescribe a liturgical life organized around the Hours. The cycle of Hours used by the canons seems only slightly less time-consuming than the Benedictine. The Rule of Porto lists seven Hours to the Benedictine eight, eliminating Prime. The number of psalms, hymns, and readings outlined in the Augustinian rule is slightly less than in the Benedictine.[86] Beyond the liturgical life of the Hours, how did the canons spend their time?

They seem not to have cultivated learning as much as the Black Monks. Chapter 18 of the first book of the Rule of Porto does not assume an entirely literate congregation and treats the hubris of the learned as a real danger. Entitled "If those, who are literate, should dare to teach something," the chapter asserts:

> If some fittingly humble canons, not arrogant according to the degree of their knowledge of erudite letters, and full of knowledge of divine scripture, thus are able to offer something useful to others, and the prior shall have approved it as just and seen it as necessary, with all kindling of hatred and jealousy at once removed, let him allow them [to teach], or urge them to labor in those things whose knowledge he will have seen as more necessary and useful.[87]

Literacy is here viewed as a potent incitement to sin, leading to pride, envy, and hatred. So great is this danger, it seems that learning should not be pursued for its own sake. Unlike the monks of San Zeno who delighted in the classical authors, the canons of San Giorgio allowed only what learning was necessary and useful.

Wary of erudition, the regular canons seem to have devoted themselves instead to the service of others in the world. In his prologue to the rule, Peter of Onesti described exactly what the apostolic life of the canons should be. He called his followers to abandon the "business of the world," but Peter's idea of abandoning the world is markedly different from the Benedictine notion. He continued:

> Therefore let them love fasting, let them comfort the poor, let them gather in guests, let them clothe the naked, let them visit the sick, let them bury the dead, let them serve the oppressed, let them console the sorrowful, let them weep with the weeping, rejoice with the joyful, let them not forsake charity, if possible let them have peace with all, let them fear the day of judgment, let them desire eternal life above all, let them put their hope in God, let them put nothing before the love of Christ, let them obey the orders of their prelates in all things, let them comply with their own bishop in all things according to the canonical institutes, and finally, let them devote work to spiritual teachings, readings, psalms, hymns, canticles and let them persevere unfailingly in the exercise of all good works.[88]

The very order of these exhortations is revealing. The liturgical life – spiritual doctrines, psalms, hymns – comes last, even after obeying the bishop and other prelates. Highest on Peter's list of apostolic callings is fasting, caring for the poor, clothing the naked, and visiting the sick. These acts of self-denial and charity are ranked even before the general exhortations to seek eternal life and put Christ before all. There is, in fact, a strong orientation toward the world and its problems in the canons' idea of abandoning the world.

These ideals seem particularly well suited to San Giorgio's location and circumstances. Its church was the *plebs* in a growing suburban neighborhood, along the road north to Trent outside the Porta San Stephano. Charters drawn up at San Giorgio give us a glimpse into this neighborhood served by the new regular canons. It was full of millers and dyers working along the river, with builders and artisans along the road to the city and the narrower streets veering off it. Many of its inhabitants labored in trades related to transit: blacksmiths, saddlemakers, and shoemakers. Butchers appear frequently, their bloody line of work relegated to neighborhoods outside the city.[89] It was in the same type of suburban quarters, among workers and the poor, that the mendicants would settle in the thirteenth century. Already in the early twelfth century, however, the regular canons of San Giorgio dedicated themselves to a life of charity beyond the city walls.

As a new interpretation of the religious life, the orientation of the regular canons toward the world reveals a new direction in medieval spirituality.[90] This new direction is even more clearly evident in the emergence of another type of institution for the religious life, the leper hospital. There were institutions in early medieval Verona, the *xenodochia* or hospices (literally *xenodochia* are institutions caring for strangers, but usually with a religious component in their foundation), that cared for the sick and the poor. These institutions, however, differed in a fundamental way from the new hospitals of the sick or lepers which emerged in the twelfth century. Such *xenodochia* or hospices of the early Middle Ages were adjuncts to religious institutions. They were nearly always physically separate from the church or monastery controlling them and juridically distinct, having their own patrimonies. They constituted only a part, and usually a minor part, of the religious life of the controlling institution.[91]

The leper hospitals of the twelfth century, in contrast, were themselves religious houses, with a religious life completely devoted to the poor and sick. They were a new type of institution representing an entirely novel interpretation of the religious life. Monasteries administered some *xenodochia*, but most were under the care of the cathedral canons. Santa Maria in Organo administered at least three, and San Zeno and San Fermo each supervised one.[92] This latter *xenodochium*, however, passed from San Fermo to the canons around the millennium. The canons also administered the *xenodochia* founded by Pacificus, Notker, Dagibert, Gotefredus, Aldo, and Arduin and one located at San Giovanni in Valle.[93] The supervising institutions would assign one or two of their members to look after the *xenodochium*. In August of 1114, for example, a priest and cathedral canon named Ilderadus was *praepositus* of the *xenodochium* at San Giovanni in Valle. Zeno, a subdeacon of the cathedral was "keeper and rector" of the same *xenodochium* in December of that year.[94]

The care of the poor and sick in the *xenodochia* was only part of the work of the institutions that controlled them and never involved all of the institutions' members. The leper hospitals founded in the twelfth century were, in contrast, independent institutions, totally devoted to the care of the poor and sick. These institutions, in their dedication to the most vulnerable and reviled members of Christian society, most clearly express the new spirituality emerging in the twelfth century.

Several leper hospitals were founded in Verona along the Adige outside the city walls during the twelfth century. Santa Croce was the earliest, founded by the fourth decade of the twelfth century. The lepers of Santa Croce first appear in a document of 1136 when a certain Crescentius bought them several pieces of land. Their hospital was located outside the city, "below San Fermo."[95] By 1141, it had its own oratory: Bishop Tebaldus consecrated the church "of the poor and infirm brothers of the hospital of the Holy Cross [Santa Croce] and of holy charity" on Sunday, April 6.[96]

Lands were purchased for the hospital through an agent and donated to the brothers of the hospital. The most revealing documentation for the early organization of the hospital, however, stems from a disagreement requiring the intervention of the bishop in 1146. Contention had arisen between a certain Lord Hugo, whom Bishop Tebaldus had appointed to administer the hospital, and the lepers who were there. The lepers claimed that they "ought to rule and divide the goods and alms which God and men gave," but the bishop, "knowing their badness, their plotting, and the fornicating going on among some of them, which had even created and generated children," said that they did not have the right to administer the goods of the hospital. They had only the right always to be fed and cared for there as paupers and guests. Tebaldus gave the rectors and administrators of the hospital the right to punish, excommunicate, and expel any who entered into plots or fornicated.[97]

This dispute reveals several things. First, there were obviously both male and female lepers in the hospital! Second, in this document and other early records of the hospital, the only distinction made is between the lepers and the administrators. This implies that the "brothers and sisters" were the lepers. The designation of those who act on their behalf also bears out this interpretation. Crescentius was identified interchangeably as "treasurer" of the "sick" and "treasurer of the brothers in the place of and in the name of the sick." That the lepers felt entitled to administer and divide the goods of the hospital was understandable: donations were addressed to "you, the brothers of the hospital of the sick."[98]

The situation became no clearer as the confraternal character of the house intensified in the second half of the twelfth century. By the 1160s both the lepers and those who assisted them were called brothers and sisters, and a remarkable document of 1164 reveals the acceptance of a couple into a confraternal relationship with the house. On a Monday in June Count Riprandus of the Gandolfingi dal Palazzo and his wife Garscenda made a sizable donation to the hospital. The following day, in the church of Santa Croce and in the presence of "many lepers," the count and countess "were accepted as brother and sister of the house of the lepers." Donations and sales continued to be made to the brothers and sisters of the hospital, and in the early thirteenth century the lepers again protested that they owned the property given to Santa Croce.[99]

Throughout the twelfth century the hospital was run by lay-persons. Not until 1156 do we find a cleric associated with Santa Croce. This priest, named Lemizo, was a constant witness to the transactions of the house from 1156 to his death in 1171. Lemizo, however, appears only as a witness: the business of the house was still being transacted by lay-persons.[100] In addition to the Crescentius mentioned at Santa Croce, a certain Adam, son of Sparello, bought lands as an agent of the "sick" in 1141.[101] A document of 1149 styled John as "*gastaldus*" (perhaps warden?) of the "sick" of Santa Croce and "*gastaldus*" of the poor.[102] By the 1160s the hospital had a "keeper and rector," a *gastaldus*, a treasurer, a warehouse-keeper, a key-keeper, and a notary.[103] By the end of the twelfth century these lay-persons assisting the lepers were called *conversi*, the term used for the lay-brothers associated with other groups like the Cistercians or Cluniacs.[104] Just as the lay-brothers of Benedictine monasteries hoped to share in the spiritual benefits of the monks by supporting their religious life, so these lay-persons hoped to share the spiritual benefits of the poor lepers by supporting them.

This suggests a very different notion of the religious life. To *be* poor and infirm was a religious life, a Christ-like life. While the monks of the early Middle Ages lived a religious life by leaving the world and praying, the lepers of Santa Croce lived a religious life by being poor and sick, by being a suffering presence in the Christian community. They did in fact provide a new spiritual center for the Christian community of Verona. Bishop Tebaldus in 1141 decreed that every year on the anniversary of the consecration of Santa Croce or within its octave:

> all Christian men and women should peacefully and devoutly come
> [to the church of Santa Croce] to pray and to ask forgiveness for their
> infirmities and they should offer something of their goods to the
> charity of the brothers and the poor and sick.[105]

The bishop's invitation to *all* Christians draws attention to another important aspect of the new spirituality Santa Croce represents: it was radically inclusive. By equating holiness with weakness and poverty, rather than with ascetic virtuosity and learning, it offered all Christians an opportunity to achieve spiritual perfection. This was a notable departure from the exclusivity that characterized religious institutions and theories of spiritual perfection in the early Middle Ages. The tenth-century Ratherius of Verona, in his *Praeloquia*, was one of the earliest theologians to envision, at least theoretically, forms of spiritual perfection lay-persons could attain.[106] Two centuries later, with the emergence of institutions like Santa Croce, the pursuit of holiness became more than just a theoretical possibility for all Christians. The institutions of the religious life, and the ideals to which they were devoted, changed in Verona over the eleventh and early twelfth centuries.

NOTES

1 *Archivio Capitolare, Verona*, hereafter *ACV*, I–5–iv (calp. mp n4); *Archivio di Stato, Verona*, hereafter *ASVR*, S. Anastasia, no. 4.

2 *ASVR*, S. Maria in Organo, nos. 28, 52.

3 *ASVR*, Orfanotrofio Femminile, no. 20; *ACV*, III–6–35 (AC 60 m4 n12).

4 Ratherius of Verona, "Urkunden und Akten zur Geschichte Rathers in Verona," ed. Fritz Weigle, *Quellen und Forschungen aus italienischen Archiven und Bibliotheken* 29 (1938–9): 1–40, here 26–7.

5 The demand for clergy to meet the needs of a rapidly expanding population also helps explain some of the abuses addressed by eleventh-century reform legislation. For instance:

> So that orders are given according to the decrees of the Holy Fathers. Namely, that no subdeacon be ordained before the age of 20, no deacon before 25, no priest before 30, unless there is great need. But even granting that, no priest should be ordained before the age of 25.
>
> (Giovanni Mansi, *Sacrorum conciliorum nova et amplissima collectio*, vol. 20, col. 400, hereafter Mansi)

The Roman Council of 1059 and the Council of Melfi in 1090 also repeated injunctions against ordaining clerics before they reached canonical age. Mansi, vol. 19, col. 915; vol. 20, col. 723. The Council of Rouen in 1074 restated the minimum canonical age for ordination to the priesthood as thirty years, but allowed that this requirement might be waived in cases of urgent need. Even then, however, bishops were exhorted not to ordain anyone under the age of twenty-five. The Councils of Gerona (1068 and 1078), Rouen (1074), Winchester (1074), Rome (1078), and Benevento (1091) all published canons with the prohibition of accepting priests without letters attesting to their ordination. Mansi, vol. 19, col. 1071; vol. 20, cols 400, 508, 520, 739.

6 Archpriests appear at many of these rural churches, suggesting that the presence of several clerics required the elevation of one to a position of authority and leadership. They appear at the *plebs* of Santa Maria in the Valpantena as early as 1010, the *plebs* of San Zeno in Roverchiara by 1041, and the *plebs* of Santa Maria in Valle Fontense by 1060. *ASVR*, S. Maria in Organo, no. 44, app.*; S. Anastasia, no. 5; Ospitale Civico, no. 53. Giuseppe Forchielli, "Collegialità di chierici nel veronese dall' VIII secolo all' età comunale," *Archivio veneto*, series 5.3 (1928): 1–117, here 58–9, also finds archpriests at San Martino in Lazise, San Giorgio d'Illasi, and Sant'Andrea di Sommacompagna.

7 Gerard Giles Meersseman, *Ordo fraternitatis, fraternite e pietà dei laici nel medioevo*, 3 vols (Rome: Herder, 1977), vol. I, pp. 113–21; quotes taken from ninth-century decree of Bishop Ricolufus of Soissons, pp. 115, 158–9.

8 *ASVR*, S. Maria in Organo, no. 54 app.*.

9 Here my findings concur with Johannes Laudage, *Priesterbild und Reformpapsttum im II. Jahrhundert* (Cologne: Böhlau, 1984), especially pp. 304–10.

10 *Verona e il suo territorio*, 7 vols (Verona: Istituto per gli studi storici veronesi, 1960–9), vol. 2, pp. 145–9, 171.

11 James Matthew Borders, "The Cathedral of Verona as a Musical Center in the Middle Ages: Its History, Manuscripts, and Liturgical Practice," 2 vols (PhD diss., University of Chicago, 1984), vol. I, pp. 199, 219, 274–6, 282, 392–3; eds Gerard Giles Meersseman, E. Adda, and Jean Deshusses, *L'orazionale dell'archidiacono Pacifico e il Carpsum del Cantore Stefano: Studi e testi sulla liturgia del duomo di Verona dal IX all' XI secolo* (Fribourg: Éditions universitaires, 1974), pp. 30–1, 54–5, 57, 66. Bishops Egino (780–803) and Ratoldus (803–40) were monks of Reichenau; Bishop Nottingus

(840–4) had strong contacts with Mainz: Guglielmo Ederle, *Dizionario cronologico bio-bibliografico dei vescovi di Verona* (Verona: Vita Veronese, 1965), pp. 26–8.

12　Gerard Giles Meersseman, "Il codice XC del Capitolare di Verona," *Archivio Veneto*, series 5, 104 (1975): 11–44, here 28–34.

13　Mansi, vol. 19, cols 245, 395; vol. 21, col. 513.

14　Bishop Norandinus in 1219 forbade priests to have concubines; Bishop Peter della Scala (1290–5) devoted one of his eighty-nine synodal canons (no. 37) to clerical marriage; and Bishop Tebaldus III repeated this same canon in the early fourteenth century. Luigi Bellotti, "Gli statuti sinodali dei Vescovi Adelardo II (1188–1214) e Norandino (1214–1224)," in *Ricerche intorno alle costituzioni del capitolo della cattedrale di Verona nei secoli XIII–XV* (Venice: La deputazione editrice, 1943), pp. 54, 59, 63. The disappearance of clerical wives from notarial documents is not due to any broad change in how couples are described, for the wives of laymen continue to appear in the same notarial formula.

15　*ASVR*, Ospitale Civico, no. 55 (1071); other examples: *Archivio Segreto Vaticano*, hereafter *ASV*, Fondo Veneto, no. 6756 (1020); *ASVR*, S. Stefano, no. 4 (1059); *ACV*, II–5–4r (AC 38 m2 n4) (1070); *ASVR*, SS Nazaro e Celso, no. 630 (1102).

16　*ASVR*, S. Michele in Compagna, no. 3 app. (1088); S. Silvestro, no. 1 (1107); *ASV*, Fondo Veneto, nos. 6857 (1111), 6852 (1119); *ACV*, II–6–6r (AC 24 m3 n11) (1122); *ASVR*, Clero Intrinseco, reg. 13 (Ist. Ant. Reg. I), fol. 19 (1124). See also *ASVR*, S. Anastasia, no. 17 (1141).

17　*ASVR*, Clero Intrinseco, reg. 12 (Ist. Ant. Reg. II), fol. 196.

18　*ACV*, I–6–2r (AC 71 m3 n5). Although a sixth-century council and several Carolingian capitularies held that the Church followed the Roman law, by the tenth century many clerics (like those in Verona) were professing the laws of their nations. In the late eleventh century, however, clerics began using Roman law again, invoking a capitulary of Louis the Pious. Thus, in 1086 Bishop Rainulfus of Chieti prefaced an exchange of lands with "as is written in the law: let every ecclesiastical rank live and act according to the Roman law." *RIS* 2.2: 1002. Simeon L. Guterman, "The Principle of the Personality of Law in the Early Middle Ages," *University of Miami Law Review* 21 (1966): 297–9. I thank Tom Head for this reference.

19　I have found no evidence that this profession of Roman law by the clergy was specifically advocated by reformers. Neither the collections of canons circulating in Italy, nor the surviving canons of the reform era councils required it, but many of the canons for these councils are lost. Paul Fournier, "Les collections canoniques romaines de l'époque de Grégoire VII," *Mémoires de l'institut national de France – Académie des inscriptions et belles-lettres* 41 (1920): 271–395; *The Collection in Seventy-four Titles*, trans. and ann. John Gilchrist (Toronto: Pontifical Institute of Medieval Studies, 1980), chs 138–59, 170–3, on priests; Anselm of Lucca, *Collectio canonum*, ed. Fridericus Thaner (Innsbruck: Librariae Academicae Wagnerianne, 1906), Liber VII, on the clergy, 2, pp. 357–434. Perhaps the general recourse to Roman law by the eleventh-century reformers strongly linked reform to Roman law in the minds of local clerics. See also Aloïs Van Hove, *Prolegomena* (St Mecheln: 1945), chs 209, 216–19, 221, 223, 231; Gabriel Le Bras *et al.*, *Histoire du droit et des institutions de l'Église en occident*, volume VII: *L'âge classique* (1140–1378) (Paris: Sirey, 1965), p. 168; *DDC* 4: 1505.

20　The chapter's patrimony was administered in common, but individual canons did hold personal property in addition to whatever they received from the chapter. The documents of the capitular archive reveal canons buying, selling. and donating their own property. A few examples: *ACV*, II–5–7r (AC 59 mp n2); III–7–3v (BC 44 mp n12) [copy in Guiseppe Muselli, *Memorie istorich, cronologiche, diplomatiche, canoniche, e critiche del Capitolo e Canonici della Cattedrale di Verona*, *ACV*, buste DCCCXXXII–DCCCXLVIII]: III–7–6v (AC 68 m5 n12); II–7–2r (AC 14 m5 n14).

An extreme faction of the Gregorian party wanted to require canons to give up their personal property, but this position was never legislated. The Roman council of 1059 required only that the goods of the church be shared communally. Mansi, vol. 19, col. 898; Cosimo Damiano Fonseca, "Gregorio VII e il movimento canonicale: Un caso di sensibilità gregoriana," *Benedictina* 33 (1986): 11–23. The canons of Pistoia also adopted the communal life but retained personal property. See Yoram Milo, "From Imperial Hegemony to the Commune: A Reform in Pistoia's Cathedral Chapter and Its Political Impact," in *Istituzioni ecclesiastiche della Toscana medioevale* (Galatina: Congedo, 1980), pp. 87–107, here pp. 95–6.

21 The changes in these redaction clauses are not related to changes in formulary or type of document.

22 *ACV*, II–5–5v (BC 53 m2 n4).

23 Luigi Simeoni, "Antichi Patti tra signori e comuni rurali nelle carte veronesi," *Atti e memorie della Accademia di agricoltura, scienze, e lettere di Verona* 83 (1906–7): 54: *ACV*, II–6–4r (BC 37 m5 u9).

24 *ACV*, III–7–5r (BC 33 m5 n2).

25 *ACV*, B–6–5v, doc I, "in refectorium canonicorum," I–6–4r (AC 12 mp m11) also mentions the refectory. For the dormitory, *ACV*, II–6–7r (BC 46 m3 n2), doc II; another reference, II–6–7v (AC 27 m4 n7).

26 Cinzia Fiorio Tedone, "Tombe dipinte altomedievali rinvenute a Verona," *Archeologica veneta* 8 (1985): 270–1. I think the changed architecture of the chapter's surroundings provides persuasive evidence of reform. Cf. Maria Venturini, *Vita ed attività dello "scriptorium" veronese nel secolo XI* (Verona: la Tipographica Veronese, 1930), pp. 45–6; Meersseman, *L'orazionale*, pp. 105–6.

27 Padua's early eleventh-century reform is precocious. For a few chapters, like those of Lodi and Aquileia, there is no evidence of the communal life until the mid to late twelfth century. For Pistoia, see Milo, "From Imperial Hegemony," pp. 87–8; for Florence, George W. Dameron, *Episcopal Power and Florentine Society, 1000–1320* (Cambridge, MA: Harvard University Press, 1991), p. 50; for Vicenza, Giorgio Cracco, "Religione, Chiesa, pietà," in *Storia di Vicenza*, eds Alberto Broglio and Lellia Ruggini (Vicenza: Neri Pozza, 1987), vol. 2, p. 382, note 142; for Aquileia, Padua, Lodi, Mantua, Bologna, and Volterra, the articles by Spiazzi, Barzon, Caretta, Montecchio, Fasoli, and Cristiani in *La vita comune del clero nei secoli XI e XII* (Milan: Vita e pensiero, 1962), vol. 2, pp. 131, 139, 151–3, 168–9, 196–7, 247. Bernold of Constance also attests that the communal life was spreading throughout the *regnum Teutonicum* in the late eleventh century; Alfred Haverkamp, *Medieval Germany 1056–1273*, trans. Helga Braun and Richard Mortimer (Oxford: Oxford University Press, 1988), p. 186.

28 *ASVR*, Clero Intrinseco, reg. 13 (Ist. Ant. Reg. I), fol. 107.

29 In an exchange dated 1103, the archpriest Boniface was joined by the priests and *primicerii* Toto, Alboynus, and Winiza. In a rental agreement of 1116 there were also three *primicerii*: Toto, Dominicus, and Blanchus. *ASVR*, Clero Intrinseco, reg. 13 (Ist. Ant. Reg. I), fols 17, 18, 107.

30 *ASVR*, Clero Intrinseco, reg. 13 (Ist Ant. Reg. I), fols 17, 18.

31 *ASVR*, Clero Intrinseco, reg. 13 (Ist Ant. Reg. I), fols 17, 18, 107.

32 *ASVR*, S. Anastasia, no. 4.

33 *ASVR*, Clero Intrinseco, reg. 12 (Ist. Ant. Reg. II), fol. 19.

34 This formation of parishes within the urban center occurred in other cities of the Veneto in the late eleventh and early twelfth centuries and the emergence of associations of the secular clergy was common in the wake of this division of the urban *plebs*. There was an association of the secular clergy at Treviso by 1078, one in Venice by 1105, and the "brotherhood of chaplains" is attested at Padua by 1136; see Paulo Sambin, *L'ordinamento parrochiale di Padova nel medioevo* (Padua: CEDAM, 1941), pp. 9–14, 23–9, and Antonio Rigon, "L'associazionismo del clero in una città

medioevale: origini e primi sviluppi della 'fratalea cappellanorum' di Padova (XII–XIII sec.)," *Pievi, parrocchie e clero nel Veneto*, ed. Paolo Sambin (Venice: La Deputazione editrice, 1987), p. 103. See also Rigon's detailed study of this institution, *Clero e città: "fratalea cappellanorum," parroci, cura d'anime in Padova dal XII al XV secolo* (Padua: Istituto per la storia ecclesiastica padovana, 1988), pp. 21–2. Many of the functions exercised by these clerical congregations in Italy (e.g. clerical appointments and discipline) were carried out by archdeacons in German dioceses. See Lawrence G. Duggan, *Bishop and Chapter: The Governance of the Bishopric of Speyer to 1552* (New Brunswick, NJ: Rutgers University Press, 1978), pp. 41–3; Karlotto Bogumil, *Das Bistum Halberstadt im 12. Jahrhundert* (Cologne: Böhlau, 1972), pp. 186–94.

35 The late twelfth-century documentation of the Congregation reveals the election and investiture of archpriests to their churches. See *ASVR*, Clero Intrinseco, reg. 12 (Ist. Ant. Reg. II), fol. 103 for the election and investiture of the archpriest of Ognissanti in 1184; G. B. Biancolini, *Notizie storiche delle chiese di Verona*, 8 vols (Verona: A. Scolari, 1749–71), vol. 4, pp. 545–7 provides the first hint we have of the existence of the *Clerus Extrinsecus*. The first direct reference to the rural Congregation does not appear until 1295. Cf. Laura Castellazzi, "Aspetti giuridici nella vita di chiese e monasteri del territorio in epoca medioevale," *Chiese e monasteri nel territorio veronese*, ed. Giogio Borelli (Verona: Banca Popolare di Verona, 1981), pp. 316–24; Antonio Spagnolo, "Il clero veronese nella elezione del vescovo, 1080–1338," *Atti e memorie della Accademia di agricoltura, scienze, e lettere di Verona* 84 (1907–8): 100–5, for 1295 document. Other clerical congregations were not as successful; see Antonio Rigon, "Le elezioni vescovili nel processo di sviluppo delle istituzioni ecclesiastiche a Padova fra XII e XIII secolo," *Mélanges de l'École française de Rome: moyen age–temps modernes* 89 (1977): 371, 385, 392–3, 404–5.

36 *ASVR*, S. Martino d'Avesa, no. 1.

37 Paul F. Kehr, *Regesta pontificum romanorum. Italia Pontifica* (Berlin: Weidemann, 1906–), (hereafter Kehr, *Italia Pontifica*), vol. 7.1, p. 246.

38 Kehr, *Italia Pontifica*, vol. 7.1, p. 278.

39 Robert I. Moore, "Family, Community, and Cult on the Eve of the Gregorian Reform," *Transactions of the Royal Historical Society*, series 5, 30 (1980): 56–7, 60, also sees a connection between the increased importance of the clergy in the eleventh century and the expansion of settlement. He points out the social importance of having a church and a priest to form a "focus of social activity and organization" in new communities.

40 Monastic foundations in nearby Padua were as numerous. Fourteen new houses emerged in the eleventh and twelfth centuries. As in Verona, some were episcopal foundations, others proprietary monasteries built by leading families. Giannino Carraro, "I monasteri benedettini della diocesi di Padova," *Benedictina* 35 (1988): 91–2, 122.

41 The founders of neither of these new female houses are known. In 1081 an inscription records the foundation of Santa Maria delle Vergine in Campo Marzio. San Pancrazio, a house subject to the older convent of San Michele, is first documented in 1133. Biancolini, *Chiese* 2: 748–9; 4: 700–1. In addition to new foundations, older monasteries for women grew in wealth and prestige. San Michele in Campagna, founded before the millennium, received numerous donations in the eleventh century. Among the rights acquired by the nuns was that of holding an annual fair; the revenues derived from this fair made San Michele a wealthy and powerful monastery in the twelfth century. Valeria Monese Recchia, "Aspetti sociali ed economici nella vita di un monastero benedettino femminile, S. Michele in Campagna di Verona dal secolo XI al periodo ezzeliniano," *Archivio veneto*, series 5, 98 (1973): 5–54.

42 BC, Mss. Lodovico Perini, b. 26, document dated September 25, 1145; Biancolini, *Chiese* 3: 320–1; "Cenni Storici," [1145 bull of Eugene III], ed. G. B. Pighi, *Bollettino ecclesiastico veronese* 6 (1919): 150–7, here p. 152; Kehr, *Italia Pontifica*, vol. 7.1, p. 301.

43 Henrietta Leyser, *Hermits and the New Monasticism. A Study of Religious Communities in Western Europe, 1000–1150* (London: Saint-Martin's Press, 1984), pp. 18–37.

44 *ASV*, Fondo Veneto, no. 6762.

45 Auguste Bernard and Alexandre Bruel, *Recueil des chartes de l'abbaye de Cluny*, 6 vols (Paris: Imprimerie nationale, 1876–1903), vol. 5, pp. 86–7 (no. 3736).

46 Verona is not unusual in this regard. See Geo Pistarino, "Monasteri cittadini genovesi," and Pietro Zerbi, "I monasteri cittadini di Lombardia," both in *Monasteri in alta Italia dopo le invasioni saracene e magiare (sec. X–XII)* (Turin: Deputazione subalpina di storia patria, 1966), pp. 248–9 (Genoa), p. 287 (Milan), pp. 295–7 (Brescia), pp. 309–11 (Como); Giovanni Tabacco, "Vescovi e monasteri," in *Il monachesimo e la riforma ecclesiastica (1049–1122) (Atti della quarta settimana internazionale di studio – Mendola, 23–29 agosto, 1968)* (Milan: Vita e pensiero, 1971), pp. 106–13; Bogumil, *Das Bistum Halberstadt*, pp. 63–76, 101.

47 Castagnetti, Kehr, and Biancolini all place the monastery's foundation in the early twelfth century and name Pellegrinus as its first abbot. Biancolini, *Chiese* 2: 568–9 and 4: 714; Andrea Castagnetti, "Aspetti economici e sociali di pievi rurali, chiese minori, e monasteri (secoli IX–XII)," in *Chiese e monasteri nel territorio veronese*, ed. Giorgio Borelli (Verona: Banca Popolare di Verona, 1981), p. 122; Kehr, *Italia Pontifica*, vol. 7.1, p. 295. They cite a document of 1133 (*ASVR*, SS Nazaro e Celso, no. 318, March 21, 1133) as the monastery's first. The document here cited, enacted at the monastery in June of 1068, is in the capitular Archive: *ACV*, I–5–5r (AC 59 m4 n8).

48 Lorenzo Tacchella, "Le origini dell'abbazia dei SS. Nazario e Celso di Verona," *Studi storici veronesi* 20–1 (1970–1): 13–14.

49 An inscription, now at the Museo Castelvecchio, was erected by the bishop along with the castle: "In the year of our Lord 1040, this code was raised at the sole expense of Bishop Walther," Gianni Faè, *Badia Calavena* (Verona: Vita veronese, 1964), pp. 6–7, and Biancolini, *Chiese* 2: 571.

50 "Cenni," ed. Pighi, p. 155.

51 *ASVR*, SS Nazaro e Celso, no. 434; Tachella, "Le origini," pp. 74–5. The bishop gave two-thirds of the manor of Corliano and several other holdings. Calavena is on the northwest frontier of the diocese and the patrimony of San Nazaro on the ill-defined western border with Vicenza. Both patrimonies are also strategically located around the stronghold of the San Bonifacio family, which at the time of both these foundations was just securing its hold on the Veronese countship. The foundations of both seem to be part of episcopal efforts to expand its influence in those regions and check the rising power of the San Bonifacio. Cf. Dameron, *Episcopal Power*, pp. 32–5, 52–3; Pistarino, "Monasteri cittadini genovesi," pp. 249, 259; Tabacco, "Vescovi e monasteri," pp. 109–11. In contrast, episcopal support of the suburban monasteries San Nazaro and San Giorgio in Braida may also have been an effort to counterbalance the power of the cathedral canons in the city. For examples of this in Mantua, Modena, and Reggio Emilia, see Paolo Golinelli, *"Indiscreta sanctitas." Studi sui rapporti tra culti, poteri, e società nel pieno medioevo* (Rome: Instituto storico italiano per il Medio Evo, 1988), pp. 72–7.

52 Faè, *Badia*, pp. 8–9; Kehr, *Italia Pontifica*, vol. 7.1, p. 296.

53 Respectively, *ASVR*, SS Nazaro e Celso, nos. 40 and 42; Tachella, "Le origini," pp. 75–6, 82–4; Count Albert, his brother Mainfred, and their mother, Richelda, ceded their rights in Corliano. *ASVR*, SS Nazaro e Celso, no. 437; Tachella, "Le origini," pp. 79–80. The widow and sons of the viscount Walfred and the "nobilissima femina" Richarda also made gifts: *ASVR*, SS Nazaro e Celso, nos. 914 and 314; the "iudex" Sentichus and his brother gave the monastery a piece of land in 1090,

and in 1118 a "vicedominus" and his sons donated lands in the Val d'Illasi: *ASVR*, SS Nazaro e Celso, nos. 1679 and 806, and no. 915. For those living in the neighborhood outside the Porta Organo: *ASVR*, SS Nazaro e Celso, nos. 628, 641, 2232; in Montorio, *ASVR*, SS Nazaro e Celso, nos. 967, 1534; in Colognola, nos. 313, 314, 315, 317; in Lavagno, nos. 627, 629, 630, 631.

54 Tachella, "Le origini," pp. 85–6.

55 Tachella, "Le origini," pp. 88–9.

56 *ASV*, Fondo Veneto, nos. 6764, 6766, 6769, 6770, 6771, 6772, 6791, 6792, 6793; Cadalus was from a family of castellans in the Veronese *contado*. His grandfather was one of the inhabitants of the castle at Calmano; another branch of the family held the castle of Sabbion. Cadalus' father, Ingo, acquired a house in Verona in 1005 and in one document was styled viscount. With his two brothers, Erizo and John, Cadalus acquired a significant amount of property in the area between Lonigo, Cologna and Orti in the early eleventh century. He first appeared in a document of the Veronese chapter in 1028 identified as "clericus." By 1030, he was a subdeacon; by July 31, 1034, he had been ordained a deacon. From 1041 he also served as the bishop's *vicedominus*, a chief administrator. By 1045 Cadalus had been ordained a priest and made bishop of Parma. Vittorio Cavallari, "Cadalo e gli Erzoni," *Studi storici veronesi* 15 (1965): 63, 95, 116–24, 130–40, 153–8.

57 When Pope Nicholas II died in 1061, one group of cardinals nominated Cadalus to the Holy See, and, following Nicholas's own decree on papal elections, sought out the Emperor for his consent to the nomination. Another faction nominated Anselm, bishop of Lucca, and enthroned him as Pope Alexander II (1061–73). Cadalus, meanwhile, received the emperor's endorsement and was made Pope Honorius II (usually considered an anti-pope, 1061–72). Neither election was strictly canonical, but three years later Alexander triumphed. Before Cadalus's election, San Giorgio had received a grant of imperial protection, donation of a mill from Verona's bishop, and a quitclaim from Cadalus's Lombard relatives; *MGH*, *Diplomatum regum et imperatorum Germaniae* (Berlin: Weidmanns, 1879), hereafter *MGH, Dipl.*, vol. 5: 407 (no. 298); *ASV*, Fondo Veneto, nos. 6805, 6800. Two documents illumine the period of Cadalus's pontificate; both concern his relatives. The first, coinciding with his election as Pope, records a promise by three cousins to stop their molestation of the monastery's lands. The second, executed a year later by one of these cousins, is in the form of a donation but is more likely a renunciation of claim to a piece of San Giorgio's property; *ASV*, Fondo Veneto, nos. 6809, 6812. More than a decade of documentary silence follows.

On the evidence of several caustic letters by Peter Damian (d. 1072) Cadalus has been characterized as an example of the kind of corruption the reformers fought: "... why do you, with your ambition (namely, that of a single man), throw the whole Church of Christ into disorder?" Damian demanded of Cadalus; he continued likening Cadalus to a sword sundering the Church: "And so in this way you who had been a son of the holy Church were made a sword used against her" (no. 88). Damian also made subtle accusations of simony in his denunciations of Cadalus (no. 89); Peter Damian, *Die Briefe des Petrus Damiani*, ed. Kurt Reindel, 3 vols (Munich: Monumenta, 1988), vol. 2, pp. 515–72 (nos. 88 and 89, to Cadalus) and vol. 3, pp. 384–92 (no. 120, to Henry IV). The charge of simony reverberates through Damian's denunciation: he chides Cadalus for succumbing to aspirations and allowing himself to be used by the Emperor to sow dissension in the Church. But Cadalus was not a simoniac, nor a "heresiarch." It was Anselm of Lucca, not Cadalus, who had to purge himself of accusations of simony at the Council of Mantua in 1064 at which Damian was present; it condemned Cadalus as anti-pope and a schismatic, not a simoniac. Mansi, vol. 19, cols 1029–31. This characterization is neither fair nor particularly helpful for understanding the eleventh-century Church. Held notably by P. Cenci, "Documents inediti su la famigla e la giovinezza dell'Antipapa Cadalo," *Archivio storico per le province parmensi* n.s. 23 (1923): 94–5, it has been dismantled by Cavallari, "Cadalo," pp. 94–101, Cadalus was, surely, ambitious. Considering his family's social pretensions, it would be surprising if he were not. At worst, Cadalus was a rather traditional churchman: not particularly ascetic in his personal piety, but a man who freed his slaves and gave them land (*ASV*, Fondo Veneto, no. 6844), a supporter of episcopal dignities and prerogatives, and a generous donor to traditional ecclesiastical institutions. His family's ties were to the Emperor but in the 1060s this was not a reactionary position. In Cadalus's recent memory, Emperor Henry III (1043–56) had brought good and pious men to the Holy See. From 1046 to 1048 the Emperor had wrested the papacy from the control of local factions. He then elevated two short-lived German clerics as Popes Clement II (1046–7) and Damasus II (1047–8), finally succeeding with the elevation of his cousin, the reformer Bishop Bruno of Toul, as Pope Leo IX (1048–54). No doubt Cadalus saw his own nomination in 1061 as the continuation of these reforms. Cavallari, "Cadalo," pp. 69–72, 97–8; Uta-Renate Blumenthal, *The Investiture Controversy* (Philadelphia, PA: University of Pennsylvania Press, 1988), pp. 92–8; and Michael Stoller, "Eight Anti-Gregorian Councils," *Annuarium historiae conciliorum* 17 (1985): 254–63.

58 San Giorgio's patrimony was concentrated north and east of the Adige on the plain around Cologna Veneta, Lonigo, Bonavigo, Sabbion, and Carpi. Just to the south and west of the Adige (especially between the Adige and the Po) were numerous lands of the house of Canossa. See the map appended to Thomas Gross, *Lothar III. und die Mathildischen Güter* (Frankfurt am Main and New York: P. Lang, 1990). Canossan interests in extending influence northward are clear. In the 1070s Countess Matilda supported the foundation of a Vallombrosian house in Verona, and in the early twelfth century the Veronese counts, the San Bonifacio, became her vassals.

59 In a *placitum* on March 13, 1077 in Verona, Abbess Richarda of San Giorgio begged that the Emperor's ban might protect her, her advocate, her monastery, and all its goods. Manaresi, *Placiti* 3: 340–1 (no. 440).

60 Reformed monasteries were one of the most effective ways Matilda and her allies spread their influence, and fear of this political infiltration, not hostility to reform, is what frustrated the spread of new reformed foundations. Under Countess Matilda, Canossan power was concentrated on the southern border of the diocese, ripe for expansion into the Veronese plain. The influence exerted by the monasteries of Farfa and Fonte Avellana opened most of the Marches to the papal party: Elisabetta Archetti Giampaolini, *Aristocrazia e chiese nella Marca del centro-nord tra IX e XI secolo* (Rome: Viella, 1987), pp. 269–85.

61 Gualbert had also recently (1068) driven the simoniac bishop of Florence from his see. On Gualbert and the Vallombrosian congregation, see B. Quilici, *Gualberto e la sua riforma monastica* (Florence: 1943); on his successful political struggle in Florence, see Dameron, *Episcopal Power*, pp. 51–5.

62 Nicola Vasatura, "L'espansione della congregazione Vallombrosana fino alla metà del secolo XII," *Rivista di storia della Chiesa in Italia* 16 (1962): 456–85.

63 The German emperor, Henry IV (1084–1105) was politically weak, beset by revolts in Germany, and Verona's bishop, Bruno (1072–80), accepted the *pallium* from Rome, and a visit from the papal supporter Countess Matilda of Tuscany (d. 1115). In August of 1073, she had ceded some contested lands to San Zeno and, according to local tradition, founded the church of Santissima Trinità. By 1077, after Henry had regained political initiative at Canossa, work on the church came to a halt, and did not begin again until political tensions were resolved later. In 1106 the Veronese Count Albert of the San Bonifacio family came to a reconciliation with Matilda and Pope Pascal II (1099–1118) in Verona, but the unfriendly climate within the city forced the countess and the pontiff to leave and to abandon plans to proceed north to Germany through Veronese territory. Ferdinando Ughelli, *Italia Sacra*, 2nd edn,

9 vols (Venice: Sebastianus Coleti, 1717–22), vol. 5, pp. 767–8; Mario Carrara, "Novecento anni di vita sul Monte oliveto," in *SS Trinità in "Monte Oliveto" di Verona* (Verona, 1974), p. 47; Andrea Castagnetti, *La Marca Veronese-Trevigiana* (Turin: UTET, 1986), pp. 37–8, 43.

64 At Canossa in 1077 the Marquis Adalben Azzo d'Este in 1077 was one of those at the side of Pope Gregory VII (1073–85) who urged the pontiff to have mercy upon Henry IV; Castagnetti, *La Marca*, p. 36.

65 *Codice diplomatico padovano*, ed. Andrea Gloria (Venezia: Deuptazione veneta di storia patria, 1877, 1881), vol. 2, pp. 58–9 (no. 71). A note at the bottom of the witness list of this document indicates that the monks were already present in 1115: "Hoc fuit actum post ingressus fratrum in predicto monasterio sex dies minus tredecim mensium."

66 *Annales Sanctae Trinitatis, MGH, SS*, vol. 19: 2.

67 Ties to the reforming monasteries of south Germany were loosely organized, usually for the life of an abbot, and then lapsing. Kassius Hallinger, "Progressi e problemi delta ricerca sulla riforma pre-gregoriana," in *Il monachesimo nell'alto medioevo e la formazione dell civiltà occidentale* (Spoleto: Presso la sede del centro, 1957), p. 272; Romuald Baurreiss, *Kirchengeschichte Bayerns* (St Ottilien, 1949–70), vol. 2, pp. 32, 112. There is, for example, no evidence that Santa Maria in Organo continued to have any ties with Benediktbeurn after the tenure of Abbot Ingelbero. *ASVR*, S. Maria in Organo, no. 23; *Chronicon Benedictoburanum, MGH, SS*, vol. 9, p. 226 (lines 33–5). Saint-Emmeram, in turn, had strong ties with Gorze, Kassius Hallinger, *Gorze-Kluny* (Rome: Herder, 1950), vol. 1, pp. 129–31, 133–6, 158–9; Cf. Constance B. Bouchard, "Merovingian, Carolingian, and Cluniac Monasticism: Reform and Renewal in Burgundy," *Journal of Ecclesiastical History* 41 (1990): 365–88.

68 A decree of 1046, however, does show Ingelbero instituting reforms at an urban church under the jurisdiction of the monastery, and one suspects a similar increase in rigor had already taken place at the mother house; *ASVR*, S. Maria in Organo, no. 54 app.*.

69 On this issue of a crisis in monasticism, see Jean Leclercq 1958 article in French, translated as "The Monastic Crisis of the Eleventh and Twelfth Centuries," in *Cluniac Monasticism in the Central Middle Ages*, ed. Noreen Hunt (London: Macmillan, 1971), pp. 217–37, and John van Engen, "The 'Crisis of Cenobitism' Reconsidered: Benedictine Monasticism in the Years 1050–1150," *Speculum* 61 (1986): 269–304.

70 André Vauchez, *Les laïcs au Moyen Age: pratiques et expériences religieuses* (Paris: Cerf, 1987), pp. 97–101.

71 *Vita S. Gvalfardi solitarii, AA:SS*, April 3, 828E.

72 *Vita S. Gvalfardi solitarii*, 829A–B.

73 *ASV*, Fondo Veneto, no. 6818.

74 *ASV*, Fondo Veneto, nos. 6821, 6822, 6827, 6835, 6836, 6837, 6841, 6842, 6843.

75 *ASV*, Fondo Veneto, no. 6843; also published in Andrea Castagnetti, *La Valpolicella dall'alto medioevo all'età comunale* (Verona: Centro di Documentazione per la Storia della Valpolicella, 1984), pp. 193–94 (no. 38).

76 *ASV*, Fondo Veneto, nos. 6848, 6853, 6854, 6858, 6859.

77 *ASV*, Fondo Veneto, no. 6876. Parchments nos. 6877 and 6894 are also refutations of fiefs and judicial rights from this same period.

78 *ASV*, Fondo Veneto, nos. 6874, 6895.

79 *ASV*, Fondo Veneto, nos. 6880, 6886; purchases: nos. 6890, 6898, 6905, 6909, 6910, 6911, 6915, 6916, 6917, 6920; exchanges: nos. 6908, 6919, 6921, 6922. The reform of San Giorgio also sparked numerous donations: nos. 6881, 6888, 6891, 6893, 6899, 6912, 6928 (all during the tenure of Peregrinus).

80 *ASV*, Fondo Veneto, no. 6886.

81 *ASV*, Fondo Veneto, no. 6886.

82 *ASV*, Fondo Veneto, no. 6886.

83 Carlo Egger, "Le regole seguite dai canonici regolari nei secoli XI e XII," *La vita comune del clero nei secoli XI e XII* (Milan: Vita e pensiero, 1962), vol. 2, pp. 9–12. See also Reginald Grégoire, *La vocazione sacerdotale: I canonici regolari nel medioevo* (Rome: Edizioni Studium, 1982), pp. 29–37.

84 *ASV*, Fondo Veneto, no. 6901; Kehr, *Italia Pontifica*, vol. 7.1, p. 260.

85 Kehr, *Italia Pontifica*, vol. 7.1, p. 264. The earliest house of regular canons in Venice, Santa Maria della Carità, also appeared in 1121, and it too adopted the rule of Santa Maria di Porto. Antonio Fabris, "Experienze di vita comunitaria: I canonici regolari," *La chiesa di Venezia nei secoli XI–XII*, ed. Franco Tonon (Venice: Studium Cattolico Veneziano, 1988), p. 76; it is not surprising that the canons of San Giorgio should have looked to those of Santa Maria in Porto for a successful model of religious life. Of the most famous early foundations, the canons of Porto at Ravenna were the closest geographically and therefore probably the best known to the Veronese. The founder of Santa Maria in Porto had just died at around the time of the reform of San Giorgio. Peter of Onesti (or Peter the Sinner), founded the canons of Porto in 1096. Just before his death in 1119, his rule had been confirmed in 1117 by Pope Paschal II (1099–1119). This rule was clearly meant to be used in conjunction with that of Saint Augustine, given the varying degrees of detail and generality on different topics. L. Holstenius, *Codex regularum monasticarum et canonicarum*, 6 vols (Augsburg: I Adami und F. A. Verth 1759), vol. 2, pp. 138–75, and 162 (book 3, ch. 1). For the history of Santa Maria in Porto, see Carlo Egger, "Canonici regolari di Santa Maria in Porto," *Dizionario degli istituti di perfezione* (Rome: Edizioni paoline, 1974–), vol. 2, pp. 147–8.

86 The standard night offices in both include at least twelve psalms, although the Augustinian Rule shows more seasonal variation (its year is divided into three parts each requiring a different number of psalms; in the Benedictine Rule the year is divided only into two periods, November to Easter and Easter to November). Lauds is considerably longer in the Benedictine Rule. It consists of four psalms, two canticles, lauds, one lesson, a hymn, a benediction, the Kyrie, and the Lord's Prayer. In the Augustinian Rule, Lauds is simply three psalms. The rest of the Hours in the Augustinian Rule usually include three psalms, a reading, and a closing prayer, whereas the Benedictine Rule requires a hymn, versicles, and the Kyrie. Benedict of Nursia, *Regula monachorum*, ed. Cuthbert Butler (Fribourg: B. Herder, 1912), pp. 41–53, chs 8–18; Adolar Zumkeller, *Augustine's Ideal of the Religious Life*, trans. Edmund Colledge (New York: Fordham University Press, 1986), pp. 283–300, Réginald Grégoire, *La vocazione sacerdorale: I canonici regolari del medioevo* (Rome: Studium, 1982), pp. 85–101.

87 Holstenius, *Codex* 2: 148 (book 1, ch. 18).

88 Holstenius, *Codex* 2: 143.

89 The charters of San Giorgio are teeming with workers of all sorts: millers (*molinarii*): *ASV*, Fondo Veneto, nos. 6982, 6996, 7002; dyers (*tinctores*): nos. 6973, 6997, 6998, 7011; craftsmen (*fabri*): nos. 6560, 6974, 6995: masons (*murarii*): nos. 6983, 7013; blacksmiths (*ferrarii*): *ASV*, Fondo Veneto, nos. 7000, 7015; a saddler (*sellarius*): no. 6560; shoemakers (*calcearii*): nos. 6995, 6996; butchers (*beccarii, masselli*): *ASV*, Fondo Veneto, nos. 7008, 7009, 7019, 7020.

90 Scholars are correct in pointing out that what distinguished the regular canons from the Benedictines was a difference of emphasis; the Veronese saw this shift in focus embodied in the regular canons as particularly suited to the work of reform. In this they seem inclined to agree with Peter the Venerable that "In the religious life it is easier to found than to restore, to make something new than to repair what has existed for a long time"; see *The Letters of Peter the Venerable*, 2 vols, ed. Giles Constable (Cambridge, MA: Harvard University Press, 1967), vol. 1, p. 43 (no. 23), and Caroline Walker Bynum "The Spirituality of the Regular Canons in the Twelfth Century: A New Approach," *Medievalia et Humanistica* n.s. 4 (1973): 19–20, who

characterized this distinction as "the quality of their [the canons'] sense of responsibility for the edification of their fellow man." The new emphasis on poverty in the institutes of the regular canons had important ideological implications, relating to the rise of the mendicant movements a century later. See Cosimo Damiano Fonseca, "La povertà nelle sillogi canonicali del XII secolo: Fatti istituzionali e implicazioni ideologiche, "in *La povertà del secolo XII e Francesco d'Assisi* (Assisi: [s.n.], 1975), pp. 151–77, and Grégoire, *La vocazione*, pp. 38–48, 124–45.

91 A *xenodochium*, in classical usage, was a hostel for travelers, but by the eighth century was a place that also cared for the poor, widows, and orphans. Most early medieval *xenodochia* were founded by clerics, usually by leaving in their wills a house to be given over to the care of the poor. In 844, for example, the archdeacon Pacificus ordained in his will that his house in Quinzano should be made into a *xenodochium*. He instructed that on the anniversaries of his and his sister's deaths 140 paupers and twelve priests ought to be fed with bread, vegetables, meat, and wine. Pilgrims were also to be fed on these occasions, and on each Saturday during Lent a certain amount of food was to be distributed to the poor. The priest Rado in 774, Bishop Notker in 921, and the deacon Dagibert in 931 also willed that *xenodochia* be established in their houses. Others were founded by the nobility: a charter of 837 mentioned two royal *xenodochia* in the city of Verona and in 908 the Veronese Count Anselm founded a *xenodochium* "for the feeding of Christ's poor." *Codice Diplomatica Veronese*, ed. Vittorrio Fainelli (Venice: Deputazione di storia patria per le Venezie, 1940–63), hereafter *CDV*, vol. 1, no. 176; *CDV*, vol. 1, no. 50; vol. 2, nos 177 and 214; one at the gate of San Fermo and another called Calaudusua: *CDV*, vol. 1, no. 147; and for quote *CDV*, vol. 2, no. 88. In the ninth and tenth centuries, *xenodochia* founded as independent institutions increasingly came under the jurisdiction of larger ecclesiastical entities such as monasteries and chapters. Vittorio Fainelli, "L'assistenza nell'alto medioevo: I xenodochi di origine romane," *Atti del Reale istituto veneto di scienze, lettere, ed arti* 92 (1932–33): 918–24.

92 The proliferation of hospitals was characteristic of the spirituality of the central Middle Ages. Their origins were diverse; often foundations were the work of lay confraternities, as Meersseman, *Ordo fraternitatis*, vol. 1, pp. 136–49, shows for after the eleventh century. Vauchez, *Les laïcs*, pp. 97–101, linked lay confraternities to a more positive valuation of penance in religious life spread among the laity by hermits and reformed Benedictine congregations. Hospitals were founded by monasteries, bishops, urban churches, individual patrons, and lay confraternities. Some hospitals do not differ markedly from early medieval *xenodochia*, but most, and especially leper hospitals, tended to be more independent. See Pierre De Spiegeler, *Les hôpitaux et l'assistance à Liège (Xe–XVe siècles)* (Paris: Les belles lettres, 1987), p. 147; John Hine Mundy, "Charity and Social Work in Toulouse, 1100–1250," *Traditio* 22 (1966): 203–8, esp. p. 239; Joseph Avril, "Le IIIe concile du Latran et les communautés de lépreux," *Revue Mabillon* 60 (1981): 21–35; and statutes for leper hospitals published in Peter Richards, *The Medieval Leper and His Northern Heirs* (Cambridge: D. S. Brewer, 1977), pp. 123–43. One of Santa Maria in Organo's was in the city at Cortalta, originally founded by Lupo, and another was near the monastery. Fainelli claims the monastery held the *xenodochium* founded by Notker, but the bishop clearly placed this foundation under the care of the cathedral canons. By 987, however, the monastery did control the *xenodochium* of San Siro. *CDV*, vol. 1, no. 178; *ASVR*, S. Maria in Organo, no. 38: *ACV*, III–5–4v (/C 8 m2 ns). For those controlled by San Zeno and San Fermo, *CDV*, vol. 1, nos. 172, 50.

93 *CDV*, vol. 1, no. 176; vol. 2, nos. 177 and 214; *ACV*, II–4–7v (BC 20 m2 n2), II–4–7v (AC 38 m5 n4), I–5–5r (BC 36 m5 n10), III–6–4v (AC 28 m2 n3).

94 *ACV*, I–6–3r (AC 52 m2 n14) and I–6–2v (AC 31 m2 n1).

95 *ASVR*, Istituto Esposti, no. 1 and S. Silvestro, no. 2. A. Rossi Saccomani, *Le carte dei lebbrosi di Verona fra XII e XIII sec.* (Padua: Antonore, 1989), was published only after I had completed the archival research for this study.

96 *ASVR*, S. Silvestro, no. 5, app. The development of Santa Croce follows a pattern similar to other leper hospitals. Lepers seem to have gathered together on unoccupied lands outside a city gate where they attracted the assistance and alms of those entering and leaving. A loose network of those assisting the lepers usually developed into a confraternity. The establishment of a chapel or the assignment of a chaplain brought the community under episcopal supervision. De Spiegeler, *Les hôpitaux*, pp. 57–60, 105–110.

97 *ASVR*, Istituto Esposti, no. 4.

98 *ASVR*, Istituto Esposti, nos. 5, 6, and no. 1, app.; *ASVR*, Ospitale Civico, no. 75 (document 2).

99 *ASVR*, Istituto Esposti, no. 9; in the early thirteenth century the bishop and the commune forced the lepers of various small hospitals to join the hospital of SS Jacopo e Lazaro della Tomba. The lepers resented being deprived of the property given to them, "malsanis et pro malsanis." See Giuseppina de Sandre Gasparini, "L'assistenaza ai lebbrosi nel movimento religioso dei primi decenni del duecento veronese: Uomini e fatti," *Viridarium floridum* (Padua: Antenore, 1984), pp. 25–59.

100 *ASVR*, S. Silvestro, no. 9, app.; only at the very end of the twelfth century do priests begin to act in the name of the sick. In 1183 a priest named Crescentius bought a piece of land for the church, but not until 1199 did a priest act "on account and in the name" of Santa Croce. *ASVR* Istituto Esposti, nos. 23 and 32.

101 *ASVR*, Ospitale Civico, no. 75.

102 *ASVR*, Istituto Esposti, no. 1, app.

103 *ASVR*, Istituto Esposti, nos. 7, 9, 12, 17.

104 The term appears for the first time in a document dated November 2, 1199, *ASVR*, Istituto Esposti, no. 32.

105 *ASVR*, S. Silvestro, no. 9, app.

106 Ilarino da Milano, "La spiritualità dei laici nei *Praeloquia* di Raterio di Verona," *Raterio da Verona* (Todi: Accademia tudertina, 1973), pp. 35–93, especially p. 75ff.

7

THE CARDINALS'
VIEW OF THE PAPACY,
1150–1300

Norman Zacour

Traditional accounts of the battle between Church and State have emphasized the conflict between two important leaders, emperor and pope, and their importance at the top of their respective hierarchies of State and Church. Popes and their supporters presented the Papacy as the sole head of both Church and State – and, in their pictorial schemes, they seem to be presenting the pope as a sole individual. Such hierarchical notions are what are represented in Figure 3.2 (p. 74), where a hierarchical diagram illustrating the writing of Gilbert of Limerick places the pope (papa) on top. More recently, there has been reconsideration and historians have insisted that theories of authority from the central Middle Ages also had strong notions about consultation. King, emperor, and pope were all seen as acting with the consultation of their advisors or councilors in court. This image of the king and his major vassals acting in concert, or of the pope acting with his cardinals, was a reflection of the image of Heaven in which Christ at the Last Judgment would act in consultation with the saints, including his mother, as we see in the cover/frontispiece illustration from the apse mosaic at Santa Maria in Trastevere, Rome. Images of the papal authority consisting of the pope acting in consultation with his court, or their justification, are what Norman Zacour investigates here. What was the Papacy and did it comprise the pope alone? Or was the bishop of Rome's local college of priests, the cardinals, part of what constituted the Papacy and its universal authority? These are not mere technicalities, but concerned the proper actions of the leader of the Roman Church.

In the central Middle Ages many cathedral canons who constituted the electors for bishops first organized themselves into a corporate chapter or college of canons, then often rebelled against the authority of the bishop and wrested agreements from him regarding their rights – for instance, to a division of revenues. This certainly was the case with the priests attached to the bishop of Rome, the cardinals, the papal electors who by the twelfth century had established themselves as a corporation with rights to a separate stream of revenues. Indeed, as Zacour explains in this chapter, the cardinals saw themselves as part of the body that called itself the Papacy. The cardinals, like many cathedral chapters, demanded their rights: to a set proportion of

*revenues, to consultation, and to the esteem of particular ceremonial attire and treat-
ment. Rarely totally united in opposition to the authority of the pope, because there
were always some who were the appointees of the current incumbent, they were
often at odds about papal elections. Although the principles of the Gregorian reform
about how Church leaders were chosen began to be enforced, the new institution of
election was not easily adopted in Rome. Who were the electors, what constituted
a majority, should only those present at a particular place have a vote, were the
votes of senior members given added weight? These issues brought with them several
serious schisms in the twelfth century (in the 1130s and again in the 1150s and
1160s) and in the fourteenth century as well. All these issues had to be addressed
both in local and papal elections. Here, Zacour considers the debates over whether
cardinals were part of the Papacy or if this consisted solely of the pope alone
and also how the cardinals viewed themselves as part of the growing power of the
Church in the central Middle Ages. He draws extensively on the views of the canon
lawyer Henry of Susa, also called Hostiensis, who died in 1271, and on those of
John the Monk, Jean Lemoine, a cardinal of the early fourteenth century. This chapter,
presented first as a conference paper at the Pontifical Institute of Mediaeval Studies
in Toronto in May 1985, first appeared in a volume called* The Religious Roles
of the Papacy: Ideals and Realities 1150–1300, *edited by Christopher Ryan
(Toronto: Pontifical Institute, 1989), where the interested reader will find more
extensive Latin notes.*

* * *

If, for the moment, we take our stand at the end of the thirteenth century,
when the college of cardinals had perhaps reached the apogee of its development, we shall find ourselves in the presence of an oligarchy of great
dignity, influential in the distribution of a large amount of patronage, exert-
ing wide political influence, and viewed at the time, whether with favor or
not, as men of great wealth and power. We shall also be confronted with
some well-developed metaphors about the successors of the apostles:[1] pillars
of the church of God; part of the pope's body; the *cardines* – the hinges – upon
which the great door of the universal church swings;[2] senators of the church,[3]
reminiscent of the senators of the Roman empire now absorbed into the
Christian body politic; *patres conscripti* – enlisted fathers – as Francesco
Petrarca (Petrarch, better known as a poet, d. 1374) would later call them,
of the Christian church. There were other more material signs of their importance: the red hat that Innocent IV (1243–54) allowed them to wear to go
with the many other symbols that marked them off from other churchmen;[4] and their display of high rank in the large number of attendants
who accompanied them in public. They were churchmen and laymen
alike, who by the fourteenth century would dress in the livery of their
masters. They enjoyed a special legal status given them by Pope Honorius III
(1216–27) who defined an attack on the person of a cardinal as *lèse majesté*
(roughly the equivalent of high treason).[5] There were also institutional

features that underlined their status, the most important being their very own common treasury or *archa*,[6] into which went half the regular revenues of the Roman church to be shared equally by all the cardinals present in the papal court.

Whatever the definition of the papacy that the cardinals now entertained, it had been shaped by their relationship with the pope over a long period of time, from the eleventh century on. Originally marked out because they performed special liturgical services in certain Roman basilicas, the cardinals acquired great importance as a group after they were given sole control of papal elections. Beginning in the reform period of the eleventh century, they were continuously in the presence of the pope, assisting and advising him. As individuals they performed missions outside Rome on his behalf; some wrote treatises in support of the reform ideas being championed by the Roman church. Pope and cardinals were in constant consultation, and it would not be long before the cardinals began to take on administrative and judicial roles which gave to their title "cardinal" a new significance.

The cardinals had two functions that determined the way in which they came to view the papal office and their part in it: as papal advisers, and as papal electors. There was never any doctrine on the college of cardinals that was universally acceptable,[7] and opinions on the precise nature of both their electoral and advisory functions would tend to change between 1150 and 1300. It was assumed by the cardinals themselves, however, that the Roman church, the head of all other churches, comprised the pope and themselves.[8] They were therefore at one with the pope in encouraging the development of the authority of the Roman church, which could only enhance their own dignity and authority. It was their union with the pope, the product of two hundred years of intimate collaboration, that near the end of our period, in the second half of the thirteenth century, would allow the great canonist Hostiensis (Cardinal Henry of Susa) (d. 1271) to say with an air of impressive authority:

> Today the Roman church holds that there is no greater dignity than that of the cardinalate, since the cardinals together with the pope judge all, but cannot themselves be judged by anyone other than the pope and their colleagues.[9]

Ecclesia romana: the Roman church

There is much evidence to indicate that the central direction of the church in the twelfth century was undertaken by the pope only in the closest cooperation with his advisers.[10] Increasingly, the papacy as such was referred to as "Pope and Cardinals."[11] While cardinals did not lack ideas about the papal office or their role as part of it, such ideas rarely received direct expression. Consequently we often have to search for them as they are reflected in events. We are fortunate, however, in one exception, a description of the cardinals as defining the Roman church, made at the very beginning of our period in the middle of the twelfth century. It was reported by Otto of Freising (d. 1158) in his *Deeds of Frederick Barbarossa*, in the midst of his discussion of the synod of Rheims in 1148. This was the synod presided over by the Cistercian pope, Eugenius III (1145–53), in which Bernard of Clairvaux (d. 1153) and others sought the condemnation of Gilbert, bishop of Poitiers (d. 1154). Bernard's activities disturbed and upset the cardinals, who complained to Eugenius "as though with one voice":

> You should know that, having been elevated to the rule of the entire church by us, around whom, like pivots [*cardines*], the axis of the church universal swings, and having been made by us from a private person into the father of the universal church, it is necessary from now on that you belong not just to yourself but to us; that you do not rank particular and recent friendships [an allusion to Bernard of Clairvaux] before those which are general and of ancient standing. You must look to the welfare of all and care for and watch over the dignity of the Roman court, as an obligation of your office. But what has this abbot of yours done, and the French church with him? With what insolence, what daring, has he raised his head against the primacy and the supremacy of the Roman see? For it is this see alone that shuts and no man opens, opens and no man shuts [Isaiah 22.22; Apoc. 3.7]. It alone has the right to judge matters of Catholic faith and cannot, even when absent, tolerate anyone impinging on this unique privilege. But look – these Frenchmen, despising us to our very faces, have presumed to write down their profession of faith relative to the articles which we have been discussing these past few days as though they were putting the last touch to a final definition without consulting us. Surely, if this business were being treated in the east before all the patriarchs – in Alexandria, say, or Antioch – they could establish nothing firm and final without our authority. On the contrary, according to the decisions or precedents of the ancient fathers, it would be reserved to Rome for final decision. How then do these men dare in our presence to usurp what in our absence is not permitted to those more distant and more distinguished? We want you therefore to stand up against this rash novelty, and punish their insolence without delay.[12]

Eugenius was reminded that he owed his office to the cardinals, that he had become part of another body greater than himself – a body comprising himself and the cardinals, the Roman church. His obligation as pope, derived from what the cardinals viewed as the history of the office, was to exalt the Roman church over the rest of Christendom. Furthermore, it was not to the synod, not to some mere gathering of local churchmen, but to this Roman church, i.e. pope and cardinals, that the definition of faith belonged, than which there could be nothing more primatial. This had been so in the distant past, when the canons of the great eastern councils of antiquity received whatever validity they possessed only because of their acceptance by the Roman see; and it was so now in Rheims.

John of Salisbury (d. 1180) reported the same controversy, in terms somewhat more favorable to Bernard of Clairvaux. He records the preliminary meeting held by Bernard and others, including abbot Suger of Saint Denis (d. 1155), Theobald, archbishop of Canterbury (d. 1174), and Henry Murdac, abbot of Fountains and archbishop of York (1147–53). It was this preliminary meeting, where certain doctrinal statements were agreed upon ahead of time, which so irritated the cardinals that they began murmuring among themselves:

> As far as I recall there was not a single cardinal except Alberic bishop of Ostia of holy memory who was not wholeheartedly opposed to the abbot in spirit and deed; .... But as the abbot could not fail to hear of the cardinals' conspiracy, he forestalled them all, and going to the pope as a friend, urged him to put on zeal and manly courage in the Lord's cause, lest the weakness of the body of Christ and wounds of the faith should be found to be in the head ... it was certain that some of the cardinals were filled with envy of him, and could not refrain from slander.[13]

What is inescapable is that the cardinals made a careful distinction between the person of the pope and the Roman church, the joint body of pope and cardinals. It was a distinction which threatened to limit the personal authority of the pope. It was not universally accepted, however, or, rather, the consequences that the cardinals would seek to draw from it were not universally accepted. It was undoubtedly to counter their views that Bernard of Clairvaux spoke to the pope "familiarly," at Rheims, and would soon insist, in his *On Consideration*, that the cardinals enjoyed no authority except that bestowed by the pope. While, at one time, when warning the cardinals about the errors of Peter Abelard (d. 1142), he would acknowledge that they were men of great influence, and had written to them in conventional fashion that "there can be no doubt that it is for you especially to rid the kingdom of God of scandals, to cut down the thorns, to settle complaints,"[14] and would even refer to them as "judges of the earth."[15] He would also tell Eugenius that they had "no power except that which you grant them or permit them to exercise."[16] And Bernard was particularly scathing when dealing with the pretensions of cardinal-deacons who, because of their proximity to the pope, claimed precedence over priests; the phrases used included: "it makes no sense," "it derived from no tradition," "it had the support of no authority."[17]

One and the same: the unity of pope and cardinals

Nevertheless, for the cardinals it was their union with the pope that defined for them the nature of the papacy. The language of this union was often cast in anthropomorphic terms, an echo of the apostle Paul's unity of all Christians in Christ (1 Corinthians 12.12), and as such was in common use. It was a language familiar to and frequently used by the canonist Hostiensis.[18] The cardinals were part of the pope's body; while the pope might be thought of as general head of the universal church and individual Christians his "members" in a general sense, he was the special head of the cardinals, who were his "members" in a special sense. He and the cardinals together formed a single body. Cardinals did not have to take an oath to the pope like other ecclesiastics, because they were all one body; they were "part of his very bowels:" that is why cardinal-legates were said to come from the pope's side – "a latere" – as though from his very body. Hence the pope loves the cardinals as "himself."[19] Between pope and cardinals the union is so close that they consult together on all things; the cardinals are so united to the pope that together they are "one and the same thing."[20]

The biological metaphor remained a popular one. Cardinal John Lemoine [early fourteenth century] saw the cardinals not only as part of the pope's body, but, in somewhat more detail, members of his "head," whereas other prelates were only members of his "body"; the union of pope and cardinals was therefore even closer than the union of pope and bishops.[21]

A different though equally effective way of describing the union of pope and cardinals could also be made in legal terms. Corporation theory, developing swiftly in the thirteenth century, especially as it was applied to ecclesiastical bodies such as cathedral chapters, allowed the Roman church, i.e. pope and cardinals, to be described as a single legal body, a corporation of head and members, whose function it was to rule the universal church. The comparison to be made between bishop and chapter on the one hand, and pope and cardinals on the other, allowed one to apply the rights of chapters within their corporation to the college of cardinals within theirs.[22] Hostiensis insisted that the cardinals were not merely a collection of individuals, belonging to individual churches, their titular churches in Rome from which they derived their titles; rather, they formed a college or corporation, "universitas" (the same term used by certain medieval guilds including universities), whose head was the pope and whose church was the church of Rome. They possessed the usual attributes of a corporation: they had their own treasury, one of the members serving as treasurer; their right of papal election was a right held in common – a corporate right, not the right of individuals; and, finally, they were generally recognized as a corporate body, and a sacred one at that.[23]

A common solicitude: sharing the papal responsibilities

These various attempts to describe and define a unique relationship between pope and cardinals undoubtedly grew out of the challenges of the twelfth century: imperial hostility, Roman rebellion, the perverse disobedience of many ecclesiastics, and below the surface of all this the constant fear of papal schism, which must have brought pope and cardinals close together as though under siege. The popes of the twelfth century seem never to have been without the company of their cardinals, and never to have acted without consulting them. In the thirteenth century, with the rapid evolution of the idea of a papal plenitude of power connoting rulership over the entire church, it was almost inevitable that some would see the cardinals sharing in that plenitude. One way of expressing this was to contrast the relationship between pope and cardinals with the relationship between pope and other prelates: the pope had a general responsibility for the church; the bishops shared only in a part of that responsibility (or solicitude) within their partic-ular dioceses. Where did the cardinals stand in such a scheme? Hostiensis maintained that they shared the pope's general responsibility for the church at large: "The cardinals shared a common solicitude with the Pope for the general state of the Church."[24] Cardinal John Lemoine, early in the fourteenth century, would follow this lead, holding that it would be absurd if chapters of cathedral churches share in the responsibilities of their respective prelates while the cardinals, "who have full solicitude," could not share in that of their prelate, the pope.[25]

The term "solicitude" to describe pastoral responsibility had a long history. Pope Leo I (440–61), oppressed by the burdens of his office, recognized the necessity of sharing his general responsibility for the church with others. It was on the occasion when one of these, a vicar in Illyricum, went beyond his mandate that Leo chastised him by reminding him that he had held "part of what is called solicitude not the plentitude of power." What began as an expression to put a papal subordinate in place would later, in the pseudo-Isidorean decretals of c.850, take on new dimensions of juridical, and ultimately theological, importance, by emphasizing the general jurisdiction of the pope over the church at large and the notion of Rome as the founda-tion of all churches. Rome exercised a plenitude of power; other churches were called to share in the pope's solicitude, or authority over the affairs of the church. In time, there emerged from all this two senses of the solicitude exercised by pope and prelates: the sense that each exercised the same kind of authority, that of the prelates limited in area, that of the pope universal, each derived directly from God – the sense reflected in Bernard of Clairvaux's *On Consideration*;[26] and the sense of an authority ordered hierarchically, whereby the power of a bishop could be explained as being derived from the pope, without, as Innocent III would have it, any diminution of the plenitude that the pope enjoyed.[27] In thirteenth-century usage the term increasingly bore this second sense,[28] in the growing awareness of the special significance now being given to the term "plenitude of power"; for example, Innocent III explained why only the pope could use the *pallium* (the ceremonial shawl) at all times, because he had a plenitude of power, while other prelates could do so only on special occasions, "because they are called in partial solicitude, not in the plenitude of power."[29]

If, then, some cardinals now describe themselves as called "in the common solicitude," it is because they see themselves as part of the papacy, partners in the government of the church, sharing fully in papal authority, participants in his plenitude of power.[30] It is true that this "common" solicitude of pope and cardinals was a conception with no real future, given the rapid growth of the pope's personal sovereignty. But its corollary, that the cardinals shared in some sense in the papal plenitude of power, would still be echoed in the fourteenth century by no less than Pope Clement VI (1342–52) who, in his sermon marking the creation of his seventeen-year-old nephew and namesake, Pierre Roger, as a cardinal deacon, turned to Job 9.13 to liken the cardinals to giants shouldering the world, bowing down only before the vicar of Christ, adding that cardinals were appointed not only to share in the papal solicitude for the church but, in a fashion, to share in the pope's plenitude of power.[31]

By the counsel of our brothers: giving counsel to the pope

In the Middle Ages there was an almost universal conviction that taking advice was important in government. "Do all things with counsel," Bernard of Clairvaux told Eugenius III; "afterwards you won't be sorry."[32] At the root of this conviction lay the idea that there was too much at stake to risk the independent decisions of one person no matter how venerable, how reliable, or how feared. It was a concern that was often expressed. When one discussed rulers and rulership one almost always had recourse to the notion that there was safety in numbers, frequently reinforced by a favorite text from Proverbs: "with much counsel, there is safety."[33] When dealing, for example, with the question whether a minor might be permitted to take up the reins of government while still under age, a fourteenth-century curial lawyer gave it as his opinion that the young ruler "cannot err because he has many assistants,"[34] a pretty example of a bureaucrat's touching faith in advisory committees.

Of all the rulers of the Middle Ages, there was none whose authority was more often discussed than that of the pope, and just as often as secular princes were urged to consult their natural advisers, their great vassals, so too the pope was enjoined again and again to consult *his* natural advisers, the cardinals. Leaving aside the personal idiosyncracies of this pope or that, they needed little urging. Often they themselves bemoaned the immense practical difficulties of their position and described their pressing need for reliable advisers who would help them not only in the performance of their many liturgical, legal, and administrative functions, but also in the wide range of ecclesiastical and political problems which constantly beset the papacy. "Since we cannot handle the entirety of ecclesiastical affairs ourselves," Eugenius III writes, "we entrust to our brethren [the cardinals], in whose discretion we have confidence, the completion of certain matters having respect to time and place."[35] John of Salisbury mentions the fact that, although as a Cistercian Eugenius generally favored his order, a request from it to restore to the priest-hood a Cistercian who had once supported the anti-pope Anacletus II (1130–8) had no success:

> Although the pope seemed to lend a favorable ear to their appeals, he always referred the matter to the cardinals; and they maintained that no concession could be made on account of the constitution of Pope Innocent [II] condemning in perpetuity all who had received ordination from Peter Leonis [Anacletus II], and the decree of Eugenius himself just promulgated in the council of Rheims.[36]

Alexander III (1159–81) would look upon the advisory role of the cardinals as so important that it could take the place of a church synod.[37] On one occa-sion, being approached by the ambassador of Frederick Barbarossa (German emperor, 1152–90) who asked for a private audience, Alexander replied that it was quite useless to speak to him privately since he would not reply without consulting his cardinals.[38] Popes frequently expressed themselves on the consultative role to be filled by the cardinals they appointed. Martin IV (1281–5), when appointing a new cardinal, cited Jethro's advice to Moses who was trying to judge his people without any assistance: "provide from all the people able men who fear God, in whom there is truth, who hate avarice."[39]

One of the clearest expressions of a pope on the subject of the advisory role of cardinals comes from Nicholas III (1277–80):

> It is fitting that the pope receive from his brethren, the cardinals of the holy Roman church, who assist him as coadjutors in the execu-tion of his priestly office, counsel freely given. It is fitting that he not vacillate in his judgment in any way, so that the fear of no secular power frighten them, no momentary passion absorb them, no alarm threaten them, nothing restrain them from giving real, solid advice.[40]

This need to recruit reliable advisers was not in itself incompatible with the growing notion of a papal world monarchy and a sovereign pope of unlimited authority. Nevertheless, the pope's regular, systematic consultation with the body of cardinals in all important matters led many to believe that he could not, in fact, act legitimately in such matters without at least first asking for their advice. It was not only the cardinals who thought so. William Durantis, bishop of Mende, for example, who was no champion of the prerog-atives of the cardinalate, said that the pope should make no important decisions or do anything of consequence without first taking the advice of the cardinals, and made the obvious comparison with the lay advisers of kings and princes: "for it is certain that those who rule in spiritual and temporal affairs are human, and being human easily fail."[41] Pope Clement IV (1265–8) would himself testify to the hold that the practice had; when recommending to the king of Naples the value of consulting trusted advisers, he had this to say about what he himself did:

> Believe me, my beloved son, I often find it the case, in this see over which I preside, unworthy as I am, that having sounded the opinions of the cardinals, I have followed their recommendations even when I thought the opposite course to be better, provided the matter was such that no sin was involved; and the reason is that I thought it rash to set my own opinion against the judgement of so many prudent men.[42]

At the very time, then, that theorists were erecting the structure of papal absolutism, the customary practices of the curia itself suggest a real limitation of the pope's personal authority by a "papacy" which still included the cardinals. In fact, by the end of our period there was no longer any question, if there had been before, that in important matters, "arduous business or cases," the pope had to consult the cardinals. Contemporaries cited as evidence the fact that Boniface VIII (1294–1303) revoked some independent acts of his predecessor because they had been undertaken without such consultation,[43] and Boniface's successor, Benedict XI (1303–4), in turn suspended some of Boniface's acts for the same reason.[44]

The strength of these ideas may be measured by the fact that well into the fourteenth century popes would refer to the custom of consultation in terms such as to indicate that they were powerless to take action without it. We may prefer to think of these protestations of incapacity as convenient fictions whereby the pope could avoid some undesirable action without giving undue offence, but this is to ignore the force of their repetition and the authority they derive from their origin. Clement V (1305–14) told Philip IV, King of France (1275–1314) that, in the matter of conceding tithes to lay princes, the pope is not accustomed to act without the advice of the college of cardinals, and that in the present instance, in 1306, he could do nothing because most of his cardinals had not yet joined him.[45] Clement VI alleged the unanimous opinion of the college of cardinals in order to justify with the sovereigns of Europe his refusal to extend the benefits of the jubilee indulgence of 1350 to someone who did not actually go to Rome.[46] Innocent VI (1252–62) referred to the translation of a bishop from one see to another as "an arduous thing,"[47] adding that it therefore was *consistorialis*," meaning that it needed the formal approval of the college of cardinals.[48] Indeed, Innocent's reputation for acting only after discussion with the cardinals and other competent persons was sufficiently well known as to be commented on in one of the major chronicles of the Avignon popes in the fourteenth–fifteenth centuries.[49] Urban V (1362–70) told a papal legate who had been negotiating with Bernabò Visconti, ruler of Milan (1363–85) that he was personally willing to accept a candidate of Bernabò's for appointment to the see of Brescia, but that he could not deal with the matter without first consulting the consistory, i.e. the cardinals.[50] On another occasion, he told King John II of France (1350–64) that it was an "old custom" that a cardinal not be sent away from the curia on business "except with the advice of the cardinals," to explain why he had to turn down the king's request for having Cardinal Talleyrand of Périgord sent to France as a legate.[51]

What was thought in the curia to fall within the category of "arduous things," such that the cardinals had to be consulted? The list is long and impressive: the summoning of church councils; the granting of tithes to secular rulers; the canonization of saints; the suspension of bishops from office; the publication of collections of papal decretals to be studied in the universities; the preaching of crusades; the appointment of papal legates and nuncios; the coronation of emperors; the appointment of senators of the city of Rome; all questions having to do with episcopal elections and translations; the authorization of new universities; all matters of political importance involving the princes of Europe; everything pertaining to possessions and incomes of the Roman church; the relations of the papacy with its feudal dependencies; and a wide range of matters of a domestic or administrative nature; in short, everything that expressed the primacy of the papacy. We have some idea of the mechanics of such consultation from Jacopo Stefaneschi (d. 1343), whom Boniface VIII appointed to the college. He had a great interest in liturgy and ceremonial, and spent much of his time revising and updating the protocol of the papal curia, describing the many rituals associated with the court and the person of the pope. He has depicted for us the manner in which the pope consulted the cardinals in consistory.[52] Unfortunately, his description is limited by his interest in the ceremonial, external aspects of the process: the placing of chairs, the order of speaking, the role of seniority in the college, and so on.

We know, however, from other sources that not only were many problems discussed in common and at length, and sometimes with a vigor bordering on violence,[53] but also that the pope would sometimes ask cardinals to put their opinions in writing. These written opinions, or *consilia*, are rare indeed for our period; but we have a dossier of such *consilia* from the 1320s having to do with an abortive proposal for a crusade which throws a great deal of light on the mechanics of pope and cardinals working together. Preliminary negotiations between Pope John XXII (1316–34) and King Charles IV of France (1322–8) had led to a French crusading proposal which the pope and cardinals discussed off and on for some six weeks, during which time John asked the cardinals to write out their opinions. We have eighteen of these *consilia*, seventeen of which carry the names of their respective authors. Their contents are of no interest here, but one or two observations can be made: many of them show distinct similarities, both of ideas and language, such that we can assume that continued discussions went on amongst the cardinals even outside consistory; there is a high degree of concurrence among all of them, despite differences in length, argumentation, and style; some cardinals had much to say, while a few were quite willing to leave the discussion in the hands of others, merely indicating their general agreement; finally, the arguments, or many of them, determined the pope's response to the king, in which we often find points repeated that are to be found in one or other of the *consilia*.[54]

It might be objected that consultation of this kind was not technically obligatory on the pope, and that therefore it was not seen as an infringement of his authority. But the fact remains that by the end of the thirteenth century popes invariably consulted their cardinals on all important matters, all those matters that marked the Roman church as the mother of all churches. They did so from long and respected tradition, from the weight of venerable opinion, and out of a conviction that the practical advantages were undeniable. Consequently, the cardinals saw themselves as necessary for the validation of papal acts in all important matters as part of the papacy.

... and with their consent?

If the pope was in practice obliged to consult the cardinals, one might ask whether the unity of pope and cardinals was such that he was also obliged to follow their advice. The question is not merely of historic interest. It was current in the thirteenth century, and became increasingly uncomfortable for those cardinals who sought to maintain the prerogatives of their order. Cardinal John Lemoine asked whether the words "with the counsel of our cardinals," – the formula invariably found in papal letters dealing with "ardous cases" – meant that such consultation depended merely on whether the pope happened to ask for it or not, or was required by some standing agreement between pope and cardinals, or was thought to be the fitting or proper thing to do, or was a legal requirement.[55] That Nicholas III had already said what he thought,[56] Lemoine seems to have overlooked, perhaps deliberately. He cited examples of papal acts being canceled because they had not been made on the advice of the college – so implying that it might be a matter of "necessity," but then on the other hand he conditioned the Roman law maxim that the prince is not bound by the law by suggesting that it was fitting that he should live according to the law, so implying instead that it was only a matter of "appropriateness"; finally he refrained from reaching any conclusion whatever!

John's question would continue to be asked by others.[57] On the surface it was merely whether the pope was required to consult the cardinals, not whether he was required to follow their advice once consulted. But the phrase "with the counsel of our brothers," when it appeared in a papal act, did not refer merely to an act of consultation, did not mean that the cardinals had simply been consulted, but that in some general sense it was on their advice that the pope was acting, that the pope and cardinals were acting together. As we shall see[58] Gregory X (1271–6) consulted the cardinals about his proposed legislation on papal elections in 1274. The finished constitution, *Ubi periculum*,* lacked the formula "with the counsel of our brothers." The reason was not because the cardinals had not been consulted – they certainly had – but because they did not approve. The appearance of the formula implied acceptance.

There was one class of cases, however, that seems to have required the explicit consent of the cardinals. When it came to questions of finance, or the alienation of the property of the Roman church, we find that not only was the pope required to consult the cardinals, but that he sought their explicit consent before acting. The reason for this lies in the principle that "what touches all must be approved by all," and in the financial history of the college of cardinals whose corporate income was drawn in large part from the regular incomes and the patrimony of the Roman church. In 1234 Gregory IX (1227–41) allowed that there would be no further alienation from the patrimony without the advice and unanimous consent of the cardinals.[59] During much of the previous year some of the cardinals had remained separated from the pope.[60] This suggests that there may have been serious disagreements between Gregory and his cardinals, possibly respecting papal policy toward Frederick II (German emperor, 1212–50). The concession that he made, in effect allowing them a veto over the alienation of property belonging to the Roman church, seems to have been the price he had to pay for a united curia.

Nor was this his only concession. About the same time, he would acknowledge that the papal states had been mismanaged by the rectors whom he had previously appointed, and now provided for their future government by the cardinals themselves.[61] This provision may never have been put into full effect. The appointment of cardinals as rectors of the papal states, which was one of the provisions of the constitution, remained a hit-and-miss affair. However, throughout the rest of the thirteenth century the college seems always to have been consulted in all matters pertaining to the papal states, probably because their incomes were affected. There is one notable exception which proves the rule: shortly before his death, Boniface VIII promulgated a statute respecting the March of Ancona without consulting the cardinals, which a few months later was withdrawn by his successor for that very reason.[62]

Meanwhile, the cardinals also received more papal concessions respecting their common income. Gregory IX set aside one-third of the income of the papal states for them.[63] In fact, his financial concessions seem to have gone

---

* Papal letters and decrees are identified by the opening Latin words, the incipits, of their texts, which often have little bearing on their content, and are often untranslatable because the words make little sense in their abbreviated form.

even further than this, for although we lack other constitutions we know that the cardinals claimed to have been given half the annual tribute of 1,000 marks that the kings of England owed the papacy ever since the time King John (1199–1216) turned his kingdom over to Innocent III and received it back as a fief.[64] We know of still other concessions made to the cardinals later. For instance, in 1272 Gregory X gave them half the Sicilian tribute;[65] soon afterwards, Nicholas III gave them half the common services.[66] There is evidence that even before this time the cardinals had some share in the common services paid by newly appointed prelates, whether half or not is not known.[67] The well-known concession of Nicholas IV (1288–92) in 1289, giving the cardinals half the ordinary incomes of the Roman church, was in large part a confirmation of concessions won by the college during the previous decades,[68] the material measure of the cardinals' share of the papacy.

Papal elections and papal power

The constitution on papal elections promulgated by Alexander III in 1179, *Licet de vitanda*, had finally settled two pressing problems, by ignoring distinctions of rank among the cardinals for purposes of the election, and by requiring a two-thirds majority. It had been a reform agreed to by the cardinals themselves, which is more than one can say about Gregory X's constitution *Ubi periculum* a century later. Gregory sought to fix the conclave as a permanent feature of papal elections. This "conclave" was the practice that had appeared in the thirteenth century, possibly under the influence of Italian communal elections, of locking up the cardinals and making life increasingly miserable for them until they produced a pope.[69] Gregory, who had not himself been a cardinal, shared the widespread indignation over the long vacancy that had preceded his election. In his constitution, among other features designed to hasten the choice of a new pope, he explicitly denied to the cardinals any exercise of papal authority during a vacancy. He not only sought to reduce their freedom of action and independence, but also subjected them to local lay authority, undoubtedly awakening fearful memories of past conclaves some of which had been brutal affairs.[70] No wonder that it lacks the formula "*de fratrum nostrorum consilio* (with the counsel of our brothers)." He had shown it to the cardinals when he had first drawn it up, no doubt in the hope of winning their approval. He met instead with strong opposition. They quarreled, and their disagreement could not be hushed up. In fact, both the cardinals and the pope canvassed the fathers of the council at Lyons (1274) for support, the cardinals claiming that they had been given no sufficient reason for consenting to such a measure, the pope demanding and getting from the prelates of the council the obedience that was his due.[71] There can be no doubt of the need for some such legislation to deal with the problem of long vacancies. In addition, however, for those who saw in the old claims of the college a threat to the personal authority of the pope,[72] that personal plenitude of power that excluded all others, here was an opportunity to get rid of the notion once and for all, that the cardinals shared the papal plenitude of power or could exercise papal authority during a vacancy.

The idea that cardinals in some way inherited the papal authority during a vacancy had long held sway in the college, and would not be easily given up. Matthew Paris (d. 1259) inserted a letter in his *Chronica majora*, written by some eight cardinals in 1243 during the vacancy preceding the election of Innocent IV, not because of the subject matter itself, but because of what the letter revealed about the question of papal authority during a vacancy, which seems to have been a question of general interest at the time. The critical clause was "We in whom the power resides when the apostolic see is vacant, wish . . ." etc.[73] In this question, as in others, Hostiensis summarized the prevailing view of the college, giving it an air of legitimacy difficult to dispel. When the pope dies, he said, his power does not die with him. It remains within the Roman church which itself cannot die. Its exercise, however, ought normally to remain dormant until a new pope is elected. It was a power held in trust, so to speak, preserved intact to be passed on to the successor, and to be exercised by the cardinals only in emergencies or in matters of great moment. The argument that such exercise of authority by the cardinals might give rise to schism, scandal, or long vacancies might be valid, he agreed, if the concession were made without any limitation, but there was really nothing to fear provided it was restricted, as he suggested, to cases of necessity and the ultimate good of the church. He was able, therefore, to preserve the sense of a college of cardinals sharing in and in some sense inheriting the papal plenitude of power, while turning aside criticism that saw an irresponsible college of cardinals doing whatever it wished, as long as it wished, during a vacancy.[74]

Gregory X's constitution, which came only a few years later, incorporated this view that the cardinals could act during a vacancy in emergencies. But it also required that to do so they had to be unanimous, which in effect paralyzed the college, depriving it of any real independence of action. Not all the cardinals would accept this. They persuaded Gregory's successor but one, Hadrian V, pope for only a few weeks in 1276, to suspend the constitution and promulgate a substitute,[75] although three of their number – which three, we do not know – wanted it kept in force. Hadrian died before he could issue a new constitution,[76] and soon after his death a rumor spread that he had even canceled his suspension. An inquiry by his successor John XXI (1276–7) failed, however, to confirm this, and John continued the suspension. He too promised a new constitution on papal elections,[77] but it was also prevented by his own early death when the ceiling of his library collapsed on him. Gregory's constitution remained in limbo for another seventeen years until by a truly farsighted act in an otherwise sorry pontificate Celestine V (July–December 1294) revived it.[78] In all of this we can dimly discern a real difference of opinion within the college itself.

In the meantime, we have a good illustration of how the cardinals conducted themselves in conformity with cardinal Hostiensis' doctrine. In 1277, during the vacancy after John XXI's death, the cardinals wrote to Rudolf, king of Germany (1273–91), to urge him to come to an agreement with the Roman church before undertaking an expedition into Italy. They were only too conscious that they were carrying on papal business without a pope. They were careful, therefore, to stress that what they were really doing was pursuing the policy of two popes, Innocent V [January–June 1276] and John XXI, originally undertaken on their own advice, and that they were doing so in pursuit of the public good and in what they called "fitting imitation" of the pope.[79] They clearly had Hostiensis' doctrine in mind.

Not even Celestine's revival of Gregory X's constitution, and its formal insertion into the corpus of canon law by Boniface VIII, would immediately unseat this doctrine. Cardinal John Lemoine, for example, would continue to hold the opinion that the cardinals inherited papal authority during a vacancy,[80] and other cardinals would do the same well into the fourteenth century. A gloss on Cardinal Jacopo Stefaneschi's metrical life of Celestine V (January–December 1294, abdicated, d. 1296), made by the author himself, is quite clear in this respect: during a vacancy the power of the pope resides in the college.[81] In Perugia, after Pope Benedict XI died, Cardinal Matteo Rosso (d. 1305) showed Vidal de Villanova, the emissary of James II of Aragon (d. 1327), a document drawn up by the cardinals in the conclave dealing, among other things, with the rights they thought they had during a vacancy. It included the claim that during a vacancy the college had all the rights of the pope, although there were many outside the college who disagreed.[82] So the quarrel was still going on in the curia.

The idea of a residual authority in the college during a vacancy continued to draw sustenance from the actual practice of the college, whose acts of "fitting imitation" during a vacancy could be confirmed by the newly elected pope. Upon his election, Boniface VIII confirmed everything the college had done during the vacancy respecting excommunication, interdict, and a fine of 2,000 marks levied on Orvieto,[83] all acts that he himself had participated in as a cardinal. Even further, however, some cardinals thought that they could take advantage of a vacancy to modify the terms of Gregory X's constitution on elections. This idea was so strongly held that Clement V (1305–14) had to legislate especially against it. In *Ne romani*, promulgated at the Council of Vienne (1311–12) and later published by his successor in the canonical collection called the *Clementines*, Clement reproved in unequivocal terms the notion that the cardinals could modify or cancel Gregory X's constitution during a vacancy before proceeding to an election, and declared invalid and inane the idea that the authority of the pope while alive could be exercised by the college after his death, except in those particular cases allowed for in papal legislation.[84]

Boniface VIII

With the pontificate of Clement V we have gone beyond our period. Already, however, in Boniface VIII's time, it would seem that the old view of the papacy as embracing pope and cardinals was losing ground even in the college itself. Boniface made it clear that he thought he could act without the cardinals if necessary. Berengar Fredoli, cardinal bishop of Tusculum in the late thirteenth century, told the ambassador of the king of Aragon not to bother presenting his case in consistory, since Boniface never brought anything up in consistory except what he chose not to do.[85] He held weekly consistories for routine matters, but reserved all important affairs to himself and a small handful of trusted colleagues, and would brook no contradiction in consistory.[86] There was clearly a growing antipathy between him and some of his cardinals, in part the residue of rivalries which had sprung up during the pontificate of Celestine V.

This came to a head during the quarrel (c. 1310) with the Colonnese cardinals, James and Peter, which dramatized a sovereignty of the pope's person so great as to leave no room for the aspirations or ambitions of the cardinals. Much of the complaint that the Colonnesi made against Boniface was based on the assumption that the status or juridical character of the cardinals was perpetual.[87] But Boniface, we are told, would have none of this:

> Some might say that the cardinals do not have status. They do and they don't, since he who is established in plenitude of power over all and has the power to loose and to bind, as the vicar of Jesus Christ, is chosen by and proceeds from their canonical election. Indeed, there is no one, after the Roman pontiff himself, who has such an elevated status as this. It is well known that they are members of our head.
>
> However, they do not have the status of preeminence that the pope has. No one else has this kind of status except the pope alone, since he is not beneath that of anyone inferior to him. But the cardinals who have status are beneath the status of the Roman pontiff, who has power to correct and to punish them.[88]

In the early stages of their struggle with Boniface, the Colonnese cardinals were not the only members of the college to oppose the pope. Several of their colleagues were in touch with King Philip IV of France, attacking Boniface behind his back. In April 1311, before an investigative commission set up by Clement V, the names of several of these emerged, the most prominent being John Lemoine, no friend of the pope. He admitted that he had told Philip IV that he thought Boniface was a heretic, presumably when he had been a legate in France, since he added that he could not remember having written to the king on the subject.[89] Rumors flew of a serious split in the college and a bitterness among those who were, for one reason or another, at odds with Boniface.[90] On the other hand there was a party of cardinals who stuck with the pope, one of whom, Matthew of Aquasparta, cardinal bishop of Porto (d. 1302) insisted that between pope and college there were no differences, no dissension, no division, but rather complete concord, peace, and agreement, since whatever the pope wished the cardinals wished and vice versa.[91]

After Boniface died, the king's demands that a general council be summoned to investigate the charges against him revealed a clear division in the college between those who favored such a council, mainly those who had schemed with the king shortly after 1295, and those who opposed it, cardinals who had been appointed by Boniface after his election. There were a few, however, who sat on the fence, like Landulf Brancacci who, when he was called in 1311 to testify about the defection of cardinals, said not only that he had not himself communicated with Philip about Boniface, but that he had never even heard of any other cardinal doing so![92]

The emergence of a party of cardinals in opposition to the pope gives some color to one of the claims of the Colonnesi, that Boniface had altered the status of the college of cardinals. The language they used was, by and large, the traditional language used in the past to describe the cardinals. They could not be deprived of their office at the whim of the pope. Their duty was to disagree with and stand up to the pope when necessary, as a kind of loyal opposition – a duty which would go by the board if they were to be dismissed "without cause."[93]

The pontificate of Boniface VIII made manifest a view of the papacy within which the cardinals were ceasing to play a central role. As late as Celestine III (1191–8) it was still the *sacrosancta Romana ecclesia* that was endowed with a plenitude of power.[94] With Innocent III, the term was coming to mean the full personal sovereignty of a ruler in his realm, albeit still the realm of the spirit.[95] It would be enlarged yet further by his successors. As expressed by Boniface VIII, the idea of the pope's personal sovereignty would have serious implications for the college of cardinals which suffered a sharp diminution of status. The following century, beyond the scope of this present study, saw two events which would reveal the role which the cardinals sought to reserve to themselves, given the limitations with which they now had to contend.

The first was the vacancy preceding the election of Innocent VI in 1352, during which the cardinals drew up a *capitulatio*, a written agreement to limit the future pope in the appointment of new cardinals, to restrict his disciplinary power over them, to guarantee their regular sources of income, to ensure their share in the supervision of the papal states, and in all such matters to require the concurrence of two-thirds of the college, or one-half, as the case might be. There was some doubt within the conclave that what they were doing was legal, for the oath that each swore, to uphold the capitulation if elected, was taken by some only with the stipulation: "thus, if and by whatever written law he had preceded in this."[96] And indeed, upon election, Innocent VI declared their agreement void, not only because it was in contravention of papal constitutions which forbade dealing with any business other than the election itself during a vacancy, but also as redounding to the "diminution and prejudice of the plenitude of power granted from the lips of God to the Roman pontiff alone."[97]

The second was the double election of 1378, by which the college sought to exploit their one privilege, so firmly embedded in canon law as to be virtually untouchable – the election of the pope.

As dramatic as these events were, and as significant for an understanding of the oligarchical tendencies of the college of cardinals, neither marks any kind of return to the concept of the papacy as a union of pope and cardinals. The first had to do with personal privileges, incomes, and the cardinals' control of the membership of their college; the second was an attempt to enlarge their electoral function to include the power to depose. While there were large forces at work during the ensuing conciliar period that sought to locate ecclesiastical sovereignty elsewhere than in the person of the pope, it was to the church at large, represented by the universal council, not to the college of cardinals, that reformers would henceforth look.

NOTES

1   Cf. Michael Wilks, *The Problem of Sovereignty in the Later Middle Ages* (Cambridge: Cambridge University Press, 1963), p. 460, n. 2.

2   So Leo IX in 1054; see Stephan Kuttner, "Cardinalis: The History of a Canonical Concept," *Traditio* 3 (1945): 176.

3   Peter Damian, in *Patrologia Latina*, hereafter *PL*, vol. 145: 540.

4   F. Pagnotti, "Niccolò da Calvi e la sua Vita d'Innocenzo IV," *Archivio della Società Romana di Storia Patria* 21 (1898): 97, cites a manuscript owned by Francesco Petrarca, who wrote in the margin at this point: "pillei rubei patrum conscriptorum." For Cardinal Luca Fieschi's white mule, see Karl H. Schäfer, *Die Ausgaben der apostolischen Kammer unter Benedikt XII, Klemens VI, und Innocenz VI (1334–1362)* (Paderborn: F. Schöningh, 1914), p. 47.

5   Charles Coquelines, *Bullarium ... Romanorum pontificum amplissima collectio* (Graz, Austria: Akademische Druck, 1733), vol. 3, p. 239, no. 76.

6   Hostiensis, *Decretalium librum commentaria* (Venice: Juntas, 1581), hereafter *Comm. ad Decret.*, 5.6.17. On the subject in general, see Johann P. Kirsch, *Die Finanzverwaltung des Kardinal Kollegiums im XIII. und XIV. Jahrhundert* (Münster: H. Schöningh, 1895); Paul M. Baumgarten, *Untersuchungen und Urkunden über die Camera Collegii Cardinalium für die Zeit von 1295 bis 1437* (Leipzig: Giesecke und Devrient, 1898).

7   But cf. Giuseppe Alberigo, *Cardinalato e collegialità: Studi sull'ecclesiologia tra l'XI e il XIV secolo* (Florence: Vallecchi, 1969).

8   Hostiensis, *Comm. ad Decret.* 2.24.4. The identification of pope and cardinals as the Roman church was already a commonplace when enunciated by the canonist Huguccio late in the twelfth century: "Romana ecclesia dicitur papa et cardinales," cited in Brian Tierney, *Foundations of the Conciliar Theory* (Cambridge: Cambridge University Press, 1955; reprint 1968), p. 42.

9   Hostiensis, *Comm. ad Decret.* 3.5.19.

10   See Werner Maleczek, *Papst und Kardinalskolleg von 1191 bis 1216: Die Kardinäle unter Coelestin III und Innocenz III* (Vienna: Verlag der Österreichischen Akademie der Wissenschaften, 1984), p. 255.

11   From the beginning of the pontificate of Eugenius III it was a rare exception when references to the pope's taking advice implied prelates other than the cardinals; see Maleczek, *Papst und Kardinalskolleg*, pp. 307–8.

12   *Ottonis et Rahewini Gesta Friderici I imperatoris*, ed. Bernhard de Simson, *MGH, SS rerum Germ.* (Hanover: Hahnsche, 1912); *The Deeds of Frederick Barbarossa by Otto of Freising*, trans. Charles C. Mierow (New York: Columbia University Press, 1953), p. 99.

13   *John of Salisbury's Memoirs of the Papal Court*, trans. Marjorie Chibnall (London: Thomas Newlson & Sons Ltd, 1956), pp. 17–21.

14   Bernard of Clairvaux, "Epistolae," in Bernard of Clairvaux, *Opera Omnia*, ed. Henri Rochais and Jean Leclercq (Rome: Editiones cistercienses, 1963–), vol. 8, esp. p. 188.

15   Bernard of Clairvaux, *De consideratione*, 4.1.1 (Rochais and Leclercq edition, vol. 3: *Tractatus et opuscula*, p. 449).

16   Bernard of Clairvaux, *De consideratione*, 4.4.9 (Rochais and Leclercq edition, vol. 3, p. 455).

17   Bernard of Clairvaux, *De consideratione*, 4.5.16 (Rochais and Leclercq edition, vol. 3, p. 461). At this time it was still held to be inappropriate for cardinal-deacons to take precedence over bishops. When Pope Eugenius III proposed to promote to the priesthood John Paparo, a cardinal-deacon, preparatory to his going to Ireland as a papal legate, John refused. Eugenius suspended him, whereupon John threatened to lead a rebellion in Rome. Finally the other cardinals prevailed upon him to make his peace with the pope and accept the priesthood, "pointing out that it was not seemly for a deacon to bless archbishops, and that the lord pope would not give the Irish legation to anyone who was not a priest"; see *John of Salisbury's Memoirs*, p. 71.

18   Hostiensis, *Comm. ad Decret.* 4.17.13. Hostiensis' several comments on the college of cardinals have been conveniently brought together by John A. Watt, "The Constitutional Law of the College of Cardinals: Hostiensis to Joannes Andreae," *Mediaeval Studies* 33 (1971): 151–7. Hostiensis' opinions, together with those of cardinal John Lemoine after him, are of particular value for us as opinions not of distinguished canonists, but rather of cardinals reflecting on the ideas and practices of their order. See especially Brian Tierney, "Hostiensis and Collegiality," in *Proceedings of the Fourth International Congress of Medieval Canon Law*, ed. Stephan Kuttner (Vatican City: Bibliotheca Apostolica Vaticana, 1976), pp. 401–9.

19   Hostiensis, *Comm. ad Decret.* 5.33.23.

20   Hostiensis, *Comm. ad Decret.* 5.6.17; cf. Martinus Laudunensis, "Tractatus de cardinalibus ad modum singularis digestus per centum quaestiones," q. 5, in *Tractatus illustrium in utraque ... iuris facultate iurisconsultorum*, 13, pt 2 (Venice, 1584), fol. 60ᵇ; Andreas de Barbatia, "Tractatus de praestantia card.," ibid., fol. 71ᵃ.

21   In his commentary on the *Extravagantes*, col. 328, on *Dudum* of Benedict XI, Pope John XXII, in a letter about the occupation by Roman noble families of houses and palaces in Rome belonging to the cardinals' churches, wrote: "cum ipsi qui fore noscuntur capitis nostri membra ...": Augustin Theiner, *Codex diplomaticus dominii temporalis s. sedis* (Frankfort: Minerva, 1861), vol. 1, p. 506, no. 669.

22   Tierney, *Foundations*, pp. 68–84, 149–53, and *passim*.

23   Hostiensis, *Comm. ad Decret.* 5.6.17.

24   Hostiensis, *Comm. ad Decret.* 5.6.17.

25   John Lemoine (Johannes Monachus), *Glossa aurea super Sexto Decretalium Libro* (Paris, 1535; reprint Aalen: Scientia Verlag, 1968), 5.11.12.

26   Bernard of Clairvaux, *De consideratione*, 2.8.15 (Rochais and Leclercq edition, vol. 3, pp. 423–4).

27   Jean Rivière, "*In partem sollicitudinis*: évolution d'une formule pontificale," *Revue des sciences religieuses* 5 (1925): 210–31.

28   William Durantis, bishop of Mende, *Rationale divinorum officiorum*, 3.1.17 (Venice, 1499), fol. 31r.

29   See Innocent III, *Decretales*, 1.8.4; also in *PL*, vol. 215: 294D. Cf. Ep. 320 (*PL*, vol. 214: 286C).

30   Hostiensis, *Comm. ad Decret.* 4.17.13. The "universality" of the cardinals' solicitude was not unknown abroad; see the letter to the cardinals from the community of Christ Church, Canterbury, in *Chronicles and Memorials of the Reign of Richard I*, vol. 2, *Epistolae Cantuariensis: the Letters of the Prior and Convent of Christ Church, Canterbury from A.D. 1187 to A.D. 1199*, ed. William Stubbs (London: Longman, 1865), p. 434, no. 469, and to cardinal Gratian in 1159 (ibid., p. 503, no. 538).

When discussing questions touching on the deposition or excommunication of cardinals, and marshalling arguments to limit arbitrary action by the pope, Hostiensis would still recognize that in the pope alone resides a plenitude of power, *Comm. ad Decret.* 3.4.2. Note that the power "resided" in the pope, not in the college of cardinals; but the cardinals shared it, i.e. they helped the pope to exercise it.

31   Paris, Bibliothèque Sainte-Geneviève, MS 240, fol. 416v-a.

32   Bernard of Clairvaux, *De consideratione* 4.4.11 (Rochais and Leclercq edition, vol. 3, p. 457), citing Ecclesiasticus 32.24.

33   Proverbs 11.14. See Innocent III in *PL*, vol. 215: 1128.

34   *Oldradi da Ponte Laudensis . . . Consilia seu Responsa* (Venice, Franciscum Zilettum, 1571), con. 52.

35   Julius von Pflugk-Harttung, *Acta pontificum Romanorum inedita* (Graz: Akademische Druck, 1880) vol. 1, p. 187, no. 204.

36   *John of Salisbury's Memoirs*, p. 43.

37   Alexander III, Ep. 34 (*PL*, vol. 200, p. 107): the matter had to do with the canonization of Edward the Confessor.

38   Alexander III, Ep. 36, *PL*, vol. 200.

39   Edmund Martène and Ursin Durand, *Veterum scriptorum . . . collectio* (Paris: Montalant, 1724, reprint New York, B. Franklin, 1968), vol. 2, p. 1283. The biblical text is from Exodus 18.21. For a discussion of the formula *de fratrum nostrorum consilio* up to and including the pontificate of Innocent III, see Maleczek, *Papst und Kardinalskolleg*, ch. 7 (pp. 297–324).

40   *Les Registres de Nicholas III*, ed. Jules Gay and Suzanne Vitte (Paris: A. Fontemoing, 1898–1938), vol. 1, p. 106, no. 296.

41   See his *Tractatus de modo generalis concilii celebrandi*, 3 vols (Paris, 1671), vol. 1, p. 17, and vol. 3, p. 278. Ptolemy of Lucca, in his *Determinatio compendiosa*, while acknowledging the unlimited authority of the pope to make new law, urged him not to change old law without taking advice. Prelates had councils, he said, just as princes had parliaments. The ancient Romans had required their consuls to consult with the Senate. Now the place of the Senate was held by the cardinals, and the pope should consult with them. See Charles T. Davis, "Roman Patriotism and Republican Propaganda: Ptolemy of Lucca and Pope Nicholas III," *Speculum* 50 (1975): 422. The *Glossa palatina*, a compilation of glosses on the *Decretum*, probably written by Laurentius Hispanus (cf. Alfons M. Stickler, "Il decretista Laurentius Hispanus," *Studia Gratiana* 9 [1966]: 461–549), had already insisted that the pope could not legislate for the whole church without the cardinals; see Tierney, *Foundations*, p. 81.

42   Edmund Martène and Ursin Durand, *Thesaurus novus anecdotorum* (Paris: Sumptibus Fr., 1717), vol. 2, p. 407, no. 380; cf. O. Rinaldi, *Annales ecclesiastici*, 14 (Rome: Delaulne, 1648), Clement IV, an. 1266, c. 21.

43   Lemoine, *Ad Sext.*, 5.2.4; cf. *Annales de Wigornia [Worcester]*, in *Annales Monastici*, ed. Henry Luard, 4 vols (London: Longman, 1869), p. 518; *Annales de Dunstaplia*, ibid., 3 (London, 1866), p. 383; *Bartholomaei de Cotton Historia Anglicana*, ed. Henry R. Luard (London, 1859), p. 268; and see Jacopo Stefaneschi's *Opus metricum*, 2, c. 10,

in Franz Xaver Seppelt, *Monumenta Coelestiniana. Quellen zur Geschichte des Papstes Coelestin V* (Paderborn F. Schöningh, 1921), pp. 69–71.

44 Theiner, *Codex diplomaticus*, vol. 1, pp. 393–4, no. 578; cf. Cesare Baronio, Odorico Rinaldi, and Giacomo Laderchi, *Annales ecclesiastici ad annum 1304* (Luca: Typis Leonardi Venturini, 1740), para. 12.

45 Georges Lizerand, *Clément V et Philippe IV le Bel* (Paris: Hachette, 1910), p. 427, doc. 4.

46 E. Déprez and Guillaume Mollat, *Clément VI: Lettres closes, patentes et curiales intéres-sant les pays autres que la France* (Paris: E. de Boccard, 1910–61), no. 4426.

47 Traditionally so, but by the fourteenth century a routine business.

48 Jean Glénisson and Guillaume Mollat, *L'administration des états de l'Église au XIVe siècle: correspondance des légats et vicaires-généraux*, I: *Gil Albornoz et Androin de la Roche (1353–1367)* (Paris: E. de Boccard, 1964), pp. 180–1, no. 497.

49 E. Baluze, *Vitae paparum Avenionensium*, new edn Guillaume Mollat (Paris: Letouzey et Ané, 1914), vol. 1, p. 329; cf. Bernard Guillemain, *La Cour pontificale d'Avignon (1309–1376): Étude d'une société* (Paris: E. de Boccard, 1962), p. 140.

50 P. Lecacheux and G. Mollat, *Lettres secrètes et curiales du Pape Urbain V (1362–1370) se rapportant à la France* (Paris: A. de Fontemoing, E. de Boccard, 1954), pp. 121–2, no. 826.

51 Lecacheux and Mollat, *Urbain V*, p. 62, no. 475.

52 When appointing a legate or nuncio, and when appointing new cardinals; see Marc Dykmans, *Le Cérémonial papal de la fin du moyen âge à la renaissance*, 2: *De Rome en Avignon ou Le Cérémonial de Jacques Stefaneschi* (Brussels and Rome: Institut historique belge de Rome, 1977), pp. 475ff.

53 Norman Zacour, *Talleyrand: The Cardinal of Périgord* (Philadelphia, PA: American Philosophical Society, 1960), pp. 25–6.

54 Anguste Coulon and Suzanne Clemencet, *Lettres secrètes et curiales du pape Jean XXII relatives à la France* (Paris: A. de Fontemoing, 1900–), vol. 2, pp. 281ff., nos. 1692ff.

55 Lemoine, *Ad Sext.*, 5.2.4.

56 *Les Registres de Nicholas III*, vol. 1, p. 106, no. 296.

57 Guillaume de Montlauzun, *Ad Sext.*, 5.2.4, who said that consultation was certainly a necessity with lesser prelates and their canons, and then went on to follow John Lemoine on the pope and cardinals, likewise without any final resolution. Cf. Guido de Baysio, *App. ad Sext.* 1: 168 (cited by Watt in *Mediaeval Studies* 33 [1971]: 144) on the continued debate in the college.

58 See section on papal elections below.

59 *Rex excelsus*, in Lucien Auvray, *Les Registres de Gregoire IX* (Paris: A. de Fontemoing, 1896), vol. 1, p. 945, no. 1715; Theiner, *Codex diplomaticus*, vol. 1, pp. 102–3, no. 124.

60 See *Ryccardi de Sancto Germano notarii Chronica*, ed. C. A. Garufi, *Rerum italicarum scriptores*, new edn, 7, pt 2 (Bologna, n.d.), pp. 184, 186.

61 See the constitution *Habet utilitas stimulo*, found only in the *Summa dictaminis* of Cardinal Thomas of Capua, published by Karl Hampe, "Eine unbekannte Konstitution Gregors IX. Zur Verwaltung und Finanzordnung des Kirchenstaates," *Zeitschrift für Kirchengeschichte* 45 (1926): 192; cf. Daniel Waley, *The Papal State in the Thirteenth Century* (London, 1961), pp. 122, 139, who feels that it may have been an unpromulgated draft, because the terms of the constitution seem not to have been observed.

62 Theiner, *Codex diplomaticus*, vol. 1, pp. 391–5, no. 571; see also Charles Grandjean, *Le Registre de Benoit XI* (Paris: E. Thorin, 1883), pp. 694–5, no. 1147.

63 Also in *Haber utilitas stimulo*.

64 Henry III of England wrote to the cardinals (February 25, 1235), rehearsing their complaint that he had not divided the latest payment of the tribute in half and sent them their share of 500 marks direct. He excused himself on the grounds that his

father's original concession had said nothing of such a division. He suggested that if he was to make such a division in future the cardinals would have to get a written mandate from the pope on the subject. Obviously Henry was not going to get mixed up in an internal squabble of the curia. See Thomas Rymer, *Foedera*, 2nd edn (London: J. Tonson, 1727), vol. 1, p. 337.

65   Johannes B. Sägmüller, *Die Tätigkeit und Stellung der Cardinäle bis Papst Bonifaz' VIII* (Freiburg im Breisgau: Herder, 1896), p. 190; Baumgarten, *Untersuchungen und Urkunden über die Camera Collegii cardinalium*, p. cxxviii.

66   See Kirsch, *Die Finanzverwaltung des Kardinal Kollegiums*, p. 6.

67   Jean Guiraud, *Les Registres d'Urbain IV (1261–1264)*, vol. 1, pp. 8–9, nos. 31–6; cf. Emil Göller, *Die Einnahmen der apostolischen Kammer unter Johann XXII* (Paderborn: F. Schöningh, 1910), vol. 1, pp. 30–1.

68   *Celestis altitudo*, in Theiner, *Codex diplomaticus*, vol. 1, pp. 304–5, no. 468.

69   See E. Ruffini-Avondo, "Le Origini del conclave papale," *Atti della reale Accademia delle scienze di Torino* 62 (1926–7): 409–31.

70   For example, see Karl Hampe, *Ein ungedruckter Bericht über das Konklave von 1241 im römischen Septizonium* (Heidelberg: C. Winter, 1913). For papal elections in the thirteenth century, Olga Joelson, *Die Papstwahlen des 13. Jahrhunderts bis zur Einführung der Conclaveordnung Gregors X* (Berlin: Kraus, 1928).

71   Giovanni Mansi, *Sacrorum conciliorum nova et amplissima collectio*, 24: 66–7.

72   Whose criticisms were met head on by Hostiensis in his comments on the rights of the college: *Comm. ad Decret.* 5.38.14 and 5.6.17.

73   *Matthaei Parisiensis monachi sancti Albani chronica majora*, ed. Henry R. Luard (London: Longman & Co., 1877), vol. 4, pp. 250–2.

74   Hostiensis, *Comm. ad Decret.* 5.38.14. Cf. Augustinus Triumphus, *De potestate collegii mortuo papa* (in Richard Scholz, *Die Publizistik zur Zelt Philipps des Schönen and Bonifaz' VIII* [Stuttgart, 1903; reprint Amsterdam: P. Schippers, 1962], pp. 501–8), who also held that during a vacancy the papal authority rested with the college of cardinals, especially since papal power is perpetual and cannot die when a pope dies; but it rests with the college in a special way as a potential rather than an effective or active power. Just as a root, however, has a threefold power of resisting opposition, of producing growth, and of sprouting, so the cardinals could (i) resist those who would injure the church, (ii) elect a new pope, and (iii) so produce flower and fruit again. It was strongly to be doubted, however, that the cardinals could do with the pope dead what they could with him alive, else why elect a pope at all? Finally, "mortuo papa non videtur quod collegium possit tollere decreta et mandata facta per papam maxime illa que ligant eos." It is therefore impossible to credit Wilks, *Problem of Sovereignty*, p. 480: ". . . we find in his [Augustinus'] *De potestate collegii* an advocacy of the complete supremacy of the College over the pope."

75   For the changes in the statute between the time of its presentation in the fifth session of the Council of Lyons on July 16, 1274 and the publication of the conciliar acts on November 1, see Stephan Kuttner, "Conciliar Law in the Making: The Lyonese Constitutions (1274) of Gregory X in a Manuscript at Washington," in *Miscellanea Pio Paschini* (Rome: Facultas Theologica Pontificii Athenaei Lateranensis, 1948), vol. 2, pp. 39–81, esp. pp. 43–4, 60–5; cf. Leonard E. Boyle, "The Date of the Commentary of William Duranti on the Constitutions of the Second Council of Lyons," *Bulletin of Medieval Canon Law* 4 (1974): 39–47.

76   For Hadrian's intention of promulgating a substitute for or an amended version of *Ubi periculum*, see *Martini Oppaviensis Chronicon pontificum et imperatorum*, in MGH, SS, vol. 22: 443; also Louis Duchesne, *Le Liber Pontificalis* (Paris: E. de Boccard, 1892), vol. 2, p. 457.

77   *Les registres de Grégoire X et de Jean XXI*, eds Jean Guiraud and E. Cadier (Paris: E. de Boccard, 1892–1960), p. 51, no. 159.

78 Auguste Potthast, *Regesta pontificum romanorum* (Berlin, 1875, reprint Akademische Druck), vol. 2, p. 1918, no. 23980; also John Lemoine (Johannes Monachus), *Glossa aurea*, fol. 63v.

79 Theiner, *Codex diplomaticus*, vol. 1, pp. 201–2, no. 356. For another case of the cardinals acting *vice* the pope, in the consecration of and giving the pallium to the archbishop of Genoa (1292), shortly after Nicholas IV died, see *Iacobi da Voragine chronica civitatis ianuensis*, ed. Giovanni Monleone (Rome: Tipographi del Senato, 1941), vol. 2, p. 404.

80 Lemoine, *Ad Sext.*, 5.11.2: ". . . penes quem [sc. cetum cardinalium] plenitudo potestatis sede vacante residet"; and again, *Ad Sext.*, 1.6.16: ". . . quia mortuo papa iurisdictio et jurisdictionis exercitium penes collegium cardinalium remanet." Cf. Johannes Andreae on the *Clementines, Ne Romani*, S.V. *Verum*, in the Lyons (1584) edition, col. 32. Peter John Olivi also held that the cardinals had the power of acting "vicem pape defuncti saltem in casibus necessariis"; see Franz Ehrle, "Petrus Johannes Olivi, sein Leben und seine Schriften," *Archiv für Litteratur und Kirchengeschichte des Mittelalters* 3 (1887): 526. Stephanus Hugoneti, long in the service of cardinal Bertrand du Poujet, held the same view in his *Apparatus super constitutionibus concilii Viennensis*. Commenting on *Ne Romani*, he followed John Lemoine's argument that since Boniface VIII restricted the cardinals during a vacancy from reinstating the deposed Colonna cardinals, the college must have general power or jurisdiction during a vacancy to have it so limited in this special case; if they had no such jurisdiction, then the limitation would make no sense. See University of Pennsylvania, MS Lat. 95, fols 9v–10r; cf. Norman Zacour, "Stephanus Hugoneti and his 'Apparatus' on the Clementines," *Traditio* 13 (1957): 456–62.

81 *AA:SS*, May, vol. 4, pp. 448–9.

82 Heinrich Finke, *Acta Aragonensia* (Berlin and Leipzig, 1908), vol. 1, p. 178.

83 Theiner, *Codex diptomaticus*, vol. 1, pp. 322–7, no. 494.

84 *Corpus Iuris Canonicus* (*CIC*), the Clementine decretals, 1.3.2.

85 Finke, *Acta Aragonensia*, vol. 2, p. 586.

86 See Lorenzo Martini's diary in Heinrich Finke, *Aus den Tagen des Bonifaz VIII: Funde und Forschungen* (Münster: Druck und Verlag der Aschendorffschen Buchhandlung, 1902), Quellen: pp. xxxviii–l; Richard Scholz, *Die Publizistik zur Zeit Philipps des Schönen und Bonifaz' VIII* (Stuttgart, 1903; reprint Amsterdam: P. Schippers, 1962), pp. 190 ff.

87 Pierre Dupuy, *Histoire du differend d'entre le pape Boniface VIII et Philippes le Bel roy de France* (Paris, 1655; reprint Tucson: Audax Press), p. 227.

88 Finke, *Aus den Tagen*, p. 79, citing *Gesta Boemundi archiepiscopi Treverensis*, in *MGH, SS*, vol. 24: 479.

89 Constantin Höfler, "Rückblick auf P. Bonifacius VIII, und die Literatur seiner Geschichte," *Abhandlungen der königliche Akademie der Wissenschaften, Historische Klasse* 3 (1841): 53; cf. pp. 48, 76.

90 From a letter of Laurentius Martinic, at the papal curia, March 1302, in Finke, *Aus den Tagen*, Quellen: pp. IL–L. Cardinal Landulf Brancacci said that it was better to be dead than to live with such a man as the pope, who was nothing but eyes and tongue in a putrefying body; ibid., pp. 106 and CXXIX.

91 Referring to a letter to Philip IV of France which Boniface VIII said was falsified by Pierre Flotte. See Dupuy, *Histoire du differend*, pp. 74–5.

92 Dupuy, *Histoire du differend*, p. 68.

93 Dupuy, *Histoire du differend*, pp. 226–7, and p. 236.

94 *PL*, vol. 206: 1075–6.

95 Gerhart B. Ladner, "The Concepts of 'Ecclesia' and 'Christianitas' and their Relationship to the Idea of Papal 'Plenitude Potestatis,' from Gregory VII to Boniface VIII," in *Sacerdozio e regno da Gregorio VII a Bonifacio VIII* (Rome: Pontifica Università Gregoriana, 1954), pp. 64–8. The decline in the number of papal acts with the

formula "de fratrum" during the pontificate of Innocent III is an indication of that pope's tendency to emancipate himself from the tutelage of the college as a whole; see Maleczek, *Papst und Kardinalskolleg*, pp. 315–16.

96 Pierre Gasnault and M. H. Laurent, *Innocent VI* (Paris: E. de Boccard, 1959), vol. 1, pp. 137–8, no. 435.

97 Gasnault and Laurents, *Innocent VI*. They also refined some of the rules pertaining to the process of papal election; see Dykmans, *Le Cérémonial*, vol. 3, pp. 57–8, n. 22.

Part III

WOMEN AND THE PRACTICE OF ASCETICISM AND CONTEMPLATION

Introduction

The most important recent change in our understanding of asceticism and monasticism in the Middle Ages has been the integration of women into the history of such medieval monastic and religious lives. With the exception of a handful of relatively powerful and important monastic women of the early Middle Ages, religious women received little attention in the traditional histories.[1] Yet monastic life was well suited to women. The monastic Office, the recitation of Psalms at regular intervals each day (completing the entire book of Psalms once a week) could be performed by nuns as easily as by monks, and women's communities needed priests only to celebrate the Mass. Although the eleventh century (as discussed by McNamara in Chapter 4) seems to have been a low point for women's monasticism in Western Europe, recent studies show that women's participation in monastic life reached new heights from the twelfth through fourteenth centuries.[2] Although historians now tell the story of religious reform in the central and late Middle Ages with women included, to do so has required rewriting the larger narrative which once denied women any role within the major twelfth-century monastic reform movements, and only a minor one among the thirteenth-century mendicants.

Most new religious communities of the central Middle Ages for both sexes derived from efforts to return to the practices of the early desert Fathers, or the communal life of the early Apostles, the *vita apostolica*. Seeking the simplicity of such "apostolic" lives, reformers left the twelfth-century towns to live in the "deserts" of Western Europe – the forested wildernesses or craggy mountain slopes.[3] Many new communities began as such communities of hermits (living in hermitages or eremitical communities), recluses or anchorites (living in anchor-holds or isolated cells). Many such monastic communities were single-sex ones, but sometimes they included whole families. Such groups of heroic, eremitical reformers were gradually rout-inized into cenobitic monastic communities. (*Coenobia* refers to the common table at which they ate; the word monastery too comes from the Greek word for a monk, *monachos*, related to the word for alone, but it had come to mean a community of shared lives.) These cenobitic monastic communities had an elected head, the abbess or abbot (prioress or prior at a priory). They followed a written rule, most often that of Benedict of Nursia (d. *c*.530), but there was also a popular rule attributed to Augustine of Hippo (d. 430), fourth-century bishop in North Africa. Each community developed its own peculiar practices or customs that often were written down in books called customaries, and sometimes shared with other new communities. Such sharing might extend to liturgical practices and prayers for neighboring communities, to the creation of small congregations of related houses, or eventually to what came to be known as religious orders.

The traditional history of monasticism tends to describe individual groups in terms of what Janet Nelson has recently described as a cyclical "tripartite drama": first, heroic reform; then, a brilliant Golden Age, and finally decadence and decline at a particular site or community, only to be followed by a new group's repeat of the cycle.[4] In its most frequent version, Western monastic history recounts the development of one or another set of local early medieval monastic practices coming together with the early tenth-century foundation of Cluny at a Burgundian site bordering Empire, France, and the road south to Italy and Rome. Cluny was a famous liturgical center offering impressive anniversary masses for the dead, its coffers filled with impressive tribute from Reconquest rulers in Spain; its leaders had close ties to men of power and prestige who led the eleventh-century Gregorian reform. With its monarchical congregation that was created out of once-independent monastic communities given to its abbot for reform, Cluny dominated tenth and eleventh-century Europe, but traditional accounts, usually drawing on the remarks of the twelfth-century Cistercians, describe a crisis in which Cluny's elaborate liturgy and ornate buildings, budget problems, and decreasing austerity led to its decadence by the late eleventh century.

In such accounts the spotlight moves from eleventh-century Cluny to the new foundations such as those at Cîteaux and Clairvaux in the twelfth century. Despite the implication that reform followed decline, however, the rise of such new reform communities had little to do with what was happening at Cluny, and the foundations of such reform communities reflect instead a general expansion of monasticism based on an increased demand for places in religious communities which could now be supported by an improving economy in the twelfth century. Such new religious communities also had new emphases that relate to societal changes at the time. For one thing, many of them attempted to live simple lives of "apostolic poverty" without liturgical elaborations, and to support themselves by manual labor rather than being "lords" of villages or living on rents from ovens, mills, tithes, or altars. Some of the new communities recruited among peasants for brothers and sisters who would labor on distant granges. Concern for souls in the hereafter was mixed with a sympathy for the sick and poor of this world, and many of the new religious foundations of the twelfth century provided specialized religious services intended to improve conditions in the here and now – founding hospices for travelers, leprosaria, and military-religious outposts in the West that would transmit funds to support the Crusades.[5]

The most successful of the new twelfth-century groups would be that which developed from the abbey of Cîteaux, the Cistercians. This reform group would become a huge international association with hundreds of affiliated communities, all exempt from local episcopal visitation, which was replaced by an elaborate system of internal visitation. Ruled by written constitutions, exhorting members to uniformity of practices, and holding annual General Chapter meetings of all abbots (and in the thirteenth century, a separate one for all abbesses), the Cistercians became the model for the organization of all religious houses into orders after the Fourth Lateran Council in 1215. As Constance Hoffman Berman shows in Chapter 8, however, this standard description is more apt for the thirteenth century than the twelfth. The leading twelfth-century spokesman for the Cistercians, Bernard, abbot of Clairvaux (d. 1153), has already been discussed, as has the fact that, despite their protests about the contemplative life, abbots like Bernard and his successors at Clairvaux and Cîteaux were important preachers against heresy, or were promoting Crusade, or in support of contenders in the papal schisms of the twelfth century.[6] As Berman shows, the Order of Cîteaux, as an institutional umbrella group which encompassed many abbeys, appeared somewhat later in the twelfth century than has traditionally been thought. There were Cistercian nuns from an early date and they cannot be dismissed as only imitating the practices of the men within that order. Despite the fact that official histories of the Cistercians have denied women's presence, the role of women within this and other reform movements of the twelfth century was an important one.

The accounts of twelfth-century monastic foundations made by flight to the desert that have characterized traditional accounts of this period of reform history are paralleled by accounts of the lives of twelfth-century individuals in which adult conversion is central.[7] Recruits to the new religious houses were not usually oblates (the children who in an earlier period had been dedicated to monastic communities by parents), but adults who entered the religious life at mid-career, or founded a new religious community after experiencing a mid-life crisis and conversion. Thus, in some cases, a secular cleric like Bernard of Clairvaux gave up the vanities of the urban schools to seek an austere life in rural seclusion as a hermit or monk – in Bernard's case entering the existing house at Cîteaux before being sent to found and be abbot at Clairvaux. Monastic *Lives* also report adult conversion to the religious life in the twelfth century by secular clerics, knights, and even merchants. In some cases these were "conversions" to a stricter religious life, like those of the group who left the "decadent" monastery of Molesme to found a stricter one at Cîteaux. A knight, like Pons de Léras, founder of

Silvanès (d. c.1140), could renounce his violence and go on pilgrimage, decide to found a hermitage, and eventually become a "conversus" (the word first meant a convert, but eventually a lay-brother), at what would become a Cistercian abbey.[8] Other knights who chose to join one of the new military-religious orders like the Templars or Hospitalers, "converted" to monasticism while remaining active as knights. There was also conversion from Judaism or Islam to Christianity, or vice versa.[9]

Men's conversion stories rarely identify the women and family members involved; despite it being her tears that had converted him, the wife's name in the Pons de Léras account is unknown. *Lives* describing men's conversions to the religious life are more frequent than those for women, and involved very dramatic changes of heart – men went from lives as knightly thugs or grasping merchants to being humble lay-brothers or hermits. In contrast, what at first looks like conversions in *Lives* of women like Christina of Markyate (d. c.1160) and Yvette of Huy (d. 1228), were not strictly speaking conversions at all, but heroic tales that parallel the plot lines of secular romances. These heroines encountered a series of trials or obstacles before finally reaching the object of their quest, to lead religious lives as they had long desired.[10] But there were also true female converts, often mentioned only in the charters.[11] Given the widespread conversion theme in so many narratives and documents of the period, it is not surprising that historians have spoken of the twelfth century as a period of "the birth of the individual."[12]

As the Cistercians, like the Cluniacs before them, became wealthy and powerful and less attractive to new recruits, they were replaced by new groups. According to the tripartite drama of medieval monasticism, thirteenth-century conversions were not to the practices of the life of the Cistercians (although there were still Cistercian foundations, particularly of women's houses). The preferred thirteenth-century choice was conversion to a life of active service within the mendicant (begging) and preaching orders. Indeed, thirteenth-century conversions were epitomized by that of Francis of Assisi (d. 1226), founder of the Franciscans, who, after being taken prisoner while fighting for his town against a neighboring one, decided that the life of the knight was not for him. He gave up the life of a wealthy bourgeois, renounced his family and their possessions – giving up even his clothing – to convert to religion, wandering from place to place, restoring churches, teaching the Gospel, and living as a beggar or mendicant. His example in Italy was paralleled by that of Dominic of Guzman (d. 1221), the originator of the Dominican Order, who decided to preach against the Cathars in southern France barefoot and in rags. Although some of the anti-establishment activities of Francis in particular came close to those of heretics, Pope Innocent III (1198–1216) wisely harnessed this new movement in support of orthodoxy by granting a preaching mission supported by daily mendicancy to Francis and his followers.

Once again, as with the Cistercians, we find in the thirteenth-century history of the new mendicant orders a tendency to refuse to give much attention to the many penitent women who constituted a great part of the new movement. But for the thirteenth century sources are slightly more full than for twelfth-century nuns. Yet the presence of mendicant women has been dismissed by many as unimportant, in part because mendicant women were soon forbidden to beg, like the men of those orders. Katherine Jansen looks at both Dominicans and Franciscans in her examination in Chapter 9 of the appeal to these new groups of the contemplative Mary Magdalen. Jansen examines not only the sermons written about Mary Magdalen as a contemplative saint, but also shows that we should neither dismiss the impact of the mendicant movement on women, nor minimize the ways in which female models of sanctity were efficacious among these new groups. Mary Magdalen, the active saint who had washed the feet of Jesus, became, from at least the thirteenth century, the contemplative saint inspiring all those who abandoned worldly vanities to retreat to the contemplative life. This legendary Mary Magdalen was depicted in art as living in a craggy wilderness in Provence, acting out her penitence by stripping herself of all possessions, even her clothing, which was replaced by the covering of her beautiful hair. She was able to inspire those mendicants attempting to meld their active mission of preaching and service to one of contemplative prayer. This is seen in the spread of religious foundations that took as their patron this former sinner, not necessarily because they were houses of reformed prostitutes (a common assumption in the past), but because these communities saw in Mary Magdalen a symbol of hope that their own repentance would bring salvation.

Mary Magdalen is closely tied to debate about whether active or contemplative lives were better. Such discussion often centered on the contrast between the biblical Martha, who had chosen to serve Jesus in the active life, and her sister Mary who chose to listen to his teachings. In the Middle Ages the contemplative Mary was often conflated with Mary Magdalen, who from at least the eleventh-century in Italy had been the inspiration for communities of penitents – often taking temporary vows and without the formal rules of monastic houses – which were a preliminary stage in what would become the mendicant orders. Thirteenth-century mendicant brothers who sought to mix the active and contemplative lives sometimes saw the women within their orders as providing a solution to the vexed question of mixing the *vita activa* and the *vita contemplativa*; as was suggested in the letters of the early Dominican Jordan of Saxony (d. 1237) to the Dominican nun in Florence, Diana of Andalo (d. 1234), gender specialization would allow the active lives of mendicant brothers to be balanced by the contemplative lives of their enclosed mendicant sisters.[13]

Related to the issue of the contemplative life, moreover, was the issue of monastic enclosure, particularly for women, an issue that became more pressing in the thirteenth century when women attempted to lead mendicant lives. From the inception of mendicant orders grave doubts had been expressed about the propriety of women's preaching or begging. At Prouille in southern France and at San Sisto in Rome, houses for Dominican nuns were soon founded, but these women were endowed like traditional nuns and were strictly enclosed. Some women who sought to follow the way of life of Francis of Assisi formed a community at San Damiano under the direction of his disciple and friend, Clare of Assisi (d. 1253). Clare agreed to enclosure, but wanted to own no property. She gained papal approval for such absolute poverty and it was agreed that the sisters would depend on the local Franciscan brothers to beg for the nuns. The permission to have no property, however, was rescinded soon after Clare's death and thereafter the Clarissans, like Dominican nuns, had to have endowment on which to live. Thereafter, women who wished to live religious lives under mendicant direction were allowed to do so only if they neither preached nor begged. They were either strictly enclosed, as members of mendicant orders but with the same enclosed lives as traditional nuns, or became Beguines or recluses under mendicant direction.

Caroline Bruzelius's work in Chapter 10 on the architecture of the churches for the followers of Clare of Assisi, or Clarissans, turns to the practical consequences of the increasingly strict enforcement of monastic enclosure for these women. In her examination of the physical setting in which Clarissans lived, Bruzelius finds that the establishment of nuns' choirs, grills, and screens to isolate the nuns from the priests celebrating Mass also limited the nuns' ability to see the Mass and the crucial moment of the elevation of the Host, when the consecrated bread and wine became the body and blood of Christ. Women were encouraged to depend on their hearing rather than on their seeing of the Mass. As the Mass and reverence for the Eucharistic wafer or Host, seen as the very body of Christ, or Corpus Christi, became more important in the later Middle Ages, nuns wanted a view of the altar and its relic. Such female Eucharistic devotion affected the configuration of space in the church of Donnaregina in Naples.

Finally, in overturning old assumptions about women and the monastic orders there is the vexing issue of whether men found it a duty and a burden to be required to provide the *cura monialium*, the care of women's souls, to enclosed religious women. Very recently, Fiona J. Griffiths has looked at intellectual history sources to re-evaluate this question, citing the letters of Abelard and Heloise, and Abelard's sermons to argue that religious men of the twelfth century, while never actually using the term *cura monialium* were attracted to the idea that caring for the needs of religious women was a means toward their own redemption. Thus as Griffiths argues in Chapter 11, some twelfth-century men, including Abelard, seemed to have embraced the idea that such care for nuns' souls was an opportunity to be embraced because it promoted their own spiritual perfection. In Abelard's case it was also a means to assure the occupation of a religious site, the Paraclete, which he had founded as an oratory before Heloise and her nuns were sent there. (Indeed Griffiths' work suggests that it may well be only the modern scholarship that has presented the *cura monialium* as an unpleasant duty.) In the case of Abelard and Heloise, that activity extended beyond the spiritual or pastoral concerns and the introduction of liturgical innovations to the provision of a rule. In its logical conclusion Abelard argued that men's communities should be attached to women's ones; Heloise did not agree that religious women should be ruled by men.

Griffiths, like Berman, Jansen, and Bruzelius, provides a gender-integrated history of monasticism that is not just about women and religion, but about women and men together creating religious orders and negotiating their rules, devoting themselves to new saints, and thinking their way through the implications of a newly developing Eucharistic devotion. That devotion, so fulfilling and important to religious women, would have profoundly different consequences for non-Christians; its further ramifications are discussed in Part IV.

NOTES

1 On these early medieval religious women, see Jane T. Schulenburg, *Forgetful of their Sex: Female Sanctity and Society, ca. 500–1100* (Chicago, IL: University of Chicago Press, 1998).

2 Important recent studies include Penelope D. Johnson, *Equal in Monastic Profession: Religious Women in Medieval France* (Chicago, IL: University of Chicago Press, 1991); Bruce Venarde, *Women's Monasticism and Medieval Society: Nunneries in France and England, 890–1215* (Ithaca, NY: Cornell University Press, 1997); and Marilyn Oliva, *The Convent and the Community in Late Medieval England: Female Monasteries in the Diocese of Norwich 1350–1450* (Woodbridge: Boydell, 1998).

3 See Henrietta Leyser, *Hermits and the New Monasticism: A Study of Religious Communities in Western Europe, 1000–1150* (London: Macmillan, 1984); Ludo Milis, *Angelic Monks and Earthly Men: Monasticism and its Meaning to Medieval Society* (Woodbridge: Boydell, 1992); Paulette l'Hermite-Leclercq, "Reclus et recluses dans le Sud-Ouest de la France," *La Femme dans la vie religieuse du Languedoc (XIIIe–XIVe s.). Cahiers de Fanjeaux* (Toulouse: Privat, 1988), vol. 23, pp. 281–98; and Ann K. Warren, *Anchorites and their Patrons in Medieval England* (Berkeley, CA: University of California Press, 1985).

4 Janet L. Nelson, "Medieval Monasticism," in *The Medieval World*, eds Peter Linehan and Janet L. Nelson (London: Routledge, 2001), pp. 576–604, esp. 583.

5 A good introduction is still Lester K. Little, *Religious Poverty and the Profit Economy in Medieval Europe* (Ithaca, NY: Cornell University Press, 1978).

6 See Beverly Kienzle, *Cistercians, Heresy and Crusade in Occitania 1145–1229: Preaching in the Lord's Vineyard* (York: Medieval Press, 2001).

7 See, for instance, Caroline Walker Bynum's "Did the Twelfth-Century Discover the Individual?" in eadem, *Jesus as Mother. Studies in the Spirituality of the High Middle Ages* (Berkeley, CA: University of California Press, 1982), pp. 92–109, or Colin Morris, "Individualism in Twelfth-Century Religion: Some Further Reflections," *Journal of Ecclesiastical History* 31 (1980): 195–206.

8 The text is available in Beverly Kienzle, "The Tract on the Conversion of Pons of Leras and the True Account of the Beginning of the Monastery of Silvanès," *Cistercian Studies Quarterly* 30 (1995): 227–43.

9 In a growing literature on such conversion, see David Nirenberg, "Conversion, Sex and Segregation: Jews and Christians in Medieval Spain," *American Historical Review* 107 (2002): 1065–93, esp. 1078ff.

10 For example, *The Life of Christina of Markyate*, ed. C. H. Talbot (Oxford: Clarendon, 1959).

11   See the story of Mayheudis:

> Who first lived as a secular woman but afterwards, being visited by the
> Holy Spirit and wishing to provide for the health of her own soul, and
> having come to realize how contrary to her soul's health were all the trap-
> pings of the World, took the garb of a monastic woman.

With the permission of her husband, Peter Beaucorps, who was still living, she
entered the Benedictine house for nuns at Saintes; then because of her good works
and holiness, she was sent to be prioress at Chapières. *Cartulaire de l'abbaye royale
de Notre-Dame de Saintes de l'ordre de Saint Benoit*, ed. Thomas Grasilier (Niort:
Clouzot, 1871), no. 67 (1163).

12   See n. 7 above.

13   See *Love Among the Saints: The Letters of Blessed Jordan of Saxony to Blessed Diana of
Andalo*, trans. Kathleen Pond (London, Bloomsbury Publishing Co., 1959).

8

WERE THERE TWELFTH-CENTURY CISTERCIAN NUNS?

Constance Hoffman Berman

The Cistercian Order was the most successful of the new reform monastic orders of the twelfth century, but its early history has been obscured by a tendency to read back its thirteenth-century practices on to its twelfth-century origins. The one exception to this has been the history of its women, who were excluded altogether from that earliest history. Indeed, it has been a truism in the history of medieval religious orders that the Cistercians only admitted women late in the twelfth century and then under considerable outside pressure. This view has posited a twelfth-century "Golden Age" when it had been possible for the abbots of the Order of Cîteaux to avoid contact with women totally. Only later did the floodgates burst open and a great wave of women wishing to be Cistercians sweep past abbots powerless to resist them. This chapter reassesses narrative accounts, juridical arguments, and charter evidence to show that assertions about the absence of any twelfth-century Cistercian nuns are not only incorrect, but are based on mistaken notions of how the early Cistercian Order developed, as well as on a biased reading of the evidence, including a double standard for proof of Cistercian status – made much higher for women's houses than for men's. In fact, evidence from which it has been argued that nuns were only imitating the Cistercian Order's practices in the twelfth century contains exactly the same language, which when used to describe men's houses has been deemed to show that they were Cistercian. If approached in a gender-neutral way, the evidence shows that abbeys of Cistercian women appeared as early as those for the Order's men. Formal criteria for incorporation of women's houses into the Order in the thirteenth century, moreover, are irrelevant to a twelfth-century situation in which only gradually did most communities of monks or nuns eventually identified as Cistercian come to be part of the newly developing institution. The argument in this chapter was extended from beyond the case of nuns in Constance Hoffman Berman, The Cistercian Evolution: The Invention of a Religious Order in Twelfth-century Europe *(Philadelphia, PA: University of Pennsylvania Press, 2000); it was originally published in a slightly longer form in* Church History 68 (1999): 824–64.

* * *

Charter and cartulary evidence

Overwhelming evidence from the documents of practice shows that women were present from the start of the religious movement that grew out of the Burgundian reform monastery of Molesme to become the Cistercian Order.[1] In documents for the house at Molesme from which Cîteaux originated, we find women not only as donors and patrons of the reform monastic movement, but also entering the abbey of Molesme as sisters. We see a charter for Molesme, for example, detailing a donor's daughter entering that abbey after 1075.[2] In another act dating from between 1076 and 1085, a donor's sister was given as a nun at Molesme.[3] A third act from c.1100 in the Molesme cartulary shows a woman entering Molesme with her son in a text mentioning the community of other nuns there.[4]

By 1113 or so Molesme had founded a house of nuns at Jully which would eventually have at least seven daughters.[5] Jully is said to have followed a rule established for it by Guy, second abbot of Molesme, along with the famous Cistercian abbot, Bernard of Clairvaux (d. 1153), and by abbots of two or three other Cistercian houses at c.1130.[6] Milo, count of Bar, gave Molesme the property at a castle called Jully on which the priory was founded, at approximately the same moment that Bernard was founding Clairvaux.[7] The bishop of Langres confirmed tithes in two villages to Jully in 1126–36, and other charters of c.1130 also confirm rents, tithes, and other properties given to the nuns at Jully.[8] A number of charters suggest the close relationship of the priory of Jully with Bernard of Clairvaux; such evidence includes a charter recording a conveyance of tithes given to the community of nuns by Humbelina, Bernard's sister, when she entered Jully in 1133.[9] Charters reveal that already in 1128 Aanolz, widow of Walter of la Roche, gave Jully a rent of ten livres when she left the world and entered that abbey. She is described as making her gift in the presence of Bernard, abbot of Clairvaux, and three of his monks, and three monks from Molesme.[10] A house at Bar-sur-Aube given to Clairvaux was transferred by Abbot Bernard of Clairvaux to the nuns at Jully, but whether the donor had explicitly intended that the gift be received by Clairvaux for those nuns of Jully is unclear.[11] Nonetheless, the relationship was still close in 1142 when Bernard himself, along with the bishop of Langres (who was present at Jully with Andrew of Baldimento and his son Guy), received and vested as nuns at Jully Andrew's daughters Mahaut and Halvide. Andrew and Guy gave the nuns a rent of forty solidi over a villa called Johei, to be paid annually at the feast of Saint Rémy.[12]

Three years later, however, when Eugenius III (1145–53) confirmed Jully's rights in a papal privilege of 1145, it was Molesme not Clairvaux that was in question. The pope confirmed the gift from Milon of Bar of Jully's site to Abbot Gerald of Molesme and the brothers "professing the regular life there," establishing that Jully and the holy nuns of that church and their properties in the dioceses of Langres and Chalons be under the management of Molesme.

Those nuns, described as following the institutes established for Jully, were to be enclosed, and the monks of Molesme were to provide for their secular business.[13] It may indeed be that this moment in 1145 marks the point when ties between Jully and Clairvaux were permanently severed. Certainly at some point between 1142, when Bernard was still overseeing the abbey, and 1145, it had been decided that, rather than have its nuns be under the authority of Clairvaux, Jully would remain tied to Molesme, the abbey which had originally founded it as a priory.

In addition to Bernard of Clairvaux's support of the women at Jully from 1113 and over the next several decades, by the 1120s we also find a house of nuns at le Tart, reputed to have been founded by the abbot of Cîteaux, Stephen Harding (d. 1134).[14] This abbey of Cistercian nuns is usually treated as an unofficial foundation made by Stephen in the 1120s, having nothing to do with the Cistercian Order, which Stephen was reputed to have founded in the previous decade. In fact much of the most reliable information about le Tart comes only from the 1140s or later. The foundation account for le Tart, presented as if it were a document of practice or charter, is probably actually a narrative composed later than the twelfth century, listing the various gifts that had been made to Elizabeth, abbess, and Maria, prioress of the house.[15] That this was a house of aristocratic women is seen by a confirmation made by Matthew, duke of Lorraine, of whatever his mother Adelaide had given to le Tart when she entered that house.[16] It is also likely that at least one daughter of the lord of Montpellier was sent to le Tart in the 1170s.[17] Le Tart had at least eighteen daughter houses by the end of the twelfth century.[18] We have a papal confirmation from 1147 in a bull, *Desiderium quod*, that parallels other confirmations by Eugenius III to Cistercian houses for men. The bull lists le Tart's site, five granges, more than fifteen other properties, and its Cistercian tithe privileges, telling us that these nuns followed Cistercian practices.[19]

For the thirteenth century there are a number of accounts of meetings of Cistercian abbesses at le Tart held under the presidency of the abbot of Cîteaux (from these documents derive a list of eighteen daughters).[20] This filiation of women's houses parallels that which the king of Castile wished to establish in the 1180s in Spain under the leadership of the royal foundation of las Huelgas.[21] There are also scattered references suggesting the existence of several other small congregations or filiations of houses of Cistercian nuns in the thirteenth century – for instance, those following the practices of the Cistercian nuns of Saint-Antoine-des-Champs outside Paris.[22]

Many other houses of early twelfth-century nuns associated with the Cistercians might be mentioned. They include foundations made by Jully and le Tart from the 1120s. Many of these have been described in traditional narratives as genuine foundations made by colonies of women sent out from Burgundy. Such references to monastic colonization in groups of six or twelve nuns with an abbess, however, reflect a widespread gestational myth of apostolic foundation among the Cistercians that sees all houses of nuns or monks as having necessarily sprung from some earlier community.[23] Certainly, many houses among the daughters of le Tart, like Fabas and Rieunette in Languedoc, were independent local foundations similar to the nunnery at Marrenz founded in 1157 by Count Raymond V of Toulouse (1148–94). This last house did not even claim to have ties to le Tart, but nonetheless did consider itself Cistercian.[24]

Such women's houses also included many independent houses of religious women that were founded locally without any impetus from Burgundy, although they may have been encouraged by the preaching of Bernard of Clairvaux to practice the *ordo* or way of life of Cîteaux and Clairvaux. There were among them some houses of women that became Cistercian only after having become attached to local communities and congregations of monks, which in turn eventually adopted Cistercian practices. For instance, in 1147 nuns at Coyroux were apparently incorporated or at least began to adopt Cistercian practices along with monks from their sister house at Obazine.[25] Nuns at l'Abbaye-Blanche and at Villers-Canivet would come to be incorporated by Cîteaux along with Savigny at an unknown date. The date of 1147 is often given for this attachment, but there is little clear evidence that this congregation was practicing Cistercian customs until the early 1160s.[26] It was into this category of incorporated communities that Gilbert of Sempringham had apparently attempted to affiliate his nuns and canons at Sempringham, possibly as early as the late 1140s, but more likely in the 1160s as is discussed elsewhere.[27] Another group of independent houses of nuns who considered themselves Cistercian in Lincolnshire and Yorkshire was founded in the middle years of the twelfth century.[28] In Spain, las Huelgas in 1187, but also Tulebras as early as 1157, might also be considered to have begun to adopt Cistercian practices independently of any men's house. This also appears to have been true of the abbey of nuns at Montreuil-les-Dames in northern France, founded in 1136 near Laon and described by Herman of Tournai in his history of that diocese of *c*.1150 discussed on pp. 229–30.[29]

Sometimes such communities of women even predated the houses of monks to which they would eventually become subject, or had early ties to one another. These include those between the nuns of Bellecombe in the Auvergne and its daughter house at Nonenque in the Rouergue. Both of these communities of nuns first appear in records in 1139 and both were later attached to Cîteaux along with the congregation of Mazan. While Nonenque and Bellecombe date to the 1130s or earlier, only later did the monks of nearby Silvanès take control of Nonenque, in this case breaking Nonenque's earlier link to another house of women, and eventually making it a dependent satellite. Possibly in response to their house's forced dependence on Silvanès, the abbesses of Nonenque eventually tried, but failed, to secede from the Order altogether.[30] Careful analysis of such examples suggests that these twelfth-century houses of nuns were as Cistercian as were twelfth-century houses of monks founded at similar dates. Their existence problematizes, however, traditional notions of just what we mean by the early Cistercian Order.

While documents of practice concerning religious women at Molesme, Jully, le Tart, and elsewhere provide abundant evidence for twelfth-century Cistercian nuns, the standard monastic histories have tended to leave out or marginalize these women.[31] This is probably because the early Cistercian narrative texts are remarkably silent about religious women associated with early Cîteaux.[32] The silence of the Cistercian *exordia* has allowed historians to apply juridical arguments about Cistercian status to these nuns that are more suitable to the thirteenth century, but not at all suitable to the twelfth-century situation, and hence to argue that twelfth-century houses of religious women were not really Cistercian. Such historians claiming that there were no twelfth-century Cistercian women – or at least that there were no Cistercian nuns before the late 1180s when abbots in General Chapter were consulted with regard to such nuns in Spain – have based their claims on a picture of the early Cistercians that is wholly unfounded.[33]

Such a reading of the medieval sources, disallowing any claims regarding religious women's participation in early Cistercian life, is in striking contrast to the standard presentation of the Cistercian Order's monks. That this is so should not be surprising given how much the discourse concerning medieval religious women was controlled by the men who wrote the earliest histories of the Cistercian Order and other orders. It was apparently men within the Cistercian Order who wrote the accounts of its earliest history in the *Exordium Cistercii*, *Exordium parvum*, and *Exordium magnum*, as well as writing and editing the *Vita prima* of Bernard of Clairvaux.[34] If we look at the origins of the Cistercian Order not according to the self-glorifying texts called *exordia*, which Cistercian men wrote and from which they excluded women, but from the viewpoint of local administrative records, we must argue for a slowly developing Order that included nuns.

A new view of the Order

Usually the twelfth-century Cistercian Order has been seen as one made up wholly of monastic men whose precociously invented institutions allowed great numbers of monks to spread out from Burgundy to colonize abbeys during the 1130s and 1140s. This outflow from Burgundy was assumed to be by a process of apostolic gestation in which mother abbeys sent out communities of twelve monks and an abbot to found daughter houses. Such language of mothers and daughters is indeed found in the earliest text of the Cistercian foundation stories, the *Exordium Cistercii*. In the model of Cistercian colonization based on that and other early texts, miraculous numbers of monks departed from Burgundy in this colonialism, taking with them Cistercian customs, to found new communities of monks in all parts of Europe. According to this view, top-down decisions were made about the creation of new houses because the Order's early corporate structure had emerged fully formed from the brain of Stephen Harding by 1119. An order was created by the foundation of a series of daughter houses like new colonies in far-flung territories. Each new monastery was the result of a positive decision on the part of a mother abbey, which sent out its surplus of monks to an unsettled place to make clearances in the wilderness where members of the new group could lead their contemplative lives.

In this explanation, abbots from the newly founded houses would return to Burgundy each year to a General Chapter to consult further on the Order's practices. Such an organization was believed to provide considerable unanimity and standardization of practice, for instance, in its creation of granges and buildings, and in the recruitment of members, as well as in the practice of the liturgy or copying of texts of the Bible. Such filiation trees of the Order, despite dating only to the thirteenth century when they became necessary for organizing the Order's practice of internal visitation, have tended to be used to support such a mythical presentation of the Order's early history. Filiation trees have distorted the actual events of the expansion of the numbers of new men's houses by their implication of a movement overflowing from the original houses in Burgundy. That implication, however, is an artifact of the tree-like structure of the Order's organizational charts created in the thirteenth-century, rather than reflecting a reality about Cistercian expansion.[35] Moreover, the moment of finding an official place on the filiation trees for women (by their reduction to satellites of men's houses) cannot be seen as the moment at which women were "allowed" into the Order.

New and considerably later dating for internal narrative accounts such as the *Exordium Cistercii* and *Exordium parvum*, and for the earliest collections of Cistercian statutes (once thought to have been in place before 1134), and for papal confirmation of a Charter of Charity (probably first done in 1165 rather than in 1119), challenges assumptions about the validity of the traditional depictions of the Order.[36] This dating is based on careful reconsideration of the twelfth-century manuscripts of these texts and the statutes, lay-brother treatises, and liturgical *ordines* which frequently accompany them. Particularly, it is from small, incremental, changes in the liturgical treatises that it is possible to construct a chronological series of such primitive Cistercian documents in surviving manuscripts and to date the *exordia* to no earlier than the 1160s.[37] These findings about the *exordia* manuscripts are confirmed by the fact that the earliest references to a Cistercian Order even in the documents of practice are first found for the 1140s.[38] There is in addition no documentary evidence for any references to either a General Chapter or to an order in the administrative sense in which we think of it today before the late 1150s.[39] The first surviving early manuscript copy of a papal confirmation of a Cistercian Charter of Charity was that by Alexander III, dating to 1163 or 1165, and may parallel demands by this pope that all reform religious groups present him with such written customaries.[40] Such recent research on the early "constitutional" documents of the Cistercians demonstrates that depictions of an early Cistercian Order refusing to accommodate women are false.

No such order existed before the second half of the twelfth century. This is not the usual way the Cistercians have been described.

There was no miraculous expansion from Cîteaux. We can now see that early abbeys directly associated with Cîteaux constituted only a tiny congregation in Burgundy united by nothing more than a vision of monastic love and equality. This tiny congregation of abbeys emanating from Cîteaux and Clairvaux in the first half of the twelfth century cannot have numbered more than a couple of dozen houses.[41] Its expansion into an order of hundreds of abbeys occurred through massive "takeovers" of independently established pre-Cistercian religious houses and congregations, which had gradually been adopting certain Cistercian practices. Such communities of monks and nuns in the earliest stages of their adoption of Cistercian practice might be described as part of a proto-order. Admiration for the way of life of the brothers of Cîteaux and Clairvaux may have increasingly motivated such independent reform communities to adopt Cistercian customs even before there was an order with which to become affiliated. But influence was not unidirectional from the Burgundian center and growth occurred not by an overflowing of reform ideals from that region, but by a complex interchange of institutional ideas which moved both toward that center and away from it.

The creation of the new twelfth-century institution, the religious order, was thus probably a more collaborative activity than historians have usually believed. Indeed, some parts of the new Cistercian institutions may not even have been invented at Cîteaux but elsewhere; Cistercians undoubtedly borrowed from other reformers and vice versa at a time when all were attempting to create larger supra-monastic structures. Such new umbrella groups of abbeys (and that is what the new twelfth-century invention, the religious order, is really about) could not have been unanimous and monolithic in the early twelfth century because structures for control did not exist at such an early date. All evidence shows that a General Chapter, written statutes, and well-developed internal visitation came for the Cistercians only after mid-twelfth century. Until then the status of many individual abbeys of such reform monks was just as ambiguous as was that of the houses of nuns that also eventually came to be recognized as Cistercian. For most, such ambiguity remained into the thirteenth century.

This is not to say that there was no Cistercian movement in early twelfth-century Burgundy, or to deny a "conversation about charity," or a "textual community" around Bernard of Clairvaux that created much enthusiasm for the practices of the brothers at Cîteaux. Nor is this to deny that a tiny congregation of houses began to appear around Clairvaux before the mid-twelfth century.[42] The semi-eremitical movement developing from Cîteaux and Clairvaux in the first half of the twelfth century might even be called a Burgundian congregation, although apparently the Cistercians themselves rarely used this term. During the movement's earliest years, training and indoctrination in its monastic customs were conducted in personal, informal, oral, and indeed charismatic ways, as apprenticeships in monastic charity which need not have excluded either lay-brothers and lay-sisters or noble women. As this small congregation became known more widely, probably principally through the preaching of Bernard of Clairvaux, houses that were still not part of any religious order or congregation began to adopt the liturgical practices and lay-brother customaries associated with Cîteaux – at this stage forming a proto-order. After *c*.1150 administrative institutions began to appear which eventually joined together all these abbeys of the proto-order into a supra-monastic government, or order, in which training in the monastic life and relations between abbeys were increasingly backed up by written statutes.[43]

The process by which this proto-order of independently founded houses gradually merged with the earlier Burgundian congregation and coalesced into an increasingly controlled and unanimous entity, the religious order, is not very clear, but it had begun by the 1160s. The new entity, the Cistercian Order as described by historians, did not come to be fully formed until the 1180s, 1190s, or even later. This is clear because the statutes of those very years reveal the process of "order-building" underway.[44] Only after this new order grew to be more administratively oriented in the last decades of the twelfth century did legislation by the Cistercian General Chapter on the incorporation of nuns appear.[45] Pressures that it articulate its policies about religious women probably arose because some abbots within the Cistercian movement (for example in Flanders) had become overwhelmed by the *cura monialium*, having large numbers of houses of women under their care.[46] It was becoming increasingly obvious as well that, although many wealthy communities of nuns were being founded, in some cases women's communities were not suitable – in all likelihood because they did not have sufficient endowment to be economically independent.[47]

That there were no such regularly established procedures in the twelfth century for the incorporation of women's houses, or those for men, that were comparable to procedures established in the thirteenth century must be viewed as an entirely normal result of how the Cistercian movement grew, even though it had included women as well as men from nearly the start. Until the articulation of the Order's administrative structures in the third quarter of the twelfth century, no formal criteria could have been in place for the admission of either women's or men's houses into the Order.[48] Moreover, that such issues became noticeable in the thirteenth century does not indicate that Cistercian nuns were not there from the beginning of the reform movement, or that Cistercian houses for twelfth-century nuns were any more problematic with regard to their juridical status than were most twelfth-century abbeys for Cistercian monks.[49] What the sudden flurry of regulation of women's houses in the early thirteenth century shows instead is the enormous surge of Cistercian foundations in the years 1190 to 1250. This later process consisted almost entirely of the creation of women's houses.[50]

The Cistercian Order must then be viewed as an only gradually established institution which later constructed stories about its own origins. That these origins were complex and now nearly untraceable has been rarely discussed by historians. Indeed, the ad hoc nature of the entire Cistercian movement has been discussed by Cistercian historians only insofar as they have discussed those irregularities about the foundation of the new monastery at Cîteaux that were treated in the standard Cistercian foundation accounts, the *Exordium parvum* and the later *Exordium magnum*. The fact that such irregularities are "confessed to" in those accounts, however, must in itself put us on guard about the veracity of such "witnesses" to early Cistercian history.

The *Exordium parvum* and later histories admit that Abbot Robert of Molesme (d. 1111) left that abbey with a group of monks for the site at Cîteaux and that he abandoned his earlier community at Molesme without episcopal permission. Such accounts assure us, however, that, although Robert may have been disobedient and broken a vow of stability in acting without episcopal permission, the abbot's waywardness had nothing to do with the validity of his foundation. Once Robert had been returned to his duties at Molesme, those of his followers who had stayed at Cîteaux were justified in having made the foundation and in their decision to stay. These accounts assure us that these men at the "new monastery" had chosen the better road, having abandoned a less rigorous life for a stricter one, and had done so with the assent, indeed the participation, of their immediate superior. Theirs was the narrower path because they had left the comforts of the community at Molesme for the harsher life of the desert of Cîteaux – these texts use such language of community and desert. Despite the confession of a weakness, the account is an occasion to describe early Cîteaux's purity in comparison to Molesme. More importantly, such an admission of Robert's fault becomes the rhetorical means of disarming readers, persuading them of the validity of the rest of this self-deprecating source.

The rhetorical aspects of the Cistercian foundation accounts are even more obvious if we look at the events from other viewpoints, including that of Molesme. Obviously the events read differently from the viewpoint of Molesme, which may well have seen the foundation at Cîteaux as that of just one more priory among many established by Abbot Robert. From Molesme's viewpoint, it was only a slight irregularity that Robert had left Molesme with monks he had sent to Cîteaux to participate personally in the foundation of a priory. It may in fact have been his intention to stay there only temporarily and then return to Molesme – we have the account only from Cîteaux's viewpoint. The "admission" that Robert of Molesme may have acted in error in leaving Molesme not only casts Cîteaux in a better light in comparison to Molesme, but probably itself reflects a slightly later sensibility about monastic stability than was that of *c*.1100, when we find many monastic reformers wandering around Europe from site to site.[51] Indeed, such concern about monastic stability makes more sense in the third quarter of the century when the first surviving manuscripts of this account appear. A greater irregularity from Molesme's viewpoint must have been the growing independence of its priory at Cîteaux. This independence appeared in such actions as its election of a head who was declared to be an abbot not a prior, and eventually in its foundation of its own daughter houses and its splitting away from the congregation of houses attached to Molesme. Readers of the *Exordium parvum* and the *Exordium magnum* often miss the extent to which only Robert was condemned by these accounts while the other monks going to Cîteaux were praised. When this is taken into account, the rhetorical argument that this is a true account because it shows the foundation "warts and all" loses validity.

Once we begin to think about Cîteaux's foundation in these terms, the *Exordium parvum*'s insistence that this was a "new monastery" rather than a new priory seems more pointed. Such references to a new monastery in that text, which historians have used to argue for its primitive nature, in fact probably only mark the moment of the height of the debate about the secession, when the Cistercians were asserting that this was not just another priory, but a monastery from the start. This terminology has to do with the issue of Cîteaux's independence from Molesme, and cannot necessarily be viewed as an accurate pointer to chronology within the early documents.

That the *Exordium parvum*'s admission of "slight irregularities" in Robert's flight from Molesme to Cîteaux may mask considerably more – the disobedience of a priory, which eventually became a successful secession from Molesme's congregation – is suggested by consideration of other sources not usually consulted. For instance, the Molesme cartulary shows the frequent foundation of such priories by Robert of Molesme in these years. Among such foundations were obviously both Cîteaux and Jully – despite the fact that the latter is attributed in the *Vita* of Bernard of Clairvaux to that abbot alone, there are charters for Jully in the Molesme cartulary. That the charters there give no indication of the acquisition of the site at Cîteaux, and that there are no early originals for the foundation or site acquisition in the Cîteaux archives either, lends credence to the supposition that certain documents were suppressed by both houses – probably in the 1140s as argued next.

Another view is to consider whether there had also been an unsuccessful attempt by Jully to secede from Molesme as Cîteaux had done. If so, was the 1145 privilege for Jully by Pope Eugenius III, former monk of Clairvaux and protégé of Bernard, made in favor of Molesme's getting control over Jully as a quid pro quo intended to end debate over the earlier secession of Cîteaux itself? Whether or not this is so, such a possibility suggests that the attachment of Jully to Molesme in 1145 rather than to Clairvaux says less about Bernard's attitudes about religious women or Cistercian ones in particular, than about the need to end the political confusion concerning Molesme's claims over the very religious house at which Bernard had made his monastic profession, Cîteaux itself.

The *Exordium parvum* is elsewhere packed full of "documents" providing a chorus of praise for the good motives of the monks who founded Cîteaux.

Authors of these letters include everyone from nearby bishops and papal legates to the popes themselves. That there are no manuscripts for the *Exordium parvum* before the 1160s, and no independent sources for any of the documents included in it praising the Cistercians and denouncing Molesme, however, is rarely mentioned by historians of the Cistercians. They have pointed to those documents as proof not only of the authenticity of the *Exordium*'s account, but also of its early date. While it is likely that the letter from Pascal II (1099–1118) recorded therein has some relationship to a real document addressed to Cîteaux, most of the other documents found in the *Exordium parvum* were concocted by the *Exordium parvum*'s authors. Even when they have been published separately, the manuscript references show that they were all extracted from the *Exordium parvum*, and there are no contemporary manuscript collections by their issuers which might confirm that they had been issued. Notable, also, is the onesidedness of this "correspondence," which presents no letters by Cistercians themselves, but only letters purported to have been written in their favor by diverse hands.

Another forgery is the purported papal confirmation of the Cistercian constitution dated to 1119 in which Calixtus II (1119–24) is claimed to have confirmed the Charter of Charity. That papal confirmation is not present along with the earliest version of the *Exordium parvum* (in Paris 4346A), but only appears in the Ljubljana/Laibach 31 manuscript where it immediately follows the *Exordium parvum* and the *Carta caritatis prior*. There is no independent confirmation of this papal document outside the *Exordium parvum* manuscripts either, and the confirmation by Calixtus II of the "Cistercian constitution" dated to 1119 is probably a forgery based on an authentic papal confirmation of the foundation of a daughter of Cîteaux at Bonnevaux in the province of Vienne with the assistance of Calixtus II while he was still bishop of Vienne.[52] Refutation of claims to the authority and authenticity of the primary "primitive" documents of the Cistercians, along with a careful rereading of the private charter record, papal privileges from the twelfth century, and such outside reports as that of Herman of Tournai at *c*.1150, suggest that traditional denials of the existence of Cistercian nuns are based on a false picture of the Order itself.

Such evidence suggests that we need to understand the evolution of the Cistercian Order as part of a slow process taking place over several generations. There was a slower break from Molesme than is usually thought, but also a slower articulation of the Cistercian administrative institutions. All this makes it less surprising that the female presence at its origins is not documented before the late twelfth century.[53] Charter evidence showing that important Cistercian abbots, including Abbot Bernard of Clairvaux and Abbot Stephen Harding of Cîteaux, had founded or had somehow affiliated themselves with houses of nuns can as a consequence be re-evaluated as well. Traditional historians have interpreted the acts of these abbots regarding nuns as peripheral to the real story of the Cistercians, and as evidence that those abbots acted in a private, unofficial, even officious capacity when they acted on behalf of religious women. Such traditional treatments have contended that, although such women were befriended by early Cistercian abbots, they should nonetheless be judged as having had nothing to do with the Cistercian Order itself. A revised dating of the Cistercian primitive documents, including the *exordia*, however, suggests that such evidence need no longer be discounted in these ways. The fact that internally generated, but anonymous, narrative accounts like the *Exordium Cistercii* and the *Exordium parvum* say nothing about nuns thus cannot be interpreted to mean that there were no Cistercian women. Indeed, this argument is strengthened by the fact that these sources say nothing about Bernard of Clairvaux either, an omission explained best by the post-1153 context in which other abbots disputed the excessive claims of Bernard's successors at Clairvaux to primacy within the Order.[54]

The literary evidence interpreted

Book 1 of the *Vita prima* in its full text, as well as the charter evidence showing Bernard's interest in Jully and its nuns, must be seen to counter any silence of the "official" *exordia* sources. In fact, the sources, other than the official Cistercian *exordia*, confirm the revised picture of the twelfth-century Cistercians and the women among them. In chapter 4 of the *Vita prima*'s book 1, written by William of Saint-Thierry *c.*1147, we read:

> In the year of the incarnation of the Lord 1113, the fifteenth year since the foundation of Cîteaux, that man of God, Bernard, at about age twenty-three, entered Cîteaux with more than thirty companions, submitting himself to the yoke of Christ under Abbot Stephen. From that day forward the Lord gave his blessing and the vines of that Lord Sabaoth gave forth fruit, extending their tendrils up to the sea and propagating beyond it. *Because some of his companions were already married, those wives took vows with their husbands for this sacred transformation. Out of concern for those women Bernard built a monastery for holy nuns in the diocese of Langres called Jully which with the aid of the Lord increased to great proportions. Jully has become extremely famous in the opinion of the religious and is now growing in both personnel and possessions so that it has expanded to other places and has not ceased up to now to produce even greater fruit.*[55]

This reference to women at Jully in the *Vita prima* written by William of Saint-Thierry (d. 1148) before 1150 (if the section in italics has not been excised, as in some printed versions of the *Vita prima*), obviates the silence about Cistercian nuns in other early sources created by the Cistercians themselves.

References to nuns in the *Vita prima* of Bernard are paralleled by those found in other lives of founders of religious communities which became Cistercian, such as the *Vita* of Pons de Léras, founder of Silvanès in the

Rouergue (written c.1170), and that of Stephen of Obazine (written slightly later).[56] The first claimed that Silvanès had founded a house of nuns at Nonenque (mentioned on p. 220); only later did Nonenque become a satellite of the men's house. The second is about what was at the outset a double community, which then developed into a house for men at Obazine and a women's house nearby at Coyroux. Both *Vitae* describe how early reformers' concerns about women's religious needs were included in decisions made by early communities about what practices their foundations should follow. In each case the men's house appears to have been part of a "double community" at the outset.

One can hypothesize that decisions to adopt Cistercian customs may have been what triggered those communities to begin treating the women's and men's components of their communities as separate entities. This conjecture seems to be confirmed by one external witness, Herman of Tournai. Herman, writing c.1150, turns out to be the only one of the four earliest external narrative witnesses to the Cistercians to mention Cistercian women.[57] From Herman's report it seems that this separation of the genders into separate houses, rather than hostility to women per se, was what differentiated Cistercians from Premonstratensian reformers. At first sight, the passages in his book in praise of the church of Laon appear contradictory on the subject of Cistercian women. Herman discusses the religious reform in the diocese of Laon in the 1130s, describing new foundations there. In commenting on the house of nuns at Montreuil-les-Dames near Laon, he remarks on the extraordinary ability of these women to work as hard as the brothers of Clairvaux, not at weaving or sewing, but in the fields. He asserts, moreover, that they followed the way of life of Clairvaux (the *ordo cistellensis*, but as it is practiced by the brothers of Clairvaux):

> There were also eight new monasteries of which three were of monks from Clairvaux and five were of clerics from Prémontré thus totalling eight reform houses of monks constructed by the Lord Bishop Bartholomew in his diocese. Also he ordained that there be added a ninth abbey bringing the number of new communities up to the number of the nine virtues of the order of the angels. This new monastery was for the feminine gender and made at a place called Montreuil where he named as abbess an extremely religious girl named Guibergis. In no other part of the world have such women as lived in this abbey been ever read about in books or heard about by ears. . . . They lived according to the *ordo* of Cîteaux which is difficult even for men . . . working hard not at sewing and weaving, which are usually women's work, but also in harvesting the fields, pulling up brush and cutting the forest, and working in the fields in the vicinity of wild beasts. Seeking their food in silence, they show themselves imitating in all things the lives of the monks of Clairvaux. This is clearly a sign from the Lord that all is possible for those who believe.[58]

Thus Cistercian nuns are attested to from the 1130s, albeit as rare examples of what women can do. It is important to note, however, that Herman does not refer to imitation of an order, or membership in an order, but *ordo* as a way of life. The term "imitating" does not mean then that these women were less Cistercian than were contemporary Cistercian monks.

A different passage (although falling earlier in Herman's text) has been interpreted as evidence that nuns were not part of the Cistercian Order. There, in contrasting the two great monastic leaders of the first half of the twelfth century, Bernard of Clairvaux and Norbert of Xanten (d. 1134), founder of Prémontré, Herman says that Norbert allowed monks and nuns to live under the same roof, while the abbey of Cîteaux had no women:

> Furthermore, the monastery of Cîteaux receives only men, whereas Lord Norbert has allowed that not only the male gender but the female as well be accepted in religious conversion; thus we see that the harsher and stricter conversions of women rather than those of men alone are seen in Norbert's monasteries.[59]

Herman's report does not say that Cistercian reformers refused to have anything to do with nuns, but that Bernard and other Cistercians favored separate communities of men and women rather than the double monasteries of the Norbertines or Premonstratensian canons.[60]

Slightly later writers have also been misread in attempts to demonstrate that Cistercian women were insignificant during the "Golden Age" of the Cistercian Order's formation. Historians of the Cistercian Order have thus preferred the witness of the anonymous Lincolnshire author of *The Book of Gilbert*. According to this author, Gilbert's request for incorporation of his reform communities was denied because Cistercians claimed they did not have authority over houses of other religious, particularly of women:

> Then [in 1147] he [Gilbert of Sempringham] went to the Chapter of Cîteaux, where Pope Eugenius of happy memory chanced to be present at that time, for Gilbert intended to entrust the responsibility for his religious houses [of women] to the care of monks of Cîteaux. . . . However, the lord Pope and the Cistercian abbots said that monks of their order were not permitted authority over the religious life of others, least of all that of nuns; and so [Gilbert] did not achieve what he desired.[61]

The author of Gilbert's *Life* was attempting to explain what he and other Gilbertines clearly saw as the slighting of Gilbert and his nuns by the Cistercians who had refused to incorporate them. The statement attributed by this early thirteenth-century Gilbertine to the abbots at a Chapter at Cîteaux in 1147 is clearly anachronistic. As historians of the Gilbertines have shown, however, there is no independent or contemporary verification of Gilbert's purported visit to a Cistercian General Chapter in 1147. Indeed, the evidence for such an 1147 meeting in Gilbertine or other sources of the time is non-existent.[62] Gilbertine negotiations with Cistercians seem to have been undertaken in the 1160s when there was at issue a Charter of Peace similar to that established at about the same time between Cistercians and Premonstratensians.[63]

Only the prejudice about admitting the possibility that there were Cistercian women has led monastic historians to prefer the thirteenth-century account of the anonymous canon of Sempringham in *The Book of Gilbert* (because it denies the presence of women) over that of the virtually contemporary prominent, university-trained theologian James of Vitry (d. 1240), who was named bishop of Acre at the beginning of the thirteenth century (who asserts their presence). James says in his *Historia occidentalis, c.*1220:

> The reverend religious men of the Premonstratensian Order, wisely attending to the assertions of experts within their own family that it was burdensome and dangerous to guard such charges, decided that they should henceforth not receive women into the houses of their Order. Thereafter abbeys of nuns of the Cistercian Order multiplied like the stars of heaven and increased enormously, blessed by God as it is said, "Increase and be multiplied and replenish the sky."[64]

One can thus hardly deny the presence of Cistercian women by that date.

Indeed, not able altogether to deny James of Vitry's positive statements about the existence of Cistercian women, Cistercian historians have eventually conceded a brief moment between 1190 and 1250 when, with the help of patrons and popes, women successfully put pressure on the Order's General Chapter for their incorporation. But they still have misread James of Vitry. They assume that an actual decision was made to admit women at the end of the twelfth century as a response to the move by the Premonstratensian canons not to admit any more sisters. This should not be inferred from James of Vitry's statement, which only says that Cistercian nuns became extremely prevalent thereafter. As evidence that Cistercian women were commonplace and highly respected (indeed more so than Cistercian monks if one looks elsewhere in this tract), and that they had been around for some time, James of Vitry's *Historia occidentalis* may be a reliable source, but it does not date the initial addition of women to the Order. Their participation dates to much earlier.

Frequent citation of James of Vitry's *Historia occidentalis* with regard to Cistercian nuns has led even the most traditionalist historians of the Cistercians, those who dismiss twelfth-century houses of nuns as not yet really Cistercian, to admit that by the thirteenth century there were houses of Cistercian nuns. Such concessions have been on a limited scale, however, and might be deemed efforts at "damage control." Thus a nearly official view, that found in Lekai's survey, concludes:

The founders of Cîteaux had no intention of establishing a new order of monks, much less of initiating an order of Cistercian nuns. Nevertheless, at a place called Tart, some ten kilometers north of Cîteaux, a foundation was made in 1125 for pious women, who were determined to imitate the austere example of the Cistercian monks. . . . There is no evidence that the Cistercian General Chapter took any responsibility for the nuns, or that monks of the order were in any way engaged in the spiritual and material care of the new community. Throughout the twelfth century the General Chapter scrupulously maintained a policy of aloofness, lest involvement in the nuns' affairs endanger the purely contemplative character of the order. . . . [B]etween 1190 and 1210, the gates of the order had been forced open for the admission of nuns.[65]

In this standard version of events, houses of Cistercian nuns existed only once there was an official procedure for their incorporation, one established by the express decision of abbots in General Chapter meetings starting around 1190. Even so, such houses are deemed somewhat unusual.[66]

Are criteria for limited membership reasonable?

Lekai supported the view that there were a few authentic houses of Cistercian nuns, but that they appeared at the end of the twelfth century and were admitted into the Order only during a very limited span of time. Lekai also qualified this concession that there was female participation in the Order by asserting that many houses of nuns claiming to be Cistercian and inspired by the practices of the brothers of Cîteaux were only "imitating" those practices, a word drawn from Herman of Tournai's comments about Laon. He asserted that, by 1228, the General Chapter had begun to discourage individual abbots from additional incorporation of houses of nuns into the Order and that papal promises made in 1251 to limit any more papal recommendations of nuns to the chapter were indeed effective in closing off the possibility of the addition of any more houses of nuns. Lekai's account, moreover, repeats the very negative depiction found in almost all earlier treatments of the entry of women into the Cistercian Order as "an overwhelming flood." The image of the pressure of women "forcing open the Cistercian floodgates," a pressure that the General Chapter's abbots were powerless to resist, is an extremely misogynous one. Such a depiction links women's admission with an onset of decadence, and treats women as uncontrollable powers, needing to be confined and enclosed.[67]

Recent standard treatments do in fact treat of thirteenth-century Cistercian women, but in those views, these women were part of the Order only because carefully controlled. Historians like Lekai assert that the most important decisions undertaken by the General Chapter at this time were that Cistercian nuns were to be strictly enclosed and sufficiently endowed so as not to prove a burden on neighboring men's houses. The number of women's communities that might be incorporated was strictly limited, and the maximum size of many individual communities was set out in charters. Neighboring abbeys of Cistercian monks should not be required to provide members of their communities as chaplains or lay-brothers to the nuns. Members of men's houses were not to demand hospitality from women's communities, for instance, from the nuns of Saint-Antoine-des-Champs in Paris. Lay-brothers and chaplains attached to nuns' communities would be received like equivalent members of men's houses when traveling. Abbesses were not to attend the General Chapter at Cîteaux, but were allowed an annual meeting at le Tart presided over by the abbot of Cîteaux. He would there announce to the assembled abbesses any decisions of note made by the earlier General Chapter of abbots. Visitation would be by father abbots rather than by founding abbesses.[68] In fact many of these practices would only come about gradually, as the result of the regularization of women's houses over the course of the thirteenth century.

More recently, Brigitte Degler-Spengler has made explicit a series of well-documented actions by which the General Chapter formalized the procedure for the affiliation of houses of nuns to the Order in the early thirteenth century, and lists criteria by which historians may identify such houses of Cistercian women.[69] These criteria are: (1) concession of freedom from episcopal visitation; (2) notice from the Order's *Statuta* showing incorporation after inspection of resources by commissioned abbots; (3) papal recommendation of nuns to the General Chapter; and (4) less explicit in Degler-Spengler, but included in other studies, documents mentioning the *ordo cisterciensis*.[70]

This list sets an unusually high standard of proof for women's houses as opposed to men's, which is possibly inappropriate given the fragmentary nature of the surviving documents dealing with women's houses. Yet many thirteenth-century houses of nuns can be found fulfilling some or all of these qualifications. Historians using a list such as Degler-Spengler's usually assume that an authentic house of Cistercian nuns founded between 1190 and 1250 would fulfill all these criteria and that houses without these documents or references in their archives were never houses of Cistercian nuns. Even if it is argued that documents in individual archives could have been lost, such treatments have assumed that the *Statuta* of the General Chapter at least would nonetheless have provided evidence for incorporation. If this evidence too is missing, a house of nuns tends to be described as having "only imitated" the Cistercians.

Many historians of religious women have assumed that such tests for determining which convents were authentic houses of Cistercian nuns in the thirteenth century are appropriate for either that time or later, and that such tests may also be legitimately applied to the twelfth century. Others have tried to sort through this web of pseudo-juridical argument on which historians have based assertions that there were no twelfth-century Cistercian nuns.[71]

Most have missed the fact that such criteria as are demanded for asserting Cistercian incorporation of women's houses have established a double standard of proof – one in which standards for authentication of women's abbeys within the Cistercian Order are not applied to men's houses either in the twelfth or the thirteenth century. What needs to be demonstrated here is that such proof of Cistercian women's status, although possibly appropriate to thirteenth-century houses of Cistercian nuns, is irrelevant to the twelfth century. Taking each of the criteria mentioned above in turn, it may be shown that they are *invalid* for determining the authenticity of a twelfth-century women's house as part of the Cistercian Order.

First, Cistercian exemption from episcopal visitation is irrelevant to much of the twelfth century. Although a hallmark of the Cistercian Order of the thirteenth century was the replacement of episcopal visitation by a system of internal visitation by father visitors, historians of the Order have known, at least since the publication of work by Jean-Baptiste Mahn in 1945, that the privilege of internal visitation was not granted to the Cistercians until 1180 or so.[72] Tithe privileges came earlier and were granted to both monks and nuns, but the issue of internal visitation was only resolved for the Cistercians very late in the reign of Pope Alexander III (1159–81). To assume that twelfth-century houses of nuns needed to have such exemption from episcopal visitation in order to be considered Cistercian, when in fact the men's houses of the Order were only just receiving that exemption at the end of the century, is to apply an anachronistic criterion for the authentication of such houses of nuns.

A second criterion, the expectation that Cistercian affiliation would have been documented by notices in the statutes of the Order, is also irrelevant to the twelfth century.[73] As is apparent from a careful study of the first volume of statutes of the Cistercian General Chapter published in 1933 by Canivez, no surviving *Statuta* concern any individual house of monks or nuns before 1190, except for the five heads of filiations which are mentioned in the 1180s.[74] If we apply such arguments from the *Statuta* in a non-gender-biased way to decide which houses were Cistercian before 1190, we might indeed conclude that there were no houses of Cistercian nuns, but equitable application of such arguments would require that we conclude as well that there were no more than five houses of Cistercian monks in the twelfth century!

Nonetheless, the argument that twelfth-century Cistercian nuns did not exist because they are not mentioned in the published statutes has been particularly convincing to outsiders to the field of Cistercian history. Such scholars have tended too often to treat the Order's published *Statuta* as a compendium in which all available – and all possible – information about any Cistercian house may be found, assuming that all entries have been critically edited and that there is coverage for all years. When making arguments from the silence of the Statutes, such assumptions about Canivez's edition and in particular his volume 1 are injudicious in the extreme. Statutes dated to earlier than 1190 are of a general nature and concern the beginnings of the enforcement

234

of uniform practices among Cistercian houses. There is no continuous series before 1179, except for the years 1157–61, and none concerning individual houses' problems until 1190.[75] There are also fewer surviving statutes than a first glance suggests. There are many years for which no records survive. For some Canivez provides extracts from Manrique's much later history of the Order, but other years are skipped over entirely. Many dates assigned to statutes, including those for 1134, 1152, 1154, and 1156, are wholly fanciful, having no basis in the twelfth-century manuscripts.[76] Indeed, the fact that the *prima collectio* cannot be dated to 1134 in the twelfth-century manuscripts, and that its contents in fact are more likely to date to *c*.1160, means that all claims about 1134 statutes being "ideals" by which abbots attempted to live are false.[77] That there is no contemporary dated evidence for a Cistercian General Chapter until 1150 or later, as discussed next, also suggests that there could be no statutes from such early dates; it is not simply that they are missing.

As for criterion three, the requirement for papal letters urging that houses of nuns be incorporated, such papal recommendation is not expected for men's houses of the twelfth century. It could not be expected for men's or women's houses before at least the mid-twelfth century, moreover, because there was no General Chapter of the annual universal sort to which such houses could have been recommended by a pope before that date. The fact, which derives from the redating of the early Cistercian documents, that there was no annual, universal General Chapter until the second half of the twelfth century, needs to be underlined here. While Cîteaux may have hosted local informal meetings which resembled somewhat the "General Chapter" held at Cluny in 1132, which was mentioned by Orderic Vitalis in his history, there is no evidence for a Cistercian General Chapter in the first half of the twelfth century.[78]

Such evidence for an annual, universal General Chapter of all Cistercian abbots does not appear until the 1150s (perhaps not coincidentally the same time as that of the first dated *Statuta*).[79] Moreover, references to it remain limited in the 1160s, only suddenly burgeoning in the 1170s.[80] What we do find for the first half of the twelfth century (although primarily for the 1140s) are papal privileges confirming properties for early houses of Cistercian nuns like le Tart, as well as for a few houses of Cistercian men, but of a General Chapter or administratively construed order there is no evidence.[81]

These papal privileges just mentioned for abbeys of women like le Tart have been misread. They have been interpreted as evidence that Cistercian women were in fact only "imitating" the Cistercian Order, that such nuns were Benedictines in Cistercian habits. This conclusion is to generalize widely the example of women like the recluse Yvette of Huy (d. 1228), who may have lived "in imitation of the Cistercians" as an anchoress.[82] Women such as Yvette who may be classed as "imitating" the Cistercian way of life were but a tiny number, while there were many houses of nuns at the time who acted like Cistercians, thought they were Cistercian, resisted efforts to deny that they should share in the privileges of the Order such as its tithe exemptions, and received papal confirmation of their Cistercian privileges. Historians have treated these women as "only imitating Cistercian practices" because papal privileges announce that they "followed the Rule of the Blessed Benedict according to the norms (mores, practices, or customs) of the brothers of Cîteaux."[83] But this is the language for all papal confirmations of Cistercian customs in mid-twelfth-century documents, whether for houses of monks or of nuns. The identical words when found for a men's house have been interpreted to indicate a house of the Cistercian Order; only with regard to women's houses do historians conclude that these abbeys were but "imitation" Cistercian. Thus, ironically, the papal privileges which best document the properties and practices of communities of Cistercian nuns like those at le Tart have been used by traditional historians as evidence that such houses of women were not Cistercian. Despite paralleling their sister houses of monks in having founders and friends who had offered them sites, endowment, recruits from among their sisters and mothers, tithe exemptions and others, confirmations by bishops, and eventually papal protection, these nuns have been declared "imitation" Cistercians. Despite possessing papal privileges in their archives which are identical to those of houses of Cistercian monks, such communities of nuns have been dismissed as being not part of the Order.[84]

As for the fourth criterion mentioned above, references to houses of nuns as part of the *ordo cisterciensis*, these again cannot be expected for much of the twelfth century given the lack of institutional articulation of an Order at all before 1150. In fact we find no authentic documentary references from before the thirteenth century to specific men's houses or women's houses identified as part of an *ordo cisterciensis*.[85] *Ordo* is a frequently discussed term in the twelfth century, inspiring whole tracts, such as the *Little Book of the Diverse Orders and Professions in the Church*.[86] While there is considerable discussion of *ordo monasticus* in pre-1150 documents, letters, treatises, and sermons, the practice of describing monks and nuns as part of a group called an Order (as opposed to their living an *ordo* as a way of life) was a new usage of the term *ordo*.

Careful study of twelfth-century sources shows that *ordo* as a term to mean "a religious group" had not come into regular usage at the time of the foundation for women of houses like le Tart in the 1120s or Jully in 1113, or even of Nonenque in 1139. It was developing over the twelfth century and was still at mid-twelfth century subject to a considerable amount of ambiguous usage.[87] Except for suspect, retrospective foundation charters, the earliest references I have found to an *ordo cisterciensis* come from William VI, lord of Montpellier, and date to 1146, and from Henry II (1133–89), as king of England, in the 1150s.[88] So this particular criterion cannot show that there were no Cistercian nuns for much of the twelfth century.

The conventional view, then, that nuns were "not admitted" to the Cistercian Order during the twelfth century is obviously in error. But this erroneous statement and all the discussion of the admission of women into the Cistercian Order, and of the date at which they were finally admitted, mask a larger misconception of the issues involved. In fact, as the above re-evaluation shows, the administrative order which we think of as the Cistercian Order emerged only gradually from an early Cistercian movement that in fact included women. That Order began as a tiny congregation to which was added a great number of pre-Cistercian foundations in some sort of "take-over" from the third quarter of the twelfth century. Such houses of monks and nuns, those not founded from any other Cistercian house, would become the mainspring of this new institution, the Cistercian Order. In those terms, the question of "admitting women" becomes ill-stated. Twelfth-century Cistercian women's houses, like men's houses, "just happened" and gradually coalesced into an Order. There was no admission of men's houses by women's or vice versa.

A new view of Cistercian nuns

How do these interpretations change our view not only of twelfth-century, but of thirteenth-century Cistercian women? First, although certainly the two generations from 1190 to 1250 saw an enormous growth of Cistercian houses for women, whose numbers came to equal numbers of the Order's men's branch, this was a second wave, for there were many twelfth-century foundations for nuns as well. Moreover, the thirteenth century saw significant changes in the status of both the newest and the earliest Cistercian women's houses. In certain cases, older, richer, more prestigious foundations of women, like that of the women at Nonenque mentioned on pp. 220 and 229, were transformed into the satellites of houses of monks which had once been their equals or juniors. Indeed, both charter evidence and statute evidence provides many indications of such transformations. In general the gradual regularization of many priories of Cistercian women into abbeys of Cistercian nuns in mid-thirteenth century may have made them less able to function independently, and more dependent on houses of men. Thirteenth-century evidence concerning maximum size of communities, or attaching them to neighboring abbots as "daughter houses," or elevating them into abbeys, however, should not be seen as marking the moment of the addition of women's houses to the Cistercian Order. In a few cases sufficiently astute patrons were successful in attaching them not to the local abbey of monks but to Cîteaux and Clairvaux, a tactic which at least deferred some of the ill-treatment.[89]

In fact, thirteenth-century records mark a time during which the Order instituted a massive regularization of houses of nuns of diverse types (some priories, some abbeys still not dependent on local Cistercian visitors, many clinging to their episcopal founders) into a single type of community, the abbey of nuns placed as "daughter-abbey" under the direction of a local abbot visitor. This was part of the continued "invention" of the Order itself, a process that was ongoing for men's as well as women's houses. Only in the thirteenth century did all men's houses take their places on filiation trees designed to allow internal visitation, and only then did all women's houses become demoted into satellites of nearby men's houses. As women's places in this hierarchical organization became more regularized, earlier visitation by bishop-founders was eliminated at the same time that all priories of women were elevated to abbey status, and maximum as well as minimum numbers of nuns (and monks) were established. Father visitors, chaplains, and confessors were assigned for purposes of discipline and liturgy. Sometimes the nuns were successful as well in claiming that father visitors must provide them with lay-brothers to undertake business with the outside world.[90] But not all lay-brothers came from outside the houses of nuns. Lay-brothers also took vows directly to the abbess of the community – kneeling down before her and kissing the Rule of Saint Benedict rather than touching the abbess.[91] Too often this thirteenth-century evidence, however, has been misread as the norm for both earlier and later, or papal decrees about all religious women which cut across the boundaries of many religious orders are read as evidence of problems specific to individual communities.

It is unfortunate that the great authority on religious women's movements, Herbert Grundmann, in his work on women's religious movements, heresy, and the use of the vernacular in the later Middle Ages, originally published in 1935, from which much later discussion stems, mistook this thirteenth-century formalization process for the beginnings of the Cistercian Order's "admission" of women.[92] Grundmann thus presented all Cistercian women's houses as part of a movement of foundation paralleling that of Dominican and Franciscan women, rather than a second Cistercian wave, which followed a first wave of Cistercian women's houses founded in parallel with the twelfth-century "double communities," such as that of Fontevrault. Grundmann was followed in this error by Sir Richard Southern who saw efforts by nuns in the thirteenth century to resist pressures to be regularized into dependencies of men's houses as evidence of resistance to the Order and its practices.[93] The assumptions of scholars such as Grundmann and Southern that there were no twelfth-century Cistercian nuns, however, began to be disproved by publications from French archival materials starting in the early 1950s, especially those by Jean-de-la-Croix Bouton and Anselm Dimier, both of whom discussed evidence for twelfth-century women's houses associated with the Cistercians.[94] A thesis by Ernst Günther Krenig attempted to incorporate this evidence, but did not really take proper account of it.[95]

Other quasi-juridical arguments have been invoked in denying the existence of twelfth-century Cistercian nuns. One of these is that all truly Cistercian houses are identifiable by unanimous practices having to do with property, or by typical material remains. Such contentions have been used to argue away much positive evidence for early Cistercian nuns by citing the negative evidence of such things as buildings or economic practices.

Historians thus have claimed that we may judge "just how Cistercian" were communities of nuns on the basis of evidence for material remains of architecture, or charters concerning endowment. By assuming an idealized image of what a Cistercian house should have been – one which no house of twelfth-century monks would have conformed to either – Cistercian nuns have been deemed "more Cluniac than Cistercian." For instance, because twelfth-century women's houses were called priories rather than abbeys, or because they owned tithes, a practice presumed contrary to Cistercian ideals, it has been argued that these nuns could not have been Cistercian.[96]

Obviously such reasoning among earlier historians is faulty inasmuch as it is founded on assumptions of a uniformity and unanimity of Cistercian practice which is untrue for the twelfth century whether applied to women's or men's houses. Conformity to regulations was not there for most of the twelfth century and it cannot be given such "gate-keeping" functions. We must hence conclude that insofar as there was a Cistercian movement in the twelfth century, local administrative records prove that if there were twelfth-century Cistercian monks, there were also twelfth-century Cistercian nuns.

Finally, it has been an assumption in all considerations of Cistercian nuns that the many new groups of religious women appearing in twelfth- and thirteenth-century Europe actually sought or desired affiliation with the Cistercians or some other order. Historians assume that the pressure for the incorporation of nuns by such groups came from the women themselves, or at least from patrons and authorities outside the Order who saw the admission or incorporation of women by the Cistercians as a desideratum. In the old view, abbots within the Cistercian Order struggled to maintain their monastic solitude by denying or carefully controlling incorporation, but were overcome by a deluge of women wishing to be admitted. This is not necessarily true. Although many patrons often successfully sought the foundation of Cistercian houses, including those for women that their daughters might enter or they themselves might retire to, Cistercian affiliation was not necessarily a good thing for nuns. This is especially true once houses of nuns were no longer treated with the equality that they should have been guaranteed by the Charter of Charity after its promulgation in the 1160s. (Of course, promulgation of legislation may actually suggest widespread problems in need of correction.)

Local evidence suggests that women sometimes actively opposed the incorporation of their abbeys when it would lead to their dependence on father visitors who were abbots of neighboring and rival abbeys of monks. Nuns preferred visitation not by abbots of rival communities, but by bishops and archbishops who were supporters and even founders of their houses.[97] Regularization was not necessarily a good thing for the filiations of women's communities either. Ties were broken between women's houses, and eventually abbesses even of le Tart and Las Huelgas no longer held General Chapters or had filiations over which they were official visitors of daughter houses.

The evidence of resistance by some nuns to having new visitors imposed on them or to having outsiders determine how many nuns they could admit suggests that becoming Cistercian was not necessarily a consummation devoutly to be wished for by all women's religious houses. Perhaps a phenomenon remarked on by many historians, of the constant shifting from Order to Order of late medieval religious women, reflects how little any existing Order provided for their needs. A related issue, although rarely discussed, is how much some abbots' willingness to accommodate the care of souls for such pious women derived from the considerable temptations presented by the property belonging to women's houses.[98] The seductive pressure to incorporate a community of nuns as a daughter because it was rich or had rival claims to tithes and property is seen, for instance, in the northern Italian example of Staffarda's attempted incorporation of tithes belonging to the nuns of Rifreddo.[99]

We must conclude that the early Cistercian Order's history with regard to nuns has been misread in the past. Arguments that denied that there were Cistercian nuns in the twelfth century, or claimed that most thirteenth-century nuns were "imitation Cistercians," were based on false premises about how the sources should be read. Such contentions have been difficult to counter because many scholars have not realized how much the central texts have lacked critical editing. Such misreading has also happened because historians looking only at women have not understood that the same lacunae in the documents for nuns' houses exist for houses of monks as well.

We also have underestimated the amount of work ahead. My work on Cistercian nuns over more than a decade has shown that women cannot just be stirred in as an extra ingredient to the broth of an existing narrative. To add nuns, lay sisters, and female patrons to the narrative of early Cistercian history means first writing the histories of individual houses of religious women which have not to date even been noted in the gazetteers. More dramatically it means rewriting the narrative of early Cistercian history itself. As this consideration of twelfth-century Cistercian women has shown, both telling individual histories and fitting women into a larger narrative often requires peeling away many layers of misinterpretation.

NOTES

1   Parts of this chapter were presented between 1995 and 1998 in Copenhagen, Lawrence (Kansas), Iowa City, and Chicago. In addition to thanks to Mary Martin McLaughlin and Suzanne Fonay Wemple, I am grateful to NEH for support in 1988, to the president and fellows of Clare Hall, Cambridge, who appointed me a visiting fellow in 1994–5, and to the University of Iowa for a Faculty Scholar Award in 1993–6 and for research travel money in 1997 and 1998; see also Constance Hoffman Berman, "Abbeys for Cistercian Nuns in the Ecclesiastical Province of Sens: Foundation, Endowment and Economic Activities of the Earlier Foundations," *Revue Mabillon* 73 (1997): 83–113, and related articles. Standard accounts such as that of Louis J. Lekai, *The Cistercians, Ideals and Reality* (Kent, OH: Kent State University

Press, 1977), pp. 347ff., have moved in the direction of less rigid exclusions of women from any role in the Cistercian Order. Perhaps the most important to date has been that of Jean-de-la-Croix Bouton, *Les Moniales cisterciennes*, vol. 1, *Histoire externe* (Grignan: Abbaye N. D. d'Aiguebelle, 1986), which has treated much of the evidence for nuns as if they were at least related to the Order.

2   *Cartulaires de l'Abbaye de Molesme, ancien diocèse de Langres, 916–1250; Recueil de Documents sur le Nord de la Bourgogne et le Midi de la Champagne, publié avec une introduction diplomatique, historique et géographique*, ed. Jacques Laurent, 2 vols (Paris: Picard, 1907, 1911), no. 126.

3   *Molesme*, ed. Laurent, no. 135.

4   *Molesme*, ed. Laurent, no. 79.

5   *Histoire du Prieuré de Jully-les-Nonnains, avec pièces justificatives*, ed. Abbé Jobin (Paris, 1881), p. 29.

6   Jean Leclercq, "Études sur Saint-Bernard," *Analecta Cisterciensia* 9 (1953): 153ff.

7   *Jully*, ed. Jobin, no. 1 (n.d.). Jean Leclercq has remarked on the similarities of economic regime between these nuns and the early Cistercians in "Cisterciennes et filles de S. Bernard à propos des structures variées des monastères de moniales au moyen âge," *Studia Monastica* 32 (1990): 139–56; and Leclercq, "La 'Paternité' de S. Bernard et les débuts de l'ôrdre cistercien," *Revue Bénédictine* 103 (1993): 445–81. Additional information on what has historically been thought to have been the economic regime of these nuns, but also on how such communities of nuns were moved from one reformed practice to another, is suggested by *Jully*, no. 12 (1155), drawn from the history of the monks of Saint John of Reomaensi, who had property in the parish of Jully; obviously this is a very problematic text since it asserts that the women were associated with Fontevrault.

8   *Jully*, ed. Jobin, no. 8 (1126–36), by Guilencus, bishop of Langres; *Jully*, no. 4 (1129), Guilencus, bishop of Langres, notes a gift by Lady Eluidis of Montregal and Ancericius her son; *Jully*, no. 5 (1130), Hato, bishop of Troyes, notes what was given for his daughter by Erlebaudus Goziaudus.

9   *Jully*, ed. Jobin, no. 6 (1133).

10   *Jully*, ed. Jobin, no. 3 (March 1128).

11   *Jully*, ed. Jobin, no. 7 (before 1137). This charter seems to have been written and sealed by Bernard himself.

12   *Jully*, ed. Jobin, no. 9 (1142).

13   *Jully*, ed. Jobin, no. 10 (1145).

14   Jean-de-la-Croix Bouton, Benoît Chauvin, and Elizabeth Grosjean, "L'Abbaye de Tart et ses filiales au moyen âge," in *Mélanges à la mémoire du père Anselme Dimier*, ed. B. Chauvin (Pupillin: Arbois, 1981–2; hereafter *Mélanges Dimier*), 2.3: 19–61.

15   *Patrologia Latina*, hereafter *PL*, vol. 185: 1409–11. Other charters follow in this publication, but the next is from the year 1142. The inclusion of a prioress in the discussion suggests drafting after the introduction of commendatory abbesses.

16   *PL*, vol. 185: 1411.

17   *Liber instrumentorum memorialium: Cartulaire des Guillems de Montpellier*, ed. A. Germain (Montpellier: Jean Marel Ainé, 1884), no. 96 (1172), will of William VII of Montpellier.

18   Bouton *et al.*, as cited in note 14.

19   *PL*, vol. 180: 1199–1200: Benoît Chauvin, "Papauté et abbayes cisterciennes du duché de Bourgogne," in *L'Église de France et la papauté (Xe–XIlle siècle)*, ed. Rolf Grosse, vol. 1, pp. 326–62 (Bonn: Bouvier, 1993), p. 351, discusses the original of this papal bull of Eugenius III for le Tart.

20   *Les Monuments primitifs de la Règle cistercíenne*, ed. Philippe Guignard (Dijon: Rabutot, 1878), pp. 643–9; Bouton *et al.*, as cited in note 14.

21   *Statuta capitulorum generalium ordinis cisterciensis ab anno 1116 ad annum 1786*, ed. J.-M. Canivez (Louvain: Bureaux, 1933), p. 1187, and see Elizabeth Conner, "The

Abbeys of Las Huelgas and Tart and Their Filiations," in *Hidden Springs: Cistercian Monastic Women*, ed. John A. Nichols and Lillian Thomas Shank (Kalamazoo, MI: Cistercian Publications, 1995), pp. 29–48.

22　On nuns being sent from Saint-Antoine to Maubuisson to found the new house, see Anselm Dimier, *Saint Louis et Cîteaux* (Paris: Letouzey et Ané, 1954); on references to nuns following the practices of Saint-Antoine in *Gallia Christiana* entries for La-Cour-Notre-Dame near Sens, and Îles-les-Dames, near Auxerre; see Constance Hoffman Berman, "The Labors of Hercules, the Cartulary, Church and Abbey for Nuns of La-Cour-Notre-Dame-de-Michery," *The Journal of Medieval History* 26 (2000): 33–70.

23　Such assumptions are present in unfounded statements such as, "Tart was established by dissident nuns from Jully with the help of Stephen Harding," in Sally Thompson, *Women Religious: The Founding of English Nunneries after the Norman Conquest* (Oxford: Clarendon, 1991), p. 95; cf. Bruce Venarde, *Women's Monasticism and Medieval Society: Nunneries in France and England, 890–1215* (Ithaca, NY: Cornell University Press, 1997), pp. 73–4.

24　Pierre-Roger Gaussin, "Les Communautés féminines dans l'espace languedocien," in *La Femme dans la vie religieuse du Languedoc (XIIIe–XIVe s.)*, Cahiers de Fanjeaux 23 (1988): 299–332, esp. 307–8.

25　*Cartulaire de l'abbaye cistercienne d'Obazine (XIIe–XIIIe siècle)*, ed. Bernadette Barrière (Clermont-Ferrand: Université, 1989), provides no references to Stephen attending the purported 1147 meeting; see also Bernadette Barrière, "The Cistercian Monastery of Coyroux in the Province of Limousin in Southern France, in the 12th–13th Centuries," *Gesta* 31 (1992): 73–5.

26　Jacqueline Buhot, "L'Abbaye normande de Savigny, Chef d'Ordre et fille de Cîteaux," *Le Moyen Age* 46 (1936): 1–19, 104–21, 178–90, 249–72, is the standard treatment; but see forthcoming work by Patrick Conyers.

27　Brian Golding, *Gilbert of Sempringham and the Gilbertine Order c.1130–c.1300* (Oxford: Clarendon, 1995), pp. 26ff.; but see also Sharon Elkins, *Holy Women of Twelfth-century England* (Chapel Hill, NC: University of North Carolina Press, 1988), pp. 133ff.; Thompson, *Women Religious*, pp. 73ff; on 1160s for Savigny, see Constance Hoffman Berman, *The Cistercian Evolution: The Invention of a Religious Order in Twelfth-Century Europe* (Philadelphia, PA: University of Pennsylvania Press, 2000), pp. 142–7.

28　David Knowles, *The Monastic Order in England*, 2nd edn (Cambridge: Cambridge University Press, 1949), p. 362, "Of the thirty-odd Cistercian nunneries which were in course of time established in England almost one-half date from the period 1175–1215," glides over the fact that most of the other half were founded earlier; see Roberta Gilchrist, *Gender and Material Culture: The Archaeology of Religious Women* (London: Routledge, 1994), p. 37, fig. 7.

29　These three houses are discussed in Brigitte Degler-Spengler, "The Incorporation of Cistercian Nuns into the Order in the Twelfth and Thirteenth Century," in *Hidden Springs*, pp. 85–134, here at 87ff.; Catherine E. Boyd, *A Cistercian Nunnery in Mediaeval Italy: The Story of Rifreddo in Saluzzo, 1220–1300* (Cambridge, MA: Harvard University Press, 1943), pp. 78–81.

30　See *Cartulaire de l'abbaye de Silvanès*, ed. P.-A. Verlaguet (Rodez: Carrère, 1910); *Cartulaire et documents de l'abbaye de Nonenque*, eds C. Couderc and J. L. Rigal (Rodez: Carrère, 1955); and Constance Hoffman Berman, "Men's Houses, Women's Houses: The Relationship Between the Sexes in Twelfth-century Monasticism," in *The Medieval Monastery*, ed. Andrew MacLeish (St Cloud, MN: University of Minnesota, 1988), pp. 43–52; Berman, "The Foundation and Early History of the Monastery of Silvanès: The Economic Reality," in *Cistercian Ideals and Reality*, ed. John R. Sommerfeldt (Kalamazoo, MI: Cistercian Publications, 1978), pp. 280–318; and Beverly M. Kienzle, "The Tract on the Conversion of Pons of Léras and the True

Account of the Beginning of the Monastery of Silvanès," *Cistercian Studies Quarterly* 29 (1995): 219–43.

31 C. H. Lawrence, *Medieval Monasticism: Forms of Religious Life in Western Europe in the Middle Ages*, 2nd edn (London: Longman, 1989), gives nuns a separate chapter.

32 On these texts (described in n. 37 for dating) see David Knowles, "The Primitive Cistercian Documents," in *Great Historical Enterprises: Problems in Monastic History* (London: Thomas Nelson, 1963), pp. 197–222; Giles Constable, "The Study of Monastic History Today," in *Essays on the Reconstruction of Medieval History*, ed. Vaclav Mudroch and G. S. Couse (Montreal: McGill-Queen's University Press, 1974), pp. 21–51; and François de Place, "Bibliographie raisonnée des premiers documents cisterciens (1098–1220)," *Cîteaux* 35 (1984): 7–54.

33 Anselm Dimier, "Chapitres généraux d'abbesses cisterciennes," *Cîteaux* 11 (1960): 268–75; Micheline de Fontette, *Les Religieuses à l'âge classique du droit canon: Recherches sur les structures juridiques des branches féminines des ordres* (Paris: Vrin, 1961), pp. 27–63; and Sally Thompson, "The Problem of Cistercian Nuns in the Twelfth and Early Thirteenth Centuries," in *Medieval Women*, ed. Derek Baker (Oxford: Blackwell, 1978), pp. 227–52.

34 See Conrad of Eberbach, *Exordium magnum Cisterciense, sive narratio de initio Cisterciensis Ordinis*, ed. Bruno Griesser (Rome: Editiones Cistercienses, 1961). Internal evidence suggests a date no earlier than 1200. The earlier *exordia* are anonymous, as are some of the editorial revisions of the *Vita prima* of Bernard of Clairvaux; on the latter see Adriaan H. Bredero, *Bernard of Clairvaux: Between Cult and History* (Grand Rapids, MI: Eerdmans, 1996), pp. 6ff.

   For centuries these texts have been taken as truthful descriptions assigned authority because of presumed early dates. Only recently has the reliability of those narratives as virtual eyewitness accounts come under question, in part because we now question the accuracy of texts which would so obviously distort the early history of Cistercian women in contradiction to the widespread evidence of their existence found in the documents of practice. Translations of the *Exordium Cistercii* and *Exordium parvum* are found in the appendices of Lekai, *Cistercians*, pp. 442ff., and more recently in *The New Monastery: Texts and Studies on the Earliest Cistercians*, ed. E. Rozanne Elder (Kalamazoo, MI: Cistercian Publications, 1998); they are based on *Les Plus Anciens Textes de Cîteaux: Sources, textes et notes historiques*, eds Jean-de-la-Croix Bouton and Jean-Baptiste Van Damme (Achel, Belgium: Abbaye Cistercienne, 1974). They have until recently been treated as accounts of *c.*1120 found in manuscripts dated to the 1140s (see Giles Constable, *The Reformation of the Twelfth Century* [Cambridge: Cambridge University Press, 1996], p. 38, n. 171), but arguments for manuscripts before 1152 are incorrect. Despite being treated by pious admirers of the Cistercians as virtual eyewitness accounts, these "documents" are retrospective accounts filled with paraphrases of the Rule of Saint Benedict, Deuteronomy, and other standard monastic exemplars (see Jean-Baptiste Auberger, *L'Unanimité cistercienne primitive: Mythe ou réalité?* [Achel, Belgium: Abbaye Cistercienne, 1986], pp. 109ff.), which have rarely been subjected to codicological or literary scrutiny; see n. 39.

35 But on this see Marcel Pacaut, "La Filiation claravallienne dans la genèse et l'essor de l'Ordre cistercien," in *Histoire de Clairvaux: Actes du Colloque de Bar-sur-Aube/Clairvaux, 22–23 juin, 1990* (Bar-sur-Aube: Némont, 1991), pp. 135–47.

36 The arguments that follow regarding the institutions of the Cistercians and their dating are made in further detail in Berman, *Cistercian Evolution*, esp. pp. 46ff.

37 There are two alternate versions of the Cistercian foundation story in the twelfth century, both dating to no earlier than the 1160s. The earlier *Exordium Cistercii* is very short, containing only a few paragraphs describing the departure from Molesme and the foundation, and is probably found in its earliest form in Paris, Sainte-Geneviève MS 1207. The longer, later narrative is the *Exordium parvum*, which

contains a series of "documents" supposedly supporting its account; later manuscript versions of it (but still dating from the twelfth century) contain a papal confirmation purported to be by Calixtus II, usually immediately following the *Exordium parvum*. On the relationship of this forged papal bull to authentic confirmations for Bonnevaux, see p. 246, note 52, below. The establishment of an accurate series of manuscripts for these *exordia* is based on establishing a series out of all the surviving twelfth-century manuscripts of the liturgical *ordines* or customaries known as the *Ecclesiastica officia*, which are found in the same manuscripts along with all the *exordia* texts with the exception of that from Sainte-Geneviève. A primitive fragment of those liturgical *ordines*, found in Montpellier H322 in a book of Cistercian usages without any *exordia* texts at all, dates the entire group to after 1160. This is in accord with the evidence of the most-cited early manuscripts of the *Ecclesiastica officia*, Trent 1711 and Ljubljana 31, which have been dated incorrectly to before 1152 by Danièle Choisselet and Placide Vernet, *Les "Ecclesiastica officia" cisterciens du XIIeme siècle: Texte latin selon les manuscrits édités de Trente 1711, Ljubljana 31 and Dijon 114*, La Documentation Cistercienne 22 (Reiningue: Abbaye d'Œlenberg, 1989), because they believed that the absence of a liturgical practice outlined in Canivez, *Statuta*, vol. 1 (1152), no. 6, made those two manuscripts earlier; in fact, the statute in question cannot be definitively dated to before 1185, and the dating of Trent 1711's *exordium* to before 1135 cannot be upheld once it is noted that this text was written on a later-added opening quire and single sheet preceding the next quire. On the wholly hypothetical dating of parts of vol. 1 of Canivez's edition of the Cistercian *Statuta* to such years as 1134 and 1152, and for further discussion of these "Institutes" or *Capitula* in manuscripts such as Paris, B. N. Latin MSS 4221, 4346B, and N. A. 430; Ljubljana 31; and Trent 1711 – which all date to between 1161 and 1185 – see Berman, *Cistercian Evolution*, pp. 46–68.

38 See discussion below at n. 86ff.

39 The dates given for the earliest Cistercian General Chapters in studies by Jean-Baptiste Mahn, *L'Ordre cistercien et son gouvernement des origines au milieu du XIIIe siècle (1098–1265)* (Paris: Boccard, 1945); Jacques Hourlier, *Le Chapitre Général jusqu'au moment du Grand Schisme: Origines, développement, étude juridique* (Paris: Sirey, 1936); and Jane Sayers, "The Judicial Activities of the General Chapters," *Journal of Ecclesiastical History* 15 (1964): 18–32, 168–85, suggests how often our attribution of these assemblies to an early date is based entirely on the misdated attribution of Cistercian statutes to the years 1134 and 1152. In published documents for Burgundian abbeys dated to before the 1170s, references thought to be to the General Chapter turn out to refer to internal chapters at Cîteaux; cf. *Chartes et documents concernant l'abbaye de Cîteaux: 1098–1182*, ed. J.-M. Marilier (Rome: Editiones cistercienses, 1961), no. 90 (1132) (which turns out to be the interpolation of a Lucius III bull from the 1180s – the surviving copy still bears the 1180s' rota), and *Recueil de Clairvaux*, ed. Waquet, no. 4 (1132), which is the authentic text which the Cîteaux charter mimicked. This authentic Clairvaux tithe privilege does not mention an Order but rather a congregation under Bernard of Clairvaux – a distinction I clarify below. The "original" cited in Canivez, *Statuta*, vol. 1 (1142), for a Charter of Peace between the Cistercians and the Premonstratensians has dating clauses which suggest an interpolation from the 1160s, but there is a possibility that such peace agreements date to the last years of Bernard of Clairvaux's life. There are three references to a General Chapter, possibly none of these from before the 1150s: *Chartes de Cîteaux*, no. 128 (1146–53); *Le Premier Cartulaire de l'Abbaye Cistercienne de Pontigny (xiie–xiiie siècles)*, ed. Martine Garrigues (Paris, 1981), no. 114 (attributed to 1156); and *Recueil des pancartes de l'abbaye de la Ferté-sur-Grosne: 1113–1178*, ed. Georges Duby (Aix-Marseilles, 1953); and no. 8 (from an act of 1158 describing earlier events).

40 This suggests that J.-B. Van Damme, "La Constitution Cistercienne de 1165," *Analecta Cisterciensia* 19 (1963): 51–104, actually concerns the earliest constitution, that

approved by Alexander III, and the first Cistercian constitution submitted to any pope. A copy dated to 1163 is Dijon, Bibl. Mun. MS 87, fols 168v–169r.

41 This congregation might have included only those nine or ten houses each of whose sites were chosen either by Bernard of Clairvaux or Stephen Harding, as shown in Auberger, *L'Unanimité cistercienne primitive*, esp. pp. 395ff.

42 Brian Stock, *The Implications of Literacy: Written Language and Models of Interpretation in the Eleventh and Twelfth Centuries* (Princeton, NJ: Princeton University Press, 1983), pp. 88ff., 405ff.; Martha B. Newman, *The Boundaries of Charity: Cistercian Culture and Ecclesiastical Reform, 1098–1180* (Stanford, CA: Stanford University Press, 1996), pp. 10ff.

43 On the more general trends see Michael T. Clanchy, *From Memory to Written Record: England 1066–1307*, 2nd edn (Oxford: Blackwell, 1993); and Ellen Kittel, *From Ad Hoc to Routine: A Case Study in Medieval Bureaucracy* (Philadelphia, PA: University of Pennsylvania Press, 1991).

44 See Canivez, *Statuta*, vol. 1, for years 1179–89; the issues addressed in those years concern the minutiae of creating an order, enforcing attendance and accommodating abbots at an annual, universal General Chapter meeting, size of abbeys, etc.

45 See de Fontette, *Religieuses*, pp. 27–63; Degler-Spengler, "Incorporation," pp. 99ff.

46 See accounts by John Freed, "Urban Development and the 'Cura Monialium' in Thirteenth-century Germany," *Viator* 3 (1972): 311–27; Simone Roisin, "L'Efflorescence cistercienne et le courant féminin de piété au 13ème siècle," *Revue d'histoire ecclésiastique* 39 (1943): 342–78; Roger de Ganck, "The Cistercian Nuns of Belgium in the Thirteenth Century Seen Against the Background of the Second Wave of Cistercian Spirituality," *Cistercian Studies* 5 (1970): 169–87; de Ganck, "The Integration of Nuns in the Cistercian Order particularly in Belgium," *Cîteaux* 35 (1984): 235–47; and Ernst McDonnell, *Beguines and Beghards in Medieval Culture, with Special Emphasis on the Belgian Scene* (New Brunswick, NJ: Rutgers University Press, 1954).

47 It is important not to lump them together as all alike; there were extremely wealthy communities of Cistercian women like that founded by Blanche of Castile at Maubuisson as described by Dimier, *Saint Louis et Cîteaux*; there were also very poor ones like Netlieu, as described by Daniel Rouquette, "Note sur la date de fondation et l'emplacement de l'abbaye de Netlieu," *Mélanges Dimier*, 3.6: 697–700.

48 Such issues about women's communities arose across the spectrum of new religious groups at this time, but the thirteenth-century history of many reform groups founded in the twelfth century, particularly of their "women's branches," has been neglected until recently.

49 This means that explanations of aberrance, such as found in Louis de Lacger, "Ardorel," *Dictionnaire d'histoire et de géographie ecclésiastique* 7 (1924): 1617–20, or of the introduction of decadence with incorporations, as found in Bennett D. Hill, *English Cistercian Monasteries and their Patrons in the Twelfth Century* (Urbana, IL: University of Illinois Press, 1968), or of a conflict between ideals and reality, as found in Louis J. Lekai, "Ideals and Reality in Early Cistercian Life and Legislation," *Cistercian Ideals and Reality*, pp. 4–29, are irrelevant.

50 Richard W. Southern, *Western Society and the Church in the Middle Ages* (Harmondsworth: Penguin, 1970), p. 317, n. 19, gives totals for the entire Middle Ages of 654 houses for women as against 742 for men, but admits his numbers for women's houses are low for some cases; more recent studies show even more houses, for instance, Brigitte Degler-Spengler, "Die Zisterzienserinnen in der Schweiz," *Helvetia Sacra* (Bern) 3 (1982): 507–74; Dominique Mouret, "Les Moniales cisterciennes en France aux XIIe et XIIIe siècles," Mémoire de Maitrise, Université de Limoges (1984); Elkins, *Holy Women*; Constance Hoffman Berman, "Fashions in Monastic Patronage: The Popularity of Supporting Cistercian Abbeys for Women," *Proceedings of the Western Society for French History* 17 (1990): 36–45; Thompson, *Women Religious*; Venarde, *Women's Monasticism*.

51 On the dating see Henrietta Leyser, *Hermits and the New Monasticism: A Study of Religious Communities in Western Europe, 1000–1150* (London: MacMillan, 1984).

52 That a confirmation of Bonnevaux's properties of *c*.1120 was used as the basis for an interpolated text dated to 1119 and turned into a papal confirmation of the Order's practices is confirmed by the fact that only the last of the twelfth-century manuscript versions of the *Exordium parvum* contain this papal bull, that there are sentences out of order in all versions of it until the *Exordium magnum*, and that only the later manuscript versions contain its dating clause. The parallels of language to the Bonnevaux document are clear, yet the entire argument for the precocious foundation of an order is based on the 1119 Calixtus document which is not even present in the earliest surviving manuscripts of the so-called "eyewitness" accounts. See Berman, *Cistercian Evolution*, pp. 281–4.

53 Such an account is in accord with the account of gradual regularization of women's houses in other reform groups, described by Penny Shine Gold, *The Lady and the Virgin: Image, Attitude, and Experience in Twelfth-century France* (Chicago, IL: University of Chicago Press, 1985), pp. 80–1.

54 Bredero, *Bernard*, pp. 248ff.; Pacaut, "Filiation"; Berman, *Cistercian Evolution*, pp. 148–51, pushes this explanation further in light of its dating of the *exordia*.

55 *PL*, vol. 185: 237; for date of William, see Bredero, *Bernard*, p. 285.

56 *Cartulaire de l'abbaye de Silvanès*, no. 470, 371ff.; Kienzle, "The Tract," *passim*; and *Vie de Saint Étienne d'Obazine*, ed. Michel Aubrun (Clermont-Ferrand: Université, 1970).

57 Both Orderic and William, when they discuss Cistercians, discuss not the Cistercians as an Order, but the monks of the abbey of Cîteaux itself; see *The Ecclesiastical History of Orderic Vitalis*, 8.26, ed. Marjorie Chibnall (Oxford: Clarendon, 1969–80), vol. 4, p. 322; and *Willelmi Malmesbiriensis Monachi De Gestis Regum Anglorum*, ed. William Stubbs, 2 vols (London: Eyre and Spottiswoode, 1887), *passim*. This is approximately the same with the *De institutione clericorum* of Philip of Harvengt, *PL*, vol. 203: 836–7, from the 1140s. See relevant parts of the *De miraculis sanctae Mariae Laudunensis* of Herman of Tournai, *PL*, vol. 156: 962–1018.

58 *PL*, vol. 156: 1001–2.

59 *PL*, vol. 156: 962–1018, cited at col. 996.

60 That Cîteaux was promoting a less syneisactic approach to the inclusion of religious women in its reform does not necessarily mean that its leaders were denouncing the inclusion of women altogether. Indeed, it even seems likely that it was only later Cistercian commentators who saw a denunciation of women or of syneisacticism in Bernard's famous sermon 65 from the collection of his homilies on the *Song of Songs*, parts of which were written after 1147. Perhaps that sermon should not be interpreted as anything more than a sermon on heretics who hypocritically called "apostolic" their living together with women. See Bernard of Clairvaux, *Sermones super Cantica Canticorum*, no. 65, in *Opera Omnia*, eds J. Leclercq, C. H. Talbot, and H. M. Rochais (Rome: Editiones Cistercienses, 1957), vol. 2, pp. 172–7. The emphasis in the text is on heretics, not syneisacticism, although this is how it is often read by modern interpreters. My reading of this sermon suggests that it reflects Bernard of Clairvaux's anxiety about the hypocrisy of heretics who pretended to be true Christians, claiming among other proofs their apostolic lives in common with women. It would later become a convenient way to avoid the *cura monialium* to claim that Bernard had said that the care of religious women was heretical. Cf. Jo Ann McNamara, "The *Herrenfrage*: The Restructuring of the Gender System, 1050–1150," in *Medieval Masculinities: Regarding Men in the Middle Ages*, ed. Clare A. Lees, with Thelma Fenster and Mo Ann McNamara (Minneapolis, MN: University of Minnesota Press, 1994), pp. 3–29, and McNamara, Chapter 4 in this volume.

61 *The Book of Saint Gilbert 5*, ed. Raymonde Foreville and Gillian Keir (Oxford: Clarendon, 1987), pp. 40–3; written by an anonymous canon of Sempringham, the account dates to no earlier than 1205.

62 There is no contemporary evidence even for that meeting of a General Chapter supposed to have taken place at Cîteaux in 1147 (when Eugenius III is said to have been present and Savigniacs and Obazine were incorporated while Gilbert's nuns were rejected); Golding, *Gilbert*, pp. 26ff., finds no evidence for that meeting earlier than the *Vita prima* of Bernard.

63 On that charter see n. 39.

64 *The Historia Occidentalis of Jacques de Vitry: A Critical Edition*, ed. John Frederick Hinnebusch (Fribourg: University Press, 1972), p. 117; dating, pp. 6, 16.

65 Lekai, *Cistercians*, pp. 347–9.

66 Dimier, "Chapitres généraux"; Degler-Spengler, "Incorporation," pp. 96ff.; Canivez, *Statuta*, vol. 2, 1213, nos. 3 and 4; 1218, nos. 4 and 84; 1219, no. 12; 1220, no. 4; 1225, no. 1; 1228, no. 16; 1233, no. 12; and 1239, no. 7.

67 Ernst Günther Krenig, "Mittelalterliche Frauenklöster nach den Konstitutionen von Cîteaux," *Analecta Cisterciensia* 10 (1954): 1–105, esp. 15ff.

68 Lekai, *Cistercians*, pp. 347ff.; on Saint-Antoine, see Constance Hoffman Berman, "Cistercian Nuns and the Development of the Order: The Cistercian Abbey at Saint-Antoine-des-Champs outside Paris," in *The Joy of Learning and the Love of God: Essays in Honor of Jean Leclercq*, ed. E. Rozanne Elder (Kalamazoo, MI: Cistercian Publications, 1995), pp. 121–56.

69 Degler-Spengler, "Incorporation," pp. 96ff., lists all but *ordo cisterciensis*.

70 Coburn Graves, "English Cistercian Nuns in Lincolnshire," *Speculum* 54 (1979): 492–9, attempted to account for the local evidence of twelfth and thirteenth-century houses of Cistercian nuns in England by creating a special category of "English Cistercian nuns." This allowed for the study of these communities, but fell into the larger misinterpretation, as is discussed at more length in the original version of this chapter in *Church History*.

71 See Berman, "Men's Houses," and Venarde, *Women's Monasticism*.

72 Mahn, *L'Ordre cistercien*, esp. pp. 148ff.

73 Cf. Thompson, "Problem," pp. 227–52.

74 Canivez, *Statuta*, vol. 1, *passim*.

75 The earliest annual statutes in a series are found in Montpellier, Bibliothèque de l'École de Médicine, MSS H322, dated in the manuscript to 1157–61. I argue at length that this predates any other series of statutes – all the others contain no dates – because this is also the earliest manuscript for parts of an early liturgical *ordo* and the earliest Cistercian lay-brother treatises; see Berman, *Cistercian Evolution*. Cf. *La Législation cistercienne abrégée du manuscrit de Montpellier H322*, ed. Louis Duval-Arnould (Paris: Champion, 1997), who contends that this is a truncated later text.

76 With the exception of a single statute attributed to 1152 in an 1185 manuscript (Dijon 114) none of the statutes dated in that publication to 1134 and to 1152 bear dates in any twelfth-century manuscript.

77 The *prima collectio* is dated in no twelfth-century manuscript.

78 *Orderic Vitalis*, ed. Chibnall, vol. 6, pp. 424–7.

79 Statutes from before 1150 have not been lost, but were simply never made; the first distribution of statutes throughout the Order only occurred in 1202; see Lekai, *Cistercians*, pp. 75–6.

80 See n. 39.

81 Bouton, "L'Établissement," pp. 98, 115; and see n. 19 above.

82 Jennifer Carpenter, "Juette of Huy, Recluse and Other (1158–1228): Children and Mothering in the Saintly Life," in *Power of the Weak*, ed. Jennifer Carpenter and Sally-Beth MacLean (Urbana, IL: University of Illinois Press, 1995), pp. 57–93.

83 Roisin, "L'Efflorescence cistercienne"; reference to imitation is found as well in the Herman of Tournai passage quoted at n. 58 above.

84 For instance René Locatelli, "Papauté et cisterciens du diocèse de Besançon," in Grosse, *L'Église de France*, p. 306, or the papal bull of Alexander III published

in *Cartulaire de l'abbaye de Silvanès*, no. 1 (1162), or François Blary, *Le Domaine de Chaalis: XIIe–XIVe siècles* (Paris: C.N.R.S., 1993), no. 2 (1153).

85 Earliest references to an *ordo monasticus* at Cîteaux or to *universus ordo Cisterciensis* appear in papal bulls of Alexander III from 1163, *Recueil de Clairvaux*, nos. 92 (1163) and 97 (1163); this is confirmed by the following CD-ROM databases: Cetedoc: Library of Christian Latin Texts: CLCLT–2, published by Brepols; Cetedoc: Corpus Diplomaticórum: Belgium Latin Text, published by Brepols; and Patrologia Latina, CD-ROM index published by Chadwick-Healy.

86 *Libellus de diversis ordinibus et professionibus qui sunt in aecclesia*, eds Giles Constable and B. Smith (Oxford: Clarendon, 1972), never discusses a Cistercian Order. Constable, *Reformation*, pp. 174–6, stresses uniformity as the issue seen as creating orders by 1215, but this is not what *ordo* necessarily meant in the twelfth century.

87 Giles Constable, "The Orders of Society," in *Three Studies in Medieval Religious and Social Thought* (Cambridge: Cambridge University Press, 1995), pp. 251ff. [and see Ch. 3, above].

88 For examples of early but ambiguous usage, see *Chartes de Cîteaux*, no. 69 (1119), and no. 85 (1131), but see no. 90 (1132), which refers to both congregation and *vestri ordinis abbatiis*. See also *Liber instrumentorum*, ed. Germain, no. 95 (1146), for the will of Guillelm VI.

89 But see Berman, "Labors," *passim*.

90 Promises of this sort to Jully are documented; see n. 7 above; Reinhard Schneider, *Vom Klosterhaushalt zum Stadt und Staatshaushalt: Der Zisterziensisehe Beitrag* (Stuttgart: Anton Hiersemann, 1994) provides the example of a count and countess of Flanders in 1238 who petitioned the General Chapter in the mid-thirteenth century to lend them three lay-brothers. This evidence suggests that the precedents for such assignment of monks and *conversi* outside their own communities may well have been in the detailing of members of neighboring Cistercian men's houses to Cistercian women's communities.

91 See Ljubljana (Laibach), State and University Library, MS 30, for example.

92 Grundmann, *Religious Movements*, *passim*.

93 Southern, *Western Society*, p. 317, cites instances from Canivez, *Statuta*, vol. 2, 1242, nos. 15–18; 1243, nos. 6–8, 61–9, and 1244, no. 8, of nuns rebelliously locking out new abbot visitors; in this he mistook resistance to local visitors for resistance to being Cistercian.

94 Jean-de-la-Croix Bouton, "L'Établissement des moniales cisterciennes," *Mémoire de la société pour l'histoire du droit et des institutions des anciens pays bourguignons, comtois, et romands* 15 (1953): 83–116; Dimier, "Chapitres généraux."

95 Krenig, "Mittelalterliche Frauenklöster," *passim*.

96 On this see both Boyd, *Rifreddo*, and Roisin, "L'Efflorescence."

97 See Martin Aurell i Cardonna, "Les Cisterciennes et leurs protecteurs en Provence rhodanienne," *Les Cisterciens de Languedoc (XIlle–XIVe siècle)*, Cahiers de Fanjeaux 21 (Toulouse: Privat, 1986), pp. 35–68; and *Cartulaire de Notre-Dame de Voisins*, ed. Jules Doinel (Orleans: Herluison, 1887).

98 Berman, "Labors"; Anne Bondéelle-Souchier, "Les Moniales cisterciennes et leurs livres manuscrits dans la France d'ancien régime," *Cîteaux* 45 (1994): 193–336; and next note.

99 Boyd, *Rifreddo*, esp. pp. 95ff., describes the "takeover" by Rifreddo and disputes over tithes; a reassessment of this evidence on Cistercian women's agriculture and tithes is found in Constance Hoffman Berman, "Cistercian Women and Tithes," *Cîteaux* 49 (1998): 95–128.

9

MARY MAGDALEN
AND THE CONTEMPLATIVE
LIFE

Katherine Ludwig Jansen

Although new nunneries continued to be founded well into the thirteenth century, many laywomen and -men were inspired to a life of penance and service within more informal communities. As was seen in the example of Verona above, already in the eleventh century such penitents coming from all levels of society joined together into small communities or anchorholds to lead exemplary lives, often without formal rules. In Italy these communities were often urban ones and many were of women; these female religious recluses (sometimes called beatae *or* pinzochere*) with their male counterparts were often transformed in the early thirteenth century into communities of the new mendicant (begging) orders, most notably the Franciscans and Dominicans. These mendicant groups sought to mix a life of prayer and contemplation, "the contemplative life," with a more active mission, "the active life." In both groups, men quickly became preaching and teaching brothers (and eventually inquisitors), as well as wandering from place to place living by mendicancy. Associated houses of nuns soon appeared, but their participation in the practice of begging for their subsistence was always more limited.*

In the book from which this selection comes Katherine Jansen traces how the penitential practices of these groups led them to identify themselves closely with Mary Magdalen, a composite of several biblical Marys. Medieval legends about Mary Magdalen, the sinner who had washed Jesus's feet and had witnessed him after the resurrection, conflated her with the anchoress, Mary of Egypt. She was also confused with the Mary of the biblical sisters, Mary and Martha, described in the Gospel of Luke and identified as sisters of Lazarus, who had been raised by Jesus from the dead. Martha represented the housewife, the practitioner of "the active life," because she had served food to Christ; her sister Mary was identified with "the contemplative life," because she had not helped her sister, but instead sat at the feet of Christ and listened to his teaching. Mary Magdalen could be both or either.

The fact that Mary Magdalen had been the first to see Jesus after his resurrection gave her an importance in the Middle Ages as an equal to the Apostles. Whereas there has been much attention given by earlier historians to the increasing devotion to the Virgin Mary in the later Middle Ages, Katherine Jansen's contribution is to show that such devotion to the Virgin was paralleled by an enormous expansion in interest in the Magdalen as well. The Magdalen would come to be considered the most powerful woman saint in heaven after the Virgin and her appeal spanned the social spectrum. Legends about her contemplative life as an anchoress in the "desert" or wilderness at La Sainte-Baume in Provence were particularly promoted by the Angevin Kings of Naples (who were also counts of Provence), and she is associated with that part of France as well because it was believed that she was one of the three Marys who set out from the East to land at the mouth of the Rhône River where the town of Les Saintes-Maries was founded.

In this selection Jansen discusses the legend of Mary Magdalen as a hermitess or anchoress saint who was patron of the contemplative life. Drawing on the many sermons on the Magdalen by Italian mendicant preachers, as well as her portrayal in pre-Renaissance art, Jansen argues for the popularization of Mary Magdalen as the archetypical penitent. Although many of the surviving sermons for the Magdalen were intended for audiences of men, women were probably those who most often identified with Mary Magdalen. Jansen also traces the Magdalen's identification as patron saint for communities of contemplative women associated with the penitential and mendicant movements. The Magdalen's example showed that even the greatest sinner could be saved. Religious men and women of the thirteenth and later centuries, deeply aware of their own failings, may have found her more appealing than the sinless Virgin. They turned increasingly to the repentant sinner, Mary Magdalen, as an aid and hope for salvation after conversions from sinfulness to penitence. Perhaps most surprising is that the Magdalen comes to be portrayed as the female counterpart of Francis of Assisi (d. 1226) in art that depicts her as a penitent of great beauty, often dressed only in her luxuriant hair. This selection comes from Katherine Ludwig Jansen, The Making of the Magdalen, Preaching and Popular Devotion in the Later Middle Ages *(Princeton, NJ: Princeton University Press, 2000), pp. 116–29, 135–42.*

* * *

Mary Magdalen's contemplative life began at Bethany – at Jesus's feet – where rapt, she sat listening intently to his every word. The Lord had commended Mary for her choice of contemplation over action with these words: "Mary has chosen the better part which shall not be taken from her" (Luke 10:42).[1] Giordano da Pisa (d. 1311) and other preachers took the relative clause in that sentence to mean that the active life, while good, was fleeting; the contemplative life, on the other hand, would endure throughout eternity.[2] This chapter examines how preachers used Mary Magdalen as the symbol of the "better part," transforming her in the process from Jesus' attentive student into a veritable medieval mystic. It also explains why the new mendicant orders identified deeply with the image of the contemplative and mystical Magdalen.

Spiritual concentration

It seems a tautology to state that the object of the contemplative life is contemplation. But, like action, contemplation has many components. At its most elementary it consists of empathetic meditation on the life, passion, and resurrection of Jesus. It also comprises listening intently to sermons or the words of holy people, introspection, reflective acts of prayer, and *lectio divina*, meditative reading. These are parts of acquired or ordinary contemplation, the lower rungs on the contemplative ladder. The end toward which the contemplative aspires is mystical union, an infused or extraordinary state in which the enlightened soul attains a personal knowledge of the divine. Supernatural states such as trances, levitation, ecstasies, visions, and revelations sometimes accompany mystical experience but are not a crucial constituent of it.[3] The *Lives* of Mary Magdalen demonstrate that eventually she scaled the heights of mystical contemplation, but it all began in a humble novitiate at the feet of the Lord at Bethany.

The Augustinian Agostino d'Ancona (d. 1328) commented that "blessed Magdalen was drawn by contemplation of the divine word even there, in the house of Martha her sister, where sitting at the feet of the Lord, she listened to his word."[4] The Dominican Aldobrandino Cavalcanti (d. 1279) emphasized that Mary's seated position denoted her contemplative state, her repose of mind, while other preachers focused on the spiritual meal of the divine word upon which Mary feasted.[5] The fourteenth-century Jacopo Capocci da Viterbo was not alone in noticing that, while Martha labored to feed Christ corporally, Mary was being fed spiritually by the word of the Lord.[6] And in a pithy maxim, Agostino d'Ancona summed up his approval of her spiritual repast thus: "Nourishing the mind is better than nourishing the stomach."[7] Thus the novice contemplative partook of a spiritual feast at the Lord's feet.[8]

As one who had received instruction directly from the master himself, the Magdalen was regarded as a model student, at least in the view of the Franciscan Matteo d'Aquasparta (d. 1302). In the first of his Magdalen sermons he used the contemplative Magdalen as an example of scholarly comportment, presumably in contrast to the imperfect examples he had encountered during his teaching career at the universities of Paris and Bologna. The text is worth citing in full. He maintained:

> We have here in Mary the ordered example of study for which three things are required: [First], the leisure of repose without distraction. This is signified by sitting, rather than students who are wandering about and running hither and thither. Second is her humility of mind, without vain display, since it is noted that she sat at the Lord's feet. This is contrary to the presumptuous and the proud who, immediately when they know something, despise all the others, and reject the positions of their elders. Third is her diligence of attention since it is understood in the act of listening. This is contrary to those who

want to speak rather than listen, or those who want to be masters rather than students. The master is the one to whom you ought to listen. Christ is in his *cathedra* (the chair of the bishop) in heaven and his school is on earth; his scholars are his members. For he himself teaches human knowledge. Whence I believe that if scholars would first consult the master through prayer they would profit more than by consulting any teacher.[9]

It is clear that the audience for this sermon was male: men in holy orders, probably university men engaged in pursuing their higher degrees in theology. By the fifteenth century, two English colleges dedicated to the Magdalen were founded in order to house university men: one at Oxford and one at Cambridge.[10]

But women too were expected to use the Magdalen as a contemplative guide. The Franciscan Bertrand de la Tour (d. 1332), who ended his career as cardinal-bishop of Tusculum (Frascati), took the occasion of a Magdalen sermon to point out to his auditors that Mary said very little, because a female religious should not be garrulous.[11] Given the common belief about her scandalous past, it would seem that Mary Magdalen was a rather unlikely candidate to become a model for cloistered women. But contrary to all expectations she became just that as preachers transformed her into a mirror for contemplative nuns. The Dominican Guillaume Peyraut (d. 1271) told his auditors that the Magdalen's feast was celebrated by everyone, but especially by enclosed nuns who lead the contemplative life of which Mary is the example and mirror.[12]

Convents of Benedictine, Premonstratensian, and Cistercian nuns were founded under the spiritual patronage of the Magdalen throughout much of Europe and the Latin Middle East by the mid-twelfth century.[13] In that century, England led the way with six foundations at Davington (Kent), Kynewaldgraves (Yorkshire), Bristol (Gloucestershire), Sewardsley (Northamptonshire), Wintney (Hampshire), and Ickleton (Cambridgeshire).[14] The convent at Bristol had a female benefactor: it was founded by the widow of Robert Fitz Harding, Eva, who may even have become the prioress of her nunnery.[15] In the same century, there were three foundations in France, one each at Orléans, Rouen, and Etrun. In addition, one community of Norbertine women was founded in Anvers and another near Prague. Neither the German Empire nor the Holy Land was bereft of such convents of contemplative Magdalens.[16]

The earliest notice for an Italian foundation is in Norman Sicily. A document of 1151 records Roger II's endowment of lands near Sciacca to Adelicia, abbess of the Benedictine convent of Saint Mary Magdalen near Corleone in the diocese of Palermo.[17] Another early foundation for Benedictine women was in 1162, at Subiaco, where Saint Benedict himself had formed his first community of monks. The new foundation was made near the cave where

Chelidonia of Abruzzo had spent most of her life, possibly in imitation of the legendary Magdalen.[18]

By the end of the next century, however, Italy had far outstripped the rest of Europe in its establishment of cloistered communities of women dedicated to Mary Magdalen; in the thirteenth and early fourteenth centuries Benedictine and Cistercian convents were founded throughout the peninsula: in Urbania, Verona, Alexandria, Recanati, San Severo, Castellaneta, Marta, Chieti, Florence, and Perugia.[19] Likewise for the more recent reformed orders. The blessed Santuccia Carabotti of Gubbio (d. 1305), who by the time of her death had founded a monastic congregation which included some twenty foundations, seems to have had a special fondness for Saint Mary Magdalen. In fact, over one-quarter of the convents in her congregations were named for the saint.[20]

The mendicant orders were no less dedicated in founding contemplative convents in honor of the Magdalen. In 1286, thirty years after the Order of the Hermits of Saint Augustine was formally organized, the first convent of Augustinian nuns was founded in Orvieto and dedicated to Mary Magdalen. Other communities of female contemplatives associated with the friars soon emerged. In the diocese of Spoleto alone there were eleven mendicant-associated convents dedicated to Mary Magdalen during the thirteenth and fourteenth centuries. No other female saint, not even the Virgin Mary, who was commemorated with ten foundations in the diocese, could claim so many titular honors.[21] Outside the Spoleto valley, female contemplative foundations emerged at Siena, Atri, Città di Castello, Forlì, Perugia, Borgo Sansepolcro, and San Gimignano, among other central Italian cities.[22]

A document dated February 20, 1334 from the convent at San Gimignano provides a glimpse of the material and spiritual life of such nuns. A certain Monna di Rufo di Petroio received a privilege from John, cardinal-deacon of Saint-Theodore and legate to the Holy See, to build a monastery complex including a church, altar, bell tower, residence, cemetery, and other necessities. The twelve nuns, of whom seven are named, followed the Augustinian rule. The abbess and enclosed nuns were able to select their own priest or suitable confessor. Their complex was dedicated to Saint Mary Magdalen.[23]

Preachers intended that the contemplative Magdalen serve both cloistered nuns and ordinary women alike. Toward this end they stressed her great wisdom acquired through listening to the word of the Lord. Nicolas de Hanappes (d. 1291), a Dominican who ended his career as cardinal-bishop of Ostia and patriarch of Jerusalem, named Mary Magdalen under the rubric, *De sapientia mulierum* (*On the wisdom of women*), in his book of *exempla*.[24] Giovanni da San Gimignano, prior of the Dominican convent in Siena, contrasted the Magdalen's wisdom with the foolishness of Eve. The imprudent woman, he argued, opens her ears to the words of lechers like the serpent – the devil – whereas the wise woman, as exemplified by Mary Magdalen, closes her ears to such types and opens them only for the word of God.[25]

Persuading certain women to listen to the word of God was no easy matter, at least according to Humbert of Romans, Dominican master general (d. 1277); according to him, some women

> are not devoted to the word of God, but rather when they are in church, they just talk, say their prayers, genuflect before images [and] take holy water. They can hardly be persuaded to go now and then to the preaching.

For these ordinary women who participated in the rituals of the faith without much reflection on their deeper meaning, Humbert advised "the example of the Magdalen, who sitting at the feet of the Lord listened to his word."[26]

Thus preachers turned to the Gospel-writer Luke's image of Mary Magdalen, "absorbed in listening and attending to words of the Lord,"[27] to promote devotion to the contemplative aspect of the saint. There was, however, another source than the Gospel for this image. There were legends that transmitted an image of the Magdalen as contemplative saint, but such representations differed markedly from that found in scripture. In the legends that formed her *vitae* Mary Magdalen became a type of desert saint, a hermit hungering in spirit, who retired to the wilderness to devote herself entirely to the mystical contemplation of God.[28]

The mystical Magdalen

The legend of the eremitical Magdalen, a conflation with the *vita* of Mary of Egypt, began circulating in Europe prior to the mid-ninth century. Honorius Augustodunensis (d. 1137), whose Magdalen homily made up a part of his *Speculum ecclesiae*, drew on the *vita eremitica* (the *Eremitical Life of the Magdalen*) to enliven his sermon. In his account of her life, after receiving the holy spirit with the other disciples, Mary Magdalen withdrew to the desert where she lived out the rest of her years in solitary reclusion.[29] Honorius's description of her eremitical life is rather laconic; the *vita eremitica*, which was a source for him, provided more detail. It narrated that Mary Magdalen secluded herself in a grotto for thirty years, taking no earthly fare; she did, however, receive spiritual refreshment at the canonical hours – when angels sent by the Lord transported her into the ether where they nourished her with divine sustenance.

Although this legend became widespread throughout Europe, the eremitical facts of her life were not accepted unanimously. A contemporary of Honorius Augustodunensis, an anonymous Cistercian, who in the early twelfth century wrote a *Life* once ascribed to Hrabanus Maurus (d. 856), dismissed the *vita eremitica* with this withering piece of source criticism:

> The rest of the tale – that after the ascension of the Savior she immediately fled to the Arabian desert; that she remained there without any

clothing in a cave; and that she saw no man afterwards until she was visited by I know not what priest, from whom she begged a garment, and other such stuff – is false and a fabrication of storytellers drawn out of the accounts of the Penitent of Egypt [Mary of Egypt]. And these tale-spinners convict themselves of falsehood from the very beginning of their story, for they ascribe their account to Josephus, that most learned historian [of the ancient world], though Josephus never mentions anything about Mary Magdalen in his books.[30]

The Cistercian's most severe censure was directed at the episode that scholars acknowledge was a direct "borrowing" from the *Life* of Mary of Egypt. But he was not entirely convinced of the angelic episode either. He suggests that it too was "an apocryphal story," but then retreats from such an exacting position by proposing that,

> if this is understood in a mystical sense it is not completely unbeliev-able, for it is a fact that admits no doubt that she was quite often refreshed by the sight of angels, aided by their services, and delighted by their conversation.[31]

Nevertheless, he is the only writer known to me who expressed any sort of skepticism in relation to Mary Magdalen's angelically assisted mystical life. By the thirteenth century most hagiographers and preachers embraced the story wholeheartedly, even using the language of mysticism to describe the events in the wilderness. Thus Agostino d'Ancona told his audience that "Mary Magdalen was rapt by the jubilation of angels."[32]

What made the figure of the eremitical Magdalen, secluded in her grotto and attended by angels, such an attractive figure to medieval preachers? I would like to argue that it is consistent with the mendicant identification with the saint as a symbol of the apostolic Magdalen, for the apostolic or mixed life that the friars lived drew equally from the wells of contemplation and action. The contemplative life was the life that spiritually restored the preachers so that they could better discharge their active ministries in the world. All too often, however, the duties of office were so burdensome that no time remained for such solitary refreshment.

The case of the Dominican Raymond of Peñafort (d. 1275) is revealing. Sometime in the period between 1231 and 1236, while he was serving as papal penitentiary, one of the personal priests of Pope Gregory IX (1227–41), Raymond wrote a letter to the prioress of the convent of Dominican contemplatives in Bologna asking to be remembered in her prayers. Here is Raymond's wistful supplication:

> Living, as I do, in the whirlwind of the court, I am hardly ever able to reach, or, to be quite honest, even to see from afar, the tranquility of contemplation. . . . So it is a great joy and an enormous comfort to

me to feel how I am helped by your prayers. I often think of this service which you and your sisters do for me, sitting as you do at the Lord's feet with Mary, enjoying the delights of your spouse, our Lord Jesus Christ, contemplating the face of him whom the angels desire to look upon. So when all is going well for you with your spouse in the secrecy of your chamber, do not forget, in your mutual uninterrupted love, to pray for me and beg alms for me in my poverty and need.[33]

Clearly, Raymond was longing to sit at the feet of the Lord with Mary but, given his manifold obligations at the papal court, he was compelled to live the life of Martha. The Catalan friar's experience was not unique. As the medievalist John Coakley has pointed out, since the friars were frequently unable to attend to their own interior lives, they often devoted themselves to recording the contemplative lives of the visionary women whom they served as confessors.[34] Women, of course, were forbidden from holding clerical office; but nevertheless, as historian Caroline Walker Bynum has vividly demonstrated, women did develop an authoritative voice in the later medieval Church through their active interior lives which were recorded for posterity in the form of *Lives*.[35] The friars, their confidants, and chaplains, were fascinated by these women's supernatural knowledge received frequently in the form of visions. Though the friars regarded such mystical gifts as signs of holiness, they were assisted in this belief by medieval medicine which suggested that such female inspiration was explained by sex differences. Medieval medical theory was based on the ancient theory of humors, which maintained that physiologically women were composed of cold and wet properties. Extrapolating from this theory, medieval theologians claimed that women's cold and wet nature disposed them toward infused knowledge – inspiration, mysticism, revelations, and visions.[36] Men, on the other hand, being constitutionally hot and dry, were considered the more rational and inclined to acquired learning, by the traditional means of study and education. Therefore, in the very restricted context of mystical perfection, being male and in clerical orders was a distinct disadvantage.[37] Recall that in the gnostic *Gospel of Mary* Mary Magdalen is the visionary, while Peter and the other apostles merely look on in wonder and envy at her prophetic gifts. But here of course the similarity ends; whereas the apostles in the gnostic text attacked the veracity of the Magdalen's visionary experience, by the late medieval period the friars were reporting in lavish detail on her mystical experiences.

Both biology and priestly office conspired to distance the friars from engaging in the sort of mystical life for which they yearned and which the eremitical Magdalen had practiced daily at the seven canonical hours. By attending to the details of that mystical life in their sermons, the preachers were able to refresh themselves vicariously in the restorative waters of contemplation. By recording it, speaking it, and preaching it, the friars were willing themselves into the contemplative life.

Thus it is not surprising that the preachers relished describing the forbidding and desolate spot that Mary Magdalen, avid for contemplation, had chosen for reclusion. It was called variously an *aspirum heremum*, *rupes*, *spelunca*, *desertum*, or *antrum*, words meaning desert or cave, all medieval shorthand for denoting "the wilderness." The late thirteenth-century Franciscan Servasanto da Faenza was not the only one to describe this place as bereft of even the slightest natural consolation: there were no streams, no trees, not even any grass.[38] Salimbene (d. 1288), the loquacious Franciscan chronicler who had actually been to the Magdalen's Provençal grotto on pilgrimage, described the region as being "secluded, uninhabitable and deserted."[39] Interestingly, although the *vita eremitica* began circulating as early as the ninth century, the precise localization of this southern French desert did not occur in legendary and homiletic material until the twelfth century.[40] Even then it was usually unnamed and reckoned in relation to Marseilles. Bertrand de la Tour referred to it as being in the *deserto marsiliense*, in the Marseillaise desert, while the Dominican hagiographer, Jean de Mailly, situated it fourteen miles from Marseilles.[41]

The saint's mystical rapture in the desert wilderness was frequently the culmination of a Magdalen sermon. The Franciscan provincial Luca da Padova (d. 1287) closed one of his sermons by describing how the Magdalen's life of ascetical contemplation fulfilled the laws of *ordo in contrarium*, "order through opposition." Before her conversion she was a base sinner, afterwards she was so precious that angels elevated her to the heavens. Moreover, one was to understand that she was not only elevated intellectually, but also corporeally. Likewise, before her conversion she dressed herself in soft and expensive finery, but afterwards no material clothing touched her at all. Finally, in regard to her alimentary habits, when she was a sinner she was accustomed to sup on delicacies, now she was refreshed by celestial fare, having rejected all carnal nourishment.[42]

The fourteenth-century Pietro de' Natali in his *Catalogus sanctorum* (*Catalogue of Saints*), observed that such deprivation of food signified that Christ wished to satisfy the Magdalen not with earthly banquets but heavenly meals.[43] Preachers and hagiographers linked the divine meals that Jesus had prepared for Mary at Bethany with the angelic sustenance he offered her in the desert. Fasting, as was known in the Middle Ages, often induced mystical experiences and accompanying supernatural states such as levitation. Domenico Cavalca (d. 1342) cited the Magdalen's mystical levitation as an "example of spiritual concentration," one of the many types of prayer he analyzed in his *Frutti della lingua* (*The Fruits of the Tongue*). He remarked that those thus engaged in such concentration are frequently rapt in the ecstasy of the mind and lose sensation; others, "through the force of an enraptured heart also levitate the body above the ground, as did Thomas Aquinas, Saint Anselm and the Magdalen."[44] Margaret of Cortona (d. 1297) also levitated, possibly in a mimetic act of self-identification with the Magdalen's "spiritual concentration." Fra Giuma, her biographer, who did not hesitate to cast Margaret as a second Magdalen, related many stories of Margaret's levitation, including one in which she experienced the ecstasy of mystical marriage. After crowning her with a diadem, and placing a ring on her finger, Jesus directed his angels to bestow on Margaret the same gift of contemplation he had given the Magdalen.[45]

The motif of the Magdalen's desert retreat was not confined to hagiography and sermons. It also found expression in the liturgy. By the fourteenth century, hymns could be found that praised the desert saint. One sung for the office of lauds said:

> Rejoice daughter of the highest king
> who is conveyed outside
> the cave at the seven (canonical) hours.[46]

One of the two *laude* (songs of praise) dedicated by Savonarola (d. 1498) to the Magdalen sang of the contemplative saint in her grotto, suspended in the air by angels. He encouraged his audience to join her at the forbidding mountain with sweet songs and a serene mind:

> Up to that harsh mountain,
> where the Magdalen contemplates,
> Let us go with sweet songs
> and a pure and serene mind.
> She is suspended in the air
> in the sweet Nazarene face.[47]

If writers exulted in imagining the Magdalen's mystical ecstasies in the desert, painters did so all the more. Almost every late medieval Italian fresco cycle of her *vita* included at least one scene representing her anchoritic withdrawal from the world; such consistency is not something that can be said about any other episode in her life, either scriptural or legendary.[48] To take Angevin Naples as just one example, in the three churches that contain late thirteenth- to early fourteenth-century fresco cycles dedicated to the saint, all three include a scene of desert reclusion. That by Pietro Cavallini (d. 1330) in the Dominican church of San Domenico Maggiore may perhaps be the finest example.[49] Many fresco cycles, such as the one at the church of San Domenico in Spoleto, represent her angelic levitation, probably borrowing the iconography from the Assumption of the Virgin Mary.[50] It must be stressed, however, that such iconography was not restricted to the fresco cycles of her *Life*; it is also found in individual "portrait" frescoes, altarpieces, panel and predella paintings, and in manuscript decoration. A devotional book, written in Latin but of German provenance, shows the Magdalen clothed in nothing more than her mane of hair, borne aloft by a fiery-red group of angels.[51]

It is worth pausing for a moment to examine the image of the Magdalen's abundant hair. Her hair and nakedness were not inconsequential in contributing to the success of this motif in both its literary and visual forms. From time immemorial female hair – loose, unbound, and uncovered – was associated with sexuality. It is revealing that in both her pre- and post-conversion lives Mary Magdalen's most predominant physical attribute was her copious and flowing hair. When she was a sexual sinner Mary Magdalen entered the house of the Pharisee, wept at the feet of the Lord, and dried them with her hair. It is significant that at the moment of her conversion it was her hair – the symbol of her sexual sin – that became the emblem of her penitence. Such multivalent symbolism also informed representation of her post-conversion life at La Sainte-Baume, the Provençal hermitage site associated with her. According to legend, after years of reclusion and harsh penitence in the desert, her clothes had fallen away and her hair had grown to cover her nakedness. On one level such representations of the Magdalen's nakedness could be construed as her post-conversion condition of innocence and purity. But, given her prior association with sins of the flesh, medieval depictions of the hair-covered and naked Magdalen did more than evoke images of the innocence of Eden: they also pointed back to the sexual aspect of her nudity, a reminder of her past as a sexual sinner. It should never be forgotten that Mary Magdalen was known in the medieval world as the *Beata peccatrix*, the Holy Sinner, a title that simultaneously evoked both sin and sanctity. Suggestive images of the naked, eremitical, hair-clad Magdalen functioned similarly. Her nakedness was at once innocent and seductive. Her mane of hair served as a veil of modesty, but nonetheless invoked female sexuality. Medieval artists, their patrons, preachers, and moralists were all seduced by the rich paradox contained in such a symbol, which no doubt contributed to making the eremitical Magdalen one of the most enduring images of the Middle Ages.

The hermit-saint also recalled images of John the Baptist. The Magdalen and the Baptist were frequently paired off together in medieval art by virtue of their association with the desert.[52] The medieval archeologist Roberta Gilchrist reminds us further that the Christian notion of "rebirth through baptism and repentance" also linked these two saints in an association of ideas.[53] Perhaps this nexus explains the city of Florence's devotion to the Magdalen, for John the Baptist was (and still is) Florence's patron saint. But the Magdalen was frequently paired with him in Tuscan art. Indeed, in Florence's Cappella della Maddalena in the Palazzo del Podestà the south wall is frescoed with the life of the Magdalen, the north wall with scenes from John the Baptist's life.[54]

Significantly, both saints were also regarded as prophets. The anonymous Cistercian hagiographer called the Magdalen the prophet of Christ's ascension, arguing:

> She witnessed the ascension on the mountain; just as she announced to the apostles the first event as soon as it had taken place . . . she showed she was equal to John the Baptist in being more than a prophet. . . . Her deeds are equal to his, write the four evangelists.[55]

The popularity of the Magdalen's eremitical model of sanctity was assisted in the fourteenth century by the great success of Domenico Cavalca's mid-fourteenth-century *Lives of the Holy Fathers*, a vernacular version of the *Lives of the Desert Fathers* made for the devotional needs of the laity. Written in Italian, it included a Life of Mary Magdalen in the section on the *Vitae matrum*, the lives of the desert mothers.[56] Cavalca's translation of this and other eremitical lives no doubt also aided the popularity in this period of all the other very early desert saints including saints Honophrius, Anthony Abbot, and Jerome.[57]

Whether or not they intended to do so, hagiographers, artists, and preachers were creating a prescriptive literature when they described in detail the Magdalen's eremitical retreat into the wilderness. In this regard the preaching of Bernardino da Siena (d. 1444) is paradigmatic. His recipe for such a life (found in a Magdalen sermon) included these redolent ingredients: the solitude of wild animals, anonymity, nakedness except for the cover of one's own hair, a body so thin that flesh clings to the bones, no human food, heavenly marriage, the ground for one's bed, and an awareness that the whole world has been abandoned and forgotten, all of which induce a wondrous intoxication of the mind.[58] Many a prospective holy person tried to live according to such a program. Margaret of Cortona seems to have intended to imitate the Magdalen's eremitical life but was dissuaded in a vision by Christ himself who told her: "Even though it is not your destiny to live in the desert (because deserts are not adapted to our times), you can live in solitude in your land *as if* you lived in the desert places."[59] Many holy women engaged in "urban eremitism," either living in cells just outside the city walls, or locked away in seclusion in the family palazzo, as did noblewomen Filippa Mareri (d. 1236) in Rieti and Umiliana de' Cerchi (d. 1246) in Florence, both early *beatae* (reclusive women who were often considered living saints) associated with the Franciscan order.

Whether they practiced metaphorical eremitism or actual eremitism, the Magdalen became a patron to anchorites and hermits. The ascetical women at Ankerwyke in Buckinghamshire dedicated their foundation to Mary Magdalen, and on their official seal, the image which represented them in the world, they inscribed a timber-framed and thatched roof hermitage.[60] On the continent women did similarly. In the early twelfth century, in the black forest of Thuringia, a solitary called Pauline built first a wooden, then a stone chapel dedicated to the Magdalen at her retreat in the wilderness. Eadmer of Canterbury reported two recluses living near the oratory of Saint Mary Magdalen in Lyons; one of them, Adelaide, experienced visions and levitated just as her patron saint had done.[61] Solitary reclusion seems to have been favored by women more than men in the Middle Ages. Medievaliast Ann K. Warren has found for England, for example, that among 780 anchorites who lived in the period between 1100 and 1539, women outnumbered men by more than two to one.[62] The numbers for central Italy are even more striking. In Perugia, in the year 1277, the commune first doled out charity to twenty female and two male recluses, and then again a few weeks later to thirty-six female anchoresses and eight male anchorites. In 1290 charitable assistance was received by fifty-six sisters and twelve brothers.[63] These small communities of female recluses frequently put themselves under the patronage of Mary Magdalen. In the Spoleto valley alone, for example, thirteen communities of penitents were founded within the last decade of the thirteenth century. Mary Magdalen was the only saint who was patron for more than one community, being patron for the penitents of Monteluco, founded in 1294, and for those of Santa Maria Maddalena "de Capatis" on Monte Çiçiano, founded in 1300.[64]

In Tuscany, hermitages at Pisa, Cortona, Chiusi, and Lucca took Mary Magdalen as their patron.[65] The one at Lucca was notable for its double dedication to Saints Mary Magdalen and Francis of Assisi. Contemplation was the theme that linked these two patrons. Both saints had experienced mystical ecstasies culminating in angelically assisted unions with Christ. It did not go unnoticed by preachers and painters that Francis received the stigmata at the rocky sanctuary of La Verna high in the Tuscan hills, while celestial care was bestowed on Mary Magdalen on a similar *altissimo monte saxoso* (high and rocky mountain), reckoned by Salimbene to be so high above sea level that three of Bologna's Asinelli towers placed each on top of the other could not reach its height.[66] Accordingly, it was entirely possible that the Franciscan theologian and preacher François de Meyronnes, a native of neighboring Digne, knew firsthand the physical layout of the Magdalen's Provençal grotto at La Sainte Baume. He associates the two grottoes (that of Francis and that of the Magdalen) in the first of his three Magdalen sermons. After discussing the Magdalen's contemplative hideaway, which he refers to as "that mountain," he goes on to consider that Francis prayed on the mountain of *alverna* (the anagram for La Verna). He explains that this is because the saint was known to say that "the spirit of the Lord is found in solitary places."[67] This textual linking of the Magdalen and Francis in their rocky retreats finds an iconographical analogue in a panel painting made in 1307 by Giuliano da Rimini for a confraternity of women in Urbania. The central image is a Madonna and child who are flanked by various saints. The saints filling the bottom register are female saints; on the top from left to right are Saints Francis, John the Baptist, John the Evangelist, and Mary Magdalen (Figure 9.1). Francis, on the far left, is shown at La Verna receiving the stigmata from a seraphim (detail in Figure 9.2), while Mary Magdalen is shown in her cave at La Sainte-Baume communing with an angel (detail in Figure 9.3).[68]

Figure 9.1 Guiliano da Rimini, *Madonna with Child Enthroned with Saints* (1307). Boston, Isabella Stewart Gardner Museum (© Isabella Stewart Gardner Museum).

Figure 9.2 Detail from Figure 9.1.

Figure 9.3 Detail from Figure 9.1.

At Fontecolombo, the hermitage near Rieti where in 1221 Francis retreated to write the rule for the order, there was, even in his time, a small chapel on the mountainside dedicated to Mary Magdalen.[69] Francis himself did not shrink from representing the eremitical life of which he was occasionally able to partake as the life of Mary Magdalen. In his rule for anchorites (c.1223–24) he suggests that those who want to undertake the eremitical life should group themselves into clusters of threes and fours. Two should take the part of mothers who care for at least one son. The two mothers should lead the life of Martha, while the others take up the life of Mary in individual cells where they can devote themselves to meditation and prayer.[70]

Writers of Franciscan devotional literature fancied their founder a second Magdalen. In one late thirteenth- to early fourteenth-century tract, the anonymous author claims that Francis, after having had a vision of the naked Christ on the cross,

> yearned to serve Christ 'til the end, naked following the naked one, far removed from the world and unknown to all people, just like one reads about Mary Magdalen and many other saints; to wit, he offered himself up to death, by preaching of the faith and by witnessing Jesus Christ to the Saracens and the other infidels, and by suffering every harsh torment.[71]

These few sentences provide a wealth of information about the mendicant mind-set. Mary Magdalen is invoked as the example whom Francis followed in following Christ. Following in her footsteps, he became a contemplative recluse, as well as the naked follower of Christ, preaching and suffering for the faith.

NOTES

1 Medieval preachers, following Gregory the Great, were of course assuming that Mary Magdalen and Mary of Bethany were one and the same person; there is further discussion of the Gregorian composite saint in the volume from which this selection came, Katherine Ludwig Jansen, *The Making of the Magdalen: Preaching and Popular Devotion in the Later Middle Ages* (Princeton, NJ: Princeton University Press), ch. 1.

2 Giordano da Pisa, *La vita attiva e contemplativa predica di frate Giordano*, ed. P. Zanotti (Verona: Tipografo Vescovile, 1831), p. 17.

3 The distinction between infused or extraordinary contemplation, and acquired or ordinary contemplation, was first drawn by Denis the Carthusian in the fifteenth century. See Edward Cuthbert Butler, *Western Mysticism: The Teaching of Augustine, Gregory and Bernard on Contemplation and the Contemplative Life* (New York: Harper Torchbooks, 1966, 2nd revised edition), pp. 213–17.

4 Rome, Bibliotheca Angelica (hereafter Angelica) MS 158, f. 122v; *Repertorium der lateinischen Sermones des Mittelalters für die Zeit von 1150–1350*, ed. Johannes B. Schneyer (Münster: Aschendorff, 1969–90) (hereafter *RLS*), vol. 1, p. 126.

5 Vatican City, Bibliotheca Apostolica Vaticana (hereafter BAV), Borghese MS 175, f. 29v; *RLS*, vol. 1, p. 343.

6   BAV Arch. Cap. S. Petri D. MS 213, col. 363; not in *RLS*. Cf. Matteo d'Aquasparta, Assisi MS 682, ff. 194v–195r.

7   Angelica MS 158, f. 122v.

8   Although a popular symbol in sermons and exegetical literature, it is worth mentioning that Mary of Bethany, the contemplative, was not a theme that inspired visual artists or their patrons. One of the few examples, completed about 1370, is found in Giovanni da Milano's Magdalen cycle in the Rinuccini Chapel at Santa Croce, the Franciscan church in Florence. Mary sits with her back toward Martha, attentively absorbed by the master's teachings. For the chapel decoration see Mina Gregori, *Giovanni da Milano in Santa Croce* (Valmorea: Comune di Valmorea, 1980). For other medieval examples of this scene, see Jane Couchman, "Action, and *Passio*: The Iconography of the Scene of Christ at the Home of Mary and Martha," *Studi Medievali*, 3rd series, 26/2 (1985): 711–19. A medieval example that she does not include, however, comes from a Florentine predella of the life of Mary Magdalen now in the Stoclet Collection in Brussels. It has been attributed to both the Master of the Fabriano Altarpiece and Giovanni da Milano. It is reproduced in Richard Offner with Klara Steinweg, *A Critical and Historical Corpus of Florentine Painting* (New York: College of Fine Arts, New York University, 1930–; reprint Florence: Giunti Gruppo Editoriale), III.5 (1947), pl. XLVI (1).

9   Assisi MS 682, f. 193v; *RLS*, vol. 4, p. 78.

10   Magdalene College in Cambridge was originally founded in 1427 as a hospice for Benedictine monks. It was refounded and dedicated to the saint in the 1540s by the Lord Chancellor, Lord Audley. It has been suggested that Audley chose the patron because his own name was contained in the dedication: "M-AUDLY-N," as contemporaries spelled the saint's name. See the concluding note in Christopher N. L. Brooke, "The Dedications of Cambridge Colleges and their Chapels," in *Medieval Cambridge: Essays in the Pre-Reformation University*, ed. Patrick Zutshi (Woodbridge: Boydell Press, 1993), pp. 7–20. Magdalene College, Oxford, was founded by Willam Waynflete, Lord Chancellor of Henry VI in 1458.

11   Padua, Antoniana MS 208, f. 332r; *RLS*, vol. 1, p. 1216. The *explicit* says: "Episcopus Salernitensis," which might indicate that the sermons were complied *c.*1320, when he still was, or at least remembered as, archbishop of Salerno. For Bertrand, see J. Goyens, "Bertrand de la Tour," in *Dictionnaire d'histoire et de géographie ecclésiastique* (1935), p. 1084. On the sin of garrulousness, see Carla Casagrande and Silvana Vecchio, *I peccati della lingua: disciplina ed etica della parola nella cultura medievale* (Rome: Istituto della Enciclopedia Italiana, 1987), pp. 150–5 and 425–40.

12   Some of his sermons were published under the name of Guillaume d'Auvergne. See Guillaume d'Auvergne, *Opera Omnia*, 2 vols (Paris/Orléans: Ludovicus Billaine and F. Hotot, 1674), vol. 2, p. 437. For Guillaume Peyraut, see Philippe Delhaye, "Guillaume Peyraut," *Dictionnaire de spiritualité, ascétique et mystique, doctrine et histoire* (1967), vol. 6, pp. 1229–34.

13   The literature on women's monasticism is quite large; see Bruce L. Venarde, *Women's Monasticism and Medieval Society: Nunneries in France and England, 890–1215* (Ithaca, NY: Cornell University Press, 1997); Penelope Johnson, *Equal in Monastic Profession: Religions Women in Medieval France* (Chicago, IL: University of Chicago Press, 1991); Sally Thompson, *Women Religious: The Founding of English Nunneries after the Norman Conquest* (Oxford: Clarendon Press, 1991); Sharon Elkins, *Holy Women of Twelfth-Century England* (Chapel Hill, NC: University of North Carolina Press, 1988); and Catherine Boyd, *A Cistercian Nunnery in Mediaeval Italy: The Story of Rifreddo in Saluzzo, 1220–1300* (Cambridge, MA: Harvard University Press, 1943).

14   *Twelfth-century England*: Davington (Daunton) (Kent) was a Benedictine priory founded in 1153 by Fulke of Newenham; Kynewaldgraves was founded before 1169; Bristol *c.*1170–3; and Sewardsley (Northamptonshire), a convent of Cistercians, was founded *c.*1173–88 by Richard of Lester. *Thirteenth century*: Wintney (Hampshire)

was a Cistercian house founded *c*.1200 by Richard Holte (de Hereard) along with his wife, Christine, daughter of Thomas Cobreth: Remsted (Kent) was a priory of Benedictine nuns founded *c*.1229–31 by Richard, archbishop of Canterbury; and Whistones (Worcester), a Cistercian convent, was founded by bishop Gautier of Cantilupe and dedicated in 1255. Victor Saxer, *Le culte de Marie Madeleine en Occident des origines à la fin du moyen âge*, 2 vols (Paris: Librairie Clavreuil, 1959), pp. 135–6, 146, 196–7. On the nuns of Whistones, referred to in the royal close rolls in 1241 as both "the white sisters of Worcester" and the "sisters of penance" of Worcester, see Sally Thompson, *Women Religious*, pp. 199–200. Roberta Gilchrist, *Gender and Material Culture: The Archeology of Religious Women* (New York: Routledge, 1994), p. 129, adds the Benedictine convent at Ickleton (Cambridgeshire). Neither this list, nor any that follows, pretends to be an exhaustive listing of foundations made in the name of Mary Magdalen in the Middle Ages. For the sake of comparison, it should be noted that in the period 1151–1216 Alison Binns has found eighteen English monastic church dedications to Mary Magdalen for male houses. Mary Magdalen was the fifth most popular titular saint for English monastic foundations in that period, tied for that honor with Saints James and John the Evangelist. Binns found six Benedictine dedications, four Cluniac, seven Augustinian and one Premonstratensian. The Virgin Mary is the only female to exceed the Magdalen in number of monastic dedications; indeed, she is the most popular titular of all. See Alison Binns, *Dedications of Monastic Houses in England and Wales, 1066–1216* (Woodbridge: Boydell, 1989), pp. 18, 34–8.

15 Thompson, *Women Religious*, pp. 45–6, suggests that Eva's foundation may have originally been a hospital which only later became a convent.

16 *France*: Orléans had a Fontevrist foundation made *c*.1113. Rouen had a Cistercian abbey called Sainte-Marie-Madeleine de Bival, which records two foundation dates: 1128 and 1154. Etrun was founded in 1142. Abbess Marie obtained apostolic protection for the convent. Monteux (Provence) was a convent of Benedictines founded in 1354 by Jean Blanqui of Avignon. *Low Countries*: The priory was founded in Anvers in 1135. *Bohemia*: This abbey of Premonstratensian nuns had a double dedication to Saints Wenceslas and Mary Magdalen. It was founded by Blessed Hroznata *c*.1196–1202 at Chotesov, in the diocese of Prague. *German Empire*: Albert de Kevernbourg founded a convent at Magdebourg, consecrated in 1231. *Latin Kingdom*: A convent of Benedictines was founded in Jerusalem by 1092; in Nicosia (Cyprus) by 1192; a Cistercian convent in Tripoli; and by 1223 a convent in Acre. See *The "Historia Occidentalis" of Jacques de Vitry: A Critical Edition*, ed. John Frederick Hinnebusch (Fribourg: University Press, 1972), Appendix C, p. 268. The other references are from Saxer, *Le culte*, pp. 116–17, 119, 122, 145, 219, 246, with the exception of Orléans which is from Johnson, *Equal in Monastic Profession*, p. 268. Again, it is worth stating that these lists do not pretend to be exhaustive.

17 Lynn Townsend White Jr, *Latin Monasticism in Norman Sicily* (Cambridge, MA: Medieval Academy of America, 1938), pp. 158–9. It was subject to Monreale in 1177; this was confirmed by the pope in 1183.

18 *Roma e Lazio, di Gaeta e l'abbazia nullius di Montecassino*, ed. Filippo Caraffa, *Monasticon Italiae I* (Cesena: Badia di Santa Maria del Monte, 1981), p. 174, n. 227: this monastery bore a double dedication to Saint Mary Magdalen and Saint Chelidonia (d. 1162).

19 The Benedictine abbey of Urbania (Marche) was founded in 1200; the Benedictine convent of Verona (Veneto) was founded in 1211; the penitents of Alessandria (Piedmont) received a papal privilege in 1247; a convent at Recanati (Marche), near Ancona, was founded before 1249; the Benedictine convent of San Severo, near Foggia (Apulia), was founded before 1258; the Benedictine convent at Castellaneta, near Taranto (Apulia), was founded by the testamentary bequest of one Magister Nicolas in 1283; Pope Nicolas IV gave an indulgence to the convent of Saint Mary

Magdalen on the island of Marta, in Bolsena (Lazio) in 1290. They claimed that Count Gherado of Burgundy brought relics of their patron to the island in the year 75(!); a Cistercian convent was founded in Chieti (Abruzzo) before 1309 while Florence (Tuscany) had its Cistercian convent of nuns at Cestello in Borgo Pinti by 1325; and, finally, Perugia (Umbria) founded a Benedictine convent in the fourteenth century. For Urbania, Verona, Alessandria, Recanati, and Chieti, see Saxer, *Le culte*, pp. 215–17, 262. For San Severo and Castellaneta, see *Puglia e Basilicata*, eds Giovanni Lundardi, Hubert Houben, and Giovanni Spinelli, *Monasticon Italiae III* (Cesena: Badia di Santa Maria del Monte, 1986), p. 48, n. 91 and p. 97, n. 281. For Marta, see *Roma e Lazio*, p. 148, n. 130. For Florence, see Alison Luchs, *Cestello: A Cistercian Church of the Florentine Renaissance* (New York: Garland, 1977). For Perugia, see Giovanna Casagrande, *Religiosità penitenziale e città al tempo dei comuni* (Rome: Istituto Storico dei Cappuccini, 1995), p. 233.

20   Don Leandro Novelli dell'abbazia de Cesena, "Due documenti inediti relativi alle monache benedettine dette 'Santucce,'" *Benedictina* 22 (1975): 237–42. The convents were: Perugia (1262), Cagli (1270), Cortona (1270), Urbino (1270), Borgo Sansepolcro (1271), and Massa di Cerbone (by 1305). For an introduction to Santuccia's reforming enterprise, see Katherine Gill, "*Scandala*: Controversies Concerning *Clausura* and Women's Religious Communities in Late Medieval Italy," in *Christendom and Its Discontents: Exclusion, Persecution and Rebellion, 1000–1500*, eds Scott Waugh and Peter D. Diehl (Cambridge: Cambridge University Press, 1996), pp. 177–203. For *Borgo Sansepolcro* (Tuscany), see James R. Banker, *Death in the Community: Memorialization and Confraternities in an Italian Commune in the Late Middle Ages* (Athens, GA: University of Georgia Press, 1998), pp. 30–1, 151. By 1271 the Santucce had moved to new quarters and another group of nuns occupied the old monastery of Santa Maria Maddalena.

21   The foundations were at Cascia (today Santa Rita), Gualdo Cattaneo ("de Mercatali"), Montefalco, Monte Martano, Norcia, Paterno, Rupino, Spello, two at Spoleto ("de Capati" and "de Colleluce"), and Trevi. See Silvestro Nessi, "Le religiosae mulieres," in *Il processo di canonizzazione di Chiara da Montefalco*, ed. Enrico Menestò (Florence: La Nuova Italia Editrice, 1984), pp. 546–55.

22   *Augustinian foundations*: For the foundations in Orvieto (Umbria) and Siena (Tuscany) in 1339, see David Gutiérrez, *The Augustinians in the Middle Ages, 1256–1356* (Villanova, PA: Augustinian Historical Institute, 1984), pp. 203, 207. (Siena had earlier founded Santa Marta [1328], also an Augustinian convent, ibid.) *Franciscan affiliations*: For Atri (Abruzzo) in 1324, see *Aprutium-Molisium. Le decime dei secoli XIII–XIV*, ed. Pietro Sella (Vatican City, 1936), items 3129 and 3368. They were evidently an order of Poor Clares who had at one point been under interdiction and excommunication. For Città di Castello (Umbria), see Casagrande, *Religiosità*, p. 296, who lists it with a question mark as a convent of Poor Clares. *Dominicans*: For Forlì (Emilia-Romagna) in 1303, see Jacques Quétif and Jacques Échard, *Scriptores Ordinis Praedicatorum recensiti*, 3 vols (Paris: J.-B.-C. Ballard & N. Simant, 1719–1934), vol. 1, p. vii, who list this as a house of Dominican nuns. *Unknown Affiliations*: For Perugia, a third Mary Magdalen dedication (thirteenth century), see Casagrande, *Religiosità*, p. 233, and for Borgo Sansepolcro see Banker, *Death*, p. 155, who mentions a "monastery of the sisters of Santa Maria Maddalena in Borghetto." The *decime*, of course, list many Mary Magdalen foundations; it is for the most part impossible to distinguish between male and female houses.

23   ASF, *Diplomatico normale, San Gimignano, agostiniane, pergamene 20 Feb. 1334*: the monastery flourished until 1570. See Diana Norman, "The Case of the *Beata* Simona: Iconography, Hagiography and Misogyny in Three Paintings by Taddeo di Bartolo," *Art History* 18 (1995): 154–84. She identifies Monna di Rufo di Petroio as Beata Simona. Unlike many female communities which suffered financial hardship, this one seems to have prospered. In 1456, Benozzo Gozzoli painted an altarpiece of an

enthroned Madonna and child, flanked by Mary Magdalen and Martha for them. It is now in the Museo Civico and illustrated in Raimond Van Marle, *The Development of the Italian Schools of Painting*, 28 vols (The Hague: Martinus Nijhoff, 1924–36), vol. 11 (1929), pp. 183–4, fig. 118.

24 *Exempla sacrae scripturae ordinata secundum alphabetum* (n.p., 1473), unpaginated. It was once attributed to Bonaventura and published under his name. For Nicolas, see André Duval, "Nicolas de Hanappes," *Dictionnaire de spiritualité ascétique et mystique, doctrine et histoire* 11 (1982), 283–4.

25 BAV Barb. lat. MS 513, f. 98r; *RLS*, vol. 3, p. 377.

26 Humbert of Romans, *De eruditione praedicatorum* in *Maxima bibliotheca*, p. 506.

27 François de Meyronnes, *Sermones de laudibus sanctorum* (Venice: Pelegrininus de Pasqualibus, 1493), p. 79.

28 It should be noted that some such as Cavalca say that she retired to the desert to do penance. Others such as Jacobus de Voragine say that it was for the sake of contemplation. Still others say it was for both reasons. Intense asceticism and mystical ecstasy are of course frequently intertwined, as was well known in the Middle Ages.

29 Honorius Agustodunensis, *PL*, vol. 172, 981.

30 *The Life of Saint Mary of Magdalene and of her sister Saint Martha: Medieval Biography*, ed. David Mycoff (Kalamazoo, MI: Cistercian Publications, 1989), p. 98.

31 *Life*, ed. Mycoff, p. 98.

32 Angelica MS 158, f. 122v.

33 *Early Dominicans: Selected Writings*, ed. Simon Tugwell (New York: Paulist Press, 1982), p. 409.

34 John Coakley, "Friars as Confidants of Holy Women in Medieval Dominican Hagiography," in *Images of Sainthood in Medieval Europe*, eds Renate Blumenfeld-Kosinski and Timea Szell (Ithaca, NY: Cornell University Press, 1991), pp. 222–46; Coakley, "Gender and the Authority of the Friars: The Significance of Holy Women for Thirteenth-Century Franciscans and Dominicans," *Church History* 60 (1991): 445–60; and Coakley, "Friars, Sanctity, and Gender: Mendicant Encounters with Saints, 1250–1325," in *Medieval Masculinities: Regarding Men in the Middle Ages*, ed. Clare A. Lees (Minneapolis, MN: University of Minnesota Press, 1994), pp. 91–110.

35 Caroline Walker Bynum, *Holy Feast and Holy Fast: The Religious Significance of Food to Medieval Women* (Berkeley, CA: University of California Press, 1987).

36 For the elaboration of medieval gender theory from sexual difference, see Joan Cadden, *Meanings of Sex Difference in the Middle Ages: Medicine, Science, and Culture* (Cambridge: Cambridge University Press, 1993).

37 For this theme in fourteenth century Umbrian and Tuscan hagiography, see Catherine M. Mooney, *Women's Visions, Men's Words: The Portrayal of Holy Women and Men in Fourteenth-Century Italian Hagiography* (PhD diss., Yale University, 1991).

38 Padua Antoniana MS 490, f. 100v; not listed in *RLS*.

39 Salimbene de Adam, *Cronica*, ed. Giuseppe Scalia, 2 vols (Scrittori d'Italia series, vols 232–3) (Bari: Giuseppe Laterza & Figli, 1966), vol. 1, p. 962. *The Chronicle of Salimbene de Adam*, trans. Joseph L. Baird, Giuseppe Baglivi, and John Robert Kane (Medieval & Renaissance Texts & Studies, vol. 40) (Binghamton, NY: Medieval & Renaissance Texts & Studies, 1986).

40 Victor Saxer, "Maria Maddalena," *Bibliotheca Sanctorum* 8 (1967): 1092.

41 Bertrand de la Tour, Sermo 217, in *Sermones Bertrandi de tempore de sanctis. Una cum quadragesimali epistolari* (Strasbourg: Georg Husner, [c.1500]), unpaginated. The Dominican hagiographer Jean de Mailly reckoned it as "approximately fourteen miles from Marseilles," Rome, BAV Vat. lat. MS 1198, ff. 69v–70v. Salimbene estimates the site being fifteen miles from Marseilles, *Cronica*, vol. 1, p. 962.

42 Padua, Antoniana MS 466, f. 270v; *RLS*, vol. 4, p. 95.

43 *Catalogus sanctorum*, 257–8.

44   *Racconti esemplari di predicatori del Due e Trecento*, eds Giorgio Varanini and Guido Baldassarri, 3 vols (Rome: Salerno, 1993), vol. 3, p. 141.

45   Cited in Susan Haskins, *Mary Magdalen: Myth and Metaphor* (London: HarperCollins, 1993), p. 187.

46   This was one of three hymns found appended to Bernardino's sermon, *Feria Quinta*, in *S. Bernardini Senensis Opera Omnia*, 9 vols (Quaracchi: Collegium S. Bonaventurae, 1950–65), vol. 3 (1956), p. 441, n. 64. It was used popularly as well; it was published as a chapbook called *Sette gaudi di Santa Maria Maddalena* (n.p., n.d.). One of these is preserved in the Capponi collection in Rome, BAV Capponi V. 686. int. 64. Other hymns using this motif are listed in Joseph Szövérffy, "'Peccatrix quondam femina:' A Survey of the Mary Magdalen Hymns," *Traditio* 19 (1963): 79–146, here 103, 141.

47   These are stanzas 1, 2, and 9 of the *lauda* which can be found in Patrick Macey, "*Infiamma il mio cor*: Savonarolan *Laude* by and for Dominican Nuns in Tuscany, " in *The Crannied Wall: Women, Religion and the Arts*, ed. Craig A. Monson (Ann Arbor, MI: University of Michigan Press, 1992), pp. 161–89; Jansen has modified his translation.

48   Of the thirteen later medieval fresco cycles (fourteenth–fifteenth centuries) representing the life of Mary Magdalen only two do not make reference to this episode of anchoritic withdrawal in her life. The first is the Magdalen chapel at Sant'Antonio di Ranverso. Since most of this damaged cycle is lost, presumably it too contained a scene referring to her eremitic reclusion. Only Giovanni da Milano's Rinuccini chapel in Santa Croce in Florence does not witness this event. (For the chapel, see n. 8 above.) Out of five scenes, four are gospel scenes and only one is a legendary scene: the Marseilles miracle. Perhaps since he had already included the contemplative scene at Bethany (a rarity), the artist did not feel obliged to make reference to the legendary contemplative as well. Among other scenes, six of them depict her preaching apostolate. (That number may have been larger as some of the frescoes at S. Lorenzo Maggiore (Naples) and S. Maria Maddalena Bergamo have been lost.) The cycles that depict this scene are: (1) Cappella Pipino (early fourteenth century), S. Pietro a Maiella, Naples; (2) S. Maria Maddalena (*c.*1370), Bolzano; (3) Cappella della Maddalena (1392–5), S. Antonio di Ranverso, Buttigliera Alta (prov. Turin); (4) Cappella della Maddalena (*c.*1400), S. Domenico, Spoleto; (5) S. Maria Maddalena (1470–97), Cusiano (Trentino); and (6) S. Maria (1495), Pontresina (Engadine). The other cycles are: Cappella della Maddalena (*c.*1295–1300), S. Lorenzo Maggiore, Naples; Cappella Brancaccio (1308–9), S. Domenico Maggiore, Naples; Cappella della Maddalena (*c.*1312), Basilica of S. Francesco, Assisi; Cappella del Podestà (*c.*1322), Bargello, Florence; Cappella Rinuccini (1360–70), S. Croce, Florence; S. Maria Maddalena (mid-thirteenth century), Bergamo; and Oratorio di S. Maria Maddalen (early fifteenth century), S. Maria del Belverde, Cetona (Siena). For Magdalenian iconography in Italy, see George Kaftal, *Iconography of the Saints*, 4 vols (Florence: Sansoni, 1965–86).

49   All three churches – San Lorenzo Maggiore, San Domenico Maggiore, and San Pietro a Maiella – were directly or indirectly patronized or connected to the Angevins, a subject further discussed in chapter 11 of Jansen, *The Making of the Magdalen*. For the decoration of the three chapels, see Ferdinando Bologna, *I pittori alla corte angioina di Napoli 1266–1414* (Rome: Ugo Bozzi, 1969), pp. 94–7, 115–46, 311–20.

50   For further examples of this motif, see *La Maddalena fra sacro e profano*, ed. Marilena Mosca (Milan: Mondadori, 1986), pp. 31–64, 218–27.

51   One can see this in a fourteenth-century miniature in a devotional book dedicated to Mary Magdalen. It contains a version of her legend, miracles, five sermons, antiphons, and hymns. The manuscript was copied in Germany by Bertholdus Heyder. It is now in the British Library, MS Add. 15682, f. 105r. The scene is also found in the Magdalen Master panel, the *Leggendario Ungherese*, BAV MS Vat. lat.

8541, f. 103v, and Botticelli's predella for his *Trinity*, discussed in chapter 6 of Jansen, *The Making of the Magdalen*.

52   An early fourteenth-century Florentine triptych epitomizes this relationship. The central panel is an enthroned Madonna surrounded by saints. The left wing is divided into two registers: the upper portion is occupied by John the Baptist in the desert; the lower part by the hirsute Magdalen, captured in an act of contemplative prayer. Offner and Steinweg, *Corpus* III.7 (1967), p. 216.

53   Roberta Gilchrist, *Contemplation and Action: The Other Monasticism* (London: Leicester University Press, 1995), p. 216.

54   See Giovanni Poggi, *Il Duomo di Firenze* (Berlin: Bruno Cassirer, 1909), pp. 99–100, fig. 71, for a trecento polyptych illustrating Florence's patron saints. The hermits Mary Magdalen and John the Baptist are among them. For the Magdalen chapel in the Palazzo del Podestà, see Janis Elliott, "The Judgement of the Commune: The Frescoes of the Magdalen Chapel in Florence," *Zeitschrift für Kunstgeschichte* 61 (1998): 509–19, who notes that there are two scenes of the life of John the Baptist in the Magdalen chapel. Tuscany did not have a monopoly on the visual pairing of the two saints, however. Among numerous examples see the fourteenth-century hair-clad saints in the baptistery in Parma, for example. For a color reproduction, see *Battistero di Parma*, texts by Georges Duby, G. Romano, C. Frugoni, and Jacques Le Goff, 2 vols (Milan: Franco Maria Ricci, 1992–3), vol. 2, p. 160. For a discussion of the possible political implications of this pairing, see Elliott, "Judgement," pp. 509–19 where she points out that Charles, Duke of Calabria, Robert's son, resided in the Palazzo during his *signoria* of Florence and that the terms of the seigneurial contract gave the Angevins control over most of the important communal offices of the city.

55   Prophetess; see *Life*, ed. Mycoff, pp. 84–5, 96. Among others who associated Mary Magdalen with prophecy are: Hrabanus Maurus, *PL*, vol. 111, 84; Peter Abelard, *PL*, vol. 178, 485; Iohannes de Biblia, BAV MS Borgh. 24. f. 63v; and Humbert of Romans, *De eruditione praedicatorum*, Lib. II, 483–4. The themes of prophecy and penance continued to inspire visual representations of both of these saints. Donatello's wooden sculpture of the Magdalen made for the baptistery in Florence, to say nothing of his similar figure of John the Baptist made for the Frari in Venice, were influenced by this eremitical model of sanctity, which was being preached by Antonino Pierozzi in Florence at precisely the time when the sculptor undertook these commissions in the mid-fifteenth century. There is no documentation regarding the commission of the Magdalen. John Pope-Hennessy, *Donatello: Sculptor* (New York: Abbeville, 1993), pp. 276–7, gives the Magdalen a date of 1454, the year when Donatello returned from Padua. Sarah Wilk, "The Cult of Mary Magdalen in Fifteenth-century Florence and Its Iconography," *Studi Medievali*, 3rd series, 26 (1985), ii: 685–98, proposes Antonino's preaching as inspiration for Donatello's Mary Magdalen. The John the Baptist was made in 1438 for the Frari in Venice. The church is Franciscan; the commission was made by the Florentine *scuola* (confraternity), explaining the presence of the only work by Donatello in Venice. Rona Goffen, *Piety and Patronage in Renaissance Venice: Bellini, Titian and the Franciscans* (New Haven, CT: Yale University Press, 1986), p. 26. Another Baptist, made for the Duomo in Siena and dated about 1457, also bears a striking resemblance to the Magdalen. It is illustrated in Pope-Hennessy, *Donatello*, figs 287 and 288. For other examples of wooden penitents from the same period and provenance, see Marilena Mosco, *La Maddalena tra sacro e profano* (Firenze: A. Mondadori, 1986), pp. 48–52.

56   For an introduction to and a reading of the lives of some of the desert saints, see Alison Goddard Elliott, *Roads to Paradise: Reading the Lives of the Early Saints* (Hanover, NH: University Press of New England, 1987). For the diffusion of this eremitical model of sanctity in medieval Italy, see Carlo Delcorno, "Le *Vitae patrum* nella letteratura religiosa medievale (secc. XIII–XV)," *Lettere Italiane* 2 (1991):

187–207, and the conference proceedings in the volume entitled, *Eremitismo nel francescanesimo medievale (Atti del XVII convegno della Società Internazionale di Studi Francescani, Assisi, 12–14 ottobre 1989) (Perugia: Università degli Studi di Perugia, Centro di Studi Francescani, 1991)*, particularly the essays by Giovannna Casagrande, "Forme di vita religiosa femminile solitaria in Italia centrale," pp. 51–94; Edith Pásztor, "Ideali dell'eremitismo femminile in Europa tra i secoli XII–XV," pp. 129–64; and Daniel Russo, "L'iconographie de l'érémitisme en Italie à la fin du Moyen Age (XIIIe–XVe siècles)," pp. 187–207. See also Anna Benvenuti Papi, "Donne religiose nella Firenze del Due-Trecento," *"In castro poenitentiae": santità e società femminile nell'Italia medievale* (Rome: Herder, 1990), pp. 593–634.

57 For the eremitical Jerome, see Eugene Rice, *Saint Jerome in the Renaissance* (Baltimore, MD: Johns Hopkins University Press, 1985). Chiara Frugoni has argued that Cavalca's translation of the *Vitae patrum* made at the Dominican house of Santa Caterina in Pisa was the source for Buffalmacco's visual representation of the *Vitae patrum* at the Camposanto in the same city. See her "Altri luoghi, cercando, il paradiso (Il ciclo di Buffalmacco nel Camposanto di Pisa e la committenza domenicana)," *Annali della Scuola Normale Superiore di Pisa* (Classe di Lettere e Filosofia), ser. III, vol. XVIII/4 (1988): 1557–1643. The late fourteenth-century frescoes depicting the lives of the hermits by Leonardo da Besozzo and Perrinetto da Benevento at the Augustinian church of San Giovanni a Carbonara in Naples are also probably indebted to the wide diffusion of Cavalca's translation of the *Vitae patrum*. See also Ellen Callman, "Thebaid Studies," *Antichità Viva* 14 (1975): 3–22.

58 "Feria quinta post dominicam de passione, De Sanctissima Magdalena (Sermo 46)," *S. Bernardini Senensis Opera Omnia*, 9 vols (Quaracchi: Collegium S. Bonaventurae, 1950–65), vol. 3 (1956), p. 436. In the same sermon Bernardino mentions the Magdalen's levitation, p. 434.

59 *AASS*, February, vol. 3, par. 46, 312. [Emphasis is Jansen's.]

60 Gilchrist, *Contemplation*, p. 155.

61 Saxer, *Le culte*, pp. 110 and 120. He also mentions two male hermits of the same period: Adjuteur of Tiron and Girard of Vienne, pp. 113 and 126.

62 Ann K. Warren, *Anchorites and their Patrons in Medieval England* (Berkeley, CA: University of California Press, 1985), pp. 18–20.

63 Mario Sensi, "Anchoresses and Penitents in Thirteenth- and Fourteenth-century Umbria," in *Women and Religion in Medieval and Renaissance Italy*, ed. Daniel Bornstein and Roberto Rusconi, trans. Margery J. Schneider (Chicago, IL: University of Chicago Press, 1996), pp. 57, 64. For the year 1290 he is citing the work of Giovanna Casagrande, "Forme di vita," p. 76.

64 Sensi, "Anchoresses," p. 78. Saint Catherine of Alexandria also receives two, but one of them is a double dedication under the title "Santa Caterina and Santa Croce de Colle Floris." It should by noted that two of the foundations listed by Sensi (Montefalco and de Capati) are listed by Nessi "Le religiosae mulieres," as convents. For *Monteluco* (1300), a hermitage of female recluses near Spoleto, see also Giovanna Casagrande, "Movimenti religiosi umbri e Chiara da Montefalco," in *Chiara da Montefalco e il suo tempo*, ed. Claudio Leonardi and Enrico Menestò (Firenze: Nuova Italia, 1985), p. 61.

65 *Pisa*: Casagrande, *Religiosità*, 44. *Le decime degli anni 1274–1280, Tuscia I*, ed. Pietro Guido (Vatican City, 1942) and *Le decime degli annia 1295–1304, Tuscia II*, ed. Martino Giusti and Pietro Guido (Vatican City, 1942). The Tuscan *decime* are the only ones that list hermitages separately from churches or monasteries. It is likely that there were others throughout Italy, but just not listed as such. The exact dedications of the *hermitoria* are as follows: *Cortona: Heremus/Ecclesia*, vol. 2, item 2846 (1302–3); *Chiusi: Heremus Sanctae Mariae Magdalenae Montis Carcianesi*, vol. 1, items 2768 (1275–6) and 2814 (1276–7); *Lucca: S. Maria Magdalena de Chifenti* Titolare: S. Maria Maddalena e S. Francesco, vol. 1, item 5073 (1260); *Hermitorium de Iunceto* Titolare:

S. Maria Magdalena, vol. 1, item 5133 (1260); and *Hermitorium S. Maria Magdalena Vallisbone de Versilia*, vol. 1, item 3835 (1275–6) and 4429, and vol. 2, item 3854.

66   Salimbene, *Cronica*, vol. 2, pp. 762–3. In his day, the Magdalen's cave had already become a noted pilgrimage site.

67   François de Meyronnes, *Sermones de laudibus sanctorum et tractatuum*, 1494), p. 79.

68   The painting is in the Isabella Stewart Gardner Museum (Boston). See Philip Hendy, *The Isabella Stewart Gardner Museum: Catalogue of the Exhibited Paintings and Drawings* (Boston, MA: Trustees of the Museum, 1931), pp. 175–8. See also the predella of the Rinuccini altarpiece by Giovanni del Biondo (1379) in which an enthroned Madonna and child are flanked by Saint Francis, John the Baptist, John the Evangelist, and Mary Magdalen. The predella painting of Francis is of the stigmatization at La Verna, the Magdalen's corresponding image is of her angelic levitation in a grotto outside Marseilles. For a color plate, see *Il complesso monumentale di Santa Croce*, eds Umberto Beldini and Bruno Nardini (Florence: Nardini Editore, 1983), p. 252.

69   Later fourteenth-century frescoes in the Magdalen chapel at Fontecolombo include one of the hair-clad Magdalen attended by angels.

70   *De religiosa habitione in eremo* in *Opuscula S. Francisci et scripta S. Clarae Assisiensium*, eds Giovanni M. Boccali, O.F.M. and Luciano Canonici, O.F.M. (Assisi: Porziuncola, 1978), p. 160. Boccali's note 3 to this text explicitly states that half of the manuscripts say *Mariae Magdalenae* instead of simply *Mariae*.

71   *Vita del povero et humile servo de Dio Francesco*, ed. Marino Bigaroni (Assisi: Porziuncola, 1985), p. 6.

10

HEARING IS BELIEVING
Clarissan architecture, c.1213–1340

Caroline A. Bruzelius

Female followers of Francis of Assisi (d. 1226) and his female friend and disciple Clare (d. 1253) began to found communities of Clarissan nuns from early in the thirteenth century. Unlike the men's houses of the order, those of women by 1219 were strictly enclosed, with outsiders excluded and its nuns rarely, if ever, leaving the monastic complex. Such enclosure was of course unthinkable for the mendicant brothers, whose mission lay precisely in their involvement with the lay community and in living as the poorest of the poor, begging for sustenance. Indeed, it had been generally honored in the breach for most monastic men and women up through the twelfth century. But the challenge presented by the new mendicant orders led to the imposition of new strictures, especially for women religious, which separated them from the clerics, lay-brothers, and secular business agents who served the practical needs of the community. The new regulations, imposed with particular force first upon the female branch of the Franciscan Order and later on all women religious, had a direct impact upon the administration of the sacraments, which were offered through a series of architectural divisions and barriers. Older buildings were modified to include turnstiles, grilles, screens, curtains, and chambered gates into which provisions were placed so that there was no visual contact between the lay-brothers or clergy and the female community. The strict enclosure of women also had specific consequences for religious women's visual relationship to the Mass, for here too screens, walls, and barriers were imposed between the monastic community and the altar. These consequences were not recognized before the 1992 publication of this selection.

Caroline Bruzelius broke new ground by recognizing that because of a need for strict gender separation, church and conventual space designed for mendicant women needed a different architectural configuration from that designed for men. Because the churches of the mendicant nuns also usually served parochial needs, it was not possible to simply separate nuns in the nave from the priest at the altar with a fence or grille, and provide a door to the outside for the priest and one to the inside for the nuns (as is seen in some monastic churches not used by the public). Because of the need to separate the women religious from both the public and the clergy, the standard architectural layout of churches and convents designed for men was often radically reconfigured for the community of women; in one case (Anagni) a choir for the nuns was created over the aisle vaults by raising the roof over this space to the level of the nave roof – the nuns could participate in the Mass only through the thin slight windows that had once provided light to the interior of the church. The arrangements for nuns' choirs developed in these structures suggest that the religious experience was to take place through the faculty of hearing rather than of seeing.

Turning to churches built for these women in Naples, Bruzelius establishes that there was an architectural shift in how women's monastic space was shaped there and elsewhere. That such a shift occurred is without question, but Bruzelius's originality lies in her description of the implications of such shifts in architectural space for mendicant women's spirituality. In buildings for Clarissan communities, such as that at Donnaregina in Naples, begun after 1297 by the Queen of Naples, Mary of Hungary, the space was designed so that the experience of the Mass was auditory rather than visual. Then Santa Chiara (originally dedicated to Corpus Domini) was built by Queen Mary's daughter-in-law, Queen Sancia of Naples (1286–1345), wife of Robert the Wise. Here the placement of the nuns' choir directly behind the altar was in order to permit a direct vision of the elevation of the host through the grilled separation between choir and church. Bruzelius argues that this shift represents an important rethinking of the spatial relationships in the mendicant churches for nuns, that this change represents the importance of Eucharistic devotion in the late Middle Ages, and in particular, Queen Sancia's own devotion to the consecrated Host. This chapter was originally published in a special volume, Monastic Women's Architecture, *of* Gesta *31 (1992): 83–91.*

*   *   *

The second verse of the hymn "Adoro te devote" by the Dominican theologian Thomas Aquinas (d. 1274), was written for the institution of the feast of Corpus Christi in 1264; it suggests that the other senses are poor in comparison to the primacy of the Word, and asserts that we approach God through Christ, as the "word" of God incarnate, as well as through hearing the reading of Scripture:

> Sight, touch and taste are not trustworthy ways to know God,
> But one can trust in hearing alone as secure
> I believe what the son of God said
> (namely that) nothing is truer than this Word of Truth.[1]

The emphasis on the importance of the "word" in this hymn may reflect a new character to the spirituality of monastic life. It also, however, illuminates some aspects of the developments in the architecture of women religious, for in the thirteenth century architecture of the Clares it was above all the sense of hearing that was privileged over the other senses through which the spiritual experience of the Mass could be apprehended.

The study of women's monastic architecture has until recently been an almost entirely neglected field.[2] Like the metaphor of death and burial so often used in the Middle Ages to describe the monastic vocation, the subject of women's monastic architecture has also been dead and buried. Rarely has the scholarship on monastic architecture included convents, and more rarely still has it considered the distinctions between male and female use of liturgical space.[3] Indeed, how often do historians of medieval architecture concern themselves with the ways in which church space was used, and how architecture not only responded to but also helped shape religious practice?[4] This is an especially important issue for convent architecture, for the strict enclosure of women imposed certain requirements in the arrangement of buildings and barriers in convents that were different from those of monasteries.[5] Strict enclosure presented additional complexities when the convent churches were open to the lay public, as was the case in the Clarissan order ("Poor Clares").[6] The presence of a lay population meant that the church had to be divided to contain two populations for the same liturgy; two populations, however, who were forbidden to see each other. But to be "dead to the world" meant further to become invisible, entombed, and withdrawn not only from the public, but also from the clergy, and therefore also from some of the sacraments.

This chapter begins with an examination of the implications of religious enclosure in Clarissan churches at the two Clarissan convents of Assisi, San Damiano and Santa Chiara, and it will trace the development of the order's church architecture to two convent churches in Naples, Santa Maria Donnaregina and Santa Chiara.[7] Through an analysis of the location of the nuns' choirs in the first three convents, I shall propose that enclosure shaped women's liturgical experiences. However, in the last of the four monuments, Santa Chiara in Naples, new ideas about liturgical participation for women were introduced, dramatically transforming earlier patterns of spatial divisions. The change reflected a distinct shift in medieval piety, especially that of women, toward veneration of the Eucharist, which brought with it an emphasis on the importance of vision of the altar and the Host placed upon it.[8] For as we shall see, the architectural evidence at San Damiano, Santa Chiara in Assisi, and Donnaregina in Naples, as well as at a number of other thirteenth-century convent churches of the order, indicates that in the thirteenth century the actions of the clergy during the administration of the sacred Eucharist were usually not visible to Clarissan nuns. What has been described as the sacred drama or theater of the Mass remained invisible to the female population for whom the convent had been founded.

Given the frequent destruction and Baroque remodelings of so many monastic churches, the reasonably good state of preservation of both San Damiano and Santa Chiara at Assisi seems especially fortunate. As the home of Clare and her first companions, San Damiano represents, albeit with numerous modifications, Francis' vision of how Clare and the "Poor Ladies" who gathered around her should live.[9] This humble complex underwent a number of changes and additions prior to Clare's death in 1253, most of which can probably be interpreted as refinements of the original spatial concepts.[10]

On the other hand, at Santa Chiara in Assisi, the *protomonastero* of the order to which the sisters from San Damiano moved not long after Clare's death, the church was intended from the outset as the mother house of the order as well as the site of the veneration of Clare's remains.[11] As is amply evident from its plan and structure, it was conceived as a pendant to the basilica of San Francesco on the other side of the city.

Whereas Francis' mission at its origin had entailed a life of social action, and was essentially transient (and hence, almost by definition, anti-architectural), it was evident from the first moments of Clare's escape to the Portiuncola (where Francis and his followers lived) that this life could not be available to her. Indeed, although she had been tutored and encouraged in her vocation by Francis, it might be suspected that Clare's actual arrival presented awkward and embarrassing difficulties which held within them the potential for compromising not only her virtue, but also that of Francis and his companions. Since the need for protection and enclosure required well-defined architectural spaces, Clare was immediately placed in the nearby Benedictine convent of San Paolo. She then moved to the convent of beguine-like recluses or penitents at Sant'Angelo in Panso, from which she was transferred to the modified complex at San Damiano. There she remained until her death in 1253. Because San Damiano also administered to a small lay congregation, a certain number of friars were also affiliated with the house. It was thus a double monastery, a pattern that recurred often in the order, but was especially well developed at the great Neapolitan convent of Santa Chiara.[12]

The succession of moves for Clare and her small retinue prior to their arrival at San Damiano suggest that the old church required modifications to accommodate a female population. These appear to have first consisted of the heightening of the walls to include a dormitory directly above the church, work which was probably done by Francis to prepare the complex for the sisters (Figure 10.1).[13] Romanini suggests that the apse and the upper chapel were added somewhat later.[14] According to this author, a third campaign consisted of the addition of the choir, known as the *coro di Santa Chiara*, which is situated on ground level at right angles to the apse (Figure 10.2).[15] This choir still contains its thirteenth-century stalls and may have extended further north than presently, so as to entirely encompass the exterior wall of the apse. It is accessible through the small doorway to the right of the altar.

Although Romanini's chronology remains tentative, the successive additions and modifications to San Damiano seem to reflect both the growth of the community and the evolution of Clarissan religious practice during the early decades of the order. Since Francis had restored the church to parish use prior to the arrival of the Clarissan community, from the outset the sisters would have needed a separate enclosed area as a choir. If the church was indeed shorter, as has been proposed by Romanini, the window in the vault on the right side of the nave that opens into one of the ancillary rooms may have permitted that room to serve this function. The first choir may thus have been located in the easternmost of these small chambers on the right side of the nave (Figure 10.2).[16] If Romanini is correct about the sequence of the additions, the enlargement of the church to the east with the addition of the present apse would then have meant that the original nuns' choir would have been too distant from the altar. The expansion of the church to the east would thus have necessitated the addition of the *coro di Santa Chiara*, the small room to the right of the altar at right angles to the axis of the nave. To facilitate hearing the service, a small opening was made in the back of the apse wall. However, this aperture did not permit vision of the Mass from the thirteenth-century stalls that are still preserved in the far end of the *coro*. The opening in the grille could have been used for the passage of the consecrated Host to the sisters.[17]

The possible succession of ancillary rooms as choirs at San Damiano reflects the arrangements found in churches to which the cells of recluses were attached. These often took the form of small rooms open to a church through a grated window.[18] Since Clare had been housed at the beguinage of Sant'Angelo in Panso, and her mission was conceived by Francis as one of meditation, the model of the anchoress and anchoritic practice may well have been a source for the arrangements at San Damiano.

It has often been noted that both Clare and Francis had a special veneration for the Eucharist, and Clare is often represented with a monstrance in

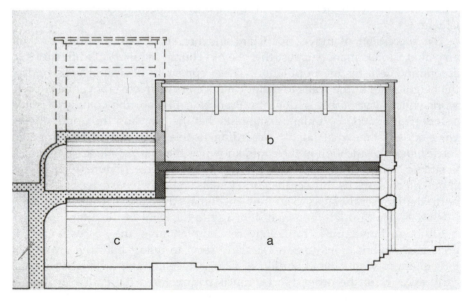

Figure 10.1 San Damiano, Assisi, longitudinal section: space a and dark hatching is original structure restored by Francis; space b and lighter hatching is dormitory added above church; space c with dotted walls is new apse on lower story, oratory above (Bruzelius after Romanini, "Il francescanesimo nell'arte").

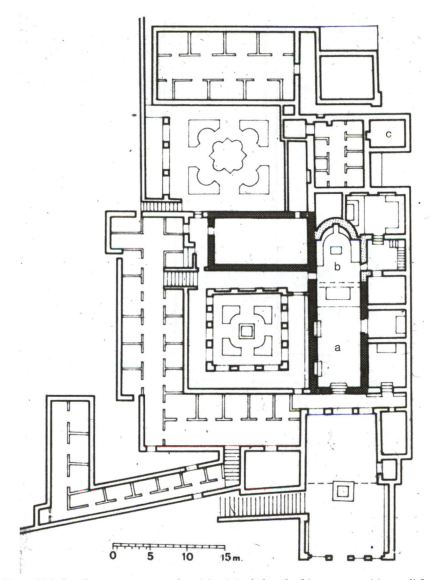

Figure 10.2 San Damiano, Assisi, plan: (a) original church; (b) new apse; (c) *coro di Santa Chiara* (Bruzelius).

her hand.[19] At San Damiano a reserved Host would have been kept in a niche in the little oratory next to the sister's dormitory on the second floor, directly above the church (Figure 10.3). This use is attested by the still-preserved wall painting representing Clare and the sisters kneeling in adoration below the niche in the oratory, which seems to have been that used for the night offices and private devotions of the sisters.

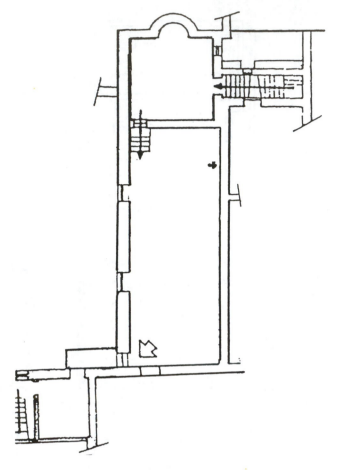

Figure 10.3 San Damiano, Assisi, plan of the dormitory and oratory (Bruzelius).

The sequence of additions at San Damiano indicate that the arrangements evolved over time to reflect the gradually shaped religious practices of the community. In the *protomonastero* of Santa Chiara in Assisi, erected from the outset for the Clarisses, however, equally frequent changes and modifications in the location of the nuns' choir suggest that there were still uncertainties as to the best place for it. One has the impression that the demands of the public cult of Clare, and the need to evoke in architectural form the basilica of San Francesco, took precedence over the spatial provisions for the nuns. The number of additions to the church of Santa Chiara indicate that a choir attached to the church was added only as an afterthought to the original design.

The site had originally been occupied by the hospital and chapel of San Giorgio, where Francis' body had been buried before the erection of the great basilica of San Francesco, and where Clare also was first interred.[20] The new church of Santa Chiara (Figure 10.4), begun at the site in 1257 and consecrated in 1263, seems to have been designed from the outset with no apparent provision for the sisters, who may at first have used the old chapel of San Giorgio, venerated for its role as a burial place for the two patron saints of the order.[21] Yet within a few decades of the completion of the church, the chapels of the Holy Sacrament and the Crucifix that flank the nave on the south side of the church were added to create a choir for the sisters. The addition of the new choir may suggest that the sisters wanted to be in closer proximity to the tomb of their foundress, but it may also reflect the need for more space than the old chapel of San Giorgio could provide, or that the latter was in ill repair. Into the new choir was brought the old cross from San Damiano, which had been so fundamental in the conversion of Francis, and

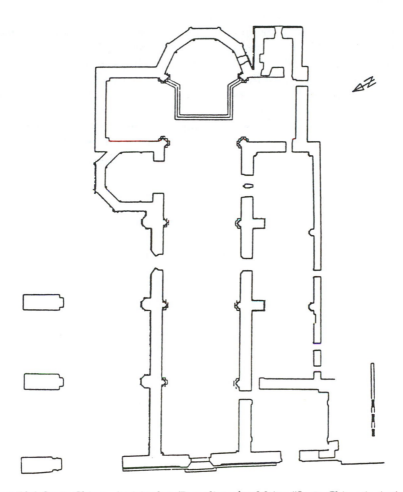

Figure 10.4 Santa Chiara, Assisi, plan (Bruzelius after Meier, "Santa Chiara in Assisi").

which can still be seen between the first and second bays of the chapel. Pressure from the public to see the cross precipitated further changes, which in time led to the opening of these lateral chapels to the public. The erection of a small gallery at the western end of these chapels (presumably as an enclosed space for private prayer in front of the crucifix) permitted the sisters to view it from an enclosed space.[22] The present nuns' choir is in a modern chapel added to the south of the easternmost bay of the chapels.[23]

The pressures of the public cult of Clare created a special situation at Santa Chiara, the implications of which were apparently not fully anticipated when the church was designed. To modern eyes there is a certain irony in the thought of a monumental convent church, decorated with important panel paintings and an impressive altar screen, yet inaccessible to the community itself.[24] Even though the dates and sequence of the construction of the successive choirs remain uncertain, one point is clear: none of the various choirs provided a direct line of vision to the altar.

Elsewhere in the order, the location and arrangement of choirs depended on the site. Since older churches were frequently remodeled for the use of the Clarisses, the disposition of the pre-existing buildings was a major determinant.[25] By the second half of the thirteenth century it was common to erect a tribune, or *matronium*, at the western end of the church, as can be seen at Santa Chiara in Anagni.[26] If the community had settled in a pre-existing monastery or convent, however, the choir was sometimes positioned in an upper room of the conventual buildings that adjoined the church, with a small hole cut through the wall so that the service could be heard within. This arrangement can be found at San Sebastiano near Alatri.[27] In none of these arrangements have I found evidence that the nuns could gaze upon the altar and the Mass.

The use of a tribune finds elegant and refined expression in the church of Santa Maria Donnaregina in Naples, rebuilt after the earthquake of 1297 with the patronage of Queen Mary of Hungary.[28] Donnaregina consists of a polygonal apse with tall and slender traceried windows (Figures 10.5 and 10.6). The western part of the nave is two-storied: the lower serves the lay population, while the upper tribune was reserved for the nuns (Figure 10.7). The prestige of royal patronage must have given this convent special allure, and rapidly made it a popular monastic retreat among the female aristocracy of Naples, for even during construction the tribune was enlarged toward the apse (Figures 10.7 and 10.8), as two of the nave windows are cropped by the extended gallery.

Yet even in a church as up-to-date as Donnaregina, there is no direct line of vision to the altar from the stalls in the nuns' choir. Not until one reaches the balustrade at the far end of the tribune does the altar become visible. The nuns in their stalls would have contemplated the frescoes by Cavallini and his school (or one another) during the services, not the liturgy being performed at the altar below. In this context, as no doubt in many other convents, wall painting therefore takes on special significance, and should be

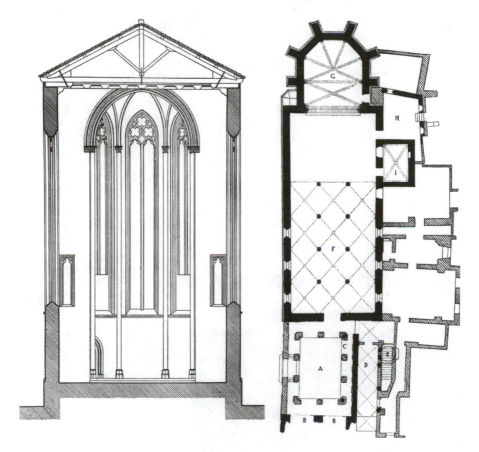

Figure 10.5 Santa Maria Donnaregina, Naples, elevation of apse (Bruzelius after Venditti, *Storia di Napoli*).

Figure 10.6 Santa Maria Donnaregina, Naples, plan (Bruzelius after Venditti, *Storia di Napoli*).

considered as providing a visual pattern for prayer and meditation that may have taken place as an accompaniment to hearing the service.[29]

Galleries as a type adhere to ancient patterns of separating women and men in church interiors and antedate Christian practice. In the great convents of the Ottonian period, such as Gernrode and Essen, the choirs were located in a variety of upper tribunes either at the entrance to the nave or above the aisles. If any evolution can be detected in the architecture of the Clarisses in the thirteenth century, it seems to consist largely of the replacement of lateral rooms at ground level based on an anchoritic model by the more traditional modes of separation in the form of tribunes between the conventual and lay population.

Almost contemporary with the reconstruction of Donnaregina, Mary of Hungary's daughter-in-law, Sancia of Mallorca, founded a second new

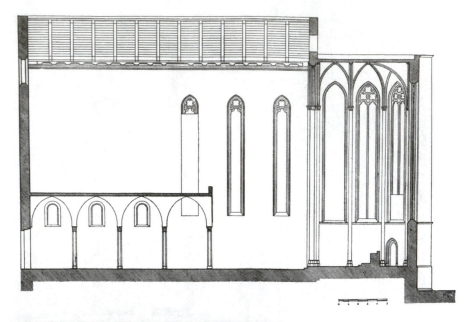

Figure 10.7
Santa Maria Donnaregina,
Naples, longitudinal section
(Bruzelius after Venditti, *Storia
di Napoli*).

Figure 10.8
Santa Maria Donnaregina,
Naples, view of the interior
from the west
(photo: Massimo Velo).

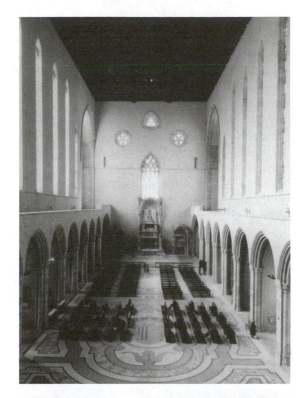

Figure 10.9
Santa Chiara, Naples, interior
(photo: Massimo Velo).

Figure 10.10
Santa Chiara, Naples, nuns'
choir (photo: Massimo Velo).

Clarissan church in Naples: the convent of Santa Chiara (Figure 10.9). This new foundation, first known as *Corpus Domini*, presents an important rethinking of the location of the choir, and, as the original name of the convent attests, is directly related to Eucharistic veneration. Established in 1310 by Sancia and Robert the Wise, the church was essentially complete by 1328, although some work continued until c.1340.[30] Santa Chiara was by far the largest Clarissan church ever erected, and was intended as the setting for state ceremony.[31] Sancia and Robert also invested Santa Chiara with an ambitious spiritual agenda, for this convent even before its construction was complete became a center for the Spiritual Franciscans protected by the royal pair in Naples.[32] Many of the schismatic brothers were housed in the friars' cloister on the right side of the church. Numerous papal letters in the 1320s and 1330s instructed Sancia and Robert to remove those "errant Franciscans who still wear short habits without precise form or color" from the cloister at Santa Chiara.[33]

For our purposes in this chapter what is significant is neither the grandiose vision of the building nor its role in the heated struggle over apostolic poverty, but the rethinking of the location of the choir for the enclosed sisters. The nuns' choir is located directly behind the altar in a retro-choir to the east, with three large grated openings that have broadly flanged edges on the nuns' side (Figures 10.10–10.12).[34] These are specifically designed to permit the sisters to view the altar and the elevation of the Host during the Mass

Figure 10.11 Santa Chiara, Naples, nuns' choir, openings toward the altar (photo: Massimo Velo).

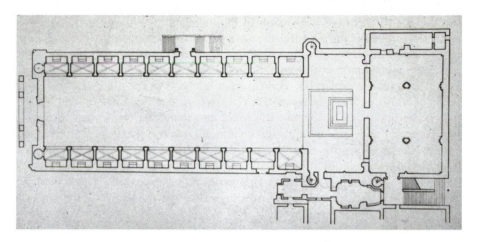

Figure 10.12 Santa Chiara, Naples, plan (photo: Soprintendenza dei Beni Culturali e Monumentali, Naples).

(Figures 10.10 and 10.11). (In order to discourage voyeurism, eight-inch spikes protrude from the grilles that separate the church from the nuns' choir toward the nave.)

Although perhaps loosely based on the location of the choir or *coro di Santa Chiara* at San Damiano, the arrangement at Santa Chiara in Naples results in a dramatic change in the organization of the church interior because of the positioning of the sisters directly facing the congregation beyond the wall. For the first time that I know of, the church plan is bifurcated: two populations face – but must not *see* – each other (Figure 10.12). The Eucharist on the altar becomes the central pivot of the plan, the hinge between the nuns' choir and the nave to the west. The officiating priest, in facing the altar and turning his back to the nave during the elevation of the Host, would have faced the nuns' choir, thus presenting the sisters with a privileged viewing of the Host at the moment of its elevation.

Why should this important rethinking of space have happened at Santa Chiara in Naples? From her many hectoring letters to the pope and the Franciscan order we know that Queen Sancia of Naples (1286–1345), who originally intended to enter the convent at the demise of her husband, had a particular devotion to the Eucharist.[35] In one of her letters, she claims inspiration directly from the Host reserved on the altar of the palace chapel.[36] The feast of *Corpus Domini*, first established after the miracle of Bolsena in 1264, was repromulgated in 1312, hardly more than a year after the beginning of work on Santa Chiara.[37] The dedication of this church to *Corpus Domini* is one of the earliest such dedications, and attests to the currency of Sancia's religious predilections.[38] As a devoted "true daughter" of Francis, Sancia not only adopted this aspect of their piety, but had a hand in reconceptualizing the character of church space to reflect the vital importance of this new dimension in medieval faith. We might nonetheless speculate whether such an important change in architectural design might have taken place if the patroness had not had such prestige and prominence.

But if Santa Chiara, or *Corpus Domini*, in Naples provided the first example I can document of a plan based on women's vision of the altar and the Host, what of those earlier Clarissan churches where such vision was excluded? Given the numerous studies of the Mass as sacred rite and drama, and the gestures of the Mass as a ritual enactment of the Passion,[39] should we conclude that enclosure entailed spiritual deprivation for women religious? For the thirteenth century, however, it is important to recall that Christianity has always contained a tradition that especially blessed are those who can believe *without* seeing, touching, or tasting. This was the lesson of the episode of Doubting Thomas, reaffirmed in the hymn to the Holy Eucharist attributed to Aquinas.[40] Until the feast of *Corpus Domini* was firmly established, and given expression in architectural form, for women in religious life, that which was most holy often came only through the ear.[41] With the explosion of Eucharistic veneration in the fourteenth century, any inability to see the elevation of the Host during the Mass might have come to have been perceived as a deprivation, which could be overcome by a reconfiguration of architectural space.

NOTES

1. The stanza begins, "Visus, Tactus, gustus in te fallitur." (And see note 40.) I owe a special debt to the sisters of the Clarissan order who discussed this project with me, in particular Chiara Anastasia in Assisi. I also thank Hank Milton, Shreve Simpson, and Therese O'Malley, in whose comforts at the Center for Advanced Study in the Visual Arts in Washington, DC, these ideas about seclusion and denial were first germinated. Bill Franklin, George Williams, Catherine Gill, Anne Prache, Lucy Freeman Sandler, Willibald Sauerländer, Jane Tibbets Schulenberg, and Grover Zinn have all also helped me greatly with their thoughts, suggestions, and reflections.

2. For example, the words of Peter the Venerable:

   The world being dead to them, they were dead to the world, and becoming unseen by all, after their vocation they laid over their eyes and faces a thick veil like a shroud. . . . Enclosed in this cloister of salvation, or rather buried alive in this sepulchre, they waited to change a temporary prison for the freedom of eternity, and to change this burial for resurrection.

   Quoted by Jane Tibbets Schulenberg, "Strict Active Enclosure and its Effects on the Female Monastic Experience (500–1000)," in *Distant Echoes*, eds John Nichols and Lillian Thomas Shank (Kalamazoo, MI: Cistercian Publications, 1984), pp. 87–114. See also the words of Innocent IV in his letter to the Clarisses of Pamplona with regard to enclosure: "When living in the reclusion of Christ you are dead to the world, that is in the monastery where you are as if buried alive." Quoted by Gérard Huyghe, *La clôture des moniales des origines à la fin du XIIIème siècle* (Roubaix: J. Verschave-Hourquin, 1944), p. 92.

3. See for an example of a volume that includes convents, but makes no distinctions between the use of space, Joan Evans, *The Romanesque Architecture of the Order of*

Cluny (Cambridge: Cambridge University Press, 1938). It should be noted that there is currently (1992) a competition on studies of Clarissan convents being organized by the Centro di Studi per la spiritualità, la storia a l'architettura Francescana in Fara Sabina that may result in a major publication of new plans, elevations, and sections of Clarissan convents.

4   One of the few exceptions is the series of articles published in the volume *Luoghi sacri a spazi della santità*, eds Sofia Boesch Gajano and Lucetta Scarafa (Turin: Rosenberg & Sellier, 1990), especially the article by Gabriella Zarri, "Recinti Sacri. Sito e forma dei monasteri femminili a Bologna tra '500 e '600," pp. 381–96.

5   The best study to date is that of Schulenberg, "Strict Active Enclosure." See also the important survey of monuments in Liliana Grassi, "Iconologia delle chiese monastiche femminili dall'alto medioevo ai secoli XVI–XVII," *Arte Lombarda* 9 (1964): 131–48. Although the treatment of the medieval convents in the second article is preliminary, and does not address the differences in liturgical practice and degrees of enclosure in different orders, the study presents an important summary of known plans, especially in Lombardy and the north.

6   The Clarissan order is particularly important for the study of enclosure, for, although far from being the first women's order to observe strict enclosure, the Clarissan constitution was the first to be authorized by the Holy See. The history of Clarissan legislation is long and complex, but a good summary can be found in Huyghe, *La clôture des moniales*, pp. 91–5. Already in the sixth century Caesarius of Arles had prohibited the entrance of nuns into the churches of their convents, which were open to the public. See Schulenberg, "Strict Active Enclosure," p. 54.

7   The basic source for medieval enclosure is Huyghe, *La clôture des moniales*, esp. 91–5 on Franciscan legislation concerning enclosure. The research for this project is part of two larger studies, one on the convent of Santa Chiara in Naples, the other on the Angevin churches of the kingdom of Sicily.

8   There are many studies on Eucharistic veneration, but for the relation of this phenomenon to women, see especially Caroline Walker Bynum, *Holy Feast and Holy Fast: The Religious Significance of Food to Medieval Women* (Berkeley, CA: University of California Press, 1987).

9   The major sources on San Damiano are L. Brocaloni, *Storia di S. Damiano in Assisi* (Assisi, 1919); Marino Bigaroni, "San Damiano, Assisi: The First Church of Saint Francis," *Franciscan Studies* 47 (1987): 45–97; and Angiola Maria Romanini, "Il francescanesimo nell'arte: l'architettura delle origini," *Francesco il Francescanesimo e la cultura della nuova Europea*, ed. Ignazio Baldelli and Angiola Maria Romanini (Rome: Instituto della Enciclopedia Italiana, 1986), pp. 181–95. As Romanini notes, our understanding of the various phases of construction cannot be resolved until excavations are undertaken and the walls are freed from plaster and other incrustations. Until that time, all conclusions must remain tentative.

10   Romanini, "Il francescanesimo," esp. pp. 191–2. Her chronology is generally convincing, though the simplicity of the structure and the covering of many surfaces with paint and/or plaster precludes precise conclusions. San Damiano exemplifies Francis' preference for restoring old churches rather than building new ones. It anticipates a pattern commonly found in Clarissan foundations, where older buildings were modified for the use of the sisters. A succinct summary can be found in John R. H. Moorman, *A History of the Franciscan Order from its Origins to the Year 1517* (Oxford: Clarendon Press, 1968), pp. 32–9.

11   The most recent thorough study of the basilica is that of Hans-Rudolf Meier, "Santa Chiara in Assisi. Architektur und Funktion im Schatten von San Francesco," *Arte Medievale* 4 (1990): 151–78.

12   San Damiano has undergone numerous changes since the removal of the sisters in the 1260s, and the original disposition of space must remain somewhat conjectural.

It seems highly unlikely that there was an extensive crypt, however, as suggested by Bigaroni, "San Damiano," pp. 45–97.

13   See Romanini, "Il francescanesimo," pp. 191–2. The heightening of the walls to include a dormitory is amply evident in the exterior masonry of the facade. The unusual arrangement of placing the sisters directly above the church can be explained by the sloping character of the site as well as the need to keep building expenses to a minimum. It is characteristic of the somewhat original, ad hoc solutions that tend to be found in Clarissan convents, since so many adopted older buildings or monastic complexes.

14   Romanini, "Il francescanesimo."

15   Romanini, "Il francescanesimo."

16   Romanini, "Il francescanesimo," states that these lateral rooms on ground level antedate the dormitory above.

17   Clarissans received communion only seven times a year. See Lázaro Iriarte, *La Regola di Santa Chiara: lettera e spirito* (Milan: Biblioteca francescana provincciale, 1976), p. 87.

18   On anchorites and recluses see Louis Gougaud, *Ermites et reclus: Études sur d'anciennes formes de vie religieuse* (Vienne, France: Abbaye Saint-Martin de Ligugé, 1928).

19   One of the most famous, and in the context of her seclusion, certainly one of the most dramatic events from Clare's life at San Damiano, was her chasing away marauding Saracens from San Damiano by holding aloft a reserved Host. See Thomas of Celano, *Vita di S. Chiara Vergine d'Assisi*, trans. Fausta Casolini (Assisi: Edizioni Porziuncula, 1976), pp. 55–6. See the collection of representations of Clare in Pablo Bisogni, "Per un census delle rappresentazioni di Santa Chiara nella pittura in Emilia, Romagna e Veneto sino alla fine dal Quattrocento," in *Movimento religiosa femminile a francescanesimo nel secolo XIII*, Atti dal VII Convengo Internazionale: Società internazionale di studi francescani (Assisi, 1980). See also B. Cornet, "Le *De reverentia Corporis Domini* exhortation et lettre de S. François," *Études franciscaines* 6 (1955): 65–91, 167–80; 7 (1956): 20–35, 155–71; 8 (1957): 33–58.

20   See Marino Bigaroni, *La chiesa di S. Giorgio in Assisi ed il primo ampliamento della cinta medioevale* (Assisi, 1990).

21   See Bigaroni, *La chiesa di S. Giorgio*, p. 34.

22   This chronology is based on my discussion with Suor Chiara Anastasia at Assisi, and I extend to her my deepest thanks.

23   I have not been able to determine the date of this addition. It is separated from the altar in the easternmost bay of the lateral chapels by a grille.

24   Yet this arrangement is reminiscent of the prescriptions of Caesarius of Arles. See Schulenberg, "Strict Active Enclosure," p. 54.

25   The adoption and adaptation of older churches also explains the dedications of the churches, which are those of the earlier institution.

26   See Filippo Caraffa, "Il monastero di S. Chiara in Anagni dall' origini alla fine dell'ottocento;" *Documenti e studi storici anagnini* 8 (1985): 39–59.

27   The convent, presently private property, appears to be unpublished, but goes back to an early medieval Basilian monastery.

28   The most complete study of Santa Maria Donnaregina is that of Ersilia Carelli and Stella Casiello, *Santa Maria Donnaregina in Napoli* (Naples: Editoriale scientifica, 1975). As a completely new structure, which is rare in the order, the church is an important example in Italy of a planned Clarissan space, and combines French tracery and structure with certain spatial concepts perhaps most prevalent in Clarissan churches in Eastern Europe.

29   This is suggested by the repetition of certain narrative elements in the subsidiary scenes behind the main event in each pictorial panel. A number of scholars have studied the paintings at Donnaregina, including Maria Prokopp at the University of Budapest and Stefan Woholijan at Harvard. There may be a parallel with

meditative texts designed for women, such as that attributed to Saint Bonaventure. See *Meditations on the Life of Christ: An Illustrated Manuscript of the Fourteenth Century*, eds Isa Ragusa and Rosalie B. Green (Princeton, NJ: Princeton University Press, 1961).

30　The most reliable studies on Santa Chiara are those by Benedetto Spila da Subiaco, *Un monumento di Sancia in Napoli* (Naples: Società anonima, 1901); Émile Bertaux, "Santa Chiara de Naples," *Mélanges d'archéologie et d'histoire*, 18 (1898): 165–98; Tomaso Gallino, *Il complesso monumentale de Santa Chiara in Napoli* (Naples: Pontificio istituto superiore di scienze e lettere s. Chiara dei fratri minori, 1963); A. de Rinaldis, *Santa Chiara, il Convento delle Clarisse, il Convento dei Minori, la Chiesa* (Naples: s.n., 1920); Don Ferrante, "Santa Chiara," *Napoli nobilissima* 11 (1902): 28–31; and Gaudenzio dell'Aja, *Il restauro della Basilica di Santa Chiara in Napoli* (Naples: Giannini, 1980).

31　The church is 82 m long, 28.3 m wide, and is 45.7 m in height. The measurements are from Spila da Subiaco, *Un monumento di Sancia*, p. 92, n. 1.

32　See the documents assembled by Spila da Subiaco, *Un monumento di Sancia*, pp. 194–277.

33　Lydia von Auw, *Angela Clareno et les Spirituels Italiens* (Rome: Di storia e Letteratura, 1979), p. 191. For an excellent overview of the spiritual question, see Duncan Nimmo, *Reform and Division in the Medieval Franciscan Order from Saint Francis to the Foundation of the Capuchins* (Rome: Capuchin Historical Institute, 1987); on habits, see pp. 13, 100.

34　Under Carlo Borromea this type of arrangement becomes codified and formalized. See Grassi, "Iconologia," *passim*.

35　See the essay on Sancia and her letters to the Franciscan order, some of which are included in translation, by Ronald G. Musto, "Queen Sancia of Naples (1286–1345) and the Spiritual Franciscans," *Women of the Medieval World, Essays in Honor of John H. Mundy*, ed. Julius Kirschner and Suzanne F. Wemple (Oxford: Blackwell, 1985), pp. 179–214.

36　Musto, "Queen Sancia," pp. 213–14.

37　See Gallino, *Il Complesso*, pp. 18–19; see also Bynum, *Holy Feast and Holy Fast*, p. 55. Bynum's work stands in the forefront on research on women and Eucharistic veneration, but it should be noted that the architectural implications of the phenomenon have never been explored.

38　By the later fourteenth century dedications to *Corpus Domini* become quite common, especially for women's houses; [see also discussion in Miri Rubin, *Corpus Christi: The Eucharist in Late Medieval Culture* (Cambridge: Cambridge University Press, 1991)].

39　For example, O. B. Hardison, "The Mass as Sacred Drama," in his *Christian Rite and Christian Drama in the Middle Ages: Essays in the Origin and Early History of Modern Drama* (Baltimore, MD: Johns Hopkins University Press, 1965), esp. pp. 37–48.

40　The authorship of the hymns on the Eucharist is in doubt; see François Baix and C. Lambot, *La Dévotion à l'eucharistie et le VIIe centenaire de la Fête-Dieu* (Gembloux: Duculot, 1964), pp. 89–91; and Frederic James Edward Raby, *A History of Christian Latin Poetry from the Beginnings to the Close of the Middle Ages* (Oxford: Clarendon, 1953), pp. 402–14.

41　Therefore the "frenzy to see the elevation of the host," described vividly by a number of authors, should perhaps be adjusted to reflect the character of the populations for whom that kind of vision was in fact possible. Given the arrangements of choir screens and other barriers in churches, one might inquire as to whether the "drama" of the Mass was not apparently intended primarily for the clergy.

"MEN'S DUTY TO PROVIDE FOR WOMEN'S NEEDS"

Abelard, Heloise, and their negotiation
of the *cura monialium*

Fiona J. Griffiths

The cura monialium, *literally "the care of nuns," is a term used to describe the
essential religious services required by female monastic communities. Every
community of nuns had to celebrate Mass, hear confession, and grant penances on
a regular basis. However, since religious women could not be ordained, they were
forced to rely on male priests to provide them with these services. Thus the* cura
animarum, *or "the care of souls," which priests provided for all Christians was
transformed for these religious women into the* cura monialium – *specifically "the
care of nuns' souls." During the twelfth century, as concern for the separation of
men and women within the religious life reached a high point, men's provision of the*
cura monialium *became a subject for delicate negotiation between nuns and their
priests. The letters of Abelard and Heloise reflect many of the issues facing male and
female monastic communities at this time: the degree to which contact between men
and women was permissible, the possible spiritual equality of the sexes, and the ideal
role played by priests in the governance of female communities.*

*In the early Middle Ages most religious women had been aristocratic, their social
status was more important than their gender, and their ability to hire priests and to
direct the male servants and lay-brothers attached to their communities was not questioned. That such issues needed negotiation between men and women like Abelard
and Heloise arises in part because women in religious communities of the twelfth
century and later were not always from the highest social strata and their qualifications for leading religious communities were those of intellect, education, religiosity,
and experience in the world before their entrance into the community (widows, for
instance, could become nuns and might bring years of worldly managerial experience to the cloister). Such qualifications, unlike aristocratic status, could only in more
subtle ways be asserted as equal to or superior to those of priestly men.*

*In this chapter Fiona Griffiths considers the negotiations between Peter Abelard,
one of the famous teachers of the early twelfth century (discussed earlier on*

pages 13–14), and his student, lover, wife, and friend, Heloise, about what the cura monialium *should encompass beyond the priestly duties that women could not provide to each other. While the scholarly discourse to date has treated Abelard as ambivalent about the care of religious women, Griffiths returns to an early sermon by him on "men's duty to provide for women's needs" to show his early focus on religious women's needs. By assessing ideas circulating at the time Griffiths challenges the assumption of most historians of medieval monasticism that the* cura monialium *was a burdensome duty for religious men and shows that for Abelard (and others) such activities were seen as a means toward their own redemption. This article appeared in* The Journal of Medieval History 30 (2004), 1–24.

* * *

Introduction

Several years after the end of their famously tragic affair, Peter Abelard (d. 1142), once a celebrated philosopher and teacher in Paris, now a humbled monk, sat down to compose a letter to Heloise (d. 1164), the woman who had been first his student, and then his lover and unwilling wife, but who was now his sister in Christ.[1] This was not the first time that Abelard had written to Heloise. Since the discovery of their affair, when Abelard as Heloise's tutor had lived in her uncle's house in Paris, their secret marriage, and the attack against him that had precipitated his adoption of the monastic life, Abelard had written several letters to Heloise.[2] However, the letter that he was about to write had little to do with their affair, its discovery, or the violence that followed it. Instead, Abelard was preparing to respond to Heloise's third letter – in which she had asked him to compose both a history of the order of nuns and a monastic rule especially for women.[3] Interest in the letters of Heloise and Abelard has tended to drop off at this point, since it is here that their personal drama, and its appeal to modern readers, is seen to have been eclipsed by lengthy discussion of the religious life.[4] However, Abelard's later letters mark the culmination – emotional as well as intellectual and spiritual – of his relationship with Heloise: their shared involvement in the project of monastic foundation and reform.[5] Together, Heloise and Abelard established a monastic community for women at the Paraclete, ensured its financial and legal viability, and produced a body of regulatory and liturgical texts to guide the women in their spiritual lives.[6] These texts reveal an ongoing dialogue concerning the roles and reciprocal obligations of men and women within the religious life, topics that were increasingly problematic for contemporary reform communities. This dialogue, and the negotiation of spiritual authority and responsibility that it represents, provides an invaluable witness to the *cura monialium* during the twelfth century and suggests that the *cura* was at once more complicated and perhaps also less contentious than has hitherto been assumed.

The *cura monialium* and "decline" for women

In his survey of medieval ecclesiastical history, Richard Southern spared few words in describing the impulses that animated reform in the eleventh and twelfth centuries, commenting tersely that "as society became better organized and ecclesiastically more right-minded, the necessity for male dominance began to assert itself."[7] Although scholars have challenged Southern's relegation of women to the historical periphery, treated within a section entitled "fringe orders and anti-orders,"[8] his idea that the twelfth century solidified the equation between orthodoxy and the assertion of male authority is one that has been widely adopted. Historians evaluating the impact of reform on women have largely followed Southern in assuming that the restructuring of the church and the extension of its influence were accompanied by increasingly rigid gender strictures, with the conclusion that the reform movement was inimical to women.[9] The leitmotif for religious women within orders during the twelfth and thirteenth centuries is as succinct as it is familiar: decline.[10]

The assumption of decline for women within the monastic life during the twelfth and thirteenth centuries is linked to their presumed intellectual and social decline: women's exclusion from the emerging universities is seen to signal their isolation from later medieval intellectual developments, while the consolidation of royal power increasingly promoted a society in which women's previously informal systems of influence are thought to have been no longer practicable.[11] Within the religious sphere, decline is predicated on the papal campaign against nicolaitism and its effect on attitudes not only toward marriage and sexuality, but ultimately also toward women. Concern to ensure clerical celibacy is generally thought to have resulted in an almost frenzied obsession with sexual purity, which could only be guaranteed through the strict separation of the sexes.[12] The most tangible manifestation of reform "right-mindedness," the drive to separate the sexes and assert male control within the religious life, is the increasing concern that accompanied contact between nuns and their priests within the context of pastoral care, the *cura monialium*.[13] Since religious women were reliant on men as priests to administer the sacraments, celebrate the divine office, and hear their confessions throughout the medieval period, such contact was as inevitable as it was troubling.

The historiography of the *cura monialium* has been marked by a number of shared assumptions: most scholars agree that it was a source of anxiety for men, who preferred to avoid the potential pollution of contact with women, and for whom it offered little tangible benefit, while for women it is seen as both a financial drain, since women's communities were required to provide their priests with remuneration, and the source of their perpetual spiritual dependence on men. The idea that religious men opposed the care of women has remained largely undisputed: the declarations of the Cistercian General Chapter and the gradual distancing of the Premonstratensians from their female members are taken as proof enough that the *cura* was an unwanted encumbrance.[14] Instead, debates have centered on such issues as the extent to which male orders accommodated women, the intensity of women's attraction to male-centered reform movements, and the ultimate impact of legislation mandating the abandonment of the *cura*.[15] Despite their importance to the histories of individual male orders, these debates do little to challenge the overarching model of male opposition to the *cura* and attendant theories of decline for women during the reform period. Moreover, since they have focused almost exclusively on the negative response of male orders to what Jo Ann McNamara has called the "clergyman's burden," such debates rarely address women's reaction to their supposed abandonment, with the result that female passivity is simply assumed.[16] Most important, these debates neglect both men's attraction to religious women and the theological and spiritual underpinnings of their attraction, thereby obscuring the many productive relations that developed between monastic and mendicant men and the women for whom they provided care.[17]

The relationship between Abelard and Heloise was unique among practitioners of the *cura monialium*; their marriage, its disastrous consequences, and the conditions under which they adopted the religious life mark them apart from the majority of contemporary monastics, as do their learning and the wealth of written material that their discussion of the religious life produced.[18] However, it is precisely this – their written record of the *cura*, what it was, and what it ought to be – that renders Abelard and Heloise so important to scholarly discussions of the *cura*. Writing in the 1130s, they provide a lively transcript of the negotiation of the *cura* at a time of acute ambivalence concerning the engagement of men and women within the religious life.[19] Their letters and other writings reveal that the *cura* was a subject of real concern both for women, who sought to secure an appropriate and willing priest, and for ordained monks, who faced widespread public, as well as personal, uneasiness regarding their service to women. However, at the same time, they demonstrate that the *cura* could be less a source of tension for men than it was a spiritual opportunity, since, as Abelard argued, they could store up treasure in heaven through their service to women on earth, while for women it was an occasion not only for dependence, but also for dialogue. That dialogue occurs, most obviously, as Heloise engages Abelard in a discussion of the care provided at the Paraclete; less evident, but no less noteworthy, is the way in which both Abelard and Heloise participate in a larger dialogue concerning women's roles within reform monasticism. For Abelard, engagement in this larger dialogue was, at least initially, largely defensive. His *Historia calamitatum*, the letter of consolation to a friend that he wrote sometime around 1132, includes a public account of his early involvement with religious women and of his attempts to negotiate, and also to satisfy, public opinion. It also provides a witness to Abelard's personal reflection on his role at the Paraclete, recording both his early ambivalence concerning the care of women and his gradual recognition of the purpose that could be served in his own life through his service to women, a subject to which he would return in his *Rule* and later writings for the Paraclete. Taken together, Abelard and Heloise challenge the traditional interpretation of the *cura* as a burden that was resented by men and that formed a source of tension between the sexes.

Private and public negotiations of the *cura monialium* in the *Historia calamitatum*

Abelard's involvement in the *cura monialium* began in 1129 when Heloise and the nuns of Argenteuil were ejected from their monastery by Abbot Suger of St Denis (d. 1155).[20] Although this crisis provoked a split in the community, with some of the nuns joining the house of Malnouë in Brie, those who remained under Heloise's authority were not homeless for long. Abelard soon invited the women to take up residency at the Paraclete, an oratory near Nogent-sur-Seine that he had founded in about 1122 but that he had been forced to leave probably by 1127.[21] In the *Historia calamitatum*, Abelard relates his involvement in the transferral of the nuns from Argenteuil to the Paraclete, intentionally privileging his concern for the oratory, and not the women, as the reason for his invitation:

> It happened that my abbot of St Denis by some means took possession of the Abbey of Argenteuil where Heloise – now my sister in Christ rather than my wife – had taken the veil. He claimed that it belonged to his monastery by ancient right, and forcibly expelled the community of nuns, of which she was prioress, so that they were now scattered as exiles in various places. I realized that this was an opportunity sent me by the Lord for providing for my oratory, and so I returned and invited her, along with some other nuns from the same convent who would not leave her, to come to the Paraclete; and once they had gathered there, I handed it over to them as a gift, and also everything that went with it.[22]

Abelard's refusal to identify himself explicitly with concern for the plight of the nuns was at least partly a function of his infamous relationship with Heloise; however, it also reflects public ambivalence concerning the involvement of men in the care of women more broadly. Certainly Abelard was aware of the accusations that had been leveled against Robert of Arbrissel (d. 1116), whose foundation for women and men at Fontevrault had institutionalized the pastoral care of women, explicitly involving them in the reform enthusiasm of the twelfth century and even placing them at its center.[23] Roscelin of Compiègne, who had been Abelard's teacher before he moved to Paris, was vociferous in his attacks against Robert, accusing him of luring wives from their husbands and holding him responsible for sexual sins that might result from the women's denial of the marital debt.[24] Although Abelard had previously defended Robert, praising him in a letter to the bishop of Paris as "an outstanding preacher of Christ,"[25] he was particularly sensitive to the sort of accusations made against him, since even in the period immediately after his castration Abelard had been accused of maintaining a lascivious lifestyle.[26] Evidently those accusations had not lost their sting: Abelard records that scandal hung over the Paraclete when he was first involved there, despite his physical inability to commit what he refers to simply as "this sin."[27] Given this climate of anxiety regarding contact between monastic men and women in general, and in his situation in particular, Abelard no doubt thought it best to circulate a history of the Paraclete that emphasized his desire to ensure the continuity of the divine office at his oratory while minimizing his concern for the fate of the women under Heloise's care. His caution may explain why Heloise, who was most likely involved in the transfer and may even have requested Abelard's help, as Constant Mews has suggested, is not mentioned as a factor in his decision.[28]

Whatever his motives, Abelard's argument – that his involvement with the Argenteuil nuns had been prompted only by concern for the Paraclete – would have rung hollow by the time that he was writing, since he had already demonstrated more interest in the community of women than his dispassionate account of its origins would suggest. Between 1131 and his return to Paris in about 1133, Abelard records that he visited the Paraclete with some frequency. If he was based at St Gildas in Brittany at the time, some 350 miles away, Abelard's seemingly casual visits would have required substantial travel time and signaled a commitment to the community that transcended concern for the oratory alone. It is possible that Abelard recognized the weakness of his argument; in any case he offers two further reasons for his involvement at the Paraclete, both of which directly undermine models of male opposition to the *cura*. The first – a striking example of contemporary ambivalence regarding the care of women – centered on his report that he had been compelled by a public outcry to assume responsibility for the community. He writes that, "all the people in the neighbourhood began attacking me violently for doing less than I could and should to minister to the needs of women . . . so I started to visit them more often to see how I could help them."[29] The obligation for men to provide care for women that is assumed in this report stands in marked contrast to the anxiety that contact between religious men and women occasioned elsewhere, most notably among the critics of Robert of Arbrissel. Abelard's report demonstrates that support, no less than opposition, could be a natural response to the *cura monialium* and that supporters of the *cura* could draw on biblical as well as patristic authority in their defense. Those who encouraged Abelard's intervention at the Paraclete may have been inspired by the examples of the Fathers and even of Christ, in their care for women;[30] or they may have believed that men's care for women was a natural obligation since, as Abelard wrote, "the weaker sex needs the help of the stronger."[31]

The theme of women's weakness, which would later inspire Abelard's discussions of women's dignity, signals the second explanation that he offers for his involvement at the Paraclete: the satisfaction that he anticipated he would derive from being needed by the women. "After much reflection," Abelard writes:

> I decided to do all I could to provide for the sisters of the Paraclete, to manage their affairs, to watch over them in person too, so that they would revere me the more, and thus to minister better to their needs. The persecution I was now suffering at the hands of the monks who were my sons was even more persistent and distressing than what I had endured previously from my brothers, so I thought I could turn to the sisters as a haven of peace and safety from the raging storms, find repose there for a while, and at least achieve something amongst them though I had failed with the monks. Indeed, the more they needed me in their weakness, the more it would benefit me.[32]

By his own admission, Abelard's decision to involve himself in the continuing life of the women's community was informed ultimately not by concern for the Paraclete, nor even by the force of public opinion, but by the benefit that he expected in return for his care. This benefit extended beyond private and personal satisfaction to include the public realization of his role as a monastic reformer. In addition to the love and respect that he wanted and the retreat that he saw for himself in the community, Abelard felt that he could achieve with the women of the Paraclete what he had failed to realize at St Gildas – meaningful reform of the religious life.

Abelard's experience of the monastic life both at St Denis and at St Gildas, where he became abbot in about 1127, had been disastrous. Having been expelled from St Denis by the other monks who resented his criticisms of their worldly living, Abelard reports that he was living in fear for his life at St Gildas, even as he wrote the *Historia calamitatum*.[33] His trials as abbot of St Gildas had prompted a serious re-evaluation of his achievements, of his "wretched" and "useless" life and of his failures as a teacher and an abbot.[34] Given the desperation of his situation, Abelard seems almost to have welcomed the expulsion of the nuns from Argenteuil since it provided him with the opportunity to reinvent himself as the founder of a monastic community and the architect of its religious life. Disappointed as he had been by his experience of the male monastery, Abelard anticipated that the women of the Paraclete would provide him with a sense of spiritual satisfaction that had been lacking at St Gildas. Indeed, it is likely that, in addition to defending his role at the Paraclete, which Mary Martin McLaughlin proposed was Abelard's purpose in writing the *Historia calamitatum*,[35] a further objective may have been to prepare for his exit from St Gildas and removal to the community at the Paraclete.[36] If this was the case, then Abelard's discussions of the pastoral care of women and explanation of his involvement at the Paraclete were not just an apology for the past, but an aggressive attempt to sway future public opinion in his favor.

Abelard and the idealized *cura monialium*

By the time that Abelard came to write his *Rule* (letter 8), in which he outlines his plan for the ideal engagement of religious men and women, and his letter 7, "On the authority and dignity of the nun's profession," he seems to have overcome many of the personal anxieties that had prevented his wholesale involvement in the early life of the Paraclete and that overshadow his *Historia calamitatum*. In these later texts, which are themselves records of his engagement with the women of the Paraclete and of his unequivocal commitment to the *cura monialium*, Abelard extended his discussion beyond the limited personal context that had formed the basis for his discussion of care in the *Historia* in order to set out daring ideas concerning the mutual dependence and reward that he argued bound all men and women together within the religious life. Where in the *Historia* Abelard had admitted the personal benefits that he expected through his service to the women of the Paraclete – love, comfort, and fulfillment – in his later writings he generalized those benefits, arguing that all monastic men could profit from their service to women and promising them an eternal reward for their efforts. The spiritual complementarity of the sexes that was at the heart of this argument provided the basis for the ideal monastic community that Abelard planned and presented in his *Rule*.

According to this *Rule*, male and female monasteries were to be paired geographically and bound in a "mutual affection" that could be strengthened by bonds of kinship between individual men and women.[37] However, the two communities were not to be equal. The women were at the center of Abelard's monastic plan, while the men were intended simply to provide for the women's material and spiritual needs. In a dramatic shift from the caution that he had demonstrated in the *Historia calamitatum*, the *Rule* includes the explicit requirement that men provide support for religious women. Writing that "it is always men's duty to provide for women's needs,"[38] Abelard now argued that men's care for the practical needs of the women's community was not voluntary, but an obligation modeled on the care that Joseph had provided for Mary and the provision made for her by Christ at his crucifixion.[39]

The centrality of the women's community to Abelard's plan and his requirement that men should provide them with pastoral care point to the most original aspect of his *cura monialium*: the inversion of traditional relations between the sexes. As in his second letter to Heloise, where he had placed her name before his own in greeting, in the *Rule* he emphasized the superiority of nuns as brides of Christ. When Heloise had charged that his address was "contrary to custom in letter-writing and, indeed, to the natural order," Abelard had responded:

> You must realize that you became my superior from the day when you began to be my lady on becoming the bride of my Lord. . . . By

the privilege of your position you are set not only over your former husband but over every servant of that King.[40]

Heloise's superiority as a bride of Christ not only solidified her nominal authority over Abelard, but also extended it over all religious men. This same belief in the superiority of the women in the celestial hierarchy governed Abelard's expectations of monastic organization. Accordingly, he set down that the abbot should "preside over the nuns too in such a way that he regards those who are the brides of the Lord whose servant he is as his own mistresses, and so be glad to serve rather than rule them."[41] The courtly relationship that Abelard envisioned between the abbot and the deaconess in his *Rule* directly mirrored his own idealized demeanor toward Heloise, to whom, in the spirit of the Church Father Jerome (d. 420), he had written, "You have as a servant me whom in the past you recognized as your master."[42] Like the steward in the king's palace, Abelard insisted that the abbot should not oppress the queen but rather treat her wisely, while the brothers were to swear an oath to the sisters not to mistreat them.[43] Finally, to ensure that oppression of the women could not occur, Abelard stipulated that all members of the monastic communities, both male and female, should be obedient to the female leader of the community, whom he calls the deaconess.[44]

Yet despite the dignity that Abelard ascribed to the deaconess, and his willingness to provide care for women and even to accept his nominal subordination to them, Abelard's discussion of governance within the monastery indicates that he opposed the inversion of real power. His final position concerning authority within the monastery, as it is outlined in his *Rule*, suggests that the implications of his devotion to the *cura* could not ultimately extend to the abolition of male headship, as at Fontevrault.[45] Men's ultimate authority within Abelard's idealized community was ensured in his declaration, "we want convents of women always to be subject to monasteries of men."[46]

Abelard's resistance to real inversion of the gender hierarchy suggests that, despite the practical commitment that he had by this time made to the *cura monialium* – at least at the Paraclete – and his sense of the centrality of the *cura* to the spiritual lives of religious men, he had not completely abandoned his earlier ambivalence regarding the interactions of men and women. Even at this point, when he was most devoted to the *cura*, Abelard stopped short of allowing women to rule over men, an arrangement that would have been the logical conclusion of his model of men's voluntary subordination to the women who were brides of their King. This is a subject on which Abelard had expressed himself forcefully in the *Historia calamitatum*. There he cited the natural weakness of women and the apostle Paul's requirement that men have authority over women, concluding:

> And so I am much surprised that the custom should have been long established in convents of putting abbesses in charge of women just

as abbots are set over men. . . . In several places too, the natural order is overthrown to the extent that we see abbesses and nuns ruling the clergy.[47]

It is possible that in his *Historia calamitatum* Abelard was trying to distance himself, and the Paraclete, from the troubles that had arisen at Fontevrault in 1126 and 1132; papal bulls from those years prohibit men from leaving the order, proof that all was not well between the men and women of the community.[48] However, in his *Rule* Abelard returned to this topic, declaring with Paul, "Woman's head is man, as man's head is Christ and Christ's is God."[49] Of course, it is possible that Abelard's insistence on male headship was designed to ensure his continuing centrality to the life of the community and to safeguard his own role as its founder. Even so, the resulting confusion of mutually rendered authority and obedience must have made Abelard's *Rule* as difficult to follow as it was impractical.[50]

Abelard's *Rule* provides an important witness to the *cura monialium* in the twelfth century, whether or not it was ultimately used at the Paraclete.[51] To Abelard, male provision of material and pastoral care was mandatory; his concern was only to guard against potential abuse, which he did by reserving to the deaconess all authority to manage the internal workings of the community.[52] At the same time, he recognized that not all men could share the personal interest that, as its founder, he took in the Paraclete, although this knowledge did not in his view alter or lessen their obligation to provide care for the women. Even while requiring that "it is always men's duty to provide for women's needs," Abelard suggested the prospect of eternal reward in men's service to women, promising that, "the more a man has humbled himself before God, the higher he will certainly be exalted."[53] As Abelard had himself discovered, men's relationships with women could enable them to explore aspects of their own spirituality and to approach Christ vicariously through his brides. If women needed men in the religious life, so too, Abelard realized, did men need women.

Heloise and the negotiation of pastoral care at the Paraclete

Abelard marshals a number of justifications for his involvement in the spiritual and material life of the women of the Paraclete: his personal investment in the continuation of worship at his oratory, the apparent weight of public opinion, and the excellent example of the Fathers, as well as his private ambitions as a monastic reformer and his need for respite from the bitter reality of his situation at St Gildas. The one factor that he fails to mention in his public letter of consolation, the *Historia calamitatun*, but which of course lay behind all of his future writing for the women of the Paraclete, was Heloise herself – not as his one-time wife now abandoned and in need of support, but as a learned and questioning woman engaged in the religious life.[54]

In the first letter that Heloise had written to Abelard after reading his *Historia calamitatum*, she had pleaded with him to comfort her in writing.[55] Her arguments were forceful. She reminded him of her utter obedience to his wishes when she had taken the veil in Paris some fifteen years before. She recalled the singular debt that he owed to her as his wife, the result of the marriage into which she had entered only in accordance with his wishes and that had marked the beginnings of their troubles.[56] In short, she tells him, "I have finally denied myself every pleasure in obedience to your will, kept nothing for myself except to prove that now, even more, I am yours."[57] Surely his debt to her was clear. Yet as much as her words have haunted modern readers, Abelard was largely untouched by their poignancy. He responded with a letter, but refused to indulge in the nostalgia from which, as he argued, his castration had effectively delivered him and which he would shortly ask Heloise to surrender as well. Heloise's third letter elicited a different response, so lengthy and dense in its historical and theological arguments that modern readers have tended simply to shy away from it. Evidently the subject of this third letter together with her request, presented on behalf of the entire Paraclete community, had affected Abelard in just the right way. Perhaps because she had read Abelard's letter to a friend, perhaps because she knew him so well, Heloise pushed all the right buttons when she presented him with her final appeal – that he should be the director of the religious life at the Paraclete, or, in other words, that he officially adopt the *cura monialium*.

If Abelard worried that he was wasting his time in the wilds of Brittany among murderous and immoral monks, Heloise offered the women of the Paraclete as willing alternatives: "While you spend so much on the stubborn, consider what you owe to the obedient; you are so generous to your enemies but should reflect on how you are indebted to your daughters."[58] If he was anxious for the future of the Paraclete as a place of worship, and for his own reputation as its founder, Heloise reminded him of the special obligation that bound him to the Paraclete community as its creator:

> It is for you then, master, while you live, to lay down for us what Rule we are to follow for all time, for after God you are the founder of this place, through God you are the creator of our community, with God you should be the director of our religious life.[59]

As she had already observed in an earlier letter, the painful truth for Abelard was that the Paraclete and the women there were all that was left to him.[60]

Ultimately, though, only three of Heloise's arguments seem to have affected Abelard. The first was that he had a unique responsibility, as Heloise reminds him, to "heal the wounds you have yourself inflicted."[61] When this obligation involved painful reminiscence, Abelard demurred. But when it suggested the possibility of securing Heloise's future "corner in heaven," Abelard was ready with pen in hand.[62] Heloise's second argument, one that was near to Abelard's own heart, was that men should support holy women.[63] So, even as she asks Abelard to compose a rule that would reflect women's peculiar position within the church, Heloise reminds Abelard of what his obligation to the nuns should be. Finally, she suggests that if he does not fulfill his obligations, a future priest may be unwilling or unable to complete the task. Here Heloise underscores the very real possibility that the Paraclete nuns might have difficulty securing a competent and sympathetic priest after Abelard's death. This was clearly a possibility that Abelard recognized as well and wished to mitigate through his provision of liturgical and prescriptive literature.[64] That Heloise saw female agency in the *cura monialium* is clear from her next, somewhat mischievous comment. She hints that, while a future priest may be willing to provide care, he might not be respected by the women and would therefore be ineffective:

> After you we may perhaps have another to guide us, one who will build something upon another's foundation, and so, we fear, he may be less likely to feel concern for us, or be less readily heard by us; or indeed, he may be no less willing, but less able.[65]

On that note, Heloise drew her letter to a close: "Speak to us then, and we shall hear. Farewell."

When Abelard did speak, which he did at great length in his letters, Heloise may have heard, but the question is, did she listen? Only in recent years has Heloise begun to be studied apart from Abelard in her own right, among other things as a capable abbess, a writer, and a philosopher. Peter Dronke has argued that Heloise had already established for herself a mature letter-writing style before she ever met Abelard. He suggested that, rather than having molded her according to his own techniques, Abelard may in truth have been influenced stylistically and intellectually by her.[66] More recently, Constant Mews has argued persuasively for Heloise's intellectual integrity and excellence quite apart from her relationship with Abelard. His work has established that Heloise's literary activity extended well beyond the letters to Abelard that appear in the collected correspondence and for which she is most well known.[67] Heloise's writings, not only in her letters, but also in the questions that she poses for Abelard in the *Problemata*, have been taken as evidence of the high level of scholarship at the Paraclete under her authority.[68] Yet Heloise's abilities were not limited to the intellectual sphere. The record of her extraordinary success as a manager of the Paraclete's properties establishes her reputation as a talented administrator, belying Abelard's insinuation that the Paraclete's solid financial situation was due only to the generosity of its donors.[69] In reality, as Bruce Venarde points out, Heloise had dramatically increased the Paraclete holdings during her abbacy.[70] If Abelard had once thought that he would be welcomed by the Paraclete women to "manage their affairs, [and] to watch over them in person too," it may just be that he had underestimated Heloise's ability to manage for herself. Left to her own devices, she not only increased the property and prestige of the Paraclete, but also gained the respect of such monastic leaders as Bernard of Clairvaux (d. 1153) and Peter the Venerable, abbot of Cluny (d. 1156).[71]

Heloise's relationship with Bernard of Clairvaux, whom Abelard seems to have credited with the failure of his school at the Paraclete and who would bring about his condemnation at the Council of Sens in 1141, further complicates the picture of the *cura monialium* that emerges from the letter collection and *Rule*.[72] Bernard's involvement at the Paraclete is recorded in two letters, the first from Abelard to Bernard and the second from Bernard to the Pope, at Heloise's request;[73] it can also be inferred through the substantial Cistercian presence in the Paraclete liturgy that has been identified by Chrysogonus Waddell.[74] Abelard's letter to Bernard indicates the intimacy of the relationship that Bernard had established with the women of the Paraclete, reporting Heloise's account of Bernard's visit to the community. Heloise had told Abelard "with the greatest joy how you had come there for the sake of a long awaited holy visitation and had strengthened both her and her sisters with pious exhortations."[75] As Constant Mews observes, the tone of Abelard's letter suggests that Heloise knew Bernard more intimately, and was on better terms with him than Abelard was himself. However, the purpose of Abelard's letter was not to flatter Bernard or to bolster his relations with the Paraclete, but to provide an explanation for a change that Abelard had introduced into the wording of the Lord's Prayer and upon which Bernard had commented unfavorably during his visit. The alacrity with which Abelard defended his modification, and by implication also the quality of his provision of the *cura*, suggests that he may have seen in Bernard a rival for the care of the women at the Paraclete. Evidence for the widespread influence of Cistercian customs at the Paraclete indicates that Abelard may have been correct in this assessment: the Paraclete may have adopted Cistercian practices from its inception, during the early years when Abelard had intentionally kept his distance. Bernard's involvement at the Paraclete challenges received interpretations of the *cura monialium* – particularly the widespread assumption of Cistercian opposition to the care of women. Abelard's description of Bernard's visit to the Paraclete as a "long awaited holy visitation" suggests that Bernard came in his official capacity as abbot of Clairvaux. Whether or not the Cistercians were prepared to support the care of women in their General Chapter, a question that has long dominated discussion of the *cura*, they certainly provided assistance to women's communities, as this episode reveals. Moreover, it hints that Abelard's relationship to the Paraclete was even more complicated than has typically been assumed; instead of condescending to provide care for the women of the community, Abelard may in fact have been competing for the privilege.

Heloise knew what she wanted from a spiritual director. She knew too that certain things might be "less readily heard" by the women of the Paraclete and, most especially, by her. The women at the Paraclete were not uncritical recipients of pastoral care. Was Heloise's observation that not all spiritual directors would be "heard" by them intended as a caution to Abelard? In fact, his own voluminous writing for the women was not all "heard" by them, at least not in the sense of being rigorously adopted. It is unlikely that Abelard's monastic masterpiece, the *Rule* that he wrote for the Paraclete, ever became the sole guide for the life of the community. Heloise's influence over the religious life at the Paraclete was substantial. Not only were Abelard's *Rule* and other works written at her prompting, and according to her suggestions, but when Abelard deviated from the script he had been given, the nuns of the Paraclete evidently stopped "hearing" him: the places in which the Paraclete *Institutes* differ from Abelard's *Rule* are at precisely those points at which Abelard had strayed from Heloise's initial suggestions. Most telling is Heloise's refusal to accept Abelard's requirement that the Paraclete be placed under male authority.[76] The Paraclete was never placed, as Abelard's *Rule* had required, under the authority of a male abbot.

Mutuality in the *cura monialium*

The example of Abelard and Heloise highlights the mutuality that both expected in their relationship as nun and spiritual director. To be sure, Abelard was motivated to some extent by self-interest, but even his self-interest implied his belief in the dignity of women, enabled paradoxically through their weakness. He believed that his monastic experiment was as valid if performed by a community of women as it would be by men, and even more worthwhile. Indeed, Abelard anticipated that he and other men would realize a hefty heavenly return on their spiritual service to women, whose weakness had gained them particular favor with their heavenly spouse.

Abelard's argument that men were under an obligation to support religious women dates to the earliest period of his involvement with the Paraclete community. At some point after the women's ejection from Argenteuil in 1129 but probably before writing his *Historia calamitatum*, Abelard had delivered a sermon soliciting donations to the struggling new community in which he argued that men ought to provide financial support for religious women, and that they might expect a spiritual reward as a result. In this sermon, "On alms for the nuns of the Paraclete" (sermon 30), Abelard took as his text the parable of the unworthy steward in Luke 16, in which Christians were encouraged to use their wealth strategically in order to gain friends who might also ultimately be benefactors.[77] Combining Jerome's belief in the superiority of religious women, who as brides of Christ were literally the mistresses (*dominae*) of his servants, with the Pauline promise that weakness could become strength in Christ, Abelard added a new element – mutuality – to traditional conceptualizations of women's potential spiritual pre-eminence. As brides of the highest King, Abelard argued that women had privileged access to Christ and had gained authority over religious men; however, he also suggested that religious men could benefit from women's supposed pre-eminence, earning spiritual reward through their service to Christ's brides first by gaining favor with Christ the bridegroom, and second by benefiting from the influence with Christ that his brides could exert. The mutuality that Abelard suggests in sermon 30 is a simple equation: men's financial support for women's prayers. However, its potential impact was considerable; although Abelard may initially have limited his understanding of mutuality to the spiritual reward that a potential donor might expect in return for his gift, the equation could also be applied to the benefit that a priest could expect by his engagement in the *cura monialium*.

The timing of sermon 30 indicates that Abelard had composed and probably preached it before he wrote a single word at Heloise's request or, according to her own testimony, offered her a personal word of consolation.[78] It suggests that Abelard's advocacy for women predated his interaction with Heloise at the Paraclete and formed a central part of his monastic vision from at least 1129, if not before. This should force a reconsideration of Abelard's sincerity as a champion of religious women since, despite the extent of his writings for women and his surprising disruption and even inversion of the gender hierarchy, his support for women has been received with varying degrees of skepticism. Abelard's arguments for the dignity of women have struck a hollow note with some, who, while noting the effusiveness of his rhetoric, doubt his sincerity.[79] Faced with Abelard's repeated references to women's weakness alongside praise for their dignity, Mary Martin McLaughlin asks: "Are we to place Abelard in the company of those Western 'fathers,' from St. Jerome to Freud, whose 'best friends' were women, but who felt nonetheless impelled to stress their inferiority?"[80]

In an attempt to reconcile the two conflicting images of Abelard – the predatory image of himself that he projects in his *Historia* and the tireless advocate for the dignity of women that he appears to be in letter 7 – scholars have been drawn to a model of conversion. Like Heloise, who is thought by some to have experienced a spiritual and emotional conversion to the monastic life, effected in her third letter and marked by her ensuing silence on personal subjects, Abelard too has been described as having undergone a conversion from "anti-feminism" at some point after he became involved in the life of the Paraclete.[81] Abelard's hypothetical conversion has been seen to provide a solution to the many inconsistencies in his advocacy of women that have plagued scholars, while at the same time neatly incorporating Heloise's supposed improving influence on him. However, this explanation fails to account for his early commitment to the spiritual priority of women. If anything, Abelard surpassed, rather than echoed, Heloise in his praise for women, his optimism for the spiritual possibilities available to them, and his unwillingness to admit gender-specificity in the religious life. Whereas Heloise had insisted on the differences that must separate religious men and women, Abelard was reluctant to abandon Paul's promise of a Christian life free from gender distinctions.[82] In his response to Heloise's requests for a monastic rule specific to women's needs, Abelard argued first that such a thing was unnecessary: "for as in name and profession of continence you are one with us, so nearly all our institutions are suitable for you."[83] The evidence of sermon 30 – in which the philosophical and theological foundations for his approach to the *cura monialium* had been laid probably before 1132 – suggests that Abelard's conversion from anti-feminism, if indeed he had one, had occurred independent of Heloise's influence.

Conclusion

Through their emphasis on a framework of decline for women religious, traditional interpretations of the *cura monialium* have tended to force a dichotomy between men's support for the care of women, as at Fontevrault, and opposition, which is generally, although not exclusively, associated with Cîteaux, meanwhile condemning women as passive characters to the periphery of the debate. The witness provided through the letters of Heloise and Abelard demonstrates that such a dichotomy is a false one, which obscures both the experiences of individual men and women and the nuances of local situations. As the example of Heloise and Abelard suggests, these individual experiences were by and large marked more by uncertainty and ambivalence than by either outright hostility or unambiguous support. Although women were undeniably dependent on men for the provision of pastoral care, it does not follow, as many recent discussions of the *cura monialium* have assumed, that men saw such dependence as burdensome or that they sought to avoid it. Instead, as Elsanne Gilomen-Schenkel concludes from her study of Benedictine houses in Switzerland within the early reform movement, much of the pastoral care for women was provided within the context of joint communities in which men and women were linked by ties of mutual obligation and benefit or between houses that were bound together by personal ties of kinship, friendship, or precedence.[84]

By the time that Abelard was writing his *Historia calamitatum* in the 1130s the first flush of reform enthusiasm had passed and with it the openness to women that had characterized many of the early reforming communities. The ejection of the women from Argenteuil came at a difficult time for Abelard, both personally and politically, although in many ways it offered him the validation that he needed to overcome his situation at St Gildas. Cognizant of the criticisms to which he was vulnerable as he engaged with the nuns of the Paraclete, Abelard provided in his writings repeated justifications for his adopted role as a spiritual director for women. In so doing, he provides for his modern reader a unique running commentary concerning his public negotiation of the *cura monialium* and its potential pitfalls. However, the *Historia calamitatum* reveals more than Abelard's public negotiation of the *cura monialium*; the text is a record too of his own ambivalence regarding his role at the Paraclete. While Abelard was uncertain as to what this role should be, he clearly saw it not as a burden, but rather as an opportunity both for personal and ultimately also for spiritual fulfillment.

Abelard was not alone in his approach to the *cura monialium* or in his sense that men's salvation could come through women. Some years after he wrote his *Rule* for the Paraclete, with its plan for the ideal relationship between religious men and women, the Augustinian canons of Marbach in Alsace adopted and then implemented some of Abelard's ideas regarding the spiritual complementarity of the sexes.[85] Although there is no evidence that they knew his *Rule*, the canons of Marbach owned a copy of Abelard's sermon 30, to which they turned for a rationalization of their involvement in the pastoral care of women.[86] Abelard's discussion in sermon 30 of women's special influence with Christ and of the benefit that men could gain through their support for religious women appears in a manuscript, the *Guta-Sintram Codex*, that was the joint effort of a female scribe from the nearby women's community at Schwartzenthann and a male artist from Marbach.[87] The placement of selections from Abelard's sermon 30 in the manuscript, which contains the communities' joint necrology, suggests that the relationship between the two houses was conceived in terms of the spiritual complementarity of the sexes that had first been proposed by Abelard in his sermon 30 and then elaborated in his *Rule*. The need at Marbach for a justification of the canons' actions indicates that the *cura* required negotiation in the second half of the twelfth century, even while it continued to attract men and offer them the opportunity for spiritual reward.

Abelard's writings for the Paraclete, composed in response to Heloise's demands and according to her suggestions, are critical to our understanding of the *cura monialium* at the mid-twelfth century. In the first instance, they reveal that women's monasticism was a serious subject for discussion – even by so renowned a philosopher as Peter Abelard. The simple fact of Abelard's writing is an indication of his particular concern for the lives of religious women, a concern that had its roots in the examples of the Fathers, but which by the twelfth century when he was writing was fraught with difficulties. More important, Abelard's writings form part of an ongoing dialogue between a monk and a nun, unusual enough in itself during the twelfth century but even more unusual given the particular relationship shared by Abelard and Heloise. Abelard's *Rule* formed an important part of that dialogue. It was written in direct response to Heloise's observation that the Benedictine Rule was inappropriate for women, and at her specific request.

Based on their marriage and the obligations that were its result, Heloise had reason to assert herself with Abelard and cannot therefore be seen as a typical nun corresponding with her spiritual adviser. Even so, her insistence and pointed requests for his writing argue against the widely held assumption that women were passive recipients of the *cura monialium*, demonstrating instead the proactive approach that women took to their own spiritual care. Not only did women monitor the content of that care, as Heloise did, but they were often forthright in their claims for spiritual support.[88] Heloise was an equal partner in the shaping and provision of spiritual care at the Paraclete. The dialogue between Heloise and Abelard that was the result of her prompting indicates that modern distinctions between "women's history" and "intellectual history," the latter of which has provided the primary context for most studies of Abelard, are artificial and bounded more by contemporary prejudices than medieval concerns. During the twelfth century, men and women were joined together in the religious life by practical considerations, but also by ties of mutuality and spiritual complementarity, if not equality. These ties are at the foundation of Abelard and Heloise's shared belief that "it is always men's duty to provide for women's needs."

NOTES

1   Debate concerning the authenticity of the letters attributed to Heloise and Abelard has long dominated scholarship, but has in recent years been largely settled in favor of authenticity, most notably by Peter Dronke, David Luscombe, and Barbara Newman. Peter Dronke, *Abelard and Heloise in medieval testimonies* (Glasgow: University of Glasgow Press, 1976); David Luscombe, "From Paris to the Paraclete: The correspondence of Abelard and Heloise," *Proceedings of the British Academy* 74 (1988), 247–83; Barbara Newman, "Authority, authenticity and the repression of Heloise," in: *From virile woman to womanChrist. Studies in medieval religion and literature* (Philadelphia, PA: University of Pennsylvania Press, 1995), 46–75. For a bibliography of the authenticity debate, see Constant J. Mews, "Peter Abelard," in: *Authors of the middle ages*, 2, ed. Patrick J. Geary (Aldershot: Variorum, 1995), 1–88, 78–81; and the more recent discussion of John Marenbon, "Authenticity Revisited," in: *Listening to Heloise. The voice of a twelfth-century woman*, ed. Bonnie Wheeler (New York: St Martin's, 2000), 19–33. I am grateful to Anna Sapir Abulafia, Julie Hotchin, Stacy Klein, Constant Mews, and an anonymous reviewer for the *Journal* for helpful comments on earlier drafts of this chapter. Particular thanks are due also to the participants of my senior seminar at Smith College in the spring of 2003.

2   The letters of Abelard and Heloise will be cited as follows: *Historia calamitatum*, ed. Jacques Monfrin (Paris, 1959) (=Epist. 1); "The personal letters between Abelard and Heloise," ed. J. T. Muckle, *Mediaeval Studies* 15 (1953), 47–94 (=Epist. 2–5); "The letter of Heloise on religious life and Abelard's first reply," ed. J. T. Muckle, *Mediaeval Studies*, 17 (1955), 240–81 (=Epist. 6–7); "Abelard's Rule for religious women," ed. T. P. McLaughlin, *Mediaeval Studies*, 18 (1956), 241–92 (=Epist. 8). The *Historia calamitatum* and letters 2–6 and 8 are translated in *The letters of Abelard and Heloise*, trans. from the Latin, intro. by Betty Radice (Harmondsworth: Penguin, 1974); Abelard's letter 7, "On the authority and dignity of the nun's profession," is in *The letters of Abelard and Heloise*, trans. C. K. Scott Moncrieff (London: G. Chapman, 1925; reprint New York, 1974), 105–42. See also Constant J. Mews, *The lost love letters of Heloise and Abelard. Perceptions of dialogue in twelfth-century France*, with a translation by Neville Chiavaroli and Constant J. Mews (New York: St Martin's, 2000).

3   Epist. 6; ed. Muckle, 241–53; *Letters*, trans. Radice, 159–79. Linda Georgianna, "Any corner of heaven: Heloise's critique of monasticism," *Mediaeval Studies* 49 (1987), 221–53; this article has been updated and reprinted in: *Listening to Heloise*, ed. Wheeler, 187–216, to which all subsequent notes will refer.

4   Neglect of the later letters is equally a function of the sharp split between the so-called "Personal Letters" and the "Letters of Direction" that was popularized by the editors of the published collection. However, as Alcuin Blamires has demonstrated, Abelard's writings for the Paraclete were intensely personal, while Morgan Powell argues that the so-called "personal" letters were concerned with matters of interest to the entire Paraclete community. Alcuin Blamires, "*Caput a femina, membra a viris*: Gender polemic in Abelard's letter 'On the authority and dignity of the nun's profession'," in: *The tongue of the fathers. Gender and ideology in twelfth-century Latin*, eds David Townsend and Andrew Taylor (Philadelphia, PA: University of

Pennsylvania Press, 1998), 55–79, 70; Morgan Powell, "Listening to Heloise at the Paraclete: Of scholarly diversion and a woman's 'conversion,'" in: *Listening to Heloise*, ed. Wheeler, 255–86, 262–3.

5   David Luscombe, "Monasticism in the lives and writings of Heloise and Abelard," in: *Monastic studies II. The continuity of the tradition*, ed. Judith Loades (Bangor: Headstart History, 1990), 1–11; Jean Leclercq *"Ad ipsam sophiam Christum*: le témoignage monastique d'Abélard," *Revue d'ascétique et de mystique* 46 (1970), 161–81; and J. M. B. Porter, "The convent of the Paraclete: Heloise, Abelard and the Benedictine tradition," *Studia Monastica* 41 (1999), 151–69.

6   A listing, now somewhat dated, of Abelard's writings and their editions is provided in Julia Barrow, Charles Burnett, and David Luscombe, "A checklist of the manuscripts containing the writings of Peter Abelard and Heloise and other works closely associated with Abelard and his school," *Revue d'histoire des texts* 14–15 (1984–5), 183–302.

7   Richard W. Southern, *Western society and the church in the middle ages* (Harmondsworth: Penguin, 1970), 310.

8   Janet L. Nelson, "Women and the word in the earlier middle ages," in: *Women in the church*, Studies in Church History 27, eds W. J. Sheils and Diana Wood (Oxford: Blackwell, 1990), 53–78.

9   See, for example, Jane Tibbets Schulenburg, "Sexism and the celestial gynaeceum from 500–1200," *Journal of Medieval History* 4 (1978), 117–33; Brenda Bolton, "*Mulieres sanctae*," in: *Sanctity and secularity: the church and the world*, Studies in Church History 10, ed. Derek Baker (Oxford, Blackwell, 1973), 77–95; and Jo Ann McNamara, *Sisters in arms. Catholic nuns through two millennia* (Cambridge, MA: Harvard University Press. 1996), 202–29, and "The 'Herrenfrage': The Restructuring of the Gender System, 1050–1150," in: *Medieval masculinities: Regarding men in the middle ages*, ed. Clare A. Lees (Minneapolis, MN: University of Minnesota Press, 1994), 3–29.

10 "Decline" is the title given by Southern to his discussion of women during the monastic revival of the tenth through early twelfth century. Southern, *Western society and the church*, 310–12. For theories of decline for religious women after the mid-twelfth century see Sharon Elkins, *Holy women of twelfth-century England* (Chapel Hill: University of North Carolina Press. 1988), 105–60; Penelope D. Johnson, *Equal in monastic profession. Religious women in medieval France* (Chicago, IL: University of Chicago Press, 1991), 248–66; and Bruce L. Venarde, *Women's monasticism and medieval society. Nunneries in France and England, 890–1215* (Ithaca, NY: Cornell University Press, 1997), 133–69, although Venarde recognizes a period of monastic expansion for women during the mid-thirteenth century.

11 See for instance Jo Ann McNamara, "Victims of progress: Women and the twelfth century," in: *Female power in the middle ages*, ed. Karen Glente and Lise Winther-Jensen (Copenhagen: C. A. Reitzel, 1989), 26–37; and David Herlihy, "Did women have a renaissance? A reconsideration," *Medievalia et Humanistica* 13 (1985), 1–22. Judith Bennett offers a thoughtful critique of the model of transformation in women's history and the emphasis on "seeming advances or declines in women's status" that it requires, in her "Confronting continuity," *Journal of Women's History* 9 (1997), 73–94, 74.

12 *Medieval purity and piety. Essays on medieval clerical celibacy and religious reform*, ed. Michael Frassetto (New York: Garland, 1998). Conrad Leyser suggests a reevaluation of the pollution language of reform in: "Custom, truth, and gender in eleventh-century reform," in: *Gender and Christian religion*, Studies in Church History 34, ed. R. N. Swanson (Woodbridge: Boydell, 1998), 75–91. For the argument that reform was "less sex-segregated than is often thought," see Constance Hoffman Berman, "Men's houses, women's houses: The relationship between the sexes in twelfth-century monasticism," in: *The medieval monastery*, ed. Andrew MacLeish (St Cloud, MN: North Star Press, now Minneapolis, MN: University of Minnesota Press, 1988), 43–52.

13   Arrangements for the provision of sacramental services to religious women are detailed in: Johnson, *Equal in monastic profession*, 180–91; Michel Parisse, *Les Nonnes au moyen age* (Le Puy: C. Bonneton, 1983), 134–43; *Les religieuses dans le cloître et dans le monde des origines à nos jours*. Actes du Deuxième Colloque International du C.E.R.C.O.R. Poitiers, 29 Septembre–2 Octobre 1988 (Saint-Étienne: Publications de l'université de Saint-Étienne, 1994), 331–91; Brian Golding, *Gilbert of Sempringham and the Gilbertine Order, c.1130–c.1300* (Oxford: Clarendon Press, 1995), 71–137; and Penny Schine Gold, *The lady and the virgin. Image, attitude, and experience in twelfth-century France* (Chicago, IL: University of Chicago Press, 1985), 76–115. Janet Sorrentino considers liturgical celebration within the Gilbertine Order: "In houses of nuns, in houses of canons: a liturgical dimension to double monasteries," *Journal of Medieval History* 28 (2002), 361–72.

14   Concerning the Cistercian response to women see: Sally Thompson "The problem of the Cistercian nuns in the twelfth and early thirteenth centuries," in: *Medieval women. Dedicated and presented to Professor Rosalind M. T. Hill . . .*, Studies in Church History, Subsidia 1, ed. Derek Baker (Oxford: Blackwell, 1978), 227–52; and the revision of early Cistercian women's history provided by Constance Hoffman Berman, "Were there twelfth-century Cistercian nuns?," *Church History* 68 (1999), 824–64; see Ch. 8, this volume. The experience of Premonstratensian women is explored in: Micheline de Fontette, *Les religieuses à l'âge classique du droit canon. Recherches sur les structures juridiques des branches féminines des ordres* (Paris: J. Vrin, 1967), 13–25; and A. Erens, "Les soeurs dans l'ordre de Prémontré," *Analecta Praemonstratensia* 5 (1929), 5–26. Herbert Grundmann outlined Franciscan and Dominican efforts to avoid the *cura monialium* during the thirteenth century, establishing a model of male opposition to the care of women that since has been widely accepted. Herbert Grundmann, *Religious movements in the middle ages*, trans. Steven Rowan (Notre Dame, IL: University of Notre Dame Press, 1995), 89–137. Significant exceptions to the model of male opposition to the care of women are provided in: Elkins, *Holy women of twelfth-century England*, 45–60, 78–91; and, for the later period, Jeffrey F. Hamburger, *The visual and the visionary. Art and female spirituality in late medieval Germany* (New York: Zone Books, 1998).

15   See, for instance, John Freed, "Urban development and the 'cura monialium' in thirteenth-century Germany," *Viator*, 3 (1972), 311–27.

16   McNamara, *Sisters in Arms*, 220. A notable exception to the assumption of female passivity is Gertrud Jaron Lewis, *By women, for women, about women. The Sister-books of fourteenth-century Germany* (Toronto: Pontifical Institute of Medieval Studies, 1996). See especially her chapter "The 'Cura monialium': The women's perspective," pp. 176–99.

17   As recent studies have demonstrated, individual religious men often sought religious women as prophets and channels of divine grace, engaging in spiritual friendships with them. Caroline Bynum argues that men "actively sought, in holy women, both a standard of piety and a window open to the divine." Caroline Walker Bynum, *Holy feast and holy fast. The religious significance of food to medieval women* (Berkeley, CA: University of California Press, 1987), 229. See also John Coakley, "Friars as confidants of holy women in medieval Dominican hagiography," in: *Images of sainthood in medieval Europe*, eds Renate Blumenfeld-Kosinski and Timea Szell (Ithaca, NY: Cornell University Press, 1991), 222–46, 225; and his "Gender and the authority of friars: The significance of holy women for thirteenth-century Franciscans and Dominicans," *Church History* 60 (1991), 445–60, 452; Simone Roisin: "L'Efflorescence cistercienne et le courant féminin de piété au XIIIe siècle," *Revue d'histoire ecclésiastique* 39 (1943), 342–78; and the discussion of relationships between religious men and women in: *Gendered voices. Medieval saints and their interpreters*, ed. Catherine M. Mooney (Philadelphia, PA: University of Pennsylvania Press, 1999).

18   Abelard is recognized as the most prolific author of spiritual works for women during the twelfth century. See Michael T. Clanchy, *Abelard. A medieval life* (Oxford,

FIONA J. GRIFFITHS

1997), 21; and Mary Martin McLaughlin, "Peter Abelard and the dignity of women: Twelfth-century 'feminism' in theory and practice," in *Pierre Abélard, Pierre le Vénérable. Les courants philosophiques, littéraires et artistiques en Occident au milieu du XIIe siècle.* Colloques internationaux du Centre national de la recherche scientifique 546 (Paris: C. N. R. S., 1975), 287–334, 292.

19   For a vivid statement of contemporary concerns surrounding the provision of care to women by male spiritual guides, see the *Speculum virginum* (*c*.1140), in which virgins are warned to be careful "lest the pastors of Christ's handmaids prove to be wolves rapacious for souls, slaying with the swords of incontinence those whom they feed with the word of truth." *Speculum virginum* 5.1029; ed. Jutta Seyfarth, *CC:CM* 5 (Turnhout: Brepols, 1990), 149; trans. Barbara Newman, in: *Listen, daughter*, ed. Mews, 291–2. The later incidence of a pregnancy and miraculous delivery, or abortion, at the Gilbertine house of Watton in England did nothing to diminish concerns regarding the interaction of men and women within the religious life. Aelred of Rievaulx, *De Sanctimoniali de Wattun*, PL 195: 789–96. See also *The Book of St Gilbert*, eds Raymonde Foreville and Gillian Keir (Oxford: Clarendon Press, 1987), liv–lv; and Giles Constable, "Aelred of Rievaulx and the nun of Watton: An episode in the early history of the Gilbertine order," in: *Medieval women*, ed. Baker, cited in note 14 above, 205–26.

20   Thomas G. Waldman, "Abbot Suger and the nuns of Argenteuil," *Traditio* 41 (1985), 239–72.

21   For a chronology of Abelard's career and writing, see Constant J. Mews, "On dating the works of Peter Abelard," *Archives d'histoire doctrinale et littéraire du moyen âge* 52 (1985), 73–134, 130–2.

22   *Historia calamitatum*, ed. Monfrin, 100; *Letters*, trans. Radice, 96. Mary Martin McLaughlin discusses the psychological importance of the Paraclete to Abelard in her article, "Abelard as autobiographer: The motives and meaning of his 'Story of calamities,'" *Speculum* 42 (1967), 463–88.

23   Concerning Fontevrault, see: Michel Parisse, "Fontevraud, monastère double," in: *Doppelklöster und andere Formen der Symbiose männlicher und weiblicher Religiosen im Mittelalter*, ed. Kaspar Elm and Michel Parisse (Berlin: Duncker & Humblot, 1992), 135–48; Jacques Dalarun, "Pouvoir et autorité dans l'ordre double de Fontevraud," in: *Les religieuses dans le cloître et dans le monde*, 335–51; Penny Schine Gold, "Male/female cooperation: The example of Fontevrault," in: *Distant echoes, medieval religious women*, 1, Cistercian Studies Series 71, eds Lillian Thomas Shank and John A. Nichols (Kalamazoo, MI: Cistercian Publications, 1984), 151–68; Gold, *The lady and the virgin*, 93–113; and Berenice M. Kerr, *Religious life for women c.1100–c.1350. Fontevraud in England* (Oxford: Oxford University Press, 1999). Despite Fontevrault's emphasis on the *cura*, contact between the sexes was strictly limited, reflecting what Loraine Simmons has called a "pervasive proximity anxiety." Loraine Simmons, "The abbey church at Fontevraud in the later twelfth century: Anxiety, authority and architecture in the female spiritual life," *Gesta* 31 (1992), 99–107.

24   Roscelin of Compiègne, *Epistola ad Abaelardum* in: *Der Nominalismus in der Frühscholastik. Ein Beitrag zur Geschichte der Universalienfrage im Mittelalter*, ed. Josef Reiners (Münster: Aschendorff, 1910), 63–80, 67. Roscelin was joined in his opposition to Robert's involvement with women by Marbod of Rennes and Geoffrey of Vendôme. Marbod, Ep. 6, PL 171, 1480–6; Geoffrey de Vendôme, *Oeuvres*, ed. Geneviève Giordanengo (Paris: C. N. R. S., 1996), no. 79.

25   Abelard, Epist. 14, in: *Peter Abelard. Letters IX–XIV. An edition with introduction*, ed. Edmé Renno Smits (Groningen: Rijksuniversiteit, 1983), 280. Cited in Mews, *Lost love letters*, 67.

26   Fulk of Deuil, Ep. 16, PL 178: 371–6; Roscelin, *Epistola ad Abaelardum*. Both letters are discussed in Luscombe, "From Paris to the Paraclete," 255–9.

27   *Historia calamitatum*, ed. Monfrin, 102; *Letters*, trans. Radice, 98. Abelard is pre-occupied in the *Historia calamitatum* with accusations of sexual impropriety from which he points out that he of all people should be immune – even more so than Christ "as far as human judgement goes," he comments bitterly. *Historia calamitatum*, ed. Monfrin, 104; *Letters*, trans. Radice, 100.

28   Mews, *Lost love letters*, 155.

29   *Historia calamitatum*, ed. Monfrin, 101; *Letters*, trans. Radice, 97.

30   The special care of the Fathers for the spiritual lives of women is a subject to which Abelard would return in his letters to Heloise, most notably in his letter on the dignity of nuns. Epist. 7, ed. Muckle, 279; trans. Scott Montcrieff, 139. Jerome, whose devotion to Paula, Marcella, and Eustochium was well known, was a perennial inspiration for both Heloise and Abelard. Mews discusses Abelard's increasing iden-tification with Jerome in Constant J. Mews, "Un lecteur de Jérôme au XIIe siècle: Pierre Abélard," in: *Jérôme entre l'Occident et l'Orient*, ed. Yves-Marie Duval (Paris: Etudes augustiniennes, 1988), 429–44. See also Alcuin Blamires, "No outlet for incon-tinence: Heloise and the question of consolation," in: *Listening to Heloise*, ed. Wheeler, 287–301. Of course, Abelard was even more strongly influenced by the example of Christ, who surrounded himself with female supporters and honored them not least by revealing his resurrection first to his female disciples. Donald K. Frank, "Abelard as imitator of Christ," *Viator* 1 (1970), 107–13.

31   *Historia calamitatum*, ed. Monfrin, 104; *Letters*, trans. Radice, 101. The paradox of woman's weakness, which appears first in Abelard's sermon 30, is at the core of his letter 7 (Epist. 7, ed. Muckle, 253–81, especially at 257). See Alcuin Blamires, "Gender polemic in Abelard's letter," in: ibid. *The case for women in medieval culture* (Oxford: Clarendon Press, 1997), 199–208; and M. M. McLaughlin, "Peter Abelard and the dignity of women," 301.

32   *Historia calamitatum*, ed. Monfrin, 105; *Letters*, trans. Radice, 102.

33   *Historia calamitatum*, ed. Monfrin, 107; *Letters*, trans. Radice, 104.

34   Abelard writes: "I had proved ineffective in all my attempts and undertakings, so that now above all men I justly merited the reproach, 'There is the man who started to build and could not finish.'" *Historia calamitatum*, ed. Monfrin, 99; *Letters*, trans. Radice, 96.

35   M. M. McLaughlin, "Peter Abelard and the Dignity of Women," 315. [The *Historia alamitatum* or *History of my Adversities* describes itself as a letter of consolation to a friend whose grief must be much less than Abelard's own!]

36   As David Luscombe has suggested, Abelard may even have tried to become abbot of the Paraclete when he left St Gildas, probably in about 1132. Luscombe, "From Paris to the Paraclete," 280. See also M. M. McLaughlin, "Abelard as autobiogra-pher," 468.

37   Epist. 8; ed. T. P. McLaughlin, 258, 259; *Letters*, trans. Radice, 210, 212. Abelard's centrality to the history of male–female cooperation in the religious life was estab-lished by Stephanus Hilpisch, *Die Doppelklöster. Entstehung und Organisation* (Münster: Aschendorff, 1928), 75–6. See also Georg Jenal, "*Caput autem mulieris vir* (I Kor 11,3). Praxis und Begründung des Doppelklosters im Briefkorpus Abaelard-Heloise," *Archiv für Kulturgeschichte*, 76 (1994), 285–304. Evidence that the Paraclete community did include male members is provided in Paola De Santis, *I Sermoni di Abelardo per le Monache del Paracleto*, Mediaevalia Louvaniensia Series 1, Studia 31 (Leuven: Leuven University Press, 2002), 125–35; and *The Paraclete statutes. Institutiones nostrae*, ed. Chrysogonus Waddell (Trappist, KY: Gethsemani Abbey, 1987), 153–5.

38   Epist. 8; ed. T. P. McLaughlin, p. 258; *Letters*, trans. Radice, p. 209. Abelard also writes:

>If the convent needs emissaries, the monks or their lay monks should supply them, for it is always men's duty to provide for women's needs,

and the greater the religious devotion of the nuns, the more they give themselves up to God and have need of men's protection.

And later, "all external affairs should be conducted for the women through men of the same religious life." Epist. 8; ed. T. P. McLaughlin, 258; *Letters*, trans. Radice, 209, 210.

39   Epist. 8; ed. T. P. McLaughlin, 258; *Letters*, trans. Radice, 210. The example of Christ's care for his mother was one that had inspired other male reformers to adopt the *cura*; the second life of Robert of Arbrissel also cited Christ's care in outlining the men's obligation to serve women at Fontevrault, as Heloise had too in her third letter to Abelard. For Robert, see *Vita altera*, 3; *PL* 162: 1063; and Jacques Dalarun, *L'impossible sainteté. La vie retrouvée de Robert d'Arbrissel (v. 1045–1116) fondateur de Fontevraud* (Paris: Cerf, 1985). Heloise provides the example of Christ's provision for Mary first in her third letter to Abelard, Epist. 6; ed. Muckle, 252; *Letters*, trans. Radice, 177.

40   Epist. 4; ed. Muckle, 77; *Letters*, trans. Radice, 127. Epist. 5; ed. Muckle, 83; *Letters*, trans. Radice, 137.

41   Epist. 8; ed. T. P. McLaughlin, 259; *Letters*, trans. Radice, 212. The idea of women's superiority to men, achieved by virtue of their position as brides of Christ, is derived from Jerome's letter to Eustochium. Jerome, Ep. 22, in: *Select Letters of St. Jerome*, ed. and trans. F. A. Wright (Cambridge, MA: Harvard University Press, 1933), 52–159. It appears in Abelard's letter "On the authority and dignity of the nun's profession" (Epist. 7, ed. Muckle, 267; trans. Scott Montcrieff, 124) and his sermon 30, *On alms for the nuns of the Paraclete (De eleemosyna pro sanctimonialibus de paraclito)*, ed. Aldo Granata, "La dottrina dell'Elemosina nel sermone 'Pro sanctimonialibus de Paraclito' di Abelardo," *Aevum* 47 (1973), 32–59, 54–9).

42   Epist. 5; ed. Muckle, 93; *Letters*, trans. Radice, 154.

43   Epist. 8; ed. T. P. McLaughlin, 260; *Letters*, trans. Radice, 213.

44   Epist. 8; ed. T. P. McLaughlin, 260; *Letters*, trans. Radice, 213. Abelard attributes quasi-clerical status to the deaconesses of the early church, writing "what we now call abbesses anciently they named deaconesses, that is ministers rather than mothers." Epist. 7; ed. Muckle, 264; trans. Scott Montcrieff, 121. See also Epist. 7; ed. Muckle, 262; trans. Scott Montcrieff, 118.

45   According to *Rule II*, thought to be part of the earliest *Rule* for Fontevrault (*c.*1116–17), the abbess was to have authority over the spiritual as well as the secular aspect of monastic life and governance. In practice, as the community's extant charters demonstrate, the less important monastic business (which Gold terms "necessary but spiritually unrewarding work") was managed by the male community. Gold, "Male/Female Cooperation," 159.

46   Epist. 8; ed. T. P. McLaughlin, 259; *Letters*, trans. Radice, 212.

47   *Historia calamitatum*, ed. Monfrin, 105; *Letters*, trans. Radice, 101.

48   Fontette, *Les religieuses*, 78, n. 8; Kerr, *Religious life for women*, 57.

49   Epist. 8; ed. T. P. McLaughlin, 258; *Letters*, trans. Radice, 210.

50   Barbara Newman comments that "Abelard's insistence on mutual service left the lines of authority muddled, making his rule unworkable in practice." Barbara Newman, "Flaws in the golden bowl: Gender and spiritual formation in the twelfth century," in: *From virile woman*, 19–45, 27. Clanchy calls Abelard's *Rule*, "worse than useless as a working document." Clanchy, *Abelard*, 222.

51   On the possible use of Abelard's *Rule* at the Paraclete, see *The Paraclete statutes*, ed. Waddell, 32.

52   Epist. 8; ed. T. P. McLaughlin, 259; *Letters*, trans. Radice, 213.

53   Epist. 8; ed. T. P. McLaughlin, 260; *Letters*, trans. Radice, 214.

54   Like his later hymns and commentary on the Hexameron, Abelard's rule and letter 7 were written in direct response to Heloise's request. On Heloise's role in commissioning Abelard's writing for the women of the Paraclete, see Joan M. Ferrante, *To*

the glory of her sex. Women's roles in the composition of medieval texts (Bloomington, IN: Indiana University Press, 1997), 55–67. Ferrante comments that Heloise is "directly responsible for much of Abelard's extant writing" (57). Mary Martin McLaughlin goes one step further than Ferrante in attributing to Heloise much of the credit for the writings for the Paraclete, which she writes were the result of "their talents." Mary Martin McLaughlin, "Heloise the abbess: The expansion of the Paraclete," in: *Listening to Heloise*, ed. Wheeler, 1–17, 2.

55   Epist. 2; ed. Muckle, 70; *Letters*, trans. Radice, 112.

56   Heloise reminds Abelard of the personal bond between them:

> you are bound to me by an obligation which is all the greater for the further close tie of the marriage sacrament uniting us, and are the deeper in my debt because of the love I have always borne you, as everyone knows, a love which is beyond all bounds.

Epist. 2; ed. Muckle, 70; *Letters*, trans. Radice, 113.

57   Epist. 2; ed. Muckle, 73; *Letters*, trans. Radice, 117.

58   Heloise makes this argument in her first letter. Epist. 2; ed. Muckle, 70; *Letters*, trans. Radice, 112.

59   Epist. 6; ed. Muckle, 253; *Letters*, trans. Radice, 178. Cf. Epist. 2; ed. Muckle, 69; *Letters*, trans. Radice, 111.

60   Epist. 2; ed. Muckle, 68; *Letters*, trans. Radice, 110.

61   Epist. 2; ed. Muckle, 69; *Letters*, trans. Radice, 111. In her third letter, Heloise repeats this idea: "you have it in your power to remedy my grief, even if you cannot entirely remove it." Epist. 6; ed. Muckle, 241; *Letters*, trans. Radice, 159.

62   Even in her first letter, when Heloise had asked Abelard for support and teaching for the new foundation of the Paraclete, Abelard had responded by inviting her to submit a specific request for his attention. Heloise writes:

> And so it is yours, truly your own, this new plantation for God's purpose, but it is sown with plants which are still very tender and need watering if they are to thrive. Through its feminine nature this plantation would be weak and frail even if it were not new; and so it needs a more careful and regular cultivation.

Epist. 2; ed. Muckle, 70; *Letters*, trans. Radice, 111. Abelard responded: "If . . . you feel that you have need of my instruction and writings in matters pertaining to God, write to me what you want, so that I may answer as God permits me." Epist. 3; ed. Muckle, 73; *Letters*, trans. Radice, 119. Already at this stage Abelard was engaged in a spiritual exchange with Heloise; he writes that he sends with his letter a Psalter which she had "earnestly begged." No record of such a request exists in Heloise's extant letters and it is possible that she had made the request in person.

63   Heloise makes that argument that true "widows," whom she defines as "women devoted to Christ," should be supported by the Church. Epist. 6; ed. Muckle, 252; *Letters*, trans. Radice, 176–7. Georgianna posits that Heloise may be responding to the unwillingness of men to minister to the practical needs of women, who were seen as idle, in her defense of contemplation as the highest form of devotion for women. Georgianna, "Any corner of heaven," 200.

64   Chrysogonus Waddell argues that Abelard's voluminous writing for the Paraclete was designed to create for the community a custom-made liturgy. Chrysogonus Waddell, "Peter Abelard as creator of liturgical texts," in: *Petrus Abaelardus (1079–1142). Person, Werk und Wirkung*, Trierer theologische Studien 38, ed. Rudolf Thomas (Trier: Paulinus-Verlag, 1980), 267–86.

65   Epist. 6; ed. Muckle, 253; *Letters*, trans. Radice, 178.

66   Peter Dronke, *Women writers of the middle ages* (Cambridge: Cambridge University Press, 1984), 112. See also Clanchy, *Abelard*, 169–72, especially 169.

67 Mews suggests that Heloise may have been the author of some of the sequences generally attributed to Abelard. Constant J. Mews, "Heloise and the liturgical experience at the Paraclete," *Plainsong and Medieval Music* 11 (2002), 25–35; and Constant J. Mews, "Hugh Metel, Heloise, and Peter Abelard: The letters of an Augustinian canon and the challenge of innovation in twelfth-century Lorraine," *Viator* 32 (2001), 59–91. See also the essays in: *The poetic and musical legacy of Heloise and Abelard. An anthology of essays by various authors*, ed. Marc Stewart and David Wulstan (Ottawa: Institute of Mediaeval Music, 2003).

68 Marenbon comments that the "*Problemata Heloissae*" [a text in which Heloise poses questions and Abelard provides answers] show even more clearly that Heloise and the nuns of the Paraclete were as eager and advanced in their studies of theology as the men Abelard was teaching in Paris. John Marenbon, *The Philosophy of Peter Abelard* (Cambridge: Cambridge University Press, 1997), 76. See also Peter Dronke, "Heloise's *Problemata* and *Letters*: Some questions of form and content," in: *Petrus Abaelardus*, ed. Thomas, 53–73; and Newman, "Authority, authenticity and the repression of Heloise," 69.

69 *Historia calamitatum*, ed. Monfrin, 100; *Letters*, trans. Radice, 97.

70 Venarde, *Women's monasticism*, 120–4; and, more recently, Mary Martin McLaughlin, "Heloise the abbess." See also Venarde's discussion of abbesses as business managers during the twelfth century. Bruce Venarde, "*Praesidentes negotiis*: Abbesses as managers in twelfth-century France," in: *Portraits of medieval and renaissance living. Essays in memory of David Herlihy*, eds Samuel K. Cohn and Steven A. Epstein (Ann Arbor, MI: University of Michigan Press, 1996), 189–205. Eugene III confirmed the holdings of the Paraclete in a papal letter of November 1, 1147. *Cartulaire de l'abbaye du Paraclet*, ed. Charles Lalore (Paris: E. Thorin, 1878), no. 6, 7–14.

71 Peter the Venerable's letters to Heloise are included in the collected correspondence: *Letters*, trans. Radice, 277–87; and *The letters of Peter the Venerable*, ed. Giles Constable (Cambridge, MA, 1967), 303–8, 401–2.

72 For Abelard's intimation that the collapse of the Paraclete had been the result of "new apostles," generally thought to have been Norbert of Xanten and Bernard of Clairvaux, see *Historia calamitatum*, ed. Monfrin, 97; *Letters*, trans. Radice, 93. For Bernard's role at the Council of Sens, see Constant J. Mews, "The Council of Sens (1141): Abelard, Bernard, and the fear of social upheaval," *Speculum* 77 (2002), 342–82; and at the Paraclete, Constant J. Mews, "Liturgy and identity at the Paraclete: Heloise, Abelard and the evolution of Cistercian reform, I," in: *The poetic and musical legacy of Heloise and Abelard*, eds Stewart and Wulstan, 19–33.

73 Abelard, Epist. 10; ed. Smits, 239–47. Bernard of Clairvaux, Ep. 278; *Sancti Bernardi Opera*, 8, eds Jean Leclercq, C. H. Talbot, and H. Rochais (Rome, 1957–), 190.

74 Chrysogonus Waddell, *The Old French Paraclete Ordinary and the Paraclete Breviary* 1, Cistercian Liturgy Series 3 (Trappist, KY: Gethsemani Abbey, 1985). Waddell has also noted significant Cistercian influence on the Paraclete customs. See *Institutiones nostrae*, ed. Waddell, 62–5.

75 Epist. 10; ed. Smits, 239; trans. in Mews, "Liturgy and identity at the Paraclete," 26.

76 *Institutiones nostrae "De obedientia*," VI; *Institutiones nostrae*, ed. Waddell, 10.

77 Abelard, Sermon 30, ed. Granata, "La dottrina dell'Elemosina," 54–9.

78 Abelard had been derelict in the early days after Heloise's entry into the monastic life in providing for her. Epist. 2; ed. Muckle, 70; *Letters*, trans. Radice, 112. Evidently he did not offer her more solace even after their reunion at the Paraclete. See Epist. 2; ed. Muckle, 72; trans. Radice, 116.

79 Both Mary Martin McLaughlin and Barbara Newman note the extreme ambivalence of Abelard's stance on female dignity and conclude that he was trapped ultimately in a *sic et non* of his own making. M. M. McLaughlin, "Peter Abelard and the dignity of women," 294, 320. Barbara Newman comments that "No one went further in the ritual praise of women than Abelard." Newman, "Flaws in the golden bowl," 27.

Blamires has challenged this dismissal of Abelard, describing Abelard's support for women as "profeminine." Blamires, *The case for women*, 207.

80   M. M. McLaughlin, "Peter Abelard and the dignity of women," 293.

81   Clanchy, *Abelard*, 253–7.

82   Galatians 3:28.

83   Epist. 8; ed. T. P. McLaughlin, 243; *Letters*, trans. Radice, 184. He makes a similar argument in his letter 7 claiming that Christ,

> as He had come to call either sex and to redeem them, so thought fit to unite both sexes in the true monkhood of His congregation, that thereafter authority for this profession might be given both to men and to women, and the perfect way of life might be laid before all, which they should imitate.

Epist. 7; ed. Muckle, 253; trans. Scott Montcrieff, 107. In the early church, Abelard writes that "women, in those things which pertain to God, or to any singularity of religion, were not separated from men." Epist. 7; ed. Muckle, 261; trans. Scott Montcrieff, 117.

84   Elsanne Gilomen-Schenkel, "'Officium Paterne Providentie' ou 'Supercilium Noxie Dominationis': Remarques sur les couvents de bénédictines au Sud-Ouest du Saint-Empire," in: *Les religieuses dans le cloître et dans le monde*, cited in note 13, above, 367–71, 368. Julie Hotchin makes a similar point in her examination of the Benedictines at Reinhardsbrunn. Julie Hotchin, "Abbot as guardian and cultivator of virtues: two perspectives on the *cura monialium* in practice," in: *Our medieval heritage. Essays in honour of John Tillotson for his 60th Birthday*, eds Linda Rasmussen, Valerie Spear, and Diane Tillotson (Cardiff: Merton Priory Press, 2002), 50–64.

85   Fiona Griffiths, "Brides and *Dominae*: Abelard's *Cura monialium* at the Augustinian Monastery of Marbach," *Viator* 34 (2003), 57–88.

86   Colmar, Bibliothèque Municipale, MS 128.

87   Strasbourg, Bibliothèque du Grand Séminaire, MS 37; *Le Codex Guta-Sintram. Manuscrit 37 de la Bibliothèque du Grand Séminaire de Strasbourg*, 2 vols, ed. Béatrice Weis (Lucerne: Éditions Fac-Similés, 1983).

88   See, for example, Lezlie Knox's discussion of conflict in 1261 between the Friars Minor and the Clarisses. The conflict had to do with the nature of spiritual care: the Clarisses had attempted to bind the Friars legally to *cura monialium*, and, as a result, the brothers withdrew from the women's communities altogether, refusing to minister to them. The situation was normalized only after Pope Urban IV recognized that the brothers provided spiritual care voluntarily and could not be bound legally to it. Lezlie Knox, "Audacious nuns: Institutionalizing the order of Saint Clare," *Church History* 69 (2000), 41–62.

Part IV

INCREASING VIOLENCE AND EXCLUSION

Introduction

Historians of European religion have given increased attention recently to the interaction between Christians and non-Christians in medieval Europe, and to how the increased power and self-assuredness of Christian authorities, particularly from the twelfth century on, had negative effects on Jews, Muslims, pagans, and those deemed Christian heretics. The history of Christian intolerance of non-Christians is not something new, but until recently much of the attention was given to groups who considered themselves Christians, but who were deemed heretics by the Church establishment. Perhaps because protestant reformers of the sixteenth century saw predecessors in some of the Christian heretics of the medieval world, considerable attention has been given to heretics and the definition of heresy within Christianity and much effort has been expended on defining just what those heretics believed.[1] The most recent work has turned from the obviously still difficult evaluation of heresy to a consideration of non-Christians.

In his introduction to *Christianity and Judaism: Studies in Church History*, the 1992 volume in which the article by Miri Rubin (Chapter 14) first appeared, Richard Barrie Dobson, an expert on the Latin West, asserted that "For historians to 'encounter' Jews, . . . [is] positively essential to a proper understanding of the structure and development of the Christian Church itself."[2] Dobson was among the earliest to assess the negative effects of Christianity on "others" in his analysis of the Jewish martyrdoms at York on the eve of the Third Crusade, showing that attacks on Jews were not simply the outcome of irrational, lower-class violence, but were promoted by an increasingly narrow-minded Christian rhetoric.[3]

Only a generation ago a textbook on medieval Europe would have discussed Jews and Judaism only as precursors of Christianity, then, reviewing the origins of Islam, would have discussed how Muslim advances in the southern half of the Mediterranean cut off Western Christendom from

317

the Byzantines, then would have described Christian advances against pagans living on the northern fringes of medieval Christendom who were systematically converted, if necessary by force. Pagan survivals were often identified in superstitious practices of poorly indoctrinated countrymen and -women. Such treatment would have described Muslims in Spain or the Levant as objects of proselytizing and conversion like the pagans on the Scandinavian and Baltic fringes and in central Europe, because, for most of the early Middle Ages, Western Christians thought of Muslims as just another group of pagans. Only in the central Middle Ages did Christians realize that Muslims shared sacred books with Christians and Jews; after that Islam tended to be treated as a Christian heresy. Despite the fact that both Jewish and Muslim communities continued to exist as minorities facing an increasing intolerance from the Christian majority, with their own religious and educational institutions, marriage practices, and sacred beliefs that were passed down by families from generation to generation, such Muslim or Jewish Europeans living under Christian rule remained undiscussed.[4]

Many historians once assumed that the early medieval centuries were ones of religious tolerance, particularly for Jews. David Nirenberg, in a recent book from which Chapter 15 is excerpted, however, argues against the historiography of an early medieval tolerance for Jews under Christian rule, followed by late medieval anti-Semitism, saying:

> (There was) the well-known argument that an early medieval "Augustinian" tolerance toward Jews was replaced by a harsher clerical intolerance which then spread to the common people. According to this view, medieval attitudes toward Jews before the late twelfth century were governed by an Augustinian paradigm that condemned the Jews but insisted on the importance of their presence within Christian society: as living reminders of the Crucifixion, of Christ's victory, and of the truth of the Christian version of sacred history.[5]

According to this view Jews in the early medieval period were treated differently from pagans and Muslims with regard to conversion, because Christian doctrine assumed the necessity of there being Jews at the Second Coming. Although it is possible to trace a growing hostility to Jews within the written sources for the later Middle Ages, as Rubin and Abulafia do, Nirenberg argues that it is impossible, given the silences in the early medieval documentation, to know for sure whether there were long periods in those centuries when Christians did indeed live with Jews, Muslims, or pagans in a situation of mutual toleration (*convivencia*).[6]

Such toleration, if it in fact actually existed, however, went only so far. A Christian concept of the "just war" to enforce orthodoxies had existed from at least the time of Augustine (d. 430), bishop of Hippo, who had allowed State authorities to use force against Donatist heretics.[7] The Merovingian King, Clovis (482–511), himself a convert to Catholic Christianity, used the excuse of their heretical Arianism as a reason for attacking his rivals, the Visigoths, and driving them from France into Spain.[8] The Visigoths themselves instituted one of the first campaigns of forced conversion of Jews *c.*600 CE, a campaign nonetheless denounced as contrary to church law by Pope Gregory the Great (590–604).[9] Charlemagne (r. 768–814) converted by force in his campaigns against the Saxons, and presumably as well against the Muslims; certainly the literary Charlemagne, fighting the forces of Saracen evil as portrayed in *The Song of Roland*, included his converting Muslims to Christianity.[10] While consequences for Muslims and pagans are only now beginning to be assessed, as for instance in the recent study of Cuman pagans by Nora Berend,[11] there is considerable literature now available on the situation of Jews within Christian Europe.

Consideration of medieval European Jews within the mainstream historiography once turned on Jewish contributions to the intellectual history of the period. Jews were responsible for some of the translations into Latin of Greek texts, coming by way of Hebrew or Arabic translations; such texts provided Christian intellectuals' access to and understanding of Greek philosophy. Despite the fact that Jewish and Muslim scholars produced many works in the thousand years of the European Middle Ages, such as important Hebrew commentaries written by Rashi (d. 1105 CE) or Maimonides (d. 1204 CE), or the works of such medieval Arabic philosophers as al-Ghazali (d. 1111 CE) and Avicenna (d. 1037 CE), only in very specialized intellectual histories are such scholars discussed along with the Christian theologians their work inspired.[12] There are also legal and economic issues about Jewish settlement within Christian Europe which are now being incorporated into mainstream history. Jewish communities in the West derived their legal status from that of Jews in the Roman Empire who had been allowed to practice their monotheism rather than being required to participate in the official rites of the Roman State. Once Christianity became the State religion, that special status for Jews was incorporated as part of the law of the Church, the canon law, which supposedly assured the protection of Jews from Christian proselytizing or forced conversion. The fact that canon law also prevented Jews from owning Christian slaves or serfs, however, limited their practice of agriculture to that of single family enterprises (often viticultural) or as Jewish tenants similar to Muslim ones living under Christian rule. Similarly, limitations of guild membership to Christians prevented Jews from practicing most crafts. Given such restrictions, many early medieval Jews had no option other than to engage in trade, an occupation made more possible by their religious networks. It was probably as an effort to encourage Jewish traders that Louis the Pious (r. 814–40), Charlemagne's son, recruited Jews from Italy, southern France, and Spain, where Jews were once concentrated, into the cities of the Rhineland and northern France. From northern France and particularly Normandy, where there was a large community in Rouen, Jews moved into England after 1066.

Carolingian charters of the ninth and tenth centuries gave special status to certain individuals who were considered the King's Jews. By the twelfth century these grants had become the model for grants of protection to entire

Jewish communities by kings, emperors, bishops, and counts. Unfortunately, such status left Jews wholly dependent on the ruler for protection. Even if such protection was effective, it was limited to the boundaries of a kingdom or province. This situation limited Jewish mobility as traders. As their ability to travel for trade deteriorated, Jews were pushed toward money-lending and provision of credit. Such credit was absolutely essential to the growing economy of the central Middle Ages because Church prohibitions against usury, which was construed as any lending at interest, prevented many Christians from lending at all.[13] As the money economy deepened, city life expanded, and taxation of Christians for foreign Crusades increased, resentment about Jewish lending and distrust of Jews increased, as did the identification of usury with Jews.

A change in mental attitudes of Christians toward non-Christians is traceable from c.1050 CE. As discussed earlier, this attitudinal change is closely tied to developments that led to the Crusades and to initial crusading victories. With the opening of the Crusades, Jews began to be attacked by mobs inspired by crusading rhetoric and sometimes led by crusading knights. Often local authorities were powerless to protect these Jewish communities. Moreover, rulers whose predecessors had protected the Jews became increasingly apt to abandon them in face of political, economic, or religious crises, or the need to be successful in Crusade.[14] The power of the clergy after the eleventh-century Gregorian Reform allowed the Church to be more repressive of individuals diverging from Catholic orthodoxy, both internally and on the frontiers. From the time of the Fourth Lateran Council in 1215, recognized sinners, such as prostitutes or lepers (whose disease was considered a result of sin), and non-Christians, like Jews, were all required to wear special clothing. They could live only in their respectively designated areas; this is the origin of separate Jewish quarters, the *ghettos* or *calls*, as well as of the red-light districts for prostitutes or isolated hospitals for lepers.[15] Periodic expulsions of Jews by secular rulers began, like that in 1182 when Philip Augustus, King of France (1180–1223), expelled Jews from all areas he then ruled. Eventually such rulers, in France and elsewhere, came to be associated with various vigilante efforts against Jews. Churchmen too were increasingly intolerant. Such ill-treatment was not confined to Jews or Muslims, but paralleled actions against all those declared by orthodox Christian leaders to be threats to public order, including heretics, witches, homosexuals, prostitutes, and lepers, who shared with Jews and Muslims their marked and ghettoized condition.

The following selections consider Christian attitudes toward Muslims and Jews in the central and late Middle Ages. The first, Chapter 12, from *Order and Exclusion* by Dominique Iogna-Prat, considers a treatise, *Against the Saracens*, written by Peter the Venerable, abbot of Cluny (d. 1156).[16] The treatise was based on a series of translations of Islamic texts which abbot Peter commissioned while in Spain. Until Iogna-Prat's analysis, most historians of medieval religion took this treatise at face value, as a disputation, and cited it as evidence of Peter's liberal-minded openness to new ideas.

Iogna-Prat contests that evaluation by a careful analysis of the translations made in preparation for the treatise and the rhetoric of *Against the Saracens* itself. He shows that the translations distorted Islamic ideas considerably, but that Peter was in no way preparing a discussion of the ideas of Islam, but only establishing a battery of arguments against it. Iogna-Prat suggests something of Peter's attitude as abbot of what had once been considered the most important monastic church in Christendom, and how he would have reacted to the version of Islamic practice and beliefs that he had in front of him. According to Iogna-Prat, the abbot of Cluny, totally confident of his place in a hierarchy of religious authority, dedicated to the life of chastity since childhood, must have found horrifying the sense of Islam as a religion of great sensuality: "What could be more insufferable to a Cluniac virgin, like Peter, who saw renunciation of the flesh as the best way to transform humanity into an angelic society, than the sexual debauchery promised in Allah's paradise?"[17] What is most clear from Iogna-Prat's analysis is that Peter the Venerable had no intention or willingness to debate Islam on its own terms.

Anna Sapir Abulafia's analysis in Chapter 13 considers a different treatise by Peter the Venerable, that called *Against the Jews*. Her analysis considers it as part of a whole group of early twelfth-century anti-Jewish "disputation" treatises written by Christian authorities. She focuses on the misunderstandings on both sides: on how Christians tended to view Jews as representing bodies, as opposed to the spiritual nature represented by Christians, but also how notions of embodiment that had become so central to Christian belief were very difficult for Jews to understand or accept. Indeed, insurmountable difficulties arose for any possible Jewish belief in Christianity's message because its central teaching was about the Incarnation, the embodiment of Christ:

> Essential to twelfth-century theological inquiries into the doctrine of the Incarnation was the question of how an ineffable, transcendent, majestic God could take on the body of a man. ... The urgency of the Incarnation as a topic of debate in this period's Jewish–Christian polemics lies in the fact that Jews were denying a doctrine which Christians were at great pains to explain among themselves.[18]

Abulafia suggests that their experiences with Jews in the emerging towns of the early twelfth century were also important in the opposition between Christians and Jews at this time. In her view, such experts on Christian doctrine as she has considered were men who faced great opportunities for social mobility or failure in this expanding society, and who must have found unsettling the extremely erudite biblical exegesis going on in the Jewish communities.[19] Was it because Jews were a source of such unease to Christian theologians' self-confidence that such uncompromising positions were developed on issues like the Incarnation and the presence of the body of Christ in the host at the moment of transubstantiation? Were doctrinal positions, such as that the consecrated Host was in fact the very body of Christ and that to do harm to any crumb of it was to harm Christ himself, defensive reactions to Jewish rejection of such ideas? Such doctrines about the Host had considerable potential for anti-Jewish consequences, as is seen in Chapter 14 by Rubin, but as Abulafia makes clear here and elsewhere, there was a second force at work. This was the development of what were considered "rational" arguments for Christian doctrine, which in fact made Christian authors increasingly impatient with the "obstinacy" of the Jews. Their ability to establish such rational Christianity, what Anselm had described as "faith seeking understanding," led Christian thinkers to assert that those who did not accept the "rational truths" of Christianity, for instance, the Jews, were less than rational, indeed less than human.

While in Chapter 13 Abulafia considers the development of beliefs about the embodiment of Christ among Christian intellectuals, Miri Rubin, in Chapter 14, turns to more popular beliefs. She considers the increased Eucharistic piety associated with Christians' belief in Christ's real presence in the consecrated Host, and the popular tales that arose about the need to protect this new relic, the Eucharistic "Host." If the Incarnate Christ was present in the consecrated Host, then it was logical to fear that any harm to the Host was harm to the very body of Christ. Rubin suggests that the difficulty that clergy had in persuading Christians of the doctrine of transubstantiation (the notion that the Eucharistic miracle caused the very body of Christ to appear on the altar where it became a relic, the consecrated Host) led to an elaboration of details making protection of the Host an impossibly difficult task. Every crumb of the consecrated Host came to be seen as the complete Christ and capable of being wounded; the image used was of a broken mirror in which each piece of glass could still infinitely reflect. Each piece must be carefully guarded. Such focus on the Eucharist created a situation ripe for the appearance of tales of Jewish Host desecration. Rubin is adept at reading the evidence of medieval art and literature that provides images of Jews attacking the Host. Medieval manuscript illustrations, stained glass, and even altarpieces depicted Jews obtaining consecrated Hosts and mutilating or destroying them; such tales are also found in collections from which medieval sermons were drawn and in the accounts of the miracles of the Virgin Mary. Such evidence seemed to justify violence against Jews who were threats to "the very body of Christ," which is what the consecrated Host had become. The anti-Judaism inspired in medieval audiences by such tales only expanded as a religious feast celebrating the Eucharistic body of Christ, or Corpus Christi, was established, and play-cycles to celebrate that feast were elaborated.

Although Iogna-Prat and Abulafia concentrate on the intellectual roots of an increasing intolerance, while Rubin emphasizes more popular media, all argue for increased anti-Judaic and anti-Islamic sentiments on the part of late medieval Christians. In contrast, David Nirenberg asks whether such Christian ethnocentrism and anti-Jewish and anti-Muslim feelings actually became more virulent in the later medieval centuries, or if they had always been there, but are only better documented for the later medieval centuries. Nirenberg's focus is on Spain, where Jews and Muslim were believed to have lived together along with Christians in a situation of tolerance called *convivencia*. As he suggests in Chapter 15, although confrontation reached the level of outright violence only on occasion, such a notion of *convivencia* is highly romanticized, and the harmonious existence of Jews, Muslims, and Christians in a state of mutual religious tolerance was probably rare. Moreover, what does *convivencia* mean in practice? Was this "living together" a life of perpetual hostility which could always, if allowed, erupt into outright violence? Nirenberg contends that Jewish–Christian, or Christian–Muslim interactions were always fraught with ambiguities – not always outright hate and violence, but not total tolerance on either side. Nirenberg investigates here the ritualized interactions that surrounded Easter Week in medieval Spain when the stoning of the Jewish quarter was a sport or drama under-taken primarily by youths and adolescents of the lower clergy who thought of it as a necessary part of their clerical rituals during Holy Week, and a means by which such young men proved or tested their Christian zeal. Although further violence against the Jews did not always occur and was opposed by the secular authorities, that such violence was anticipated is clear from the fact that Jewish communities were taxed for guards to protect them against it. Nirenberg's evidence for Easter actions against Jews comes from the fourteenth and fifteenth centuries, but he suggests that it can be read as evidence of well-established practices. It thus looks backwards to a consid-erably earlier, widespread, but often wholly under-reported, phenomenon.

NOTES

1   On different heresies' appeal to women, for instance, see Peter Biller, "Cathars and Material Women," published in *Medieval Theology and the Natural Body*, eds Peter Biller and A. J. Minnis (Woodbridge: York Medieval Press, 1997).

2   *Christianity and Judaism: Studies in Church History*, ed. Diana Wood, vol. 29 (Oxford: B. Blackwell, 1992), p. xv.

3   Richard Barrie Dobson, *The Jews of Medieval York and the Massacre of March 1190* (York: St Anthony's Press, 1974).

4   David Nirenberg, "Muslims in Christian Iberia, 1000–1526: Varieties of Mudejar Experience," *The Medieval World*, eds Peter Linehan and Janet T. Nelson (London: Routledge, 2001), pp. 60–76: Marc D. Meyerson, *The Muslims of Valencia in the Age of Fernando and Isabelle: Between Coexistence and Crusade* (Berkeley: University of California Press, 1991); Olivia Remie Constable, *Housing the Stranger in the Mediterranean World: Lodging, Trade and Travel in Late Antiquity and the Middle Ages* (Cambridge: Cambridge University Press, 2003).

5   See p. 398.

6   Cf. Jessica A. Coope, *The Martyrs of Cordoba: Community and Family Conflict in an Age of Mass Conversion* (Lincoln, NE: University of Nebraska Press, 1995).

7   Peter Brown, *Augustine of Hippo* (London: Faber, 1967), pp. 233–43.

8   For the story of Clovis and the Visigoths, see J. B. Bury, *The Invasion of Europe by the Barbarians*, ed. F. J. C. Hearnshaw (New York: Norton, 1967), pp. 247–53.

9 On forced conversions in Visigothic Spain and Gregory the Great's response, see Kenneth R. Stow, *Alienated Minority: The Jews of Medieval Latin Europe* (Cambridge, MA: Harvard University Press, 1992), pp. 47–54, and Bernard Bachrach, *Early Medieval Jewish Policy in Western Europe* (Minneapolis, MN: University of Minnesota Press, 1977).

10 Richard W. Southern, *Western Views of Islam in the Middle Ages* (Cambridge, MA: Harvard University Press, 1962).

11 Nora Berend, *At the Gate of Christendom: Jews, Muslims, and "Pagans" in Medieval Hungary, c.1000–c.1300* (Cambridge: Cambridge University Press, 2001).

12 Marie-Thérèse d'Alverney, "Translations and Translators," in *Renaissance and Renewal in the Twelfth Century*, eds Robert L. Benson and Giles Constable (Cambridge, MA: Harvard University Press, 1982), pp. 421–62; and Stow, *Alienated Minority*, esp. pp. 135–46.

13 Stow, *Alienated Minority*, pp. 29–101.

14 For attacks by Christian knights on Jewish settlements in the Rhineland, where Jews who resisted forced baptism were murdered, and many Jewish leaders martyred themselves and their families rather than convert, see J. A. Watt, "The Crusades and the Persecution of the Jews," *The Medieval World*, eds Peter Linehan and Janet L. Nelson (London: Routledge, 2001), pp. 146–62; Stow, *Alienated Minority*, pp. 102–20; Robert Chazan, *European Jewry and the First Crusade* (Berkeley, CA: University of California Press, 1987), esp. pp. 50–84; and *The First Crusade: The Chronicle of Fulcher of Chartres and Other Source Materials*, ed. Edward Peters (Philadelphia, PA: University of Pennsylvania Press, 1997).

15 On the Fourth Lateran Council and Jews, see Stow, *Alienated Minority*, pp. 242–51.

16 *Against the Jews* and *Against the Petrobrusian Heretics* are treated by Iogna-Prat in the longer work.

17 See p. 342.

18 See p. 348.

19 This argument is debated by Robert I. Moore, *The Formation of a Persecuting Society: Power and Deviance in Western Europe, 950–1250* (Oxford: Blackwell, 1987) and Robert Chazan, *Medieval Stereotypes and Modern Antisemitism* (Berkeley, CA: University of California Press, 1997), esp. pp. 78–88.

12

THE CREATION OF
A CHRISTIAN ARMORY
AGAINST ISLAM

Dominique Iogna-Prat

Increased suspicion by clerical and monastic authorities of "the other" within Christian society was matched by an increased awareness and suspicion of "others" at its borders. In particular, there was great fear and antipathy toward the Muslims or Saracens, as twelfth-century Christians often called them. Whereas, in later eras, warfare seemed the only effective response to these "followers of Islam," some twelfth-century Christians claimed to believe that it was possible to persuade Muslims, or indeed Jews, of their errors and to successfully convert them to Christianity, and some works were written that present dialogues or conversations between Jews and Christians as if they were actual exchanges on a level playing field. It is as such works of persuasion for the conversion of heretics, Jews, and Muslims that the three treatises by the abbot of Cluny, Peter the Venerable (d. 1156), Against the Jews, Against the Petrobrusians, *and* Against the Sect of the Saracens *(Contra sectam Sarracenorum), have usually been treated by Western historians.*

French medievalist Dominique Iogna-Prat suggests a very different interpretation of Peter's three treatises in the book from which this consideration of Against the Saracens *has been taken. According to Iogna-Prat, the treatises by Peter the Venerable were less well intentioned than they have been taken to be. Peter's* Against the Saracens, *like the other two treatises, is a work of considerable prejudice and dissimulation. Despite rhetorical flourishes about conversion, it was a work not really intended to convert, but to "arm against" Islam by preparing the reader with information (most of it in fact misinformation as it turns out) about that most vile religion.*

Iogna-Prat shows that Peter the Venerable was remarkably ill-informed about Islam and its history, despite the fact that he had commissioned translations of Islamic works for his own use. But, despite protestations to the contrary, Peter was very willing to use whatever rhetorical tools were at hand to argue against Islam, even when those arguments were based on a false reading of Islamic practice and history. Moreover, as Iogna-Prat shows, abbot Peter applied to the hoped-for conversion of the Muslims very inappropriate expectations about group conversions drawn from the writings of Bede the Venerable, who described the conversion of Ethelbert, the Anglo-Saxon king, and, with him, his tribe.

Iogna-Prat concludes that Peter's treatise had little lasting effect insofar as it survives only in a couple of manuscripts and was not widely copied or cited, but that it is important nonetheless in its reflection of an attitude that was prevalent among monastic writers at places like Cluny, whose self-opinion was high because they thought of themselves as operating at the very pulse-center of Christendom. Their tendency to deride and berate, rather than to attempt to understand their opponents, is a serious one because they saw themselves as so important.

Whether or not we agree wholly with Iogna-Prat about Cluny's twelfth-century importance, it is clear that Cluny and its abbot Peter the Venerable were well placed for the creation of "a Christian armory" of debating tools in the form of treatises not only against Islam, but against Jews and heretics as well. This selection comes from Dominique Iogna-Prat, Order and Exclusion, Christian Society Faces Heresy, Judaism and Islam, 1000–1150 *(Paris, 1998; Cornell, 2002), pp. 338–57; notes have been renumbered and many Latin quotes omitted.*

* * *

By a happy chance, we know how the abbot of Cluny, Peter the Venerable (d. 1156, became abbot in 1122) and his secretary, Peter of Poitiers (d. 1215), prepared and conducted the war of ideas against Islam. Between March and October 1142, Peter was on a long visit to Spain. There he visited Cluny's dependencies and saw Alfonso VII (d. 1157), the "victorious emperor" of Castile-León, whom he reminded of his family duty to give tribute to the church of Cluny.[1] On the battle-front of the Christian Reconquest, Alphonse was at the focal point in the struggle between the two branches of Abraham's descendants: the line of Hagar and Ishmael on the one hand versus that of Sarah and Isaac on the other, a scene that is represented on the tympanum of the southern door of the church of Saint Isidore at León.[2] During his stay, Peter encountered two men of letters who had learned Arabic to further their work on astronomy, Robert of Ketton (or Chester) (fl. 1143) and Herman of Dalmatia (d. 1154).[3] Investing an important sum in the enterprise, the abbot of Cluny decided to commission a translation of the Koran into Latin together with other books documenting "the heresy of Muhammad."[4] Meanwhile literate Muslims in Baghdad and the Islamic West had seen Arabic versions of the Christian Scriptures for over two centuries.[5] When Peter sent the translation of the Koran to Bernard of Clairvaux, encouraging him to "refute that pernicious error," he justified his initiative by the need to make available a "Christian armory."[6] This armory consisted of a corpus of texts on Islam usually referred to as the *Corpus toledanum* or *Collectio toledana* after the founder of the Spanish "school" of translation, Raymond, archbishop of Toledo (1125–52).[7] The corpus is made up of the following items:[8]

1   the *Fabulae Sarracenorum*, translated by Robert of Ketton from an unknown Arabic original, comprising a collection of Judeo-Muslim legends on the creation of the world and mankind, a chronology of the patriarchs and prophets, the story of Muhammad, and biographical sketches of the first seven caliphs;

2   the *Liber generationis Mahumeth* of Kitab Nasab Rasul Allah de Sa'id ibn-'Umar, translated by Herman of Dalmatia, recording the legend of the "prophetic light" passed down from Adam to Muhammad via Noah;

3   the *Doctrina Muhammad* of Masa'il 'Abdallah ibn-Salam, translated by Herman of Dalmatia, telling the story of four Jews led by Abdia who asked Muhammad one hundred questions about the Jewish Law;

4   the *Lex Sarracenorum*, the Koran as translated by Robert of Ketton; and

5   the *Epistola Sarraceni et Rescriptum Christiani*, a translation by Peter of Toledo (fl. 1120–60) and Peter of Poitiers of the *Apologia* or *Risala* of al-Kindi, possibly written in the first half of the ninth century and summarizing the main points of Islamic doctrine in the form of correspondence between a Christian and a Muslim.[9]

The *Collectio toledana* survives in complete form in Paris, Arsenal Library, manuscript 1162, accompanied by two texts by Peter the Venerable that serve to introduce it. The first of these, the "Letter About his Translations," was addressed to Bernard of Clairvaux (d. 1153). Its contents appear in extract form in another of Peter's letters (no. 111 in Constable's edition); this contains material on various subjects and was similarly addressed to Bernard.[10] Peter evidently wanted Bernard to be the first to read his translation; he sought to persuade Bernard to follow in the footsteps of the Latin Fathers and fight against heresy. Peter asserts to Bernard the useful nature of this "Christian arsenal" and invokes the examples of Solomon and David. Solomon helped to preserve the republic by building up arms in advance, though his own days were peaceful; David devoted resources to "ornament" in the form of a Temple for God. Although their preparations, argued Peter the Venerable, seemed of little immediate use, they had turned out to be of enormous value. Modifying Paul's words in II Corinthians 10.5, Peter tells Bernard that it is essential to fight with the spoken and written word against "every knowledge that exalteth itself against the height of God." Even if it fails to win converts, the effort at refutation ought to strengthen the least secure members of the Church.

The second text by Peter the Venerable in the Arsenal manuscript is entitled "Summary of All the Heresies of the Saracens" (hereafter referred to as "Summary"). It encapsulates the manuscript's contents. A short introductory rubric sets the tone. Muhammad is "the greatest forerunner of the Antichrist and the Devil's chosen disciple;" his genealogy "most foul and false;" his life and doctrine "impure and unspeakable;" his "fables . . . utterly derisory and insane."[11] Rubrics and marginal notes, written in a contemporary hand, maintain this unpleasant, indeed vengeful, theme throughout the manuscript. The

"Summary of All the Heresies of the Saracens" is, as its title clearly shows, a compendium of the "absurdities" to which "the most wretched and most impious man, Muhammad ... has delivered ... almost a third of humanity."[12] Peter begins his eighteen-part argument with the most serious charge. The Saracens or Ishmaelites reject the Trinity and acknowledge only God and his soul; the God of the Koran expresses himself in the first person plural, as "we" ("Summary," 1). Christological deviations follow ("Summary," 2). Muhammad's followers deny that Christ is the Son of God, because it is impossible to be a father without begetting. Jesus, they say is simply a sinless prophet, born of Mary without a father. He did not die, but escaped the murder planned for him by the Jews and flew to heaven, where he now lives bodily in the Creator's presence until the Antichrist should come. At that time he will come and kill the faithless with the power of his sword; he will convert the remainder of the Jews and restore the Christians, who, after the death of the apostles, turned aside from the teaching of the Gospels. Like all creatures Jesus is destined to die and then to be resurrected. At the Last Judgment, he is to assist God in his work, though he himself will not judge.

The essential part of the "Summary" is a succinct presentation of Muhammad's vile doctrine and life ("Summary," 3–16). Peter's announced intention is not to use untrue allegations, like the legend declaring that Muhammad was a Nicolaitan* ("Summary," 3), but the abbot of Cluny depicts Muhammad as a man of low extraction, uneducated, scheming, and violent, who sought to rule through terror ("Summary," 4). Realizing that he could not attain his ends by the sword, he tried to become king under the cover of religion, declaring himself to be God's prophet. The Arabs, though ignorant of idolatry, were not led by Muhammad to know the true God. They were simply led astray into the illusions of his heresy ("Summary," 5). Using a Nestorian heretic called Sergius as his intermediary, Satan had conveyed to Muhammad a corrupt reading of the Scriptures, which taught that the Savior was not God, and other apocryphal fables ("Summary," 6). The perdition became total when the Jews, too, contributed their nonsense. For Muhammad based his conceptions on the "best" Jewish and heretical Christian doctors, maintaining that Gabriel, whose name he knew from Scripture, transmitted the Koran to him "volume by volume" ("Summary," 7). His Christological teaching is, continues Peter, laughable. It fails to take account of the mystery of the Incarnation, for Muhammad sees Jesus as simply the greatest of the prophets and not God. At the hour of Judgment, Jesus, like Muhammad himself, simply intervenes to defend humankind ("Summary," 8). Paradise is not an angelic society unified in the vision of God and the supreme good, but a place flowing with milk and honey, a sensual world of infinite couplings with virgins and magnificent women.

* Nicolaitans, Arians (after Arius), Donatists, Eutychians, Macedonians, Manichaeans (after Mani), Nestorians, Pelagians, Sabellians (after Sabellius) were all ancient heresies; Petrobrusians were medieval heretics against whom Peter wrote.

A whole series of notes copied further on in the manuscript, in the margins or between the lines of the translation of the Koran, reveals the extent of the scribe's (or a reader's) incomprehension. When, in the opening section (Sura 2.23), the Koran speaks of "wives of perfect purity" inhabiting this paradise, a well-informed observer has clarified, "purified of menstruation and excretion." The implied objection, which quickly became a classic of Christian criticism of Allah's paradise, derived from reading literally the Koran's description of human existence there.[13] If the blessed feasted in the afterlife, what did they do with their bodily waste products? Encounters with Islam thus revived Christian discussion about the materiality of the resurrected body. In the tradition of the Latin Fathers, particularly Augustine, the clerics of the West gradually evolved the concept of a glorious resurrected body that was wholly physical, one possessed of all its members. Yet they emphasized that the Resurrection would change that body, in some way "shutting it down," rendering its sexual and alimentary functions obsolete.[14]

Peter's "Summary," meanwhile continues with Muhammad, the devil's creature, who represents the sum of all heresies. Like Sabellius, he denied the Trinity; like Nestorius he denied the divinity of Jesus. Finally, like Mani, he put the Savior to death ("Summary," 9). With the practice of circumcision, said to be taken from Ishmael, Muhammad unleashed all kinds of lasciviousness, setting a polygamous example with his own eighteen wives. As he evokes these damnable teachings and practices, Peter the Venerable also recalls Muhammad's piety in teaching charity and showing mercy. Rather like the unnatural monster depicted by the poet Horace, Muhammad has a human head with an equine neck and bird feathers.[15] Indeed, as Marie-Thérèse d'Alverny has pointed out, a small ink drawing is inserted at this point in Paris, Arsenal manuscript 1162, depicting "a long rectangular head extending into a feathered body and ending in a sort of fish's tail."[16] Muhammad was able to persuade rustic and uneducated populations to abandon their multiplicity of gods to worship a single God only ("Summary," 10). He thereby managed to become a king, mixing good and evil, truth and falsehood, providing fuel for the everlasting fire. After the fall of the Roman empire and with the consent of him "by whom kings reign" (Proverbs 8.15), the Arabs and Saracens took over most of Asia, the whole of Africa, and a part of Spain, all subjected to the empire of Muhammad and his error ("Summary," 11) – ruling "now almost half the world."[17]

Are Muhammad and his sectaries heretics or pagans? Peter acknowledges that they share several points of belief with Christians and proclaim several truths about the Lord. But the teachings they propagate are essentially false; they do not recognize baptism, the sacrifice of the Mass, penance, or any other Christian sacrament. They have therefore rejected more than any other heretics before them ("Summary," 12). Muhammad stands between Arius and Antichrist. The long rubric prefacing the "Summary," in Paris, Arsenal manuscript 1162 describes Muhammad as "the greatest precursor of Antichrist" and "the devil's chosen disciple." Like Arius, Muhammad refused to see Christ as the true son of God. Although the Antichrist will accept Christ neither as God, as Son of God, nor even as a good man, Muhammad did at least believe the Savior to be a prophet ("Summary," 13). Yet Peter sees this as a further cause for mistrust, since Augustine taught that the subtleness of the Evil One led him always to speak some truth and good about the Savior ("Summary," 15).

Peter ends his "Summary" by stating its aims. These notes, he tells us, are meant not as debating material but in order to sound an alert, to brief anyone willing and able to write against this heresy. Response is essential, for Muhammad's teaching is the only heresy to have gone thus far unopposed, even though it affects the greater part of the world. No one has even taken the trouble to define it ("Summary," 17). Hence Peter's acceptance of the task. He explains that he has taken advantage of visits to Spain to commission, at great expense, translators who will expose "that entire impious sect and the execrable life of its most wicked inventor." Peter had waited for a long time for another person to take up the pen, but in vain. In the end, it has fallen to him to raise a Christian voice against Muhammad and his followers ("Summary," 18).

The final words of the "Summary" are perhaps a passing shot at Bernard of Clairvaux, who, in spite of Peter's urging, had failed to launch into the expected refutation. Having supplied Bernard the fundamental texts of Islam in translations which he declared to be "very faithful," the abbot of Cluny believed that the main obstacle to a response had been overcome.[18] Information would lead to refutation. Yet Peter's optimism was ill-judged. Modern criticism has shown that the *Collectio toledana* texts are far from faithful to the Arabic originals. In particular, the translation of the Koran by Robert of Ketton, though never completely incorrect, was sufficiently inexact to lure Latin commentators into unfortunate interpretations. One instance, mentioned by Norman Daniel, will suffice to show the scale of the problem. Robert of Ketton never managed to translate the word "Muslim;" he avoided it by resorting to circumlocutions mostly drawn from the verb *credere* (to believe). He failed to understand that in Islam a "Muslim" "surrendered," "resigned," or "submitted" to God. He could only conceive of a Muslim as adhering to a body of beliefs.[19] His translation also contained some significant changes and omissions. Thus the Prophet's "unchanging word [that] has never harmed men" was truncated by Robert to simply the Prophet's "unchanging word." Robert could not conceive that Muhammad's preaching was capable of anything but harm.[20]

Peter of Poitiers' "Capitula"

Peter the Venerable had no option but to work on the long hoped-for refutation himself. It was his final work, written at the very end of his life.[21] His secretary, Peter of Poitiers, who had revised Peter of Toledo's translation of al-Kindi's *Apologia*, mapped out the treatise for him in a text called the

"Capitula," envisaging four books divided into a varying number of chapters. The first task was to defend the validity of the Jewish and Christian Scriptures, which had never been lost and whose tradition was extremely trustworthy. Then the abbot of Cluny would proceed to a personal attack on Muhammad, who was no prophet but a deviant, homicide, parricide, adulterer, and sodomite. Third and fourth, the treatise was to note the total lack of miracles performed by Muhammad and define precisely what his purported prophecy was. Thereby it would be proved that Muhammad's activity was not prophetic and that his "writing" consisted simply of variations on already known heresies, especially Manichaeism, and of nonsense found in the Talmud. The treatise was to end with an exhortation to conversion. A letter by Peter of Poitiers accompanied this sketch. In it the secretary made clear that the "Capitula" was only a plan, which his master could expand or prune as he wished. He hoped that the abbot of Cluny would not be shocked by the chapter concerning the "shameful abuse of women" attested both in the Koran and in the daily practice of the Saracens in Spain.[22] He ended by stressing the importance of refuting Christ's enemies as a whole. Since Peter had already written treatises that refuted the Jews and the "Provençal heretics" (the Petrobrusians), this proposed refutation of the Saracens would close the series.

Contra sectam Sarracenorum[23]

It is hard to say whether Peter the Venerable fully accomplished the task sketched out in Peter of Poitiers' "Capitula." There is no obvious answer. The abbot Peter's extant treatise, *Against the Saracens*, or *Contra sectam Sarracenorum*, consists only of two books, whereas the secretary's sketch called for four. It was long believed that two books had been lost. The scribe who copied the collection of Peter the Venerable's work contained in manuscript 381 of the Municipal Library at Douai notes at the end of the treatise (folio 195r2): "Two books are missing, which I have not been able to find." The sixteenth-century *Chronicon cluniacense* actually speaks of a treatise in five books.[24] Modern criticism has come to reject these venerable observations, concluding that the known version of *Against the Saracens* most probably contains the totality of Peter's text.[25] Did the abbot of Cluny perhaps leave the work unfinished when he died? Commentators generally think so. Medievalists Jean-Pierre Torrell and Denise Bouthillier have pointed to several internal references to later material that does not actually appear. They observe that *Against the Saracens* is barely a third of the length of either of his other two polemics, *Against the Jews* (*Adversus Iudeos*) and *Against the Petrobrusians* (*Contra Petrobrusianos*).[26] Without reopening the problem here, it is nevertheless noteworthy that, compared with Peter of Poitiers' sketch, the supposed gaps in the text as we have it would scarcely constitute two more books; far from it. On the contrary – though this is only a working hypothesis – it would seem that Peter the Venerable actually did complete his set task. Once he had demonstrated the robustness of the Jewish and Christian Scriptures and given lengthy treatment to the nature and history of prophecy, Peter had also dealt with the essential issue, Muhammad's "imposture." Having established that Muhammad was no prophet, what need had he to discuss further? The lack of biographical detail could be explained by the desire on Peter's part not to get enmeshed in personal attacks against Muhammad and thereby give gratuitous offense to the Saracens. Hence the neglect of Muhammad as homicide, parricide, adulterer, and sodomite, and, more generally, of the "shameful abuse of women." This absence is all the more understandable since the "Summary" had already said what needed communicating in criticism of Saracen morals, and the question of "Saracen lasciviousness" had already been raised in *Against the Jews*. If this hypothesis is valid, then *Against the Saracens*, with its limits and silences, should be regarded as the work Peter the Venerable intended. Such, in any event, is the reading offered here.

The impossibility of silence

The prologue to *Against the Saracens* (here identified as *CSS* for *Contra sectam Sarracenorum*) sets out to justify the long-contemplated enterprise of refuting Muhammad and his sectaries, those "most dreadful adversaries" (*CSS*, 1).[27] Having called upon the spirit of wisdom and the Paraclete (the Holy Spirit), Peter refers to the tradition of the Church Fathers who, possessed by the Spirit, "subverted, trod down, destroyed" anything "inimical" to the knowledge of God. He begins with an inventory of the chief heretics who were answered by the Fathers: Manichaeans, Arians, Macedonians, Sabellians, Donatists, Pelagians, Nestorians, Eutychians (*CSS*, 3–4). Relying on Jerome's (d. 340) *On Illustrious Men* (*De viris illustribus*), he pictures the men who became illustrious in their defense of orthodoxy: he labors to show that never in the Church's history did any heresy go unanswered (*CSS*, 5–7). Although he knew of no refutation of Sabellianism – the heretical belief in a single divine person with three names – those who fought the Arians have sufficiently answered it. Moreover heresies can contradict one another. Thus the Arians and the Macedonians were in opposition to the Sabellians; the first two groups acknowledged only the Father's divinity, while the last named repudiated the divinity of the Spirit. Alongside the Fathers gathered in Church councils, the illustrious men of orthodoxy even opposed those erring thinkers whose ideas had not been successful enough to attach their names to sects: Jovinian, who denied that virginity was a higher state than marriage; Helvidius, who argued against the perpetual virginity of Mary; and Vigilantius, who mocked the veneration of holy bodies and relics. Peter, then, describing himself as acting in the name of Church unity, made real in one faith, one baptism, one God, and one life eternal, asserts that it is impossible to do less than these illustrious predecessors. Following in their traditions means doing battle as they did. The iron law of tradition obliges Peter the Venerable and his contemporaries to fight against Islam, just as the Fathers fought heresy. The Fathers, he says, were never silent; they refuted all error, even the "barely heretical." Otherwise the Church, identified with the bride of the Song of Songs 4.7, could not be presented to Christ as "fair" and "spotless" (*CSS*, 8–9). Peter believes it to be even more dangerous to remain silent now, inasmuch as Muhammad's "error" is more widespread than was Arianism, though that heresy contaminated numerous barbarian and Roman princes in many countries. Muhammad's "frenzy," more dangerous than all other known heresies put together, has gained kingdoms for the devil in three parts of the world, especially in Asia. Now Europe is at stake; Spain is already affected (*CSS*, 10–11).

Yet these "dreadful adversaries," are they "of us"? Are they such as "went out from us" (1 John 2.19)? Ought one simply to answer errors arising within the Church and ignore "alien, extra-ecclesiastical errors"? Indeed, though, how are Muhammad and his sectaries to be characterized? Are they heretics or pagans? There is no clear answer. They are like heretics when they lose themselves in Christological deviations; they are like pagans when they reject and deride the Church's sacraments. Peter had already touched on this issue in *Against the Petrobrusians*, when he noted that the Muslims did not sacrifice.[28] The question therefore remained open. Now, Peter decides to adopt a dual strategy: oppose Muslims as heretics and resist them as pagans. Again, Peter explains that tradition in the shape of Justin, Irenaeus, Augustine, and many other Church Fathers offers numerous examples of resistance, with their various writings "against the Pagans" (*CSS*, 12–16).

Within the perspective of a dual struggle thus defined, however, is not the linguistic barrier insurmountable, given the Latins' ignorance of their heretical and pagan adversaries' language? Peter is undaunted. Ignorance means inability to resist and the overriding necessity of answering the Muslims had driven him directly to the Arabic sources themselves, translation of which he commissioned in 1142, while visiting Spain.[29] Moreover, what can work in one direction might also work in the other. Peter's own treatise could possibly be translated into Arabic and help to bring Muhammad's followers out of their errors. For, he argues, are not the Scriptures translated into Latin and Latin Fathers translated into Greek (*CSS*, 19)? Peter's declaration of intent does not seem to have been accompanied by a real effort to have his *Against the Saracens* translated into Arabic.[30] Even so, the translations he has had made into Latin will serve the Church as a "Christian armory" to aid in the struggle against the "hidden thoughts" of Christians inclined to the view that the impious Muslims are not absolutely without piety or wholly outside the truth (*CSS*, 20). Here Peter acknowledges the temptations of Islam and hints that the Christian body is already infected here and there by the Islamic disease. He does not specify, but no doubt had in mind, the zones of contact between Christians and Muslims, especially in Spain, where adherents of the two religions lived side by side.[31] There, combatting Islam was a matter of internal policing. Peter recognizes that "the Spirit breatheth where he will" and the success of his refutation is in the hands of God. Yet Peter, the abbot of Cluny, does not doubt that he will succeed. Following his predecessors on this inspired route, he cannot imagine being mistaken and his work fruitless. It will be a means of conversion, a help in fighting the enemy, or simply useful to Christians (*CSS*, 21).

The impossibility of not hearing

The main aim of the first book of *Against the Saracens* is to determine the bounds of the argument. On what ground are Muslim and Christian to meet? Such is the question Peter begins with, having briefly introduced himself as "Gallic by tribe, Christian by faith, abbot by office" and declaring a real willingness to meet Islam across the geographical, religious, and cultural divide:

> It seems strange, and perhaps indeed it is, that I, a man in a place far from you, speaking a different language, divorced from you by creed and customs, leading a life alien from yours, should write from the farthest corners of the west to you, the men in the east and south, addressing in words those whom I have never seen and perchance never shall see. I do indeed address you, not as our men often do, with arms, but with words, not with violence but reason, not with hate but love.[32]

This declaration of his intentions, the touchstone of a rose-tinted legend of Peter the Venerable as the apostle of nonviolence, is too famous and has been too often over-interpreted to be allowed to pass without some placing of it in context. What lies behind the appeal to "words . . . reason . . . love"? Peter immediately proceeds to explain the two driving forces behind his expression of "reasoned love" (*CSS*, 24–33). First is the need to obey the "Christian authority" that teaches that the Creator loves his creatures before they come to know him; as Matthew 5.45 says: "[God] maketh his sun to rise upon the good and the bad." Second is the need to conform to reason. Scripture says (Ecclesiasticus 13.19): "Every beast loveth its like; so also every man loves him that is nearest to himself." Animate beings, like man, "seek out [*consectantur*] those whom they sense to be similar or of like form to themselves."[33] The use of the verb *consector*, a form of *consequor*, is significant: it means as much "to seek after eagerly" as "to pursue," "to chase," "to follow with hostility." The desire to seek out those who are like oneself thus has as much to do with attraction within the species as with rejection of those outside it. Peter addresses himself to his adversaries as to fellow "rational men," who will not by their nature be deceived, not even because of the strong ties of friendship and kinship or passionate love. Do not the arts, he says, teach as much? Beginning with philosophy, as practiced in Greece and among the Latins, Persians, or Indians, we find that all the sages do not keep silent but talk and argue in their seeking after truth, the nature of God, and the "non-created essence." Such, too, is the message of Christ, who, through his apostle

334

Peter (I Peter 3.15), urged his followers to be ready always "to satisfy everyone that asketh you a reason of that hope which is in you."

The search for truth is an open matter. Error alone seeks to hide. The refusal to discuss leads to darkness. Does not this exactly describe the situation of Muhammad and his followers? The rumor is that they will hear nothing that goes against their laws and customs, and that the merest word is met instantly with stones and swords.[34] Their very law forbids discussion: "Do not argue with those possessing the law. For bloodshed is better than a dispute." Peter says much about this recommendation, which he holds to be "asinine stupidity," contrary to human reason (*CSS*, 35–48). In fact, Peter's horror stems from a misunderstanding. The first sentence quoted, "Do not argue with those possessing the law," comes from al-Kindi's *Apologia*.[35] The second, "For bloodshed is better than a dispute," is a faulty reading of Suras 2:191 and 2:217, portions of the Koran which in reality are far from recommendations to kill infidels rather than debate with them.[36] Peter wonders who these "possessors of the law" might be. They cannot be, he says, the pagan Saracens who lived before Muhammad; nor the Greeks and Romans, who had simple human laws to keep order and help run the republic. The law referred to here is the divine law; therefore only Jews and Christians are referred to. So, the words are Satan's, for who else could declare "such absurdities"? Satan knows that he cannot effectively challenge the divine law, even with arms. He is familiar with both the constancy of the Maccabees and the valor of the Christian martyrs. He knows that nothing can oppose the outward spread of the divine word, as taught by Psalm 18 (19).5 and the apostle Paul's words in Romans 10.18. All Satan can do is to interpose arms and thereby remove those who might have heard and been saved. This is why Satan-Muhammad teaches that "bloodshed" is better than "disputation." Moreover, says Peter, this assertion defies the rules of logic: it is possible to compare two good things or two bad things, but not a good thing with a bad thing or a bad thing with a good thing.

Having drawn strength from this argument, Peter prevails on his adversaries not to impede the free circulation of that "charity" that unites all men, not just Christians. His opponents are not asked to agree, but simply to listen without resorting to stones or arms. It is sufficient to follow the example of the Christians who argue with the Jews, he says. Hearing the Jews blaspheme, the Christians do not get into a fury, but listen patiently and make scholarly, wise replies (*CSS*, 49–50). Displaying a most sanguine view about the treatment of slaves in the Christian world, Peter goes so far as to mention Muslim prisoners of war: they may have lost their freedom to return home, but they have not forfeited their freedom of speech.[37] All he seeks is a hearing, along the lines so often seen in the history of Christian missions. Drawing liberally on Chapter 25 of the first book of the Venerable Bede's (d. 735) *Ecclesiastical History*, Peter cites the example, virtually contemporary with Muhammad's own lifetime, of the conversion of the English under King Ethelbert who ruled in the years 560–615. He reports in detail how the mission, sent by

Pope Gregory the Great (590–604) and led by the Roman missionary Augustine (d. 604), was received in England. When the missionaries landed on the Isle of Thanet, Ethelbert received them in the open air, taking care not to let them enter anywhere where they might commit sorcery. In response to Augustine and his companions' enthusiastic news of eternal bliss in heaven, an endless paradise, the king replied that these were very fine promises but "new and uncertain" and that he could not abandon overnight what he had long since honored. Even so, Ethelbert offered to let the missionaries stay in his country at his own expense and preach conversion as they wished. The story is a godsend to Peter. From it he is able to argue that Ethelbert's example exemplifies the behavior of all kings. There is no reason why the Saracens should exempt themselves from this universal rule and refuse a hearing to the Christians' missionary appeal (CSS, 51–4).

Defense of the Scriptures

Now that Muhammad's followers have been forced to listen by Peter's argument, "combat" can begin.[38] Peter starts by attacking Muhammad's law, now available to him in his own language. How astonished he is to discover this mixture of borrowings from the Laws of the Hebrews and that of the Christians! But if Muhammad accepts some part of the Scriptures, then why not all of them? Either the Scriptures are bad, in which case they should be wholly rejected; or they are true and should be taught. Unlike the fallible, perfectible laws of humanity, the law of God is to be accepted or rejected in its totality (CSS, 55–7).

Next, Peter answers an objection put out by his adversaries concerning the reliability of the Scriptures. They allege that the original text was lost long ago and that the modern text is a reworking by subsequent generations, mixing truth and falsehood (CSS, 58–86); an early task of Islam was thus to filter out the true and condemn the false. Peter was probably aware of the boast by educated Muslims, like al-Bayi, that the whole of Islam, regardless of geography, read the same "Book" – "without adding a single word, diverging by so much as a vowel or a diacritical mark."[39] The Muslims saw the Christians as corrupters or, as the anonymous marginal hand of Arsenal manuscript 1162 put it, "variatores".[40] What is the basis, asks Peter, for this assertion that the Christian Scriptures have been falsified? In the collection of translated texts at his disposal, Peter can see no foundation for such talk. What he does see, however, is a collection of fables unworthy of men so expert in the things of this world. The first of these ludicrous fables tells the story of the Jews' loss of their sacred books on the way back from captivity in Babylon: the ass "carrying the Law" having wandered off (CSS, 64). Now suppose, for argument's sake, says Peter, that this absurd story were true. The obvious question to ask then would be whether in the entire exiled Jewish world there was no other written copy of the Law. Would a single volume have been enough to serve so many scattered people? The example of contemporary European Jewry, he says, contradicts this hypothesis. Peter asserts that every community of fifty, even twenty Jewish inhabitants, keeps a complete copy of the Law, the Prophets, and other Hebrew writings in their synagogue. Long before the destruction of the place of sacrifice, the Temple, by the Romans and their expulsion from Jerusalem, the Jews had copies of their sacred books in cities throughout the Diaspora. One might as easily suggest that the Koran is to be found only at Mecca (CSS, 66–9)! Moreover, Scripture itself proves the story of the errant ass to be a fable. In Nehemiah 8.1–6, moreover, Ezra, one of the erstwhile captives, is depicted opening and reading the book of the Law of Moses. Are we to deem the holy Ezra a falsifier? If the story is a fable, why do people go on pretending that Scripture, which is so old and widespread, has been falsified? And where is the falsification supposed to be: in the Law, in the Prophets? Muhammad refers to both. Peter thus arrives at the "probable and necessary" conclusion that the rumor casting doubt on the validity of the Old Testament is baseless (CSS, 74–5).

What is true of the Old Testament is equally so of the New. Peter now addresses the false notion that the foundation scriptures of Christianity were lost during the persecutions of the early centuries, then rewritten on the basis of surviving scraps and conjecture centuries later (CSS, 77). To be sure, says Peter, there were persecutions, particularly under Diocletian, who required by edict the destruction of churches and Christian books. Yet can we believe that all the books were destroyed? When the edict was made, did no one think to hide a copy? There were Christians throughout the empire. What about those in the kingdoms of the Persians, Medes, Arabs, and other places not subject to Rome? No part of the world remained ignorant of the Gospel message, which was spread in every language and written down everywhere (CSS, 80). So abbot Peter asserts that the texts of the evangelists and apostles have been transmitted without interruption down to his own day and "by most sure intermediaries."[41] The apostle Peter, instructed directly by Christ, and Paul, the beneficiary of an invisible revelation, spread the Gospels of Mark and Luke from Jerusalem to the far reaches of the west. The Gospel of John was revealed in Asia Minor, and the Gospel of Matthew in the regions of the south. Rome, "the head of the world's churches," kept these writings pure of all falsification from the time of the apostle Peter down to the present (CSS, 81–2). The same is true of the apostles' writings; these had been dispersed throughout the world, have come down to the present, and must be preserved "as long as the heaven hangeth over the earth" (Deuteronomy 11.21). In so far as all or any part of the universally diffused Christian scriptures have suffered corruption, this can have occurred only among some, not among all the peoples of the earth. Otherwise the conclusion would have to be that all the earth's books have been corrupted and no one realizes except – an even greater absurdity – the Saracens: "The Saracens know the business of others, while the Christians don't even know their own!"[42] Declarations of this sort, says Peter, are but "the emptiest of jests" (CSS, 83–5). Finally, if the Gospel is false, it must be admitted that the Koran must be too, since a falsified book can only spread errors. At the end of Book 2 of *Against the Saracens,* Peter will return to this matter, maintaining that it needs only one falsehood to contaminate the totality of a text. Peter's all-or-nothing logic is intended to force the Saracens to accept the books in the Jewish and Christian canons, from which Muhammad himself drew inspiration. Basing his argument on these writings, whose authority he believes he has now fully established, abbot Peter now prepares to demonstrate to his opponents in Book 2 that their law is false and that Muhammad is neither a prophet nor an envoy of God, but a falsifier (*CSS,* 87–8).

What is prophecy?

Book 2 opens with an appeal to the humanity of those to whom it is addressed, according to the principle enunciated earlier, that man seeks out those like himself (*CSS,* 89). Out of love for humanity, Peter the Venerable echoes Isaiah 44.18–21 to warn his interlocutors against the sin of idolatry. He admits that Muhammad's followers do not worship wood or stone; but those who follow Satan will inevitably drift in that direction, as so many Jewish and Christian examples testify. Failing to worship the true God or ceasing to obey him amounts to idolatry. It is a guilty deed that will end in the same darkness and reign of Antichrist, which will swallow up pagans, Jews, and heretics alike (*CSS,* 90–3).

Peter's aim is to show his adversaries their error so that they may realize the risks they run. He goes to the heart of the debate. Was Muhammad really a prophet, the "seal of the prophets," the transmitter of revelation, the Lord's messenger? Peter, abbot of Cluny, means to prove the opposite and he calmly proceeds to define what prophecy is.[43] He begins with his namesake, the apostle Peter, who, drawing strength from the Lord's transfiguration and resurrection, taught that prophetic inspiration lay not in the human being but in the Holy Spirit (2 Peter 1.21). Building on this, Peter the Venerable gives prophecy a broad definition that goes well beyond the etymological:

> Prophecy is the proclaiming of unknown things, be they past, present, or future, made not by human invention but by divine inspiration. ... The prophet is the one who manifests to mortals unknown things of past, present, or future time, not having been taught by human cognition but inspired by the Holy Spirit.[44]

As an example of retrospective prophecy, Peter cites the example of Moses speaking of the Creation. As "a certain great man of ours" – Gregory the Great – put it, "A man has spoken about that time when there was no man" (*CSS,* 98).[45] The Book of Numbers reports Moses' prophecies about the then present, accurately predicting, first of all in Numbers 16. 30–3, the damnation of Korah, Dathan, and Abiram (*CSS,* 99). Then the episode ends in verse 46 with Moses announcing to Aaron, "Already wrath is gone out from the

Lord," a statement vindicated by events. Regarding future prophecy, Peter has a wide choice of examples from before and after Moses: Enoch, Noah, Jacob, Joseph, Samuel, David, Isaiah, Elijah, Elisha, Jeremiah, and many others (CSS, 100–1). Among them Isaiah prophesied "from afar" the coming of the virgin-born Lord, as well as Christ's baptism, miracles, and passion (CSS, 104–5).[46] Isaiah and Jeremiah both prophesied events that took place before and after their own deaths (CSS, 107–8). A little later, Peter cites the example of Elisha, in 2(4) Kings 6.8–12, warning the king of Israel about traps set by the king of Syria. Peter points out that Muhammad's inability to foresee the outcome of his various military exploits is a perfect counterexample of this (CSS, 118–19).[47]

The Koran, says Peter, contains no prophecy by Muhammad. Does his prophetic reputation rest on some other text? According to Muhammad's "genealogy" – Peter's reference is to the Liber generationis Mahumeth – the "Prophet" is supposed to have foretold that twelve caliphs would descend from his family and to have given the names of the first three of them, Abu-Bakr, 'Umar, and 'Uthman. Yet the Koran, says Peter, contradicts such a prophecy. Actually, what Peter cites as a warning from the Koran comes from al-Kindi's Apologia: "Reject everything that does not concur with these words."[48] As the Koran contains no prophecy, Peter maintains that the episode from the Liber generationis Mahumeth should be rejected as inconsistent with the revelation. Even if he had had access to other sources, like the hadith [the traditional accounts of Mohammed's life], reporting signs intended to prove the sincerity of Muhammad's prophecy, Peter would still have held to the same negation based on the Koran. Schooled in the Christian continuum between scriptural miracles and extraordinary signs recorded in the hagiographic tradition, Peter manifestly failed to conceive that Islam could distinguish between the Muhammadan prophetic model, which essentially allowed little space for miracles, and hagiographic models.[49]

Then comes the supposed Muslim defense: that God did not have Muhammad accomplish any miracles because his audience would not have believed in them. Peter again relies on al-Kindi's Apologia: "They would not have believed these, just as they did not believe the others."[50] The abbot of Cluny makes an immediate challenge. What "others" are these? Surely not Moses or Christ, for these both accompanied their prophetic words with signs (CSS, 124–6). In any case, such could not be the will of God, since it is impossible to get anyone to believe by simple faith in words. In Peter's view God's word needs to be efficacious and accompanied by tangible proof. In Against the Jews Peter had already declared his complete perplexity at Islam's success in the absence of any miracles.[51] How could such empty verbiage command belief? Because it promised sensual pleasure in all its forms in paradise? Peter denies that Muhammad was a prophet, even if he did claim to be one; indeed, real prophets, like Amos, have refused the name of prophet out of humility.[52] Muhammad has revealed nothing about things that have happened or are to happen. His views on the "sensual pleasures" of heaven or on hell are not based on any proof. What witnesses, dead or alive, did Muhammad advance to support his prophecies about the Last Things? Peter, a specialist on miracle accounts and visions of the afterlife, sometimes false and sometimes believable, knows this territory. Hence the efforts deployed in *Against the Petrobrusians* to distinguish false from true visions and the precautions taken in his *On Miracles* to verify the reliability of testimonies to the supernatural.

Since he was no prophet, Muhammad cannot, says Peter, have been the "seal of the prophets." Book 2 of the whole treatise (in the state in which we have it, at least) ends by examining this matter. Peter clarifies and widens the definition of prophecy given earlier. Good prophets, he says, need to be distinguished from bad. Bad prophets lead blameworthy lives and their preaching is false, even if they manage to speak truth on occasion, as do diviners, augurs, sooth-sayers, or magicians. Good prophets, whose lives are praiseworthy and whose preaching is true, fall into three categories: those who announce universalities, those who predict particular events, and those who are capable of both, such as Isaiah, Jeremiah, and Daniel. Their common feature is that their pronouncements are borne out by events (*CSS*, 131–2). Bearers of universal truths speak of universal salvation: namely, the work of Christ (*CSS*, 133). From the time of Christ to the end of time, says Peter, there can be no further universal prophecy. With the Savior, all universal prophecy was given; some things were accomplished then, and some events are yet to come. The "seal of the prophets" was not therefore Muhammad but John the Baptist, whom the Saracens call "the son of Zacharias" (*CSS*, 136–7). The only prophets that were left were those prophets whose pronouncements were intended for certain people or individuals, such as the apostle Paul, who foretold many events that have happened or are yet to come in the Church of Christ. Among the things that have happened, abbot Peter points to Paul's prophecy in II Timothy 4.3–4: "There shall be a time when they will not endure sound doctrine," a prediction that the "fables" of Muhammad and of the Talmud have proved right (*CSS*, 138).

Having spoken of the apostle Paul, Peter the Venerable says that he will not speak of the many other examples of particular prophecy that he could mention. His pretext is that his opponents would refuse to believe him; they do not even believe in God (*CSS*, 139–40). Beyond these convoluted justifications, it is possible to suspect, along with Jean-Pierre Torrell, some embarrassment on Peter's part in the face of the ever-vexed question of prophecy in the post-apostolic age, after the Church became institutionalized and there were fewer inspired voices.[53] But his silence nevertheless begs the question of why the majority of the prophets cited are Hebrews. Peter extricates himself with a remark that to him seems sensible. He explains to his opponents [the Muslims] that these prophets are in fact their prophets as well. Ishmael, their forebear, was born, like Isaac, of Abraham, who had sired Ishmael by Hagar and Isaac by Sarah. Thus ties of consanguinity – not to mention language, writing, and the practice of circumcision – included the Saracens in the prophetic tradition of the Hebrews (*CSS*, 145–6). Yet again

Peter's all-or-nothing logic comes into play: the teachings of the prophets are to be either accepted in their entirety or totally rejected. Peter then finishes his long discussion on prophecy by concluding that Muhammad cannot have been a prophet in either the universal or the particular sense, or else he was a bad prophet, depraved and false (*CSS*, 151–4).

A debate of the deaf

The medievalist Norman Daniel has successfully traced the history that made meaningful debate between Islam and Christianity an impossibility in the Middle Ages. He points to the "air of unreality" in Latin literature concerned with the Muslims.[54] The debate between "fellows," the meeting of minds sought by Peter the Venerable between men united by reason and charity, was actually unrealizable. The "discussion" was abortive almost from the start. The necessary conditions for a proper exchange were far from being fulfilled. Peter thought that obtaining a translation of the corpus of Islam's fundamental authorities would put him in a position to challenge his adversaries. Yet he demonstrably failed to see the limitations inherent in his approach. As the noted scholar of medieval Arabic manuscripts Marie-Thérèse d'Alverny has commented, moreover, the rubrics and glosses accompanying the texts compiled in the *Collectio toledana* were "inspired by a spirit of systematic denigration," which betrays a manifest lack of serenity in the face of the adversary.[55] Lacking accuracy, his translations led Peter into some dire misunderstandings. Above all, he seems not to have gauged the necessity of two expository efforts that were indispensable if he was to have an even minimal chance of making intellectual contact with his interlocutors. Unable to gain an overall view, Peter always quoted the Koran out of context and failed to distinguish, in the Islamic legacy, between revealed text and tradition.[56] Peter behaved like that "monk of France," whom al-Bayi had refuted in the 1080, charging him with moving quotations "out of their proper place" and "using them outside of their meaning."[57]

It is, as medievalist Jean Jolivet thinks, unclear whether the abbot of Cluny was involved in an "exchange" of views – which would imply the recognition of an opponent.[58] Debate was an unrealistic expectation. Peter does not hide his irritation in the blocking procedures that, by an extremely eloquent projection mechanism, he attributes to adversaries supposedly unwilling to engage in debate. The circumstances leave him with no alternative but to verbally abuse these cowards and, incidentally, enrich the rhetorical arsenal necessary to Latin Christendom in order to defeat Islam or at least resist it. Contrary to the pacific declaration of his intentions placed at the start of Book 2 and cited ad nauseam by historians of the twelfth-century Renaissance – words rather than arms, reason not force, love not hate[59] – Peter sees himself compelled to make war. For a twelfth-century Christian intellectual and a Cluniac monk, there was only one war, the fierce, always uncertain war against the devil. Regardless of the dialectical nuances that here and there adorn *Against the Saracens*, the struggle with Islam could be reduced in the end to demonizing Muhammad and his followers. In a mental universe that was divided, in anticipation of the Last Things, into "good" and "evil" parts, to fail to follow the path of obedience to the true God was to fall into the territory of the Evil One. There was no room for fine distinctions: Jews, heretics, and pagans all belonged in the bottomless abyss of all the abominations. Compared with this, did it really matter if declared monotheists were presented as idolaters?

In the history of demonizing the other in the West, Peter the Venerable's treatment of Islam is interesting from two points of view. First, he shows the place ascribed to Islam on a progression of gradually increasing power attributed to the Ancient Enemy. Muhammad represented an intermediate stage between Arius, the worst of heretics, and Antichrist. That final satanic manifestation before the last great unloosing at the End of Time was Peter's justification for dealing with Muhammad and his followers by a process of summation. In accordance with a conception developing in Hispanic apocalyptic thought since the ninth century, Islam was thus presented as the accumulation of all heresies.[60] It contained every possible bad influence, including Christian heresies and Jewish Talmudic fables. With their ambiguous identity, the Muslims were at once heretical and pagan. One sees therefore why Peter could not avoid confronting these worst possible enemies. Despite his generally steely personality, Peter was eaten up by anxiety when he beheld in his opponents the inverse image of himself. Not negligible as a member of the Church establishment, the abbot of Cluny found himself brutally confronted by a religion with neither priests nor sacramental mediation. Moreover, what could be more insufferable to a Cluniac virgin, like Peter, who saw renunciation of the flesh as the best way to transform humanity into an angelic society, than the sexual debauchery promised in Allah's paradise? Entering the monastery as a child, Peter was the living incarnation of the sexual phobia of monastic men: contemplatives, men of the spirit, intent on keeping women beyond the bounds of the monastery and repressing any sexual awakening among the boys trained there.[61] The demons pervading Peter's *On Miracles* cause lay-folk to commit adultery in the world and adults inside the monasteries to fornicate with their young charges.[62] Obsession with Islam as a religion "of the lascivious" reflects his own insecurity of identity. Would the blessedness of the afterlife perhaps not include the sublimation of sex? It would be centuries before this heavy burden would lift, enabling nineteenth-century French poet Paul Verlaine (d. 1896) to sing of "endless harems" and Victor Hugo's (d. 1885) near contemporary ficitional character Grantaire to proclaim that "Mahom has some good."[63]

As he watched for signs of Antichrist's advance, Peter the Venerable revealed on several occasions how worried he was about the gains made by Islam; it had already come to dominate half, if not two-thirds, of the earth. His preoccupation was all the greater because Islam's expansion was coming to block Christian proselytizing during a period when the Latin West was also in a fully conquering phase. Several times in *Against the Saracens*, Peter defines Christianity as a universal religion. In his "Sermon on the Transfiguration of the Lord," he thrills to the voice of God sounding from the clouds (Matthew 17.5) and exhorts not simply the faithful but pagans and infidels to hearken to so clear a message.[64] Within this perspective, Peter's war of ideas against Islam came down to one proselytism against another. What was important for him was to have an "arsenal" of information and proven responses at hand in case there was a confrontation. This was far from a missionary effort, which did not come to the fore before the activities of the mendicant orders in the thirteenth century. This was an attempt to steady the faithful.[65] Hence his reaffirmation of the basic principles of the "Unity of the Church" – to imitate the Fathers in fighting the least deviation and, above all, acknowledge the Church's deep roots in a body of writings faithfully transmitted by tradition. Whatever Peter's intentions for his writing *Against the Saracens*, it was for internal consumption by Christians. Yet even on this limited front, Peter's impact seems to have been faint. The medieval reception of *Against the Saracens*, of which there are only two known surviving manuscripts, was very limited.[66] The attempt at an interpretative, reasoned approach to Islam by teaching was short-lived. Though his resources were more sophisticated than those of many other twelfth-century clerics, the abbot of Cluny, too, ended up feeding the stereotypes of Islam as an empire of the devil.

NOTES

1   Charles J. Bishko, "Peter the Venerable's Journey to Spain," in *Petrus Venerabilis 1156–1956* (Rome: Herder, 1956), pp. 163–75; Damien van den Eynde, "Les principaux voyages de Pierre le Vénérable," *Benedictina* 15 (1968): 58–110. The title "Emperor Victorious" used for him by Peter the Venerable in *Contra sectam Sarracenorum*, ed. Reinhold Glei, in *Petrus Venerabilis Schriften zum Islam*, Corpus Islamico-Christianum, series latina I, pp. 30–225 (Altenberge: CIS Verlag, 1985), hereafter *CSS*, 17, p. 54, lines 25–6 had been adopted since the reign of Alfonso VI (1055–92).

2   John Williams, "Generationes Abrahae: Reconquest Iconography in León," *Gesta* 16 (1977): 3–14, connects the iconography of the tympanum with Peter the Venerable's activities and work, although it is impossible to say whether the tympanum's iconography influenced Peter or the writings of Peter influenced the tympanum. Everything depends on the tympanum's date: Williams dates it to the late 1140s, while most art historians place it in the 1110s.

3   On Herman, see *A History of Twelfth-Century Western Philosophy*, ed. Peter Dronke (Cambridge: Cambridge University Press, 1988), pp. 386–404.

4   Peter the Venerable, *Summa totius haeresis Sarracenorum*, ed. Reinhold Glei, in *Petrus Venerabilis Schriften zum Islam*, Corpus Islamico-Christianum, series latina I, pp. 2–22 (Altenberge: CIS Verlag, 1985), hereafter "Summary," 18, p. 20; *CSS*, 17, p. 54, lines 14–22.

5   In his reply to the "monk of France," al-Bayi confirms that he has read the Gospels translated into Arabic; see Abdel Majid Turki, "La lettre du 'moine de France' à al-Muqtadir Billah," *Al-Andalus* 31 (1966): 73–153, here 140, and n. 130 for earlier attestations.

6 Peter the Venerable, *Epistola de translatione sua*, ed. Reinhold Glei, in *Petrus Venerabilis Schriften zum Islam*, Corpus Islamico-Christianum, series latina I, pp. 30–225 (Altenberge: CIS Verlag, 1985), pp. 22–8, ch. 4, p. 26, lines 7–8.

7 On the "school" of Toledo – or rather the nebula of translators somewhat arbitrarily grouped under this common head – see Roger Lemay, "Dans l'Espagne du XIIe siècle: les traductions de l'arabe au latin," *Annales: Économies, Sociétés, Civilisations* (hereafter *Annales ÉSC*), 18 (1963): 639–68; Marie-Thérèse d'Alverny, "Translations and Translators," in *Renaissance and Renewal in the Twelfth Century*, eds Robert Louis Benson and Giles Constable (Cambridge, MA: Harvard University Press, 1982), pp. 421–62, here 444ff.

8 On this collection, see Marie-Thérèse d'Alverny, "Deux traductions latines du Coran au Moyen Age," *Archives d'histoire doctrinale et littéraire du Moyen Age* 16 (1947–8): 69–131.

9 For more details on this corpus, see Reinhold Glei's introduction to his edition, *Petrus Venerabilis Schriften zum Islam* (Altenberge: CIS Verlag, 1985), pp. xv–xix. The *Apologia*'s date of composition – ninth or tenth century – is controversial.

10 The relationship of Letter 111 to the *Epistola de translatione sua* and *Summa* is controversial – see *CSS*, p. xix, and Constable's Appendix F in *The Letters of Peter the Venerable*, ed. Giles Constable, 2 vols (Cambridge, MA: Harvard Historical Studies, 1967), hereafter Peter of Cluny, *Letters*, vol. 2, pp. 275ff.

11 Paris, Arsenal MS 1162, fol. 111:

> If you want to know who the greatest forerunner of Antichrist and the devil's chosen disciple, Muhammad, was or what he taught, read this prologue attentively, in which are briefly contained all this book's contents: his most foul and false genealogy, his most impure and unspeakable filth and doctrine, and the utterly laughable and insane fables produced by him and his followers.

12 "Summary," 2, p. 4, il. 22ff. The following analysis refers directly to the paragraphs of Reinhold Glei's edition, *Petrus Venerabilis Schriften zum Islam*, pp. 2–22, which follow the original: Paris, Arsenal MS 1162.

13 Paris, Arsenal MS 1162, fol. 26r2. On this question, see Norman Daniel, *Islam and the West: The Making of an Image* (Oxford: One World, 1997), pp. 172–6.

14 Peter directly tackles the question of the incorruptibility of holy bodies in his sermon on Saint Marcel's relics: "Sermo cuius supra in honore sancti illius cuius reliquae sunt in praesenti,"ed. Giles Constable, *Revue Bénédictine* 64 (1954): 265–72, here 266 and 269. On the history of this complex problem, see Caroline W. Bynum, *The Resurrection of the Body in Western Christianity*, pp. 200–1336 (New York: Columbia University Press, 1995). The term "shutdown" is used by Jérôme Baschet in his excellent review of Bynum's book in *Annales ÉSC*, 51 (1996): 135–9, here 138.

15 Ovid, *Ars poetica*, 1–4, many editions.

16 D'Alverny, "Deux traductions latines du Coran," p. 81.

17 "Summary," 16, p. 18, line 13. On Latin Christendom's obsessive fear in the face of the Muslims' great numbers, see Daniel, *Islam and the West*, pp. 152 and 211.

18 *CSS*, 17, p. 54, line 17.

19 Daniel, *Islam and the West*, p. 43.

20 D'Alverny, "Deux traductions latines du Coran," p. 101.

21 Yvonne Friedman, in an attempt to elucidate the textual relationship between *Adversus Iudeorum* and *CSS*, proposes two dates for *CSS*, namely 1148 or 1154 (in her edition, *Adversus Iudeorum*, p. lxiii), cited in note 23, and referred to by Iogna-Prat as *Adversos Judeos*. She does not appear convinced by her own arguments for the earlier date. We shall therefore keep to the later date, long held by historians of Peter the Venerable.

22 *Epistola Petri Pictavensis*, 3, in *Petrus Venerabilis Schriften zum Islam*, p. 228, lines 8–14; *Capitula Petri Pictavensis*, 2.6, in ibid., p. 234. On this, see Daniel, *Islam and the West*, pp. 164ff.

23 The present analysis refers to Reinhold Glei's edition in *Petrus Venerabilis Schriften zum Islam*, which is based on one manuscript, Douai, BM 381, fols 177–95, copied between 1156 and 1166. *CSS* is also partially transmitted in a fifteenth-century manuscript, Madrid, BN 4464 (Conde del Miranda, 144), used by a mendicant active in Spain (on this, see introduction to Peter the Venerable, *Adversus Iudeorum inveteratam duritiem*, ed. Yvonne Friedman, *CC:CM* 58 [Turnhout: Brepols, 1985], pp. xxxviii ff.).

24 *Bibliotheca Cluniacensis*, eds M. Marrier and A. Duchesne (Paris: 1614, Mâcon: 1915), col. 591c.

25 James Kritzeck, "Peter the Venerable and the Toledan Collection," in *Petrus Venerabilis 1156–1956* (Rome: Herder, 1956), pp. 176–201, here 188–9, and Kritzeck, *Peter the Venerable and Islam* (Princeton, NJ: Princton University Press, 1964), pp. 155–6.

26 Jean-Pierre Torrell and Denise Bouthillier, *Pierre le Vénérable et sa vision du monde* (Leuven: Spicilegium Sacrum Lovaniense, 1986), pp. 182–3.

27 The numbers in parentheses refer to the textual divisions in Reinhold Glei's edition of *CSS*, pp. 30–224.

28 Peter the Venerable, *Contra Petrobrusianos hereticos*, ed. James Fearns, *CC:CM* 10 (Turnhout: Brepols, 1968), p. 161, lines 10ff.

29 *CSS*, 17, p. 54: here, Peter is speaking of 1141.

30 Daniel, *Islam and the West*, p. 278.

31 On conversion to Islam, see Daniel, *Islam and the West*, pp. 294–6.

32 *CSS*, 24, p. 62, lines 1–8.

33 *CSS*, 25, p. 64, lines 9–10.

34 *CSS*, 29, p. 68, lines 10–14.

35 *Apologia del Cristianismo*, ed. José Muñoz Sendino, in *Miscelanea Comillas*, 11–12 (Comillas: Santander Universidad Pontificia, 1949), p. 426.

36 See Glei's commentary, *CSS*, n. 278, pp. 273–4.

37 *CSS*, 50, p. 98, lines 11ff.

38 *CSS*, 55, p. 104: "Now to the main points, and first against the worst enemy let aid be furnished for the battle by the spirit of God."

39 Turki, "La lettre du 'moine de France,'" p. 141.

40 Paris, Arsenal MS 1162, fol. 89r2: "He calls the Christians variers of the laws, meaning that they have corrupted the Gospel and changed it at will."

41 *CSS*, 80, p. 138, lines 12–15.

42 *CSS*, 85, p. 144, lines 4–5.

43 The best clarification of the issue is Jean Pierre Torrell, "La notion de prophétie et la méthode apologétique dans le *Contra Sarracenos* de Pierre le Vénérable," *Studia monastica* 17 (1975): 257–82, reprinted in *Recherches sur la théorie de la prophétie au Moyen Âge: XIIe–XIVe siècle. Études et textes* (Fribourg, Switzerland: Dokimion, 1992), pp. 75–100.

44 *CSS*, 97, p. 158, lines 9–11, and p. 160, lines 17–19. Peter relies on Gregory the Great's classic definition of the prophecy given in his first Homily on Ezekiel (see next reference).

45 Gregory the Great, *Homilia in Ezechiel*, 1.1, ed. Charles Morel (Paris, Éditions du Cerf, 1986), pp. 50–2.

46 Respectively Isaiah 7.14, 35.5–6, 53.7–12. Regarding the baptism of Christ, Peter confuses Isaiah with Ezekiel 36.25.

47 *CSS*, 119, p. 186, lines 1–3.

48 Peter of Cluny, *Letter* 410, lines 7–9.

49   On the prophetic signs of Muhammad discussed in a polemic context, see the refutation of the "Monk of France" by al-Bayi in Turki, "La lettre du 'moine de France'," pp. 126ff. On the distinction between the Muhammadan prophetic model and hagiographic models in Islam, I am indebted to stimulating ideas heard at the colloquium "Les saints et leurs miracles à travers l'hagiographie chrétienne et islamique (IVe–XVe s.)," Paris, November 23–5, 1995, organized by Denise Aigle; proceedings published as *Miracle et Karama: hagiographies médiévales comparées*, ed. Denise Aigle (Turnhout: Brepols, 2000).

50   Peter of Cluny, *Letter* 408, lines 5–6, 27–8.

51   *Adversus Iudeorum*, ed. Friedman, 4.1448–52. Quoted and commented upon by Torrell and Bouthillier, *Pierre le Vénérable*, p. 189.

52   On criticism of Islam, general on the part of Latin commentators, and for the absence of miracles from the life of Muhammad, see Daniel, *Islam and the West*, pp. 88–99.

53   Torrell, "La notion de prophétie," p. 269.

54   Daniel, *Islam and the West*, p. 287.

55   D'Alverny, "Deux traductions latines du Coran," p. 99.

56   Daniel, *Islam and the West*, p. 56.

57   Turki, "La lettre du 'moine de France,'" p. 151.

58   Jean Jolivet, "Philosophie au XIIe siècle latin: l'héritage arabe," and Jolivet, "L'Islam et la raison, d'après quelques auteurs latins des XIe et XIIe siècles," in his *Philosophie médiévale arabe et latine. Études de philosophie médiévale* (Paris: J. Vrin, 1995), pp. 47–76, here 47–9, and 155–67, here 164–7.

59   *CSS*, 24, p. 62.

60   Paul Alphandéry, "Mahomet-Antichrist dans le Moyen Age," in *Mélanges Hartwig Derenbourg 1844–1908. Recueil de traveaux d'érudition dédiés à la mémoire d'Hartwig Derenbourg* (Paris: Ernest Leroux, 1909), pp. 261–77, esp. 261–2; Bernard McGinn, *Antichrist: Two Thousand Years of the Human Fascination with Evil* (San Francisco, CA: Harper, 1994), pp. 85ff.

61   On this point see Isabelle Cochelin, "Enfants, jeunes et vieux au monastère: la perception du cycle de la vie dans les sources clunisiennes (909–1156)," doctoral thesis, 2 vols, typescript, University of Montreal, 1996, vol. 1, pp. 295ff.

62   Peter the Venerable, *De miraculis libri duo*, ed. Denise Bouthillier, *CC:CM* 83 (Turnhout: Brepols, 1988), 1.14, p. 46.

63   Paul Verlaine, "Résignation," in *Poèmes saturniens* (1866), many editions; Victor Hugo, *Les Misérables*, 4.12.2, many editions.

64   Peter the Venerable, "Sermo de transfiguratione domini," *PL* 189: 968B.

65   Claude Cahen, *Orient et Occident au temps des Croisades* (Paris: Aubier Montaigne, 1983), p. 187; Daniel, *Islam and the West*, pp. 140ff; Christoph T. Maier, *Preaching the Crusades: Mendicant Friars and the Cross in the Thirteenth Century* (New York and Cambridge: Cambridge University Press, 1994).

66   See n. 18. The weak influence of Peter the Venerable's work is noted by Daniel, *Islam and the West*, pp. 259–60, and recalled more recently by M. Vandecasteele, *Étude comparative de deux versions latines médiévales d'une apologie arabo-chrétienne: Pierre le Vénérable et le rapport grégorien* (Brussels, 1991), pp. 81–134. My thanks to Benoît-Michel Tock for obtaining this work for me.

13

BODIES IN THE JEWISH–CHRISTIAN DEBATE

Anna Sapir Abulafia

It is not surprising that the central tenet of the Christian faith, the Incarnation, the embodiment of Christ, or God assuming flesh, was a subject of considerable anxiety among Christian thinkers. It had become rhetorically not just something that had happened in the past, but as represented in the sacrament of the Eucharist, a relic and a constantly reappearing miracle. Here Anna Abulafia considers how the notion of the Incarnation, of God becoming man, was of great concern to Christian intellectuals of the twelfth century because it was the central theological point on which they distinguished themselves as Christians from non-Christians, including from the Jews in their midst. The fact that Jews refused to accept the notion of the Incarnation despite sharing certain sacred texts with Christians, had become increasingly more frustrating to Christian thinkers at this time, particularly as they came to argue for more proofs of Christian belief based on "reason" rather than "revelation." Here Abulafia traces ways in which Christian notions about Jewish bodies and Jewish notions about Christian bodies, not least of them the body of Christ, created insurmountable misapprehensions between the two. Even when honest debate was attempted it was doomed to failure because Jews and Christians were talking at cross purposes. The fact that Jews could not accept the Christian notion of God embodied as Christ caused Christian intellectuals to conclude that Jews were obstinate, irrational, and less than human. Abulafia summarizes the theological debate between Christians and Jews on bodies and embodiment, but also suggests how the social interactions of Christians with Jews created increased tension in the twelfth century. Abulafia's ability to move back and forth between Jewish and Christian viewpoint is one of the hallmarks of her important work on how Christian notions of Jews became more intolerant in the twelfth-century and later. This chapter originally appeared in Framing Medieval Bodies, *eds Sarah Kay and Miri Rubin (Manchester: Manchester University Press, 1994), pp. 123–37. It is also reproduced in Anna Sapir Abulafia,* Christians and Jews in Dispute *(Aldershot: Variorum, 1998).*

* * *

347

I

It is hardly customary to broach the topic of "the body" in an analysis of the Jewish–Christian debate. Scholars of Jewish–Christian polemics usually concentrate on the clearly visible components of that debate. These are the disagreement between Jews and Christians about the true conception of God and the acrimony arising from the Christian doctrine of Incarnation; the competition between Jews and Christians for the cherished status of *Verus Israel* or the Chosen People; and the vituperative discussions concerning the correct method of interpreting the Holy Scriptures. Yet if one looks closely at the underlying issues of these components, one finds that the concept of "the body" did in fact enter the debate in various guises. In its most obvious form "the body" was an issue when the Incarnation and the Virgin Birth came up for discussion. In conjunction with the human bodies of Jesus Christ and his mother the humanity of the Jews, who did not believe in Jesus, became a subject of debate. Finally, the body of Christ in its relationship to the mystical body of Christian believers, the *communitas Christi*, is an issue of vital import-ance. The purpose of this chapter is to see how these guises of "the body" emerged in anti-Jewish polemics of the first half of the twelfth century. An attempt will be made to show that looking at that period's Jewish–Christian debate from the viewpoint of the body can actually help to explain how and why attitudes toward Jews deteriorated so much in the course of the twelfth century.[1]

II

Essential to twelfth-century theological inquiries into the doctrine of the Incarnation was the question of how an ineffable, transcendent, majestic God could take on the body of a man. How did God become man and, even more pointedly, why should God have wanted to become man in the first place? The urgency of the Incarnation as a topic of debate in this period's Jewish–Christian polemics lies in the fact that Jews were denying a doctrine which Christians were at great pains to explain among themselves. And the reason why so much new work was needed to make that doctrine intelligible was that twelfth-century thinkers were rapidly taking on board large chunks of classical philosophy. This new pagan knowledge demanded a precise recon-sideration of old Christian doctrine. Reason was hammering at the gates of the realm of faith.

One of the best minds to face this challenge was Anselm of Canterbury (d. 1109), who tackled the problem of the Incarnation in his *Why God Became Man* (1095–8).[2] Anselm believed that faithful and obedient Christians could perceive with their reason the necessity and the feasibility of the Incarnation. To Anselm faith was the prerequisite to understanding; without the light of faith showing the way, reason could not hope to solve any of the issues at hand. The logical inference of Anselm's approach to the relationship between faith and reason would be that no Jew (or any other non-Christian) could be convinced of the truth of Christianity through reason alone. Nonetheless, a number of thinkers, who clearly bear the mark of Anselm's influence, did bring rational arguments into their anti-Jewish polemics.[3] Others, who developed their own ideas about the role of reason, did so too. But however much recourse these thinkers had to philosophy, they did continue to attach great weight to the value of scriptural arguments. The Bible retained its central role in the debate.

Odo, bishop of Cambrai (d. 1113) used many of Anselm's arguments in his anti-Jewish disputation, which he wrote between 1106 and 1113. Yet he seemed to expect that these rational arguments should be able to convince Jews of their error, at least if they would be prepared to use their reason. The meaning of reason in the hands of Odo and of many of his contemporaries is a very stoical one. It denotes what was believed to be the innate faculty of human beings to perceive truth. To be human is to possess reason; the bond between men is their common possession of reason.[4] Odo's confidence in reason is particularly apparent in the second part of the disputation where he argues against what he understood the Jewish criticism of the Virgin Birth to be. Odo claims that anyone using their reason should be able to understand the spiritual dimensions of the doctrine. Even though their senses are repelled by the thought of a woman's belly and all the waste passages it contains, their reason would inform them that the Virgin Mary's body was spotless because it was free of sin. Its sublime purity made it the ideal place for God to assume man.[5] (Earlier in the disputation Odo had explained how the one person of Jesus Christ consisted of two natures, one human and one divine, with neither impinging on the other.)[6] Christians, as human beings who use their reason, understand all of this. Jews bear more resemblance to animals because they rely solely on their senses to teach them about what is true. Odo in fact does not stop short from wondering whether Jews are animals rather than human beings.[7]

Guibert, abbot of Nogent (d. c.1125), who emphasized how much Anselm's teaching had meant to him, wrote a vicious attack on Jews and their Christian sympathizers in his treatise *On the Incarnation in Answer to the Jews* (c.1111).[8] Much of what Guibert wrote betrays his deep concern about his own body and about bodily impurities in general. In his tract against the Jews he scoffs at Jewish rejection of the idea that God could take on the baseness of a human form. Bodies are pure as long as they lack sin; unlike all other human beings, there was not even a hint of sin in Jesus Christ. His body was as pure as can be. No opprobrium can be attached to the fact that like other men he too covered his private parts by wearing breeches. And because he had to eat and drink, his body would have functioned in the same way as that of all humans. And in any case even in sinful bodies there is help at hand. Within the framework of faith, reason is there to curb appetite and to keep the material aspect of the body under tight control. Jews do not curb their material instincts; they are a people who delight in the literal meaning of the Old

Testament. When understood at that primitive level, the Old Testament has no spiritual message to offer. All it seems to offer are material rewards. Indeed, Jews are concerned solely with making money and crippling the poor with their usury. Their mouths, which they stuff with lies and the excesses of luxury, are filthy in comparison to the purity of the Virgin's privy parts.[9] Guibert was particularly devoted to the Virgin Mary. Indeed his devotion forms part of the history of the developing cult of the Virgin. Like Odo he was at great pains to dispel any possible doubts about the propriety of Mary's body as the place for God to become incarnate. Thus we see him here being so explicit in his assertion that the parts of Mary which engendered Jesus Christ were purer than the mouths of those whom he accuses of being her detractors.[10]

Peter the Venerable, abbot of Cluny (d. 1156), shakes off Jewish criticism of the Incarnation as being crude in his diatribe against the Jews, *Against the Jews*, which he completed by 1147.[11] He asks whether Jews really believe Christians have not worked out for themselves that there is a gulf separating God's sublimity from man's humanity. But whereas Jews condemn the idea that God became man on account of the imponderability of such a thing ever happening, Christians seize on the element of wonder in the thought that God assumed flesh, and they believe in it. They do not believe that God labored, was hungry and thirsty, suffered, died, and was buried. To read that in the doctrine of the Incarnation is to approach it in a carnal, animal-like fashion. The essence of God was not affected by the impurities of the human condition. In Jesus Christ there was the unity of one person made up of diverse substances. Different actions of his belong to the properties of these different substances. Thus the assumption of human flesh did not compromise the deity of Christ. But his flesh was exalted by the fact that God had assumed it.[12]

Thus Odo of Cambrai, Guibert of Nogent, and Peter the Venerable defended the doctrine of the Incarnation by pointing to its spiritual meaning. God did not simply change into man; human nature was assumed by God without effecting a change in the divine nature of God. Because the full implications of God becoming man go beyond anything human beings can experience or see for themselves, these thinkers insisted that only the spiritual side of man could grasp that the Incarnation truly happened. The bodily or sensual component of human beings on its own is incapable of taking on board this mystery. Because Jews refused to accept the doctrine, they were viewed by these Christians as lacking spiritual qualities and being dominated by their bodies. But an interesting new twist was brought to the discussion about God by Peter Alfonsi, an early twelfth-century convert from Judaism, which in turn was taken up by Peter the Venerable in the final part of his work against the Jews.

As we have seen, the Jews accused Christians of demeaning God by asserting that the man Jesus was the son of God. This, in Jewish eyes, was tantamount to blasphemy. Peter Alfonsi and Peter the Venerable proceeded to turn the tables on the Jews by accusing them of blaspheming God because they (and not Christians) gave God a body. The two Peters did this by isolating anthropomorphic descriptions of God in rabbinic literature and by assuming that all Jews took these words at face value. Because Jews refused to accept the spiritual christological meaning that Christians discovered in the Old Testament, Christians accused them of having regard for the literal sense of Scripture only. The perceived dearth of Jewish capacity for spiritual understanding led Peter Alfonsi and Peter the Venerable to believe that Jews were incapable of reading any text allegorically. In addition to this Peter Alfonsi, who had been a Jew, had experience of anthropomorphic tendencies among some of his former Spanish co-religionists.[13]

Peter Alfonsi composed his *Dialogue* between Peter (himself) and Moses (his former Jewish self) between 1108 and 1110 in order to explain and justify his motivations for converting.[14] Peter claimed that the Jewish "learned men" err against God because they refuse to read the words of the Prophets allegorically, even when those words, taken literally, clash with reason. Reason, says Peter, dictates that there is a God, who is the prime maker of all that exists. This creator must be simple and unchangeable. It is therefore impossible to suppose that he bears any likeness to the creatures he himself created. All of this means that it is nonsensical to read passages of the Bible which refer to the body of God (e.g. Isaiah 62.8: "The Lord hath sworn by his right hand, and by the arm of his strength") literally. Even worse are the stories in the Talmud which have God weeping, being angry, residing in a particular part of the heavens, and so on. All this would mean that God is a composite corporeal substance behaving in the same way as men do. This is patently absurd. People with any knowledge of the make-up of the created world would not dream of thinking such unworthy things of God. Peter concludes that Jews clearly have no understanding at all of the true nature of God and his world.[15] Peter goes on to say that, where the Bible speaks of God as a man, Jesus Christ, who was God and man, is prefigured. His human nature did not impinge on the divine nature of his person.[16] Thus these passages bear no insult to God's majesty. On the contrary, they contain substantial truths, provided they are understood as they should be, i.e. on a spiritual level and not a carnal one. In other words, Peter has Jews making a nonsense of God by reading texts literally, while he has Christians making perfect sense precisely in that area where Jews accuse them of getting it so wrong: the belief that Jesus Christ is both God and man.

Peter the Venerable devoted a whole section of his anti-Jewish polemic, *Against the Jews*, to an attack on the Talmud. Some of his material is similar to that of Peter Alfonsi, and it seems reasonable to suppose that he knew of Alfonsi's work. Yet Alfonsi could not have been Peter's only source, for his treatise contains more Talmudic material than Alfonsi's *Dialogue* does.[17] The Talmud serves to reinforce Peter the Venerable's conception of Jews as animal-like beings. In the first four chapters of his treatise he incessantly accuses Jews of being less than human. It is as if this is the only way he can put into words why it is that Jews refuse to understand that the words of the Bible tell them that Jesus Christ is God and man and the Messiah who was foretold by the prophets. According to Peter, any other reading of the text contradicts reason and authority. Peter writes:

> I really do not know whether a Jew is a man, given that he does not yield to human reason, nor does he assent to the divine authorities which are his own. I know not, say I, whether he is a man from whose flesh the stony heart has not yet been removed and to whom the heart of flesh has not yet been given and in whose midst the divine spirit has not yet been placed, without which no Jew can convert to Christ.[18]

Elsewhere Peter emphasizes what he sees as the animal-like qualities of Jews by asking his imaginary Jewish opponent why he supposes the miracles of the Exodus from Egypt and the wonders related by the Prophets occurred:

> So that you, Jew, could . . . stuff your belly with a variety of foods? So that you could get drunk . . . and snore in a drunken stupor? Did these things happen so that you could give such great rein to your desires . . . [and] abandon yourselves to your lusts? So that you could abound so greatly in riches and fill chests with gold, silver and many treasures and so that you could elevate yourself with proud and dominating arrogance over inferiors? No! May this be far from human minds, may it be absent from souls capable of reason and may it be remote from all those who know God. Reason does not support this and justice herself denies that man, who was placed before all irrational creatures by the Creator, should be compared to animals in all things and made similar to them, even though in some things man and beast are connected . . . if God had conferred only worldly goods on man, what more would puny man possess than a cow, a donkey or the vilest worm?[19]

It is clear to Peter that reason, which demarcates man from animal, simply does not operate in Jews. For in his eyes Jews are only interested in worldly goods. But the crucial question still remains. *Why* does reason not function in Jews? What is it that shuts down the working of reason in a Jew's mind? And it is here that Peter introduces the Talmud. According to him the fables of what to him is a hideous, bestial book overshadow the hearts of Jews and obliterate Jewish capacity for reason. Jews are somehow caught up in a vicious circle of depravity. According to Peter, it is on account of their sins and the crimes of their fathers that they are being punished by having their minds taken over by the Talmud. The resulting insanity provokes them to blaspheme God and to be impervious to all reasonable arguments proving that Jesus Christ is God. Without escaping the vice of the Talmud no Jew can hope to glimpse the truth.[20]

The passages of the Talmud which Peter the Venerable ridicules are again narrative sections in which the rabbis explored what one might call the give-and-take relationship between God and his chosen people. To illustrate their points the rabbis used anthropomorphic language to describe God. Thus at one point God is seen to mourn the captivity of his children. At another he is involved in a scholarly debate between students of the Talmud and, as any wise father would be, he is proud when his sons defeat him.[21] Peter, however, lacks any appreciation for these texts. He does not doubt for a moment that all Jews read all these words in a purely literal sense. According to him Jews reject metaphors and allegories which make it possible to use anthropomorphic language when speaking about God. Where the Bible uses such modes of speech, Jews pervert the text by reading only the "killing letter."[22] According to Peter, Jews are the stupidest of all peoples, because they believe their rabbinic legends to be literally true. The Greeks and the Latins were much wiser; as rational beings, they never believed the inanities of their myths. They, unlike the Jews, interpreted their stories in a useful way.[23]

Peter the Venerable does not only take the text of the rabbinic stories which have come his way literally; he makes changes and twists their contents to prove his point even better.[24] In Peter's version of the tales the rabbis are incredibly rude to God and treat him as if his wisdom is barely on a par with their own. They even imply he is a fool and a liar.[25] In Peter's hands, then, the legends of the Talmud prove that Jews have stripped God of his omnipotence and transformed him into a vulnerable man, who can cry and can be outsmarted in a debate. Peter wonders who except a Jew would not shudder to think that God could be so "wretched"? He calls the Jews a "truly wretched people" because they imagine the divine essence to be human, ascribing as they do to God human and even animal-like roaring and weeping.[26] In other words, we could say that Peter accuses the Jews of regarding God in the same way that Jews thought Christians regarded him. For we now have both sides of the Christian–Jewish debate insisting that the other has encumbered God with a human body in a totally inappropriate way. In Jewish eyes Christians were the blasphemers because they claimed that God had a son, who was God and who suffered and died like a man. In Peter's eyes Jewish blasphemy against God has earned them the opprobrium of God and their fellow men. Their "blaspheming mouth which constantly vomits out curses over men and pours out abuse over God" justly marks them for shame in this world and the next, where they can look forward to being a plaything for the demons of hell.[27]

III

We have seen how doctrinal differences between Christianity and Judaism encouraged twelfth-century Christian polemicists to transpose the generally accepted polarities of mind/body, spirit/flesh, and man/beast on to the existing opposition between Christians and Jews. According to the developing paradigm, reason, which should control the mind, is what Christians care about; the body, with its bestial qualities, is the domain of Jews. We have seen how this theoretical doctrinal exclusion of Jews from the realm of reason presumed that Jews were concerned with material affairs only. It is therefore worthwhile to pause for a moment to consider Christian attitudes toward Jews which arose from the social and economic realities of the period.

The late eleventh and the twelfth centuries in northwestern Europe were a period of rapid economic expansion. A society that had been primarily a gift economy began to reshape itself as a monetary one. The economic and social changes which took place were not beneficial to everyone. Those left out of the general increase of prosperity were bitter about the innovations they were experiencing. Beyond this Christian moralists were faced with the fundamental challenge of working out whether it was indeed a good thing for a Christian society to seek monetary profits rather than the poverty which the apostolic Church had extolled. All this affected Christian attitudes to Jews. The Jews of France, England, and Germany were visible in this period as entrepreneurs and moneylenders. They were certainly not the only people occupied in this way, but there can be no doubt that their economic activities did boost the growing economy. Thus unease about the making of money was often expressed by Christians by attacking the Jews for doing just that. And the disappointment of those who were not as successful as they wanted to be was often translated into condemnation of any economic success Jews were seen or thought to have.[28] The economic stereotyping which grew out of these attacks was used to pinpoint what was seen to separate Jews from Christians. The similarities between economic anti-Jewish stereotypes and the doctrinal exclusion of Jews from matters spiritual is significant. For one thing the two types of stereotyping were mutually reinforcing. For another the overlap between the stereotypes served to marginalize the Jews even further.

Peter Abelard (d. 1142) describes the economic position of the Jews rather sympathetically. In his *Dialogue of a Philosopher with a Jew and a Christian* (written by the latter half of the 1130s)[29] he states that Jews are not permitted to own land and the only occupation they can have is that of lending money at interest. This leads Jews to be hated by those who feel oppressed by them.[30] Abelard's unbiased reporting of Jewish moneylending should not, however, blind us to the fact that one of the conclusions of his *Dialogue* is that Jews, however much they mean to, do not in fact serve God correctly. Jewish refusal to exchange the ceremonial details of the Law of Moses for a christological figurative signification means, in Abelard's eyes, that Jews do not have access to the inner spiritual truth which would direct them to true love of God.[31]

354

And Abelard, too, resorts to animal imagery when he writes that Jews are "animals and sensual and are imbued with no philosophy whereby they are able to discuss reasoned arguments."[32]

We have already seen Guibert of Nogent connecting Jewish hermeneutics with Jewish morals. Just as Jews cannot rise above the letter of the law, so they do not seek anything in life that will not give them material gain. In his treatise against the Jews, the Jews are stereotyped especially as thieves and usurers. Bogged down as they are by these crimes they are incapable of perceiving something as spiritual as the Virgin Birth.[33]

Not surprisingly, Peter the Venerable had little sympathy for the economic position of the Jews. On a theoretical plane he saw Jews as so keen on material and ephemeral things that they cast aside the heavenly eternal goods on offer to them and everyone else.[34] Here, in a way not dissimilar to Guibert, Peter's view is informed by his conviction that Jews misread the Bible by taking it literally. But on a more practical level Peter is no less scathing. And here too his words are sparked off by religious fire. In his letter to Louis VII concerning preparations for the Second Crusade, he suggests to the king that the Jews should bear the brunt of the cost of the expedition. Peter writes that the Jews are far worse than the Saracens; Muslims and Christians have at least some beliefs about Jesus and the Virgin Mary in common. Jews believe Jesus was nothing special. They blaspheme him and his mother, rejecting and deriding all the sacraments of human redemption. The only reason they should not be wiped off the face of the earth is that God wishes them to live a fate worse than death. A good way to achieve this would be to take away from the Jews the money they make out of their reprobate business affairs. Instead of performing and holding useful and honest economic positions, Jews, according to Peter, function as "fences," making a living from the stolen goods Christian thieves bring them from churches. "The vessels of the body and blood of Christ [are divided] among the killers of that body and the spillers of the blood of Christ." And to make matters worse, they desecrate the holy objects before making a profit out of them.[35] However much Peter's views were colored by the difficult financial position of Cluny in this period, it is plain that his attitude to Jewish moneylending was inexorably bound up with his ideas about Jews as religious adversaries. The occasion of the Crusade, which he himself could ill afford to support, could only serve to bring out his feelings more strongly.[36]

IV

The question of otherness in the doctrinal and socio-economic spheres and the overlap between the concepts used in both spheres impinge in their turn on another facet of "the body" in the Jewish–Christian debate. Jews were not only seen as a people denying that God assumed flesh; they were not only seen as a separate economic group. They stood accused of crucifying the very body through which God was supposed to have become incarnate.[37]

Christians for their part not only venerated that body, they believed they had a share in that same body when they partook of the Host. And it was through their participation in the Eucharist that they conceived themselves to be united in the body of Christ, becoming his holy Church.[38]

The expressions concerning Christian unity, which we find in our sources of the first half of the twelfth century, must be interpreted against the backdrop of the developing ideology of a universal Church or Christian society which was put forward so forcefully by papal reformers from the middle of the eleventh century onwards. One of the pressing questions of this period was to work out whose authority – the pope's or the emperor's – should have supremacy in this "republic." The problem became even more urgent in the course of the thirteenth century when temporal authority could use for its own purposes the political theory of Aristotle.[39] But whether temporal authority or ecclesiastical authority was given precedence in this notional body politic, the "republic" remained Christian. And it seemed as if in that Christian society there could only be less and less room for Jews.

These sentiments emerge very clearly from the work of Rupert, abbot of Deutz (d. 1129), who was an outspoken protagonist of papal reform. In Rupert's work a direct connection is made between the Jewish rejection of Christ and the supposed enmity of Jews toward Christians. Rupert represents Jewish hands as dripping with the very blood that serves Christians for their spiritual food and consequent salvation. He writes in his *Dialogue Between Christians and Jews*, also called the *Anulus* or *Signet-Ring* (1126), and elsewhere, that the Jews conspired to and consented in the death of Christ and cruelly crucified him. But what is even worse than killing him is that they continue to malign Christ in their synagogues, which are part of the Synagogue of Satan. Thus Jews continue to be covered in Christ's blood because they do not distance themselves from the crime of their ancestors by recognizing Christ as the son of God. The reason the prophets had to speak in such enigmas was that they would have been murdered if their Jewish listeners had been able to understand that they were preaching salvation to the nations through Christ. Rupert is adamant that Jews believe that only the circumcised can be saved. That is why he thinks Jews jealously keep circumcision to themselves. He sees the Jews as the antithesis of Christians. Where Christians are generous and do all they can to bring salvation to the whole of mankind, Jews are a mean and particularist people. They are the greediest nation on earth, dispersed throughout the world. Rupert is convinced that pride in their status as God's chosen people is what determines the attitude of Jews to non-Jews. They live in contempt of all non-Jews and are jealous of their salvation and plot against them.[40]

As far as Christians are concerned, Rupert's vision of the Church is a united one pivoting around the body of Christ. Rupert believes in a very literal way that partaking of the Eucharist gives the faithful the chance to be one with Christ.[41] He identifies himself explicitly with Christ, whose crucified body he adores on the cross.[42] Heterodoxically he asserts that the salvific Eucharist was instituted by Christ at the time of his passion.[43] In such a view it really does become hard to find a decent niche for Jews.

Peter the Venerable's worldview is no less Christian than Rupert's. But, writing at a time when a second crusade had to be preached to buttress the victories of the first, Peter could not be unaware of the vast numbers of persons who were inimical to Christendom. In addition to this his visit to Spain in the early 1140s had exposed him to a society in which Judaism and Islam were still vibrant forces. Moreover his own writing against the Petrobrusian heretics (the followers of Peter of Bruys) betrays his awareness of the existence of heresy within Christendom.[44] Nonetheless, in his polemic against the Jews he maintains first that Christendom is universal, both in theory and in reality, and second that Judaism is so in neither.

The universality of the Christian faith is of course based by Peter on the Gospel's message of salvation for all who believe in Christ. In Peter's eyes the universality of Christ's rule was presaged in the Old Testament. Peter tries to defend the reality of this by asserting that, even though there are lots of Muslims, Jews, and pagans about, they are not everywhere, whereas Christians are:

> The Christian faith did not, in the manner of errors, subject to itself only bits of the world; because it is the truth, derived from ultimate truth, which is Christ, it conquered the whole world. I have said the whole world because although pagans or Saracens exercise dominion over some parts and although Jews skulk amongst Christians and pagans, there is not any part, or a significant part, of land, not of the remotest island of the Mediterranean or the ocean itself, where Christians do not live either as rulers or subjects. So it is shown to be true what Scripture says of Christ: "And he shall rule from sea to sea, and from the river unto the ends of the earth" (Psalms 71.8); and what our Apostle says: "In the name of Jesus every knee shall bow" (Philippians 2.10). So what if the Mohammedan error corrupted part of the world after the law was given by Christ? There were many heresies among the Jews after the law of Moses; after the Gospel of Christ many heresies were born in Christendom. ... There is no comparison between this Satanic falsehood and the divine truth of the Gospel, because although that prevailed among many, this ... prevailed universally.[45]

According to Peter, Judaism not only lacks the universal appeal of Christianity, it does not have any universalistic ambitions. The only universalism it contains is the message of universal Christendom, and this is precisely what Jews resolutely deny. It is this denial that Peter must combat. For although Muslims constituted a formidable military challenge to Christian attempts to put their universal ideas into practice, it was the Jews who seemed to challenge the very content of that universal message. Thus we see Peter arguing that one must be stupid and "thinking" like a beast of burden to imagine that God, the Creator of the whole world, would ignore everyone else and only look after the Jews, giving only them hope of salvation. Peter asks how one could imagine that God would narrowly confine his mercy by choosing this tiny quarrelsome ungrateful people while rejecting and damning the infinite number of other people. In the event he is convinced the opposite has occurred. The nations of the world have been saved, whilst it is the Jews who have been rejected and damned.[46]

It is clear that Peter sees the concepts which Jews possess about their own peoplehood and about the existence of a special bond between them and God as an affirmation that Jews are happy to see all non-Jews damned. To Peter, as to Rupert, this constitutes an affront to the all-embracing Christian faith. Thus he urges the Jews to stop being so arrogant and to cease bragging about the singularity of their law. They must understand that everyone is saved by the grace of Christ's Gospel and they must understand that this is exactly what the Hebrew Bible says.[47] In the eyes of Christian polemicists like Peter the Venerable the refusal by Jews to accept the role in which they were cast not only placed them outside the Christian body; Jews were seen as threatening that very body by blaspheming Christ and by steadfastly denying the salvation his body was supposed to bring to all those who believed in him.

V

The close of the eleventh century inaugurated a period in Western Christian thought that revealed a great fascination for the human nature and body of Jesus Christ. At one end of the spectrum we see this interest in theologians like Anselm and Abelard, who studied the Incarnation and its implications. At the other end we find it in the fervor of crusaders to win back for their Lord the land they believed he trod as a man. In all of this we sense that Christians concentrated on the special relationship they felt they had with God's son in order to feel closer to God. For in so many texts which expound the reason "Why God became man" a great deal of emphasis is put on the brotherly bond which was created between Christ and humanity on account of his willingness to die in order to save man. And that bond was made explicit again and again when Christians felt united in the body of Christ through their veneration of and participation in the Eucharist. Interwoven into these discussions was the attempt to explain how it was possible for a transcendent God to become man and how Jesus Christ could be both man and God. We have seen how these philosophical ramifications were discussed on the assumption that all human beings have a share in reason. And we have seen how this concept of human universality was made to overlap with the Christian one. Those who refused to have a share in the salvation universally offered to man by Christ were thought to lack a human share of reason. Refusing to enter the perimeters of "true" belief, which was tantamount to refusing to become a member of Christ's body – for a time at least – became synonymous with quitting the perimeters of reason.

It will be patently obvious that the concept of universal Christendom was an illusion. But that did not make it any less real as a goal worth aspiring to. Jews were, of course, not the only people to run afoul of this goal. Muslims, heretics, and other social misfits joined them. But the Jews did hold a special position among what we might call the medieval outcasts.[48] Unlike Muslims living in Christendom, they had no autonomous Jewish territory they could ever turn to. Indeed the loss of their land was interpreted as a sign of their failure and obsolescence. Judaism, unlike Islam, was seen as a threatening negation of the very essence of Christianity. Unlike heretics, Jews formed a self-perpetuating social group that defined itself not in opposition to the established Church, but without reference to the Church at all. As non-Christians, Jews not only could not play any part in the religious manifestations of the Church. They could not participate in the social activities generated by that religious ritual. To make matters worse that ritual often entailed a great deal of anti-Jewish sentiment. After all, each time the Eucharist was celebrated thoughts could easily turn to those who were accused of killing Christ.[49] And in Northwestern Europe the special economic position of Jews could only marginalize them further.

One did not have to be a twelfth-century Jew to be called an animal. The wording of a number of biblical texts had encouraged Christians to use the word against Jews long before that. Moreover, Christians were happy to use the insult against their own co-religionists when it suited them.[50] But what we have seen in the anti-Jewish polemical material of the first half of the twelfth century is that the accusation was used against Jews as an all-encompassing reproach. Jews were not only being accused of reading the Bible literally as they always had been. Jews were being accused of blaspheming God and of being implacable enemies of Jesus Christ and his mother. Jews stood also accused of separating themselves from the domain of reason to which all other human beings belonged. And Jews were increasingly being accused of day-to-day animal-like behavior. Examining the role of "the body" in the Jewish–Christian debate of the first half of the twelfth century has helped us to uncover how and why these accusations began to interlock. And it is the interlocking of these different aspects of anti-Jewish feeling that, I believe, contributed to the deterioration of the position of the Jews in the course of that century and beyond.

NOTES

1   The writing of this article coincided with my supervision of David Behrman for his dissertation for the diploma of historical studies in Cambridge entitled "Parallels between Christian critique of rabbinic literature and Jewish critique of the Christian faith in the twelfth and thirteenth centuries." Thinking with him about the topic of his research has certainly contributed much to my thoughts for this chapter.

2   *S. Anselmi Opera Omnia*, ed. Francis S. Schmitt (Edinburgh: 1946), vol. 2, pp. 37–133.
3   See Anna Sapir Abulafia, "Christians disputing disbelief. St Anselm, Gilbert Crispin and Pseudo-Anselm," in *Religionsgespräche in Mittelalter*, eds Bernard Lewis and Friedrich Nimböhner (Wiesbaden: Harrassowitz, 1992), pp. 131–48. For Richard W. Southern's view on the background to the *Cur Deus Homo? (Why Did God Become Man?)* see his *Saint Anselm. A Portrait in Landscape* (Cambridge: Cambridge University Press, 1990), pp. 197–205.
4   See, e.g. Cicero, *De Officiis* 1.4, trans. Walter Miller (Cambridge, MA, and London: Loeb Classical Library, 1975), pp. 12–17 and Cicero, *De Legibus*, 1.7.23, trans. Clinton W. Keyes (Cambridge, MA, and London: Loeb Classical Library, 1977), pp. 320–3. Both these texts were widely read in the twelfth century; see Michael Lapidge, "The Stoic inheritance," in *A History of Twelfth-century Western Philosophy*, ed. Peter Dronke (Cambridge: Cambridge University Press, 1988), p. 92.
5   Odo of Cambrai, *Patrologia Latina* (hereafter *PL*) 160, cols 1110–12. Odo's obvious disgust for the female body is part of the story of medieval attitudes toward women.
6   Odo of Cambrai, *PL* 160, col. 1108.
7   Odo of Cambrai, *PL* 160, col. 1112; see Anna Sapir Abulafia, "Christian imagery of Jews in the twelfth century: a look at Odo of Cambrai and Guilbert of Nogent," *Theoretische Geschiedenis* 16 (1989): 383–91.
8   Guibert of Nogent, *De Incarnatione contra Iudeos*, *PL* 156, cols 489–528.
9   Guibert of Nogent, *De Incarnatione contra Iudeos*, *PL* 156, cols 489, 492, 496–7, 498, 519–24. See also Anna Sapir Abulafia, "Theology and the commercial revolution: Guibert of Nogent, St Anselm and the Jews of Northern France," in *Church and City, 1000–1500. Essays in Honour of Christopher Brooke*, eds David Abulafia, Michael Franklin, and Miri Rubin (Cambridge: Cambridge University Press, 1992), pp. 23–40.
10 In this matter too, Guibert and Odo seem to have been under the influence of Anselm; see Jaroslav Pelikan, "A First-generation Anselmian, Guibert of Nogent," in *Continuity and Discontinuity in Church History. Essays presented to George H. Williams*, eds F. Forrester Church and Timothy George (Leiden: Brill, 1979), pp. 71–82, and 77ff.
11 *Petri Venerabilis adversus Iudeorum inveteratam duritiem*, ed. Yvonne Friedman, *CC:CM* 58 (Turnhout: Brepols, 1985); see Friedman's introduction on the dating of the text, pp. lxiii–lxx.
12 *Adversus Iudeorum*, ed. Friedman, 2, lines 426–603, pp. 28–33.
13 M. Kniewasser, "Die anti-jüdische Polemic des Petrus Alphonsi (getauft 1106) und des Abtes Petrus Venerabilis von Cluny (+1156)," *Kairos, Zeitschrift für Religionswissenschaft und Theologie* 23 (1980): 47–9. See also Norman Roth, "Forgery and abrogation of the Torah: a theme in Muslim and Christian polemic in Spain," *Proceedings of the American Academy for Jewish Research* 54 (1987): 203–36.
14 On Alfonsi (1062–1110) see John Tolan, *Petrus Alfonsi and his Medieval Readers* (Gainesville, FL: University of Florida Press, 1993).
15 Peter Alfonsi, "Dialogus," *PL* 167, cols 541–67.
16 Peter Alfonsi, "Dialogus," *PL* 167, cols 577, 617–19.
17 Friedman discusses the relationship between Peter the Venerable and Peter Alfonsi in her edition, pp. xiv–xx. See also Kniewasser, "Die anti-jüdische Polemic," 34–76.
18 *Adversus Iudeorum*, ed. Friedman, 3, lines 564–70, pp. 57–8; cf. Ezekiel 36.26.
19 *Adversus Iudeorum*, ed. Friedman, 3, lines 757–72, p. 63; cf. Psalm 48.13.
20 *Adversus Iudeorum*, ed. Friedman, 5, lines 1–83, pp. 125–7. Peter speaks of the shadows which had cast Egypt into darkness now occupying the hearts of Jews.
21 On the content of some of these legends see *Adversus Iudeorum*, ed. Friedman, intro. pp. xviii–xx.
22 *Adversus Iudeorum*, ed. Friedman, 5, lines 989–1002, p. 153; cf 2 Corinthians 3.6.
23 *Adversus Iudeorum*, ed. Friedman, 5, lines 1106–40, pp. 157–8.
24 On Peter's use of the Talmud, see *Adversus Iudeorum*, ed. Friedman, intro., p. xx.

25   *Adversus Iudeorum*, ed. Friedman, 5, lines 357–9, p. 134.

26   *Adversus Iudeorum*, ed. Friedman, 5, lines 1022–32, p. 154.

27   *Adversus Iudeorum*, ed. Friedman, 5, lines 611–20, pp. 141–2.

28   Lester. K. Little, *Religious Poverty and the Profit Economy in Medieval Europe* (Ithaca, NY: Cornell University Press, 1978), pp. 3–57.

29   Eloi Marie Buytaert, "Abelard's collationes," *Antonianum* 44 (1969): 33–9. There is disagreement about the dating of the dialogue; see Anna Sapir Abulafia, "*Intentio recta an erronea*? Peter Abelard's views on Judaism and the Jews," in *Medieval Studies in Honor of Avrom Saltman*, eds Bat-Sheva Albert, Yvonne Friedman, and Simon Schwarzfuchs (Ramat-Gan: Bar-Ilan Studies in History, 1995).

30   Peter Abelard, *Dialogus inter philosophum, Judaeum et Christianum*, ed. R. Thomas (Stuttgart-Bad Cannstatt: Frommann, 1970), pp. 50–1; in English translation, *A Dialogue of a Philosopher with a Jew, and a Christian*, trans. Pierre J. Payer (Toronto: Pontifical Institute of Medieval Studies, 1979), p. 33.

31   See Abulafia, "*Intentio recta an erronea.*"

32   Peter Abelard, *Dialogus*, ed. Thomas, p. 90; trans. Payer, p. 39.

33   Guibert of Nogent, *De Incarnatione contra Iudeos* 2, 5, *PL* 156, col. 506.

34   *Adversus Iudeorum*, ed. Friedman, 3, lines 19–25, p. 42.

35   *The Letters of Peter the Venerable*, ed. Giles Constable, 2 vols (Cambridge, MA: Harvard University Press, 1967), letter 130, pp. 327–30.

36   Yvonne Friedman, "An anatomy of anti-Semitism: Peter the Venerable's letter to Louis VII, King of France (1146)," in *Bar-Ilan Studies in History*, ed. P. Artzi (Ramat-Gan, 1978), p. 100. See also Jean-Pierre Torrell, "Les Juifs dans l'oeuvre de Pierre le Vénérable," *Cahiers de la Civilisation Médiévale* 30 (1987): 339–42. Friedman states that there is no proof that Peter borrowed money from the Jews (pp. 98–9); Torrell disputes this (pp. 332–3). See also Gavin I. Langmuir, "Peter the Venerable," in *Toward a Definition of Antisemitism* (Berkeley, CA: University of California Press, 1990), pp. 200–3.

37   On the idea developing in the course of the twelfth century that Jews did not crucify Christ out of ignorance, see Jeremy Cohen, "The Jews as the killers of Christ in the Latin tradition, from Augustine to the Friars," *Traditio* 39 (1983): 1–27.

38   On the Eucharist, see Miri Rubin, *Corpus Christi. The Eucharist in Late Medieval Culture* (Cambridge: Cambridge University Press, 1991).

39   Walter Ullmann, *A History of Political Thought: The Middle Ages* (Harmondsworth: Penguin, 1965), pp. 192–5. Ullmann stresses that the debate between *regnum* and *sacerdotium* could only move forwards when those defending temporal authority had non-biblical language at their disposal. But in my view the use of Aristotle did not make these polemicists and the society, in so far as it was their own, any less Christian.

40   *Dialogue* or *Anulus*, ed. Rhabanus Haacke, in Maria L. Arduini, *Ruperto di Deutz e la controversia tra Christiani ed Ebrei nel secolo XII* (Rome: Instituto storico italiano per il Medio Evo, 1979), pp. 189–204, 238; Rupert of Deutz, *Commentaria in XII Prophetas minores in Amos Liber III*, *PL* 168, cols 339–42; Rupert, *De Sancte Trinitate*, 29, *In Hieremiam* 81, ed. Rhabanus Haacke, *CC:CM* 23, pp. 1633–4; Rupert, *In Iohannes Evangelium* 7, ed. R Haacke, *CC:CM* 9, p. 391; Rupert, *In Genesim* 8.26, ed. Rhabanus Haacke, in *De Sancta Trinitate et operibus eius CC:CM* 21, p. 513; Rupert, *De Sancte Trinitate, In Librum Psalmorum* 5, ed. Rhabanus Haacke, *CC:CM* 22, p. 1356; David E. Timmer, "The religious significance of Judaism for twelfth-century monastic exegesis: a study of Rupert of Deutz *c*.1070–1129," PhD dissertation, Notre Dame University, 1983 (UMI reprints), pp. 59–70. See also Anna Sapir Abulafia, "The ideology of reform and changing ideas concerning Jews in the works of Rupert of Deutz and *Hermannus quondam Iudeus*," *Jewish History* 7 (1993): 44–50.

41   Gary Macy, *The Theologies of the Eucharist in the Early Scholastic Period. A Study of the Salvific Function of the Sacrament according to the Theologians c.1080–1220* (Oxford:

Clarendon, 1984), pp. 66–7; John H. van Engen, *Rupert of Deutz* (Berkeley, CA: University of California Press, 1983), p. 140.

42 Van Engen, *Rupert of Deutz*, pp. 105–16; *Dialogue* or *Anulus*, ed. Haacke, pp. 232–6.

43 *Anulus*, ed. Haacke, pp. 224–6; Van Engen, *Rupert of Deutz*, pp. 148–9.

44 Langmuir, "Peter the Venerable," pp. 197–204.

45 *Adversus Iudeorum*, ed. Friedman, 4, lines 1464–85, p. 109. See James Muldoon, *Popes, Lawyers and Infidels* (Philadelphia, PA: University of Pennsylvania Press, 1979), pp. 119–25, 132–5, for what happened when Christians later discovered areas like the Canaries, which were untouched by Christianity.

46 *Adversus Iudeorum*, ed. Friedman, 3, lines 835–51, p. 65.

47 *Adversus Iudeorum*, ed. Friedman, 4, lines 1244–65, p. 103.

48 Essential for an understanding of the phenomenon of medieval outcasts is Robert I. Moore, *The Formation of a Persecuting Society* (Oxford: Basil Blackwell, 1987).

49 In the late thirteenth century Jews were accused of desecrating the Host in an attempt to make Christ suffer yet again at their hands; see Gavin Langmuir, *History, Religion and Anti-Semitism* (Berkeley, CA: University of California Press, 1990), pp. 300–1, and Miri Rubin, Chapter 14, this volume.

50 Torrell, "Les juifs," pp. 337–8; Abulafia, "Christian imagery," p. 388.

14

DESECRATION OF THE HOST

The birth of an accusation

Miri Rubin

Eucharistic belief was an important aspect of Christian religion in the central Middle Ages. From at least the eleventh century there was considerable debate about the actual presence of Christ within the newly consecrated bread and wine of the Eucharist. By the end of the twelfth century Christian belief in the miracle of transubstantiation, the transformation of that bread and wine into the body and blood of Christ through a miracle that occurs every time a priest celebrates the Mass, had been thoroughly established. Using distinctions between "substance" and "accidents" derived from Aristotelian philosophy, theologians described the bread and wine being consecrated as miraculously becoming the "substance" of Christ himself, although continuing to have the "accidental" appearance of mere bread and wine. Each scrap of the Eucharist was Christ himself – just as every part of a broken mirror still reflected an entire image. While the wine was used up during the service (and was increasingly reserved for the priest alone), the consecrated bread was distributed to parishioners and some reserved for the sick. As these consecrated wafers came to be considered relics of Christ himself, they received increased devotion, including the establishment of a feast for this body of Christ, Corpus Christi. As the Host became more venerated, as a relic of Christ, who had left no earthly relics because he had ascended to heaven, Christian concern about protecting the Host increased.

In this chapter Miri Rubin considers tales of desecration of the Host, the miraculous body of Christ. These increased fear of disrespect, desecration, and violence against the Eucharist which then justified Christian violence and hatred against Jews. Implicit in the anti-Jewish tales of Host desecration that Rubin examines are other Christian anxieties epitomized in age, class, and gender stereotyping. Thus it was always Jewish males who attacked the Host, while it is often a poor, ignorant, frequently elderly Christian woman who handed over the Host to the Jews, and Christian or Jewish children who were respectively sacrificed or saved. This chapter originally appeared in Christianity and Judaism: Studies in Church History, *ed. Diana Wood, 29 (1992), pp. 169–85.*

* * *

A new tale entered the circle of commonplace narratives about Jews which were known to men and women in the thirteenth century: the tale of Host desecration. This new narrative habitually unfolded as (1) an attempt by a Jewish man to procure (buy, steal, exchange) a consecrated Host in order to (2) abuse it (in re-enactment of the Passion, in ridicule of bread claimed to be God), (3) only to be found out through a miraculous manifestation of the abused Host, which leads to (4) punishment (arrest and torture unto death, lynching by a crowd).[1] The tale was a robust morality story about transgression and its punishment, and it always ended with the annihilation of the abusing Jew and often of his family, neighbors, or the whole local Jewish community. It was a bloody story, both in the cruelty inflicted on the Host/God and in the tragic end of the accused abuser and those related to him. This basic narrative was open to myriad interpretations and combinations, elaborations at every stage of its telling. It is a particularly interesting narrative inasmuch as it was often removed from the context of preaching and teaching, of exemplification, into the world of action and choice. The Host-desecration tale was not only a poignant story about Jews, it was also a blueprint for action whenever the circumstances of abuse suggested themselves in the lives of those who were reared on the tale. The story's fictionality was masked from the very beginning of its life: it was always told as a report about a real event, with no irony or explicit elaboration. It was a concrete, new tale, which provided tangible knowledge about Jews and, through the actions of Jews, about the Eucharist.

It is usually claimed that the archetype of the Host-desecration tale is that of Paris at Easter of 1290.[2] A Jew named Jonathan, who lived in the parish of Saint-Jean-en-Grève, approached a woman who had come to redeem some pawned clothes around Eastertime. He offered to hand over the clothes "without taking any of her money" if she would bring him the Host which she would receive at Easter Communion.[3] The covetous woman was tempted to do so and provided the man with the Host, who then proceeded to abuse "the meritorious person" in it. He threw it into a boiling pot of water, then pierced it with a knife, only to find that the Host was not destroyed and that the water "became bright red as if mixed with blood."[4] An elaborate Latin version of the case imputed to the Jews a desire to ridicule that which Christians claimed to be their God.[5] They pierced it with knives and pins and saw it bleed (see Figure 14.1), threw it into boiling water, only to see it turn into a figure of the crucified Christ hovering over the boiling cauldron.[6] Here the Jew, his wife, son, and daughter looked on when the figure of Christ appeared above the boiling cauldron. The desecration was revealed when the Jew's son ran into the parish church and called out to the Christians there that they were wrong to think that Christ was on the altar, since he was being killed at his own home, by his own father.[7] A woman of the congregation came forth, and after making the sign of the Cross came to the Jewish house and saw the scene of abuse. She had the parish priest called, and the Host

Figure 14.1 "Two Jews desecrating the Host with knives." London, British Library, MS
Harley 7026, folio 13r, marginal illustration (© British Library).

recovered, after which the Jew was arrested; and in another version the bishop
of Paris, Simon de Bucy (1290–1304), was alerted, and two sergeants were
called to arrest the Jew.[8] It goes on to say that the regent professors of theology
were consulted, and together with the judgment of the people this led to a
verdict of death by fire, while the Jew's family converted, and his daughter
joined the monastery of les Filles-Dieu.[9] The Jew's house was confiscated, and
by 1295 a license was granted by Pope Boniface VIII (1294–1303) for the
building of a chapel on the site of the Jew's house.[10] A cult soon developed
there, around the miraculous Host, as well as in the parish church of Saint-
Jean-en-Grève, which held the "holy knife" with which Jonathan was said to
have perpetrated the desecration. It attracted pilgrims and the attentions of
a branch of the Carmelite Order, which settled and ran the miracle chapel.
The chronicle of Saint-Denis and the court chronicle soon helped spread the
story in the monastic milieu of the Île-de-France. By 1294 the chronicler, John
of Thilrode of Saint Bavo's abbey, in Ghent, recorded the tale in the early
version which placed a maid in the Jewish household as the accomplice.[11] By
1299 a royal ordinance for the south of France relating to Jewish "perfidy"
included among the Jewish offences the desecration of the Host:

> Jews provoke Christians as a result of their heretical depravity and
> with their abominable hands they have wickedly presumed to handle
> the most holy body of Christ and to blaspheme the other sacraments

of our faith, by seducing a very great number of simple folk and by circumcising those who have been seduced.[12]

Yet there are reasons to question the uniqueness of the attribution of an origin in Parisian circles. Further to the east, in the Rhineland, Alsace, and Franconia, we encounter already earlier in the century the development of narratives about Jewish abuse which come just short of the full-blown Host-desecration accusation. There is the case of the young man of Cologne, son of a convert, who received the Host and took it out of his mouth in the churchyard, only to find the Host turn into a tiny infant on the palm of his hand. Mysterious voices threatened him in utterances made up of scriptural verses. When he buried the little creature and hoped to get away he was stopped by the Devil. He finally gave up and called a priest, to whom he confessed, convinced of the truth of Christian faith.[13] This tale is the product of a reworking of more traditional material, which was common in the early Middle Ages and which had the Jew act as a witness to, and a conduit for, the manifestations of faith which ultimately swayed him and his to join the faith. Here, though, was not a Jew, but a convert's son, and a witnessing of miracles served to strengthen the young man's faith and fortified that of the future audiences of the tale. Some time in the 1280s it was told in Saint-Dié, near Épinal, that a Jew had procured a Host and was apprehended by the parish priest just in time, before the abuse had taken place. Two of the eight glass medallions in the local church describe scenes related to the planned abuse: one shows the Jew in a burgess's house, giving the Christian a box in which to place the Host, and another shows a suspicious priest catching the Jew.[14] Some time in the late 1280s an accusation of Host desecration in Büren (Westphalia) resulted in the killing of Jews and the building of an expiatory chapel.[15]

Within the secular and the religious legal systems an awareness of this category of activity becomes evident in these very decades. The Council of Vienne of 1267 required Jews to stay indoors behind closed windows and doors from the time of the sounding of the bell which announced a procession with the Eucharist to the sick.[16] In 1281 King Rudolf of Austria sat in judgment during a visit to Vienna in the case of a Jew who had thrown stones at a priest carrying the Eucharist to the sick.[17] Godfrey Giffard, Bishop of Worcester (b. 1235–d. 1301), sent a mandate to the archdeacons of Westbury and Bristol to pronounce excommunicate the Jews of the city, following a case of injury inflicted on the Host as it was being taken to a sick person by the priest of Saint-Peter's parish, passing by way of the Jewish quarter.[18]

So a preoccupation with the contact which Jews might have with the Eucharist provided the insight at the heart of the newly evolving tale of abuse, and determined the possibilities of punishment and redress inherent in it. The emphasis in the tales will move from witness to transgression and its punishment, from the possibilities of inclusion and absorption of the doubting Jew to the insistent need to purge him and his effects out of the Christian body.

It is interesting to note that the Jew was always the male Jew, and, in particular, the Jew as father. Already in the early Middle Ages a fascination with the hard-hearted, stubborn Jewish male encapsulated the whole attitude to Jews. Whereas Jewish children in their purity could be made to see the light of Christian truth, and the tender mother might be swayed by her son's insight, the Jewish father stood in the way. The Jewish father stood for the Law in its cruel and unyielding nature; whereas the woman/mother was assimilated into the image of female gentleness, seen as a person easily influenced, and more readily moved by affective manifestation, the person who might convert through miraculous illumination, together with her children, as in the most important tale of the early medieval repertoire, that of the Jewish boy. In this tale a Jewish boy, who went to school with Christian boys, saw the child Christ in the consecrated Host while attending and receiving Communion at Christmas with his friends.[19] When the boy returned home and was asked by his father of his whereabouts, he said that he had been in church and had seen a little boy given to each communicant. This incites the Jewish father to anger and moves him to commit the worst sin of all – infanticide – by throwing his son into a furnace (see Figure 14.2). The Jewish mother cries out, and her wailing summons Christian neighbors, who peer into the oven only to find the boy intact. The boy told of a lovely lady in whose lap he had rested secure within the fire, the woman who had appeared painted in the altarpiece he had seen earlier that day. The mother and son and many

Figure 14.2 "Jewish boy thrown into the furnace," Queen Mary Psalter. London, British Library, MS Royal B VII 2, folio 208r, *c*.1310 (© British Library).

other Jews were moved to conversion, while the father received the punishment, justly inverted, of being thrown into the same furnace. For him, there was no hope, no redress. It is this type of male, paternal Jew who is the active and evil actor of the new type of tale – the Host-desecration tale. This was a typical early medieval tale which moved in the sixth century from Greek material into the hagiographical work of Gregory of Tours (538–93), *De gloria martyrum*, a tale which came to be used in the ninth century as a central miraculous proof in debates about the Eucharist and subsequently was enshrined in the popular genre of Marian tales collected and distinctively codified in the twelfth century.[20]

So the Host-desecration accusation was developing throughout the thirteenth century out of the Eucharistic lore and the tales about Jews. The Eucharist raised so many difficulties and doubts, not only in the minds of theologians, but in the questions of simpler folk and in the context of pastoral practice, and these were often treated through the genre of tale, through miraculous exemplification, through edification by recounting of prodigious proofs of Eucharistic truth.[21] The Host-desecration tale also came to live another life: one of action and violence, as it provided a line of action against real Jews, who had allegedly committed the abuse described so carefully in the tale. The powerful Eucharistic awareness and the peculiar vulnerability of Jews in late medieval towns, as well as the political and legal settings which constructed their modes of existence, all combined to create the circumstances which made the Eucharistic desecration tale a tale of life, applicable to being enacted and re-enacted. Its immediacy and relevance was universal, just as was the sense of the Eucharist's vulnerability, and of Jewish otherness. This is not to say that such sentiments were entertained by all, or that all accusation against Jews succeeded, but rather to say that, to the phobic psyche, and to the poor parish priest, and to poor townsfolk, and to indebted knights, participation in the narrative could be constructed as an act equally pious and advantageous.

How does a new story travel, how does it become established among the commonplaces of a culture, so as to suggest a routine, a truth about the actions of, in this case, Jews? Tracing the tale through its Italian vernacular route is a good example. Out of the many possible transmissions we can trace two: one in the preaching of Giordano da Rivalto, the Florentine preacher (d. 1313) whose vernacular sermons in the city squares were popular, and much excerpted and copied.[22] In November 1304 he was able to tell of recent massacres of Jews following a Host desecration: a Jew had sent his maid to church to get a Host and rewarded her with payment or some other evil, and when she returned he began to abuse the Host, which turned into a little boy. Though his numbers are exaggerated (he claims the death of 24,000 Jews), and details sparse, he knew that a regional pogrom following the abuse of the Host had touched the Jews in another region (he is probably referring to the Franconian massacres of 1298–1300). Now the Dominican Giordano may well have been privy to the early fourteenth-century account of a Dominican friar, Rudolf, prior of Schlettstadt in Alsace, who produced a series of tales about those events, the *Historiae memorabiles*.[23] He may also have heard it on the grapevine of an international order such as his, or even from Florentine merchants who had visited the Rhineland. Giordano told it authoritatively, and with interpretation. He linked these events with others concerning his order, the expulsion of Jews from Sicily, following the intervention of the Dominican Bartholomew of Aquila and his influence on Charles II, King of Naples (1285–1309) to introduce the inquisition to Apulia, with special attention to Jewish crimes, and to force Jews to convert or to go into exile.[24] He told it not as a miracle tale, but as a relevant and stirring event woven into his homiletic structure of the sermon for Saint Saviour's Day. Three decades later Giovanni Villani (d. 1348) told the story as part of his historical account under the year 1290, as "a miracle which occurred in Paris," recounting the tale as it had crystallized there, a tale of a usurer who procured and abused a Host through a simple and poor woman.[25] Giovanni had spent years in the service of the Bardi firm in Flanders between around 1304 and 1312 and, as the tale was known there, could he not have learnt it during his stay in the north, only to use the poignant story in his rich and varied history? It was exactly the tale of Villani which provided the narrative behind a new drama, a "sacred representation," known to us only from the fifteenth century, which provided the version which animated the mind and the eye of Paolo Uccello when choosing the scenes for the six *predella* scenes (a narrative sequence on the edge of an altarpiece) commissioned of him by the confraternity of Corpus Domini of Urbino between 1465 and 1468.[26]

So the Host-desecration accusation moves dynamically between the world of tales, the self-conscious recounting and listening to stories, experienced at leisure, or in the ritualized event of a sermon, and the world of action, as a useful narrative came to be applied and followed in a specific context. By 1294 an accusation was made against Jews in Laa (Austria) for the theft and burial of a consecrated Host in the manure of a stable, an accusation which destroyed the lives of some members of the Jewish community and banished others from the town.[27] Some of the cases recounted by Ruldolph of Schlettstadt are highly instructive: for example, his account of the regional persecutions in Franconia which have come to be known as the "Rintfleisch" massacres, and which lasted for the three years 1298 to 1300, and saw the annihilation of some 146 communities and at least 3,000 Jews.[28] Rudolf identified the spark which set off the terrible blaze in a Host desecration perpetrated in Röttingen, on the river Tauber. Here, the sense of misdeed arose when the cries of a child emanated from a Jewish house inhabited by a childless couple. Children at play who had heard the sound alerted their parents, and the parish women approached the house only to find the scene of abuse, in the course of which the Host manifested itself as the Christ-child and wailed in agony. The local priest was called to acknowledge the events and pronounce the miracle, while a man, called Rintfleisch, sometimes identified as a butcher, but most likely a knight from the vicinity, led a crowd

369

which set out to avenge the wrong in a collective punishment of the Jews by death.[29] The group led by Rintfleisch furthermore carried the events over into the countryside, where massacres of Jews in the villages and small towns around Röttingen were habitually followed by the discovery of abused Eucharistic species in nooks and crannies of smoldering Jewish houses.[30] Thus an explanation and justification of the terrible violence is constructed through the presentation of an almost instinctively motivated vengeance. The regional aspect of massacres following Host-desecration accusations was also grounded in the very tropes of Eucharistic understanding.[31] The Eucharist was, after all, the species whole and perfect, without limit to its quantity, divisible and yet powerful even in its smallest fraction. The Eucharist was eminently divisible, made to be parceled and portioned, by the consecrating priest at the altar, but also by the abusing Jew. In Enns (Upper Austria) in 1420 a Host-desecration accusation was made which ultimately led to the great expulsion of Austrian Jewry in 1421. The rich Jew, Israel of Enns, was said to have procured from the Church of Saint-Lawrence "many little pieces of the sacrament," which he sent to his Jewish associates in the region. The arrests, confiscations, and expulsions under ducal mandate then followed the route of this alleged dissemination.[32]

So we observe in this story of the origin of the events of 1298–1300 an enactment of a narrative of abuse and its punishment, but also the creation of a blueprint for future action. In these dramas certain characters play an important role: the neighbors observing the evidence, the parish priest pronouncing the miracle, the local leader, in Germany most frequently a knight from the lower gentry of the region, and the Jew's accomplice in the figure of a Christian woman. Women played an important part in the narrative: they were represented as weak links in the Christian armor, accomplices and procurers of Hosts for Jews. A maid in a Jewish household was the most common provider of the Host for Jewish pleasure, in other cases a poor sexton persuaded by his wife, a female convert, or a female debtor. The fourteenth-century Egmont Chronicler, William the Procurator, describes the woman as "a certain woman, daughter of the devil," chosen by the Jews of Rymagen about 1323 to bring them the Host after Christmas Communion.[33] Female agency could be very active. In Metz about 1385 a Christian woman and a Jew were burnt. The rich widow had consulted a Jew in pursuit of the lucrative sale of her corn, and he agreed to help her on condition that she bring him Christ's Body ("if she could bring him the sacrament of the holy body of our Lord, we would help her"). She feigned illness and received Communion, fulfilling her part in the bargain. But having put the Host in a box in her cupboard, her servants later discovered that it turned into a toad, and later into a little child.[34]

So the Host-desecration narrative provided voices, roles, and gestures for its actors, but it could also be contested, and its very applicability to local circumstances could be brought into question. In Pulkau a bloodied Host was found on the threshold of a Jew's house and was taken to the local church. A massacre of the Jews ensued. But the narrative of Host-desecration was contested. Responding to local doubts and pressure from the Duke of Austria, the Bishop of Passau set up an investigation into the affair.[35] He was sufficiently anxious to place a consecrated Host side by side with the "miraculous" host, to save simple worshippers from the danger of idolatry if the "discovered Host" turned out to be false. In 1341 the investigator Frederic, a canon of Bamberg Cathedral and doctor of canon law, handed in his report, a tract which was no less than a tract on the Eucharist in ten points, which wholly endorsed any miraculous manifestation by a Host as an obvious proof of the alleged preceding abuse.[36] He further claimed that any magnate who wished to absolve the Jews of the crime was surely acting for the basest of financial motives, greed which had ensnared them into Jewish debt. So the local cult lived on, and in 1396 the *Blutkapelle* or Bloodchapel was built even as the very truth of its miraculous endorsement was in doubt.

Now the investigation in Pulkau was made in a very special context, and it is undoubtedly the exception; most accusations of Host desecration and the ensuing massacres passed with little subsequent comment, and usually without punishment, to be noted only by the chronicler as "in town X a certain number [often specified] of Jews were burned," and in the heart-rending verses of Jewish laments. But in Pulkau some very important local knowledge had come to bear on interpretations of the accusation. Some forty years earlier in the same diocese and not very far away, in Korneuburg, near Vienna, a similar Host-desecration accusation resulted in the establishment of a Eucharistic cult and in a massacre of Jews in 1305. A Jew, Zerkl, a school master, had been caught by a Christian baker and accused of blasphemy and abuse of the Host over a period of three years.[37] The Hosts were recuperated and began working miracles. Yet some doubts had existed as to the nature of the abused Host: had it already been consecrated or was it simply a piece of baked dough? The investigator, the early fourteenth-century Cistercian scholar, Ambrose of Heiligenkreuz, raised some doubts. But the evidence brought to him by witnesses was overwhelming. Miracles took place in front of the Eucharistic particle salvaged from the Jews: candles being lit up spontaneously, the lame beginning to walk, and the blind gaining sight.[38] Ambrose's doubts were not shared by the local community, and he passed on the investigation to a higher instance, a papal investigator. Yet there must have been some further assessment of the case of which we have no remaining evidence, since in his letter of 1338 authorizing the investigation into the Pulkau events, Pope Benedict XII (1334–42) recounted the recent case of Korneuburg as a precedent of fraudulent action.[39] Indeed, some of the contemporary local chroniclers telling the story of Pulkau recounted it as a fraud perpetrated by a poor parish priest, like John of Winterthur, who explained the priest's motivation, "for reason of his indigence."[40] A Host stained red with blood, found on the threshold of a Jewish house,

provided sufficient material for the remaking of the Host-desecration narrative, which ends badly, in death to the perpetrator and to his fellow Jews.
And then this, in turn, became a famous case, to be told and retold by
preachers and chroniclers.

To say that the Host-desecration accusation was a blueprint for action is
not simply to suggest some inexorably self-fulfilling force to it; it is rather to
suggest that authoritative narratives in any culture provide patterns within
which actions it is to be understood, and its shapes appreciated. Every accusation and every massacre which followed it were products of specific
contexts; yet they sought to fulfill the requirements for legitimation suggested
by the Host-desecration narrative. The events which prompted the second
large regional massacre in southwest Germany, the "Armleder" movement of
1336–8 is a good example.[41] It was told as the consequence of an offence
planned by Jews as they saw the Eucharist carried by a priest passing in the
streets. A knight, Arnold of Ussingheim, whose brother had been murdered
by a Jew, and who was in town for a court hearing, appointed himself leader
on a tour of revenge. A well-known local trouble-maker, Arnold had been
banished from the region by the territorial lord, and his gift for arousing
armed crowds is manifest in the events of 1338. He led a group of armed
townsmen (named after the leather arm-guards which they wore), joined by
knights, on a rampage which all but annihilated Franconian Jewry. His forces
were finally stopped around Kitzingen, and he was arrested, tried, and
executed. Yet Arnold's tomb quickly became a site of pilgrimage as his body
was reported to work miracles. And another leader took over as "King" or
"Rex" of the "Armleder" and led the second and then the third waves
throughout Franconia, Alsace, and Bavaria.[42]

So the universal tale, told all over Europe, conveyed in collections of *exempla*
(stories suitable for preaching), in chronicles, in wall-paintings, in religious
drama,[43] and enshrined in the chapels and pilgrimage sites commemorating
specific desecrations, spread near and far, even to England, from which the
Jews were expelled in 1290.[44] The spread of accusations is striking: there were
recurrent massacres in the centers of Jewish settlement in the Rhineland, in
southern imperial lands, and in Austria by the last years of the thirteenth
century, in Polish lands from the 1320s, a single case in the Low Countries,
in Brussels, in 1370,[45] and a few cases in Spain, in Hueca in 1377, and in
Segovia in 1410.[46] Bohemia, which had been comparatively untouched by the
massacres of the Black Death, experienced the accusation in Prague in 1398.[47]
By the fifteenth century Host-desecration crises could directly cause the end
of Jewish settlement with mass killings and expulsions from a region; in some
cases it simply provided the final spur in towns where the citizenry had been
agitating for expulsion of the Jews over decades, like Regensburg and
Nuremberg.[48] By the late fifteenth century, when most of Western Europe was
empty of Jews (most of France, Spain, England, the Low Countries, some
Italian towns), the story grew even more fantastic as it came to be super-
imposed upon the ritual-murder accusation. The most infamous late medieval

accusation, that of the ritual murder of the child Simon of Trent (in 1475), followed by a trial whose copious records have survived, developed into an accusation of Host-desecration.[49]

The cases of Rintfleisch, Pulkau, and Armleder show us that the universal narrative was always told and unfolded within the immediate context of power and politics of a town and its region. That this was not the only course of action, and that there may have been dissenting voices and unsuccessful "tellings" of the narrative is evident from the eloquent testimony of a case like that of Pulkau, where the narrative was not believed by all, or in a city like Regensburg, whose town council stopped the Rintfleisch crowds from entering and injuring its Jews.[50] The tale's force derived from the rich world of Eucharistic knowledge and myth which was being imparted as the very heart of the religious culture, and it was bolstered by an ongoing tension between the Eucharistic claims and the realities or appearances which most people apprehended in and around it. It also derived from the strange vulnerability of Jews: even when legally protected, and their status was very clearly defined in those very imperial lands in which most accusations took place, their lives were always liable to be transposed on to a wholly different plane, into the heart of the anti-Jewish discourse which turned them from neighbors, friends, and business partners into polluting, bestial, and life-denying creatures whose very existence depended on a cost or a loss to the non-Jews. The Host-desecration tale was a narrative produced within this discourse, and the unfolding of a Host-desecration accusation was the creation of a script for the enactment of gestures and the making of utterances learnt and legitimated within it. Versed in these roles, women, priests, children, dukes, and Christian knights all had compelling parts to play.

To concentrate on the birth of a single anti-Jewish narrative is simply to set a single context through which some larger questions can be asked. It points us toward the investigation of the power of narratives within the culture and the element of agency and choice as actors in the past supported or accepted them. It seeks to problematize the complexity of Jewish existence at the heart of the mysteries of Christian culture and in the heart of towns and villages and to suggest some of the terrifying mechanisms which move or facilitate that awful transformation of neighbor into persecutor, of community into murderous crowd, of tolerated other to the object of all phobic energy and destructive desire.

NOTES

1   For a general survey of the Host-desecration accusation see P. Browe, "Die Hostien-schändungen der Juden im Mittelalter," *Römische Quartalschrift* 34 (1926): 167–97.

2   For accounts of this event see, "De miraculo hostiae a Judaeo Parisiis anno Domini MCCXC multis ignominiis effectatae," *Recueil des historiens des Gaules et de la France* (hereafter *RHGF*) 22, pp. 32–3; "Ex brevi chronico Ecclesiae S. Dyonisii ad cyclos paschales," *RHGF* 23, p. 145; "Extrait d'une chronique anonyme finissant en

MCCCLXXX', *RHGF* 21, pp. 123–30; "Extrait d'une chronique anonyme française, finissant en MCCCVIII," *RHGF* 21, pp. 132–3; "Chroniques de Saint-Denis depuis 1285 jusqu'en 1328," *RHGF* 20, pp. 654–724; *Les Grandes chroniques de France*, ed. J. Viard (Paris, 1934), vol. 8, pp. 144–5. See William C. Jordan, *The French Monarchy and the Jews: From Philip Augustus to the Last Capetians* (Philadelphia, PA: University of Pennsylvania Press, 1989), pp. 192–4.

3 "Extrait d'une chronique," p. 133.
4 The descriptions in the "Grandes chroniques," pp. 144–5, the "Extrait d'une chronique," p. 127, and the "Chroniques de Saint-Denis," p. 658, all give very similar versions of the tale. A Latin account claims that a group of Jews had perpetrated the desecration in 1289. It also places the piercing with knives before the boiling in water: "Ex brevi chronico," pp. 145–6.
5 On the imputation of intentions or beliefs to the Jews in cases of Host-desecration see Cecil Roth, "The mediaeval conception of the Jew," in *Essays and Studies in Memory of Linda R. Miller*, ed. Israel Davidson (New York: Jewish Theological Seminary, 1938), pp. 171–90, here pp. 180–2.
6 "De miraculo hostiae," p. 32.
7 "De miraculo hostiae," p. 32.
8 "Extrait d'une chronique," p. 133.
9 "Chroniques de Saint-Denis," p. 658.
10 *Les Registres de Boniface VIII*, 4 vols (Paris, 1884–93), vol. 1, no. 441. See also "De miraculo hostiae," p. 32, and *The Apostolic See and the Jews. Documents: 492–1404*, ed. Schlomo Simonsohn (Toronto: Pontifical Institute of Medieval Studies, 1988), no. 175, pp. 283–4.
11 "Iohannis de Thilrode Chronicon," *MGH, SS*, 25, ed. J. Heller (Hanover, 1880); or in *RHGF* 23, pp. 145–6.
12 Gustave Saige, *Les Juifs du Languedoc antérieurement au XIVe siècle* (Paris: Picard, 1881), no. 20, pp. 235–6, at p. 236. See Sophia Menache, "Faith, myth, and politics – the stereotype of the Jews and the expulsion from England and France," *The Jewish Quarterly Revue* 75 (1984–5), pp. 351–74, p. 364. See also Robert Chazan, *Medieval Jewry in Northern France: A Political and Social History* (Baltimore, MD: Johns Hopkins Press, 1973), pp. 182–3.
13 Told in the *Viaticum narrationum* of Herman of Bologna, *Beiträge zur lateinische Erzählungs-literatur des Mittelalters: III. Das Viaticum narrationum des Hermannus Bononiensis*, ed. A. Hilka (Berlin: Weidmannsche, 1935), no. 72, pp. 100–2.
14 The sequence is enshrined in the stained-glass windows of the abbey church of Saint-Dié of *c*.1280, described to me by Professor Meredith Lillich, whom I warmly thank. [The material has since been published as Meredith Parsons Lillich, *Rainbow like an Emerald: Stained Glass in Lorraine in the Thirteenth and Fourteenth Centuries* (University Park, PA: Pennsylvania State University Press, 1991).]
15 See the document on the foundation of a chapel in *Westfalia Judaica: Urkunden und Regesten zur Geschichte der Juden in Westfalen und Lippe*, eds Bernhard Brilling and Helmut Richtering (Stuttgart: Kohlhammer, 1967), no. 31, p. 56 (1292).
16 Karl-Joseph van Hefele and Henri Leclercq, *Histoire des conciles* (Paris: Letouzey et Ané, 1914), 6, 1, p. 138.
17 "Heinrici de Heimberg Annales," *MGH, SS*, 17, ed. G. H. Pertz (Hanover, 1861), p. 717.
18 *Register of Bishop Godfrey Giffard*, ed. J. W. Willis Bund (Oxford, 1902), vol. 1, p. 71.
19 On the story and its development and dissemination see Theodor Pelisaeus, *Beiträge zur Geschichte der Legende vom Judenknabe* (Halle: s.n., 1914); T. Nissen, "Zu den ältesten Fassungen der Legende vom Judenknabe," *Zeitschrift für französische Sprache und Literatur* 62 (1938–9): 393–403.
20 Richard W. Southern, "The English origins of the 'Miracles of the Virgin,'" *Mediaeval and Renaissance Studies* 4 (1958): 176–216.

21   Miri Rubin, *Corpus Christi: The Eucharist in Late Medieval Culture* (Cambridge: Cambridge University Press, 1991), pp. 109–20.

22   Giordano da Rivalto, *Prediche del B. Giordano da Rivalto recitate in Firenze*, ed. Domenico Moreni, 2 vols (Florence: Magheri, 1831), vol. 2, pp. 227–8; on this report see Jeremy Cohen, *The Friars and the Jews: the Evolution of Medieval Anti-Judaism* (Ithaca, NY: Cornell University Press, 1982), pp. 239–40. On Giordano see Daniel R. Lesnick, *Preaching in Medieval Florence: The Social World of Franciscan and Dominican Spirituality* (Athens, GA: University of Georgia Press, 1989), pp. 103–8, 111–33, 257–8.

23   Rudolf of Schlettstadt, *Historiae memorabiles*, ed. E. Kleinschmidt (Cologne: Bohlau, 1974); on the author, pp. 9–12.

24   Giordano da Rivalto, *Prediche*, vol. 2, pp. 231–2. On the introduction of the inquisition into Jewish matters in France, see Maurice Kriegel, "La Jurisdiction inquisitoriale sur les juifs à l'époque de Philippe le Hardi et Philippe le Bel," in *Les Juifs dans l'histoire de France: premier colloque international*, ed. Myriam Yardeni (Leiden: Brill, 1980), pp. 70–7.

25   "Croniche di Giovanni, Matteo e Filippo Villani," *Bibliotheca classica italiana secolo xiv* (Trieste: 1857), vol. 21, c. 143, p. 166.

26   Marilyn A. Lavin, "The Altar of Corpus Christi in Urbino: Paolo Uccello, Joos Van Ghent, Piero della Francesca," *Art Bulletin* 49 (1967): 1–24, here 1–10.

27   "Continuatio Zwetlensis tertia," *MGH, SS*, 9, ed. A. Wattenbach (Hanover, 1851), p. 658.

28   On the massacres, Friedrich Lotter, "Hostienfrevelvorwurf und Blutwunderfälschung bei den Judenverfolgungen von 1298 ('Rintfleisch') und 1136–1338 ('Armleder')," in *Fälschungen im Mittelalter* (Hanover: Hahn, 1988), vol. 5, pp. 533–83, here 548–60; Friedrich Lotter, "Die Judenverfolgung des 'König Rintfleisch' in Franken um 1298. Die endgültige Wende in den christlich-jüdischen Beziehungen im Deutschen Reich des Mittelalters," *Zeitschrift für historische Forschung* 15 (1988): 385–422. For a map of the massacres see *Germania judaica*, ed. Zvi Avneri (Tübingen: J. C. B. Mohr, 1963) 2, 1, at end. See the Jewish sources in *Das Martyrologium des Nürnberger Memorbuches*, ed. Siegmund Salfeld (Berlin: L. Simion, 1898), pp. 162–200, 231–6.

29   Rudolf of Schlettstadt, *Historiae memorabiles*, c. 6, pp. 49–51.

30   Rudolf of Schlettstadt, *Historiae memorabiles*, c. 6, pp. 49–51.

31   See the report of *Chronica S. Petri Erfordiensis*, ed. Oswald Holder-Egger, *MGH, SS rerum Germ.*, 42 (Hanover, 1899), p. 319.

32   Thomas Ebendorfer, *Chronica austria, MGH, SS*, new series, vol. 13, ed. Alphons Lhotsky (Hanover, 1967), bk 3, pp. 370–1. Such a pattern also falls in with that of the ritual murder, which in the Norwich version imputed to the European Jewry an annual rotating schedule of child murder by which a community was chosen annually to murder and provide the blood for the Paschal ritual; on this myth see Gavin I. Langmuir, "Thomas of Monmouth: detector of ritual murder," in *Towards a Definition of Antisemitism* (Berkeley, CA: University of California Press, 1990), pp. 209–36.

33   William the Proctor, *Chronicon comitum et nobilium Hollandiae ab 1206–1332*, ed. A. Matthaeus (The Hague, 1738), vol. 2, pp. 496–718, at p. 611.

34   Paris, BN, MS nouv. acq. 4857, fol. Q262. On this case see Joseph Weill, "Un Juif brulé à Metz vers 1385 pour profanation d'hostie," *Revue des Études Juives* 53 (1907): 270–2.

35   *The Apostolic See*, ed. Simonsohn, pp. 372–4.

36   Vienna, Austrian National Library, MS 350, fols 1ra–17vb.

37   *Urkundenbuch des Stiftes Klosterneuburg bis zum Ende des vierzehnten Jahrhunderts*, ed. Hartmann Zeibig (Vienna: Hof und Staatsdruckerei, 1868), pp. 172–5.

38   On the case of Korneuburg see Klaus Lohrmann, *Judenrecht und Judenpolitik im mittelalterlichen Österreich* (Vienna: Böhlau, 1990), p. 105; see also the case of Saint- Pölten,

p. 106; see also with a reproduction of the altarpiece *Die Zeit der frühen Habsburger. Dome und Klöster 1279–1379* (Vienna: Amt d. Niederosterr, 1979), no. 119, p. 364; Lotter, "Hostienfrevelvorwurf," pp. 559–60.

39   *The Apostolic See*, ed. Simonsohn, p. 372.

40   *Die Chronik Johanns von Winterthur*, ed. Carl Brun and Friedrich Baethgen, *MGH, SS rerum Germ.*, new series, vol. 3 (Berlin, 1924), pp. 142–3.

41   On which see K. Arnold, "Die Armledererhebung in Franken 1336," *Mainfränkisches Jahrbuch für Geschichte und Kunst* 26 (1974): 35–62.

42   Arnold, "Die Armledererhebung," pp. 44–53.

43   In the fifteenth century Alfonso da Spina claimed that the tale decorated many a French chapel, *Fortalitium fidei* (Lyons, 1511), bk 3, *consideratio* 9; Lynette Muir, "The mass on the medieval stage," *Comparative drama* 23 (1989–90): 314–30, here 317–18.

44   On the English version of the drama of Host-desecration, see S. Beckwith, "Ritual, Church and Theatre: medieval dramas of the sacramental body," in *Culture and History, 1350–1660: Essays on English Communities, Identities and Writings*, ed. David Aers (Detroit, MI: Wayne State University Press, 1992), pp. 65–89.

45   For a short account and a bibliographical survey see Jean Stengers, *Les Juifs dans le Pays-Bas au moyen-âge* (Brussels: Palais des académies, 1950), pp. 24–7, 132–47.

46   J. Miret y Sans, "El procés de les hosties contra les jueus d'Osca en 1377," *Anuari de l'Institut d'Estudis Catalanas* 4 (1911–12): 59–80; Joshua Bruyn, *Van Eyck Problemen* (Utrecht: Kunsthistorisch Instituut der Rijksuniversiteit, 1957), pp. 143–4.

47   F. Graus, *Struktur und Geschichte. Drei Volksaufstände im mittelalterlichen Prag* (Sigmaringen: J. Thorbecke, 1971), pp. 50–60.

48   On the process of expulsion from late fifteenth-century Imperial territories, see Markus J. Wenninger, *Man bedarf keiner Juden mehr. Ursachen und Hintergründe ihrer Vertreibung aus den deutschen Reichsstädten im 14. Jahrhundert* (Vienna: H. Bohlaus, 1981).

49   Willehad P. Eckert, "Beatus-Simoninus – aus den Akten des Trienter Juden-prozesses," in *Judenhass – Schuld des Christen?!*, eds Willehad P. Eckert and Ernst L. Ehrlich (Essen, 1964), pp. 329–58; Willehad P. Eckert, "Aus den Akten des Trienter Judenprozesses," in *Judentum im Mittelalter*, ed. Paul Wilpert (Berlin, 1966), pp. 283–336. Professor R. Po-chia Hsia is currently investigating afresh the contents and influence of the Trent affair. [See his *Trent 1475: Stories of a Ritual Murder Trial* (New Haven, CT: Yale University Press, 1992).]

50   See "Eberhardi archidiaconi Ratisponensis annales," *MGH, SS*, 17, ed. G. H. Peru (Hanover, 1861), p. 597.

15

THE TWO FACES
OF SECULAR VIOLENCE
AGAINST JEWS

David Nirenberg

David Nirenberg's work contends that the violent acting out of hatred and distrust of "others" within medieval Christian Spain was a complicated phenomenon, character-ized by local activity rather than universal trends, ebbing and flowing according to local circumstances, rather than moving always toward ever more hateful violence. His account of activities against the Jews during Holy Week is that of ritualized activity. Such attacks on Jews also manifested conflict between civil and ecclesiastical authori-ties that might precede, or even act as a substitute for, violence between the commun-ity and the Jews. In this activity it was primarily clerics, but often very young ones – adolescent and prepubescent males, tonsured and in minor clerical orders – who cre-ated a virtual "office" of the stoning of the Jewish quarter in certain cities in the king-dom of Aragon. Such a ritualized drama was both a demarcation of the exclusion of Jews from Christian society and served to integrate young Christians into their com-munity by allowing them to "prove themselves" in acting against a common "enemy."

The Jews described here were members of a corporate community called the aljama *and they live within the established boundaries of Jewish quarters, the* calls, *which were often located quite close to the cathedral. The fact that Jewish quarters were in close proximity to Christian sacred spaces became most worrisome to Christians during Holy Week, when the riots' ritualized violence recalled that these "others" had been implicated in the Crucifixion of Christ. At most times, the populace seems to have accepted that Jews were to be protected from attack. That protection often was by Christian civil officers who taxed the* aljama *for this policing activity.*

The prevalence of such riots, and the increase and decrease in such violence from year to year, suggests that religious tolerance in Spain, its famed convivencia, *was not always sure. There is no clear evidence – only the arguments from silence in earlier centuries – that violence against Jews saw a sudden upswing in the later Middle Ages; more likely it was a constant.*

This selection opens with a Muslim writer's assertion that, in the Middle Ages, Jews were treated better in Muslim than in Christian lands, but Nirenberg does not attempt here to determine whether or not this was true. The selection comes from

David Nirenberg, "The Two Faces of Secular Violence," Chapter 7 from Communities of Violence: Persecution of Minorities in the Middle Ages *(Princeton, NJ: Princeton University Press, 1996), pp. 200–30.*

* * *

The Muslim polemicist Ahmad ibn Idrīs al-Qarāf ī (d. 1285) reports:

> In the remainder of the cities of the Franks they have three days in the year that are well known, when the bishops say to the common-folk: "The Jews have stolen your religion and yet the Jews live with you in your own land." Whereupon the commonfolk and the people of the town rush out together in search of Jews, and when they find one they kill him. Then they pillage any house that they can.[1]

For the Egyptian al-Qarāf ī this annual event, the attacking of Jews during Holy Week, was emblematic of the intolerant depravity of European Christians, and he used it (despite what his Iberian coreligionists said differently) to draw an unfavorable comparison of Christian violence against minorities with Muslim tolerance.

Critics today might disagree about the overtly polemical comparative element of al-Qarāf ī's claim,[2] but his reading of Holy Week attacks as emblematic of intolerance is in line with that of the most up-to-date historians. In those few moments when Easter riots surface from the footnotes of modern scholarship, they mark a transition from tolerance to intolerance. The only existing extended commentary on such riots that I know of, on the attack of 1331 in Girona, provides a good example:

> [The riot was] symptomatic of the state of mind beginning to form among some sectors of Christian society in Catalonia during the first half of the fourteenth century, a state of mind increasingly unfavorable to the Jews ... the first symptoms of an anti-Semitism that would gather momentum throughout the fourteenth century, and would pour into the catastrophe of the Jewries, in the year 1391.[3]

The imagery in this passage makes its assumptions clear: Holy Week riots are the tremors that preceded an earthquake, signs of escalating stress at the fault lines of society.[4] In this model, acts of violence are treated as symptoms of increasing intolerance and strung together to create a narrative culminating in tragedy. Such narratives generally focus on the changing power of persecuting discourses, with the violence itself treated as little more than a voltmeter. Hence readings like that of Jean Delumeau's *Fear in the West*, where Holy Week violence (specifically the events of 1331) serves as evidence for the transformation of the "theological discourse" about Jews as Christ-killers from a specialized and local phenomenon into a generalized popular hatred of the Jews.[5]

While modern critics agree with al-Qarāf ī in treating Holy Week riots as uniformly negative signs of intolerance, their approach is at the same time more sophisticated and less well informed than his was: more sophisticated because they place the riots in a Christendom whose intolerance is evolving historically, whereas for al-Qarāf ī such intolerance was rather a defining and monolithic characteristic of (Western) Christianity; less well informed in that they achieve this evolutionary explanation only by ignoring what al-Qarāf ī himself tells us: that Holy Week riots were annual, customary, and quasi-liturgical, not some aberrant symptom of a system gravely ill. Though both equate violence with intolerance, the tension between them is that between the diachronic and the cyclical, between the periodizing interpretations of historians and the rhythm and formal repetition of ritual life.[6]

Because Holy Week riots self-consciously represented a violent ritual paradigm for a level of Christian toleration of Jews, one that persisted with little formal change over a period of centuries, their analysis can uncover some of the assumptions and tensions implicit in our (and al-Qarāf ī's) understanding of medieval violence and intolerance. First, however, we need to reconstruct Holy Week riots themselves: their frequency, their participants, their scripts. Only then can the search for contexts and meanings begin. The plural is deliberate, for the world of Holy Week violence was one in which the sacred was physically experienced, relations of power were criticized, the past became the present, and urban space was transformed. In and through these transformations and extravagances, Holy Week violence argued for the continued existence of Jews in Christian society, while at the same time articulating the possibility of and conditions for their destruction.[7]

When al-Qarāf ī used the word "Franks," he meant by it Western European Christians, not just Frenchmen. The religious riots[8] he described extended throughout most of the Mediterranean basin, that is, from the Iberian Peninsula through southern France and into Italy.[9] He was right, too, in stressing the sense of annual tradition, for Holy Week riots were an ancient phenomenon even in al-Qarāf ī's time. Variants of such attacks were recorded in Toulouse in 1018, and an accord purporting to *end* the "custom" in Béziers was dated 1161, while Cecil Roth believed that the practice may have dated to antiquity.[10] Antique, perhaps, but with a long future as well. In a folklorized form the Holy Week "killing of Jews" has survived in parts of Europe, especially Iberia, to the present day. In modern Tortosa, for example, *matâ judiets*, "killing the Jews," was until recently part of the liturgy of Holy Thursday, with children banging sticks and raising bedlam at certain points in the services.[11] Similar festivities have been customary throughout Iberia. In modern Asturias the children would shake their rattles and sing a song with distinct echoes of al-Qarāf ī's episcopal exhortation: "Marrano Jews: you killed God, now we kill you. Thieving Jews: first you kill Christ and now you come to rob Christians."[12]

We can get a sense of the density of these traditions by returning our gaze to the medieval Kingdom or Crown of Aragon. Though the editors of the

1331 inquests described the Girona riots as an anti-Semitic novelty, this type of violence was in fact documented long before 1331 in Girona and elsewhere in the Crown of Aragon. Peter III (1276–85) remembered that, during the reign of his father James I (1213–76), the king had spent a Good Friday in the city of Girona. Members of the clergy nevertheless rang an alarm or tocsin from the cathedral belfry, then attacked the Jewish quarter, so that King James I was forced to take up arms to defend his Jews. Peter III himself complained on several occasions to the bishop of Girona about the behavior of the clergy during Holy Week, most vehemently in 1278, when clerics and their familiars again stoned the Jewry of Girona from the cathedral's belfry at about Easter time. Jewish vineyards and gardens were damaged, and, when the town crier ordered the rioting clergy to cease in the name of the king, the perpetrators laughed and mocked him.[13] The events of 1278 may have been especially troubling to King Peter because property was destroyed. Unless extensive damage occurred, people were injured, or Jewish communities asked for special protection, Good Friday riots were tolerated, and their mention often omitted from any chancery documentation.

That they nevertheless occurred frequently is evident from more local records. In or about 1302, for example, and again in Girona, clerics attacked the *call*, or Jewish quarter of the town. A young boy named Nicolas, the stepson of a silversmith, was injured when he was struck on the head by a slingshot swung by Simon, a fifteen-year-old cleric. Nicolas died some days later. As the cause of death was uncertain and could constitute an impediment to Simon's promotion into major orders of the priesthood, an inquest was held. Among the witnesses a doctor named Berenguer Sariera testified that,

> as far as his memory goes, which is some twenty years and more, he has seen in the city of Girona, as well as in Barcelona and Valencia, and in other places of Catalonia, that students and adolescents threw rocks at the Jews . . . on Good Friday . . . and he thinks that this aforesaid custom and observance has gone on thirty years and more, in most places of Catalonia.[14]

Clearly 1331 was no "anti-Semitic novelty" but one in a long series of annual Holy Week attacks on the Jewish *call* of Girona.[15]

Such attacks were even more widespread geographically than Berenguer Sariera thought. A cursory survey documents these events throughout the Crown, in Barcelona, Vilafranca del Penedès, Camarasa, Pina, Besalú, Daroca, Alcoletge, Valencia, Burriana, Apiera, and Teruel.[16] Obviously many more riots occurred than survive in the documentation: all the witnesses at the Girona inquest of *c.*1302 swore the riots had been annual for decades, though only a very few surface in royal archives before that date. The Jews themselves seem to have been reluctant to appeal to the king unless matters got out of hand. A short time before the Gironese riot of 1331, a group of children dancing to the music of a *jongleur* named Bernard de Campdara had been incited by the *jongleur* to throw stones at a Jewish funeral procession. The bailiff arrested Bernard but later released him at the request of one of the secretaries of the Jewish community, or *aljama*, who refused to press charges.[17] It was a Christian widow, not the Jews, who complained of the riots in Burriana. A house she rented to a Jew had been damaged by the rioters, and she wanted compensation.[18]

Even in years for which we have no evidence of riots, we know they were anticipated. Sometime in the decade of the 1370s, for example, a visitor to the *call* of Girona on Good Friday found it guarded by a number of lower-level royal officials (*curritores* and *sagiones*). The level of alert seems not to have been very high: the anonymous visitor was apparently so scandalized by the carousing of the officials and the Jews that he reported it to the Inquisition. According to the accusation, the officials ate, drank, and gambled with the Jews. When the bailiff came by on patrol and saw these activities, he fined the Christians for gambling outside of approved premises but took no further action. Bailiff and officials both were denounced.[19]

The hiring of guards, usually lower officials, to protect Jewish *aljamas* during Holy Week was customary. For Zaragoza, where I have found no record of riots, it may be significant that the salary of guards for Good Friday and a provision for alms to be distributed on Easter were listed among those expenses most necessary for the *aljama*, along with payments of debts owed, taxes, maintenance of the royal lions, the salaries of rabbis, and Christmas presents for royal officials.[20] The earliest document I have found attesting to the use of Christian guards, from 1287, ordered officials of Besalú to ensure that the guards protecting the Jews were not molested on Good Friday.[21] Some two centuries later, in 1473, the Jews of Castellon refused to pay the customary protection fee to the lieutenant of the justice of that town, arguing that, instead of protecting them on Thursday, Friday, and Saturday of Holy Week, the lieutenant had stoned them himself and incited others to do so as well.[22]

If such hired police officials proved insufficient protection, a community would be obliged to defend itself. Vigorous self-defense had its dangers, however, since it could involve the Jews in feuds, retaliatory attacks, and royal fines for death or loss of limb. Perhaps this difficulty was behind the privilege issued by Infant Alfonso (d. 1468) to Jewish settlers in Alcoletge:

> If perchance anyone, Christian or Muslim, impelled by audacity, wishes or attempts to invade or rob those Jews, their houses, or their goods . . . the Jews can defend themselves . . . against the aforesaid invaders and injurers, whosoever they be and of whatever status. And that if in said invasion or conflict the invaders are hit or injured, even if death is the result, no petition or demand can be made against the said Jews. . . . And if the friends of one thus injured or hit wish

vindictively to inflict harm or damage upon those Jews, we and our officials are bound to defend and maintain the Jews and their goods.[23]

The phrase "Christian or Muslim" in this edict is not accidental. Muslim attacks against Jews during Holy Week are documented in Daroca (1319) and Pina (1285); others may have occurred. Muslim participation might suggest that the religious specificity of Holy Week riots against Jews had been worn down through custom and repetition. More likely it reflects the fact that, at least in their polemics, Muslims in Christian Spain attacked the Jews for rejecting Jesus's revelation. Through Holy Week violence Muslims aligned themselves with the Christian majority as avengers of Christ.[24] Ahmad ibn Idrīs al-Qarāf ī would have been most surprised.

Before we can talk of what these riots meant, how they functioned, or how they could be manipulated, we need to know what actually occurred in them. For the twentieth-century historian, haunted by memories of the pogroms of the Pale and Kristallnacht, it is easy to imagine a scene of uncontrolled and murderous fury, violence, and looting such as this from Kiev:

> At twelve o'clock at noon [in April 1881], the air echoed with wild shouts, whistling, jeering, hooting, and laughing. An enormous crowd of young boys, artisans and laborers was marching. The entire street was jammed with the barefoot brigade. The destruction of Jewish houses began. Windowpanes and doors began to fly about, and shortly thereafter the mob, having gained access to the houses and stores, began to throw upon the streets absolutely everything that fell into their hands. Clouds of feathers began to whirl in the air. The sound of broken windowpanes and frames, the crying, shouting, and despair on the one hand, and the terrible yelling and jeering on the other, completed the picture. . . . Shortly afterwards the mob threw itself upon the Jewish synagogue, which, despite its strong bars, locks and shutters, was wrecked in a moment. One should have seen the fury with which the rill-raff fell upon the [Torah] scrolls, of which there were many in the synagogue. The scrolls were torn to shreds, trampled in the dirt, and destroyed with incredible passion. The streets were soon crammed with the trophies of destruction. Everywhere fragments of dishes, furniture, household utensils, and other articles lay scattered about.[25]

Consider how different from this image is the picture that emerges from eyewitness accounts of royal officials present during the Girona riot of 1331:

> On Holy Thursday, the bailiff "heard that clerics were attacking and invading the walls and gates of the aforesaid *call*, and . . . immediately went to the said gate, and . . . saw many tonsured students or

clerics ranging in age from ten to twelve years, who fled when they saw this witness . . . with them there were a few boys between fifteen and eighteen years of age. . . . (He) then inspected the said wall and gate and saw that . . . some few stones had been removed from it. . . ." Similarly, the next morning, he "went with some other officials of the said court to the said *call*, and when he got there, he saw nobody over twelve years of age, and he saw there a large rock wedged against the door. . . . Later that day . . . he heard that the *call* was being invaded and attacked, and he went to the *call* immediately but saw no one there, and he inspected the said wall and gate and saw that the props of the gate were moved away from the gate toward the wall, and this witness immediately had it pushed back. . . ." He also heard that "the aforesaid gate was set afire by a tonsured son of Raymond Alberti, some fourteen years of age, and by a son of the said vicar, a tonsured cleric . . . some twelve years of age, and by another tonsured cleric some twelve years of age, which fire was extinguished by the Jews of the *call* . . . and no evil resulted from this." Another witness out for a stroll saw "many clerics . . . throwing rocks against the *call*."[26]

The "attack and invasion" of the *call* of Girona in 1331 was an attack upon its walls and gates. This is what is meant by the phrase "they stoned the Jewish *call*" that appears in this and other documents.[27] This type of attack was not limited to Jews: people often threw stones at the houses of their enemies, or at official buildings. King Alfonso, for example, angrily ordered the justice of Ejea to announce a sixty-shilling fine for anyone who dared throw rocks against the walls or roof of the royal palace in that city.[28] What is emphasized in the 1331 accounts from Girona is not the sense of invasion, but of perimeter and boundary.[29]

Even when attacks were limited to stoning the walls of the Jewish quarter, they were dangerous and frightening. Jews could never be sure that officials would defend them, or that customary restraints would prevail. Furthermore, thrown stones could prove deadly:

It was reported to the bailiff that, during the holiday of Easter, a group of youngsters was playing next to the castle of the Jews of Daroca, and that Pero Xomonez, son of Don Xomen de Palaçio, who was with them, threw a rock over the wall of the castle that injured a Jewish woman, from which injury the woman died. The bailiff pressed charges and the case came before the lord King. . . . [Fine received:] five hundred shillings of Jac.[30]

Nevertheless, although Jews were injured and terrorized, these attacks (at least as reported by Christian witnesses) lacked the face-to-face brutality we tend to associate with pogroms.

To Bertrand de Lauro, vicar of Barcelona in 1308, it was not so much the actions of the attackers as the noise they made that was noteworthy:

> On the Sunday on which this last Feast of the Palm Branches was celebrated, at about dusk, it occurred in the city of Barcelona that some men with rocks stoned and attacked the *call* of the Jews of Barcelona, for which reason there was tumult and a very great noise emitted, at which tumult and noise I immediately went out in order to put down and proceed against those found to be guilty. . . . They intend to pretend that in that event a woman who was one of those who were emitting the sounds was hit by a blow of a stick by one of my retinue.[31]

Verbs of noisemaking run through the account of the 1335 riot in Barcelona as well: "bell-ringing," "making a report or rumor," "they sounded the alarm-bell, the *viafors*."[32] In Vilafranca, the crowd was "clamoring."[33] The bells, too, could be pealed in an alarm or tocsin, as occurred during James I's visit to Girona. Throughout much of the surviving documentation, Holy Week violence against the Jews seems a matter of noise and the stoning of the walls that enclosed the Jewish quarter.[34]

More extensive Holy Week violence did occur. Much of it, however, was directed not at the Jews but at the Christian officials who protected them. Our most detailed source for this is the inquest carried out in 1331 after the attack on those officials who intervened to protect the Jews of Girona.[35] What follows is a narrative composite of the most important testimony.

On the Thursday of Holy Week the bailiff of Girona, Bernat de Bas, had it cried throughout the city that anyone who harmed or insulted the Jews would be fined one hundred shillings. At about ten o'clock on that Thursday, the bailiff together with seven or eight police officials (*sagiones*) walked around the *call* to make sure that no one was harming the Jews. The officials confiscated weapons from clerics they encountered and ordered groups of clerics and children who were throwing stones at the *call* to disband. Near the cathedral, the bailiff saw some twenty armed clerics, servants of clerics, and students who were throwing rocks at the *call*. When they saw the bailiff, the clerics ran into the church; when questioned about their intentions, they complained that the Jews, who should have been shut up in the *call*, were still walking about the city and had fought with the clergy, a charge that the officials denied. When an official tried to take a knife from one of the clerics, the clerics attacked, throwing stones, making a great noise, and yelling. A knife-wielding cleric hit the head of an armed citizen who was trying to help the bailiff and it looked like a mortal stroke, but since he used the flat of the knife and not the edge, the citizen was not injured and went home. Another cleric threatened the bailiff with a dagger to his chest but did not stab him. Two police officials fled into the house of a cleric of the cathedral chapter, where they were found and surrounded by their attackers. Two canons of the cathedral, apparently leaders of the clerical group, pushed up to them and said:

> You dog, son of a dog, what are you doing here, you people, you come to disturb our "office" or "liturgical ritual." You will have an evil day, you and the others, and we will give you so many stab wounds that it will be an evil day for you.

And one of the canons drew his dagger.[36] The abbot of Saint Feliu of Girona, seeing this, restrained the canon and drew him back, and the two officials fled back to the court. Meanwhile, the rest of the officials saw that they were outnumbered and retreated back to the court.

During this first installment of the 1331 riot, the officials seem not to have expected too much trouble. They were lightly armed, confident enough of their authority that at one point the bailiff sent one of his men to disband a group of clerics. Official action was limited to confiscating weapons and ordering groups that were forming in front of important religious buildings to disband. Among the children and young clerics throwing stones, no one was arrested.

When conflict erupted in front of the cathedral, it began with words. The clerical attack itself was not as violent as at first appeared. For example, the bailiff was not stabbed, and the seemingly fatal knife blow to the head of one participant turned out to have been a strike with the flat part of the knife. The two officials who were cornered and threatened with death were allowed to flee. All the participants showed their willingness to act violently: weapons were displayed, insults were shouted, people took up aggressive stances. These were actions that if carried through seriously would have resulted in severe injury to the officials. In fact, the actions were restrained, punches were pulled, and only minor injuries or humiliation resulted. The participants seem to have been following informal protocols, or rules of engagement, that prevented excessively brutal violence. In this sense, the confrontation between clergy and officials can be called "ritualized aggression."[37]

There are indications in the above account that the stoning of the *call* was a ritual event *for the Christians* as well. Virtually all participants in the stone-throwing were clerics or from the retinues of clerics. These ranged from ten-year-old children to beneficed clergy, canons, and abbots. All the attacks occurred in front of religious buildings (the archdeacon's house, the bishop's court, the cathedral) fronting on the *call*. According to the clerics, the conflict began over a ritual transgression: the Jews refused to remain within their quarter during Holy Week.[38] The clerics thus presented themselves as enforcing the purity of a religious festival. Most suggestive is the cleric Vidal de Villanova's complaint against the two trapped officials that they had come to disturb the clerics' "offices," or "liturgical ritual," an offense which, Vidal threatened, would cost them their lives. For Vidal and his colleagues, stoning the *call* was an important part of the Easter service and the divine office.

The ritual, even ludic or playful, aspect of the violence is evident in the terms contemporaries used for it. Both officials and clerics referred to various aspects of the events of Holy Thursday 1331 as *jochs*, that is, games, jokes, or plays. The bailiff was most explicit: "By my faith, sir, we are dealing with evil people. You see what a game the clerics are making for us, that they do not wish to be prevented by us from stoning the Jews." One of the clerics had already justified the clerical attack upon the *call* by complaining ironically, "You see what a beautiful game this is, that the Jews are still walking through the town."[39] The word *joch* was used to describe the re-enactment of the Passion on Good Friday as well, as in the ledger entry for expenses "necessitated by the representation of the Good Friday games."[40] This vocabulary, imprecise as it is, reminds us that we are not far from the world of play and carnival invoked by Mikhail Bakhtin in his treatment of "monkish pranks" and "Paschal laughter."[41] As testimony to the importance of fulfilling these offices and rituals, and the dangers inherent in failing to do so, consider the anxieties of the town council of Castellón de la Plana when their Corpus Christi procession was canceled because a local official had been excommunicated: "For they understood that our Lord God would not conserve their health nor multiply the fruits and harvests which had been commended to the earth."[42] To call these events an "office" or "ritual" is not to deny that they might be terrifying or brutal. They were, however, stylized, restrained, and significant.

The events of Holy Thursday 1331 did not end with the bailiff's flight. The bailiff asked the subvicar for support, and then, hearing that the *call* was again under attack, both returned with about twenty-five armed men to the cathedral. As the bailiff discussed the events with the noblewoman Elionore de Cabrera, who was also there, he heard a great noise and saw that his men were fighting with the clerics; they were striking each other with knives and throwing rocks. The clerics were shouting, "Kill them, kill them." One official entered the church while fleeing from two clerics with knives. There some clerics tried to stab him, though one intervened on his behalf and he escaped. The attackers had yelled, "Kill him, kill him, for he is of the bailiff's company." The officials retreated and the clerics locked themselves in the church. The hue and cry was raised, and the vicar arrived with his men to support the bailiff. Together the officials went to the cemetery, where they saw clerics among the tombs preparing stones to throw at them. At this point the sworn men of the city and other leading citizens came to support the royal officials. Finally, because of the great scandal that might result from a confrontation on holy ground, the officials returned to the court, declaring that the king would soon be in Girona and would settle this dispute. The vicar again spoke to the archdeacon and some canons; then the clergy came down from the tombs, and the citizens who had come to help the bailiff, along with other officials, went back to the city. Back at the court, they heard several reports that the *call* was being attacked, and each time found minor damage to the walls.

The protagonists are now more heavily armed, the stakes higher, but controls on the violence are still visible. Though the clerics chanted, "Kill them," when they actually cornered an official he was permitted to escape. At the point when serious injury seemed inevitable, the officials raised the hue and cry, calling all officials and the citizenry to their defense. The arrival of reinforcements did not result in a defeat for the violent clerics, however. They immediately took refuge in the church and demanded that the officials leave consecrated ground. With the emphasis shifted from a siege of the *call* to a siege of the cathedral, the parties spontaneously disbanded, and resolution of the confrontation was put off.

Each phase of the Girona riot had its own protocols and controls. During the first phase, which consisted of throwing rocks against the walls of the *call*, officials themselves were the main instrument of control, confiscating weapons that might cause severe injury and disbanding crowds. When, perhaps because of a misstep by an official, physical confrontation occurred, the actors emphasized aggressive actions and postures, but restrained themselves and one another from excessively violent behavior. Finally, at the very verge of chaos, the populace could intervene to avert the danger. Despite a narrative of considerable violence, virtually no serious injuries resulted from the riot of 1331.

This, then, was a ritual of escalating violence and excitement barely held in check. Controls could fail, or protocols be violated. The reaction of the bailiff of Girona when this occurred in 1320 is telling:

> Some people, in contempt of royal authority and against the announcement issued by order of Bernat de Olzeto, bailiff of the same city, threw rocks and harmed Jews of that city this past Good Friday. And when the said Bernat, as he ought, prevented them in this, these people, in even greater contempt of the royal eminence, rose up against the said bailiff, and seeking to kill him put him to flight . . . intending to inflict harm and an insidious death upon him. And when the same bailiff had the hue and cry raised throughout the city, no one came to help and defend him, so that the bailiff, frightened by the aforesaid, wishes to abandon his office.[43]

While the pattern followed by the 1331 riot in Girona seems to have been widespread, other patterns were possible. One such occurred in Barcelona in 1335.[44] With the knowledge and consent of the archdeacon of Lleida, tonsured and lay members of his household dug a secret tunnel into the Jewish *call* from a nearby house. The diggers were intimidated by the guards of the *call* and so did nothing on Holy Thursday and Good Friday. But on that

Saturday, after the bell rang for divine service and "when the gates of the *call* stood open, with the guards, as is the custom, far away," they broke through in two holes large enough for two armed men to enter. Once through, they ran into the *call* and straight to a certain synagogue, where they smashed the lamps. Then they removed the Torah scrolls from their cabinet and injured a Jew who was present. After this they broke into a neighboring house, punched the couple living there and stole their money, smashed a coffer belonging to those Jews, and made off with a bag containing loan documents. Back in the streets, they screamed and yelled, fired slingshots at some Jews who came to resist them, and tried to excite the populace against the Jews. At this point the Jews raised the hue and cry, but none of the royal officials came to their aid, much to the displeasure of the king, who ordered judicial proceedings against the perpetrators.

This type of attack, too, had a history. In 1285 the Jews of Pina complained to King Peter that some Christians and Muslims of the town had penetrated into the synagogue and stolen some objects from the compartment where the Torah was kept. The date of the complaint suggests that the incident occurred during or just before Holy Week.[45] In their execution, such attacks differed from the Gironese model in that confrontation with the authorities was deliberately avoided. The breaching of the wall had of necessity to be clandestine if the attack was to attain its goal: the humiliation of the Old Law by the followers of the New. Once this was achieved, the yelling and screaming could begin. These attacks were also more dangerous for the Jews because they involved face-to-face confrontation. With its guards, tunnels, sorties, and walls, the 1335 documentation reads like an account of siege warfare, and so in some ways it was.

With these reconstructions of the riots in hand, we can ask what they resonated with, from what contexts they drew their meanings. One such context is obvious. Hence most analysis of Holy Week begins and ends with the statement that violence occurred because medieval Christians saw the Jews as deicides:

> The medieval Christian believed that the Chosen People was respon-sible for the *deicide*. The Jews constantly suffered reproaches, insults, vexations and other excesses arising from this strange, anachronistic accusation, specifically on the most noted days of Holy Week.[46]

But it is not enlightening, though it may be humane, to call these accusations strange and anachronistic. For contemporaries, deicide was not a matter of the distant past but an annual event.

Medieval re-enactments of the Passion have received a good deal of critical attention, particularly from historians of the theater.[47] These representations generally receive the blame for whipping up the emotions of the mob, inciting the populace to attack the Jews.[48] Both Passion plays and the traditional forms of Holy Week violence that followed them can, however, be viewed in a different light, as ritualized combative games or agonistic events re-enacting and encapsulating the foundational history of Jewish–Christian relations.

Good Friday Passion cycles were one of a number of medieval ceremonies that demanded the participation of Jews, either real or impersonated by Christians. Medieval account books and stage directions are full of references to such roles. Expenses for the Passion re-enacted in Vilareal (Valencia) in 1376 included:

> masks for the Jews, which we had brought from Valencia by Mr. Johan Renau, nine shillings . . . *vayres* painted on paper for the use of the Rabbis, and the painting of the costume of the devil, and four masks for the devils, to the painter of Burriana, five shillings.[49]

For the festival of the Assumption in Tarragona, "first, the Jews are to build a beautiful pavilion, where they will be. Similarly Lucifer and the other devils are to build another."[50]

Of course there is no reason to believe that these parts were played by Jews: Lucifer was not played by Lucifer.[51] Nevertheless, these "Jews" represented for spectators the Jewish role in sacred history. When medieval Christians watched representations of the Passion, they witnessed the sacrificial act from which their history originated. They recognized that this history was affiliated with that of the Jews, that the Jews fulfilled a function in Christian genealogy and society. Far from demanding their excision from the body social, these ceremonies assigned the Jews a fundamental place in the Christian community. In this very restricted sense, Passion cycles could be termed (from the point of view of Christian spectators) "integrative."[52]

Yet in contemporaries' understanding, the Jews' crime had not gone unpunished: of this both history and their immediate present were proof. Christians did not need to be theologians to know that the fall of Jerusalem and the initiation of the Diaspora had been both divine vengeance and evidence of the immanence of Christian empire: they could read this in the numerous epics and apocrypha that sprang from Josephus's *The Jewish War* (written *c.*79 CE), hear about it in stories drawn from these sources, and in some towns even see it re-enacted in "plays of the destruction of Jerusalem."[53] Consider the Catalan epics, *The Destruction of Jerusalem* and *The Vengeance That Vespasian and His Son Titus Inflicted for the Death of Jesus Christ*. These chivalric epics, recently edited by the modern scholar, Josep Hernando i Delgado, vary only slightly from the many other examples of the *Defense of the Savior (Vindicta salvatoris)* genre.[54]

In these epics Vespasian, pagan emperor of Rome and flower of chivalry, was afflicted with the cancer of leprosy by God's command.[55] Once cured by a relic of the Crucifixion, Vespasian swore that he would be baptized with his people, and embarked on the siege of Jerusalem. In the climactic battle the sun stood still, as it had done for Joshua and would do for Charlemagne, that the enemy might not find its escape in darkness. Tunnels and ditches were built against the walls of the city so that the Jews were trapped inside and began to die of starvation. It had been prophesied that Jerusalem would not fall until no stone remained upon another and a mother ate her own child from hunger.[56] To fulfill this latter clause, an angel visited an African queen who lived in Jerusalem and instructed her to eat her child. The odor of the roasting flesh was so sweet that it comforted all who smelled it.

Pilate had ordered all the Jews to eat the treasure, gold, and jewels with which the city was filled, that they might not fall into the hands of the Romans. When the Romans entered the city, they seized all the Jews, and the Emperor sold the Jews, just as the Jews had sold Jesus, though Jesus had cost thirty pennies, while Jews were thirty for a penny. One knight bought thirty Jews, brought them to his tent, and proceeded to disembowel them, but as he removed his sword from the body of the first Jew, the gold and silver the Jew had eaten poured out. All the knights then hurried to buy Jews and disembowel them, until, out of 80,000 Jews, only 180 Jews, that is six pennyworth, remained: these the Emperor kept for himself, so that in their descendants the passion of Jesus would be remembered whenever the Jews were seen. The walls of Jerusalem were torn down, and the surviving Jews were put aboard three ships in Acre, sixty to a ship, and set to the mercies of the wind. Because Jesus wished his passion remembered, and wanted the Jews to serve as examples for all of us, one boat came to Narbonne, another to Bordeaux, and the third to England.[57]

This account of the fall of Jerusalem presents the event as sacrifice, vengeance, and the foundation of Judeo-Christian history in the Diaspora.[58] Like the Passion, vengeance needed to be re-created and remembered: "Present violences resonated with violences past and eternal, and a local topography transmuted into a sacred landscape: the familiar, reiterative astonishing miracle of ritual." The stoning of the Jewish quarter during Holy Week constituted this "miracle."[59]

This second unit of the Holy Week cycle was far from integrative. Its aim was to make brutally clear the sharp boundaries, historical and physical, that separated Christian from Jew.[60] A "theater of conquest," it re-enacted the defeat and humiliation of the Jews.[61] Yet it did so in a stylized and restrained fashion, with participation limited to the clergy.[62] If the Vengeance cycle was a re-enactment of the "sacrificial crisis" at the foundation of the Judeo-Christian encounter, it was nevertheless a ritualized one, a "pugilistic event that evokes the rivalries inherent in the sacrificial crisis."[63] Read as a "ritual sacrifice," Holy Week violence served to reinstitute differences and emphasize boundaries while displacing violence from the interior of the community. By alluding to and containing the original act of vengeance at the foundation of Christian–Jewish relations in the Diaspora, Holy Week attacks flirted with but ultimately avoided the repetition of that violence in contemporary society.[64]

Insofar as it concerned Jews, the Christian Holy Week ritual contained at least two parts: the re-creation of the Passion, a re-enactment of the sacrifice binding the two communities; and the stoning of the *call*, emphasizing vengeance, difference, and boundaries.[65] Neither of these called in any transparent way for the extermination of the Jews. Even the latter could be used to establish a common historical foundation for Iberian Christian and Jewish culture, as when one Jewish chronicler began a chapter on the tribulations suffered by the Jews of Sepharad with Ferdinand I's desire to translate the bones of Saint Isidore, bishop of Seville (d. 636) to Leon in the eleventh century, and used this as a segue into a legend of the destruction of Jerusalem. According to him, Titus was accompanied to Jerusalem by Isidore's father, the latter acting as representative of the king of Seville. While pillaging the city, Isidore's father found an old man shut up in a large house full of books, reading. The wise man had long ago foreseen the siege and gathered all these books together against that day. Marveling at his prophetic wisdom, Isidore's father brought the man back to Seville to be his son's tutor and built him a house there that, according to the chronicler, still stands. Here, the fall of Jerusalem and the resulting diaspora is treated as a "transfer of wisdom," with displaced Jewish erudition and prophecy providing the foundation for the learning and prophetic skills of Saint Isidore, a "founding father" of subsequent Iberian-Christian culture. This was surely not a popular interpretation, but it serves as a reminder that even the fall of Jerusalem could be read in ways that stressed the common history of the two religious communities.[66]

Notwithstanding such idiosyncratic readings, the destruction of Jerusalem as ritually re-enacted in the violence of Holy Week was meant to delimit the space for Jews in Christian culture, not expand it. If the use of the term "ritual" here seems disturbing, it is in part because we have been taught that ritual

> tends to be inclusive, not exclusive, and seeks to bind rather than sunder. Indeed, many anthropological theorists have noted, despite their differing vocabularies or emphases, that participative drama seems to require harmony and good-will among participants for such events to have any magico-religious efficacy.[67]

In contrast, Inga Clendinnen has noted that "interludes of vigorous male action" (contests, battles, games) can be constitutive of sacred action, "however little such episodes square with our notions of sacred etiquette."[68] It was this sort of competitive action in which our stone-throwing clerics were engaged.

The competitive energy coursing through these "vigorous interludes" is one alien to our modern sporting sensibilities. Open-ended competition is obvious in the games of ball that raced up and down the streets of Valencia city on Christmas and other holidays.[69] It is not so evident in the Holy Week battles between clergy and officials, where a clear winner seldom emerged. And it seems completely absent from those moments when the dominant majority ritually defeated a subordinate minority. In the Christian stoning of the Jewish call, for example (or in the Christians' defeat of Muslims in the festival battle of "Moors and Christians"),[70] the winners were preordained. Yet such ritualized and reiterated victories remained both necessary and competitive because the struggle was far from over: until the end of days all victories were insecure. Indeed, Christian competitive anxieties were never greater than during Holy Week and the period surrounding it.

The sharp increase in accusations of blasphemy against Jews during the Jewish festivals of Passover and Purim, and, most especially, the Christian Easter is evidence of such feelings. A revealing one of many examples occurred during Holy Week 1367, in the village of Villanova de Cubells (province of Lleida), where a Christian youth was reading an account of the Passion. Vidal Afraym walked past, and the youth hailed him: "Look, Jew, what a joke your ancestors played on Jesus Christ." When Vidal asked what joke that was, he was told, "They crucified him," to which he responded, "In good faith, had I been there, I would have done so myself . . .!"[71] Vidal's story reflects the fact that at this time of year Jews were suspected of re-enacting the Crucifixion, just as the Christians were doing. But Christians thought that the Jews' intentions were the opposite of their own. Hence some Jews of Sogorb were accused of molding the crucified Jesus out of bread dough and burning him in an oven.[72] In a world where past violences needed to be remembered, Christians tended to assume that Jewish ritual memory was as good as theirs.[73]

Just as Christians could imagine Jews repeating the Crucifixion, they worried as well that the Jews might re-enact the defense of their besieged "Jerusalem" against Christian attack by staging sorties and armed excursions from their quarters during Holy Week. It is in this vein that we should interpret the accusation against some Jews of Zaragoza of building a tower on to their home so that they could watch services in the neighboring church, and of throwing meat bones from it on to the facade gallery of the church on Good Friday.[74] The same sense of a belligerent Judaism is evident in an alternative version of the 1331 Girona riots discussed on pp. 378–87. In a separate lawsuit under ecclesiastical jurisdiction pursued by clerics against those very same royal officials whose testimony we have already heard, it is the Jews whose armed excursions seem to threaten even the Cathedral of Girona. Not surprisingly, this account denied the participation of any clerics other than schoolboys in the stoning of the Jewish quarter. Instead the blame was placed on the Jews, who, it was said, had opened the gates of the *call* and lounged about them bearing arms, thus violating the law. Other clerics added that the Jews had paid the bailiff to attack the cathedral, hiring him to avenge wrongs done them. Still others went further, testifying that the Jews had emerged armed from the *call* and marched to the stairs leading to the cathedral, intending to support the bailiff in his attack upon the clergy.[75] These clerical versions differed slightly from one another, but in this at least they all agreed: the Jews were not toothless enemies. This was an ongoing war, and once a year the Jews and their mercenaries needed to be defeated.

The claim that royal officials were mercenaries of the Jews was not an afterthought, a mere waving of hands to distract as part of a legal defense. The connection between Jews and royal government was at the heart of Holy Week violence and accounts for some of its most stabilizing and its most subversive aspects at one and the same time. Some of the subversion is obvious. The opprobrium that the clerics heaped upon officials in 1331 ("He is of the bailiff's court: kill him, kill him") was extreme, much greater than that directed against the Jews, and the citizens who intervened portrayed the conflict as one between court and clergy, not clergy and Jews ("It is evil, it is evil, that the court is treated this way"). Even in the many years when violence against officials did not erupt, the stoning of Jews contained implicit criticism of the king. We have seen how in *The Destruction of Jerusalem* the emperor claimed the remaining Jews and disposed of them as he willed. The Jews were his slaves.[76] In this, the epic conformed to medieval juridical reality. The Jews were the king's "coffer and treasure," or "slaves of our chamber," and under royal protection. For any lord the ability to protect dependants was evidence of power, while infringements on that protection were a defiance of that power. This is what King John of England meant in his much-quoted edict forbidding attacks on Jews: "If I give my peace even to a dog, it must be kept inviolate."[77] Attacks upon the king's Jews were attacks on royal majesty, and time after time the Crown condemned them as such. One did not need to be a lawyer to understand this. A ban on violence against the "king's Jews" was proclaimed before Holy Week by town criers throughout the realm. When clerics attacked Jews during Holy Week, they knew full well that they were attacking the Crown. A clerical anti-royalist carnival was emerging within the privileged sphere of a sacred festival.

If attacks on Jews during Holy Week implied a criticism of the Crown, they also provided a forum for struggle between local elites. In the Gironese example, official intervention led to a battle in which the clerical hierarchy confronted royal officials, the municipal council, and the town's "leading men," the very people, incidentally, with a financial interest in the protection of the Jews.[78] This battle of the elites could even supplant "killing the Jews" as the focus of Holy Week violence. Events in Valencia provide a case in point.

In 1320, Jews from various areas of Valencia kingdom complained that Christians stoned them on Good Friday, and that officials were insufficiently watchful in protecting them. In 1321, the Jews of Valencia city again complained that their quarters were invaded during Holy Week. The king ordered them to be specially protected, since they were "slaves of our chamber," and ordered the gates of Caragol and the cemetery of the hospital to be closed during Holy Week to protect the Jews.[79]

By 1322 royal officials had had enough. I have found no record of a clerical attack on the Jews that year. If it occurred, it was probably overshadowed by the other events that took place during Holy Week. The police officers (*sagiones*) of the criminal justice of Valencia, perhaps in their function as guardians of the Jews, argued with men of the bishop's family on Good Friday, though they parted without fatal violence. On Easter Sunday, these officers gathered before the bishop's palace, rang the bells, incited the populace, and then attacked the palace together with the mob, killing some of the bishop's men and injuring others.[80] Protocols that would barely restrain the violence in Girona in 1331 failed in the Valencia of 1322. The fact that the result was not a violent pogrom against the Jews, but rather unrestrained violence between local clerical and official elites, suggests that the dispute between secular and sacred, between monarchy and clergy, could be as large a component in Holy Week violence as the dispute between church and synagogue.

The events of 1331 in Girona, or 1322 in Valencia, are striking to us (and were recorded by contemporaries) because their violence, ritualized though it may have been, far exceeded the norm. Much more typical than these battles between adults were the juvenile festivities that so delighted the young Nicolas and cost him his life in 1302. An earlier observation bears repeating here: what is most conspicuous about Holy Week violence is its limits. In town after town, year after year, crowds of children hurled stones and insults at Jews and the homes of Jews without inciting broader riot.[81]

The integrity of these limits was due in large part, I believe, to the fact that the stoning of Jews during Holy Week was not only a game, but a children's game. The 1302 inquest in Girona, cited at the beginning of this chapter, makes clear the primary role of children and adolescents in the festivities. More specifically, this was a game for tonsured children, referred to in the documents as "clerics" and "students." Medieval towns abounded in such children. A great many parents tonsured their children to protect them from the severity of the civil courts, a shaving that was not tied to any consecration, though it signified an "inclination to the ecclesiastical condition" and was often linked to education in cathedral schools and universities.[82] These children were the only participants in Holy Week violence whose actions were fully protected by the ritual context in which they took place. This protection is explicit in the letter James II wrote to the "university" at Lleida forbidding doctors, poets, grammarians, and artists to dance dressed as Muslims or Jews during the festivities for Saint Nicholas and Saint Catherine, but expressly allowing children (presumably students) under the age of fourteen to do so.[83] The participation of older clergy (as in 1331) may have been ritualized, but it was not "customary" or necessarily approved of. Moreover, even the children's liberties were temporally circumscribed, limited apparently to Holy Week. This is not to deny that clever strategists might seek to expand these boundaries. In Barcelona Jews were required to swear a public oath in front of the Church of Saint-Just before suing a Christian debtor. Some debtors decided to gather crowds of young students there to intimidate the Jews into forgoing the oath, leading on one occasion to the stoning of a Jew and of the bailiff. The king's reaction is instructive. He not only forbade such activities but exempted the Jews from taking oaths at Saint-Just at all, permitting them the safety of the vicar's court instead. It appears that the prerogatives of children were not easily manipulated by adults.[84]

Why children? I have no answers, only partial suggestions. Of course the legal immunities discussed above played a role,[85] but these may themselves have been partly predicated on social immunities. Children were "the raucous voice" of "the conscience of the community," a voice that could speak pure truth because it was thought to speak from outside the networks of social relations within which adults were caught and their utterances compromised.[86] As René Girard would put it, children articulate most frankly a society's "persecutory mythopoesis."[87] Why this might be so is again unclear. Bruno Bettelheim has maintained that children's tendency toward polarization and projection represents a necessary stage in the process of psychic maturation. Only through this process of dividing the world into good and evil, then destroying the evil and rewarding the good, can children "sort out ... contradictory tendencies" and gain the psychic stability to avoid being "engulfed by [the] unmanageable chaos" and ambiguities of adult life. According to this model, childhood clarity prepares one for the compromises and complexities of life in the world. If our tonsured children were involved in such a process, then this is yet another way in which Holy Week violence stabilized Jewish–Christian relations.[88]

An explanation grounded more in medieval than modern psychology might stress the relationship between childhood and memory. It is well known that in the early Middle Ages children were often made to act as witnesses to transfers of land and fealty. In an oral culture where memory was the sole guardian of contract, children had the advantage that, as Marc Bloch put it, "memory was ... the more enduring the longer its possessors were destined to remain on this earth."[89] In Bloch's example, children might be hit or slapped to give them something to remember the ritual by, to imprint what they were seeing indelibly on their minds. Violent games might be used to a similar effect. Note how children marked a contested boundary between the towns of Andújar and Jaén in 1470:

> On Monday 7 May the Constable assembled as many people as possible ... concentrating particularly on securing a large number of youths and children. His objective was to beat the agreed bounds. ... At the first landmark, which was a well, the Constable threw a lance inside it, then ordered a young aspiring knight to jump in fully dressed, and finally let the youths and children indulge in a water fight. At the next landmark the children played a game called "Mares

in the Field" and then had a fist-fight until the Constable stepped in and parted them. At the third earthen landmark the youths and children . . . killed a ram, cut off its head, and buried the head in the middle of the landmark. At the fourth and final landmark the Constable organized a bullfight. . . . The express purpose of all these events was "to establish a memory so that in future times there would not be any doubt or debate about the said boundaries."[90]

In much the same way children and their Holy Week games may have served to beat the boundaries between Christian and Jew and to preserve them in memory.

Neither Bettelheim nor Bloch would object to calling these activities "educational," in the sense that they were intended to instill in children (and perhaps in the adult audience as well) a sense of the divisions that constituted their world. They were educational too in that tonsured children may have participated in this violence as part of an apprenticeship, a step of their career path in which character could be proven and prestige gained. Like the youthful javelin-throwing games of future warriors,[91] Holy Week riots provided an age-specific way for young tonsured boys to show their zeal. We can detect several roles among the participants in the Girona riot of 1331. Ten-year-olds threw stones and launched a multitude of minor attacks against the walls and gates of the *call*, fleeing upon detection. Older boys might lead such groups, or engage in exploits of limited daring, such as lighting a small fire beneath the gates. In Girona, as we have seen, this apprenticeship shaded into the careers of adult clerics, but the same stratification is evident even within the more brutal registers of a grown-up world. Some men participated in the ritual battles with officials, yelling and throwing stones. Among these, a handful were the most daring and aggressive, engaging in hand-to-hand combat and professing a willingness to kill their opponents, or perhaps executing bold sorties into the *call* in the quest for trophies. The senior clergy – archdeacons, abbots, and the like, men with no reputations to secure – provided the face-saving compromises and restraints that averted real bloodshed, pulling back the most aggressive and negotiating with the authorities. Participation in Holy Week games thus took place within a hierarchy of roles, as did participation in the Mass, or any other clerical office. The hierarchy of ritualized violence need not, of course, overlap with those of other clerical offices. In this sense, the games could be termed an alternative "career" where prestige could be gained.[92]

It would be wrong, however, to see this career as part of a deviant subculture, the creation of frustrated youth alienated from mainstream clerical institutions by chronic underemployment, few opportunities for advancement, and a severing of ties with the secular world.[93] Men of such weight as canons and abbots do not normally partake in a culture of anomie. In Girona, it seems to me, and probably elsewhere in the kingdom, participation in Holy Week violence was part of mainstream clerical culture. It was indeed an "office" or ritual. Through such participation the clergy rearticulated divine history, defined its sacral role, provided a critique of secular structures, and created a space for militant, even apostolic, Christianity. Holy Week violence belongs at the center, not the sordid margins, of clerical culture in the Crown of Aragon.

The previous pages depict Holy Week riots against Jews as a long-lived popular ritual of extraordinary persistence over centuries of Jewish life in Iberia (at least). They also stress a range of multiple meanings inherent in the violence, some of which we might call stabilizing, others the contrary. On the one hand, this clerical re-enacting of foundational historical narratives, reinforcing of boundaries between groups, and ritualization of sacrificial violence all contributed to conditions that made possible the continued existence of Jews in a Christian society. On the other, Holy Week stonings can be read as a clerical gloss on *convivencia*, a warning that the toleration of Jews in a Christian society was not without its dangers and costs. It was also a comment on the nature of power, establishing as it did an opposition between uncorrupted sacred power and the many compromises of political and economic power. Both these latter readings emphasized choice and the existence of alternative models of society, what Victor Turner calls "anti-structure."[94] There would be moments (such as the advent of the Black Death and the massacres of 1391) when these alternatives achieved momentary and tragic dominance. Most of the time, however, they would only be hinted at year after year by guardians of the sacred hurling stones at the walls of the *call*.

These conclusions have implications for the periodization of intolerance toward minorities in medieval Iberia and in Europe more generally. At a minimum, they ask us to question the traditional use by historians of episodes of violence in their attempts to periodize the ebb and flow of intolerance. In the historiography of Iberian Jews, for example, the fourteenth century marks what Yitzhak Baer called the "age of decline" in the Crown of Aragon, a decline graphed through points of violence like that of 1348, dropping inexorably to the massacres of 1391.[95] Those few Holy Week riots that have attracted the attention of historians have been used by them to connect these cataclysms, to give them a linearity they do not otherwise possess.

Such a seismic model makes little sense of Holy Week riots, in part because it ignores their rhythmic and ritualized aspect. Henri Hubert and Marcel Mauss theorized long ago that the rhythmic time of repeatable rituals and the linear time of successions of events could coexist, and argued that rituals impose elements of rhythm and circularity on linear events at the same time that they draw meaning from them.[96] Further, the seismic model treats violence as oracle. Holy Week violence was not predictive of future intolerance. It expressed a variety of alternative visions, but prophetic vision was not one of them. To treat Holy Week riots as signs or symptoms of a linear march toward intolerance is to deny their character as repeated, controlled, and meaningful rituals, and to ignore the possibility that violence can bind and sunder in the same motion.

In much the same way, the persistence of this popular ritual undercuts the well-known argument that an early medieval "Augustinian" tolerance toward Jews was replaced by a harsher clerical intolerance which then spread to the common people. According to this view, medieval attitudes toward Jews before the late twelfth century were governed by an Augustinian paradigm that condemned the Jews but insisted on the importance of their presence within Christian society: as living reminders of the Crucifixion, of Christ's victory, and of the truth of the Christian version of sacred history.[97] This tolerant paradigm, we are told, was replaced in high and late medieval polemics by an insistence that medieval (rabbinic) Jews had strayed from the truth of their own ancient tradition, that they were irredeemably evil and inveterate enemies of Christendom, and that they should be eliminated from the Christian community.[98]

Holy Week riots suggest that, while it may be true that the style of Christian anti-Jewish polemic changed between the twelfth and fourteenth centuries,[99] we should be cautious about overschematizing Christian–Jewish relations on the basis of such evidence. We need to be less relentlessly bleak about the fate of Augustinian tolerance in the later Middle Ages. It is in this period of what we are told is its twilight that we find the greatest evidence for a widely distributed clerical ritual which in good Augustinian fashion used the Jews to re-enact the triumphant place of Christianity in sacred history, while at the same time circumscribing for and assigning to the Jews a place in Christian society.[100] But just as rumors of the Augustinian ideal's death have been exaggerated, so too with accounts of its life. We should pause for breath in our panegyrics when we realize that one of the most ancient, most popular, and clearest articulations of the Augustinian paradigm in the Middle Ages turns out to be predicated on an act of violence. It is this double register of rituals like the Holy Week stoning of Jews that gives them their greatest value in explaining both *convivencia* and cataclysm. The violence contained within them made possible both stasis and explosive historical change. The same idioms that provided stability by ritualizing the sacrificial conquest of "Jerusalem" gave ritual form to the massacre of Jews in 1348 and 1391, and of Muslims in 1455.[101]

NOTES

1 *Al-ajwiba al-fākhira 'an al-as'ila al-fājira*, p. 4, cited by Mark Cohen, *Under Crescent and Cross: The Jews in the Middle Ages* (Princeton, NJ: Princeton University Press, 1994), p. 191.
2 Al-Qarāf ī represents an early shot in the polemical debate over the relative tolerance of Muslim and Christian societies, a debate in which Cohen's book, cited in previous note, is the most recent salvo.
3 José M. Millás Vallicrosa and L. Batlle Prats, "Un Alboroto contra el call de Gerona en el año 1331," *Sefarad* 12 (1952): 297–335, reprinted in *Per a una història de la Girona jueva*, ed. David Romano (Girona: Ajuntament de Rigona, 1988), vol. 2, pp. 501–41, here p. 501.

4 Compare J. Riera i Sans, "Els avalots del 1391 a Girona," in *Jornades d'història dels jueus a Catalunya* (Girona: Ajuntament de Girona, 1987), pp. 95–159, here p. 111.

5 Jean Delumeau, *La peur en occident (XIVe–XVIIIe siècles)* (Paris: Fayard, 1978), p. 281; he cites the events of 1331 in Girona as a concrete example.

6 For a classical statement of a tension between diachronic and cyclical in the analysis of ritual, see Henri Hubert and Marcel Mauss, "Étude sommaire de la réprésentation du temps dans la religion et la magie," in their *Mélanges d'histoire des religions* (Paris: Felix Alcan, 1929), pp. 189–229. I am not arguing for continuity in meaning where there is continuity in form.

7 Natalie Z. Davis, "The Reasons of Misrule," in *Society and Culture in Early Modern France* (Stanford, CA: Stanford University Press, 1975), p. 123: "The carnival form can . . . act both to reinforce order and to suggest alternatives to the existing order."

8 By "religious riot" I mean "any violent action, with words or weapons, undertaken against religious targets by people who were not acting *officially* and *formally* as agents of political and ecclesiastical authority." See Davis, "The Rites of Violence," in *Society and Culture*, p. 153. All appearances to the contrary, Holy Week riots were never officially sanctioned by the Church.

9 For France and Iberia see pp. 379–94. For Italy, see Brian Pullan, *The Jews of Europe and the Inquisition of Venice, 1550–1670* (Totowa, NJ: Oxford, Blackwell, 1983), pp. 163–4; Kenneth Stow, *Alienated Minority: The Jews of Medieval Latin Europe* (Cambridge, MA: Harvard University Press, 1992), pp. 240; and especially Ariel Toaff, *Il vino a la carne: Una communità ebraica nel Medioevo* (Bologna: Il Mulino, 1989), pp. 224–5. If we accept the colaphization (striking on the face) of Jews as related, then violent Easter rituals are even more widespread.

10 See *Recueil des historiens des Gaules et de la France*, 12: 436; Ademar of Chabannes, *MGH*, *SS* 4: 139; Cecil Roth, "European Jewry and the Dark Ages: A Revised Picture," *Hebrew Union College Annual* 23 (1950–1): 151–3. Other traditions of "ritual pillage" were almost as long-lived. See Carlo Ginzburg *et al.*, "Saccheggi rituali: premesse a una ricerca in corso," *Quaderni storici* 65 (1987): 615–36, and add to their examples that of Albi, where ritual pillaging of episcopal property was banned in 1144; see Clement Compayré, *Études historiques et documents inédits sur l'Albigeois, le Castrais, et l'ancien diocèse de Lavaur* (Albi: s.n., 1841), p. 143. Such pillaging usually occurred following the death of a bishop. Cf. the examples of funerary pillaging collected by Robert Hertz in *"Death" and "The Right Hand,"* trans. Rodney Needham and Claudia Needham (Glencoe, IL: Free Press, 1960), p. 49.

11 For Tortosa see Joan Moreira, *Del Folklore Tortosí* (Barcelona: Imprenta Querol, 1934), pp. 559–62, who provides an explanation of the liturgical role of the ceremony; but compare M. Casas Nadal, "La litúrgia en una canònica de la diòcesi d'Urgell a l'edat mitjana: Sant Vicenç de Cardona," in *Miscelània Hommenatge a Josep Lladonosa* (Lleida: Institut d'Estudio Ilerdenes, 1992), pp. 238ff.; and Joan Amades, *Customari Català el curs de l'any*, 5 vols (Barcelona: Salvat, 1950; reprint, 1989), vol. 2, pp. 750–1. In Urgell during the civil war, men dressed as the twelve apostles would beat the riverbanks with sticks in a ceremony called "killing the Jews." See Violet Afford, *Pyrenean Festivals: Calender Customs, Music and Magic, Drama and Dance* (London: Chatto and Windus, 1937), p. 38. For additional Catalan examples see Joan Amades, *Las danzas de Moros y Cristianos* (Valencia, 1966), pp. 752–4.

12 For the Asturian example, see Maurice Kriegel, *Les Juifs à la fin du Moyen Age dans l'Europe méditerranéenne* (Paris: Hachette, 1979), pp. 35–6. The resemblance between the song's "Thieving Jews" and al-Qarāfī's "the Jews have stolen your religion" is striking. Could it derive from a reading of Genesis 27 ff., the story of Jacob and Esau?

13 For King Peter's letters to officials in Girona and to the bishop of Girona, see Arxiu de la Corona d'Aragó, Cancelleria Reial (hereafter ACA:C) 40: 79r–v (1278/4/3), published in *España Sagrada, teatro geográfico-histórico de la iglesia de España,* (52 vols),

ed. E. Flórez *et al.* (Madrid: Antonio Marin *et al.*, 1747–1918), 44: 297–9 (= Jean Régné, *History of the Jews in Aragon: Regesta and Documents (1213–1327)* [Jerusalem: Magnus Press Hebrew University, 1978], nos. 695, 696). See also J. Amador de los Rios, *Historia social, politico y religiosa de los judios de España y Portugal*, 2 vols (Madrid: Aguilar, 1960), vol. 1, pp. 359–63.

14 Arxiu Diocesà de Girona (hereafter ADG), Serie C, Lligall 69, Processes, fol. 5r–v. Other witnesses had even longer memories, reaching back almost half a century.

15 For other examples of Holy Week riots in Girona, see ACA:C 242: 141v, 145r (1315/5/5 and 1315/5/15); this is published in Johannes Vincke, *Documents selects mutuas civitatis arago-cathalaunicae et ecclesiae relationes illustrantia* (Barcelona: Balmes 1936), pp. 163ff.; ACA:C 171: 73v–74r (1321/1/13); ACA:C 428: 123v–124r (1328/1/25). Local archives provide even more extensive evidence. See, *inter alia*, ADG, LL. Ep. 26is, 122x–v (1327/3/31), which explicitly states that the attacks are annual; Arxiu Històric de la Ciutat de Girona (hereafter AHCG), Llibre Verd, fol. 300r (1333/3/26); ADG, LL. Ep. 10, 185r (1347/3/19); ADG, LL. Ep. 21, 222v–223r (1353); ADG, LL. Ep. 60, 71x–v (1370), and Christian Guilleré, *Girona al segle XIV*, vol. 1 (Girona: Ajuntament de Girona, 1993), pp. 128–30.

16 Barcelona: ACA:C cartes reials (hereafter cr.), Jaume II, box 27, no. 3477 (1308/4/22); ACA:C 434: 49v–50r (1329/5/9); ACA;C 434: 701r (1329/5/19); ACA:C 530: 162v–163r (1335/5/8); ACA:C 654: 128v–129r (1349/2/26). Vilafranca: ACA:C cr. Jaume II, box 57, no. 6974 (1322/3/21); ACA:C cr. Jaume II, box 134, no. 10 (1323/2/13). Camarasa: ACA:C 40: 30r (1277/10/24) (= Régné, *History*, no. 689). Pins: ACA:C 56: 62v (1285/4/8) (= Régné, *History*, no. 1335), not explicitly identified as Holy Week violence. Besalú: ACA:C 70: 77v (1287/3/23) (= Régné, *History*, no. 1710). Daroca: ACA:C 245: 121r (1319/4/30). Alcoletge: ACA:C 383: 40r–42r (1320/8/1) (= Yitzhak Baer, *Die Juden im christlichen Spanien*, 2 vols [Berlin: Institute Kirche und Judentum, 1936; reprint, London, 1970], vol. 1, no. 175), not explicitly identified as Holy Week violence. Valencia kingdom: ACA:C 170: 295v (1320/12/4). Valencia city: ACA:C 171: 155r (1321/1/13). Apiera: ACA:C 457: 224v (1333/3/21). Teruel: ACA:C 171: 271v (1321/4/8). Burriana: ACA:C 173: 77v (1321/5/7). For brief discussions of such events in Valencia, see José Maria Doñate Sebastiá and José Ramon Magdalena Nom de Déu, *Three Jewish Communities in Medieval Valencia* (Jerusalem: Magnus Press, Hebrew University, 1990), pp. 51–2; Montalvo J. Hinojosa, *The Jews in the Kingdom of Valencia: From Persecution to Expulsion: 1391–1492* (Jerusalem: Magnes Press, Hebrew University, 1993), p. 162.

17 ADG, box 24, A, no. 7, published in Millás and Batlle, "Un Alboroto," p. 317 (1952)/p. 521 (1988).

18 ACA:C 173: 77v (1321/5/7).

19 Unfortunately the accusation is undated. See Jean Régné, "Rapports entre l'inquisition et les juifs d'après le mémorial de l'inquisiteur d'Aragon (fin du XIVe siècle)," *Revue des Études Juives* 52 (1906): 224–33, here 226–7. See also M. Omont, "Mémorial de l'inquisition d'Aragon à la fin du XIVe siècle," *Bibliothèque de l'École des Chartes* 66 (1905): 261–8.

20 ACA:C 939: 99r–103v (1382/3/7), transcribed by Baer, *Die Juden*, vol. 1, no. 342, pp. 512–18, here 515. In a similar document limiting what expenses and bribes the secretaries of the *aljama* of Barcelona were authorized to pay, specific exception was made for the "salaries of the Good Friday guards, as is customary," ACA:C 948: 114v–122v (1386/4/2), transcribed by Baer, *Die Juden*, vol. 1, no. 381, pp. 580–93, here p. 589.

21 ACA:C 70: 77v (1287/3/23) (= Jean Régné, *History of the Jews*, May 6, 2003, no. 1710). Bonanasch Escapat, *elemosinarius* of the Jewish *aljama* of Vilafranca, testified in 1299 that he had been required to pay the royal judge of Vilafranca and the castle guards one maravedi each Easter, "as is the custom, for protection during Holy Week." ACA:C Procesos 506/1, discussed by Elena Lourie in her important article "Jewish

Moneylenders in the Local Catalan Community, c.1300: Vilafranca del Penedés, Besalú and Montblanc," *Michael* 11 (1989): 60–1.

22 AR V Bailía, 1155, fol. 58sv (1473/5/20), published by Doñate and Magdalena, *Three Jewish Communities*, pp. 148ff., and discussed on p. 52. The bailiff of Castellón had charged a Jewish official one hundred maravedis for nonpayment of the protection fee.

23 ACA:C 383: 40r–42r (1320/8/1). For the Latin text, see Baer, *Die Juden*, vol. 1, no. 175, pp. 217–18.

24 See chapter 6 on "Muslim Jewish Relations," of David Nirenberg, *Communities of Violence: Persecution of Minorities in the Middle Ages* (Princeton, NJ: Princeton University Press, 1996), esp. pp. 251–2 and 265–8.

25 *Razsvet* (St Petersburg), 19 (May 8, 1881), translated and published as an eyewitness account of the Kievan pogroms by Stephen Berk, *Year of Crisis, Year of Hope: Russian Jewry and the Pogroms of 1881–1882* (Westport, CT: Greenwood Press, 1985), pp. 35–6.

26 ADG, box 24, A, no. 7, testimony of Bernat de Bas, bailiff of Girona, and of Bonanat Tornavellis, citizen of Girona, transcribed in Millás and Batlle, "Un Alboroto" pp. 316–17 (1952)/pp. 520–1 (1988).

27 For example, ACA:C cr. Jaume II, box 27, no. 3477 (1308/4/22).

28 ACA:C 523: 97v (1330/8/21). For attacks on official buildings as a form of resistance to authority, see Christian de Mérindol, "Mouvements sociaux et troubles politiques à la fin du Moyen Age: essai sur la symbolique des villes," in *Actes du 114e Congrès National des Sociétés Savantes* (Paris, 1989): pp. 291–2. The throwing of rocks at the doors and houses of one's enemies was specifically forbidden in several law codes, e.g. the *fuero* of Teruel. See *El Fuero de Teruel*, 2nd edn, edited by J. Castañé Llinás (Teruel: Ibercaja, 1991) no. 284, p. 323.

29 The throwing of stones could even acquire a ritualized role in the law as a means of contesting property boundaries. Thus the formal denunciation of construction that infringed upon one's rights in Salamanca involved the hurling of nine stones against the structure. See M. Echániz Sans, "Las Mujeres de la Orden Militar de Santiago: el monasterio de Sancti Spiritus de Salamanca (1268–1500)" (PhD diss., University of Barcelona, 1990), vol. 4, doc. no. 143 (dated 1449/4/7).

30 ACA, Reial Patrimoni (hereafter ACA:RP), MR 1688: 39v (1311), published by José Ramon Magdalena Nom de Deú, "Delitos de los judíos de Aragón a inicios del siglo XIV (1310 a 1312): Aportación documental," *Anuario de Filología* 5 (1979): 221.

31 ACA:C cr. Jaume II, box 27, no. 3477 (1308/4/22).

32 ACA:C 630: 162v–163r (1335/5/8).

33 ACA:C cr. Jaume II, box 57, no. 6974 (1322/3/21).

34 Compare Claude Lévi-Strauss's discussion of "Instruments des tenèbres" in *Du miel aux cendres* (Paris: Plon, 1966), pp. 348ff., where noise is used to mark transitions in ritual performances. Lévi-Strauss specifically mentions medieval European Holy Week rituals, though not attacks against Jews.

35 See note 3; for a different and unpublished version of the same events, see ADG, Procesos, no. 120, discussed briefly at note 75.

36 Millás and Batlle, "Un Alboroto," pp. 324–5 (1952)/pp. 528, 531 (1988).

37 For this formulation of ritualized aggression, see Peter Marsh, Elisabeth Rosser, and Rom Harré, *The Rules of Disorder* (London: Routledge, 1978), pp. 24–7.

38 Many of the witnesses in the 1302 inquest into a death during Holy Week riots in Girona stated that they believed the stones were thrown to keep Jews inside their *call*. Jews were required by both ecclesiastical and secular law to stay within their quarter during Holy Week. See Kriegel, *Les Juifs à la fin du Moyen Age*, p. 22; Millás and Batlle, "Un Alboroto," p. 299 (1952)/p. 503 (1988). See also ACA:C 384: 101r (1321/4/22), in which Prince Alfonso ordered the prosecution of Jews of Vilafranca accused of violating this rule.

39 Millás and Batlle, "Un Alboroto," pp. 312, 314 (1952)/pp. 516, 518 (1988).

40 Archivo Municipal de Vilareal (hereafter AMVil), no. 209, Clavería de Arnau Ayç, 1368–9, fol. 18v, published in José Maria Doñate Sebastiá, "Aportación a la historia del teatro, siglos XIV–XVI," in *Martinez Ferrando Archivero. Miscelánea de estudios dedicados a su memoria* (Madrid: Asociacion Nacional de Bibliotecarios, Archiveras y Arqueologas, 1968), doc. no. 9. Though in each of these cases the meaning of *joch* is slightly different, there is clearly always a ludic element in its usage.

41 Mikhail Bakhtin, *Rabelais and His World*, trans. Hélène Iswolsky (Bloomington, IN: Indiana University Press, 1984), pp. 13ff., 84, and especially his treatment of the *Cena Cypriani* on pp. 286–9. The *Cena*, a text associated with Easter, is the account of a banquet to which a king invites the salient figures of sacred history. The characters at the banquet act, dress, and eat in accordance with their biblical roles (Judas, for instance, provides the silver; Jesus gets drunk on raisin wine [a play on *passus/passio*]). Each also brings the king a gift, and when some gifts are stolen, the king orders all the guests tortured (Jonah is thrown into the sea, Jesus is crucified). Guilt is assigned to Achan, son of Carmi (not Hagar, as Bakhtin has it, p. 288), the same Achan who brought the curse of God upon the Israelites for his theft of an impure object in Joshua 7. He is delivered to the others, who execute him appropriately (e.g. Thecla tears his clothes off, David hits him with a stone, Eleazar transfixes him with a lance, etc.), bury him, and then return home. The point here is that the work presents sacred history more as a drunken game than a deadly competition. (Its culmination in sacrifice will also be relevant to the argument below.) For the text, see *MGH, Poetae Latini aevi carolini*, vol. 4, pt 2, ed. Karl Strecker (Berlin: Weidmannas, 1923), pp. 857–900, where some of the extant fourteenth-century Iberian manuscripts of the work are listed. For a fictional version of the *Cena* see Umberto Eco, *The Name of the Rose* (New York: Harcourt, Brace, Janovich, 1984), pp. 517–24.

42 The document, dated June 16, 1409, is published in José Sánchez Adell, "Castellón de la Plana en la baja edad media," *Boletín de la Sociedad Castellonense de Cultura* 54 (1978): 310–43, here 335–6. Jews were represented in this procession, p. 339.

43 ACA:C 406: 59r–v (1320/4/5).

44 The description of this event is drawn from ACA:C 530: 62v–163r (1335/5/8).

45 ACA:C 56: 62v (1285/4/8) (= Régné, *History*, no. 1335).

46 Doñate and Magdalena, *Three Jewish Communities*, pp. 51–2 (emphasis in the original).

47 For research on Catalan Passion plays, see Jesus F. Massip, *Teatre religiós medieval als països catalans* (Barcelona: Edicions 62, 1984). For other regions, see the bibliography in *The Staging of Religious Drama in Europe and the Later Middle Ages*, eds Peter Meredith and John Tailby (Kalamazoo, MI: Medieval Institute, 1983), pp. 15–32. The cathedral of Girona was a particularly active center of "colorful liturgical customs," including stagings of Easter cycles, and even re-creations of the stoning of the apostle Stephen by the Jews, complete with fake stones. See Richard B. Donovan, *The Liturgical Drama in Medieval Spain* (Toronto: Pontifical Institute of Medieval Studies, 1958), pp. 98–119.

48 See, for example, Rafael Narbona Vizcaíno, *Pueblo, poder y sexo. Valencia medieval (1406–1420)* (Valencia: Diputacio de Valencia, 1992), p. 55, who sees Holy Week re-enactments of the Passion unleashing a "semi-lynching." Cf. Jean Delumeau, *La peur*, p. 279; H. Pflaum, "Les scènes de juifs dans la littérature dramatique du Moyen Age," *Revue des Études Juives* 89 (1930): 115; Millás and Batlle, "Un Alboroto," p. 299 (1952)/p. 503 (1988); M. Lazar, "The Lamb and the Scapegoat: The Dehumanization of the Jews in Medieval Propaganda Imagery," in *Anti-Semitism in Times of Crisis*, ed. Sander Gillman and Steven Katz (New York: New York University Press, 1991), pp. 38–80, here p. 53.

49 AMVil, no. 214, Clavería de Arnau Bosch, 1375–6, Papeles no. 24, published by Doñate, "Aportación a la historia del teatro," pp. 157–8.

50 For the text of the Assumption drama, see J. Pié, "Autos Sagramentals del sigle XIV," *Revista de la Asociación Artístico-Arqueológica Barcelonisa* 1 (1896–8): 673–83 and 726–44. The passage translated here is quoted in J. F. Massip, "Notes sobre l'evolució de l'espai escénic medieval als països catalans," *Acta historica et archaeologica mediaevalia* 5–6 (1984–5): 142.

51 Based on documentation from Vilareal, Doñate claimed that Jews participated in Passion plays. See his "Aportación a la historia del teatro," p. 158. David Romano, though he first accepted this claim ("Figurantes judíos en representaciones sacras [Villareal, siglos XIV y XV]," *Sefarad* 29 [1969]: 75–6), has since rejected it ("Judíos hispánicos y mundo rural," *Sefarad* 51 [1991]: 353–67, here p. 360, n.30). Nevertheless, Jews did participate in other types of religious processions. The church council held in Valladolid in 1322 forbade the practice of bringing Jewish and Muslim musicians into churches to help celebrate nocturnal vigils. See Ramon Menendez Pidal, *Poesía juglaresca*, p. 97. In Avila a council condemned the practice, "monstrous to the body social," of Jews and Muslims dancing in Corpus Christi processions, and forbade priests to officiate at any funeral where they saw Jewish or Muslim women wailing or mourning. See A. García y García, "Jews and Muslims in the Canon Law of the Iberian Peninsula in the Late Medieval and Early Modern Period," *Jewish History* 3 (1988): 41–50, titles 7.6 and 7.2. The council was held in 1481 but repeated older material. On Jewish women as mourners in Christian funeral processions see *She'elot u-teshuvot bar Sheshet* (Responsa of R. Isaac ben Sheshet Perfet), no. 508 (for Zaragoza); Baer, *Die Juden*, vol. 1, p. 313 (for Seville); E. Camera Montenegro, "Actividades socioprofesionales de la mujer judía en los reinos hispanocristianos de la baja edad media," in *El trabajo de las mujeres en la edad media hispana*, eds Angela Muñoz Fernández and Cristina Segura Graiño (Madrid: Associación cultural Al-Mudayna, 1988), p. 339.

52 Compare Bruce Lincoln's analysis of "ancestor invocation and segmentary lineages" and "myth and the construction of social boundaries" in his *Discourse and the Construction of Society* (Oxford: Oxford University Press, 1989), pp. 18–23.

53 For a sense of the range of the topos in Iberian letters, see Maria R. Lida de Malkiel, *Jerusalém: el tema literario de su cerco y destrucción par los romanos* (Buenos Aires: Univ. de Buenos Aires, 1972). For plays about the fall of Jerusalem (though not specifically Iberian), see Pflaum, "Les scènes de juifs," p. 120; and most recently Stephen Wright, *The Vengeance of Our Lord: Medieval Dramatizations of the Destruction of Jerusalem* (Toronto: Pontifical Institute of Medieval Studies, 1989). There was also a Christian liturgical commemoration of the fall (which did not coincide with Holy Week), on which see A. Linder, "The Destruction of Jerusalem Sunday," *Sacris Eruditi* 30 (1987–8): 253–92.

54 Biblioteca de Catalunya, MS 710, *Destrucció de Jerusalem*, and MS 991, *La venjança que féu de la mort de Jhesuchrist Vespasià e Titus son fill*, ed. J. Hernando i Delgado, "La Destrucció de Jerusalem," in *Miscel.lània de Textos Medievals* 5 (1989): 1–116. These particular manuscripts are from the fifteenth century, but fourteenth-century versions exist, such as that published by Prospero de Bofarull Mascaró, *Documentos literarios en la antigua lengua catalana (siglos XIV y XV)* (Barcelona: Impr. del Archivo, 1857), pp. 9–52.

55 In Jewish traditions, which obviously interpret the fall of Jerusalem differently from Christian ones, God also inflicts illness upon the emperor, by sending a fly up Titus's nose to devour his brain as punishment for besieging Jerusalem and desecrating the Temple. See *Bereschit Rabba* 10; *Gittin* 56b; and I. Lévi, "La Mort de Titus," *Revue des Études Juives* 15 (1887): 62–9.

DAVID NIRENBERG

56 In this version the prophecy is attributed to Jesus upon his entry into Jerusalem on Palm Sunday, but compare Rupert of Deutz, *In Ieremiam prophetam commentariorum Liber unus*, ch. 86, *PL* 167.1416 for an alternative attribution.

57 Like all of the elements of this narrative, the story of the three ships had a venerable pedigree in both Christian and Jewish tradition. One fourteenth-century Catalan variant maintained that, since Titus had put no women aboard the ships, the male Jews had had to marry Muslim women, so that they were no longer real Jews but bastards with no claims to inherit the Jewish birthright. See J. Hernando i Delgado, "Un tractat anònim *Adversus Iudaeos* en català," in *Paraula i Història, Miscel.lània P. Basili Rubí* (Barcelona, 1986), p. 730. See also the older Latin polemic, edited by Jose M. Millás Vallicrosa, "Un tratado anónimo de polémica contra los judios," *Sefarad* 13 (1953): 3–34, here p. 28, where the Jews, aboard four ships in this version, take idolatrous women to wife. For a Jewish example of the tradition, see *Midrash rabbah Lamentations*, where the ships are loaded with Jewish captives bound for Roman brothels. Cf. also *Gittin* 57b.

58 The divinely ordained cannibalism, the immolation of the captured Jews, and the fact that the Crusade was an offering of thanksgiving for the emperor's cure, all suggest that the conquest of Jerusalem was a sacrifice as well as vengeance. Cf. René Girard, "Generative Scapegoating," in *Violent Origins: Ritual Killing and Cultural Formation*, ed. Robert G. Hamerton-Kelly (Stanford, CA: Stanford University Press, 1987), p. 107.

59 Inga Clendinnen, "Ways to the Sacred: Reconstructing 'Religion' in Sixteenth Century Mexico," *History and Anthropology* 5 (1990): 119, writing, of course, of a very different context. For another example of stoning as sacrificial rite, see Henri Hubert and Marcel Mauss, *Sacrifice: Its Nature and Function* (Chicago, IL: University of Chicago Press, 1968), p. 83.

60 The importance of Holy Week riots in demarcating physical space should not be underestimated. In a city like Girona, where the Jewish quarter was surrounded by ecclesiastical properties, stoning may have been a way of insisting on the maintenance of physical barriers (walls) that were breached and contested with increasing frequency in the course of urban development. For legal examples of such contestation in Girona, see, e.g. AHCG, cartes reials, box 1 (1293–1334), 1331/9/3 (= Gemma Esetibà and Maria Frago i Perez, *Documents dels jueus de Girona, 1124–1595* [Girona: Ajuntament di Girona, 1992], no. 117); AHCG, Ordinations dels Jurats, Lligall 4 (1340–2), vol. 1340–1, fol. 64r, 1341/7/23 (= ibid., no. 178); ADG, Pia Almoina, pergamins, Girona no. 187, 1345/4/26 (= ibid., no. 228). Further, the danger posed by Holy Week riots became the primary argument used by Jewish communities seeking permission to build walls around their neighborhoods, or to prevent Jews and Christians from perforating existing ones. See, e.g. ACA:C 491: 105r–v (1328/3/12).

61 Compare Richard Trexler, "We Think, They Act: Clerical Readings of Missionary Theatre in Sixteenth Century New Spain," in *Understanding Popular Culture: Europe from the Middle Ages to the Nineteenth Century*, ed. S. Kaplan (Paris: Mouton, 1984), pp. 189–227.

62 Even as late as the eve of the massacres of 1391 the clergy still had a monopoly on Holy Week violence against the Jews in Girona. See ACA:C 1827: 87v–88r, 88v–89r (1387/4/2) and ACA:C 1839: 92r (1389/3/23), cited in Riera, "Els avalots del 1391," p. 111.

63 René Girard, *Violence and the Sacred* (Baltimore, MD: Johns Hopkins University Press, 1977), p. 93. Girard believes that sacrifice evolved as a form of ritualized vengeance (p. 13). V. A. Kolve suggests that medieval Corpus Christi dramas had a competitive, gamelike quality in their portrayal of the crucifixion. See *The Play Called Corpus Christi* (Stanford, CA: Stanford University Press, 1966), ch. 8.

404

64 Following this interpretation of "ritual sacrifice," I disagree with Delumeau's claim (in *La peur*, p. 281, quoted above, n. 5) that Holy Week violence is a symptom of the transformation of "theological discourse" about Jews as Christ-killers into a generalized popular hatred of the Jews. If these attacks are in some sense a liturgical office, then they remain strictly within whatever Delumeau means by "theological discourse."

65 Anthropologists have paid little attention to these types of contrapuntal rituals, in which "communitas" is succeeded by violence. In the modern Sierra de Alava (Basque country), inhabitants of some dozen villages that share pasture lands gather at a shrine to the Trinity, where each village hears Mass separately, and then all attend a common Mass. The next morning the youth of each village gather at the shrine and fight the youths of other villages. The violence is real, though it is governed by "sporting" rules. See Carmelo Lisón Tolosana, *Invitación a la antropología cultural de España* (La Coruña: Editorial Adare, 1977), p. 96.

66 *Sefer ha-Qabbalah* of Abraham bar Selomoh [of Torrutiel], trans. Y. Moreno Koch, *Dos crónicas hispanohebreas del siglo XV* (Barcelona: Riopiedras, 1992), p. 95. Abraham, exiled from Spain in 1492, wrote his book in North Africa and completed it in 1510.

67 Timothy Mitchell, *Violence and Piety in Spanish Folklore* (Philadelphia, PA: University of Pennsylvania Press, 1988), p. 14.

68 See Clendinnen, "Ways to the Sacred," pp. 118ff., which analyzes violence as transition marker in Meso-American ritual.

69 Narbona, *Pueblo, poder y sexo*, pp. 46–7, on the ball games documented at the end of the fourteenth century, and on the violent *joch o solaz del Rey Passero appelat* played at Christmas time.

70 Though the festival of "Moros i Crestians" is in some ways a Muslim parallel for Holy Week, it is not dealt with here because it is sparsely documented in the fourteenth century. For historical and anthropological treatments of this festival in Valencia see, *inter alia*, the *Actas del I congreso national de Fiestas de Moros y Cristianos (Villena 1974)* (Alacante, 1974); Adolf Salvà i Ballester, *Bosqueig històric i bibliogràfic de les Festes de Moros i Cristians* (Alicante, 1958); Amades, *Las danzas*; and Antoni Ariño Villarroya, *Festes, rituals i creences* (Valencia: Institució Valenciana d'Estudis i Investigacio, 1988), pp. 25–123.

71 For the case of Vitalis, ACA:C 1708: 123v (1367/7/23), in Baer, *Die Juden*, vol. 1, no. 285, p. 407. For a Jew of Biel charged during Holy Week with having (earlier) blasphemed by asserting that the Virgin Mary was an adulteress and Jesus a bastard magician, see ACA:C cr. Jaume II, box 87, no. 396 (1305/4/30) and ACA:C 137: 5v (1305/9/29), in ibid., no. 157, p. 188.

72 The original accusation was against Mosse, son of Jucef, a tailor of Sogorb. He seems to have fled, for an order was issued to return him dead or alive: ACA:C 246: 172r (1321/2/17); 246: 211r (1321/5/4). The accusation seems to have broadened to include others, since one Jew from the town took the precaution of obtaining a safe-conduct stating that he was not implicated: ACA:C 385: 161r (1322/4/5).

73 There is evidence (and this should not surprise us) that Jews could use ritual violence to criticize the Christians in whose lands they dwelled. An obvious example is Purim, on which see Elliott Horowitz, "The Rite to Be Reckless: On the Perpetuation and Interpretation of Purim Violence," *Poetics Today* 15 (1994): 9–54, esp. 27–37; and for a late medieval Iberian example, Sam Levy, "Notas sobre el 'Purim de Zaragoza,'" *Anuario de Filología* 5 (1979): 203–17. Compare ACA:C 86: 6r (1291/7/30) and 90: 12v (1291/8/28) (= Régné, *History of the Jews*, nos. 2380, 2385), where the Jewish community of Vilafranca is accused of "excesses" committed during Purim. But Christian concern on this score was doubtless amplified by the anxieties of the dominant about the resentments of the weak, a fear of, as George Eliot put it in *Daniel Deronda*, "the hidden rites of vengeance with which the persecuted have a dark vent for their rage."

74 Açach Avenaçfora and his sons Vital and Abrahaym were the accused. The church in question was that of Saint Lawrence. See ACA:C 393: 4r (1326/9/5), in Baer, *Die Juden*, vol. 1, no. 147, p. 171. Muslims were also accused of displaying undue curiosity about what went on in Easter services. For a case in which several Muslims of Valencia were accused of concealing themselves in hoods in order to enter churches during Holy Week, see ACA:C 522: 250v–251r (1330/1/20).

75 ADG, Procesos, no. 120 (1331). The manuscript contains partial testimony in the case, but no judgment. On the Jews' exit from the *call* bearing arms see fols 1v, 3r (which lists their weapons, including lances and shields), 3v, 4v. For the claim, reported twice, that the bailiff was paid by the Jews to attack the clerics as revenge, see 4v. The clerics may have been referring to the customary bribes and remuneration paid by the Jews to royal officials in exchange for protection during Holy Week, on which see p. 381.

76 The origins of Jewish "serfdom" in Vespasian's actions was noted in the Middle Ages by, among others, Eike von Repgow, author of the *Sachsenspiegel*. See S. Cassel, "Juden (Geschichte)," in Johann Samuel Ersch and Johann Gottfried Gruber, *Allgemeine Encyklopädie der Wissenschafter und Künste*, 2nd sec., vol. 27 (Leipzig, 1850), pp. 83–5. On the subject of Jewish serfdom in general, the best treatment is that of Gavin Langmuir, "'Tanquam servi': The Change in Jewish Status in French Law about 1200," in *Les Juifs dans l'histoire de France*, ed. Myriam Yardeni (Leiden: Brill, 1980), pp. 25–54, reprinted in Gavin Langmuir, *Toward a Definition of Antisemitism* (Berkeley, CA: University of California Press, 1990), pp. 167–94. For Spain see Baer, *Die Juden*, vol. 1, pp. 85–6.

77 Quoted in Cecil Roth, *A History of the Jews in England* (Oxford: Clarendon Press, 1964), p. 33.

78 J. Riera demonstrates the financial links between Jews and the municipal elite of Girona very nicely when discussing the events of 1391. See Riera, "Els avalots del 1391," pp. 98–9. For a detailed study of tensions between the city councillors and other sectors of society see Christian Guilleré, *Diner, poder i societal a la Girona del segle XIV* (Girona: Ajuntament di Girona, 1984), pp. 67–100. On p. 100 Guilleré asserts that these tensions led to the pogrom of 1391 against the Jews.

79 ACA:C 170: 295v (1320/12/4); ACA:C 171: 155r (1321/1/13).

80 ACA:C 174: 207r (1322/4/5); ACA:C 175: 69v (1322/5/13).

81 These limits are especially striking in light of Peter Loizos's argument that "when forms of marriage between antagonistic groups are treated as unthinkable," restrictions on violence tend to be minimal. See his "Intercommunal Killing in Cyprus," *Man*, n.s., 23 (1988): 639–53, here 650.

82 Bronislaw Geremek, *The Margins of Society in Late Medieval Paris* (Cambridge: Cambridge University Press, 1987), pp. 136–47, here p. 136.

83 The edict, dated 1300, is published by Jaime Villanueva, *Viaje literario*, 16: 231. Cf J.-R. Juliá Viñamata, "El estudio general de Lérida a finales del siglo XIV: Las reformas de Martín el Humano," in *Miscel.lània Homenatge a Josep Lladonosa* (Lleida: Institut d'estudis Llerdencs, 1992), pp. 323–48, here pp. 342ff. Students at Lleida also participated in direct violence against Jews. See, for example, the fight that took place in 1483 between the vicar's men and students attempting to stone the Jews, reported in Josep Lladonosa i Pujol, *L'Estudi General de Lleida del 1430 al 1524* (Barcelona: Institut d'Estudis Catalans, 1970), pp. 85, 89, 172–3. See also Lladonosa i Pujol, *Història de Lleida*, vol. 1 (Tàrrega: F. Camps Calmet, 1972), p. 671, where the Jews complain in 1420 that children regularly stone the walls of their quarter, though these are not stipulated as students.

84 The fullest account of the affair is in ACA:C 437: 130r–130v (1330/6/24). Cf. the brief mention of the document in Josefa Mutgé Vives, *La ciudad de Barcelona durante el reinado de Alfonso el Benigno (1327–1336)* (Barcelona: Consejo Superior de Investigaciones Científicas, 1987), p. 202. The court of the vicar is stipulated as the

appropriate venue in order to avoid such incidents in the earlier ACA:C 434: 263r-v (1329/7/1). Even earlier, ACA:C 433: 33v (1328/10/15) forbids the gathering of students by debtors for the purposes of intimidating the Jews, but does not mention this particular incident. Admittedly the later ACA:C 450: 114v–115r (1332/2/24) calls into question the effectiveness of all previous, since even at this date the king is ordering officials to protect the Jews when they take their oaths at Saint-Just.

85 Aside from the privilege of clergy tonsured children enjoyed, childhood then as today carried with it some diminished legal responsibilities, but this seems not to have been relevant to the issue at hand. See, e.g. *Furs de València* 2.13.6 (2: 217), where minors (under the age of twenty) are not excused from the consequences of crime by reason of age unless they are seven years old or younger.

86 Davis, "The Reasons of Misrule," in *Society and Culture*, p. 108, for the raucous voice. See also Richard Trexler, "Ritual in Florence: Adolescence and Salvation in the Renaissance," in *The Pursuit of Holiness in Late Medieval and Renaissance Religion*, ed. Heiko Oberman and Charles Trinkaus (Leiden: Brill, 1974), pp. 200–64; and Trexler, "From the Mouths of Babes: Christianization by Children in Sixteenth Century New Spain," in *Church and Community, 1200–1600*, ed. Richard Trexler (Rome: Edizioni di storia e letteratura, 1987), pp. 549–73, for examples of children being taught by clerics to attack pagan religious ceremonies in Mexico.

87 On the persecutory tendencies of children, see Julio Caro Baroja on infantile "mythomania," *Las brujas y su mundo* (Madrid: Alianya Editorial, 1973), pp. 310–13; and Caro Baroja, "Las brujas de Fuenterrabía," *Revista de Dialectología y Tradiciones Populares* 3 (1947): 200–204. Girard believes that children mimetically reproduce the persecutory fantasies of their environment and thus confirm them. See his *Des chases cachées depuis la fondation du Monde* (Paris: B. Grasset, 1978), p. 171. See also Mitchell, *Violence and Piety*, pp. 66–70.

88 Bruno Bettelheim identified children's destructive projections of good and evil as a necessary part of healthy cognitive development in *The Uses of Enchantment* (New York: Knopf, 1976), pp. 7–10, 66ff., 74–6, 144. His formulation is provocative here, though I doubt that the psychological model underlying it can easily be applied to the Middle Ages. It is worth the irony to note that, in psychosocial terms, it was once fashionable to think of medieval society as a whole as caught in this "childlike" state of polarization and projection, and to use this as an explanation of medieval violence toward minorities (as some still do). Cf. T. J. Jackson Lears, *No Place of Grace: Antimodernism and the Transformation of American Culture* (New York: Pantheon, 1981), pp. 149–81.

89 Marc Bloch, *Feudal Society*, 2 vols (Chicago, IL: University of Chicago Press, 1961), vol. 1, p. 114. Medieval theories abounded about the impressionability of children's minds and the ease with which they memorized.

90 Angus MacKay, "Religion, Culture, and Ideology on the Late Medieval Castilian-Granadan Frontier," in *Medieval Frontier Societies*, eds Robert Bartlett and Angus MacKay (Oxford: Oxford University Press, 1989), pp. 217–44, here pp. 235–6. The events are recorded in *Hechos del condestable don Miguel Lucas de Iranzo*, ed. Juan de Mata Carriazo (Madrid: Espasa-Calpe, 1940), pp. 425–31. For a study of games and ritualized violence in the *Hechos del condestable*, see L. Clare, "Fêtes, jeux et divertissements à la cour du connétable de Castille, Miguel Lucas de Iranzo (1460–70): les exercices physiques," in *La fête et l'écriture: théâtre de cour, cour-théâtre en Espagne et en Italie, 1450–1530* (*Colloque international: France–Espagne–Italie, Aix-en-Provence, 1985*) (Aix-en-Provence: Université de Provence, 1987), pp. 5–32.

91 Games long popular, and always dangerous. For the case of a youth accidentally killing another during such a game, see ACA:C 221: 124r (1321/11/23). The accidental killing in Daroca c.1300 of a Christian boy by his Muslim playmate may have been similar. See Toribo Campillo y Casamor, *Documentos históricos de Daroca y su comunidad* (Zaragoza: Imprinta del Hospicio Provincial, 1915), no. 119, p. 378.

For antique examples of such games and of such accidents, see Antiphon, *Tetralogies*, and Plutarch, *Pericles*, 36.

92 Compare, among groupings of soccer fans in England, the "Novices" (ages 9–12), the "Rowdies," and, within the grouping of Rowdies, "Aggro Leaders," and finally, "Graduates." See Peter Marsh, "Identity: An Ethogenic Perspective," in *Persons in Groups: Social Behavior as Identity Formation in Medieval and Renaissance Europe*, ed. Richard Trexler (Binghamton, NY: Medieval and Renaissance Texts and Studies, 1985), pp. 25–7. This "career" (in Erving Goffman's sense) did not appear in practice to be as antithetical to the clerical calling as we might think. Clerics were in fact frequent participants in late medieval urban violence, both as individuals and in groups, and the retinues of bishops and abbots were a potent force in urban feuds.

93 Such is the model suggested by Geremek, *The Margins*, p. 135. For a rapid overview of the sociological literature on "strain theories" of this type, see D. Downes, "The Language of Violence: Sociological Perspectives on Adolescent Aggression," in *Aggression and Violence*, eds Peter Marsh and Anne Campbell (Oxford: Saint-Martin's Press, 1982), pp. 30–3.

94 "Anti-structure" represents "the latent system of potential alternatives from which novelty will arise when contingencies in the normative system require it," while "the normative structure represents the working equilibrium." Victor Turner, *From Ritual to Theatre: The Human Seriousness of Play* (New York: Performing Arts Journal Publications, 1982), p. 28, citing from B. Sutton-Smith, "Games of Order and Disorder" (paper presented to the Symposium on Forms of Symbolic Inversion, American Anthropological Association, Toronto, December 1972), pp. 18–19.

95 Compare the imagery of Angus MacKay, "The Jews in Spain During the Middle Ages," in *Spain and the Jews: The Sephardi Experience 1492 and After*, ed. Elie Kedourie (London: Thames and Hudson, 1992), pp. 33–50, here p. 33: "Moreover, toward the end of the thirteenth century and during the fourteenth century *convivencia* broke down, and a rising tide of intolerance and persecution culminated in widespread and horrific massacres in 1391."

96 Hubert and Mauss, "Étude sommaire," pp. 189–229.

97 This paradigm was most influentially articulated by Augustine of Hippo in the fifth century. See his Augustine "De civitate Dei," *CC:SL*, vols 47–8, 18.46, 20.29; *Enarrationes in Psalmos CC:SL*, vols 38–40, 58.1.21–2; *Tractatus adversus Judeos, PL*, vol. 42: 51–67; and *Sermo, PL*, vols. 38–9: 200.2 – texts cited constantly by medieval Christian writers on the Jews.

98 The clearest exponent of this argument is Jeremy Cohen in his *The Friars and the Jews: The Evolution of Medieval Anti-Judaism* (Ithaca, NY: Cornell University Press, 1982).

99 A shift well noted by Amos Funkenstein, though he situates it differently than Cohen and draws different conclusions. See his "Basic Types of Christian Anti-Jewish Polemics in the Middle Ages," *Viator* 2 (1971): 373–82; and Funkenstein, "Changes in the Patterns of Christian Anti-Jewish Polemic in the Twelfth Century," *Zion* 33 (1968): 125–44 (in Hebrew).

100 This increased volume of evidence in the late thirteenth and fourteenth centuries does not, however, indicate increased incidence. It is primarily a function of the expanding record-keeping abilities of secular and ecclesiastical authorities.

101 Nirenberg's *Communities of Violence*, epilogue, pp. 231–49 treats the massacre of Muslims in 1455.

INDEX

Numbers in *italic* type indicate illustrations.